EDUCATIONAL
PSYCHOLOGY
AND ITS
CLASSROOM
APPLICATIONS

M. Daniel Smith

University of New Hampshire

Allyn and Bacon, Inc.

Boston · London · Sydney · Toronto

EDUCATIONAL PSYCHOLOGY AND ITS CLASSROOM APPLICATIONS

SECOND EDITION

Library of Congress Cataloging in Publication Data

Smith, Maurice Daniel.
  Education psychology and its classroom applications.

  Includes bibliographical references and index.
  1. Educational psychology. I. Title.
LB1051.S63 1978   370.15   77-26224
ISBN 0-205-06025-0

Contents

Introduction

WHOM IS THIS BOOK FOR?

The individual interested in education

The study of educational psychology is valuable to citizens in our society. Education is one of our major industries; adults pay great sums of money in taxes to support it. Parents agonize over the progress their children make in school, their problems with teachers and administrators, and the way things are taught, as well as what is taught. Politicians deal with the taxation problem, school board members attempt to understand what is going on and how it might go better, architects try to design better environments for learning, and nutritionists make decisions about the food that is served in cafeterias. The content of this book relates to the fundamental tenets and principles on which all of the procedures and policies and budgets are based, although traditionally very little attention is paid to these fundamentals—they are taken for granted.

Parents as educators

Parents are educators as well as citizens, and they teach their children by example, by precept, by choice of environment and facilities and materials in the home, by their attitudes toward children, and how they treat them. There are many places in this book where research and practice are related to styles and philosophies of "parenting": there are many aspects of teaching which require parents' support and backing and cooperation.

Classroom teachers—All levels, all subjects

Teachers teach mainly as they were taught, or as they have observed other teachers during their teacher-education programs and thereafter, or as they are required or pressured to teach by the school climate and environment and prevailing policies and traditions. One basic assumption of this book is that educational psychology is applicable to teaching in many ways, but that such applications are more difficult to create and try out than we have suspected in the past. Examples of applications are given throughout the book to serve as models.

Another basic assumption of this book is that teaching processes at different levels have more in common than is usually realized, and furthermore, that teaching processes in different subject matters have more in common than is generally recognized. The assumption that teaching is quite different from one level to another, and from subject to subject, is another barrier to the application of the concepts and principles herein, one that has to be overcome through honest attempts to apply and develop applications.

Traditional specialists

The concepts and principles of this book are basic to the work done by traditional specialists in the schools. Psychologists and guidance counselors employ educational psychology as a basic discipline: they usually emphasize the material in development and individual differences, particularly in relation to emotional problems. Special education teachers also have a firm grounding in psychology, with perhaps more emphasis on aspects of abnormal psychology, as well as behavior problems. While the emphases and languages and particular interests differ, the fundamental concepts of learning and development and individual differences are common to all specialists.

Newer specialities

While each of these specialties has its own literature and its own theories, they are based upon theories of learning, development, personality, and individual differences. They utilize common research techniques as well. Occupational therapists have become involved in various learning disabilities, particularly those of younger children related to motor problems as well as problems of posture and body image; they also deal with certain personality problems which seem related to tactile defensiveness and poor central nervous system processing resulting in lack of balance, lack of bodily awareness, and hyperactivity. Physical therapists and adaptive physical educators approach learning problems from the aspect of motor and psychomotor skills, and tend to assume that learning problems are based on awkwardness and lack of coordination and balance. Language pathologists of course emphasize aspects of language acquisition: they have gone beyond their traditional role of speech therapists to deal with receptive language (to be explained), which is closely akin to intelligence. Learning disabilities specialists are relatively new arrivals on the scene: their background is partly special education, partly language problems, and partly general learning theory, but they have a unique approach.   In all of these cases, remedial processes are based on fundamental principles of learning and teaching.   However, these specialists don't always use the same language.

Administrators

Principals and superintendents are nominally the instructional managers and leaders of our schools.   In practice, unfortunately, they devote relatively little time to these matters.   This is partly because the management and administration of a school demand attention to problems of scheduling, bussing, discipline, substitute teachers, assemblies, athletics, and the like.   The administrative (and general) tendency is to assume that teaching as we know it is the way teaching should be, so teaching is not a topic for debate and discussion.   The fact is that our schools are not doing as well as they might, for the amount of money spent on them, and more attention should be given to how teachers teach.   The concepts and processes in this book should be the basic determiners of how schools are organized and run, and administrators should know these concepts and processes even better than the teachers and specialists in the schools.   Only when the requirements of good learning and teaching become our guiding principles will we have the truly efficient and enjoyable and productive kinds of schools that are possible.

Educational technologists

Now thought of as media specialists and projector-schedulers and repairmen, educational technologists are also becoming the engineers of the educational process. Educational technology has to do with the implementation of basic principles of learning and teaching in the form of more productive and enjoyable instructional systems.   These systems emphasize the role of teachers as guides and helpers, and develop more mature and responsible learners.

Education-related and teaching-related functions in other organizations

Teaching and learning take place outside of schools and homes, of course.   Many education-related functions are part of business and industry, hospitals, and private and public human service agencies.   Community education and life-long learning programs are becoming more important, as are education and training programs for the handicapped and the aged.   This book deals with concepts which are basic to such endeavors.

**How the content of this book
relates to you**

Development.   The study of physical, social, and cognitive development is relevant
to you as an individual, and may explain some things about yourself that you hadn't
understood before.   It is also basic to teaching, counseling, special education, and
all the other specialties.   The manner in which various human capabilities emerge
and develop, the question of the interaction of heredity and environment, and the
implications of developmental processes for dealing with various age groups are all
fundamental to helping processes.

Individual differences, including learning disabilities.   Obviously the study of individual
differences is important in any specializations which deal with individual learners
and have to make allowances for such differences.   This relates to classroom
teaching because even with groups involved teachers deal with individuals as well,
and they have to interpret differences in reactions to discipline and tests and
authority figures and schedules and the like.   Obviously differences in learning
abilities are of concern to specialists and parents as well.   Administrators deal with
individuals also—not only individual learners, but individual teachers.   Some discussions of the effects of parent styles on the later personality of children is relevant
to how you go about "parenting" and to the development of "parent effectiveness."
They also relate to teacher effectiveness.

Teacher characteristics.   Teachers aren't the only ones concerned with the characteristics of good teachers: parents are continually dealing with teacher-student
interactions—or their indirect results—and citizens and school-board members
need some basis for evaluating teaching and identifying the nature of weaknesses
which may or may not be remedied.   The characteristics of good teachers apply to
Sunday School teachers and scout leaders as well.   As a student you have some
interest in the nature of the characteristics of good college teachers.

Characteristics of groups and social psychology.   While educational psychology has
traditionally dealt with learning theories and research in teaching, the equally relevant areas of social psychology and group dynamics have not found a place in the
education of teachers until recently.   Interpersonal relations and the influence of
groups is of great importance, particularly in the large schools of today where clubs
and groups and cliques are so general and powerful.   A class is a group: so is a scout
troop or a division of some business.   Leadership of groups is an important function
in all organizations; teaching classes is just one example of it.   While many of the
specialists mentioned previously deal with individual learners, they must understand the functions and pressures and dynamics of group operations if they are to
understand the environment in which their clients live and learn.

Motivation.   Obviously an understanding of the theories of motivation and, more
importantly, of practical approaches to motivating people is an asset in any under-

taking that involves people, whether they are young or old. It is, however, a more pressing problem for the teacher working with groups of learners over many months than for a specialist who works one-on-one. Nevertheless, a major part of the specialist's task may be to motivate the disabled learner.

Learning theories and teaching theories.   Theories of learning and teaching, and applications of them, are related to therapy and to dealing with handicaps as well as to conventional teaching. They suggest ways of dealing with learners in the home or hospital or in a team sport as well. It may come as a surprise to you, but few educators examine seriously the assumptions underlying our most common teaching methods, or evaluate them to find out whether or not they actually work! It is time for a more objective look at how we go about teaching, and what it produces. This begins with a study of basic conditioning processes, fundamental to traditional and modern therapies as well as to classroom and individual teaching; conditioning is a kind of learning, and a very important one, although you are more accustomed to relating learning to academic subjects. Then we will deal with elementary verbal learning research because it is enlightening in relation to such important factors as remembering and forgetting, memorizing, the distribution of practice, and making things meaningful. Concept learning and concept teaching are obviously important because it is through concepts that we cope with the tremendous amount of information that bombards us in our complex modern world. Finally, problem solving is studied because it is an important part of learning, a necessary skill in our society, and also the key to a very effective and motivating approach to teaching.

Managing, motivating, and instructing reviewed and summarized.   In two of the later chapters of this book many of the previous processes and concepts related to the management of learning and the motivation of learners are reviewed, and basic teaching processes are summarized. Educational psychology being a complex integration and synthesis of findings from a number of other disciplines, and this being your first time through it, some recapitulation of the basic themes of earlier chapters—with some variations and additions for interest—should be helpful.

Learning systems and teaching technology.   Teaching as we know it has developed empirically; in recent years, some people have taken a more systematic approach to the design of instructional processes. It has become apparent that more carefully designed teaching systems are needed to support individualized instruction as well as to cope with the information explosion. We will review some traditional systems, take a look at some new ones, and discuss briefly the theory behind instructional system design. You might think of this as the "engineering" of teaching, as compared with the theory covered previously.

Testing and evaluation.   Testing and evaluation are often viewed as separate topics, not as an integral part of teaching and learning. This is most unfortunate. It is partly the result of putting these topics last in such books as this, and this is perhaps because they customarily follow the "teaching." However, testing is an integral part of teaching. It is also a lot of other things as well. These last chapters are designed to acquaint you with the range of uses of testing and to discuss the effects of testing *on* teaching. A brief, simple introduction to measurement and statistics is also given.

The organization of the book by chapters

In order to help you take this subject a step at a time, and in order to make it possible to select some parts and not others for study or emphasis, each chapter is presented relatively independently of other chapters. In each chapter you will find introductory material which relates the content to your interests and concerns, points out some problems you might have in studying that material, and gives you a rationale for the inclusion of the content in the book and course. There is also material at the end of each chapter which is designed to help you review the major concepts, understand new terminology (the glossary), check your own knowledge through questions on the chapter, apply the content to realistic educational situations, and find additional reading beyond the references given in the body of the chapter. Your instructor will have suggested answers for the questions at the end, as well as points to be considered in applying the content. Generally, I hope that you will find the book informative and enjoyable, and worth the effort you need to put into it in order to obtain significant benefits.

PART

I

THE
LEARNER:
DEVELOPMENT,
INDIVIDUAL
DIFFERENCES,
LEARNING
DISABILITIES

1

Physical and Personal-Social Development

CONTENTS

3

ABOUT CHAPTER 1

How you will benefit from this chapter

You can derive a number of benefits from this chapter. One is a better understanding of yourself, since this chapter deals with stages of physical and social development that you have experienced, and it shows how problems at those stages can affect your attitudes and behavior later on. By the same token, you will be better able to understand learners of different ages, and their feelings and behaviors, in dealing with problems of discipline, motivation, and attitudes. Another benefit may be a better understanding of the overall direction of growth, and how various aspects of early development relate to later personality. Of course, if you are dealing with a particular age group, you will want to read more about that particular age.

What might bother you about this chapter

It is easy to say that everyone should understand more about his or her own development and that of others, but it is not always easy to confront facts that apply to you personally, or that may remind you of things you would rather forget. Anyone can be "hung up" at some stage of earlier development, and this can make it more difficult to read about such "hang-ups" and to understand them. You may find that certain parts of this chapter seem boring, although your friends find them interesting; this could mean that you are defending against this topic, because it hits too close to home. Another problem you may confront is a great deal of new terminology; if this is the case, stay with it, because many of the new terms and concepts are discussed again later in the book, and there is also a glossary at the end of the chapter for your assistance. On the other hand you may find some terms and ideas too familiar; if this is the case, don't assume you know them all, because there are many different theories covered and some of the terms may be used differently than you anticipate.

Some reasons for understanding development

There is an old saying, "As the twig is bent, so grows the tree." A modern view is that children are not just small adults, but are different at each stage of growth, and you need to know something about these stages and these differences if you are to deal with them effectively. If you are trying to improve your teaching potential, or studying to be a better specialist or parent, you should view this chapter as part of your basic preparation. Just as the medical student studies anatomy and physiology and the law student studies torts and corporation law, so the educator studies educational psychology; neither the medical student nor the law student is necessarily fascinated with these basic subjects per se, but they realize that such a foundation is important and necessary. So it is with physical and social development: there is plenty of interest in them, but there is also good reason to understand them regardless of how much they motivate you personally.

Assuring successful learning

You can exemplify the kind of preparation characteristic of successful teachers and parents by putting time and effort into learning, understanding, and applying the concepts and relationships presented in this chapter, through study, note-taking, discussion, and observation. What you learn here won't guarantee success as a teacher or parent or specialist; however, the way you go about learning will help establish a pattern of behavior and personality that will carry over into your later work. You also need to believe that you *can* learn this material if you invest effort; you don't need a previous background in psychology, or experience in teaching or being a parent, in order to understand this content.

Objectives for chapter 1

The development of physical and social capabilities from birth through high school is a tremendously important area of study and research. One of my objectives is to give you a foundation in this subject. I would like you to know what to expect of children at different ages, and how they progress from one stage or set of characteristics to another. You will not get to the point where you can identify these stages easily and accurately, since that takes practice, but you will recognize that many aspects of development proceed by fairly predictable stages and sequences. I would like you to begin to structure your observations of learners and also label some ways in which they are advanced or slow in developing. You will begin to form opinions as to whether a weakness is significant and serious, calls for special intervention, or is one of those individual traits that will take care of itself in time. Finally, you can begin to appreciate the many different ways in which developmental processes can be classified, and thus see how all individuals can go through the same processes and still have unique personal combinations of characteristics.

RATIONALE AND BACKGROUND OF CHAPTER 1

Our changing concepts of human development

Mary is in seventh grade. She is becoming very self-conscious about her early physical development in comparison with her friends', who have begun to leave her out of some of their activities and she doesn't know why. Her mother, who was a late-maturing adolescent, seems not to notice the problem, and her father notices it but doesn't know how to handle it.

There are many ways in which developmental problems manifest themselves at home and in school.

Greg is a preschooler who seems to be having some heavy emotional problems. He does a lot of things to get his mother's attention, including being naughty, crying at night, and picking on his younger sister. If his father tries to intervene Greg acts as though he doesn't want his father around, particularly when his mother is present. He watches his father closely when he is home, but doesn't seem to be as friendly with him as he was a year ago; on the other hand, he seems to follow his mother around, and dotes on her where he was always trying to get away from her before.

Bill is in high school. He has rejected his parents, and he only uses his home to sleep and get an occasional meal. He has been in trouble a couple of times, and his parents have become very upset about it, lectured him at length, and continually refer back to it. Each time, he seems to wait a while and then do something else that gets him in trouble. However, his parents never seem to set any penalties for this behavior, nor have they reacted in the past.

These are just a few of the kinds of problems of physical and personal-social development that you can run into, and probably have.

Contrary to eighteenth-century artists' representations of them, children are not just small adults, either physically or mentally. In fact, their ways of sorting out and thinking about the world seem oddly slow to develop, even in comparison with other young mammals whose potential is less but who learn most of what they need for survival quite early. During the nineteen sixties the "Head Start" program for increasing the readiness of pre-school children was considered very experimental and innovative, although Maria Montessori had organized a similar program successfully in 1912. In the seventies it became widely accepted that the major foundations for the development of language and of cognition generally are laid during the first three years (Pines, 1971[1]): evidently, Head Start was itself too late! On the other end of the spectrum, investigations suggest that intelligence increases into late adulthood, although it was formerly thought that it decreased after adolescence (Barton et al., 1975). The study of development is not just a study of theories and research related to teaching; the *object* of education *is* development, not skills and knowledge for their own sake (Kohlberg, 1976).

Some people regard the learner as a growing, unfolding organism whose destiny is predetermined by inherited characteristics. In this view, the learner needs only a warm, supportive, enriched environment for attaining full potential. This is a "maturation" or "nature-oriented" view. Others regard the learner as an organism which is molded and shaped by its environment, by creating within itself mental and sensory images of its experiences. The teacher and parent need to create an environment that will make the learner productive rather than destructive, intelligent rather than superstitious, and social rather than antisocial.

1. The name in parentheses refers to the source of this information; the bibliography at the end of the book will give you publication information by which you can look it up.

Accelerate or wait until ready?

Knowing about development and knowing what to do about it are two different things.

Some of the most widespread and emotionally charged debates in education have dealt with development and its implications for teaching. Some feel it permissible and desirable to intervene in the growth process; they point to the precociousness of children who are given very early training and contrast this experience with the retardation that results when children are brought up in deprived environments (such as in old-fashioned orphanages or in countries decimated by war). Other theorists disagree, arguing that we cannot intervene successfully in the growth process because it is inherent in the organism; they feel that such intervention may upset the natural unfolding of human abilities. They point to experiments that prove that early training makes no difference, such as studies of twins where one was taught to read early and the other was not, and where the untaught twin caught up quite easily when taught at a later age. However, it seems obvious that *persisting* environmental factors *do* have effects. Changes in height, weight, intelligence, and personality are closely related to the environment in which a person lives (Bloom, 1964). Bloom has suggested that each factor he mentioned has its own "critical" period and that supportive and helpful intervention will have its greatest effect at that time, although it may have lesser effects at other times as well.

Accelerate or wait until ready?

Heredity versus environment, and Konrad Lorenz

Q

What used to be
"heredity vs. envi-
ronment" is now
"heredity and
environment work-
ing together."

As you have probably heard, a great controversy has raged over how much of a child's development arises from the genetically inherited brain and nervous system, and how much comes through experience with the environment. The question, of course, has not been settled, although you may want to formulate some answers of your own as you read this part of the book. One valuable contribution to the solution has been made by an ethologist whose writings on the interaction of heredity and environment draw a fascinating parallel between the adaptive function of learning in an animal or human *lifetime,* and the survival function of genetic mutations that span *centuries* (Lorenz, 1965).

One method used by ethologists is the "deprivation experiment," which involves keeping essential experiences from an animal until it is mature, while giving it an otherwise normal upbringing. For example, suppose you raise ducks normally in every respect except that you deprive them of access to a body of water large enough for swimming. Then, when they are grown, you take them to a pool. You would see them exhibiting all the behaviors of ducks raised near a pond—ducking, paddling, fluffing and wetting their feathers—and you could conclude that those behaviors must have been "blueprinted" in their genes, since they could not have been learned through experience. In this case, the water is called the "releasing stimulus," in that it is the initial cue needed to bring out or "release" instinctive behaviors. As soon as this hereditary behavior emerges or is released, however, the ducks begin to "learn": they adapt their behavior to the particular situation, including the size of the pool, obstacles in the water, the best route from their pen to the water's edge, and how to tell whether water is in the pool or not.

Lorenz uses the term "blueprinting" to speak generally of the unknown processes whereby these behaviors are transmitted from generation to generation. A special case of this, called "imprinting," made him quite famous when it was first publicized. He found that young ducklings separated from their mother attach themselves to another animal or person and follow it as though it were their own mother. This happened only during a brief, critical period in the early development of the ducks. After that, no matter what kind of a mother-substitute was offered, they would not follow it.

Deprivation experiments are not performed on humans, for obvious reasons. However, they sometimes occur naturally; for example, people have been born blind and had their sight restored. Where sight has been restored, it is usually possible for the child to learn simple perceptions and discriminations between shapes and faces, but this depends partly on the age at which the restoration takes place (Hunt, 1961). In some of these cases, even such simple learning is impossible. As another example, children deprived of opportunities to exercise, speak, and interact have been found incapable of simple learning, and they are sometimes unable to walk as well (Spitz, 1945). Again, the age at which normal opportunities are restored is an important element—the later they are, the less the chance of recovery.

Konrad Lorenz (as imprinted parent). (T. McAvoy, LIFE Picture Service.)

The equivalent of a deprivation experiment with humans would be exposure of a learner to a task that he had never met before, some kind of problem that is not typical of his environment. Swiss psychologist Jean Piaget has taken such an approach in over forty years of research into the processes by which the mind develops (Piaget and Inhelder, 1969). He found that early development involves sensory and motor learning.

You may have reservations about experimenting with human subjects, so let me assure you that the experiments to be discussed have enriched the lives of the learners involved, and they have also contributed greatly to the enrichment of education generally for children all over the world. Furthermore, they have increased our understanding of the development of personality, since our personalities are in part an expression of the capabilities and limitations of our cognitive processes.

EARLY DEVELOPMENT: THE SENSORIMOTOR
PERIOD AND JEAN PIAGET

Jean Piaget is a Swiss scientist in his eighties who has devoted his career to the study of the development of thinking in children. Piaget brought an innovative approach to educational research, a basically simple one: he observed children, one at a time, reacting to various types of problems. He regarded each child as a unique individual trying to understand the environment with an intellect that was not fully formed or mature. From the similarities and differences between their responses, and between their responses and those of learners who are older and younger, he identified common thought patterns used to deal with the problems by learners of roughly the same age. He concluded that all children show certain early thought patterns, and that they graduate from one stage to another, with each stage showing more depth and complexity of thought. He said that no one skips stages, although some go through them more quickly than others.

Piaget named the earliest period of cognitive development the "sensorimotor period." During this period, physical (motor) activities became integrated with seeing and hearing and feeling, to form a foundation for later motor, personal-social, and cognitive development (Piaget and Inhelder, 1969).

Schema

Almost immediately after birth a child can recognize familiar things, including his (or her) mother's face and regular events associated with feeding. The child's behavior patterns suggest that he does not recognize himself as something separate from the environment, however; to his brain, his own hand reaching out in front is no different from the mother's hand reaching toward him, or the sides of his crib. But a child does begin very early to form basic, simple concepts of the environment; for example, he begins to recognize similar things when they recur and he relates them to other events such as eating and drinking. You can tell this is so by his regular reactions to these recurring events.

These fundamental learnings combine what a child sees, hears, and feels, and what he does himself into an internal impression or record of experience that Piaget calls a "schema." For example, by gradually coordinating hands and arms with eyes and ears, the child develops basic schema related to such matters as reaching for a cup, his mother's appearance and feel at feeding, the size and contour of his crib, and later on, familiar and unfamiliar people. These schema are combinations of motor, tactile, auditory, and visual sensations. Some are related to feelings—fear, hope, love—and are developed by a procedure that we will describe later under the title "classical conditioning," in Chapter 8. Other schema involve the concept of what behavior gets certain effects, e.g., crying when wet or hungry, and these relate to "operant conditioning" discussed in the same chapter.

Seeing and reaching and touching and mouthing and feeling—all of these together form an infant's basic building blocks of learning throughout life.

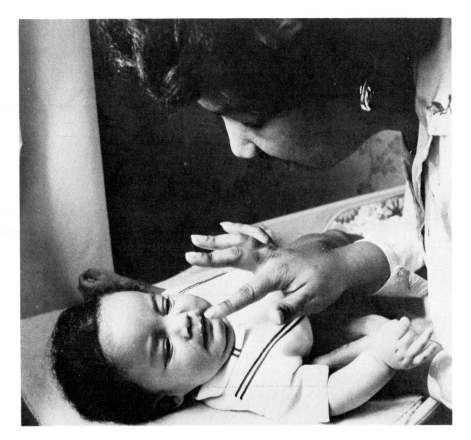

Developing schema related to feelings.

The importance of active learning

The infant seeks stimulation by lights and sounds, and tries to prolong interesting experiences and to manipulate things for the pleasure of it. Piaget and his followers have concluded from this that learning is an active process, not a passive one. (This in turn implies that learners should be put in situations where they can seek knowledge actively and independently.)   Gradually an infant develops internal representations of the world he or she experiences—schema—and they become the basis for thought. Evidence of this comes when a child continues to look for something that has disappeared, showing that he or she has a mental image of what was there. (This ability to think about things that are not present will take another giant step later on in adolescence.) During this sensorimotor period, physical, social, and cognitive matters are all practically one, with most of the social development related to the mother (or nurses) and how they treat the child. Children who are put into foster homes or placed for adoption probably experience deprivation feelings during this period which will affect them later on. Children who are born in hospitals and taken from their mothers very early—or for a large part of the day—may also suffer some deprivation effects. One study has shown clearly that this early separation policy has significant effects on the behavior of the mother toward the child which lasts for years; it may be that similar effects will be sought and found in the infants themselves (Bronfenbrenner, 1976).

Experiments involving both animals and humans have shown that the interrelationship between motor behavior (activity) and perception is an important one. In one experiment, adults were given eyeglasses made of prisms that distorted their view of the world and required a period of adaptation before they could function adequately. Adults who were wheeled around in a wheelchair during the adaptation period did not adapt as well as those who walked around on their own (Held, 1965). Thus, when put in the infantile situation of learning to "see," the amount of motor interaction with the environment made a significant difference in the adults' ability to adapt, i.e., to learn.

Effects of sensorimotor learning on the brain

There is some research with animals that suggests that if you provide an environment with things to explore and to master and to solve, you may encourage greater development of the nerve cells which make up the brain, and this may in turn increase later ability to learn. For example, providing rats with an environment rich in opportunities to explore holes and climb over boxes and do other things that rats are adapted to results in greater growth of their brains (Krech, 1970). Formal training such as teaching the rats to press a lever in response to a signal, or to run a maze, also produces changes, but to a lesser degree. Whether similar experience produces physiological changes in human brain structure is debatable, but as you will find in later chapters (particularly Chapters 2 and 3) early enrichment of learning experiences does result in better performance in school and on intelligence tests.

The changes in the brains of animals described previously take place not only through increases in the number of nerve fibers in the brain, but also in the size of synapses. Synapses are the junctions where one nerve cell transmits signals to a neighboring nerve cell, as shown in Figure 1–1. The process is a combination of electric and chemical phenomena.

MICHELE MOVES A MOBILE

Michele, as a baby, had a colored ball hanging over her crib, so that she could reach it with her hands. Very early in her life, at about 3½ months, she would study the ball as it swung about from an accidental hit that she gave it. Not long after that, at about five months, her mother noticed that she would set it swinging quite often, too often to assume it was entirely accidental. Her mother began to watch more closely, and noted that it was a sort of game for Michelle; she would set the ball in motion and watch it in a way that indicated she enjoyed doing it and had mastered the skill of making it swing when she wanted it to. She did not watch it as intently as she had earlier, however, and this seemed to indicate that she knew in advance what was going to happen, and that it was not anything new or important. Evidently she now assimilated the experience into her mental schema, where earlier it was something strange which she couldn't assimilate, and therefore had to try to accommodate to. This was a form of learning, then, where something that was initially strange and attention-getting was now something familiar and understood, although she still enjoyed playing the game, and thus evidently liked to demonstrate her mastery of the situation (adapted from Piaget, 1952).

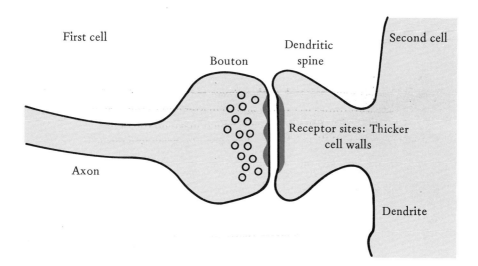

First cell

Bouton

Dendritic spine

Second cell

Axon

Receptor sites: Thicker cell walls

Dendrite

Figure 1–1. *Synaptic junctions of the brain. The vesicles in the bouton at the end of the axon of one nerve cell contain a chemical that transmits the signal to the next cell. When an electrical signal (i.e., a change in the number of electrons present) is transmitted from the center of the cell out through the axon to the end, this chemical is released. It moves across the gap between the two cells and acts on the receptor sites in the dendrite; this chemical action sets up an electric impulse that travels along the dendrite of the next cell to its center and out its axons, where the same communication process takes place with the other cells. (Adapted from M. R. Rosensweig, E. L. Bennett, and M. C. Diamond, Brain changes in response to experience, Scientific American, © February 1972. All rights reserved.)*

PHYSICAL DEVELOPMENT

Physical growth and nurturance

Each of us develops physically according to genetic (inherited) characteristics that determine whether we will be short or tall, fat or thin, or early or late maturing. However, within limits, the environment determines our growth as well: whether we have good nutrition, whether we exercise and thus promote bone growth at points of stress, or whether we have illnesses that retard growth of certain parts at certain critical periods.   More than that, there are emotional involvements also. For example, infants who have been neglected over a long period of time do not develop certain physical and mental abilities as well as normal children (Spitz, 1945).   As another example, some cases have been found where one of two siblings (i.e., brothers or sisters) has been deprived of love and attention by his or her parents, but the other has not; this has resulted in failure of the deprived child to grow in comparison with the other.   This growth loss has been reversed by placing the child in another, more nurturing home (Gardner, 1972).   (Lack of growth may be related to inadequate secretion of a hormone; this, in turn, seems to result from lack of normal sleep brought about by the deprivation of love and attention.)

In normal growth, the development of muscular strength and stamina is obviously dependent upon both natural endowments and the degree to which events have called for the use of those endowments, generally or specifically.   Talented athletes would not think of competing without a long regimen of training beforehand, no matter how much natural ability they have.   Records in swimming and track and other sports are broken yearly because training begins earlier and becomes more efficient.

General trends of physical growth

There are common trends in physical development, as well as great individual variations.

Physical development is usually irregular, occurring in spurts and plateaus, with occasional backsliding.   (A "plateau" is a level place on a graph that is drawn to show the growth pattern visually.)   These regressions and plateaus can result from a number of factors, including hereditary patterns, illnesses, nutritional deficiencies that stunt growth, and other factors not thoroughly understood.   These factors apply to cognitive development as well, as you will see in Chapter 2.

You will find also that physical as well as cognitive differences between children tend to *increase* as they grow older, when all information is taken into account.   Children who are slightly shorter at a given age will, on the average, be noticeably shorter later on (although some will be late maturing and will catch up or surpass the others).   Similarly, differences in very young children in walking age are only a matter of a few months, but differences in the age of reaching sexual maturity sometimes amount to several years.

Still another general characteristic of physical development is that the less refined, more general actions or responses that are characteristic of people generally

Growth occurs in spurts and plateaus among children of the same age.

appear first; the more refined and limited ones appear later. This is especially evident in the development of athletic skills, where a person may show a rough overall version of some skill initially and only later develop this into a smooth movement.

A number of characteristics of growth are observable when measurements are taken of many children. For example, although growth is a continuous process, it proceeds unevenly, and different parts of the body grow at different rates. The body as a whole grows quickly from birth until about five, then slows down though still growing, and then speeds up again at about fifteen. The brain, on the other hand, grows rapidly up to about seven, then levels off and stops growing at about ten. The genitals and internal reproductive organs do not grow much at all until adolescence.

In addition, it is important to realize that different aspects of growth may be dominant in different people at a given time: Johnny's dental growth may be advanced and his wrist-bone growth retarded, while Billy may have the reverse pattern. Everyone matures in a unique pattern, yet according to unvarying general processes.

Evaluation of physical (motor) development

In dealing with children who have difficulty with physical tasks, or what are called "motor" tasks, teachers and psychologists use a number of screening and evaluating

Table 1–1. *Some gross-motor and fine-motor abilities correlated with age.*

Gross	Age	Fine
Lifts head when lying on stomach Rolls over	0–½	Puts hands together Grasps rattle
Stands holding on Pulls self to stand Gets to sitting position Walks holding furniture	½–1 yr.	Bangs two blocks together Thumb-finger grasp of small object
Walks Walks up steps Kicks ball forward Throws ball overhand	1–2 yr.	Builds tower of blocks Dumps something from a bottle Scribbles spontaneously
Balances on one foot one second Jumps in place	2–3 yr.	Copies a circle with a crayon or pencil Copies a cross

Adapted from the Denver Developmental Screening Test.   Reprinted with permission.

instruments.   Among these are the Denver Developmental Screening Test, which is used to identify children who may experience motor problems, the Purdue Perceptual Motor Survey, and the Oseretsky Tests.   Table 1–1 presents some of the abilities examiners are looking for when screening with the "Denver"; it gives you an idea of the actual abilities that we can expect at different ages.   Table 1–2 lists some of the kinds of abilities that are surveyed in the Purdue (altered slightly so that the security of the test will not be jeopardized) and similar facsimile tasks for the Oseretsky battery.   These tests have been "standardized" by trying them out on large numbers of children of different ages, recording individual performances, and then using these data to develop "norms" or average expectancies for different ages. As a result, you can give the tasks to one child and determine how that child performs in relation to others of his or her age or grade group.   However, you should not expect any individual child to be equal to or above his or her age group norm on all tests, since these are average performances, not minimum ones.

MS. HOLMES HANDLES A PROBLEM

Ms. Holmes was upset because Ron was giving her trouble, both in and out of class.   He was in the wrong place, or extremely bellicose for no reason at all, or did not want to do anything he was supposed to do.   He seemed indifferent to success or failure.   She talked to Ms. Hildebrand about this, saying, "If he weren't such a peewee I'd really land on him, but he's so small I hate to give him a hard time myself—the other kids do that already."   Ms. Hildebrand did not seem too upset or surprised.   She told Ms. Holmes that children this age often went through such periods, especially if they were a bit on the short side.   She said the best thing to

Table 1–2. *Some facsimiles of tasks from the Purdue Perceptual Motor Survey.*

The examiner asks the child to walk along a board two inches in width and raised a few inches above the floor.

The examiner asks the child to skip across the room and back.

The examiner asks the child to touch his right ear with his left hand.

The examiner assumes an odd position and asks the child to imitate it.

Some facsimiles of tasks from the Oseretsky Tests of Motor Proficiency.

For ten-year-old girls: Throw a plastic ball at a circle drawn on the wall two yards away.

For thirteen-year-old boys: Balance a baseball bat on the palm of the hand for six seconds.

For fifteen-year-old girls: Stand on one foot with eyes closed for fifteen seconds.

For fifteen-year-old boys: Balance on the left foot with the right leg extended forward and eyes closed for fifteen seconds.

do would be to treat Ron as if he were six feet tall and two hundred pounds, and to give him attention in a way that implied that he was important and equal to the other boys his age. She said that it was all right to get after him if he did not perform, as long as it was done just the same way as with the other, bigger boys. Ms. Holmes tried this out, and also relaxed a little bit and did not get so uptight about Ron's behavior. She talked to Ron with a slightly different tone in her voice: more person-to-person than adult-to-child. Ron did not change overnight or become perfect, but he relaxed a bit and also began to get a few things done and to cause less difficulty. It seemed that Ms. Holmes' recognition of the nature of the problem was a step toward a solution, even though she could not put her finger on exactly what she did or said that made the difference.

Growth spurts

The adolescent growth spurt is related to sexual maturity, and shows great variations in onset time. It has effects on personality and self-concept.

Speed of growth decreases consistently after birth, and is slowest between the ages of eight and eleven. Then it picks up again as the learner heads into a growth spurt which signifies adolescence. Along with this increase in speed of growth comes development of the genitals in boys and breasts in girls, and of pubic hair in both. The development of musculature follows roughly the same pattern. As shown in Figure 1–2 there are great differences in the timing of this growth spurt from one learner to another. For girls it may reach its peak as early as ten and a half and as late as fourteen and a half; in boys, as early as twelve and as late as seventeen. Thus, one boy might complete his spurt at thirteen and a half, and have neared his adult height, while another may not begin until he is fifteen.

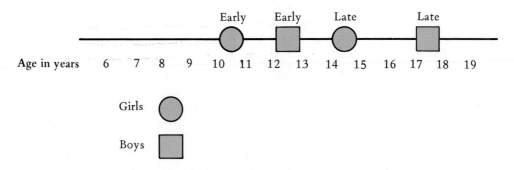

Figure 1–2. *Age at which early-maturing and late-maturing adolescents have their highest rates of growth (i.e., their growth "spurt").*

Developmental disabilities

Some particular aspects of the very complex subject of early physical development are worth mentioning here because they relate closely to problems that children have in the early grades. For example, infants are generally nonsymmetric in their movements; they don't reach for things with both hands or coordinate their left and right limbs well. They orient themselves in space only gradually. By the age of four, however, most are able to reach for toys with both hands at once. Some may not show such lateral balance even at five years, and others may develop one side far beyond the other (of course, we all do this to an extent), or they may not develop a preferred side at all. Also, some children are unable to reach across an imaginary line down their middle; they can't reach for things on their left side with their right hand (this is called "crossing the mid-line"). Such children may have difficulties later on in being competitive in playground games and in learning to read from left to right, or they may reverse letters and words in writing. They may need special attention of a type discussed further in Chapter 4 (Learning Disabilities).

Some children have difficulty skipping or they cannot jump without keeping one foot touching the ground ("earthbound"). Some, if placed on their hands and knees and then asked to turn their heads, cannot keep one of their arms from collapsing as their head turns. This is a primitive adjustment mechanism that affects more complex motor skills.

In a similar way, some children cannot lie prone (on their stomach) and lift their heads, arms, and feet off the floor. Others can do so for only a few seconds. Other developmental difficulties include poor equilibrium reactions that make it difficult to keep balance and tactile defensiveness that makes the learner very sensitive and resistant to being touched or hugged. There are remedial procedures for helping such children, and in many cases they can be brought to a level of ability that supports more complex motor learning, as well as adequate school learning. Some of these remedies are presented in Chapter 12.

Disabilities related to development, many of them involving the central nervous system of the body, have been classified in recent years as "developmental disabilities." This classification is practical because many of these disabilities call for the same kind of remedial systems (therapies, facilities, equipment), and because a particular child will often have more than one of them.

The relationship of physical development and personal–social development

The physical development of the learner relates to her or his personality in many ways: strength, coordination, physique, facial appearance, impulsiveness, susceptibility to disease, resistance to extremes of temperature and other climate conditions, and early or late maturation during adolescence. (More about this last matter later on.)   Personality development also has to do with cognitive development; your cognitive stage, discussed in the next chapter, affects the ways in which you deal with peers and adults.   Personality, however, is more than physical characteristics or mental abilities or moral development.   It is the combination of all these factors.   In order to study such a complex matter, it is necessary to break it down somewhat, and that is what we will do next.

THEORIES OF PERSONAL-SOCIAL DEVELOPMENT

Is development embryonic or hierarchical?

Before birth the fetus goes through a number of stages characterized by the increased growth and development of certain parts of the body; poor maternal nutrition or other "insult" (e.g., addiction to heroin) will be especially damaging to whichever part of the fetus is in its critical period of development when this occurs. This exemplifies "embryonic" development: each part has "its day," but does not depend on the development of other parts before it or contribute to development of other parts after it (Loevinger, 1966).   Freud's theory of personality development, discussed in the next section, parallels this type of development.

Another kind of development is "hierarchical."   Here each stage *is* dependent on the completion of a previous stage, and contributes directly to a following stage; an organism does not skip stages.   Piaget's theories of cognitive development are of this type, as are theories of ego development and moral development described later in this chapter.   There is an ongoing debate about hierarchical theories. Some theorists claim that there is not sufficient evidence to assert that stages cannot be skipped and that a given order is necessary (Phillips and Kelly, 1975).

Freud's oral, anal, and Oedipal stages

Freud's developmental theories are relatively ancient, yet basic to modern theories.

Freud (1949) dealt with people of many ages, and one of his primary methods was to delve into their memories of childhood and its problems.   From his experience with many patients, he developed a theory of early childhood development that involved three distinct stages which he called "oral," "anal," and "phallic" or "Oedipal."   In the "oral" stage babies get their primary gratification from sucking and eating; Freud pointed out that this was a "receiving" relationship between the child and her or his mother or nurse.   He theorized that emotions connected with this stage formed basic patterns for adult feelings and behaviors in "receiving" situations.   For example, if an infant should be thwarted or inadequately satisfied in her feeding, she might grow up to be a heavy eater or drinker as a result.   More generally, she might develop an extreme need for, or dependence on, other people. This inability to develop beyond the needs and patterns of a particular stage is referred to as a "fixation," and the adult is said to be "fixated" at that stage.

The "anal" period comes next; here urinating and defecating at the right time and in the right place are important skills to be mastered. These body functions involve giving out, or expelling, rather than taking in and receiving as in the oral stage. Thus they give the child an opportunity to thwart his or her parents by holding in or by letting go at the wrong time. The way parents go about toilet training, and how they react to "accidents," will affect the grown child's attitudes toward *future* situations that involve withholding and expelling. Perseverance, conscientiousness, and stubbornness are said to be traits strengthened by the experiences of this period.

The third stage was called the "phallic" period, beginning at about the third year. Here the child begins to become aware of boy-girl differences, and attitudes toward sexual organs are established. Also, a boy may experience the beginnings of unconscious competition and conflict with his father for the love and possession of his mother, while a girl may experience the converse. Freud called this conflict between son and father for the love of the mother the *Oedipal conflict*. The normal resolution is for the boy to accept the status quo and identify with the father, postponing his gratification until he matures and can have a woman of his own. A boy who is unable to come to terms with his Oedipal conflict and continues to compete, or who gives up completely without hope of someday assuming the father's role himself, is destined to have difficulties in adolescence, in coming to terms with his sexual maturation, and in assuming masculine roles.

After the phallic stage, Freud asserted that the child enters a "latency" period that extends from about age six to ten. During this period he concluded there were no significant changes or crises of a sexual nature until the onset of puberty (the "genital" stage).

Psychologists and psychiatrists today utilize many of the basic concepts of this theory without accepting its simplistic predictions and relationships. Many modern theories reflect the basic assumption that if a person is unsuccessful in resolving the conflicts of one period in his (or her) life, that person may become fixated at that stage, and his development will be incomplete, and so will his adult personality. Freud's emphasis on the importance of understanding past experience in dealing with the present has been widely accepted and applied: only in the last twenty years has it been challenged by behavioral approaches which deal with present behaviors and feelings without trying to clear up concerns and feelings in relation to the past. These behavioral principles are discussed in several places in this book, particularly in Chapters 8 and 12.

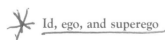 Id, ego, and superego

Another of Freud's theoretical contributions was his treatment of the mature personality as a balance between three imaginary forces called the "id," the "ego," and the "superego." Freud derived this "model" of personality from many experiences with adult patients in which he discussed their early lives and tried to identify the effects of early experiences on subsequent behaviors and feelings. Just as scientists in more traditional fields—physics, chemistry, and the like—develop models to explain the things they observe, so Freud developed a system involving three forces to explain what he observed in human personalities and behavior. One of the three was a basic drive for survival and satisfaction of selfish desires; Freud called it the "id." Another was an inhibiting, idealistic force that opposed the tendencies of the id; he called it the "superego." Finally, Freud hypothesized that there is an internal arbitrator between the id and the superego, one which integrates them in order to cope with reality; this he called the "ego." Your id tells you to do something because you want to, because it will be pleasurable, because you need it and deserve it; your superego inhibits this drive because it may lead to trouble, or because it does not match your image of ideal behavior; the ego considers the reality of the situations, your needs, and the possible good and bad results of behaving in the way in question, and then makes a decision that is for the good of yourself generally, i.e., it adjusts the inclinations of the id and superego to reality. Neurosis or neurotic behavior arises from dominance of the superego: the neurotic personality is beset by anxieties, fears, and guilt, as well as by fantasies of power and living up to high ideals. Psychosis, on the other hand, represents a domination by the id; a psychotic can find many rationalizations, sometimes bizarre, to justify selfish behavior and to avoid the guilt and anxiety caused by selfish, inconsiderate actions, or he may simply ignore the needs and requirements of society and do whatever occurs to him at the moment. Another kind of problem involves an ego that is too weak to balance the id and superego, even though neither dominates the other. This

BILLY'S WEAK EGO

Billy had a problem of balance. He could not resist certain temptations to "let himself go." For example, if he were given a record player and a set of records, he had to start flipping them around the room like Frisbees, and if he were given some ping-pong equipment and a table, he would then throw the ping-pong ball at whoever was around, rather than playing the game. He could not use things for what they were intended; everything became a means of attacking the world. Then, afterwards, he would seem to shrivel up and pull his head into his shell, overcome with remorse, ready for punishment, contrite, and in an anguish of remorse and guilt. This would last for a while—until the next outburst! His id would govern one moment, and then his superego would take over and punish him internally. He could not control either—

life was a cycle of recurrent misbehavior-guilt sequences.

A long process of treatment began eventually to help Billy monitor his behavior and begin to bring it under effective control. The treatment involved a number of things: opportunities to take out his aggressions in harmless ways; being treated by adults in a way that deemphasized guilt, remorse, and fear of punishment; training in thought processes that involved matters of looking ahead, controlling behavior, and considering consequences in advance; and generally considerate, supportive, warm, affectionate, but not overindulgent treatment. It was a slow process, and it was not clear whether Billy would ever develop the kind of ego that other children had acquired, but it was an improvement.

has been called a "pauperized ego" (Redl, 1944). Sometimes it results from overuse of punishment by authoritarian figures, or from domination by parents so that the person never learns to make independent decisions. People with weak egos will vacillate between selfish and unrestrained acts on the one hand, and great guilt and anxiety over having committed these acts on the other. They have a hard time postponing gratification, e.g., waiting their turn or saving money for something they want.

Loevinger's stages of ego development

According to a modern ego-psychologist, intellectual development, ego development and psychosexual development are almost indistinguishable during the early years (Loevinger, 1966). Loevinger's analysis of the development of ego gives us insight into stages of personal and social growth. In her view the first stage is an "autistic" one, where the infant is preoccupied with self, and only slowly begins to differentiate between self and non-self. In this stage there is no social behavior, and animate things are not differentiated from inanimate. Later in this stage, however, the infant forms a concept of self which includes his or her mother, with everything else being non-self.

The second stage is an "impulsive" one, where the infant begins to exercise his or her own will, with little impulse-control. To the impulsive-stage child actions are bad only because they are punished, and interpersonal relations are essentially exploitative, although not consciously so; that is, people are seen as sources of supply. The infant is concerned with sex and aggressive drives, so that preoccupation with bodily functions is typical, as in Freud's oral, anal, and genital stages.

The third of Loevinger's stages is an "opportunistic" or "self-protective" stage. Rules are obeyed in terms of immediate advantage; morality is expedient. What is "bad" is to be caught. The child is beginning to be able to delay action when it is to his or her immediate advantage. However, there is no real superego, i.e., the child does not experience *shame* for doing wrong.

The fourth stage is "conformist"; the child begins to internalize rules and identify with authority to some degree. She or he also begins to feel shame over doing wrong, indicating the development of a superego. However, rules are obeyed primarily because they are rules, not for any higher reason. Genuine interpersonal reciprocity is now possible; the Golden Rule is paramount. However, this reciprocity and trust may operate within a narrow group only, with prejudice evidenced against out-groups. Friendliness and social niceness are important; individual differences are scarcely perceived. (Loevinger feels that the majority of people in our society are "fixated" at this conformist stage; they do not progress beyond it.)

Her fifth stage is a "conscientious" one, where the person is concerned over inner feelings and moral guidelines, and preoccupied with obligations, ideals, and achievement as measured by inner standards. Conduct is seen as the result of enduring propensities, rather than of pressure to conform, or of punishment and

Loevinger's theories are a modern outgrowth of Freud's, and tell us what to expect of personality at different ages.

". . . animate things are not distinguished from inanimate . . ."

reward.   High school seniors and college students are apt to be in this stage; they can see multiple possibilities in every situation, partly because they have reached a new stage of cognitive development as well, the "formal operational" stage.   This is discussed in Chapter 2.

The sixth is an "autonomous" stage.   Here impulse control has been attained, and the major problem is coping with inner conflicts, conflicting duties, and conflicting needs.   There is toleration for those choosing different solutions, where these people would have been condemned on moral grounds earlier.   Mutual independence and the need of others for autonomy are recognized.   There is a preoccupation with individuality and self-fulfillment.   Relations with others become deeper and more intense and begin to be seen as incompatible with the striving for achievement and excessive moralism and responsibility that were typical of the conscientious stage.

Loevinger has also proposed that there is an ultimate stage which is quite rare, where the reconciliation of conflicting demands, renunciation of unattainable objectives, and appreciation for individual differences all come about.   She relates this to the concept of the "self-actualized" person described by Maslow, presented in Chapter 6.

You may want to think of your own personality development in terms of Loevinger's stages, and review these stages to improve your concept of "ego."

Learning requires a sense of self and of confidence in oneself in order to tolerate the insecurity and anxiety involved in changing one's thinking and behavior; this means a well-developed ego.

MR. SMITH OVERMORALIZES

Mr. Smith was teaching a fifth grade class in social studies, and he found that the children were cheating "all over the place" on his tests. He became somewhat upset, and got the class together and discussed with them the concepts of faith, and trust, and being honest with themselves. He stressed the idea that we do right because we want to be true to ourselves, and we do not want to act in a way that jeopardizes others, either. Furthermore, he said, we want to realize our own potential, and cheating will confuse this quest and make us something less than we might be.

The children listened politely; they seemed to have some respect for what he said, and to be considering it carefully. There was less cheating on the next quiz, but later it began to pick up again, until it was right back where it started.

You might see this as a failure on Mr. Smith's part to recognize the ego stage of the students. Since they were pretty much in the conformist stage, and since abstract concepts of honesty, trust, and the like were a bit beyond them, it should not have been surprising that they did a little backsliding. Perhaps he should have gone at them with a "conformist" approach, i.e., discussed how in our society there are certain things one does and certain things one does not do. (Of course, he might not have convinced them of that, since evidently their peer group permitted such things, or saw them as part of normal behavior.) He might also have success in going back to "self-protective" strategies, i.e., invoking rules and penalties for cheating on the one hand, as well as rewards (perhaps bonuses), for doing tests without cheating, on the other.

Stages of moral development: Kohlberg

Kohlberg's theories have received wide attention partly because moral development is a serious current concern of society.

The developmental process just described represents a composite of views of personality theorists since Sigmund Freud, so it is less sexually oriented and less focused on the basic id-ego-superego model than Freud's. Another theory of development which resembles this one is based on Jean Piaget's work on moral development. The theorist is Lawrence Kohlberg, who takes what he calls a "progressive" view of education, thus acknowledging the influence of John Dewey as well (Kohlberg, 1976). According to Kohlberg, the aim of education is to bring the child to attain higher levels or stages of development in adulthood than he or she might if things were left to chance. The basic strategy for achieving this is to arrange the learner's environment so that it presents genuine problems or conflicts for the learner to resolve. In solving these problems, the learner makes progress toward a higher stage of development. The force which organizes the environment and leads to development is the child's active thinking, and such thinking is stimulated by confronting problems. (This approach anticipates later discussions of problem solving as a method of teaching, in Chapters 10 and 12.)

Kohlberg divides moral development into three main stages: preconventional, conventional and postconventional. Each of these has two substages. In the preconventional stage, the child is dominated by his or her own egocentric desires. The first substage is a primitive one (typical of children up to about seven) where "right" is what authority figures (parents, teachers) ordain to be right. Children behave in order to avoid punishment (i.e., due to fear of punishment, such as spanking or withdrawal of love). The second substage of the preconventional period is one where children begin to seek rewards and have their favors returned. This is typical of preadolescents, roughly seven through ten. A young girl at this stage may dress neatly, but will also expect some kind of reward, be it an approving word from her mother or father, or something more tangible. Kohlberg calls this the "back-scratching" stage.

In the conventional stages, first "conformity" and then "law and order" are the guidelines. These stages are based on a recognition of the rules laid down by society. In the conformist substage, from about eleven to thirteen or fourteen, "good" is behavior that is approved of by others, including peer groups. Intentions are also taken into account. Thus early adolescents may fail to meet accepted standards of behavior at home partly because they are trying to gain approval of a peer group; if they are late for supper because a football game was still going, they may excuse it by saying that they really *meant* to live up to them! In the second substage ("law and order") the source of approval may be somewhat more interna-

In conventional stages, cheating is against the rules.

lized; they may do things because they are "right," or in order to show respect for authority. The law takes precedence over personal needs, intentions, or conformity to the group. Cheating is out because it is against the rules, regardless of group norms or the danger of flunking if you don't cheat! The reasoning which evidently is behind this is that you should maintain the social order rather than accede to personal wishes, good intentions, or conformity to group norms; thus prisons are necessary and right, even though they may have undesirable characteristics, because they are a part of the system for keeping our society functioning. This morality, according to Kohlberg, is typical of most American *adults*.

The postconventional stages go beyond the "law and order" morality described above, to place emphasis on the general rights of the individual as guaranteed by society through such documents as the Constitution, particularly in the Bill of Rights. Kohlberg has estimated that only one out of five Americans has achieved this level, which he terms the "social contract" stage. The problems of the individual in relation to big government and ongoing debates concerning individual rights and freedom and their protection involve this level. The responsibilities of individuals toward their society and government are also implicit in this debate, but the next stage of moral development involves itself more deeply in this matter.

At this next level, called the level of "universal principles," the individual chooses principles of justice for himself or herself and makes decisions on the basis of them. The principles are comprehensive and also consistent with each other. At such a level, a citizen might conscientiously oppose certain laws that conflict with a personal set of principles, even though it means imprisonment or death to do

A MORAL PROBLEM AND KOHLBERG'S STAGES

Suppose a person wants to steal some medicine to help his sick mother, because he cannot afford it and the pharmacy will not give him credit. A preconventional person would consider this act as to whether he would be punished and whether people would disapprove. A conventional person would judge it as to whether or not it is the "right" thing, and he would weigh the rightness of helping his mother against the wrongness of stealing. The postconventional person would consider whether or not he would earn the respect of others and of himself, and would judge this against his standards of honesty and of helping others.

Suppose a person is in the conventional stage, and that you are trying to help him handle a problem. Suppose this problem involves something he or someone else has done, as in the case of stealing the medicine. He may have come to the conclusion that he did the wrong thing, because stealing is just not done, no matter what the reason. Then you would want to bring him out of this conventional stage and into a postconventional stage—at least, you might want to *try*. Kohlberg's theory implies that this would be a waste of your time in most cases, because chances are he would not be ready to pass or mature into the next stage, and there would not be anything you could do yourself, for or with him, that would get him *to* the stage. A more likely strategy, then, would be to work within the conventional stage, and try to bring him around to seeing that what he did was the "right" thing, in terms of the way most people act.

⑦

so. Kohlberg mentions Socrates, Mahatma Gandhi, and Martin Luther King, Jr., as examples.

There have been projects designed to apply Kohlberg's theories in public schools and to encourage the progress of learners toward higher stages. Some of these have the conservative objective of moving learners up to stage four (law and order) by the end of high school. Teachers are trained in discerning levels of moral response, and they are shown how to present students with stories illustrating moral dilemmas for discussion. They assume that any class will have students of higher as well as lower levels, and therefore the teacher can react more positively to statements that represent higher levels. Through such methods, some students at lower stages may come to realize that they can solve troubling moral dilemmas by adopting a higher stage of moral reasoning. Kohlberg has also been experimenting with special "intentional" school communities where the students draw up and try to abide by their own social contracts. Experiments so far have not been as effective as had been hoped, and peer pressure has turned out to be the chief motivation for adolescent behavior.

⑧

Stages of psychosocial development: Erikson's hypotheses

Erik Erikson (1968) has developed a theory about social development which he calls "psychosocial development," indicating a parallel to Freud's psychosexual stages. Erikson's eight stages represent an attempt to identify the most crucial concerns of people throughout their lives, from early childhood to old age.

Erikson's theories identify the most crucial needs of learners at various ages, and suggest what one might do about them—even for post-adolescents and adults.

Erikson's first stage comes in infancy, and he sees its basic problem as one of developing *trust versus mistrust* of others. This attitude is based on the infant's close contact with his or her mother; if a mother reduces the quality of her care during the first year, then the baby will feel a more traumatic sense of loss than if it happened later. This might result in a basic sense of mistrust lasting throughout life. The second stage comes during early childhood, where Erikson feels that the basic problem for the child is that of *autonomy versus shame and doubt*. At this time of his life a child is exploring his world and his family relationships, and if he is defeated in his attempts to assert his role in the family structure, he may learn to expect defeat and may fail to develop a sense of autonomy. This can happen if parents are extremely authoritarian and keep the child constantly "down." The third stage comes in the preschool and early-school period and is characterized by an expansion of the child's horizons beyond the family and by the development of clearer family relationships; the central problem is *initiative versus guilt,* or the establishment of conscience. The development of a conscience is of course a necessary process, but if too strong a conscience is created, the result may be either inhibition and guilt, or overreaction through vindictiveness. The fourth stage occurs during school ages, when the child decides between *industry and inferiority*. He (or she) wants to learn to make and do things with others, but he needs to receive rec-

ERIKSON AND THE ADOLESCENT IDENTITY TRAP

When you begin to deal professionally or parentally with adolescents, the problem of delinquency or illegal behavior is one of the hardest things to cope with and understand. Stealing, drinking, taking drugs, and breaking traffic laws are among the most frequent of these violations. What do you do, you may ask, when a student whips out a knife in an argument, or when your son is arrested for drug possession, or when you find heroin equipment in your daughter's room? By taking into account Erikson's theory that the adolescent can unwittingly be trapped in an identity that he happens to "try on for size," you may begin to understand that what seem to be self-destructive or rebellious tendencies are actually the result of the person's trying to find himself. For example, suppose a young boy takes a girl for a ride in somebody else's car, which he intends to abandon rather than steal. This boy may have decided that the only way he can attain any identity, to *be* somebody, is to go this route. Calling him a criminal, punishing him, or scolding him will not affect this concern. In a sense, the fact that he is holding onto a definite, active identity of any kind may be healthier for him, in terms of his overall development, than withdrawing into complete conformity and frustration. In other words, some boys and girls who get into serious trouble actually show more strength and potential for contributing to our society than do others who conform excessively or who become neurotically defeatist about their dreams and hopes and needs. Erikson calls such phases of development as the stealing behavior "psychosocial moratoriums," which are periods of delay in the overall process of assuming adolescent commitments. He does not suggest extreme permissiveness or lack of standards generally, but he does call for different standards of treatment for adolescents going through this phase. *The Car Thief*, by Theodore Weesner (1972), is one book which deals with such problems.

ognition for his efforts and needs the tools and raw materials for "making" and "doing." When these are absent, he may develop a sense of inferiority and a lack of initiative. The fifth stage comes during adolescence, and the problem is to form an identity rather than have the identity diffused and lost; thus *identity versus identity diffusion.* The adolescent must integrate earlier concepts, schemes, and patterns with emerging adult roles and new biological drives. This often results in a diffusion, i.e., a loss of identity, which can prevent the youth from finding himself or herself. One result of this is an adolescent's fixation on a negative self-concept, with attempts to become anything *but* what his parents and society want him to be. The sixth stage, during young adulthood, involves the problem of *intimacy versus isolation.* Some young adults cannot enter into an intimate relationship, partly because they have not established their identity sufficiently to risk losing it in this way. Yet, ironically, this stage comes at a time when it is customary to marry. In the seventh stage, during adulthood, the problem is *generativity versus self-absorption.* The mature person is interested in establishing and guiding the next generation, but some people remain self-absorbed instead. The eighth stage comes in old age, or senescence, and the problem is one of *integrity versus disgust.* Here the successful person is one who is able to maintain his or her own identity and sense of satisfaction in the face of increasing physical deterioration and dependence upon others.

The search for identity.

Generally Erikson stresses a moving outward: from mother to family to neighborhood to strange environments and different people. He observes that we tend to blame parents for many problems that are actually the result of other elements in the environment, and that we ignore the problems of aging.

Early development and later learning—and teaching

Erikson's view of psychosocial development is embryonic, like Freud's; Loevinger's, Kohlberg's, and Piaget's (continued in the next chapter) are hierarchical. Erikson assumes, as did Freud and other personality theorists, that different phases of development have times of special importance for them alone; an example is Freud's "oral" stage when the infant is preoccupied with taking in and spitting out and biting. If the parent or teacher cannot completely avoid problems during one of these periods, he or she can try to provide the necessary conditions for full development in each case.

What of a child who does not develop a sense of trust in the first year of life? Learning requires trust in the parent or teacher! It requires the learner to risk being "wrong," to take a chance on a new answer or way of doing something. Erikson asserts that experiences connected with feeding are a prime source for the development of trust, with the mother setting the model for dependability,

31

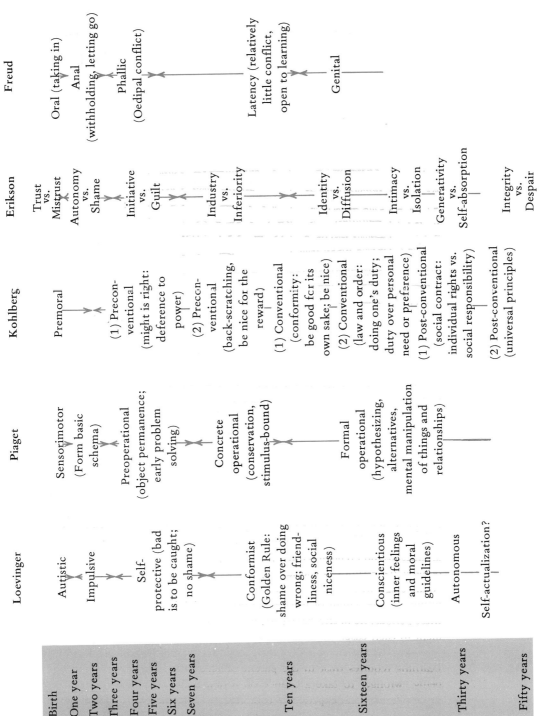

Figure 1–3. *Chart of developmental stages. Limits (beginnings and endings) are not absolute and are not always clearly stated by the theorists themselves. The sequence is more important than the ages.*

warmth, lack of punishment, and the like. Games of "peek-a-boo" during the early months teach the infant that things reappear when they go away, and that they aren't lost forever. This too can develop trust.

Infants deprived of care and affection do not develop a sense of trust, and they have a weak sense of responsibility later; they are listless, immobile, and unresponsive, not characteristics of good students at any level! The trust-mistrust period becomes most critical at about six to nine months when the child begins to move out of the "autistic stage" (Loevinger): infants who are separated from their mothers during this period react very badly, as if their faith has been shattered and there is nothing left.

In a similar manner, the development of *autonomy* in the young learner relates to his or her later ability to carry out work independently, as does the development of initiative in the four to five year old. This is crucial to the development of achievement motivation, which will be discussed in Chapter 7. Also related to achievement motivation is the development of the sense of industry during the school years; this puts great responsibility on schools and teachers to provide the kind of materials and learning tasks that encourage such development.

RESEARCH IN PERSONAL-SOCIAL DEVELOPMENT

Harlow's monkeys

There is a whole world of research and theory about child development which can only be touched upon here: Harlow's experiments represent one classic series of experiments.

The theories you have studied so far have been based on observations of children at various ages and stages, except in the case of Freud, who made his deductions on the basis of recollections of adult patients. There is a great deal of research on development, some of it using animals in order to have more control over the conditions under which development occurs. I cannot describe the whole range of such research, but I can discuss some representative studies.

In experiments during the 1950s and 1960s monkeys were raised in social isolation from birth. Such monkeys failed to develop appropriate play behavior, and they also lacked sexual, aggressive, and maternal behaviors characteristic of their species. Instead, they exhibited abnormal patterns such as hugging themselves and rocking back and forth in their cages (Harlow and Harlow). These behaviors are similar to those of children who are called "autistic." Early experiments designed to rehabilitate these monkeys were not successful; they carried these traits into adulthood. Later attempts were more successful; the isolated monkeys were encouraged to interact with normal monkeys three months younger, and as a result they began to develop normal social behaviors and came to be relatively normal (Suomi and Harlow, 1972). It is tempting to draw a parallel between the isolated monkeys and the stereotype of the overprotected child who has difficulty fitting in socially with his or her peers in normal play and school activities; one is also tempted to generalize the "cure" and suggest that such children be put into social situations with younger children, to see if they improve. However, autism in humans seems to be more complex than this.

In other experiments, Harlow raised monkeys from birth without their natural mothers. In the place of mothers, as "surrogates," he put an artificial "mother" made of wire to which the baby could cling, and from which he could feed from a nipple (Harlow, 1959). There were two kinds of surrogates: one of bare wire, and the other wire covered with soft fur. This made a great difference in that the babies with the warm, cuddly mothers would cling to them, retreat to them when something unfamiliar was introduced into their area, and would treat them as true surrogates. These babies developed normally, while those with wire mothers were more fearful and less well-developed socially. Again, then, it was demonstrated that early experience has a strong, formative effect on personality and social ability. As before, the question of how completely one can make up for early deprivations of this type is not settled.

Do early problems mean difficulty later on?

Studies of development of delinquent adolescents and unsuccessful adults have found developmental problems and assumed that such problems lead to the kind of troubles the subjects have had. However, longitudinal studies which follow children over many years (rather than looking back at a later time) have found that some early experiences which seemed damaging and predictive of later problems actually turned out to be learning and maturing experiences, and the person involved turned out quite well in spite of them. Some people did not achieve ego-identity (in Erikson's terms) until marriage and parenthood forced them to it, and presented an opportunity to fulfill a role that gave them a sense of worth. Some overdependent children became relatively independent and nurturant parents, without overdoing it and without spoiling their own children as their parents had them (Macfarlane, 1963). Another observation from one of these studies was that the best-adjusted people during childhood and adolescence were not necessarily the most interesting or dynamic adults, and that sometimes those who had many problems earlier turned out to be the most active and productive adults. Thus, learning that takes place early in life and forms the personality of the child can also take place later in life. Personality is a dynamic rather than a static thing. Observations of longitudinal development in another country (Guatemala) support this view (Kagan and Klein, 1973).

SOME SPECIAL GROWTH PERIODS

Changes occurring between five years and seven years

The period between the ages of five and seven seems to be one of important basic changes that are particularly significant for learning and progress, socially and in school (White, S., 1970). Some of these are described briefly and independently below. While they don't seem to hang together in a general pattern, each has implications for later development.

The period from five to seven years is evidently one involving important changes.

- By age seven the child's IQ (as indicated by intelligence tests) has become quite stable (this is discussed further in Chapter 3).
- Until the age of five, the child is particularly vulnerable to a variety of physiological ailments and handicaps, e.g., diabetes, convulsions, childhood autism, and the debilitating effects of hospitalization when it occurs; between five and seven the child becomes much less susceptible to such things.
- The child before five has slower reactions, and is less susceptible to the conditioning of reflexes and emotions and slower to become habituated to unusual conditions (conditioning processes are described in Chapter 8).
- During the five-to-seven period children show a sharply improved ability to act according to some proposition (i.e., a set of directions, or a certain role that they are asked to play); they are also able to maintain this activity over a period of time. This means they are more amenable to teaching, and they are more persistent in learning.
- There is an increase in certain kinds of memory, and in awareness of verbal and voluntary processes; i.e., they seem to be able to retain information better, and therefore to understand better.
- There is a decrease of emotional dependence on adults, and increased competition with their peers.
- Cross-modal integration of sensory information improves, i.e., relating sights and sounds and what they touch; this enables children to develop communication through language, where previously their language has been more imitative in nature (language development is discussed more extensively in the next chapter).
- During these ages there is a peak incidence of "tics," facial twitches and the like. Animal studies suggest that such tics evidence restraint of motor behavior. This suggests that at this period the child is learning restraint and internalizing actions rather than acting everything out.
- There is a diminution of stealing and lying after age six; this may evidence the development of a superego (conscience).
- The child from five to seven learns to reproduce order, develops perceptual constancies (this is explained in Chapter 2), learns sex roles, and becomes sensitive to racial identifications.

Preadolescence

The transitional period from childhood to preadolescence cannot be clearly delineated, although around nine years is the time in which the child now moves from a strong aca-

The particular
needs and concerns
of pre-adolescents
and middle-school
or junior high
learners has re-
ceived increased
attention in recent
years.

*demic being to a social being.   Many of his heretofore predictable behavioral patterns
start becoming less predictable.   Similarly, the well-defined values taught by parents
may begin being challenged by the child as the focus on attitudinal and value sources
moves more toward his peer group.   The changes that the preadolescent undergoes are,
in fact, distinct enough that the identification of preadolescence as a developmental
period seems warranted.   It is, however, recognized that developmental psychologists
may take issue with this viewpoint, as it is attested to by the fact that this ambiguous
developmental period is often referred to as late childhood or early adolescence in many
well-written psychology textbooks.   (Thornburg, 1974, pp. 4, 5)*

At age ten girls are slightly more advanced sexually; for both sexes fears and
anxieties are minimal, and there is increasing interest in parents, teachers, and
peers.   Sex differences in friendships emerge, and active participation in group
activities begins.   By age eleven this activity shows a distinct increase, and both
sexes are curious and eager for new things to happen.   They are beginning to exert
independence from parents and form friendships around mutual interests.   Girls
begin to show interest in the opposite sex, which becomes romantic interest at age
twelve (although boys still prefer the company of other boys).   Twelve year olds
are outgoing, enthusiastic, and generous, asserting adolescence by becoming competitive with parents in athletics and intellectual games.

Junior high or middle school years

At about thirteen adolescents begin to become preoccupied with themselves, frequently sulk and become angry.   They often reject attempts by adults to get them
to discuss problems.   Boys still show relatively little interest in girls, but girls increase dating over the previous year.   Overall this age is not as happy a one as heretofore, and these children seem to need more privacy and independent activity.
Boys mature and grow very rapidly in spurts.   Awkwardness and self-consciousness
accompany this fast growth.
     You should treat both errors of coordination and social relations with great
sensitivity, even though they appear minor to you.   You should expect more
refinement and sophistication in athletics and crafts, but since individuals mature
at different rates, be selective in your expectations and look for some to be way
behind.   Erikson's advice about identity traps is important: a consistent, firm assertion of guidelines for behavior must be coupled with an acceptance of each individual as potentially good, even though some of his or her behavior is "way-out"
and cannot be allowed.   A charitable hypocrisy is often helpful, in that you outwardly expect everyone to conform to expectations and you are obviously fair and
consistent, but privately you make allowances for individual differences along a
variety of dimensions.   You also have to allow for heavy peer influence in all your
dealings with these ages: they are not their own people, but they are continually
aware of and concerned with how their behavior appears to their group.

Varying views of adolescence (thirteen years through eighteen)

The study of adolescents is a complex field, with many different points of view; this is appropriate for a complex and sometimes chaotic period.

Anna Freud (1958), daughter of Sigmund, devoted much of her research and professional service to the problems of adolescence. According to her, during the preadolescent and adolescent years a growth spurt takes place, and sexual forces assert themselves strongly. This leads to a reawakening of urges that were experienced years before in the genital stage of development, for instance, competition with one parent for the love of the other. Since the adolescent is now bigger, stronger, and more intelligent, and thus has greater potential for competing with a parent, these urges are very threatening—there is the capability of following through, of actually winning the competition! Since this is threatening and causes guilt feelings, the adolescent seeks the company of others his or her own age or slightly older and stays away from the family. This is a normal, healthy solution, but it is seen by many parents as rejection. Some adolescents who are not accepted by their peers become prisoners in their own homes, unable to communicate with their parents but also unable to break away and join the social life of others their own age. Other adolescents overemphasize the values of their subculture and, driven by biological forces, go to extremes in conforming to peer group activities. This behavior sometimes gets them into trouble with society.

Another view of adolescence deemphasizes this concept of its being a turbulent period, and emphasizes instead the need to solve the social problems that are unique to adolescence (Adelson, 1970; Bandura and Walters, 1959; Havighurst, 1976). Some parents and local groups of parents make allowances for adolescent needs by supporting a special culture or society that involves athletics, clubs, dances, hiking trips, and the like. In such societies parents become the allies and sponsors of adolescents and provide social settings in which their needs are at least partly met. When a counterculture develops that rebels against this kind of parental support, it is hard to determine whether it is expressing dissatisfaction with such support as a solution, or dissatisfaction with the nature of the support (activities, facilities) that have been made available to them. Often it is a combination of the two, with some adolescents feeling that adults should stay out of it, while others feel that there is nothing for them to do and nowhere to go.

Adolescent personality characteristics

Dealing with adolescents requires that you understand their interests and needs.

The average adolescent demonstrates wide swings in mood and behavior. In addition to changes that are physical and sexual, cognitive changes take place which will be discussed in the next chapter. These changes result in increased ability to deal with ideas, and to compare life as it is with ideals the adolescents were taught previously. The combination results in varying moods of depression over their own inadequacies and weaknesses and elation over their new maturity and ability to deal with the world. They come to look for greater openness and honesty in dealing with social problems, particularly problems related to sex. They value tolerance, flexibility, and empathy in others, also liveliness, cheerfulness, good nature, and a sense of humor.   They want others to act "naturally" and self-confidently without being conceited, and to possess initiative, enthusiasm, drive, and plans for group activity.

Late-maturing boys.   Earlier in this chapter you found that the adolescent growth spurt comes at different times for different individuals; this has more than academic import.   One source has summarized some of the characteristics of later maturing adolescents, particularly boys, as compared with their earlier maturing peers (Mussen et al., 1974).   *Late* maturing boys are significantly higher or stronger in the following:

> *Attention getting behavior, restlessness, talkativeness, affectation and tenseness in manner, eagerness, feeling of inadequacy, negative self-concepts, feelings of rejection, feelings of domination, persistent dependency needs, rebellious searching for autonomy and freedom from restraint*

Late maturing boys are weaker or lower in the following:

> *Popularity with peers, leadership, self-control, responsibility*

Early maturing boys are more reserved, more self-assured, more matter-of-fact, more likely to engage in well-modulated and socially appropriate behavior, and more able to laugh at themselves.   Generally, this implies that socially they are more successful.   Late maturing boys as college students are higher in feelings of guilt, inferiority, depression, generalized anxiety, need for encouragement, sympathy, and understanding from others than the early or average maturing boys in college.   They are also lower in needs for leading, controlling, or dominating, are more anticonventional, mildly rebellious, and autonomy-oriented.   Generally they act as if they have not resolved the adolescent independence-dependence conflict.

Adolescent girls.   The characteristics that set late maturing boys apart are also true for girls, but to a lesser extent; with girls, the situation is evidently more complicated.   For one thing, early maturing girls find their condition something of a social handicap in the early grades, when other girls have not begun to mature and are not interested in the same things.   On the other hand, in junior high school, where the other girls are maturing rapidly, the early maturing girls become very popular and serve as models for the others.

    Data from almost eight hundred schoolgirls over ten years in an eastern suburban town indicated that there is great variability in the onset of sexual maturity (menstruation) in girls (Zacharias et al., 1976).   This study also found that while the age of menstruation (called "menarche") has decreased steadily from about eighteen years in the early 1800s to about thirteen in the 1940s, it has not changed significantly since then at least in this geographical area; the average age was 12.8,

Adolescents want to act naturally and self-confidently.

about the same as in the 1940s. (The study also found that girls were about the same height and weight as in the 1940s and 1950s.) However, girls from thirteen on up have been having an increasing problem in coping with increasing sexual permissiveness in society, and this has resulted in a greater frequency of teenage pregnancy. Some are against abortion, others not, but the debate goes on and is a real problem; ethics are involved, relating to the question of whether abortion is a form of murder, whether it is ethical to leave a child to someone when you have no control over who it is and don't know where it is going, and other such questions. Teachers and parents should be aware of the possibility of such situations occurring, and should not be taken by surprise or try to avoid confronting the matter. On the other hand, they should not be overly solicitous or overly rejecting when these incidents do occur.

Dealing with adolescents. Because of their new physical, social, and cognitive maturity, adolescents are likely to find weaknesses in their parents, to question their values, to compare them with other more understanding parents, and to accuse them of hypocritical inconsistencies. At the same time, because they are

AN ELUSIVE IDENTITY

Ray was an adolescent, a sophomore in high school, and he was having problems handling the transition from youth to adulthood. He had high aptitude scores, but he did not do very well in school. His parents were very uptight about things that he did, and they watched him very closely. They also subjected him to many questions about where he had been and what he had done every time he came home after being out in the evening. This was partly because he occasionally got into minor scrapes with the town police. Ray's parents were constantly reminding him of school work that had to be done, like tests coming up, projects due, and the like. His mother was very anxious about his grades, and she talked a great deal about his going on to college. His father, on the other hand, emphasized athletics. Ray was a reasonably well coordinated boy, but his father would criticize his play after each game and urge him to try harder or show more aggressiveness. Both parents were concerned about the kinds of friends Ray had as well. They acted as though the boys he picked to be with were not good enough.

As Ray came into adolescence, most of the boys his age outgrew him, and he was slow in becoming interested in girls. His major interest was hiking and camping, but these activities were also associated with smoking pot and drinking. Family conferences which were designed to get into discussions of his interests and problems and to straighten things out usually ended in family arguments, as often as not, between his mother and father.

In his junior year, and going into his senior year, therefore, Ray seemed to have an increasing dislike for school. He participated in athletics, but he didn't seem to have his heart in it. His main objective was to get out of school, and discussion of college was only attractive in relation to other places in the country that he might go. He seemed to be down on life generally, and to be carrying a burden of what might have been resentment or guilt or hostility or sadness—it wasn't clear which. He had good friends, and a number of girl friends, but he didn't seem to have "found" himself—he didn't seem to have a good feeling about himself or his life. Though he loved his parents, he seemed to need to be away from them and on his own, while simultaneously wanting to be dependent on them as well, and unable to plan ahead for himself.

going through a period of adjustment to greater personal potential and greater independence and mature functioning, adolescents need more opportunities than before to talk things out, to explore possibilities and alternatives, to discuss matters which relate either directly or indirectly to popularity, sexual relations, roles in society, and the like. A background of democratic treatment will stand them in good stead during this period, since communication in such a family is less subject to serious or permanent disruption. A background of authoritarian treatment by parents often leads to difficulties, since communication has already been strained. In considering the roles of parents and teachers during this period, you also have to consider *their* past adolescent difficulties: for many these were quite painful experiences and they may not want to bring them to mind all over again. For example, a late maturing father may be threatened by his late maturing son's resentment against society, or he may feel jealous of a son who is early maturing and confident and effective at everything he does. On the other hand, a father may have mixed feelings toward a daughter who is maturing rapidly and obviously becoming a woman; he may not be able to resolve those feelings or to cope with her popularity with boys, because of his own rigid upbringing and his questions about the morals of today's younger generation.   Similarly, a teacher who had difficulty socially in middle childhood, or as an adolescent, may have definite inferiority feelings in respect to the more mature boys and girls in his or her high school classes, and may overreact as a result of this, and may thus be more restrictive or more permissive than is good for the class and for the school.

College years

In college students you find adolescent problems in their later stages, with some cases of arrested development or fixations from earlier stages, and with problems involving frustrations in social, athletic, and academic endeavors—in short, the full range of adult behavior.   These are people who are mature but not yet in the mainstream of society because of the pressures of that society for further training and specialization.   Many, if not most, of you who read this book will be in this level or age.   Professors, counselors, and administrators should recognize the needs of post-secondary learners to maintain their identities in the face of increasing pressures to become cogs in the machine, part of the faceless mass.   Bereft of home ties and high school identities, they search for a new way of being somebody.   A survey at Princeton University (Pervin et al., 1966) some years ago showed that more than fifty percent of incoming freshmen expected to make the Dean's list academically, yet only the top ten percent of any class was actually selected—frustration is thus built into the situation.   Such reductions in numbers apply to athletics, social prominence, fraternities and sororities, and other social settings.   This results in a general anomie accentuated by large classes, where professors have difficulty learning names and recognizing students, not to mention coming to know them and help them as individuals.   This applies to dormitory supervisors, counselors, health service personnel, and others.   Professors, instructors, and administrators who make a point of getting to know individual students find a tremendous need for such close attention and interest by those students, as evidenced by the way they respond.

The study of college students and post-adolescents generally, and of later developmental periods, has gathered momentum only recently.

Adulthood

A recent investigator of adult development has concluded that there are predictable stages and crises for adults.   One example is the common cycle of relationships between married couples.   "During the twenties, when a man gains confidence by leaps and bounds, a married woman is usually losing the superior assurance she once had as an adolescent.   When a man passes 30 and wants to settle down, a woman is often becoming restless.   And just at the point around 40, when a man feels himself to be standing on a precipice his strength, power, dreams, and illusions slipping away beneath him, his wife is likely to be brimming with ambition to climb her own mountain" (Sheehy, 1977). The same investigator has outlined the general adult developmental ladder as follows:

- "Pulling up roots"—post-adolescence, college, military service, short-term travels
- "The trying twenties"—taking hold in the adult world, shifting from interior turmoil of late adolescence to preoccupation with externals, doing what one should
- "Catch-30"—tearing up the life one put together in the twenties, striking out on secondary roads toward new visions
- "Rooting and extending"—buying houses, climbing career ladders, "making it"
- "The deadline decade"—halfway mark, crossroads, time starts to squeeze, loss of youth is felt, fading purpose
- "Renewal or resignation"—mid-forties, regaining of equilibrium and a new stability or resigning oneself to what is

Adult learners. Adult learners tend to be more anxious about their learning ability, having been away from school for some time in many cases, and they pay more attention in class and ask more questions than college students in the same subjects or classes. Yet they find examinations more difficult, and have more difficulty in remembering large arrays of facts. Although they have a richer fund of experience to draw on and therefore can respond to concepts with examples from a variety of sources, at the same time that experience sometimes interferes with their learning. Their preconceived notions often conflict with or confuse their understanding of new concepts which seem initially to be related to what they already know, but which turn out to be quite different.

Whether teaching adult learners high school subjects, college, or graduate level material, there are some guidelines which can be kept in mind. One is to maintain respect for the adult's self-concept as an independent, not a dependent, learner. Another is to allow for and utilize the great store of experience that the adult learner brings to a learning situation. You should also encourage adult learners to take a greater role in choosing their learning goals and the kinds of learning experiences that they feel are most appropriate for them and that they are most adapted to.

Summary outline with key concepts

> ☞ *Child once* seen as small adult, now seen as different, and as changing by stages / Acceleration of learning versus letting learner mature and grow according to own pace / Deprivation experiments show abilities emerge without learning, but learning adapts to them once emerged / Hereditary mechanisms called "blueprinting" by Lorenz / There may be a critical period for acquiring specific skills most efficiently.

☞ *Infant begins* to coordinate senses and physical abilities during sensorimotor period of development, according to theory of Piaget / Characterized by egocentrism / Infants develop combinations of senses and feelings and motor skills that reflect internally the experiences of the learner; they form the foundations for later learning / Infant learns actively, develops internal representations of experience, which are what have been called "schema" / Disabilities and handicaps appear first as slowness in development; early identification and remediation helps / Early learning probably has an effect on the amount of brain growth, judging from results of animal research.

☞ *Physical growth* dependent on nurturance as well as nutrition and heredity / Occurs in spurts, with plateaus between / Differences between learners increase with time / Gross and large-muscle abilities appear first / Growth begins at head, proceeds outward to extremities / Screening instruments for physical and motor development include Denver, Oseretsky, Purdue / Most important growth spurt at adolescence; sexes mature at different times; some learners mature earlier than others / Signals indicating early developmental problems include poor balance, inability to skip, inability to lift head and feet while lying on stomach.

☞ *Freud postulated* early psychosexual stages including oral, anal, and phallic (Oedipal) latency, and genital fixation at one stage affects adult personality / Freud also postulated id, ego, and superego; the last balances the first two / Neurosis is dominance of superego; psychosis dominance of id; normal behavior comes from a balance of the two by the ego / Loevinger postulated stages of ego development including autistic, impulsive, opportunistic, conformist, conscientious, and autonomous / Kohlberg postulated stages of moral development including might-is-right, back-scratching (both preconventional), conformity, law-and-order (both conventional), social contract, universal principles (both postconventional) / Erikson postulated psychosocial stages, including trust vs. mistrust (infancy), autonomy vs. shame and doubt (early childhood), initiative vs. guilt (play age), industry vs. inferiority (school age), identity vs. loss of self (adolescence), intimacy vs. isolation (young adulthood), generativity vs. self-absorption (adulthood), integrity vs. disgust (senescence.)

☞ *Monkeys raised* in isolation were maladjusted as adults; so were monkeys raised with a wire surrogate mother without cloth covering, while those who had a cloth-covered surrogate were more normal / Humans with early difficulties and traumatic experiences are not doomed to maladjustment, and sometimes make more interesting adults.

☞ *During ages* five to seven, maturation quickens, several outcomes are observed including increased resistance to ailments, maturing of mental and behavioral patterns, increased independence, more adult morality / Junior high learners become preoccupied with selves, often sulk, reject attempts to get them to discuss problems; boys little interest in girls, girls increase dating; generally neither is as happy as earlier; awkwardness due to growth increases; need consistent firm assertion of guidelines for behavior; need to be accepted as potentially good in spite of deviant behavior; nutrition has to be watched; need guidance in forming realistic goals; cliques and group pressures becoming stronger / Adolescence is variously seen as a time of storm and stress (one view) and a time of emerging into adult world with help and support of parents (another view); adolescents have wide swings in mood and behavior, have an increased ability to deal with abstract ideas, are often depressed over own inadequacies and incensed over inadequacies of the world; value tolerance and flexibility and empathy in others (including teachers and parents) / Late maturing adolescent boys very poorly adjusted and unhappy / Some adults have difficulty relating to adolescents due to their own problems during that period of development / Senior high girls are women, early-maturing boys are men, but both still developing social and moral patterns and concepts; concerned about personal appearance, have difficulty focussing on academic matters; premarital sex increases; concerned about the world they are moving into nevertheless; need relationships between current subjects and their society; subject also to economic pressures since subculture is an economic force in society / College students deal with vestiges of adolescence, also anomie of new big community, pressure of academics; need attention to individual problems, relevance of knowledge to own future, and treatment as mature individuals / Adults, beginning with college students, go through stages of pulling up roots, the trying twenties, Catch-30, rooting and extending, the deadline decade, and renewal or resignation, according to a recent analysis / Adult learners need recognition of their unique experience, opportunity to relate them to the subject, and encouragement to exert effort and compete with recreational habits they have acquired since college.

Glossary

Achievement motivation: A pattern of motivation discussed in Chapter 7.

Anal stage: Stage where child is preoccupied with urination and defecation (Freud).

Autistic stage: Early egocentric stage of ego development (Loevinger).

Autonomous stage: Stage of coping with inner conflicts (Loevinger).

Autonomy: Reliance on self, ability to progress independently.

Autonomy versus Shame and Doubt: Early childhood stage of psychosocial development (Erikson).

Back-scratching: Late preconventional moral development—right is what satisfies one's own needs (Kohlberg).

Blueprinting: Hypothetical mechanism by which capacity for doing certain things is passed on from one generation to another.

Conformist stage: Loevinger's fourth stage involving some shame, identification with authority; Kohlberg's early conventional (third) stage, being a good boy or good girl, being well liked are motives.

Conscientious stage: Concern over inner moral guidelines; Loevinger's fifth stage.

Conventional stages: Middle two stages of moral development, including "conformity" and "law and order" (Kohlberg).

Cross-modal integration: Relating what one sees and hears, internally (see Chapter 4).

Deprivation experiment: Animal deprived of some experience or situation from birth, reacts in mature fashion to it (without learning) when exposed to it in maturity.

Developmental disabilities: A number of handicaps related to development that have been classified together, including retardation, cerebral palsy, epilepsy, autism.

Ego (Freud): The reality-facing, balancing force in Freud's personality theory.

Ego (Loevinger): Sense of self-identity, confidence in oneself, understanding of one's role and place.

Ego psychology: Psychology which explains human behavior in terms of the development and operation of the ego and interactions with other aspects of personality (e.g., id and superego in Freud's case).

Egocentricity: Behaving as though the world revolved around oneself.

Embryonic: Development theory in which stages are not dependent on each other or do not evolve from each other.

Fixation: Problem in adult personality resulting from problems at early stage of development.

Genital stage: Puberty, early adolescence (Freud).

Generativity vs. self-absorption: Psychosocial development problem in adulthood (Erikson).

Hierarchical development: Each stage comes out of the previous one; order is set.

Id: The survival, selfish force of personality (Freud).

Identity: A sense or concept of self, knowledge of where one fits in the scheme of things, perception of the role one fills or should fill.

Identity vs. identity diffusion: Adolescent psychosocial development problem.

Impulsive stage: Early ego development, bad is what is punished (Loevinger).

Industry vs. inferiority: School age of psychosocial development (Erikson).

Initiative vs. guilt: Psychosocial development, play age (Erikson).

Intimacy vs. isolation: Young adulthood stage of psychosocial development (Erikson).

IQ: Score on an intelligence text (*see* Chapter 3).

Mid-line: Imaginary vertical line down the middle of the body between right and left; some learners can't reach to other side of mid-line with one hand.

Neurosis: Fearful, inhibited behavior; domination of superego according to Freud.

Nurturance: Giving of love, attention, and support, as well as food.

Opportunistic stage: Loevinger's third stage of ego development: bad is to be caught.

Oedipal stage: Stage where child is preoccupied with genitalia and sexual feelings.

Oral stage: Stage where infant is preoccupied with taking in through the mouth (Freud).

Pauperized ego: Ego which is too weak to balance forces of id and superego.

Peer: A person of same age or status.

Phallic stage: See Oedipal stage.

Plateau: A period of no or slight growth or progress, as during learning.

Postconventional stages: Last two stages of moral development: "social contract" and "universal principles" (Kohlberg).

Preconventional stages: Early two stages of moral development: "right is might" and "back-scratching" (Kohlberg).

Primary process: Feelings, instincts, drives.

Psychosexual: Freud's stages of development, including oral, anal, and phallic.

Psychosocial: Erikson's eight stages of development, including infancy, early childhood, etc.

Psychosis: Selfish, uninhibited behavior, domination of the id.

Right is might: Early preconventional moral development; deference to power (Kohlberg).

Secondary process: Cognition, rational thinking, planning.

Sensorimotor: Earliest period of cognitive development (Piaget); senses become coordinated with physical and motor abilities.

Schema: The most basic, initial, learned units; akin to concepts; form basis for all later learning; acquired in sensorimotor period.

Screening: Evaluation for purpose of identifying problems in learning and development.

Schizophrenia: A form of psychosis.

Social contract: Early postconventional moral development; problem of individual vs. society (Kohlberg).

Social learning: Learning by observation and imitation, rather than by being told or by being rewarded for correct responses.

Surrogate mother: Mother substitute made of wire or wire-and-cloth which dispenses milk to baby monkeys and serves as something to cling to.

Synapse: The extremity of a nerve cell pathway where signals are communicated to a neighboring nerve cell.

Universal principles: Late postconventional moral development: individual chooses principles by which he operates (Kohlberg).

Trust vs. mistrust: First stage of psychosocial development: infancy (Erikson).

Law and order: Late conventional moral development; doing one's duty, respect for authority (Kohlberg).

Superego: The inhibiting force, including conscience, in Freud's personality theory.

Integrity vs. disgust: Senescence in psychosocial development (Erikson).

Identity trap: Where adolescent becomes fixed in a certain role that he or she was initially just experimenting with.

Questions for thought and discussion

1. How do "heredity" and "environment" oriented views of development differ, and what would a combined view be like?
2. How are "schema" formed and how do they relate to later learning?
3. Can emotional deprivation affect physical growth? How?
4. Describe some early indications of physical or motor problems.
5. In the Oedipal stage of development, who competes with whom?

6. How would a person in the "conscientious" stage react to a point-system for achieving a grade?

7. How have attempts to change moral stages worked out? How does this relate to the environment vs. heredity debate?

8. How do the "conformist" stages of Loevinger and Kohlberg compare?

9. What does a learner at the industry vs. inferiority stage need?

10. What interrelationship of id, ego, and super-ego results in neurosis?

11. What has research on isolated monkeys to do with human learners?

12. What are some personal characteristics valued by adolescents?

13. How do adult learners differ from college students?

14. How do high school seniors differ from freshmen?

15. What stage is a ten year old in? (according to Freud, Kohlberg, Loevinger, Erikson)

Situations calling for applications of facts and concepts

1. If you were used to dealing with fourth graders, either in a classroom or as a leader of a scout group or in some similar capacity, in what ways would you change your methods to deal with seventh graders?

2. How would you advise a friend whose son or brother is caught in an adolescent identity trap, i.e., how should that person go about helping the adolescent? Or should he or she try to help?

3. As a parent or a teacher, or in a team made up of both, what kinds of environment and experiences would you try to provide a seven year old girl, taking Freud, Loevinger, Kohlberg, and Erikson, and research in personal-social development into account. Assume that this youngster has no obvious developmental handicaps and that she passed through the sensorimotor period in a normal fashion.

Suggested activities

1. Observe learners at a given age or stage, and keep diary of their activities and patterns of behavior. Compare what you observe with what you are supposed to see according to the various theories and developmental sequences discussed, and also with the lists of characteristics given for the various grade levels.

2. Observe adults who are successful in working with adolescents, and note whether they demonstrate the attributes which adolescents are supposed to value, and what variations or added characteristics they show.

3. Work with learners at the sensorimotor level of development, note how they explore and actively learn about their environment, also note how they react to any new or puzzling situations.

4. Design a set of learning and growth activities for a specific age group in some context which exists in your locality, then get permission to try these out to see whether they are appealing to the learners and whether the regular teacher or supervisor feels that they are potentially beneficial.

Suggested readings

References given in the text are found in the bibliography; you may want to read more deeply in one or more of these areas.   There are some very comprehensive texts on child development; one well known one is that by Mussen, Conger, and Kagan. There is a short, very readable book by Elkind called *The child from birth to sixteen.* There are also journals, including the *Journal of Child Development.*   Research in this field is reviewed at intervals of some years in Carmichael, found in the bibliography. Perhaps it is well to advise you not to become discouraged at the amount of literature in this field; it is very extensive, but if you are interested you have to begin somewhere.

2

Cognitive
Development

CONTENTS

ABOUT CHAPTER 2

How you will benefit from this chapter

You will be better prepared to deal with the thinking of learners of different ages, and you will know some of the things they can and can't do, after reading about different stages of cognitive development and some aspects of language development. You will recognize thinking that is different from adult thought, and you will understand some of the relationships between thought and language. This will provide guidelines for teaching at different ages and stages of development. You will also have a better understanding of your own "mental self," and how you learn concepts and handle new problems.

What might make this material difficult to learn

You may feel that the development of cognition and how learners think are topics which are overemphasized, since the task of parents and teachers is to teach children to think as adults. You may feel that the main requirement for teaching is to know the subject matter and present it clearly, but this chapter will say something about what is "clear" at different ages. You may think that some of the ways of thinking described here are foreign to you, and that your own point of view on learning seems much simpler and practical; for example, that the important thing is to make things meaningful. Studying problems of language development also might make you uncomfortable if you had a problem with language or had a relative or friend who did.

Some reasons for studying cognitive development

To be effective with learners you have to consider the limits of their cognitive abilities at any given age, and what might be interesting to that age. The way in which learners at different ages think determines, in part, how you will present experiences and information, and how much and what kind of understanding you can expect.

Assuring successful learning

Again the primary ingredient for success will be effort and persistence, coupled with a curious and open mind. If you can convince yourself it is worth doing and rid yourself of any "hang-ups" about the topic (such as were suggested above), then you should find learning that much easier. In either case, you have the ability to do this work, and you should not feel that a prior basic course in psychology is a necessity.

RATIONALE AND BACKGROUND OF CHAPTER 2

How do you study thinking?

Studying cognitive development calls for careful detective work.

You can't see a brain grow or mature, and you can't observe directly the effects of learning and experience, but you know they are there. How can you deduce the strategies of thinking that will help learners deal effectively with facts, concepts, problems, and such? This chapter will introduce you to some ways of analyzing and classifying cognitive growth and development.

Changing views of cognitive development

In the 1800s there wasn't much question about whether or not a child thought as an adult, or how he or she learned. However, the exploitation of the younger generation during the industrial revolution led to a reaction that emphasized the purity and potential growth and development of children. Rousseau was one philosopher who led the way. As a result people began to look upon children as something to be understood and dealt with in appropriate ways. However, in the early 1900s people became preoccupied with individual differences in intelligence, and tests were devised to determine who should be given the benefits of schooling, and who was unable to profit from it, i.e., "retarded" children. Currently, we not only regard the young learner as someone with quite different thinking processes from adults, but we also regard children of different abilities as having equal right to education and the opportunity to learn. Some go further and regard the child as something of a philosopher as well, as indicated by this quotation:

> The two most basic things which Piaget found out were that the child was a philosopher and that his philosophy went through stages. Freud had found that, just like grown-ups, children were interested in birth and death and sex. But Piaget found that children were largely interested in birth and death and sex because they were bothered by the origins of things, by what is space and time and causality and reality and good and evil, by all the things that are the concerns of the grown-ups called philosophers. To be a philosopher is to be concerned about the basic categories of experience and this is just what young children are interested in. To go through stages is to have qualitative transformations in these categories, changes in world view or philosophy. (Kohlberg, 1976)

Information processing and cognition

One way to think of cognition is as part of our way of processing information and responding to it.   Messages come in to us from the environment—auditory, visual, and other—and they are received by the brain and processed.   After processing, some active response may be made, or the information may be stored for later use. The processing of the information involves related memories that are called up from some kind of storage; it also involves reviewing these memories and associations, and selecting or focusing on patterns and feelings that seem most significant in relation to the situation at hand.   Another thing that is often necessary is to select appropriate responses from among those that are available, either physical, verbal, or other kinds.

What we call "cognition" is usually considered to be different from processes by which you perceive incoming information, and from processes by which you act upon your environment physically and verbally.   However, it is often difficult to determine where perceiving or receiving leaves off and thinking begins, or where thinking leaves off and action begins.   Given that difficulty, it is still possible to conceive of an information processing system in the manner portrayed in Figure 2–1.

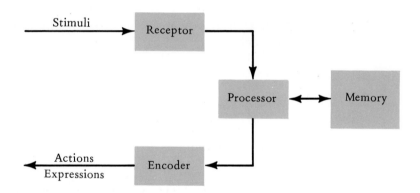

Figure 2–1. *A schematic diagram showing how theorists visualize the operation of human information processing systems.   (Adapted from Allen Newell and Herbert A. Simon,* Human problem solving, *© 1972.   Reprinted by permission of Prentice-Hall, Inc., Englewood Cliffs, N.J.)*

LANGUAGE AND COGNITION

Early language acquisition

The infant's earliest language involves babbling, which begins at about six months. Babies of different nationalities babble in about the same range of sounds, the earliest sounds being consonants like p, m, b, and t.   The average American child says

Are you born with
a language capabil-
ity, or must it be
taught you piece
by piece—or how
do you acquire it?

his or her first word about the end of the first year, often by repeating syllables as in "ma-ma" and "bye-bye." One-word sentences develop into three-word units between eighteen and twenty-four months. This development accelerates very fast: by the age of four or five the rules of grammar are essentially complete in most learners.

A child will say "Daddy go" but not "go Daddy;" later she will say (with pauses as indicated) "Give . . . the ball . . . me" but will not pause as in "Give the . . . ball me." These patterns suggest that some inherited cognitive structuring or conceptualization guides language development; it is not just trial and error. Psycholinguists, those interested in the psychology of language, feel that such evidence indicates that there are hereditary mechanisms that enable us to develop language, and that these mechanisms are what differentiate us from animals. Another indication of this is the fact that although children imitate adult speech, the frequency and nature of their sentence patterns don't follow those of their parents precisely (Brown, Cazden, and Bellugi-Klima, 1969).

As the child matures, his (or her) own speech begins to control his behavior. Also his speech becomes "covert," that is, the child ceases talking to himself out loud, and begins to talk within himself. Eventually this "inner speech" becomes automatic, something he may not be entirely aware of, and resembles what we usually call "thinking." This does not mean that it is the same as cognition, much of which is subconscious, but there is an increasing amount of interaction between thought and language.

Inherent language learning processes

The growth of language in the normal child is so rapid and extensive that it seems to theorists that there must be some inherited language acquisition mechanism at work within the learner. Since language acquisition occurs when we are very young, it is hard to look back and remember what it was like. Something of this kind of inherited ability may have been described by Helen Keller, the woman who was born deaf, dumb, and blind, yet learned to talk and "hear" and write. As she described the learning of her first word, her tutor held her hand under a stream of water and spelled "water" into her other hand in finger language. She writes: "Suddenly I felt a misty consciousness of something forgotten—a thrill of returning thought, and somehow the mystery of language was revealed to me. I knew then that 'w-a-t-e-r' meant the wonderful cool something that was flowing over my hand . . . I left the well-house eager to learn. Everything had a name, each name gave birth to a new thought" (Quoted in Lerner, 1976, p. 207).

Language learning through imitation

Another powerful process that is continually at work in developing language is referred to as "modeling," or learning by imitation. (Modeling is also discussed in Chapter 8). Children observe adults and older children using language. They see the situations in which certain phrases are used, and they observe the consequences of using those phrases. Then they are able to use similar phrases in the appropriate contexts; it is not necessary for them to try all the phrases and sentences out themselves and to be rewarded or ignored or punished depending on how effective they are, as some theorists assert (Bandura, 1969). During early years, actually, children imitate language as a sort of game (like playing house or doctor), and only gradually do they bring language into use to express their own thoughts.

To summarize, language is acquired through hereditary mechanisms, through imitation of adult language, and by trying out utterances and being rewarded or not rewarded for their use. All of these processes are involved in language development.

Language and cognition—are they the same?

Q 1

Can you think without language? Do these skills develop together or separately?

One Soviet theorist, named Vygotsky, feels that there are two distinct developmental processes involved in language development and cognitive development: a prelinguistic stage in the development of thinking, and a pre-thinking stage in the development of language (they may occur at the same time, of course). It is only after the child has begun to acquire speech, at about the age of two, that the thought processes and the speech processes begin to interact. Another Soviet theorist, named Luria, maintains that the brain (particularly the cortex) develops patterns or circuits to reflect the internal and external world of the learner; it is *not* a matter of hereditary mechanisms emerging as the child matures. The ability to regulate activity is the first "learning" to develop, according to this theorist, and is similar to the development of "ego" in Freudian theory. Later, a second level of organization develops that combines the sensory processes which developed first into a more complex perceptual system; then a third level develops that combines the secondary systems into more complex processes. It is this third level which supports language development, including speaking, listening, reading, and writing (Luria, 1968).

How language learning becomes a necessity

Q 4

As you can see there is some question about the degree to which language affects thinking or behavior before the period between five and seven years. The infant deals with the world through sensorimotor interaction and visual and auditory observation, and he or she develops schema which are adequate to the simple life of the baby. However, this "thinking" is not sufficient for many tasks, and as the child matures, these tasks become important (Blank, 1974). Pointing to things is a very effective way of communicating when they are visible; when they are out of sight or absent, however, some other communication vehicle is needed. To develop this skill, the child must be a kind of detective. When you ask a child "Why is Ann crying?" there isn't enough information for her to understand, as compared

Modeling is a powerful process at work in developing language.

with, "Where is the block?" The child will try out sensorimotor responses, like pointing to the child or repeating "cry" or touching the child, but she gets the idea that these aren't appropriate. She is forced to produce terms in a "why" or questioning context before she understands them. Again if an adult says "that's a nice song" she may say "why." The adult is usually unable to explain, which pushes the child to more complex questions such as "why song," in which for the first time she is using the word without knowing what it is—thus expression is preceding reception! However, this doesn't work very well either, so the child graduates to "why singing the song" when an adult says "he is singing a song." This kind of language is obviously not based on full understanding, but it functions as a vehicle for conceptual development. This is why interchanges with mature speakers are important for developing cognition, as well as the active involvement with the environment described previously under sensorimotor learning. In both cases, the child acts as a problem-solver, and his or her imitations of adult behavior are a form of hypothesis-testing.

Surface and deep structures

One interesting concept in psycholinguistic analysis of language is that of the difference between "surface structure" and "deep structure." For example, consider two sentences with the same surface structure:

1. Billy is easy to hurt.
2. Billy is eager to hurt.

If we use a different structure to paraphrase them, only one is correct:

1. It is easy to hurt Billy.
2. It is eager to hurt Billy.

Another structure is correct for the second one:

1. "Easy to hurt" describes Billy's desire.
2. "Eager to hurt" describes Billy's desire.

Thus the first two had similar surface structure but different deep structure.

Noam Chomsky, the originator of this analytic approach, suggests that children could not possibly master such translations from surface structure to deep structure merely by observation or imitation, by having certain utterances rewarded and others not, or by a combination of these events (Chomsky, 1972). He feels that there must be complex hereditary mechanisms that give us the capacity for this kind of translation, and that humans have the capacity to develop language even when they don't have patterns to imitate. The author has observed what seems to be an example: in two separate families, identical twin boys developed their own language for speaking to each other, a language that their own parents could not understand!

HOW WOULD YOU TEACH A CHILD TO SAY A SIMPLE SENTENCE?

How would you bring a child to say "fix my bicycle" for the first time? One way would be to have her observe you when you take your bicycle to a shop and ask the repair person to "fix my bicycle, please." She might then repeat the sentence in the same situation at a later time, if the subject came up. Another way would be to define "fix" and tell her to generate a sentence using "fix" and "bicycle." Another way would be to have her observe other people saying such things as "fix the tire," "fix the TV," or "fix the toilet," and then put her in a situation where she wants someone to fix her bicycle, perhaps inventing a game where she plays a role like this. Then she might say "fix my bicycle" even though she had never heard the entire sentence before. Another way would be to teach her to put words together into sentences, and as one exercise in this, give her words "fix," "my," and "bicycle." Still another way would be to have her repeat after you, many times, "fix my bicycle"; however, the sentence might not have much meaning for her in such cases, since it isn't associated with an actual bicycle or with the need to get one fixed. What if you failed at all of these methods? You might decide that she isn't ready to form such a sentence—perhaps she doesn't yet comprehend what it means to fix a bicycle, and therefore has no need to use such a sentence, even when you create an artificial situation or when she observes you actually asking someone to do it. In such a case you might need an artificial incentive, such as giving her praise and recognition for forming sentences of this type, or rewarding her when she happens to do so with praise or some kind of thing she likes, such as a toy.

Stages of language development

Language development is a neglected subject in the area of educational psychology, and the theories of language development are in an early developmental stage. The beginning of one such theory, espoused by Roger Brown, will give you some ideas concerning the possibilities for future progress in this field.

According to Brown, the first stage of language development is one in which children acquire a set of meanings which convey basic roles occupied by persons or things described in sentences that they hear, and a simple grammar by which they can express relationships among the meanings that have been acquired in this way. Some children have entered this stage as early as eighteen months and as late as twenty-seven months. It is characterized by the use of two-word sentences such as "all broke," "more boat," and such, sometimes referred to as "holophrastic phrases" by linguists. These two-word sentences have an astonishing variety of uses and functions, and a child can do a lot with them. However, they are ambiguous: "Bobby toy" can mean "that's Bobby's (my) toy," "give Bobby (me) the toy," or "where did Bobby's toy go." One theorist, in discussing this stage, points out that it relates closely to the development of sensorimotor thought (described in the previous chapter). The main accomplishment of the sensorimotor stage is the recognition that objects endure over time and across different locations. These sentences seem to concentrate on variations of that theme, as in "where goggie," indicating that the doggie must be somewhere even though it has disappeared (Brown, as described in Henderson and Bergan, 1976, p. 230).

Stage Two, according to this theorist, is the stage of grammatical morphemes and the modulation of meanings. (Morphemes are units of sound with a meaning: "pob" is not a morpheme, but "pots" is.) Here the learner acquires small grammatical units involving articles, prepositions, and such, and uses them to alter the meanings of sentences. He or she also begins to utter three-word sentences.

This stage theory is still being developed, so we cannot describe subsequent stages as yet.

Receptive, expressive, and inner languages

Earlier in this chapter an information processing view was given which emphasized the difference between input, output, and processing (cognition). Analyses of language development have come to discriminate similarly between receptive language (comprehension), expressive language, and inner language. Inner language is a somewhat vague term for the idea that language, once developed, becomes a vehicle for thought; this has already been discussed in respect to the theories of Vygotsky and Luria, and will be discussed again in Chapter 9 in respect to verbal mediation. The best way to describe receptive and expressive languages is to present examples of each as you can see in Tables 2–1 and 2–2.

Receptive language is, in the opinion of some theorists, more closely related to what we call "intelligence," which is discussed in the next chapter. As you will see when you inspect Tables 2-1 and 2-2, expressive language development is more obvious, and it isn't surprising that sometimes parents are unaware of deficits or retardation in receptive language development. Extreme difficulties of this type are referred to as receptive or expressive "aphasia"; expressive aphasia is inability to

Does everyone understand as much as he or she can express? Does understanding follow or precede expression?

Table 2–1. *Behavior that show typical receptive language development at various ages, integrated by Bryan and Bryan from language development and intelligence scales by Bzoch and League, Binet, and Gesell.*

0–12 months: (B&L)
Recognize and distinguish familiar sounds and voices.
Respond appropriately to some simple commands, questions, and statements in a manner that indicates some discriminate language decoding skills.

12–24 months (B&L)
Increased interest in names of things.
Increased ability to understand some new words each week.
Ability to identify one familiar object from among a group of several familiar objects when the object is named.
Understand and carry out three requests combined in a single utterance.

24–36 months (B&G items)
Listens to simple stories, especially liking those heard before.
Identifies by name: dog, cup, shoe, house, flag, star, leaf, basket, box (i.e., points to pictures of them)

36–48 (B&G)
Memory span lengthening; recalls events of yesterday.
Generalizations common: in, on, under.
Can be reasoned with verbally.

48–60 months
Can single out one word and ask its meaning (formerly reacted to sentence as a whole).
Understands some abstract words (connectives, colors).

Adapted from T. Bryan and J. Bryan, *Understanding learning disabilities*, Alfred Publishers, © 1975.

Table 2–2. *Behaviors that show typical expressive language development.*

0–12 months
Cries frequently with some variety in force and pattern.
Specific differentiated cry or vocal pattern when hungry.
Communicates several states of pleasure or discomfort or pain through vocal signals aimed at mother.

12–24 months
Expresses wants and needs by using some true words along with other vocalizations and gestures.
Combines words into short, simple sentences.
Speaks regularly in sentences of two or more words toward end

24–36 months
Often talks while acting and acts while talking.
300 words in vocabulary; reaches about 450 in this period.
Expresses intention and action in same sentence (e.g., Peter slide down).
Language beginning to be used as communication of wants, needs, ideas.

36–48 months
Indulges in soliloquy, dramatic play, to match his words and phrases and syntax.
Combines acting and talking; suits action to one word and vice versa.
Uses language easily to tell a story or relay an idea.
Complete sentences.

48–60 months
Vocabulary 1,900–2,200 words.
Can count 10 objects.
Can tell his or her age.
Can carry a plot in a story and repeat a long sequence accurately.
Dramatic play full of practical dialogue and commentary about everyday functions.

Adapted from T. Bryan and J. Bryan, *Understanding learning disabilities*, Alfred Publishers, © 1975.

talk well despite a good understanding and good vocal motor control; it seems to be an "encoding" difficulty.

To return to the matter of inner language again, it is appropriate at this point to note that Jean Piaget, whose theory was introduced in Chapter 1, believes that the child's intellectual development is basically nonlanguage at first; language develops separately and then comes to be used in thinking. Thus, as you will see, his experiments in cognitive development utilize problem situations that are primarily concrete, although he asks the learners involved to verbalize their solution processers as a help to analyzing their thought processes at different stages.

Piaget's experiments on cognition

A number of Piaget's experiments reveal different stages of children's development. In one such experiment, a group of four- and five-year-old children were shown ten

Jean Piaget did the first detective work on how children develop intellectual abilities through very clever experiments.

sticks in varying lengths. Each child was later asked to draw these sticks from memory. Some of the children were asked to draw them immediately; those under four drew a line of sticks of roughly equal length, while older children drew pairs of equal length with some pairs unequal to other pairs. Other children were asked at a later date to draw what they had seen (without having seen them again). At about five years, they began to draw three groups: large, medium, and small. Some months later, still another group drew a series of ascending length, but it was incomplete. Finally, the group that was asked to reproduce the sticks at about the age of six was able to draw them correctly.

Since all the children drew the sticks from memory without any review, the correct image must have been "stored" in their minds, even after a year. Since the drawings improved as the children grew older, you have to conclude that their ability to "process" or interpret the stored image changed. Perhaps the day-to-day experience they accumulated taught them how to do this; perhaps their mental functions matured with age; perhaps both. Piaget's explanation is that a memory image does not stem from perception alone, which is complete from the beginning, but from internal "operational schemas" that control the remembered image, dominating and coloring what has been seen. These "schemas" become more sophisticated with age.

Another of Piaget's experiments, called the "three-mountain problem," is diagramed in Figure 2–2. It demonstrates how the child's view of the world begins "egocentrically" and gradually expands to include the views of others. A child sits in one of the chairs at the table in Figure 2–2. Before him are three conical "mountains." In another chair sits a doll. He is asked to draw, describe, or select a drawing that represents the *doll's* view of the "mountains." For some children the task is impossible: they are at the "preoperational" stage of cognitive development, where their own view of the world is the only one that exists. (You remember that they were even more egocentric at the earlier "sensorimotor stage," Chapter 1). Other children rearrange their own views to account for the doll's different perspective, although this process is erratic at first. They are maturing into the "concrete operational" stage of development.

The experiment with the ten sticks, where learners drew them from memory at different intervals, described the concept of cognitive operation, or the application of a cognitive "scheme." The three-mountain problem illustrated a change in cognitive "self-centeredness." Another characteristic of cognitive growth identified by Piaget is the development of "conservation." This is the realization that a substance remains constant in volume or mass no matter how its appearance may change. In the famous "juice glass experiment," juice is poured from a short, wide glass into a tall, thin one (see Figure 2-3). A child is asked whether there is more, less, or the same amount of juice as before. A child in the "preoperational" stage of cognitive development will state that the amount of liquid *changes* as it enters the tall, thin glass, and that there is now more juice. At the concrete operational stage, however, she "conserves," i.e., she realizes that the amount remains constant. As she moves toward the next stage, called the stage of "formal operations," she will even be able to predict the new juice level, roughly, before it is

Figure 2–2. *Piaget's three-mountain problem.*

poured—she can reason in symbolic terms on the basis of past experience and can predict what will happen.   When well into the formal operational stage, she will probably be able to tell the results without having any juice glasses present, i.e., she can manipulate ideas without concrete objects present.

Another fundamental thought process that develops in stages is that of "reversibility," or the recognition that some things go "both ways."   For example, a "preoperational" four year old may be asked, "Do you have a brother?"   If he says that he does, then he is asked, "What is his name?"   Suppose he says "Bob."   Then he is asked, "Does Bob have a brother?"   To this he may well answer "No."   To

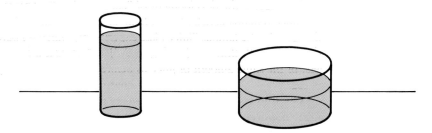

Figure 2–3. *Piaget's juice glass experiment.*

Conservation?

Piaget, this comic exchange indicates that the relationship is simply one-way, or egocentric, to the child.   Therefore, it is "irreversible."   Reversibility is also involved in the juice glass problem, in that some children do not realize that if you poured the juice back, it would come to the same level as before.

Assimilation, accommodation, and equilibrium

Piaget developed a theory of how we learn, as well as how our intellect develops.

Piaget views learning as a process in which the human mind attempts to remain in cognitive balance with its environment, just as the body maintains a temperature balance by sweating when it is hot and by becoming very active when it is cold. When your mind perceives a novel situation, it tries to assimilate this new information into previously formed structures of schemes; that is, you try to see things as you have learned to see them, to transform them into something familiar.   What you are able to see or perceive—the schemes that operate on your perceptions—is what you have learned in the past, thanks to your hereditary abilities to learn those things.

Suppose, however, that a situation occurs where you *cannot* assimilate what you perceive, where some elements of the situation conflict with the expected, and thus pose a cognitive problem, or "discrepancy."   If this is an "optimal" discrepancy that is neither too great nor too slight, then your mind somehow restructures itself or reorganizes itself to *accommodate to the difference, and this process* of accommodation results in learning. In fact, the accommodation and the resultant change *are* "learning." During early stages this accommodation involves changes in motor (physical) responses to adapt to new situations, i.e., it is "sensorimotor." During later stages the accommodation becomes more balanced between cognitive scheme changes and motor changes. As a learner goes from concrete operational to formal operational, he performs more of the integrations and manipulations in his head, without having to try them all out.

After you have accommodated and thus restructured your mind, or adopted or formed a new scheme, you attain a new balance, or *equilibrium*. This equilibrium state is not permanent, since it will yield to new discrepancy where new accommodation must be made, a new set of schemes formed, and then a new equilibrium reached with a new capacity to assimilate the environment.

Sensorimotor thought

During the sensorimotor period, as was described in Chapter 1, the child forms basic schema and comes to be able to solve very simple problems. One important achievement is the development of perceptual "constancies"; for example, a baby of seven or eight months will turn its bottle around if it notices part of the red rubber nipple in the background, but will not do so if it doesn't see the nipple but only the base of the milk-filled bottle. This implies that the child does not attribute a constant form to the bottle. However, at the age of nine months, the infant will turn the bottle around no matter how it is presented. Piaget and Inhelder have suggested that this may be related to the concept of "object permanence" since this is about the same time that the infant looks for an object when it is moved behind a screen; earlier he acts as if it has ceased to exist. At about six months, a child who is trained to choose the larger of two boxes will continue to choose correctly if you move the larger box further away, so that its retinal image is smaller. This is referred to as "constancy of size."

Preoperational thought

There are some things that pre-operational learners cannot do, some ways they cannot think—you should be aware of them.

The second stage is the "preoperational" period; this takes place roughly between two and seven years. The absolute ages of these periods are not as important as the fact that they occur in this sequence. Learners do not skip stages, or go through them in reverse order.

Symbolic thought, what Piaget terms the "semiotic" function, appears during this period. One symptom of this is exemplified by a girl of sixteen months who saw a playmate become angry, scream, and stamp her foot. An hour or two later, after the playmate had left, she imitated the scene, laughing when she did it. This was the beginning of cognitive representation, or the semiotic function. Her imitative gestures showed that she carried an internal representation of what had gone on, and that she was able to differentiate between what was real and what was not real (i.e., what was imaginary, a memory of what had occurred).

As she matures this learner "internalizes" this process; that is, she carries out many of the imitations covertly, in her mind, rather than physically. Eventually she will substitute a verbal version, for example, saying "bow wow" after a dog has left the room, or saying "Dada byebye" and pointing to the door where her father has left some time before. Gradually, representation by action (overt imitation) changes to internal representation in thought. Finally, language begins to function as a more powerful version of this internalized imitation, providing contact and communication with others, which is more effective than imitation, and a way of thinking, which is more efficient than internalized images alone. Thus language *follows* thought in Piaget's view.

Drawing is also a semiotic function. Piaget considers it to be halfway between symbolic play and the mental image; that is, it is a closer imitation of the real than other forms of symbolic play. Children's drawings give insight into the way they conceive of things—rather than how they perceive them—particularly during the preoperational period when children's drawings are not particularly "realistic" in the usual sense. For example, they will picture a profile of a person with a second eye (as did Picasso), rather than with one eye as one would see a profile in reality. This also relates to children's spatial intuitions, which are topological rather than geometrical. They will draw squares, rectangles, circles, and ellipses as closed curves without straight lines or angles, thus showing that they conceive of them as similar in a topological sense (as closed curves) rather than from the point of view of straight and curved lines or angles. It is not until eight or nine or ten years that the child begins to draw things with straight and curved lines (unless taught otherwise); it is also at this age that the child begins to be able to view things from other perspectives, as in the three-mountains problem shown previously.

Exceptions to Piaget's rules

Piaget's assertions about abilities and stages have been rather dogmatic, and some experimenters have questioned them. For example, if a preoperational child is

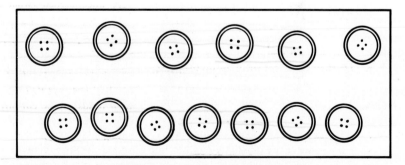

Figure 2–4. *Testing stages with buttons.*

shown two rows of buttons, with the wider-spaced (longer) row actually having *fewer* buttons, she will point to the longer row if asked which has more. A number of experiments have demonstrated this response. However, in one experiment this task was done once with buttons, and then again with M&M candies; in the latter case, the child chose the shorter, fuller row. This is one illustration of an important fact about learners, particularly handicapped learners, that teachers need to keep in mind: performance does not always reflect capacity, and a change in the learning situation can often bring out greater capacity than has been assumed. Another example of this fact is found in an experiment where young learners were given the following problem:

> There are thirteen boys and ten girls in the class; are there more boys or children?

When this question was given orally only 10 percent of the six-year-old learners answered correctly; when it was given in written form, 70 percent showed they could handle it! (Kagan and Kogan, 1970). Yet Piaget has asserted that six year olds cannot solve such a problem.

AN EXAMPLE OF PRE-LOGICAL THINKING

A theorist in the field of cognitive and social development describes two incidents involving his son, Jimmy. In one, Jimmy, who recently had his fifth birthday, came out with one of those seemingly unrelated, spontaneous observations that children of this age make: "I can be a girl, you know—I can wear a wig and have my throat so I can talk like a girl." Later on, in talking with his father, he made the following sequence of responses.

K Do airplanes get small when they fly away in the sky?

J Yes, they get real tiny.

K Do they really get small, or do they just look small?

J They really get small.

K What happens to the people inside?

J They shrink.

K How can they shrink and get small?

J They cut their heads off.

The theorist-and-father uses these incidents to compare two approaches to interpreting child behavior. In a Freudian explanation Jimmy's thinking would be called an intrusion of fantasy into his ordinary communication. The reason given for such fantasy-thinking would be that he is motivated by emotions. However, this would mean that in the first case he is very concerned or involved with the cognitive or logical content (sex differences) while in the second he was very unconcerned (what happens to people). This seems like having it both ways. An alternative explanation would be that Jimmy is simply at a prelogical level of thinking; his cognitive structures or operations do not cope with the actual situations involved. His belief that he can be a girl, and that the people can shrink or their heads can be cut off, is preoperational in Piaget's language; these conclusions are no more strange, actually, than assuming that the amount of juice increases as you pour it from a fat glass into a thin one (Kohlberg, 1976).

Concrete operational thought

How does it help
to be able to "con-
serve," or to "de-
center," or to
"reverse"?

Intelligence begins to evolve into its adult form with the attainment of a new cognitive level called the "concrete operational stage." In part this is the product of the development of the "semiotic function," which is the internalization of concrete processes. This means that children only gradually develop the ability to represent mentally what they have already learned on the action level. For example, while young children are able to find their way easily to and from some place in town, in the preoperational stage they cannot reconstruct their path when given a model of the buildings and streets and other landmarks and asked to show the route. Another mental "skill" that must mature for the concrete operational stage is the achievement of further "decentering," or freedom from ego-centeredness. This decentering begins much earlier, during the sensorimotor period, but once language has been formed and the semiotic function established (during the preoperational) there is a whole new set of interpersonal and social concepts and relationships to be learned. These involve the reactions of others, not just the actions of the learner. These are similar to the relationships involved in Kohlberg's "pre-conventional" stages of development, as well as Loevinger's early stages; they are characterized by increasing awareness of others and awareness of rules and what is expected, as you no doubt recall.

These motor and cognitive developments of previous periods also provide a foundation for developments in "affectivity" (i.e., feelings) and in social relations. During the sensorimotor period an object is significant to the emotions and feelings of the child only while there is direct contact; when the child develops mental images and language (during the preoperational period) the object of his (or her) emotions may be present and active in his mind even though it isn't actually there. This results in the formation of lasting sympathies or antipathies toward other people and toward the self (related to the ego). These sympathies and antipathies are evidenced during the "anal" and "genital" periods of psychosexual development (Freud), and they are also evidenced in the "impulsive" stage of ego development with its negativeness (Loevinger). Since this growth of affect comes at an egocentric time, the child is primarily interested in winning other people's affection and esteem, and/or manipulating people for his or her own ends (without necessarily realizing it). At the *concrete* operational level, however, the child begins to be able to deal with the concept of cooperation (or "conformity" in Kohlberg's terms). Again, however, these concepts are still concrete; they are not based on abstract ideas as in the later "law and order" or "conscientious" stages. For example, when preoperational learners are observed while playing games, they seem to play according to their own rules, unconcerned with what others do, and they don't understand "winning" or "losing." Concrete operational learners play games according to rules which tell them (concretely) what to do and what not to do, but they don't *question* the rules, or make up their own.

These cognitive operations of the seven and eight year old are still tied to the immediate concrete situation, however. They are not abstract propositions that can be generalized to many situations, as they will be in the next stage of "formal operations."

Preadolescent development—early formal operational thought

Why do adolescents get so impatient and dissatisfied with society and with their parents? They can think of alternatives!

Another type of progression of cognitive operations emerges toward the *end* of the concrete operational period, in the preadolescent stage of physical and sexual development, at about the age of eleven or twelve. (The onset of adolescence varies with sex and with the individual, as you know.) This is an increase in ability to imagine potential *combinations* of concrete objects and processes. For example, if you ask a nine-year-old learner to combine colored counters in twos, threes, and so forth, or to make all the combinations of colors including those in different sequences (i.e., red-blue-green differs from red-green-blue), he or she will not make a complete list or find all possibilities. At about twelve years, however, the learner manages this quite well by developing a method that exhausts all the possibilities.

Another example is an experiment where there are five jars, A through E, of colorless liquids (see Figure 2–5). The combination of jars A, C, and E produces a yellow color; jar B has a chemical which changes the yellow back to colorless, and jar D is just water. The learner is shown the final result, i.e., the yellow solution, and asked to find the combination which produces it. During the concrete operational stage, between ages seven and eleven, the learner will try combinations of two jars—although probably not all combinations—and then will skip all other possibilities and try all five together. After the age of twelve the learner will proceed methodically using all possible combinations of one, two, three, and so forth, and will thus solve the problem.

By this and other improvements in ability to deal with concrete situations, the learner ultimately comes to the final step in the development of intelligence which Piaget calls "formal operational thought." This kind of thought can be illustrated by the process of discovering the relationships involved in a balance beam to which two different weights can be attached at different distances from the fulcrum or pivot point (see Figure 2–6). At the formal operational stage of development, the learner is able not only to comprehend the relationship between equal weights and equal distances from the pivot, and the relationship between unequal weights and unequal distances, but he or she is also able to formulate the hypothesis or proposition that there is a proportion involved, i.e., that $W(1)/W(2) = L(2)/L(1)$ [or $W(1) \times L(1) = W(2) \times L(2)$]. This implies the learner can predict that if you increase the weight, you have to decrease the distance to maintain balance, and for a given change in weight can *predict* what the change in distance will have to be. This goes beyond the concrete situations which can be found (by trial and error) to produce a balance, and formulates a proposition about things that have not yet happened, i.e., it goes beyond the concrete existing situation, into the realm of the possible but not yet existing.

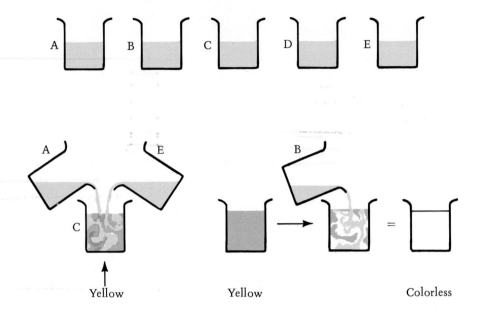

Combinations of twos: A+B, B+C, A+C, B+D, etc.
Combinations of threes: A+B+C, B+C+D, A+C+D, A+B+D, . . . etc.
Combinations of fours: A+B+C+D, B+C+D+E, . . . etc.
Combinations of fives: A+B+C+D+E

Figure 2–5. *Combination of elements experiment.*

The abilities to conceive of things that have not occurred, to imagine many possible outcomes from different combinations of events, and to imagine many hypotheses or possible ways of looking at a problem also enable adolescents and post-adolescents to handle more complex subject matter, such as calculus, philosophy, sociology, and other subjects which emphasize abstract formulations. It also makes it possible to develop the later stages of ego (a la Loevinger), morality (Kohlberg), and personality (a la Erikson).

One important message that Piaget and Inhelder emphasize concerning development is the relationship between cognitive processes and affect (feelings, desires, motives). As they put it, affect (feelings, etc.) motivates behavior patterns just as the "id" energizes personality generally. However, just as the ego and superego are needed to balance the id, social perceptions and comprehensions are needed to balance and modify feelings. Behavior is therefore all one: cognitive structures don't explain the motives or drives, nor do drives account for the cognitive processes needed to satisfy them. They operate together, and both must be considered in any teaching strategy.

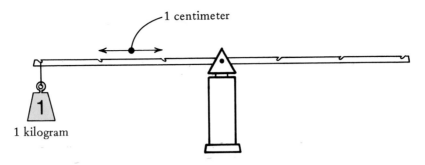

1 centimeter

1 kilogram

Where would you put a
3 kilogram weight to balance it?

$$1 \text{ kg} \times 3 \text{ cm} = \underline{3} \text{ kg} \times \underline{?} \text{ cm}$$
$$W \times L = W \times L$$

Figure 2–6. *Relationships in a balance beam experiment.*

A CONCRETE APPROACH TO DISEQUILIBRIUM

Ms. Evans is teaching sixth-grade social studies. The current topic is the legislative process, how a bill is brought before Congress. The text is fairly readable, and Ms. Evans describes the process in some detail to the class to prepare the students to read the book and understand it. After they have read the book, she asks them some questions like, "If you were a legislator, how would you go about getting a bill passed?" The response is very thin: one of her best students, who is always prepared and ready to volunteer, hesitantly raises her hand and asks if maybe the answer is to give the bill to the Speaker of the House. It becomes quite clear that in spite of her explanation and their reading, the process is not all clear: some of them have it mixed up with elections, which are coming up next month, and others have it mixed up with the Presidency—they feel that the President has to introduce the bill, and so you would go to the President.

Ms. Evans decides that the abstract treatment that she has been giving the topic is not adequate, even though these children are supposed to be entering the formal operational stage of cognitive development. Furthermore, their lack of interest seems to indicate that the way she is presenting the information is wrong also. Therefore, she decides to make two basic changes: one, to deal with the topic in more concrete terms; and two, to present it as a discrepancy which (she hopes) will be optimal, and therefore get them interested in mastering the subject in order to reduce the discrepancy. However, she finds that neither of these is very easy to do. First, to make it concrete, she has to develop a simplified model of the process, so she designs a simulation project where the learners take the part of congressmen, with a Speaker of the House, and where they have two parties, and each member of the class has a role to play. This is fine in theory, but working out the simulation takes her two weeks of writing and rewriting, in her spare time! Then she has to figure out some discrepancy: so she develops an imaginary situation related to conservation of resources (which they are all interested in) and as a part of this situation they need to draft a bill in order to make sure that factories along a river in the state do not continue to dump industrial waste into the water. This takes another week of spare-time work to incorporate into the simulation. She figures that they will have to practice the simulation a bit first, and then try the environmental problem after they have rehearsed their basic roles in the legislature. When Ms. Evans tries this out, it bombs completely the first day. Confusion is everywhere; the students have never done anything like this before, and there were a lot of things she hadn't thought of. However, in spite of the confusion and anxiety which this causes, she finds that the students are very much involved. When she asks them if they want to do it some more the next day, almost all want to go on. So the "concrete" part did have a payoff! They get some of their simple introductory roles down a little better the next day (running through some basic routines) and they tackle the environmental issues. Again there is confusion, but the discrepancy does turn out to be reasonably close to "optimal," i.e., most of the learners are "turned on" by the problem, and they show that they are willing to do some additional research during and out of school in order to help Ms. Evans work the problem through. Despite the many weaknesses of the project, she decides that it has been worthwhile, and feels that she has brought the learners into closer involvement with the subject matter.

Implications of Piaget's theories for teaching

The implications of Piaget's theories have been summarized by one interpreter as follows:

> Teaching involves setting up situations which are new to the learner, and which cause her to think about it in terms of the mental operations that are available to her: in accommodating to the situation, the learner's cognitive structure may be modified. These situations should not be precisely what the learner is accustomed to, nor should they be so far different that the learner "turns off" and withdraws, either in her actions or in her thinking or both. That is, the situation should represent an "optimal discrepancy," something which almost, but not quite, matches the learner's present cognitive structure. Since it is the nature of the learner and of his cognitive processes to be active, to make the discrepancy optimal is to motivate the learner. The only reward or reinforcement that is needed is feedback (information returning) from the situation itself as the learner operates on it, which tells her that progress is being made, or that the altered response is more adequate—i.e., indications of success in dealing with the problem. This is sometimes referred to as "intrinsic reinforcement." (Phillips, 1969)

If a situation, an environment, or an assumed "learning situation" is completely compatible with the established mental structure or expectations of the learner—then he (or she) does not learn from it. If, on the other hand, the situation does not fit into his mental structure at all—if he is completely baffled by it—he does not learn from it either, since he cannot begin to assimilate it, and therefore cannot accommodate.   The best learning task is one where the child's cognitive structure almost but not quite matches that of the problem.   If such a task is presented, since the brain is naturally active, learning will occur without urging, threatening, or offering rewards.

It is not possible to teach a learner who is in the beginning or middle of one stage to adapt or cope with situations that require abilities of the next higher stage. You may get a "right answer" from the learner, but it will not represent real understanding.   He (or she) will not be able to understand it, that is, to transfer it to other situations of the same type, until he is at the next stage.   You can, however, arrange a rich variety of experiences that "exercise" the student's cognitive abilities at the present level and prepare the foundation for moving on when he or she is ready.

As the learner grows older, more and more of the reasoning is done internally, through imagination, so that fewer and fewer overt responses have to be made. The learner is able to try out solutions in his head, as well as think of many combinations or permutations of things and processes, and to imagine how they might work out.   Therefore, as the learner comes into the formal operational stage, learning and problem solving are not overtly trial and error, but rather consist of "thinking," which is in a sense covert trial and error, but on a more sophisticated level and using more complex relationships or concepts and anticipating results without actually trying out each possibility.

STIMULATING EARLY LEARNING

Experiments that increase cognitive ability

Can you make a child more intelligent? How? Do you want to?

Is it possible that by early stimulation of the learning processes, one can expand the ability of a person to learn later in life?   D. O. Hebb (1949) was one of the first psychologists to create a theoretical model of the brain that could account for such an increase.   In his model, a perception of the environment was registered as a relationship between nerve cells, in the form of reduced resistance to transmission of impulses between these cells.   This makes it more likely that incoming signals of the same type will travel that same path rather than the other possibilities.   Hebb envisioned networks of such low-resistance paths as responding to particular types of stimuli and thus forming mental images of the outside world.   This was his physical counterpart to "learning," his way of explaining how events in the environment might be registered in the brain.   More sophisticated models of such processes have been constructed since then, of course, but this gave a conceptual basis for believing that early experiences determine to some extent what and how much can be learned later on.   In the 1960s reviews of research on early learning also suggested that the first three years of life are very important to the formation of intelligence or the ability to learn (Hunt, 1964).   The 1960s also saw a series of experiments in which young rats were raised in rich and challenging environments, with swings, wheels, push toys, and other things to explore.   They showed more noticeable increases in brain weight, displacement (volume), and structural composition (determined through autopsies) as compared with "deprived" rats who had no such advantages (Kretch, 1969).

It is interesting to note that these experimenters tried a number of different types of education for their rats, and found only specific ones to be effective in altering their brains.   Among those that did *not* have this effect were (a) sheer exercise or physical activity alone, (b) varied *visual* stimulation, (c) handling or taming or petting (the researchers commented on this by quoting the title of a book by Bettelheim, i.e., *Love Is Not Enough*), (d) the presence of another rat in the cage with a deprived rat.   One approach that had a small effect was teaching the rats to press levers in order to receive food (a traditional operant conditioning process for demonstrating learning).   The only exercise they found to be really effective was freedom to roam around in a large object-filled space; to a lesser extent,

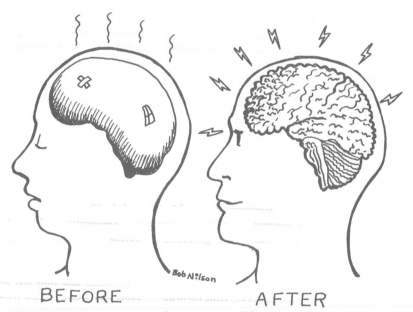

BEFORE   AFTER

E.J. of Peoria writes: "Before I took your course I was mentally flabby. My cortex was smooth as a boiled egg. Now – thanks to your easy one-semester course – I have more convolutions than others in my class, and am able to think really deep thoughts. Heartily recommend your course to all who would like to think good."

Some views of cognitive development assume we begin life with nothing in our brains and proceed to develop knowledge through experience.

giving the young rat continuous and varied maze problems to solve would develop the brain also.

GIVING A YOUNG CHILD A HIGH IQ

How can you go about making sure that a young child has a high IQ? First of all, you need to identify the nature of the tasks that define IQ—you need to know what kinds of abilities and skills are called for on an intelligence test. Then you need to give the child a great *variety* of experience in accomplishing these tasks and skills. This can begin when the child is very young, although you have to adapt the tasks to his (or her) age and cognitive stage. For example, one task on intelligence tests—or on many of them, at least—is counting objects; that is, given a set of things, the child is supposed to count them. For example, you could make up a game in which the child is expected to put a ring on each of a set of pegs, or another in which the child holds up a finger every time *you* hold up a finger. The challenge of such tasks is usually enough motivation, plus the attention involved from an adult. If these are not enough, you can reward the child initially for participating with things he likes, like food and toys, and then gradually substitute approval by you for the concrete rewards.

Another way to increase intelligence, to make sure that the child develops to his fullest cognitive potential, is to invent games where he is required to observe things and keep in mind where they are stored—say, by covering them up and having him find them, or by storing something and then having him remember where it is stored. Another type of task is sorting—putting things into different categories, such as putting all square blocks in one pile and all round ones in another. Still another task would be to put together puzzles that make various shapes or objects—like a number of blocks of wood which, when assembled correctly, form the outline of a person. You could vary this by having the child identify missing elements, such as a drawing of a person without a head or an arm. Ultimately, he would learn to put a person together, given all the parts—arms, legs, etc. One very common task on an intelligence test is to draw a picture of a person. Part of the scoring of the test relates to what the child leaves out, as well as how he draws them, and how close he is to the correct proportions.

Most intelligence tests require some reading. Therefore, teaching a child to read will increase his "intelligence," i.e., his score on an IQ test. Beyond just reading, the child should be taught to interpret what he reads and to judge whether what he reads makes sense. There are a variety of games you can make up to do this.

Another type of task is holding facts in mind—such as repeating lists of numbers, letters, or words. You can give the child practice by having him remember things—like sets of directions, lists of things to get at the store, and the like.

Generally speaking, frequent excursions beyond the home or the neighborhood add to a child's intelligence, partly because they add to the different examples of things that he experiences and thus add to his fund of concepts and facts. Thus, trips, excursions, outings, and general exposure to richer environments in and out of the home will contribute.

Finally, just talking with the child, getting his ideas, asking him to make judgments and predictions, and listening to his reasons for things will contribute greatly to his intelligence. This not only gives him mental tasks with a variety of requirements, but also reinforces his thinking processes by giving them attention and making them part of his relationship with you.

Early enrichment: Montessori

One of the first
woman doctors,
and an early pre-
school program.

In the early 1900s the first woman doctor in Italy, Maria Montessori, designed a special curriculum for teaching retarded children to read, write, and do arithmetic. When she realized that normal children in conventional schools were not doing as well as her retarded children, she tested her approaches in a child-care center in a housing development in Naples.   There she demonstrated that three- and four-year-old children were able to learn to read, write, and do arithmetic, and that they enjoyed these tasks using the carefully designed and sequenced materials, tasks, and games that she had developed.   Many educators felt that she was wrong to intrude and "force" young children to learn before they were "ready," and similar reactions are found today to carefully sequenced and tested programs for early learning.   If you read Montessori's books, you may be struck by the modern tone of her writings, by her educational philosophy, which was humanistic and child-centered, and by her interest in making learning more productive and involving for the children.

Actually, encouragement of early learning has a long and successful history; one source for a discussion of the matter as well as suggestions for bringing about early intellectual development is a book entitled *Give Your Child a Superior Mind* (Englemann and Englemann, 1966).   One unique approach to early learning came

Maria Montessori

in the 1950s and used an electric typewriter as the vehicle and motivator. O.K. Moore, then of Rutgers, had seized upon this device as one aid in helping his daughter recover from an operation and make up normal learning, in which she was behind. He developed a method which proved to be effective in teaching letters and words and reading to three and four year olds: he would stand behind the child while she played with the keyboard, and he would give the letter name (or the sound, or both) for each letter that was struck. This proved to be very motivating, and three and four year olds would go on playing this game for long periods, up to an hour or more at times. Ultimately they would start giving the names and sounds themselves, and would progress from there to reading simple words. When asked once by the author whether these children at five or six understood the rather complicated things they were reading, he suggested that the publication of their own newspaper indicated that they did!

Jerome Bruner and early learning

A man who has had impact on how we try to teach, and how we construct curricula.

Perhaps the best known exponent of enriched early learning experiences for children was Jerome Bruner, a psychologist who made his reputation initially in research in concept learning (something which will be dealt with at length in Chapter 10). After Russia launched Sputnik I, the first satellite, in the late 1950s, a large group of scientists concerned with science education (and a smaller group of psychologists and educators) began to consider the existing knowledge about science teaching as well as to explore their own intuitive feelings about how science should be taught. Through a series of conferences, they came to some general basic conclusions about these matters, which Bruner reported in a book titled *The Process of Education* (1960). This book was widely read and had a far-reaching impact on educational reform. Bruner became one of the major spokesmen for the new era in science education and in education generally as well. Some of the scientists involved in the initial group went on to organize and direct large projects for curriculum revision and rejuvenation, the first of these being the Physical Science Study Committee (PSSC), and others being the School Mathematics Study Group and the Biological Sciences Curriculum Study (SMSG and BSCS, respectively). Bruner himself turned from his previous research in concept learning and cognition generally to working with elementary and secondary curricula that exemplified his concepts of teaching and learning. Later, he went back to the study of learning, concentrating on learning in very young infants.

One of the main themes of *The Process of Education* is that it is possible to teach *any* subject or concept to children at *any age,* as long as one does it in a manner appropriate for that age. Bruner's conclusions were in part an extension of Piaget's research. Piaget himself had no intention of demonstrating that children could be taught concepts of science at a younger age, but his use of scientifically oriented problems in his research (as well as his identification of different cognitive stages) led Bruner and others to this conclusion, i.e., that if one presents problems to children in a way that matches their cognitive stage, they can learn from them.

12

According to Bruner, readiness is learned and can be taught.

One physicist later carried out this principle when he designed a successful unit for first grade science based on the theory of relativity!

Another hypothesis which emerged from this work was that readiness, or the ability to learn a certain concept or skill, is not just something that comes through maturation.   Readiness is learned, and therefore it can be taught.   This does not mean that maturation is unimportant, just that it is not sufficient in itself.   If one waits until certain kinds of learning just "happen," one might wait a very long time, and the learning might not happen at all, regardless of the learner's maturity.

One of Bruner's most challenging books is *Toward a Theory of Instruction* (1966), in which he foresees the development of teaching theory as a major study in education.   In this book and in other writings, Bruner advanced his own developmental stages.   These included an "enactive" level where the very young child learns through active involvement with the environment, as with Piaget's preoperational and concrete operational stages.   The next level uses semi-abstract symbols such as diagrams and pictures that still resemble the concrete world.   Bruner referred to these diagrams as "iconic" stimuli, and called this stage the "iconic" level. Finally, the child arrives at the "symbolic" level, where he or she is able to deal with abstract presentations of the real world, such as words.   These developmental stages are roughly parallel to those of Piaget, i.e. "enactive" covers sensorimotor and early preoperational; "iconic" covers late preoperational and early concrete; while "symbolic" refers to late concrete and formal operational stages.

In addition to identifying these developmental stages of cognitive growth, Bruner outlined some other aspects of development that have implications for teaching and learning. He saw cognitive growth in the increasing independence of the response of the learner from the particular stimulus, which in turn implies a greater degree of cognitive processing and mental representations beyond the immediate sensory data (as in the later concrete operational stage and the formal operational stage of Piaget). Bruner also saw language as the key to cognitive development, and he placed emphasis (as did Piaget) on the language of the learner as an indicator of the ongoing cognitive processing. Bruner saw cognitive growth as being marked by increasing ability of the learner to deal with a number of different alternatives simultaneously, to perform a number of activities concurrently, and to attend to a number of different situations by switching attention rapidly from one to the other.

Accelerate or wait until ready?

Whether to try to get learners to learn earlier, or to wait until they are "ready"—and what "ready" means—is a modern debate.

Some of the pros and cons of emphasizing early learning, and of emphasizing the importance of teaching learners to be ready for more complex concepts and learning skills, have been summarized ably in an educational psychology text (Craig, Mehrens, Clarizio, 1975). Among the pros given there are:

- There is a critical period for intellectual development which must be taken advantage of or it is lost. (The occurrence of this period seems to be considered to be earlier and earlier as time goes on.)
- A head start means later superiority, and intellectual superiority means economic advantages as well as a happier life.
- An early conceptual foundation facilitates later assimilation of more abstract, general, and precise presentations.
- Early learning insures one against acquisition of misconceptions.
- Early learning fosters the development of favorable attitudes and social behaviors.
- Early learning fosters increased self-confidence, a more mature personality.
- While instruction might be more efficient at a later age (critical period?), the child would miss many things if we waited.
- Certain skills are needed earlier, even though they might be learned more easily later.

Among the cons (against) are the following:

- A facility in rule learning, rather than the kind of rote learning that early learning usually emphasizes, is the most important thing in instruction.
- Instruction is more effective when given to older children.

- According to research studies, those who start late usually catch up.
- Language concepts (sentence structures, grammar) develop naturally, through maturation and everyday exposure.
- Piaget has indicated a reluctance to endorse early learning; he feels that we don't understand the natural evolution of cognition well enough to alter it without creating damage.
- Some research on lower organisms related to problem solving (Harlow, others) suggests that habits of problem solving adopted by younger animals can hinder the development of more effective and sophisticated strategies when they are older, as compared with other animals who have not been given the problems earlier.
- You can't speed up stages of cognitive development (Piaget, also Kohlberg).
- Enrichment of an already adequate environment has little impact on a child's intelligence (Elkind).
- Most of the research on critical periods has been done with lower organisms, and may not apply to humans.

Summary outline with key concepts

☞ *Cognition as* processing of information; differs from receiving (perceiving) information, and from producing physical or verbal responses: involves memory, relationships, coordination of input from different senses.

☞ *Language related* to cognition but not identical / Early babbling becomes words and words and sentences built quickly, with most of language complete by age four / Acquisition partly imitative, partly trial-error, partly guided by inherited mechanisms evolved for this purpose / Some feel that language develops separately from thought, and thought develops separately from language; others feel that language is a vehicle for thought. They are probably separate during early years; integrated from about age two on / There is thinking without language, however / Psycholinguists assert that translation of surface structures into deep structures requires some hereditary capacity or aptitude; the process is too complex to explain through trial-error learning or imitation / Stages of language development proposed by one theorist relate primarily to number of words in average sentence / Expressive language not the same as receptive; one can be normal while the other is retarded, e.g., good expression but poor receptive development, or comprehension / Just as concrete actions become internalized (in the sensorimotor period) so language becomes internalized; older children talk to themselves less, "think" thoughts instead.

☞ *Piaget feels* that cognition is developed before language / Piaget interested in how thinking develops as compared with "IQ" / Piaget against accelerated learning / Piaget's experiments exemplified by ten-sticks experiment, three-mountain problem, juice glass experiment; these demonstrate differences between preoperational, concrete operational, and formal operational stages / Assimilation of incoming information is part of normal processing: if situation is unusual or different, i.e., if learner

the way of thought processes and learning abilities, and what materials and aids you might need for this. Also consider the question of how you would determine whether the discrepancy you choose is "optimal."

2. You have a friend whose three-year-old daughter talks a blue streak. Your friend is very proud of her daughter's precocity, and shows her off at every opportunity. You notice, however, that her daughter doesn't seem to be able to understand things you say to her, at least not as well as your son of the same age; furthermore, she has trouble following simple directions. She also seems to have trouble getting along with other children; your son says she doesn't know what they are talking about. How would you explain this possible problem to your friend, how would you check on whether there is a problem of language development, and what might you suggest she do about it if there is a problem?

3. A parents' organization is considering the possibility of a very early childhood cognitive-learning program to make their children brighter and ultimately more successful both in school and generally. You are asked to present some pros and cons. What would you tell them?

Suggested activities

1. Observe learners at different ages in schools or learning centers, and look for evidence of the various stages of cognitive development and language development. Note exceptions and contradictions as well as stages that are parallel to the theory.

2. Use the receptive and expressive language development checklists to determine the developmental level of one or more children.

3. Try out some of the Piaget tasks on learners of different ages and observe their responses; try to determine what stages they are in. Don't assume that college students are all at the formal operational level in every task.

4. Interview some early childhood educators and get their opinions on early enrichment, Montessori, Bruner, and others who have become involved in this level of education. Don't be surprised to find wide differences in opinions.

Suggested readings

The readings referred to in the text are numerous and worth consulting. There are many books on Piaget; don't overlook Piaget's books themselves, particularly the more recent ones, some done with Inhelder (his associate). Bruner's books are also well-known and well-read; the *Process of Education* is a classic, while the *Toward a Theory of Instruction* is found to be hard reading but rewarding by many students. Early childhood education has become a field in itself, of course, and there are many sources to consult. There is no one source to refer to on cognitive development because there are so many diverse approaches, theories, and levels.

3

Individual Differences

CONTENTS

ABOUT CHAPTER 3

How will this chapter benefit you?

After studying this chapter you will be able to compare people along a number of dimensions that might not occur to you otherwise: socioeconomic status, personality characteristics, intelligence, and creativity, to mention only a few. This information should increase your appreciation of each individual as a complex array of traits and attributes. It should also enable you to deal more completely and effectively with learners of different ages, because these traits are often constant over many years. You will also become more aware of certain characteristics of minority groups which make learning difficult for them, and you will be better able to assist them.

What might make it difficult to learn

You may have a negative reaction, either conscious or subconscious, to thinking about individual differences; you may be compensating for certain problems of your own, or you may have been taught that it is not right to dwell on such differences. However, if you are to help learners effectively, including your own children if there should be some, you need to recognize and allow for these differences even though you don't acknowledge them outwardly. You may also find some topics here that strike rather close to home, and you may want to avoid thinking about things that are so personally involving. Again, however, you will need to rise above this if you are to be able to deal with others effectively.

Some reasons for understanding individual differences

This has been dealt with above; however, in general, it seems fair to say that you need to understand, recognize, and be able to deal with individual differences if you are going to be working with individuals as well as groups, whether as a parent, teacher, group leader, or specialist. Another compelling reason, of course, is that studying individual differences means learning more about yourself and your friends.

Assuring successful learning

If you can convince yourself that people are interesting, and that you can learn something about them from reading as well as from observing and interacting with them, then you shouldn't have too much trouble here. However, a few terms may confuse you because I won't have had an opportunity to explain them, and don't want to take time out now; the glossary will help. Of course, one good guideline is to seek help when you are confused, first from fellow students, then from your instructor or other faculty members.

Objectives for Chapter 3

My objectives are to improve your understanding of learners and to build a foundation for understanding theories of teaching and group management that will be discussed later. However, not everything presented here can be incorporated later, nor can I explain the applications or implications of every bit of information given here. Therefore, I would like you to be able to handle the various types of questions given as well, as a means of firming up your knowledge and storing it for use in the future when needed.

RATIONALE AND BACKGROUND OF CHAPTER 3

People develop in similar ways, but are different from each other

People develop in similar ways, but at any given age or time there are differences among individuals that parents and teachers need to recognize.

Though every person goes through periods of development, certain patterns of characteristics tend to define individuals throughout their lives even as they go through all the same processes that others do. A very anxious child is apt to be an anxious adolescent and adult; a creative adult is likely to have been a creative student in seventh grade. Such enduring differences are the focus of the study of personality. In recent years, there has been some progress in changing basic elements of individuals' personalities, but generally such traits are considered unchanging through life.

Individual differences affect learning and teaching

Sex differences are very obvious, yet their effects on learning and teaching are often overlooked. Socioeconomic differences—differences in "moneypower," as it were—can make a difference in the way a learner or group of learners will respond to teaching. Personality differences interact with learning processes and, more importantly, with the motivation to learn.

Individualized instruction

Teaching which makes allowances for individual differences is one of the most important developments in recent educational history. Many different techniques and organizational approaches have been developed for this purpose: Individually Prescribed Instruction, Individually Guided Instruction, Open Learning, and Project-Centered Classrooms, to name a few. All are based on a recognition of individual differences and on the assumption that there are ways of adapting teaching and learning to these differences. Whether this assumption is entirely justified is a matter of some debate, but an understanding of some of the dimensions along which learners differ is an essential foundation for such teaching and learning processes.

PERSONALITY CHARACTERISTICS RESULTING FROM DIFFERENT PARENTAL TREATMENTS

In recent years studies of effects of parent styles and ways of treating children have shown consistent relationships to resulting personality traits.

During the last ten or fifteen years an increasing amount of information has become available from research on parent and child characteristics, particularly from research which follows children over a period of years, rather than days or weeks. We will discuss the personality types that are most evident in these studies, and relate them to the type of parent treatment that seems to "breed" them. These types are oversimplified, however, as any classification of human behavior must necessarily be.

The independent, outgoing, self-assertive,
achievement-oriented learner

These adjectives describe a somewhat ideal kind of learner, obviously. Home climate and treatments which produce this admirable combination have three basic characteristics:

1. The parents are warm, accepting, and nurturant; they are not hostile or rejecting;
2. The parents are democratic and communicative, and they do not intrude into the learner's "psychological space" by demanding to know what he or she is thinking, or whether he or she has remembered to do various things, or is ready for some particular responsibility (this relates to Becker's views [1964] of "calm detachment vs. anxious emotional involvement" as an important dimension of development);
3. The parents exert firm but appropriate behavioral controls, rather than being lax and permissive, and they expect an appropriate level of effort to achieve.

There is some evidence that the most successful parents tend to set the example in these things, rather than lecture or advise.

The aggressive, overassertive, disobedient child

Where this kind of behavior exists in moderate amounts, it seems to reflect a lack of control in the home. Freud would see it as an expression of a normal "id" which has not internalized parent controls to form adequate "superego" (see Chapter 1). This can result from a democratic home where autonomy and involvement of the child in discussions and decisions is encouraged, but where there has not been a balancing emphasis on the kinds of limits that early moral and social stages require (see Kohlberg and Loevinger, Chapter 1).

Where aggressiveness and disobedience are regular and extreme, you will often find hostility and rejection in one or both parents, in addition to the lack of control just mentioned. This results in a counter-hostility on the child's part.

Ⓠ

A recent conclusion regarding aggressiveness is that it results from permissiveness as well as from rejection.

THERE YOU ARE - ALL DRESSED SO YOU WON'T GET A CHILL... **NOW** YOU MAY GO OUTSIDE AND **PLAY** BUT DON'T OVERTIRE, AND DON'T PLAY WITH BILLY. MAKE A SMALL SNOWMAN. USE STONES FOR EYES AND A CARROT FOR A NOSE. I'LL HAVE HOT CHOCOLATE FOR YOU IN TWENTY MINUTES. BUT MAYBE I SHOULD HELP YOU. WAIT IN THE YARD FOR ME. THIS IS GOING TO BE FUN! WHY DON'T YOU SAY SOMETHING?

Bob Wilson

The warm, restrictive parent.

Where parental discipline control is weak, this counter-hostility is taken out on the parents and on others in the family; when the parental discipline is strong, then the counter-hostility is taken out on people outside the family, including teachers, or it is discharged through fantasies.   When parents are inconsistent in their behavioral control, occasional discipline serves to express their hostility and rejection, and makes things worse rather than better.   Extreme aggressiveness and disobedience are referred to generally as a "conduct disorder."

There is a special case of this kind of behavior which is caused by biological and neurological makeup, usually in boys.   Such boys are trying and difficult from birth (the "difficult child"), and their parents may become hostile and rejecting without realizing it, yet be accepting toward their other children.   They may also feel guilty, and thus be lax in behavioral control.   Such learners are sometimes called "hyperactive."   This subject is treated further in Chapter 4.

The withdrawn, neurotic child

Many children are unsocial, self-blaming, and have a "poor ego" or "poor sense of self."   One type of parent behavior that leads to this is overcontrol, both psychological and behavioral.   If this is also accompanied by parental hostility and rejection, it can lead to a level of self-blame that is neurotic.   Such children are unable to express counter-hostility; therefore they direct their hostility to themselves. This makes them overconscientious, guilt-ridden, and anxious.

Boys who have social, emotional, and cognitive difficulties

Some boys have problems "across the board" without featuring aggressiveness or delinquency as described above.   Such boys are often from homes where fathers are absent as a result of divorce, or death, or being away in such jobs as the merchant marine.   Such boys are likely to be impulsive and to have difficulty delaying gratification and assuming social responsibility.   They are less likely to be socially self-assertive and competent, also.

Children who are withdrawn and non-assertive, rather than over-aggressive, are generally said to have a "personality disorder," in the language of emotional disabilities.

The dependent, unmotivated, unsocial child

This kind of girl or boy is most often the product of overcontrol of both psychological and behavioral kinds, coupled with warmth and acceptance rather than hostility and rejection.   Either the parents keep the child too bound to them cognitively, through questions and warnings and guidance and never letting the child think for himself or herself (psychological "intrusiveness"), or they keep the child too bound up in strict rules and restrictions, or both.

The child with a good self-concept and high self-esteem

This aspect of personality is very dependent on the model set by the parents. If the parents have high regard for themselves, are stable and resilient in the face of adversity as a result, and able to deal realistically and effectively with others, then their children are usually the same. This kind of personality usually is warm and accepting of others, including their own children later on. (Not **all** parents are warm and accepting to their own children, strange as this may seem to those who have warm, accepting parents.)

A WARM, RESTRICTIVE PARENT

Ms. May was very affectionate toward her five-year-old daughter, Trudy, and gave her a lot of attention, read to her, and thought up many things for her to do. She kept her quite close, and seldom left her to herself for very long. When Trudy would go out to play, Ms. May would quiz her on where she had been and what she had done at some length. When Trudy would want to play on the swing or climb a tree or go sliding in the winter, her mother usually had a number of reservations and restrictions and made it clear to Trudy that she would be worried about her and didn't want her to take any chances. When Trudy would start to build something with blocks or build a snowman, Ms. May would be right there with ideas of what to build or things to use for the snowman, and would often suggest that Trudy had done one thing long enough when she was just "getting into" the play. Ms. May would also arrange for Trudy to visit friends, and for friends to visit, and pick them up and take them back at appointed times; Trudy didn't seem to have the initiative just to go out and play with whomever she wished or whoever was around. Other mothers in the neighborhood considered Trudy a bit shy and withdrawn, and wondered why she never seemed to be able to "get out of herself" and enjoy play. She also seemed anxious at times, and worried about getting home and was unsure of herself when away from home. Trudy exhibited, then, some of the characteristics of children whose parents are warm and accepting, but also restrictive.

Some tentative conclusions regarding parent (and teacher) behavior

Here are some tentative conclusions concerning ways of producing behavior and personality characteristics. (Since parent treatment is a long-term thing, this does not mean that you can modify or reverse the effects of such long-term experience in a short time.)

Ⓠ₃

First, warmth and acceptance provide a good foundation for other behaviors; they modulate other treatments, making bad ones better and less damaging. However, they are not sufficient in themselves; as Bruno Bettelheim said in the title of one of his well-known books, "Love is not enough."

Hostility and rejection result in hostility, dissatisfaction, and poor self-concept. They inflict a kind of continuous frustration which can result in aggressive behavior as well, depending on the amount of control exerted by the parent. Hostility and rejection are very difficult to deal with, because the parent or teacher who expresses them does so indirectly for the most part, and that parent or teacher cannot recognize the source of his or her behavior as such. Such behavior is unconscious, and rationalized as something else: protecting the child, being for his or her own good, protecting other children or adults, observing the rules or the law, avoiding spoiling the child, and so forth.

Lack of control breeds lack of self-control in the child, and encourages aggressiveness and other antisocial behavior where there are other causes for it. However, too much control results in overinhibited behavior, lack of self-assertiveness,

Affection and discipline are important for the preschool child.

and inability to compete socially.   Encouragement and support of achievement re-sults in a high level of achievement; lack of it results in a low level.   The same is true of creativity.

There are also patterns of interaction with very young children that seem to produce happier, more competent children.   One investigator of the comparative behaviors of mothers of preschool children has given the following guidelines:

1. Provide access for exploration of living areas—make the house safe for chil-dren and allow them to explore it;
2. Be a firm, effective disciplinarian, but also show great affection for the child;
3. Be very responsive to interaction-seeking behavior, whether for help, com-fort, or to share something the child is interested in;
4. Learn to be perceptive concerning the current interests and concerns of the child—know how she or he is feeling;
5. Communicate verbally with the child and emphasize the use of language rather than gesture or facial expression.

SEX DIFFERENCES

How the sexes differ in their reactions to school

Similarities between men and women, as well as differences, have received much attention due to "women's lib" and "affirmative ac-tion."

Janice Jones is consistently prompt in handing in her assignments and almost an-noyingly eager to help you out, while Billy Brown seems to be hypnotized by some-thing in the other side of the window and defiantly forgets to bring a pencil to class. You have encountered an age-old mystery of classroom differences: the boy-girl an-tithesis.   Although you will have to devise your own answers for preventing girls from becoming too smug or self-effacing, and boys from feeling inferior and overly peer-oriented, it might be useful to know why the difference exists at all.

A strange transformation occurs when elementary school children call a halt to the war of the sexes and begin to become interested in one another.   The achievement balance seems to shift from high-achieving girls and reluctant, rebel-lious boys, to self-effacing young ladies (the "play dumb" syndrome) and more ag-gressive young men.

In the elementary grades, girls outperform boys in all areas; the ratio of boys to girls with reading problems ranges as high as six to one.   One theorist feels that this is because boys see school as a feminine, emasculating place to be, where female teachers reward feminine traits of obedience and suppressed aggression, and femi-nine activities like painting, coloring, and singing.   _Adolescent girls, however, begin to take on their female role in society.   They begin to see academic work as a form of inappropriate aggressive behavior since it involves competition with peers (whether boys or girls)._   Since many girls are brought up to feel that it is "unlady-like" to be competitive, they inhibit intense intellectual stirring and begin to backslide (Kagan, 1969).

Differences in aptitudes and traits

Boys have superior spatial ability, according to some research, and some feel that their later superiority in mathematics is based in part on this. Boys also are slightly more flexible in trying new approaches to solving problems; this may be related to their greater willingness to take risks. A comprehensive review of sex differences in intellectual functioning does not, however, give one the impression that these differences are major or highly significant in themselves (Maccoby and Jacklin). There are no dramatic differences in general intelligence. Girls learn to talk a bit earlier, and up to about the age of ten they do better in tests of spelling and grammar; however, this could be a reflection of the greater tendency to conformity which our society has been instilled in girls somewhat as a matter of course. This is not true of verbal reasoning and comprehension, however.

Girls are more *predictable* than boys; at a given age one can make better estimates of their future intelligence and achievement. Another way to put this is that boys are more variable (and thus less predictable) in their future performance and development than girls. How much of this is a result of environment is not known; it may again be the result of the greater freedom and autonomy given to boys, which allows them more room for such variation. One study in the 1960s found that German boys had fewer reading problems than German girls, while the reverse has always been true in America; this study also pointed out that there are more men in elementary school teaching in Germany than in America, and that reading and learning are considered "masculine" activities (Preston, 1962).

Boys are more aggressive, and this is linked to the presence of certain hormones during and immediately after pregnancy. There are cases where girls have received too much of a male hormone when in the womb, and they are born with certain exterior male sexual characteristics, although internally they are still females. There is some evidence, though not conclusive, that such girls are more masculine in their behavior later on, preferring the company of boys and boys' games to those of girls (Beach, 1975). The reverse condition, males with more than normal female hormones, or less male, seems to occur frequently also.

Teaching sex roles and behaviors

A number of investigators have observed sex-role influences of parents and teachers on the behavior of boys and girls. One study indicated that mothers seemed to encourage physical activity in three-week-old boys more than in girls of the same age, while they encouraged verbal behavior and social interaction in girls (Moss, 1967). A study of nursery school behavior found that boys reinforced other boys (through attention and approval) for boyish behavior, and girls reinforced other girls for girlish behavior. The *teachers*, however, reinforced feminine related play activity most often for *both* sexes. This may explain why boys are found to be maladjusted, inattentive, and rebellious far out of proportion to their relative numbers

Sex roles are often the result of adult influence.

(Fagot and Patterson, 1969). Studies of older boys and girls do not show such clear differences in parental treatment, except that boys are not allowed to show any feminine-type behavior although girls are allowed quite a range of boyish behaviors (i.e., girls can be tomboys, but boys can't be sissies) (Maccoby and Jacklin, 1974).

One recent study of students and teachers found that teachers perceived girls as calmer, more careful, more mature, higher achieving, more persistent, happier, more attractive, more likely to maintain eye contact, and more cooperative. The teachers were also more likely to mention girls as students to whom they were attached and less likely to name them as students about whom they were concerned (Brophy and Evertson, 1976). Observers (not teaching) who were in the same classrooms found the same kinds of differences, but they did not find them as great or as extensive as the teachers did: they saw boys as more active and less cooperative. They also described boys as more athletic, and girls as quieter, more dependent, bossier, and more likely to have good relations to the teacher. The more extreme differences seen by the teachers, therefore, appear to be based in part on attitudes conditioned by the different types of interactions that they have with boys as compared with girls. It was observed, for example, that one-to-one contacts with boys by teachers were more apt to be related to schoolwork, and more often involved criticism, while girls more often sought teacher approval for finished work. It would appear that when dealing with boys, teachers (usually female) were apt to fall into the "criticism trap" which is discussed in Chapter 11 in relation to behavior modification.

Women as achievers

In the 1970s much was written about the symbols of sexism in schools, such as the omission of women from history books, and the effects of using "he" or "his" when referring to students generally. The portrayal of males as strong and adventuresome and females as dependent and nurturant in elementary readers, the preponderance of males as administrators and females as elementary teachers, and the concentration of males in vocational classes were all subjects of criticism. Some felt strongly that this aspect of the climate of schools needed to be changed, and suggested strategies for bringing this about (Hahn, 1976).

A major problem in achievement by adult women is the reaction of society, particularly male society, to such achievement. The intelligent woman in the past had to learn to play dumb, because bright women threatened men and therefore were less able to "get" a man. The barriers to achievement in business were nearly insurmountable, and they are still high. This has led to a fear of success in some women. Intelligent boys aspire to high levels of achievement, but intelligent girls shrink from intellectual and other challenges because they see it leading to negative rather than positive outcomes.

One key to feminine personality, incidentally, is found in types of parents and their effects, already discussed. If one assumes that parents are generally warmer and more restrictive toward girls than boys, then one can predict that girls in general will have the characteristics of children brought up by warm, restrictive parents! This would include obedience, conformity, passivity, neuroticism, and inability to cope. For parents and teachers, then, perhaps the best advice in dealing with girls—and with learners generally—is to give support and encouragement, and to show reasonable expectations, along with moderate warmth and permissiveness. Such treatment would produce, assumedly, more independent and aggressive girls who would go on to achieve more than has been the norm for women.

However, you should expect a normal distribution of energy and aggressiveness among women, so only a relatively few women would (under these better conditions) have the drive and energy and intelligence to achieve *eminence* in their fields. Such achievement would not necessarily be intellectual; in the past it has been the *less* bold and impulsive *boys* who are the intellectual achievers, although it takes high boldness for girls to achieve intellectually (Maccoby and Jacklin, 1974). If girls are brought up with the same achievement motivation as boys, they will have greater aggressiveness, and will go on to achieve in nonacademic areas.

Taboos regarding sex-typing

Many common habits have sexist implications, and they need to be avoided if teachers or parents are to reduce sex-typing.   They include:

- Asking boys to do the heavy work, carrying things.
- Asking boys to lead groups, girls to be secretaries.
- Having boy-girl competitions.
- Being reluctant to suggest careers or technical professions for girls.
- Using different standards for male and female job-applicants.
- Channeling girls into certain courses (home economics) and away from others (shop).
- Expecting administrators in schools and other organizations to be males.
- Using textbooks that model sex-typing.
- In your writing using such terms as "when man first discovered fire. . ." or "when the lawyer put on his robe" or "if the teacher wishes to improve her communication. . . ."

DIFFERENCES RESULTING FROM SOCIOECONOMIC FACTORS

What are students from low socioeconomic status families like?

Whether it is right or fair, being poor also means being less able to learn— and making others less able to learn.

Much as we hate to confront the issue, money makes a difference, and learners from families and neighborhoods and areas that are "economically depressed" or "poor" are different in some ways from learners who come from "middle class" families or families with more than enough money.   If you come from a middle class or upper middle class background, it will be difficult for you to understand children from the poverty belt or the ghetto.   You will find them as a group less eager to learn, less likely to follow directions accurately, more likely to be hostile and aggressive, and generally less motivated to do the kinds of things that are expected of them in schools.   There will be exceptions, however, both individual ones and entire classes which are well prepared and motivated to learn.   You will find also that there are many behavioral and motivational problems involved in teaching middle and upper middle class children.   When we talk about social or economic group differences, we are talking of trends and probabilities and common characteristics, not of individual cases.

The Coleman report

In the 1960s concern over the nation's poor led to extensive federal programs to reverse the effects of poverty.   Special programs were developed to give low-SES (socioeconomic status) preschoolers extra preparation for school and to help high school students who would not otherwise have aspired to college to gain admission to higher education institutions. These programs were expensive, of course, although not on the order or magnitude of military appropriations. As a result they became political issues in which conservatives tended to question the value of such programs and liberals would support them as a means of providing equality of educational opportunity. Several extensive studies were conducted to gather data and determine whether or not the funds were well spent.

In one such study researchers set out to discover whether or not inadequate facilities and materials and teachers' salaries contributed to pupils' failure to learn (Coleman, 1961). Factors such as students' socioeconomic status and racial background, funds available for school facilities and equipment, and teachers' salaries were studied, and a host of other things of interest as well. The final results of this study, often referred to as the "Coleman report," surprised many people. It suggested that inadequate facilities, equipment, and teachers' salaries were not a highly significant factor in determining the differences in achievement between schools. Where students from lower socioeconomic backgrounds predominated, the achievement in the school was low, regardless of how new the school was or how well paid the teachers. Thus, a student placed among others from impoverished homes is likely to fare poorly in academic achievement. Poor children, a majority of whom are black, and newly-arrived ethnic groups such as Latin-Americans, suffer because they live in neighborhoods where only disadvantaged children attend the schools.

Another finding of the Coleman study was stated as follows:

> The special importance of a sense of control of environment for achievement of minority-group children and perhaps for disadvantaged whites as well suggests a different set of predispositional factors operating to create low or high achievement for children of disadvantaged groups . . . for (them) achievement or lack of achievement appears closely related to what they believe about their environment: whether they believe the environment will respond to reasonable efforts or whether they believe it is instead merely random or immovable.

The Coleman report was not without its critics, of course. One complained that the statistical results typical of such studies give incomplete information, and that these were misleading (Jencks and Reisman, 1968). It was pointed out that from these data you could only predict student achievement with about 50 percent accuracy: this means that about half of the variation in achievement is due to factors other than economic level. Another critic of the report asserted that the sample of schools used didn't really represent the range of types in this country (Deutsch and Deutsch, 1974).

There have been many studies of the effects of social class and economic level on achievement, one of particular interest done by Miller in England in 1970. Miller found that there were key factors in student achievement which cut across social classes, among them (1) the student's desire to get an education; (2) the positive or negative view of school held by students; (3) an attitude toward intellectual enterprise (positive, of course); and (4) the amount of indulgence shown the learner by the parents (less indulgent parents produced higher achieving children).

Language differences of special groups

Are certain minority groups and "ghetto" groups held back by their language itself, or just by having to use accepted language?

Special groups develop their own languages, due to circumstances which bring them to depend on and communicate with each other more than with outsiders. I have has already referred in Chapter 2 to the occurrence of special languages among identical twins that their parents cannot understand. A similar pattern has developed among black people in large cities; the language is called "Black English." Some theorists consider it a restricted and inferior communication process (Bernstein, 1960, 1961). Bernstein feels that such speech is characterized by incomplete and poorly constructed sentences (making discussion of complex matters difficult), few conjunctions so that logical qualifications and emphases are not easily expressed, infrequent use of impersonal pronouns making the language less objective, over-use of trite idioms which emphasize social and emotional content and deemphasize logic and explanations. Others feel that it is a rich and expressive language which is merely different from that used in schools. One of them has observed:

> Language forms are themselves transparent; we hear through them to the meaning intended. But teachers . . . have somehow gotten into the habit of hearing with different ears . . . We hear only the errors to be corrected. One value of knowledge about language—its development and its different forms—is not to make the language of our children more salient to our attention . . . it lets language forms recede into the transparency they deserve, enabling us to talk and listen in the classroom as outside, focusing full attention on the children's thoughts and feelings that those forms express. (Cazden, 1976, p. 10)

Those holding this view feel that learners with different languages will gradually adopt English as they proceed in the grades, and will continue to be more or less bilingual. (The author, who was brought up in New Hampshire, has been somewhat bilingual in the sense of being able to revert to country dialect, and I have observed Hawaiian school boys and girls in the 1950s who were bilingual in that they could change into "Pidgin English" at will.) These linguists suggest that schools should concentrate on teaching concepts, facts, and skills, and that language should be treated as a *vehicle* for this learning, not as an end in itself. Some linguists suggest that "school English" (or what they refer to as "middle-class English") could be taught as a second language for such learners, just as we have traditionally studied French or Spanish, or as European students study English.

It may not be appropriate to compare Black English to foreign languages, however. Consider some samples:

- He over to his friend house.
- He be here (meaning "he will be here" or "he is here").
- What you hit him for? He tell you what he do, man?
  (Labov, quoted in Mussen, Conger, and Kagan, 1974)
- He bih daw (not "He's a big dog").
- One-pluh-tuic'k-three (one plus two equals three).
  (Bereiter and Engleman, quoted in Gage and Berliner, 1975)

These samples aren't evidence of tremendous departures from the language we ordinarily use. One rather amusing caricature of this language was given in an article in *Newsweek* of December 8, 1975, reflecting the writing of high school students:

Shakespearean	Standard	Dialect
Alas! Poor Yorik I knew him, Horatio; a fellow of infinite jest, of . . . most excellent fancy; he hath borne me on his back a thousand times, and now, how abhorred in my imagination it is!	Poor Yorick! I really knew him, Horatio—a man of great good humor, of . . . imagination, he helped me through many hard times, and I feel terrible about this.	My man Yorick. We was real tight Horatio. I mean, the dude was crazy . . . but he saved my ass many times. What you think, man? It really took me on out.

There are some practical problems related to Black English. For example, in second or third generation black families in Washington, D.C., children's speech is much closer to the speech of newer immigrants from the South than to their parents' speech. This suggests that they learn more of their language behavior from their own peer group than from their parents. Such language learning makes it more difficult for them to learn to read, just as children who are natives of foreign countries have difficulty learning to read English. One investigator found that in Mexico and Sweden children were more successful if taught to read in their native language, and then changed to English, rather than beginning reading in English early (Dale, 1972). This suggests that we should have primers in Black English and in Puerto Rican and in Spanish for our school children, and then teach them conventional English later. But this seems unlikely, considering the expenses involved and the opposition that one would find from parent groups and school boards.

Implications for teaching and learning

Low SES and minority students are less prepared to learn, both in terms of facts and concepts, and in terms of strategies and motivation and encouragement from home.   Therefore you have to encourage them rather than challenge them, support them rather than let them go on their own, explain and guide rather than let them discover and solve.   You have to be conscious of behavioral limits and problems and set up very clear, consistent patterns for these students.   You have to enforce rules and reinforce good behavior frequently, even though it detracts from time needed for dealing with cognitive problems, for without the security and protection of a well-ordered and managed environment, you won't be able to teach at all.   Guidelines for managing and teaching generally, with specific references to these special situations, are introduced in Chapter 5 in relation to teacher characteristics, and then more extensively in Chapters 11 (Management and Motivation) and 12 (Teaching Processes).

DIFFERENCES IN PERSONALITY

Some personality traits

Personality is a global term, but differences in personality are of interest to everyone—and important to learning as well.

One developmental view of personality was presented in Chapter 1 (Freud's).   Another early personality theorist, Carl Jung, felt that we inherit wisdom from past generations in the form of a "collective unconscious" which contains beliefs and myths and basic concepts of society common to mankind.   (This is a somewhat mystical parallel to Lorenz' "blueprints," discussed in Chapter 2.)   Among these broad concepts, or "archetypes," are "mother," "father," "man," and "woman."   Jung also conceived a condition he called "mental health," characterized by a balance between conscious and unconscious forces, and the concepts of "introversion" and "extroversion."   An introvert is someone who is preoccupied with his or her personal subjective feelings, while an extrovert is interested primarily in the external world.   (This dimension of personality appears in many personality tests, as well as in common language, and in other theories.)

Another theorist, Alfred Adler, emphasized the importance of the ego and of conscious reason.   His concept of our basic motivation or drive was a striving for superiority.   Constant failure and deep feelings of inadequacy resulted in an "inferiority complex."   Since success is rare and failure relatively common, inferiority complexes are common also.   However, Adler said that you *cause* inferiority complexes by setting unrealistic goals, and this leads to being neurotic since they make failure inevitable.

A later theorist, Henry Murray, emphasized the area of individual differences according to what he postulated as basic "needs."   One need, for example, is for "nurturance," i.e., taking things from others.   Another is the need for "abasement," a need to consider oneself inferior, and to have others treat you as such.   Still another is a need for "power," and also "affiliation."   These needs were evaluated through a "projective" test called the "Thematic Apperception Test"; here the examiner asks a person to write stories about scenes pictured on cards, e.g., a man looking down on a young boy and frowning.   From these stories, or "protocols," the examiner deduces the personal needs of the person writing the story.   Someone

Individual differences may reflect "needs."

with a "need for achievement" might see the man-boy situation as one where the boy had failed to pass a course, while someone with "need for nurturance" might see it as a situation where a father was rejecting his son rather than giving him affection and support.

Testing personality

Another investigator of personality used tests made up of hundreds of objective questions relating to various aspects of human behavior and concerns (Cattell, 1966). Then he analyzed the results statistically in such a way as to identify a number of clusters of items that correlated highly with each other. He assumed that these clusters represented some aspect of life or behavior that was important to

Table 3–1. *Some of the needs postulated by Murray (1938).*

Need for Dominance: Need to influence or control others, to lead and direct.
Need for Affiliation: Need to form friendships and to cooperate and be part of groups.
Need for Achievement: Need to overcome obstacles and succeed for the sake of success.
Need for Orderliness: Need to arrange and organize things, to keep things neat.
Need for Abasement: Need to be dominated by others, to comply, to accept punishment.
Need for Rejection: The need to exclude or reject others, to be aloof.
Need for Autonomy: Need to resist domination or coercion or constraints upon one's way of life.
Need for Nurturance: The need to nourish or protect others.
Need for Succorance: Need to seek aid and nurturance, to be protected and aided.
Other needs include recognition, failure-avoidance, contrariness, defensiveness, aggression, deference, inviolacy, exhibition.

a group of people; he called them "factors of personality." This is an empirical approach to investigating personality, not one based on a theory that someone has created first. The test from which these factors are derived is about two hundred questions long, and has such items as the following. (These are facsimiles.)

(1) When someone criticizes me unfairly!
   a. Don't feel at all guilty
   b. Feel in between
   c. Feel guilty nevertheless
(2) I would rather stop and listen to someone singing on a street corner than to watch two people having a fight.
   a. True
   b. Uncertain
   c. False

Cattell's analysis of data from these questions yielded sixteen basic factors which make up personality. Some of these factors are named and described in Table 3–2. If you were to take the test yourself, the examiner would use a special key for evaluating your answers, and would then be able to tell you how you scored on each factor compared with others who took it before you; this would give you a "profile" of your personality.

Table 3–2. *Sample personality factors evaluated by the Cattell 16 PF Test (1957).*

A. Reserved, detached *vs.* outgoing, participating
B. Less intelligent *vs.* more intelligent
C. Affected by feelings, emotionally less stable *vs.* emotionally stable, calm
D. Mild, accommodating *vs.* assertive, independent
E. Sober, prudent *vs.* happy-go-lucky, enthusiastic

Defense mechanisms and personality traits

Your ego copes
with ambiguities
and threats
through a variety
of subconscious
mental tricks.

The Freudian model of personality involving the id, ego, and superego was explained in Chapter 1. The ego was the reality-facing and coping mechanism; it had to balance the id (selfish drives) and the superego (where the conscience resided), to maintain a positive, productive approach to life's many vicissitudes. To do this it uses "defense mechanisms." For example, the ego must deflect instinctual drives into permissible channels: sex, hate, and the like. This is done through "sublimation," such as music, games, or appreciation of nature. When a group of adolescent boys start throwing Christmas tree ornaments at each other, they are failing to sublimate!

Another defense mechanism is "repression," where instincts and desires are denied entrance into conscious thought, and the energy in back of them remains and builds up. This repression is unconscious: you are not aware of things you repress. As an adolescent, for example, you might have been sexually attracted to your opposite-sex parent, but you would repress this and would be very upset if someone suggested that it were true. On the other hand the repressed energy

Intellectualization is a defense mechanism.

would still be there, and thus might come out in other ways, perhaps as a crush on a movie star who reminds you of your parent.

Another such mechanism is "reaction formation," where you act in the way opposite from what you unconsciously wish: if you desire sex, you act as though sex were uninteresting. Still another strategy is "rationalization." If a golfer misses a putt he may blame his new lightweight putter or a stick that got in the way; a student who wants to go to the movies reasons that it will relax him and make him better able to cope with tomorrow's quiz.

If a golfer comments on the details of other golfer's techniques in a critical way, he may be "projecting" onto others his own feeling of inadequacy and concern about his golf swing. An aggressive child may act unnaturally friendly, or a potential homosexual may express extreme disgust at effeminacy in other men; both are defending against their own fears, and projecting them onto others.

We all occasionally withdraw from threatening situations mentally, physically, or through fantasies. Another way to avoid meeting obligations and resolving conflicts is "intellectualization," when we build towering theories about problems in order to escape dealing with them. Compulsive people often make lists of faults or things to do simply to cope with day-to-day living.

These defense mechanisms are not facts to learn by rote or memorize for a test: they are given here in order to acquaint you with some of the variety of human coping behaviors, so that you will not take these things as personal attacks or willful bad behavior when they occur. Learners of all ages use all of these mechanisms in a variety of ways. However, you should also be alert for overuse of one or two of these by an individual, because sometimes learners get "trapped" into a pattern of defense, just as they get trapped into a poor identity in adolescence (Chapter 1, Erikson).

OVERUSE OF A DEFENSE MECHANISM

Mary rationalizes. She spends the evening reading *Mad* magazine instead of doing her homework and says that *Mad* gives her needed relaxation and is much more relevant to life today than her social studies or language arts. She takes her younger brother's sweater to wear to a game and explains that she did not want to tear her good one and that he always wears his jacket anyway. She forgets to do the dishes when it is her turn and says that she had something very important which could not wait and thus was not able to get to them. Generally speaking, it seems to her parents and to the school counselor that she has made such a habit of finding reasons for doing wrong things or not doing right things that she is beginning to lose touch with reality.

Many approaches can be taken to this problem. The main point of this discussion is that there is a problem, and that it may become a part of Mary's adult personality rather than something she simply outgrows. On the other hand, if it is one of those developmental oscillations that were discussed previously, one does not want to fixate her in it by overreacting. One way to go at this is to notify, privately, all her teachers and club leaders and then have everyone begin very gently to point out to Mary that her rationalizations are not going over—in such a way that she is not terribly threatened by their reaction, and so that the attention she gets does not reinforce this behavior (i.e., reward it, so that it increases), and yet in such a way that she begins to find a difference between reactions to good reasons and reactions to rationalizations. If pointing out her error this way does seem threatening or is getting the wrong effect, then perhaps all concerned might try ignoring the rationalizations, and reward or punish the related behavior, whether good or bad. If this does not help, some counseling might be in order, i.e., nondirective therapy. Then, as a last resort, it might be necessary to go to either behavior therapy or psychotherapy.

SOME PERSONALITY TRAITS THAT ARE IMPORTANT TO LEARNING

Differences in anxiety

Certain personality characteristics affect learning more closely than others. One is anxiety. An article in the *Chicago Tribune,* for example, describes a study by Dr. Richard Shekelle in which he found that high-school students who had hypertension (high blood pressure) were more likely to be in the top 10 percent of their classes academically than those who did not. They also dated less, had fewer "steady" romances, and went steady for the first time at older ages than the students in the normal blood pressure group (*Boston Evening Globe,* Friday, June 25, 1976). He also found that the parents of children with normal blood pressure seemed to be more interested in getting their children involved in outside activities and in encouraging them to date.

Everyone is anxious about one thing or another. The sweaty-palmed monster called anxiety can attack at any time, during a job interview or a heavy date. However, some of us are more anxious generally than others, developing migraines, stomach cramps, or other ailments whenever something or someone seems the least bit threatening. If you have been exposed to a series of failures, you naturally begin to expect that everything will turn out badly. You become overly anxious, and the self-fulfilling prophecy clicks into operation. Still others do not seem to worry about a thing (*Mad* magazine's Alfred Neumann, "What, me worry?"). Either extreme can have its drawbacks, of course. In the one case you are too jumpy to take any risks, and in the other you may forget to prepare for tomorrow. Such debilitating effects of basic anxiety are frequently observed in low SES children, because they are placed in so many situations where they can't help but fail.

Research on anxiety reveals some suggestive relationships between it and various teaching styles, course organizations, and matters of time pressures and testing conditions. For example, children with low anxiety do better on a *timed* test than anxious children, while the anxious ones do better on an untimed test (Sarason et al., 1960). In another case, anxious students were more successful than nonanxious ones on highly structured tasks, while less anxious students were superior on less structured tasks (Grimes and Allensmith, 1961). It would be easy

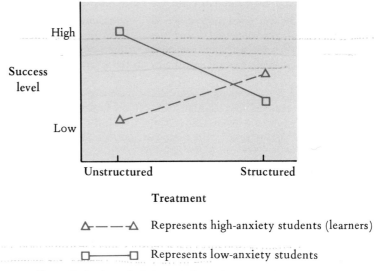

Figure 3–1. *A graph showing results similar to those found by Grimes and Allensmith, for the purpose of demonstrating what is called a "trait-treatment interaction."*

to conclude that anxiety *causes* certain academic problems; however, correlation does not imply causation, and it may be that the same basic conditions cause both the anxiety and the poor school work.

Anxiety can result from experiences of failure, punishment, pressure for achievement from parents, threats from peers, or lack of security in social achievement. In Chapter 1 it was pointed out that late-maturing boys tend to be anxious; certain types of parental treatments discussed earlier in this chapter lead to anxiety. Anxiety can be reduced by success, by security, by a relaxed and ordered atmosphere, and by a curriculum and schedule that are well organized, dependable, and nonthreatening. Anxiety can also be reduced by therapeutic processes which deal with the causes of anxiety, i.e., psychotherapy, and it can also be reduced by processes which desensitize the person to anxiety-causing things through counter-conditioning and modeling. This last approach will be described in Chapter 8.

ABLE, POPULAR—BUT ANXIOUS!

Cornelia was a good student, and she was also fairly popular with other girls in her high school senior class. She dated with average frequency, and had a relatively happy home life with her parents and one brother and sister. They were reasonably well off. Cornelia was not happy, however, and some of her friends and her mother worried a bit. She was always worried about what was going to happen: about flunking the quiz on Friday (she never did), about whether she was going to spill something or say the wrong thing or somehow be the object of attention at the dance Saturday night, whether she would make it in time to the bus for the field trip on Thursday, or whether she would feel sick in church and have to get up and leave in front of the whole congregation (or actually be sick in church!). None of these things happened, but Cornelia was anxious about them nevertheless. Her mother did her best to reduce her anxiety: she would remind her several times before it was time to leave for the bus, and would ask her if she had her papers, her lunch, and so forth; she would coach her on what to say at the dance, how to act, and how not to appear to be different. Each Sunday night she would ask Cornelia what tests or quizzes she had coming up the next week, and then remind her of them on Monday and Tuesday so she wouldn't leave the studying until too late. No matter how much her mother tried to help, however (and her mother had been doing this for

years!), and no matter how "ready" Cornelia always was, she never was at all confident or relaxed about anything she did.

Cornelia could have been a boy; anxiety is no respecter of sex. She was doing pretty well despite her problem, but there isn't any sign that she is becoming able to handle her anxiety, except by letting everything go! The problem is that when she gets out on her own—if she does, perhaps in college—she is going to have great difficulty disciplining herself to work independently with the anxiety riding her continually as it does. Of course, some anxiety is needed to keep us going; however, Cornelia's seems to be "debilitating," i.e., it seems to be so high that it interferes with her ability to order her life productively without outside help. Some approaches to dealing with anxiety described later, in Part III, might be helpful to Cornelia.

Differences in cognitive style: field dependent and independent

How influenced are you by things or people around you? Your response makes a difference in your ability to learn, among other things.

Personality differences have traditionally been treated as separate from cognitive processes. However, one experimental approach to classifying people seems to be something of a combination of the two. This is a classification according to "field dependence" and "field independence" (Witkin, 1962). There are three basic tests for determining where a subject fits in these categories. One is the "Body Adjustment Test" (BAT), where you sit in a chair whose orientation can be changed; the room is either completely dark or tilted at one of several angles. Your attention is directed to a pattern of parallel lines that are not quite perpendicular. Your task is to try to overcome the influence of those parallel lines (and of the room, if it too is tilted) to bring yourself to a true vertical position by adjusting the orientation of the chair.

A second test, called the "Rod and Frame Test" (RFT), involves a lighted frame with a lighted rod within it. The frame is not oriented perpendicularly to the ground, and you try to adjust the rod to the true vertical in spite of the misleading cues from the frame around it. All other cues are eliminated by blacking out all but the rod and frame.

The third test is the "Embedded Figures Test," where you try to find a certain shape in a picture but the shape is so much a part of something else that it is difficult to find or see. Figure 3–2 presents a fairly simple example of this test.

Figure 3–2. *An example of an embedded figure (a circle embedded in the line drawing of a racing car).*

The closer you come to the vertical on the BAT and RFT tests, and the more embedded figures you find, the less field dependent, and more field independent, you are. There are some interesting things about FDI and FD people. Field independent people have higher intelligence and higher school achievement. Field dependent people, on the other hand, are more alert to social stimuli, and they do better in incidental memory of social words and in memory of faces. They also come to a consensus quicker in a discussion, and they are more accommodating to the personalities of others (maybe they have better "social intelligence"!). However, these same field dependent people have a higher decrement in performance under conditions where they are disapproved of; that is, they are more disrupted by unfavorable emotional climates.

WARREN: BIOLOGY, GEOMETRY, AND CLUBS

Warren was a fairly good student, and he worked as hard as other students in the tenth-grade biology class, but his work didn't result in understanding as often. When he would be given a fairly straightforward assignment like learning the sequence of steps in mitosis or drawing a cell with nucleus and Golgi bodies and such, he would do a good, thorough job, but when he was asked to find relationships between such things as capillary action and the conversion of food into energy he would usually be able to offer only pat definitions, not comparisons or connections. Warren seemed to be unable to separate his thinking from the most obvious things. His social behavior was similar: he seemed to be governed by whatever others said or did, and he seldom initiated any activity or contributed anything of his own to a discussion. He was quite sensitive to the feelings of others,

however, and he seemed to understand when someone was feeling upset or needed someone to talk to. As a result, he had a reasonable number of friends. He seemed to have special problems in geometry; it was a very traditional course, and he had a great deal of difficulty seeing figures within figures. For example, when trying to prove that the perpendicular lines from the two equal angles of an isosceles triangle drawn to their opposite sides were also equal to each other in length, Warren would have to show that the two right triangles thus created were congruent, and he couldn't visualize those two triangles. He also had some difficulty doing "proofs," because he couldn't see how a new situation was a new case of some old situation (i.e., he couldn't apply old theorems to new problems or theorems). On the other hand, Warren was very active in various organizations in school, and he seemed to understand the social interactions and give-and-take that such groups emphasized; he even joined the mathematics club for a while, but had to give it up because it conflicted with his basketball practice.

From Warren's pattern of strengths and weaknesses, you might guess that he would be relatively field-dependent; one particularly suggestive piece of evidence is his difficulty with embedded figures in geometry. His social awareness also suggests field-dependence. However, you would need more information from tests—for example, the RFT or the BAT—before drawing a definite conclusion.

Impulsivity and reflectivity

Another dimension of individual differences that has been shown to be related to learning has to do with the amount of time a learner reflects on a problem or on his or her answer to it, and the persistence the learner brings to the learning situation. Some learners are impulsive rather than reflective, and they tend to jump to conclusions and not inspect either problems or their answers to determine whether they are on the right track and whether their answers seem reasonable (Kagan, 1965). Such people are found to be sociable and gregarious.

An interesting and more recent parallel to this impulsive-reflective dichotomy has emerged independently in some studies of the writing of seven year olds (Graves, 1975). This study identified two types of writers who were dubbed "reactive" and "reflective." Reactive children showed erratic problem-solving strategies, proofreading at the word unit level, a need for immediate rehearsal in order to write, and rare contemplation or reviewing of products. Reflective children showed little rehearsal before writing and little overt language to accompany writing, wrote rapidly and silently, and proofread in broad written units. Thus the reflective writers showed a greater tendency to evaluate their own work, and the reactive ones could be described as more impulsive, as in the Kagan dichotomy. However, the report observed that most of the reactive writers were boys, and most of the reflective ones girls. There are two possible interpretations of this trend: it may be a sex-linked difference, perhaps due to cultural pressures or perhaps due to innate differences; on the other hand, it may simply be a maturational difference, reflecting the generally greater maturity of the female and anticipating the wide sex differences in the onset of puberty.

Differences in creativity

Being creative is a fine thing—but it can also be a liability!

Although creativity is considered to be a desirable trait, especially in young learners, it is currently surrounded by confusion and contradiction. Creativity has been associated with artists or writers primarily, and to some extent with scientific theorists, but we all possess it to some degree, that is, the ability to give unique but appropriate responses. The teaching of creativity is regarded by many as a way to

Everyone possesses some degree of creativity.

free thought and to enable us to rise above the essentially convergent processes that dominate thinking and culture. "Mind-freeing" workshops and courses have taught people to think beyond the stereotypes and limits of their old conceptual structures, and to see new ways of living. Some processes of this kind are described in Chapter 6.

There is quite general agreement that schools as we know them tend to squelch creativity in favor of conformity quite early in the process. To give a rather simple example, a first grader might be instructed to color a fish in his workbook purple. He decides that he would rather have a goldfish with black spots and thus uses his black and yellow Crayolas. His teacher might scold him mildly for diverging from the instructions, whereas he is actually expressing himself creatively at a very early age.

Creative individuals tend to give more different responses to a given stimulus than others. Partly because of this, they are more likely to give unique ones. However, they also have the capacity (through learning, heredity, or both) to give responses that others recognize as interesting and appropriate, but that never would have occurred to them. This can be an asset at times, a liability at others. For example, creativity does not pay off when you are following a cake recipe or solving an equation: you may wind up with an amorphous blob of flour and water, or a ridiculous answer.

One way to define creativity is to examine tasks that are used to test it. One such task is given below (adapted from Torrance, 1966).

Below you will find a piece of colored felt that has a certain shape to it. It has some sticky material on the back so that you can stick it to the blackboard. Put it on the blackboard, and then with chalk draw lines to and from it and around it so that you can create a picture with the shape as some important part of it. Try to think of a picture to make that nobody else will think of making. Then think up a name for it and write it underneath. Make the name unusual and clever also.

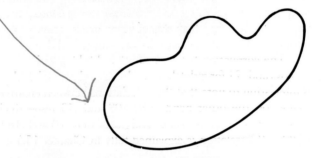

By its nature creativity is difficult to quantify or to define in operational terms, and therefore it is difficult to study objectively. One type of task which is also used, and which has become recognized as accepted practice, is to present some very ordinary object like a brick and ask the learner to give as many different uses as he or she can, including unique ones like "throwing it through a shop window to let smoke out when the shop is on fire." Such tests are scored for both fluency (number of answers) and uniqueness; creativity is regarded by psychologists as a combination of these two basic attributes or abilities.

Intelligence and/or creativity

Intelligence will be discussed in the next part of this chapter, but since it is often compared with creativity we will mention it briefly here. Intelligence is thought of as a "convergent" skill, i.e., an ability to "zero in" on an answer, while creativity is thought of as a "divergent" skill involving thinking of many possible answers (Guilford, 1967). One study of creativity and intelligence found that learners who were high in *both* qualities were able to exercise within themselves both control and freedom, and could be both adultlike and childlike in their behavior (Wallach and Kogan, 1965). Those *low in both* seemed basically bewildered, and they utilized a variety of defensive and compensating behaviors, including intense social activity and psychosomatic ailments. Those high in intelligence and low in creativity were compulsive school achievers who feared academic failure. Those who were low in intelligence and high in creativity found school unpleasant and were often both angry over school and unhappy with themselves; however, when free of the stress of school, they showed the ability to succeed unexpectedly where cognitive skills as well as creativity were required.

In a recent study of creativity, the investigators used tasks that called for (1) alternate uses of familiar objects, (2) giving meanings to abstract patterns, (3) similarities between things, and (4) meanings for simple lines of various configurations. The answers were scored for (a) ideational fluency, (b) number of discrete responses given, and (c) unusual or rare ideas. These investigators compared the scores of learners for creative *thinking* (from this test battery) with their scores for creative *performance*. Creative performance was determined through a self-report questionnaire regarding the nonacademic talented accomplishments of these learners in their four high school years: music, science, fine arts, social leadership, writing, community service, drama, sports, and dance.

The correlation between creative thinking and creative performance was .35 for boys and .21 for girls; these are low correlations, but they are still significant. It is interesting to note that the correlations between creative performance and *intelligence*, on the other hand, were .08 and .13 respectively, and the correlation between creative performance and *grades* were .03 and .16 (Milgram and Newman, 1976). (Correlation is explained fully in Chapter 15.)

Encouraging creativity   — Torrance

You probably feel that the encouragement of creativity is an important part of teaching, just as encouraging problem solving, the development of accuracy, and physical skills. Before listing some of Paul Torrance's guidelines, however, it seems appropriate to warn you that not all students react well to creative opportunities. Recalling the discussion of anxious learners, you should keep in mind that freedom of expression and lack of structure can be terrifying to some highly anxious students, and can be very confusing to others who have always been told exactly what to do and how to do it. While giving the few highly creative children in your group a chance to blossom, you should not forget that there are others who will feel threatened without more structure to lean on. You may feel that they are the ones who need encouragement the most, but your attempts can backfire on you and bring criticism. Therefore, it may be best to "shape" this behavior carefully, i.e., to require very small amounts at first, to reward small steps in this direction, and then to make rewards contingent upon larger amounts of creativity as they become able to give it, and as they learn to tolerate the insecurity of the creative situation. Here are the guidelines:

1. Encourage manipulation of and sensitivity to objects and ideas.
2. Try to be tolerant of new ideas, no matter how farfetched they may be.

3. Be flexible in setting up lessons; permit some brainstorming.
4. Maintain a relaxed classroom, tutoring, or therapeutic atmosphere.
5. Help the child who is creative learn to get along with other children.   He or she may get under their skin!
6. Present controversial problems and challenge accepted opinions.
7. Teach the basics of problem solving and creative processes.
8. Teach children not to underrate their own creativity: dispel the sense of awe of masterpieces (Torrance and Myers, 1965).

FOURTH GRADE CREATIVITY—AND FIFTH GRADE CREATIVITY— AND THEN, CREATIVITY

Mr. Welch is a fourth-grade teacher who is very interested in creativity. He feels that schools stifle this trait in students, and that if students were encouraged to be creative, they would be more interested in and knowledgeable about things that they are now expected to learn. Mr. Welch therefore tells his students that creativity is desirable, and he tries to react positively to it when it occurs. For example, when Johnny turns in a project on insects which consists of a large poster with a bug in red on a background of blue, he acts very pleased, congratulates Johnny and puts it up for all to see. On the other hand, he doesn't react in any particular way to Sally's rather lengthy report in which she gives examples of various insects and describes their characteristics and how they relate to other living things in the food chain. Mr. Welch also encourages unique answers to questions in class, and the students vie with each other to come up with the most way-out relationships and ideas. For example, when they are studying arithmetic Connie volunteers some thinking she has done about numbers, how things come in pairs or threes, and how the number of raindrops in a rain storm can't be counted but the number of lightning bolts can. Mr. Welch reacts very positively to this, but he does not encourage Frank when he observes that some numbers can be divided by two evenly but others can't, since this seems a bit mechanical and uncreative to Mr. Evans.

The next year in fifth grade these children have Mrs. Graves. She is quite interested in creativity, too. She feels that creative students are more likely to be able to solve word problems well, and she calls students "creative" when they give good answers to questions involving arithmetical reasoning. The learners who were considered most creative the previous year, however, don't seem to be as creative this year, and when Johnny turns in a poster with many different numbers on it in a sort of balanced but uneven arrangement, she tells him that this isn't exactly what she considers a creative solution to the problem, which had to do with process of calculating profits in a grocery store. Martha, who has calculated all the profits exactly and presented the result in a nicely bound report with a neatly lettered cover, is praised for having the most creative project in the class. Meanwhile, Frank has gone one with his own experiments in even and odd numbers, and has discovered that there are some numbers which are not divisible by *any* other number—he calls these "non-divisibles," and he asks his mother if anyone knows how many of these "indivisibles" there are. He doesn't ask Mrs. Graves, because she has told him that these ideas aren't part of what they are studying, and she urges him to finish his report on the grocery problem. Frank's mother also tells him he better make sure he finishes his report.

INTELLIGENCE

Intelligence and personality

What is intelligence? Is it important? Is it hereditary, or can it be changed?

Personality theorists assume that there are processes which monitor behavior and solve problems so that the basic needs of the individual are satisfied rather than frustrated. They don't usually delve into the nature of those processes but take them for granted. Freud's "ego" is an example of such "intelligence." Developmentalists, in a similar manner, assume the emergence of some kind of monitoring and guiding processes at around four or five years and maturing about ten or eleven. One group calls these "executive processes" (see Mussen, Conger, and Kagan, 1969, Chapter 7). They coordinate perception and memories and relate past experiences and future possibilities to the present in order to select strategies for solving problems. Piaget's problem-solving episodes bring out "personality" in the children he works with, and his concept of the formal-operational stage sounds like the "executive process" in mature form. The interaction of certain personality factors with intelligence test performance, as well as with performance on achievement tests, is well known; for example, "test anxiety" has been the subject of some research and concern (Sarason et al., 1964). Other elements of personality seem less involved with cognition, however; for example, the Oedipal complex, or the need for power. The way in which a learner evaluates his or her own performance is also an important consideration in everyday life, and in scoring well on intelligence tests. For example, some learners are impulsive (as was described earlier) and fail to reflect on their responses; their scores (and thus their measured intelligence) are lower as a result.

Much of our motivation is unconscious. If intelligence enables you to cope with problems, you might assume that intelligence will assist you in your unconscious objectives as well as your conscious ones. Perhaps your intelligence helps you in directions that you are not aware of! Suppose you have an unconscious need for "succorance," i.e. a desire to be taken care of (from Murray's needs, Chapter 1); suppose your intellect (intelligence) is assisting you unconsciously to achieve this goal. Then you might consistently make a mess of things, or fail in competition even when you know you are better than your opponent, because your intelligence is directing you to fail so that you can look to others for help! What seems rather stupid on the surface may reflect highly intelligent—but unconscious—strategies. In a similar manner, very intelligent students sometimes appear to be stupid because their goal is *not* to succeed, sometimes because their peer groups will ostracize them if they do, sometimes because their family has a tradition of doing poorly in school and their parents feel threatened by a "scholar." Perhaps *you* have some unconscious goals which your intelligence is helping you achieve, and you are wondering why it is that you can't achieve your conscious goals as a result! Generally, the point is that intelligence is closely related to and involved in personality.

The origin of "intelligence tests"

Alfred Binet, a French psychologist, was asked by the Paris government in the early 1900s to devise a test to indicate which children could profit from schooling and which could not. He set out to find a relatively brief set of tasks which would be easy for children who did well in school and difficult for those who did not. He laboriously tried out task after task, accepting those that differentiated between good and poor students and rejecting those that did not. The result was the first intelligence test: it was not the result of any theory, but of an empirical search. It worked well not only in France, but in other countries after it was translated; that is, it differentiated between good students and poor students. Many people assumed that it measured some innate, hereditary characteristic of the learner, one which could not change. Binet himself did not feel this way, however; he said the idea that intelligence was a fixed quantity was deplorable, and called it "brutal pessimism." He regarded a child's mind to be like a field which an expert farmer could change from a desert to a harvest. He saw the ideal education as changing the capacity of the child to learn, and this changeable quantity was what he thought of as "intelligence." Others, however, used his test primarily to separate the wheat from the chaff, as it were.

Currently, an opposite trend is evident in this country; retarded children are being taken out of special institutions and special classes and being "mainstreamed" into regular public school curricula. Such strategies are based in part on evidence that we *can* change minds "from desert to harvest," to use Binet's words. In the 1940s, for example, thirteen of twenty-five infants who had been raised in an orphanage until the age of two were transferred to a home for mentally retarded people; there, each of them was cared for by an older mentally retarded girl. The twelve left behind were "matched" with these in age, intelligence, and medical histories; each "control" child (not transferred) had a counterpart in the "experimental" group. Of course, all of them had been developmentally retarded to begin with, a condition which has been observed in orphanages around the world in the past.

After about $2\frac{1}{2}$ years, the children cared for individually in the retarded home showed an average increase in IQ of about thirty points, while those who remained in the orphanage lost on the average of about twenty points. Twenty years later, all of the members of the experimental group were self-supporting and had completed an average of twelve years of school. The average educational level of the others was fourth grade, and many were still in state institutions (Skeels, 1966).

There have been other examples of the potential for change and improvement in intelligence since this experiment. They do not indicate how far you can change the intelligence of learners who are *not* deprived initially, of course (probably much less). On the other hand there is a long tradition of early education of preschool children for the purpose of giving them greater intellectual ability (Fowler, 1962). A demonstration of the effect of early teaching on IQ is found in the fact that children who are enrolled in preschool programs usually show a positive change in IQ as a result, in comparison with children who do not attend preschool (Wellman, 1945).

What kinds of tasks are on intelligence tests?

The Stanford-Binet test is given individually, and has a different set of tasks for each age group ("Stanford-Binet" means the Binet test as adapted at Stanford University for use in this country).   Some of the tasks for age two, for example, are:

- The learner places three forms into the correct recessed areas on a form board.
- The learner locates an object after it has been hidden under a box, and the box has been screened from view for ten seconds.
- The learner is asked to name eighteen common objects pictured on cards.
- The learner is asked to point to various body parts (e.g., the face) on a paper doll.

Some tasks from the test for six year olds are:

- The learner is asked to tell the differences between specific animals and objects, such as a ball and a block.
- The learner is asked to define words ranging in difficulty from easy to hard.
- The learner is shown a series of pictures and asked to determine what part is missing from each one.
- The learner is given twelve blocks and asked to count out a certain number of them.

The learner's performance is scored by starting with the year at which he or she does all the tasks correctly, then adding months for each task he or she does correctly in tests for later years.

The Wechsler Intelligence Test for Children is also given individually.   The tasks are divided into a verbal group (all of which require verbal responses to questions asked orally), and a performance group (all of which require nonverbal responses to tasks primarily visual in nature).   The "verbal" tasks are as follows:

- The learner is asked to answer questions about facts.
- The learner is asked to answer questions involving common sense, e.g., "what do you do when you cut your finger?"
- The learner is asked to do arithmetic problems in his or her head.
- The learner is asked to tell how two things are alike.
- The learner is asked to tell the meaning of words, ranging from simple to difficult.

The "performance" tasks are:

- The learner is asked to tell what is missing in a series of pictures.
- The learner is asked to arrange sets of pictures in proper order to tell a story.
- The learner is asked to put together pieces to form a two-dimensional shape, e.g., a face.
- The learner is asked to make designs by arranging colored blocks, the design being put in front of him or her.
- The learner is given a code for numbers one through nine (each number has a mark or design paired with it). Then, as fast as possible, the learner puts the correct code mark just below each number in a series of numbers arranged in random order.

These tasks are important to keep in mind when talking about "intelligence" because they are the behaviors that are interpreted as intelligence. As you can see they are somewhat prosaic taken individually, and certainly not very mystical, deep, or sophisticated as test tasks go. However, from responses to such questions, taken collectively, you can make fairly good estimates of the individual's ability to learn in school. Also, it is from a learner's responses to such tasks that decisions are made concerning his or her placement in different "tracks" or in special classes or institutions outside the school, such as schools for the retarded. Other factors are considered, of course, but this is one of the main kinds of information used.

The Stanford-Binet has tasks for younger children, as you have seen, and there is an infant version of the Wechsler. Here are some tasks from the Bayley Scales of Infant Development. Notice that they emphasize motor and perceptual-motor tasks more than the other tests, as one would expect for a test that deals with the sensorimotor and preoperational stages of cognitive development. Age is given in months and is the age at which one half of the children show the behavior named.

- 1.9 months: Blinks at a shadow of something passed in front of its eyes.
- 3.2 months: Head follows something that is going out of sight.
- 5.7 months: Picks up a small cube directly and without fumbling.
- 12.5 months: Imitates words.
- 14.2 months: Says two words.
- 24.0 months: Names two objects.

(There seems to be a lack of *receptive* language tasks, as emphasized by Tables 2-1 and 2-2 in Chapter 2.)

Piaget's research problems, such as the juice glass experiment or the ten-sticks problem (described in Chapter 2), can be used as measures of intelligence also. Such tasks generally correlate at about the .43 level with traditional intelligence tests (Elkind, 1971). This correlation is not very high and suggests that they aren't measuring the same abilities.   One team has gone to some lengths to produce an evaluation instrument that is compatible with Piaget's theories (Pinard and Laurendeau, 1964); their scale has been reported to correlate higher than .43 with other IQ tests.   However, since it is based on Piaget-type problem situations (see Chapter 2) it takes much longer to administer than a Stanford or a WISC.

Guilford's structured view of intellect

In intelligence testing and research there are theoretical views without prior or subsequent testing to validate them, and there are tests without theories behind them. In the case of J. P. Guilford, theory and testing go hand in hand: test results lead to theory which is then backed up by empirical research using more extensive testing. These approaches go beyond the tasks used for practical purposes in such tests as the Stanford and the WISC.   Guilford's theory is rather comprehensive, and I won't try to present the entire model here.   To get a feeling for it, however, examine the following categories which he considers basic to intelligence:

- Contents: Figural (F), Symbolic (S), Semantic (M), Behavioral (B)
- Operations: Cognition (C), Memory (M), Divergent Production (D), Convergent Production (N), Evaluation (E)
- Products: Units (U), Classes (C), Relations (R), Systems (S), Transformations (T), Implications (I)

Guilford's theory is that intelligence is actually a number of different abilities, and each of these is a combination of a content, an operation, and a product.   If you do your mathematics, then, you will find quite a few abilities, i.e., rather a large number of possible combinations (content × operation × product).   Guilford claims to have actually identified over eighty of these abilities, with many left to be "found."   As an example of one of them, let's take symbolic content, cognition as an operation, and classes as a product, i.e., (S × C × C).   There are many examples of this ability, for instance, the ability to deal with symbolic content, to consider it abstractly, and to produce classifications with it.   One actual task of this type would be a requirement to recognize the common properties in sets of symbolic information, such as classifying the following two mathematical (symbolic) expressions as the same:

$$a(b + c) = ab + ac$$
$$x(m + n) = xm + xn$$

If you are up on your mathematics, you will recognize these as expressions of the property of distribution of multiplication over addition.

Guilford's search for these many different abilities, or combinations of content and operation and product, is a little like the chemist's search for elements to fill in the periodic table that went on most intensely during the first half of the twentieth

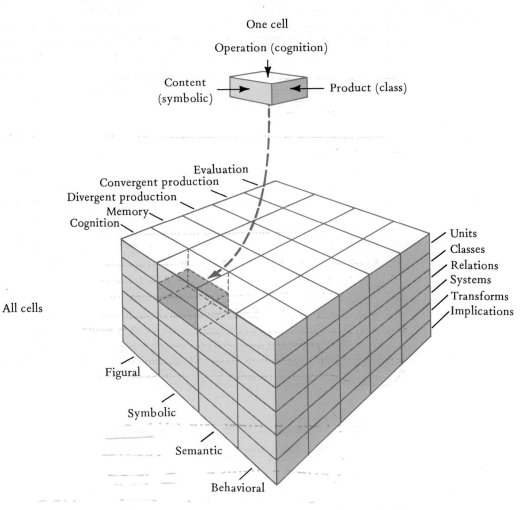

Figure 3–3. *Guilford's structured view of intellect.*

century. His theory can be demonstrated graphically by the diagram in Figure 3–3.

 How much of intelligence is inherited?

Many people feel that you can't change intelligence, and they refer to data collected in studies of identical twins (siblings who come from the same egg and therefore are of the exact same heredity). Any differences in intelligence between such twins must be attributed to the environment, since their heredity is the same. Identical twins reared together have been compared with identical twins reared apart; the latter are less similar to each other in intelligence, showing the effects of a different environment; however, those reared apart and those reared together are more alike in their intelligence than nonidentical twins reared apart or together. (Nonidentical twins are those born at the same time, but not from the same egg; thus their genetic components are not identical.) Thus, environment does make a difference, but comparing the two cases shows that heredity plays an important part in determining intelligence also.

The question that has been debated widely and hotly in recent years has been about the proportion of influence or importance of heredity as compared with environment in determining intelligence. There is no final answer. Recently, some of the data comparing the two types of twins has been shown to be faulty, and so a reassessment of the matter is under way. One statement that has been accepted fairly generally asserts that environment determines from 20 to 40 percent of the variability that you find in people's intelligence, while heredity determines from 60 to 80 percent. However, this does not tell us how significant the percentage determined by environment is in relation to success in life or success in school.

Another way of judging the relative effects of environment and heredity on intelligence has been to compare parents with their foster children and parents with their own children. If heredity is more important, then the similarities would favor the true parent, but should environment make the major difference, there wouldn't be any differences in the similarities, or they would be only slight.

Actually, parents and their own children correlate at about .50, while parents and foster children correlate at about .18, showing the strong effect of heredity in determining intelligence (Bodmer and Cavalli-Sforza, 1970).

I have described some projects in which the intelligence of the learners increased, due to an enriched and supportive environment; I have also given data to show that intelligence is largely determined by heredity.   Is there a contradiction here, or are both assertions true?   The latter is the case; the researchers who found raised intelligence worked intensely with a few children over a long period of time, and the children had been deprived to begin with.   The experiments comparing twins and others comparing foster children give the results of ordinary, chance living experiences, and thus tell what happens in normal circumstances.   However, one aspect of the twin studies makes it difficult to be sure of their implications: often, when twins are reared apart, they are reared in similar family circumstances (i.e., similar socioeconomic status, similar cultural interests, and such); therefore, some of the similarities of identical twins reared apart are due to environmental similarities, and not all can be attributed to hereditary equivalence.

One more observation is significant.   Correlations show similarities and one can compare correlations to get an idea of the relative contributions of heredity and environment, but correlations don't say anything about the magnitude of the differences that do exist.   For example, identical twins reared apart were more alike than other twins reared apart, but the differences between the identical twins still averaged about ten IQ points.   Now we have to ask "how much practical difference does ten IQ points make in school achievement or success in life?"

What can you predict from IQ?

If you know a learner's IQ, can you predict his or her achievement? His or her success in life?

If you give an intelligence test to a two or three year old you shouldn't expect it to predict what the child will achieve on such a test at age eighteen.   However, if you give it to a seven year old, the prediction will be much better, and your chances of being right about the score at age eighteen will be about four out of ten.   If you give it to a ten year old, your chances are five out of ten.   Table 3–3 shows the correlations of tests taken at various ages with scores at age eighteen.

If you give the same intelligence test to the same person several times, you will get slightly different scores, just by chance.   The test-retest change that you can expect on individual IQ tests like the Stanford or the Wechsler is usually around five points.   That means that chances are two out of three that the second score

Table 3–3. *Relationship between IQ score at age 18 and IQ scores at earlier ages.*

Age 4	.31
Age 8	.70
Age 12	.76

These are correlations (see Chapter 15). The data are drawn from a table prepared by Honzik, Macfarlane and Allen in 1948, and adapted by Mussen, Conger, and Kagan, 1974.

Table 3–4. *IQs of two different learners at different ages, showing variations from year to year.*

Age 3	Learner A, 125	Learner B, 100
Age 6	Learner A, 85	Learner B, 110
Age 9	Learner A, 70	Learner B, 100
Age 12	Learner A, 80	Learner B, 115

These figures indicate that different learners' IQs vary to different degrees and in different ways. The data are drawn from a report by Honzik, Macfarlane, and Allen in 1948, and reproduced by Mussen, Conger, and Kagan in 1974.

will be within five points of the first.   However, this means giving the retest fairly soon under similar conditions, including the physical and emotional condition of the learner.   People change from time to time, and their motivations and emotional states and outlooks vary also.   As a result, IQ scores vary quite a lot from year to year and period of life to period of life.   Table 3–4 shows the variation for two different learners over a long period of time.

Grade predictions are not reliable either; correlations with grade averages run around .7, which means that you will be right about half the time.   Predicting individual subject grades is even riskier.   Here are some correlations found in one study (Mussen, Conger, and Kagan, 1974, quoting Bond, 1940):

- IQ and English Usage, .59
- IQ and History, .59
- IQ and Biology, .54
- IQ and Geometry, .48

This means that in predicting individual subject grades you might be right a little more than one quarter of the time.

Some things IQ does not predict well at all; one important one is the ability to learn to identify concepts (Glaser, R., in Gagne, 1967).   Therefore, you can expect important differences in individual abilities in any subject that are not predicted or suggested by intelligence quotients.   Measures other than intelligence may prove to be more useful for predicting success in a particular kind of learning. This is the reason for "aptitude" tests, which sample abilities more closely related to the particular field, such as "Law Aptitude," "Mechanical Aptitude," and "Language Aptitude" tests.

In predicting how well a high school student will do in college, or how well a college student will do in graduate school, grades are the most reliable single measure; if a learner has earned a B average, she is likely to maintain a B average. Scholastic aptitude tests, which are more oriented toward academics than basic intelligence tests, add some validity to the prediction, but not a great deal (e.g., .55 over .50).   Furthermore, there are questionnaires on motivation and interests which predict future general success in college just as well as either intelligence or aptitude tests.   One review of the relationships between learning and individual differences has concluded that we need to have a much better understanding than we have now of the relationships between "entering variables" (characteristics of the learner at the beginning of learning) and learning success over a significant period of time (units, semesters, years).   We need to take into account the previous history of the learner, hereditary abilities, demonstrated learning abilities, and other individual characteristics.   General intelligence from this point of view is not a useful scientific concept for characterizing the potential of a person to learn (Glaser).

Does intelligence assure success in life?

In the 1940s Terman and Ogden reported that gifted children in their study (students with high intelligence test scores) were also above average in physical, social, and intellectual development; furthermore, they were healthier, lived longer than average, achieved greater social and occupational success, and suffered less from mental illness.   From this description, educators derived a general concept of the all-around "gifted" person, who is successful in life.   From a number of separate measurements of the comparative intelligence of people in different professions and with different incomes, it is also evident that the higher the income or status of the job, the higher the intelligence of those who are found in the job.   One theorist has claimed that if upward and downward social mobility were to be increased, and people were given an equal chance at education, we would soon have a "meritocracy" of the highly intelligent: all of the above-average intelligence people would rise to the top!   However, there are other contrary views on this; it isn't as simple as it sounds.   For example, another theorist says:

> The primary reason some people end up richer than others is not that they have more adequate cognitive skills.   While children who read well, get the right answers in arithmetic problems, and articulate their thoughts clearly are somewhat more likely than others to get ahead, there are many other equally important factors involved . . . if two men's IQ scores differ by 17 points . . . (the typical difference between IQ scores of individuals chosen at random) . . . their incomes will typically differ by less than $2,000.   That amount is not completely trivial, of course, but the income difference between random individuals is three times as large, and the difference between the best-paid fifth and the worst-paid fifth of all male workers averages $14,000.   There is almost as much economic inequality among those who score high on standardized tests as in the general population.   (Bane and Jencks, 1972)

This suggests that there are other elements in success, such as energy, persistence, personality, and luck.   Predicting success by IQ is not too satisfactory!

Intelligence testing and disadvantaged learners

Low socioeconomic status learners, including blacks, do not score as well on intelligence tests as learners from middle and upper SES backgrounds. It has often been suggested that this reflects a bias in the tests themselves, and that if this bias were removed the low-SES learners would have the same average score. In the 1950s one group developed such a test in order to demonstrate this; the tests were called "games" and required reasoning about everyday events. The tests were in the form of a comic strip, and they were administered as if they were part of a game. In spite of these efforts, however, middle-class learners still did better than lower class learners (Davis and Eells, 1953). More recently a sociologist has devoted extensive effort to the design of methods whereby intelligence test scores of minority groups can be interpreted reasonably in view of their special cultures and environments (Mercer, 1974). In her "System of Multicultural Pluralistic Assessment," Mercer has developed a process in which each child is given two test sessions instead of one, and the mother or principal caretaker is interviewed to gain information about the occupation, education, urban or rural background and size of the family, and about crowding in the home. In addition, a health history and impairment inventory are also taken. The testing itself includes a physical dexterity task first, then a test where the child is to draw (copy) figures, and then a Wechsler Intelligence Scale for Children.

Through use of the information about the child's family, Mercer has developed equations which take the IQ score that the learner achieves and translate it into the score the child probably would have received if he or she had been a white, middle-class learner. Thus it is possible to determine how the child's IQ compares and what the child's "true" potential is for development. For example, Juan, a young Mexican-American, might have a score on the WISC which would ordinarily put him at the twentieth percentile in relation to all learners across the country who have taken the test previously. However, if he were to be compared with others of his nationality living in the same conditions as he, his score might turn out to be at the sixtieth percentile (this means that 60 percent of other learners taking the test were below him, rather than 20 percent).

Some parts of intelligence tests seem less influenced by social class than others. Subtests that rely less on verbal processing of information, such as the "digit span" test, are among these. There are tests composed of nonverbal, visual tasks (e.g., The Ravens Progressive Matrices) which are used to compare intelligence of different national groups as well as subgroups such as minorities; however, none of these is completely free of cultural bias. Some people feel that we are actually measuring cultural bias itself when we measure intelligence.

Some research on the relationships between intelligence and social class suggests that the lower scores of low SES and minority groups may result from their different lifestyles and sense of discipline rather than from inferior understanding (Golden and Birns, 1969). The Cattell Infant Scale and the Piaget Scale were given to children from three levels of social deprivation and organization. As much as 25 percent of the lowest group had to be seen twice or more in order to get them to complete the tests, while 18 percent of the middle group and 6 percent of the higher group had to be seen twice. You can imagine that if the test were given only once, the lower-income group would show up poorly (regardless of the content of the test). What is important here is that when the lower-income children completed the test, there were no significant differences between the averages of the different groups. Thus the time allowed and the persistence of the learner are important matters in evaluating "intelligence."

Summary outline with key concepts

☞ *People mature* in similar ways, but they still differ from each other in many ways, over extended periods of time; such differences are what we mean by "personality" / These differences affect learning, particularly when instruction is individualized, and thus they also affect teaching.

☞ *Outgoing, assertive,* achieving learners are produced by warm-accepting-nurturant, democratic-communicative, and behavior-controlled parent treatment / Aggressive, overassertive, disobedient learners are produced by weak-controlling, overpermissive parent treatments; hostility and rejection exacerbate this effect / Withdrawn, neurotic learners are produced by overly-controlling parents; this involves behavioral and emotional controls / General difficulties are often produced by father-absent homes, or homes where the father is seldom present and/or is quite ineffective and uninvolved / Dependent, unmotivated, unsocial learners are produced by a combination of warmth-acceptance and overcontrol (again both behavioral and psychological) / Learners with good self-concepts are produced by parents who have good self-concepts, the parents who "model" this attitude / Thus warmth and acceptance are desirable attributes; hostility and rejection are not; appropriate behavioral control is positive; permissiveness is negative; democratic-supportive-communicative behaviors are good if not coupled with overpermissiveness and lack of behavioral limits and controls.

☞ *Girls outperform* boys in elementary grades; boys outdo girls at the secondary level / Adolescent girls often reject academic competition and superiority / Boys have superior spatial ability, are more flexible in problem solving; girls talk earlier, do better in spelling and grammar / Girls are more predictable in their growth patterns / Boys are more aggressive; this is related to hormonal differences / Elementary school teachers encourage feminine behaviors, discourage masculine ones, and favor girls over boys / Society encourages male achievement, discourages female achievement / Equal treatment of sexes would produce a normal distribution of achievement in women / Sexist habits include having boys do heavy work, not suggesting careers or technical professions to girls, guiding girls away from shop courses, expecting school administrators to be male.

☞ *Students from* low socioeconomic status (SES) families achieve less, are less motivated, need more help and support / The Coleman report found that the SES makeup of the student body determined the achievement of the school / The same report found that minority groups felt that achievement was due more to chance than to effort and responsibility, i.e., that environment would not respond to effort on their part (external locus of control) / Another study found that attitudes of good students were consistent across social classes / Minority groups, especially blacks in large cities, have their own languages; some feel that these will gradually become conventional English, others fear that they interfere learning and understanding.

☞ *Individuals have* unique patterns of traits, i.e., unique personalities / Personality traits are considered unchanging, but there is evidence of changes over time / Some concepts related to personality, derived from various theories, are introversion and extroversion (preoccupation with self or with others), inferiority complex (feeling of inferiority to others), and an explanation of personality in terms of needs (such as need for power, need for abasement, need for achievement) / Personality tests are used to advise individuals on characteristics that may hamper their progress or may indicate desirable jobs or professions / Defense mechanisms are aspects of personality when they become habitual; they include rationalization, projection, reaction formation, and intellectualization / When overused, they can become maladaptive and part of neurotic or psychotic behavior.

☞ *Anxious learners* need structure and support, may outperform nonanxious under those conditions; nonanxious need autonomy and challenge, and do better under those conditions / Field-independent learners achieve higher academic intelligence and achievement; field dependent learners have higher social intelligence and are more other-directed / Impulsive learners do less well than reflective ones, academically, but they are more social / Creative learners may find their creative behavior unappreciated or unrewarded in typical school settings; they tend to give more responses and more unique responses than other learners, and this may upset teachers and other students / Creativity should be encouraged, but with limits.

Intelligence is involved in personality, but it is usually thought of as a score on an intelligence test / The tasks on such tests are chosen for their (collective) ability to predict school achievement / Guilford sees intelligence as many combinations of content, operation, and product / Intelligence is largely inherited, but the difference made by environment can be quite significant / IQs (scores on intelligence tests) change from year to year, and early scores (up to age six) are not very predictive of adult intelligence / IQ scores don't predict subject matter grades (individually) very well / Individual intelligence tests are preferable to group ones / Intelligence tests classify low SES and minority learners in the low levels, possibly due to test bias, but also due to the less-effective test-taking behaviors of these learners / Other considerations impinge as well.

Glossary

Acceptance: A type of treatment of others, particularly children, which implies that their concerns and ideas are significant.

Aptitude: Potential for doing well in a certain subject or skill or profession, often measured by tests whose tasks have been chosen in such a way as to make predictions more dependable; e.g., "law aptitude tests" for determining the potential of a student for doing well in law school;

Archetype: An innate (inherited) concept or knowledge of certain basic entities such as "mother," "father" (Jung).

BAT: Body Adjustment Test, for FDI-FD.

Behavior Controls: Limits to behavior exerted either by verbal rules or by demonstrating through reward and punishment what should and should not be done.

Convergent Thinking: Thinking leading to one answer only, or a very few answers.

Correlation: A statistical way of showing relationships between measures given the same learners; i.e., if those high on one test are high on the other, and those low on one are low on the other, then the correlation is high.

Democratic: A kind of treatment which considers the rights and privileges and interests of the other person, giving him or her a say in things to the degree that is appropriate.

Defense Mechanism: Internal mental process by which one avoids recognition of something that is threatening, either something outside yourself or within yourself.

Divergent thinking: Thinking leading to alternatives.

EFT: Embedded figures test.

Embedded Figure: A common figure that is part of another figure, and thus difficult to recognize.

Extrovert: One who is preoccupied with external things rather than self (Jung).

Factor(s): Statistical term referring to several test items or questionnaire items or types of questions that correlate highly with each other—suggesting that they have something in common.

FD-FDI: Field dependence-independence.

Fraternal twins: Twins not coming from the same egg, but conceived at the same time and born at the same time.

Gifted Learners: Learners with high aptitudes across a large number of types of tasks, thus of high intelligence as well.

Hyperactivity: A behavior pattern which involves distractibility, disorganized activity, and often disruption of the learning processes of others; it also results in poor learning for the learner himself.

Identical Twins: Twins conceived from the same ovum, or egg, and thus having identical hereditary traits or capabilities.

Impulsivity: Tendency to respond without careful consideration.

Inferiority Complex: General feeling of inferiority, of unlikeliness of success, of being less able or worthwhile than others (Adler).

Intellectualization: Pretending that understanding of something equals facing it or doing something about it.

Intelligence: Either a score on an intelligence test, or a level of intellect which is demonstrated by the ability of a person to solve problems and recognize relationships and such.

Interaction: Outcome of an experiment where different combinations of variables give different results.

Introvert: One who is preoccupied with his or her personal feelings (Jung).

Mainstreaming: Placing retarded and other handicapped learners in regular classrooms with normal learners.

Matching: Choosing two groups for an experiment in such a way that each person in one has a counterpart in the other.

Mental Health: Balance between conscious and unconscious forces, and between id and superego; not neurotic or psychotic, generally able to cope.

Neurotic: Anxious, inhibited, obsessed with certain concerns, unable to let go and enjoy.

Nurturance Need: Need to be taken care of (Murray).

Operation: Thinking or remembering or producing alternate answers or finding the one answer or evaluating something (Guilford).

Other-directed: Personality trait where you are subject to the norms of a social group.

Predictive Correlation: Correlation between a score on a test and achievement scores or grades later on, used to predict later achievement from one's score on the earlier test.

Products: The outcomes of thinking, including units, classes, relations, systems, transformations, and implications (Guilford).

Projection: Seeing your own faults in others.

Psychological Autonomy: Allowing children to think for themselves, to express questions and different thoughts; permitting them to think freely and individually.

Psychological Intrusiveness: Intruding upon children's psychological space by asking what they are thinking, what they intend to do, whether they have fulfilled their obligations.

Random, Randomness: Things chosen by chance, without plan, or happening by chance without exerting control.

Rationalization: Seeing a desirable motive for doing something rather than a lack of discipline.

Reaction Formation: Acting in the opposite way to how you feel.

Reflectivity: Tendency to respond only after some consideration.

Reactive: Type of responding showing little contemplation or reflection.

Reinforcing, Reinforcement: Events occurring right after some response, resulting in the response increasing in frequency, i.e., happening more often.

Restrictiveness: Not allowing latitude or independence; over-control; setting too many or too narrow limits; applying the rules too generally or when they are not appropriate.

RFT: Rod and Frame Test, for FD-FDI.

Sample: The learners or schools that are selected to be studied for some purpose, and to represent the whole country or all learners of schools of a certain type.

Self-concept: The view you have of yourself, how you see yourself; e.g., you may be a better-than-average athlete yet see yourself as clumsy and useless.

Self-esteem: Esteem of the self, good self-concept, high opinion (without being swelled-headed or feeling superior).

SES: Socioeconomic status, economic level; whether rich or well-to-do or poor.

Siblings: Children of the same mother and father; brothers, sisters.

Stanford: The Stanford-Binet individual intelligence test.

Sublimation: Turning basic id drives into approved channels.

Test anxiety: Anxiety which occurs when you are taking a test.

Warmth: A type of response to others, particularly children, which is the opposite of cold or rejecting, and which indicates a positive feeling toward the child.

WISC: The Wechsler Intelligence Scale for Children.

Questions for thought and discussion

1. What combination of parent traits seems to produce aggressiveness and overassertiveness?

2. How do you go about fostering self-esteem in a learner (or in your child)?

3. What parental trait seems to ameliorate or make less serious other errors in handling the child?

4. How does achievement motivation of girls and boys compare in early school years? During adolescence? How could these differences be reduced?

5. Give some example of sexist behavior on the part of teachers at various school levels.

6. What are some of the problems women have in seeking success in business and in professions?

7. What were the main outcomes of the Coleman study?

8. Does Black English interfere with or aid school learning? Should such learners be taught to speak "good" English, or allowed to go on with their own language?

9. Give an example of each of the following defense mechanisms: rationalization, projection, reaction formation.

10. An adolescent boy is very mean to his mother when he is home, but stays away from her most of the time, living away from home for long periods. A Freudian explanation would be that . . . ?

11. What kind of teaching strategy would be appropriate for a learner with high anxiety?

12. How would you teach arithmetic in such a way as to foster creativity?

13. In an embedded figures task what is the "field" which a learner is either dependent on or independent of?

14. Did Binet consider intelligence innate and unchanging? Do you? Give pros and cons.

15. Describe some of the tasks which one finds on intelligence tests; choose them so they show the variety involved.

16. What if your two-year-old daughter scores 110 on an IQ test? Will she be bright or not bright at age eighteen? How sure can you be?

17. Does IQ determine success in school? in particular subjects? in life?

Situations calling for applications of facts and concepts

1. Mr. and Mrs. Brown want to raise their daughter Ann to have high intelligence and to be independent, outgoing, and achievement-oriented as well. What guidelines would you give them for bringing this about when Ann is age four?

2. Billy is a slow student, and comes from a very poor family. What levels or types of intelligence, anxiety, creativity, and other personality attributes would you expect to find in him, and what ones would you want to deal with first in order to help him improve?

3. What levels or degrees of the following individual traits would you expect would be desirable or optimal for high achievement in a high school or college course (either or both) in English literature: intelligence, creativity, anxiety, field-dependence-independence, impulsivity-reflectivity, socioeconomic status, type of parental treatment.

Suggested activities

1. Design your own test of creativity, or find one in your curriculum library or testing center, and give it to some of your friends, or some students in a local school. Compare different learners' responses, and rate them as high or low in creativity. Then ask them about their creative performance, as described in this chapter, and note whether this correlates with their scores on your test.

2. Give an anxiety questionnaire to some of your friends, or some students in a local school. Score it according to the directions in the manual, and determine whether the group is anxious generally and whether there are individuals who are anxious. Relate this to their academic performance if possible, and note whether the more anxious students prefer more structured courses or achieve better in them.

3. Make up an "embedded figures" test and give it to some friends. Compare their responses, and relate the results to their personalities as you know them. Are those who find fewer of the embedded figures more gregarious or less academic? Are there other differences?

4. Make up your own intelligence test, a short one involving several kinds of tasks that you think must be related to intelligence. Give this to a group of your friends whose IQs are known, or whose academic performance you know. See whether your test correlates with known IQ and/or academic performance.

4

Learning Disabilities

CONTENTS

ABOUT CHAPTER 4

How you will benefit from this chapter

You will be able to recognize specific learning problems that are more basic than just not knowing how to do something like long division or research about the Civil War. You will recognize problems involving auditory perception, visual comprehension, motor coordination, and behavior disabilities. You will also recognize such syndromes as hyperactivity and dyslexia. You may also recognize some of these difficulties in yourself or one of your own friends, and be able to take appropriate action to compensate or remediate. Thus you will add to your repertoire of helping abilities in the field that is sometimes called "psychoeducational teaching."

What might make this difficult to learn

Traditionally, if someone didn't learn in school he or she was either of low intelligence or had some emotional problem. You may assume that if you don't have either of these problems, there isn't anything wrong except lack of effort. If so there wouldn't be much point to studying learning disabilities. On the other hand, you may be subconsciously aware that you have certain disabilities and prefer not to discuss such matters, lest you be tempted to use this as an excuse for poor performance. This is a laudable feeling, but not one that a good parent or teacher can afford. Some learners really can't progress without this kind of help, even though they try very hard.

Some reasons for understanding learning disabilities

There are many learners who are not retarded or emotionally upset but who cannot learn specific things or types of things. Obviously they need help, and teachers and parents should have some idea about giving first aid until the specialist can take over. Furthermore, the study of such problems and their treatment sheds light on how normal students learn as well, and research in remedial processes often results in methods that are effective for all learners. In many cases teachers who have been trained to deal with classes of learning disabled students, through individualized instruction, often continue to used the same approaches when they are given "normal" classes to teach. Finally, in the study of behavior disabilities you will find some reasons for the kinds of behaviors that drive teachers up a wall, and also some suggestions for dealing with them.

Assuring successful learning

To be successful with this material you will have to maintain a tolerance for new terminology, and convince yourself that this is not difficult but only occasionally confusing. If you are one who likes to have everything carefully defined and well related, your anxiety may provide more of a barrier than the difficulty of the material itself. Make frequent use of the glossary, note down questions to ask your instructor, and don't become discouraged.

Objectives for Chapter 4

My purpose is to introduce into this book something new to the field, something that is relevant to problems of parents and teachers and others who work with learners, and that adds to the study of this subject. It is also to prepare readers for changes in education in the future, including the development of new specialties and functions in the school related to specific learning disabilities, and to other handicapping conditions and the mainstreaming of children with handicaps.

RATIONALE AND BACKGROUND OF CHAPTER 4

What are "learning disabilities?"

Sometimes learners with perfectly good intellect have surprising difficulty learning some particular thing— such as reading!

There are disabilities within individual learners that neither they nor their parents or teachers may be aware of. For example, suppose you are a boy of six who is about to start school. You have been active, have friends, and have seldom found anything that other children can do that you can't. You enter school, and after a while you find you don't "get" your letters and sounds as well as others, and you are not learning to read. The teacher gives you extra help but it doesn't make things much better. Some of the other children begin to tease you a little, your parents become worried and take you to a clinic where they give you some tests, and then nothing happens; you just get further behind. You begin to avoid schoolwork because you can't seem to master it. Your teacher tells your parents that you have good intelligence and are not retarded, but that you must have "dyslexia," whatever that is!

Consider another example. Billy is a normal child, into everything, and has many friends. He scores average or a little above on aptitude and intelligence tests. He has a little trouble with reading, but not a great deal. He seems to prefer a "look-see" or whole-word approach to reading, and has difficulty with phonetics. His teachers often become exasperated with him because he doesn't follow directions. If they ask him to hang up his coat and take his books out and start studying, he ends up doing only the first thing or two things. Several of his teachers feel he is trying to get them angry, but others—and his parents—say that he isn't like that at all. Either way, he is doing poorly in school, partly because he isn't organized, doesn't know what he is supposed to do next, and doesn't understand oral directions and explanations.

Let's look at another type or pattern of difficulty experienced by Grace.

Grace is a sophomore in high school. She has always had difficulty in keeping up with her academic work, but through extra help from parents and teachers and a bit of effort on her own, she has managed to get by. She reads adequately but not well, and she does fairly well in mathematics except for geometry, which she barely passed. Socially, she often seems "out of it." For example, when she goes to a basketball game with friends, she doesn't seem to know what is going on in the game, although she has been attending basketball games for some time. Sometimes her friends will explain what has happened so she can understand a good play or a foul, but generally she either covers up her confusion or jokes about her inability to understand sports. However, in physical education classes she is well coordinated and does her part in field hockey or other such games. Her teachers notice that she is not very good at describing things she has seen or in drawing pictures of things that are not actually there to copy.

Grace seems to have a problem with remembering or understanding things that she sees. Just as Billy could hear well, Grace's vision appears adequate, since her eye tests don't indicate a need for glasses.

What learning disabilities are not

A learning disabled child is one who is *not* retarded, who is *not* organically or physically handicapped, who does *not* have poor hearing or eyesight, who is *not* emotionally disturbed, and who does *not* have cerebral palsy, multiple sclerosis, spastic paralysis, or a number of other such conditions—but who cannot learn in some specific way. The following learners are *not* learning disabled:

- Mary has trouble learning because she is so anxious and upset over the fact that her parents are physically punishing her and her brother, each day after school.
- Johnny's IQ is 75, which suggests he is retarded. While he has been "mainstreamed" to avoid labeling, his teacher hasn't the faintest idea what to do with him since he is so far behind everyone else in the class.
- Alice can't control her muscles well enough to hold a book or write, or even to concentrate on what the teacher is doing, so she can't learn anything.

The kinds of learning disabilities that will be considered in this book are not emotional in nature, nor are they due to personality problems or physical handicaps. Generally, children with learning disabilities relate well to other children and do not have particularly serious adjustment problems. In school their main difficulty usually involves academic achievement.

For a long time people have tended to assume that if a child was unable to learn, it was because of some social or emotional adjustment problem, or a bad home life.   Of course many learning problems have such roots.   However, learning disabilities represent an assumption that inability to learn is due to specific problems related to the process of learning itself, and that emotional upsets are as likely to be caused *by* learning problems as the other way around.

Learning disabilities and more serious handicapping conditions

In defining learning disabilities emphasis is placed on what they are not as well as what they are.   This can hide some relationships between learning disabilities and more serious conditions.   One source has suggested the following connections (Clements, quoted in Lerner, 1976):

- Impairment of fine motor movement or coordination, in extreme forms, becomes what is called "cerebral palsy."
- Fluctuations in behavior and intellectual functioning in their extreme form may be what is called "epilepsy."
- Poor attention, poor impulse control, and lack of social behavior or lack of feeling for others, in their extreme forms, become "autism."
- Perceptual deficits, visual and auditory, which result in inability to process information, in extreme form become "retardation."
- Expressive difficulties in their extreme forms become "aphasia."

An overlooked source of learning problems or disabilities

Often learners have specific difficulties due to missing some learning experiences along the way, perhaps through absence due to illness, from emotional upset over a certain period of his or her life, or due to an experiment in educational innovation that didn't work out as well as it was expected to.   Such problems require going back and reteaching the missing skills, which can be very time consuming.   You should keep this possibility in mind when trying to identify the source of a disability, since diagnoses related to the problems discussed in this chapter may be in error under such conditions.

THREE TYPES OF DISABILITIES: INPUT, OUTPUT, AND PROCESSING

Bobby has trouble with addition because he cannot seem to copy the numbers down in the correct order; he doesn't perceive them correctly, and thus he has an input problem.   Sally has trouble with addition also, because she can't write the numbers legibly and therefore can't read her own work; she has an output problem.   Johnny has trouble with addition because although he copies clearly and correctly, he gets the wrong answers when he adds or multiplies; his processing is weak, although his input and output abilities are strong. The three stages in the processing of information (as was discussed in Chapter 2 in relation to an information processing model) are the input stage, the cognitive processing stage, and the output stage. However, the divisions between these stages are difficult to define simply. There are probably several stages of input processing, each one a little more "cognitive" than the preceding one, and there may be more than one stage of output processing. Input problems are usually more basic and serious than output ones, just as the development of receptive language precedes and is more basic than the development of expressive language. We will begin by describing input problems, therefore: first auditory ones, then visual ones.

INPUT PROBLEMS

Auditory perceptual disabilities

Wendy is a freshman in high school. When you talk to her, she has the odd habit of looking away, rather than straight at you. When you ask her to pay attention, she does, but she doesn't seem to hear what you say. If you give her oral directions for doing something, she gets mixed up or forgets some of them. Once she was referred for a hearing test, but the results were normal.

Some learners can hear perfectly well—but they can't understand what you tell them.

Wendy seems to have limits on what she can "take in" or "process" through her auditory channel. By looking away when someone is speaking to her, she seems to be able to interpret what she hears without having it confused by what she sees at the same time. Evidently she has to concentrate on translating messages and is easily overloaded with other information. An example of someone with a similar difficulty is Mary.

Mary is a very creative girl of about ten, who enjoys painting and drawing and such activities. She sews doll clothes very well, although she doesn't know the names of the stitches or materials, and she seems to prefer to create them without consulting any directions. In art class she is occasionally unable to follow oral directions, but she is talented enough so that it doesn't affect her grade. In other classes, when the teacher reads or makes a presentation, she often appears to be dreaming, and sometimes even covers her ears as if to shut out the sounds. She also "acts out" occasionally. Once, when she was trying to draw a person running, she got up and ran around the room, then sat down and finished the drawing. She shows some odd responses in her written work: she writes "whichs" for "which is" and "un able" for "unable," for example.

Mary seems less able to process information by ear than by eye. She has difficulty paying attention in classes where the teacher talks a lot, and you would be correct in suspecting that she doesn't do as well as she might in those subjects. Her acting out seems contradictory; it suggests that she has difficulty in imagining how things *look*, rather than how they sound.   You would have to give Mary some special tasks to determine whether she can visualize things, or "auditorize," or if she has problems with both.

   A clear description of the importance of auditory processing in reading is found in the following quotation ("dyslexic" means "unable to read":)

> Many dyslexic children show deficits in auditory perception, memory, and integration which make it difficult for them to acquire skills in phonic analysis.   They may be unable to hear the similarities in the words "toy" and "tag," or "hit" and "pit."   Others are unable to hear the double consonant sounds in consonant blends: rust, bent, sift.   Some may not be able to discriminate the short vowel sounds in pen, pin, and pan.   Many of these children have difficulty with analysis and synthesis of words. They cannot break words into syllables or into their individual sounds; when given the word "table" they cannot separate the syllables, or when given the one-syllable word "cat" they cannot dissect it into its individual sounds.   Disturbances in auditory analysis will affect both spelling and reading.   Those with problems in synthesis cannot combine parts of words to form a whole; consequently, when trying to sound out a new word, they cannot retain each of the syllables and blend them together.   Difficulties in sequentializing will often be reflected in spelling errors like "spot" for "stop." . . . There is evidence to suggest that all dyslexic children may demonstrate some difficulties in processing auditory stimuli and that their reading problem may be related specifically to an auditory involvement rather than to an intersensory difficulty or to visual perceptual problems.   (Zigmond, 1969)

Some common auditory test tasks

A test of auditory discrimination would be to give the learner (orally) two words like "tap" and "top" and ask the learner to say whether they are the same or different.   The Wepman test, popular in the late 1960s and early 1970s, is made up of such tasks.   In a more sophisticated test (Lindamood), learners arrange colored blocks to show how many sounds they have heard (number of blocks) and whether they were the same or different (by using same or different colors).   There are also tests of auditory understanding; Figure 4–1 contains some visuals adapted from one type of task (the Developmental Learning Materials tasks on Auditory Imagery). This has instructions recorded on tape to be played to the learner, e.g.:

- "Put a blue line around the picture that relates to the situation where I was in a big hurry to go up to my room."
- "Put a red line around the picture of the thing that I couldn't drink from because of a crack where I put my mouth."

Actually, this material is for *practice* on auditory imagery where a preliminary test has identified it as a problem.   If you were to use the test to diagnose learning disa-

Figure 4–1. *Sample visuals from an auditory-imagery task.*

bilities, you would have to be sure first that the learner was strong in visual understanding, since this requires the student to pick out the correct picture once he or
she understands the auditory message.

You may think that this is rather obvious, and that anyone would have to be
rather stupid to use such a task as a test.   However, consider the possibility of a

learner who has poor auditory understanding but good visual understanding, who takes the Wechsler Intelligence Test for Children.   All of the "verbal" tasks are given orally, i.e., the learner has to *listen* and understand.   The learner with poor auditory understanding might do very poorly on this test, even though he or she might be able to do similar tasks quite adequately if they were given visually. Would such an intelligence score be valid?

Visual perceptual disabilities

Some learners can see perfectly well—but they cannot understand what they see!

Just as certain learners have difficulty processing information that comes to them by sound, other learners have difficulty in processing visual information.   These learners have good vision in terms of being able to see things in an "eye test," just as the auditory perceptual disabilities were more than just hearing deficits.   Here are some examples of the kinds of symptoms that learners with visual perceptive difficulties show.

> *Roger is in the third grade.   He doesn't care much for picture books, since he has a hard time identifying pictures of objects.   When he is reading in his reader, the pictures do not help him understand the text.   When he is asked to arrange a set of pictures in their proper order (showing a series of events like a person climbing a tower and then jumping off a diving board) he has trouble getting them right.   Sometimes he does it better if the teacher asks him to tell her what he is doing and how he is going about it, while he is doing it.   Also, if the teacher makes a gesture which means "come here" or something of that kind, he may not respond; however, if she says "come here" he will come.*

It is probably clear to you that Roger does not process *visual* information well. After dealing with a number of cases of auditory problems, you may feel that this is a relief, but of course it is a real problem for Roger.   The world is passing him by. He doesn't know what is going on.

Here is another case exemplifying this kind of problem.

> *Lois is in the eighth grade.   She can't seem to learn to play games as other children do; she doesn't seem to make sense out of games when she observes them.   She also seems to be unable to tell how other children—or adults—feel about things or about her, or how they react to what she does or other situations.   She doesn't seem to "dig" common facial expressions—anger, surprise, anxiety and so forth.   On the Wechsler Intelligence Scale for Children, she had one of her lowest scores on the Picture Arrangement Test, where she was supposed to arrange a set of pictures in an order which made sense.   Lois converses fluently and her overall score on the WISC was above average.   However, she doesn't do well socially because she just isn't "with it."*

Lois's problem seems to be basically one of comprehending visual information. She can't read emotions and feelings in other people, and she doesn't know how they feel about her or things from their expressions. She can't understand games and other activities without having them explained carefully or joining in and playing for a while with guidance.

There are tests for visual problems, as you might suspect. Some examples of tasks found in these tests are illustrated in Figure 4–2.

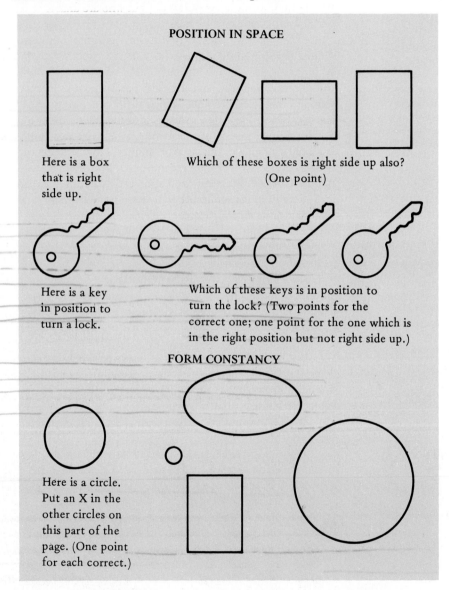

POSITION IN SPACE

Here is a box that is right side up.

Which of these boxes is right side up also? (One point)

Here is a key in position to turn a lock.

Which of these keys is in position to turn the lock? (Two points for the correct one; one point for the one which is in the right position but not right side up.)

FORM CONSTANCY

Here is a circle. Put an X in the other circles on this part of the page. (One point for each correct.)

Figure 4–2. *Some visual-perceptual tasks commonly used in diagnosing learning disabilities. These are similar to the tasks used on the Frostig Developmental Test of Visual Perception.*

DYSLEXIA

inability to read

What is dyslexia?

Dyslexia—some think of it as *the* learning disability, but it really means inability to read.

There are children who have a good vocabulary, who know what words mean, and who can use words in conversation, but who are unable to learn to read. They are said to have "dyslexia." There are two basic kinds of dyslexia: visual and auditory.

A child who is a *visual dyslexic* has difficulty translating written letters into sounds. Such a child may also have difficulty in discriminating between two similar letters, e.g., "b" and "d" or "n" and "u," when they are written in text form. This often extends to difficulty in recognizing the difference between such printed words as "cat" and "cap" or "tap" and "tip." This form of dyslexia involves difficulty in translating visual symbols into meaning.

A child who is an *auditory dyslexic*, on the other hand, has difficulty in translating *sounds* into meaning. Sometimes this shows up as a difficulty in discriminating between sounds that are somewhat similar; a child with such a difficulty will not discriminate between "bat" and "cat" when they are given orally. He or she may also fail to recognize the similarity between "milk" and "silk." A child with

Some children need help with reading or writing problems.

auditory dyslexia may also have difficulty remembering things told to him or her orally.

A visual dyslexic will have difficulty learning to read whole words, as well as pronouncing letters. It seems probable that, once the child learns to translate letters into sounds, it will be better to have him or her learn to sound out the words rather than recognize them on sight, i.e., use phonetics. An auditory dyslexic, on the other hand, might be expected to have difficulty in blending the letter sounds into whole words, and thus might learn better by recognizing whole words by sight, i.e. "look-see." However, for long-term development of reading facility, the auditory dyslexic should acquire some ability to sound out words as well.

Factors related to dyslexia

One report of research on dyslexia has identified visual-spatial organization as being associated with dyslexia (Kershner, 1975); another says dyslexics are strong in visual-spatial abilities (Bannatyne, 1971). Still another study reports that the basic difference between dyslexics and nondyslexics involves automatic *responses* (Whiting, Schnall, and Drake, unpub.). This demonstrated that the performance of poor readers on tasks requiring simple but repetitive skills is inferior to that of good readers.

Other theorists feel that dyslexia reflects a lag in the maturation of the brain, delaying the skills which are in primary ascendance at certain ages (i.e., which affect certain critical periods); this is an embryonic view of development, as described in Chapter 1. Lags in development of early abilities are related to central nervous system processing, and test tasks have reflected such processing. These tasks have turned out to be rather accurate in predicting which learners will have serious reading difficulties later on. Some of the tasks are:

1. Telling which finger is touched by another person, when you can't see that hand ("finger localization test");
2. Ability to recite the alphabet, and ability to tell what day of the week it is;
3. Visual-motor integration tasks such as copying figures. (Satz, 1974)

Another practitioner treats dyslexia as a problem of remediating serious reading difficulty through carefully prepared sequences of tasks that engage the subject's attention and enable him or her to be successful from the beginning. This approach emphasizes techniques which enable the learner to recognize and pronounce letters and letter combinations easily and quickly, and then to begin to blend them into words. Prereading skills which are taught in this approach include learning letter-name sounds ("i" as in "item" or "ice," "a" as in "acorn" or "ailment"), instead of the usual phonic approach of pronouncing the "i" in "in" or "image" (Durrell, 1976). However, the emphasis is on the sequence of learning tasks, i.e., programming as described in the section on helping learners with disabilities (page 148 ff).

HELPING A CHILD WITH VISUAL DYSLEXIA

It is one thing to identify a problem such as visual dyslexia and another to do something about it. Basic guidelines for teaching are given in another part of this book, but at this point it may help to preview some of those guidelines as applied to this particular kind of difficulty. One thing to determine is whether or not the learner can discriminate between different shapes, and particularly letters. It may be that a "b" and a "d" look the same to her, or that the "n" and the "m" are no different to him. It may also be that the learner sees no difference between "bat" and "bit." If this is the problem, then you will want to give the learner discrimination exercises, beginning with very simple visual differences and proceeding very gradually toward more difficult ones. At the same time you will want to notice whether there is a very general problem, or whether only a few basic types of difference cause trouble. If it is the latter, then focus on those. One way to do this is to present a letter or a word, and then present three or four others that resemble it, including one which is the same. Reward the learner for choosing the correct one, and note if there is an error, so that you can go back to that one and to others with the same type of difficulty.

Another type of difficulty is where the learner can discriminate between shapes and thus letters and words, but where he or she cannot translate these symbols into sounds. Here you find the overlap between visual and auditory dyslexia. To teach the sounds, you may have to do some auditory discrimination teaching, that is, give a sound and then several others, and have the learner practice picking out the one which is the same, just as you did with the visual. Even when the discrimination is all right, or after you have taught it, you may then have to teach the learner to "re-image" or remember the sound: auditory imagery is something which can be taught and improved, as has been attested to by famous musicians as well as people who work with remedial problems. What you have to do here is give a sound and ask the learner to recreate it for himself, i.e., to recall it or imagine it, or hear it in his mind. Then you sound it again, and ask him or her whether it is the same one that was imagined (of course, this ability to say whether it was or not is based in part on the auditory discrimination you just read about). Once the learner is able to do this, then the problem is to get an association between a visual symbol and a sound. This can be done generally by associating the symbol and the sound, then presenting the symbol without the sound and having the learner try to recreate the sound within her or his head.

SOME OTHER CHARACTERISTICS OF LEARNING DISABILITIES

Overloading

Suppose you present a learner with a word written in large block letters on a card, and ask her to pronounce it and tell you what it means. She may be able to do this easily and accurately. However, when the same word is presented in a sentence, where she has to visualize the meaning of the word in relation to the others and to make "sense" out of it, she may be unable to cope with the task. Her ability to interpret visually has been "overloaded."

Another type of overloading occurs when a learner is taught by being shown a word, by hearing it at the same time, and perhaps also being given a picture of the

thing to which the word refers or allowed to touch the actual object. Some teachers feel that giving information simultaneously through a number of channels will
help the learner understand. Research indicates that such an approach can be
more confusing than helpful, especially to learning disabled children. This seems
to indicate a rather low overload threshold in that particular task or type of task
(Johnson and Myklebust, 1967).

Everyone has "loading" limits of this type, but learning disabled children have
lower limits. Practicing on simple tasks may bring the learner to a point where he
or she can handle them in more complex situations; however, ability to do the
simpler task does not guarantee the more complex ability, generally speaking.

Cross-modal disabilities

As you read the words in this book most of you are translating them into sounds in
your heads, and those sounds into meanings. Some people "see" words in their
imagination when they are asked orally to spell them, while others "hear" them,
and some both. All of us acquire language auditorially at first, and all of us learn a
great deal about our environment through visual and motor exploration, as in the
sensory-motor period described in Chapter 1.

Motor proficiency can increase children's self-confidence.

arithmetic and history.   However, *motor* problems often cause the learner more distress.

Since motor abilities are among the most malleable and teachable, and since basic skills and activities are well classified, it would seem reasonable to teach these skills for their own sake, regardless of their potential effects on cognitive learning. Furthermore, a child who feels better about himself in relation to other children as a result of improved physical ability is likely to be more effective in his academic work as well.   The greater basic security and need-fulfillment that results is likely to make him or her more susceptible to motivational factors related to school learning.   Furthermore, there are hundreds of small motor tasks involved in normal classroom and school activities, most of them going unnoticed because they are performed automatically by most children.   Walking around desks, hanging up coats, carrying materials for study, building things—all require motor ability, and

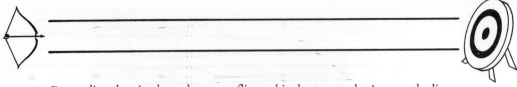

Draw a line showing how the arrow flies to hit the target: don't cross the lines above and below its path.

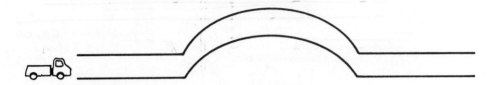

Draw a line to show how the truck goes in order to stay on the road, without going off to either side.

Figure 4–4. *Visual-motor coordination tasks.*

the child who has to concentrate on them has less attention left for dealing with other children and for socialization, or for listening to directions, or for reading. Thus remediation of motor difficulties can remove indirect barriers to learning, and thus have a positive effect on cognitive achievement as well.

Kinesthetic responses and feedback

Kinesthetic communication is communication to the brain from muscles and bones; it gives the brain information as to the position of the arms and legs and fingers, their state of motion, stress on them and such. Through kinesthetic information you can tell (without looking) roughly what position your limbs are in, what direction your head is turned, or how high your arm or hand is raised. As far as your brain is concerned, this information is produced by stimuli originating in those limbs and muscles.

Fine motor and gross motor activities

Motor activities such as lifting, running, throwing, moving your body into various positions—those using primarily large muscles of the back, legs, and arms—are called "gross." "Fine" motor activities include tying shoelaces, writing, drawing pictures, knitting, and others which use the smaller muscles and operate within a smaller space. An important relationship to know, however, is that *fine* motor activities are supported by (and have their roots in) gross motor activities. For ex-

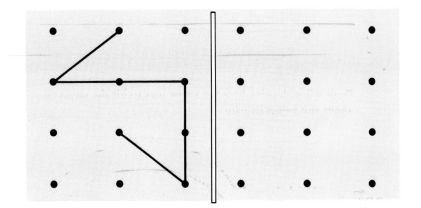

There is a picture on the left of the wall: it is a line which goes in different directions.

Copy the picture on the right of the wall, making it look like the one on the left. (One point for each of the four parts.)

Figure 4–5. *A perceptual-motor (visual-motor) task similar to tasks on the Bender Gestalt test which is often used for analyzing learning disabilities as well as emotional problems. Sample drawings you might expect from normal students at various ages follow.*

ample, playing the piano seems like a fine motor activity, exclusively, since it involves the fingers so completely, yet the way the pianist sits and moves his trunk and shoulders and arms to support the work of his fingers is crucial.

Classroom observation of integration and coordination

There are certain cues you can look for in the classroom or on the playground regarding the learner's motor integration and coordination. If the child looks tilted or doesn't sit straight, his back muscles may be weak and in need of exercise. Some children also show "winging," that is, their shoulder "blades" stick way out from their backs, and they have trouble balancing or stabilizing their back muscles. If a learner tends to move his whole head when following a moving object, instead of just his eyes, then he may need exercises to strengthen and balance his neck muscles. If he can't reach for something on the left with his right hand, or vice versa (called "crossing the midline"), then he may need exercises to improve his coordination before he can go on to learn more complex motor skills (Ayers, 1972).

Laterality and directionality

Some learners have difficulty establishing right and left, and in telling the difference between their left and right feet, or identifying the correct shoe for the correct foot and such. They seem confused about directions, and this confusion may be limited to left and right, or may include up and down as well as front and back. Some learners write certain letters and numbers backward, and some even write words and sentences backward.

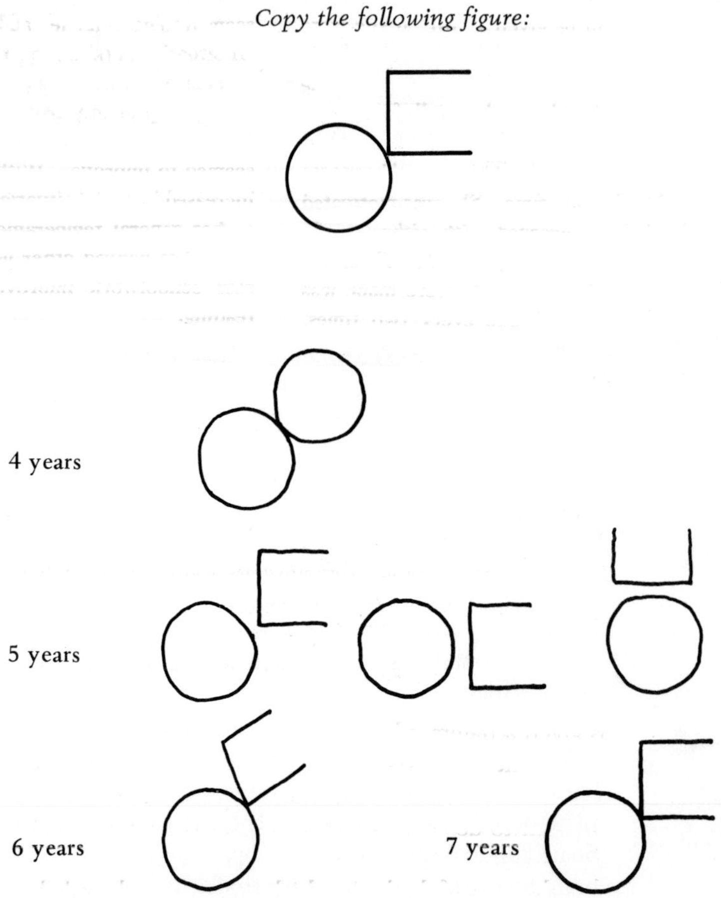

Copy the following figure:

4 years

5 years

6 years   7 years

Figure 4–6. *Sample visual-motor task.*

LELA'S MOTOR PROBLEMS

Lela was a girl of about six who was generally normal, happy, able to handle most school tasks, had friends, was considered highly intelligent by her teacher, and was well-adjusted in her neighborhood, although as the youngest child she was a bit overprotected and spoiled. However, she had difficulty learning the sounds of letters and putting them together into words. She also was not as well-coordinated as her peers and was a bit immature socially. She tended to play with girls somewhat younger than she, since she was better able to keep up with them.

Since her motor coordination was not quite up to par, her teachers thought her general achievement might be given a "lift" if she were to improve the motor problem in some basic ways. She was given exercises on the walking beam, where she first learned to walk forward—with some difficulty at the beginning—then backward, then sideward. This caused her some anxiety and took some time. She was motivated in part by being rewarded with either candy or pennies every time she "made it" across the beam; later, these rewards were made less frequent—she received one every two times, or every five times, etc.

At the same time, she was given a "hoppity-hop," i.e., a large rubber ball with a rubber ring built into it. She would hold onto the ring, sit on the ball, and bounce around on it—like a pogo stick, except sitting! At first she could not do this very long, but after a while she "got in shape" and drove her parents and brother and sister to distraction by her continuous bouncing around the house.

One result of her walking-beam training seemed to be that she had better balance in similar situations and more confidence in those contexts as a result. Also, her legs seemed to gain strength (probably from the hoppity-hop) and, from this perhaps, her general coordination seemed to improve. With that, her confidence increased in social situations with peers, as well as her general temperament, but she was still somewhat behind other girls in these respects. Her schoolwork improved, and with it her reading.

Apraxia

Several forms of motor difficulty are found in people who have suffered damage to their brains. One group of these, called "apraxia," or "verbal apraxia" (Geschwind, 1975), shows some of the complexities of motor behavior which we usually take for granted. A person with this problem will be able to perform a certain movement under one set of conditions and not under another. For example, if he is given a hammer he will be able to hammer something with his left hand; however, if he is asked to demonstrate (without a hammer) how he would go about using a hammer with his left hand, he would not be able to do so. If you were to ask him to demonstrate this with his right hand, however, he would be able to, showing that he understands what you ask of him. The explanation seems to be that the area of the brain which processes such verbal requests is in the left hemisphere, and that normally the request is translated into a message to the right hemisphere, which then controls the left side of the body. However, in this kind of brain damage the communication pathways between the left and right hemisphere have been damaged, so the verbal communication does not get through. However, the right hemisphere has sufficient autonomy to interpret the more basic visual and kinesthetic messages, and thus the person can grasp and use an actual hammer with his left hand.

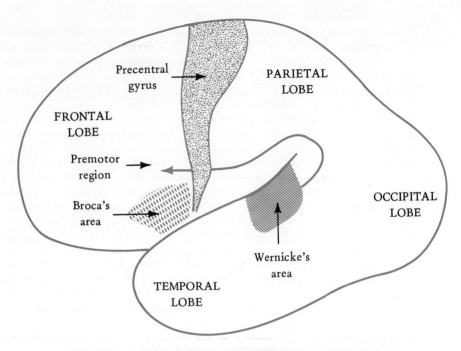

Figure 4–7. *Side view of the human brain, left hemisphere, showing the four lobes and the pathway used in the performance of motor acts by the right limbs and the cranial muscles in response to verbal command. (Adapted from N. Geschwind, The apraxias: Neural mechanisms of disorders of learned movement, American Scientist, March/April 1975, 63, 188–195.)*

BEHAVIORAL DISABILITIES

How behavior disabled learners appear to teachers, parents, and other children

Robby is a problem. His mother says that he always has been. He cried more than her other children and wouldn't feed easily or in a relaxed manner. He has always gotten into some kind of difficulty, and has never been willing to leave things as they are. He is always on the go, yet often too tired to get up in the morning. He is always breaking things, yet without enough energy to clean up his room. He often has fights with other kids and doesn't have close friends. He picks on his younger sister and fights with his older one. He can't seem to get down to work; always taking another trip to the pencil sharpener or the washroom or fidgeting with something small and noisy under the cover of his desk. He can't seem to complete an assignment given him; he doesn't concentrate on it long enough. Yet his aptitude tests say he's highly intelligent, and teachers are always talking about his "potential."

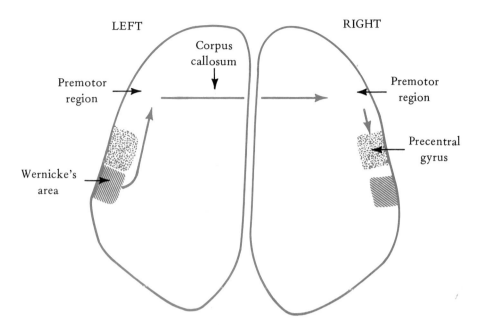

Figure 4–8. *Top view of human brain showing the pathways used in carrying out movements with the right or left limbs in response to verbal command. (Adapted from N. Gerschwind, The apraxias: Neural mechanisms of disorders of learned movement.* American Scientist, *March/April 1975, 63, 188–195.)*

There are patterns of behavior that cause problems, both disciplinary and learning.

Parents of children who have been identified by teachers as "learning disabled" often recall that it was difficult to control the behavior of these children when they were younger. The reasons aren't always clear. Some say that the learner was overactive and destructive as a young child; others say disobedient and difficult to discipline. Others say he or she resisted their authority and tried to boss other children, or that she was difficult to communicate with and didn't want to listen—and sometimes didn't express herself well. Many say that these children are more anxious than others in the family and that they weren't able to accept affection easily. Yet they are often reported as having been more dependent on their parents, as well as less considerate of others. Some summarize these observations by describing them as spoiled brats; others say they have autistic tendencies; that is, they are less able to give and receive affection and have less control of their impulses. Sometimes they are termed "hyperactive."

Teachers often find these children less cooperative, occasionally aggressive toward other children, less attentive, less responsible, and generally having a poor attitude toward teachers and school. One study found that teachers responded to behavior disabled children less frequently, while another found that when they did respond to them, it was in relation to academic matters more often than not, while their responses to other children were more apt to involve sending them on errands or asking them to help other students.   Behavior disabled learners are also less popular with other children and more often rejected by them.   Other children perceive them as being worried, frightened, messy, and not very attractive.   This does not seem to be related to their physical appearance per se, but to how they interact with others and perhaps how they present themselves physically (Bryan and Bryan, 1975).   There is also some evidence that the home environment of behavior disable learners is different from that of other learners.   Their families appear to be less well organized in respect to activities and schedules (Owen et al., 1971).

Emotional disabilities or emotional disturbance

In Chapter 3 you read of the effects of parental treatment types on children. Parents who were permissive and also hostile/rejecting bred children who were aggressive and antisocial.   Such children are often typed as "conduct disordered," which is regarded as primarily an emotional disability or disturbance.   On the other hand, parents who were overcontrolling and also rejecting bred children who were withdrawn and unassertive, and such problems were labeled "personality disorders."   Other personality disorders were noted there also, but they had overinhibition and withdrawal as common symptoms.   These too are often seen as emotional disturbances.   Such emotional disturbances are also, indirectly, learning disabilities, since they are barriers to effective learning behavior in the school. They are treated currently as one of many handicapping conditions in legislation which mandates adequate help from schools for handicapped children, but the identification or diagnosis of such conditions is not as easily defined or described as that for learning disabilitiess or retardation.   Often state laws require examination by a psychiatrist or a psychologist.   Treatments include special residential centers. in-school alternative programs, special classes, and resource centers.   These are discussed further in Chapters 11 and 12; the basic learning processes whereby emotional problems are acquired are discussed in Chapter 8.

Hyperkinetic impulse disorder, or "hyperactivity"—A group of symptoms

Behavior disabilities seem to be a combination of a number of characteristics; they are often lumped under one term such as "hyperactivity," "hyperkinetic impulse disorder," or "minimal brain disfunction."   We will describe these separately, although they occur together in clusters.

Hyperactivity means excess of activity; hyperactive learners either "fidget" a lot, run around without seeming to stop, knock things over clumsily, or exaggerate normal motions.   Sometimes such "whirlwinds" become very tired and hypoactive; sometimes, they are unable to sleep. or sleep very little.

Distractibility involves inability to concentrate. Whether it is due to lower ability to screen out extraneous stimuli, or a tendency to avoid work which is difficult and on which children have failed, or lack of communication of sufficient input information to their brains, is not clear. Some theorists link this to poor figure-ground discrimination also.

Impulsiveness has been discussed in Chapter 3; in this context it accompanies both hyperactivity and distractibility.

Social negativeness or defensiveness is another characteristic of these learners, seemingly due partly to their inability to "read" the feelings and intents of others, either adults or children. This could evidence ego-centeredness (thus lower maturity, as discussed in Chapter 1), or failure to receive or process sufficient information about others, or lack of training in social skills.

Disinhibition, characterized by speaking out of turn and moving around when one is supposed to be seated, may result from lack of discipline, immaturity or distractibility, or a combination of these factors. It may on the other hand show a seeking for stimulation and information from the environment, due to insufficient information reaching the brain (Ayers, 1972).

Hypoglycemia

An eighteen-year-old girl was doing poorly in school, couldn't concentrate, had emotional problems, worried, felt worthless, and was depressed and unresponsive to her friends. She was frequently thirsty, and had to go to the bathroom frequently at night. She was taken to a pediatrician who recommended a special test. This test showed that when she was given sugar to eat or drink, the level of glucose in her blood went down drastically, robbing her of energy since glucose is the source of our energy. This was what was responsible for her symptoms: she would eat sugar and carbohydrates to regain energy, and lose even more, leading to her anxiety and depression and emotional upset and the other things. The doctor recommended a diet free of sugar and low in carbohydrates: she followed it (unwillingly, with loud complaints) for two weeks. Her friends began to remark on how much friendlier and more fun she was, even though she grouched about the diet a lot. She began to sleep through the night without going to the bathroom. She also began to do better in school.

This short story gives the basic facts about this condition, as well as the "cure," which is dietary. Hypoglycemia is found more frequently in people who are behavior disabled, alcoholic, and schizophrenic than in the normal population.

Prescribing for behavior disorders

There are several kinds of remedial techniques for dealing with hyperkinetic impulse disorders and behavioral disabilities. In one, the learners are given an environment where there is very little stimulus input, so they can concentrate. In another, they are given drugs which reduce their distractibility and impulsiveness and allow them to concentrate.   In still another they are given behavior modification, a type of therapy described in Chapters 8 and 11.   Another approach is to change their diets so that they avoid sugar, carbohydrates, and additives, and substitute high doses of certain vitamins and minerals.   Still another technique is to treat them as allergic, and control their diets accordingly (Hilsheimer, 1974).   It seems probable that the treatment of preference in the future will involve an integration of several or all of these.

Schizophrenia and autism

While this is not a book about abnormal psychology, there are certain characteristics of a psychotic disturbance called "schizophrenia" which resemble some of the characteristics of hyperkinetic impulse disorder described here.   Schizophrenia is characterized by restlessness, hyperactivity, and impulsiveness; avoidance of the use of "distance" receptors of vision and audition and preference for "proximal" receptors of touch, taste, and smell; failure to respond appropriately to others, including difficulty in recognizing others; inability to localize sources of sounds or hear them; distorted perceptions in which time goes very slowly or very quickly, and where pictures look real while people look like pictures; inattentiveness and difficulty in sustaining effort; nightmares, hallucinations, and day-dreaming. Schizophrenia is regarded increasingly as a biochemical disorder, and is treated with vitamins and minerals and nutrition control.

      Another condition related to these problems is autism.   This is characterized by extreme lack of communication with others and extreme preoccupation with self.   Autistic children will sit for long periods of time without showing any behavior, then they will stimulate themselves repetitively by head banging or handling toys or yelling.   They will fail to respond to questions or requests, or simply echo the request or question rather than answering it.

Alcoholism and other drugs

Alcoholism is an increasingly prevalent problem or disability in the young, especially adolescents and preadolescents.   It seems to be a result of several factors: a more permissive society; a lack of structure and of acceptable roles for people of that age; foods which are very high in carbohydrates and additives; and finally a metabolism or physiological condition which is susceptible to (allergic to) digesting alcohol.   Experiments indicate clearly that animals with poor nutrition are more susceptible to alcoholism than healthy animals.   It is also recognized that alcoholics are malnourished and there is evidence that a greater proportion of alcoholics are hypoglycemic than the normal population.   Finally, they are also more likely to be low in certain trace minerals, particularly zinc; it is not clear whether this is a cause or a result of regular drinking.   The cumulative effect of regular drinking on the system can be seen in doctors' requirement that patients with symptoms suspected

of being alcohol-related refrain from drinking for six weeks, the time it takes for alcohol to be processed out of the system.   The effects of alcoholism include many of those typical of hypoglycemia, including loss of motivation, lack of energy, and forgetfulness.

Technically, the behaviors involved in taking drugs, including procuring them, are *reinforced* by the effects of the drugs; this is another way of saying that the probability and frequency of these procuring and taking behaviors increases due to their effects.   Thus, the habit is easily established.   Once established, it is hard to break because it is difficult to find reinforcers which are so effective that you can use them to establish other competing behaviors.

Allergic reactions

Within twenty minutes of eating a banana, a young girl would have violent temper tantrums.   She reacted to all sugars except maple sugar, as well.   When her grandmother wanted to give her some candy made out of regular sugar, the mother warned her, but she (the grandmother) went ahead—and had a temper tantrum on her hands within thirty minutes.

Just as a swelling of the skin often develops in response to some substance which gets into a scratch or cut, so it seems possible that swelling occurs in areas of the

Recent discoveries indicate that a learner's reactions to certain foods or need for certain vitamins and minerals can cause learning problems.

brain that contain the neural connections that control aggression, with dramatic and immediate results. It may make neural areas that produce aggression more sensitive, or it may deactivate areas that normally inhibit aggressive behavior. People who have this kind of allergic reaction are often called "impulsive," "combative," "unruly," "perverse," or "quarrelsome." The allergens which can cause this range from pollens and drugs to many foods, including milk, chocolate, cola, corn, and eggs (Feingold, 1974; Hilsheimer, 1974).

 ## Megavitamin therapy

The hyperkinetic impulse disorder syndrome has been treated successfully through administration of extremely large doses of certain vitamins, mostly from the B-group, but including C as well. This treatment was first used for schizophrenia, in which hyperactivity is one of the frequent symptoms. The effectiveness of this treatment is still being debated. From 500 to 1,000 milligrams of Vitamin C three times a day, 500 milligrams of B3 three times a day, and B6 in similar amounts are used in such treatments. This treatment is often ineffective unless the learner is treated for hypoglycemia as well, through the appropriate diet. The effects may show up within several weeks or a month, but the full benefits may not be apparent for up to a year or more. Mineral supplements (zinc, calcium, magnesium) are often found to be helpful also.

Some feel that hyperkinetic impulse disorder or "MBD" (or "hyperactivity" as it is sometimes termed) is a preschizophrenic disorder. Megavitamin treatment of schizophrenia is gaining wider acceptance, partly through testimonials by nonmedical people who have been helped this way (e.g., Vonnegut, 1975). The practice of dealing with mental disease through nutrition has come to be known as "orthomolecular psychiatry"; such theorists point out that a disease similar to schizophrenia, called "pellagra," was very common up until the early 1900s when Vitamin B-3 (Niacin) was introduced into white flour used in making bread because of laws passed for that purpose. These same theorists feel that if one could introduce larger amounts of B3 as well as C and B6 into the regular diets of everyone, schizophrenia could be eliminated as well (Hawkins and Pauling, 1973). Such treatments are based on the recognition that, while everyone has average requirements for various minerals and vitamins, people differ radically in their individual needs for and tolerances of these chemicals. Thus, one person may need less than the "minimum daily requirement" of some mineral or vitamin, while another person may need ten or a hundred times that arbitrary amount.

TESTING FOR LEARNING DISABILITIES

You may wonder how visual, auditory, and motor disabilities are identified objectively. One test which has been and still is very popular for diagnosing learning disabilities is the Illinois Test of Psycholinguistic Ability, or ITPA. It uses tasks that require only one ability at a time; for example, its auditory tasks require no visual interpretation, and only minimal ability to express an answer, e.g., saying "yes" or "no" or giving one word to complete a sentence, or saying a complete word when only part of it is given. It samples the three major channels—auditory, visual, and motor abilities. Also, it samples on two levels, one very basic or "automatic" and the other more complex, cognitive, or representational. There were strong criticisms of the ITPA in the early 1970s, though it is well established as a diagnostic tool and widely used. One of the strongest criticisms was that none of its subtests correlated with achievement in any of the common school subjects.

The tasks of the ITPA are:

1. The learner is asked "Do airplanes fly?" and "Do cars cry?" and "Do daughters marry?" and such questions. This is called ability to "decode" through *auditory reception*.

2. The learner is shown a stimulus picture, say a table, and then it is removed and he or she is asked to find among four comparison pictures the one most like it: the correct choice may be a square table instead of a round one. This is called ability to "decode" through *visual reception*.

3. The learner is asked to complete a sentence given to him or her orally, such as "I sit on a chair; I sleep on a _____." This is called *auditory association*.

4. The learner is asked to select from among four pictures one which "goes with" a sample picture, i.e., the sample might be a hammer and the correct choice is a nail. This is called *visual association*.

Figure 4–9. *"Visual association" as on the ITPA: The learner looks at the central figure, then points to the one which "goes with" it, i.e., the saucer in this case.*

5. The learner is asked to tell about simple objects such as a ball, an envelope, and the like; his or her ability to describe the items in a number of unique and meaningful ways is scored here and this is called *verbal expression*.

6. The learner is asked to express through gestures the use or meaning of an object, for example, a hammer; the test administrator says "Show me what you should do with this." This is called *manual expression* or *motor encoding*.

7. The learner is told "Here is a bed, and here are two _____." His or her ability to give the word in the plural is called *grammatic closure*.

8. The learner is shown a drawing of something like a bottle or a puppy, then asked to find others like it in a complicated picture where the bottles or puppies are partly hidden and thus not shown completely. This is called *visual closure*.

9. The learner is asked to repeat correctly a sequence of digits (same as "digit span" on other tests). This is *auditory sequential memory*.

10. The learner is asked to reproduce a sequence of visual patterns, given small plastic squares, each one with one of the patterns on it. He or she has a few seconds to view the sequence, then it is taken away. This is called *visual sequential memory* (Kirk and McCarthy, 1961).

The WISC as a learning disabilities test

Since many students with learning problems are given a WISC as part of a program of evaluation in a school system or special education setting, the subtests of the WISC are often used for diagnosis. However, you need to keep in mind that the verbal tasks of the WISC all involve auditory input—they are not balanced between auditory and visual like the ITPA—while the performance tasks all involve visual input. Thus a difference between "verbal" and "performance" scores may actually represent a difference in auditory and visual ability.

HELPING LEARNERS WITH DISABILITIES

Basic strategies

Prescribing for learning disabilities is less than a science—but more than guesswork; here are some basic guidelines.

There are three basic strategies for helping learners who have specific learning disabilities: (1) bypassing, (2) programming, and (3) guiding or prompting. These techniques will be described individually below, with brief examples. General teaching processes and specific methods for particular types of problems will be taken up in Chapters 11 and 12 of Part IV.

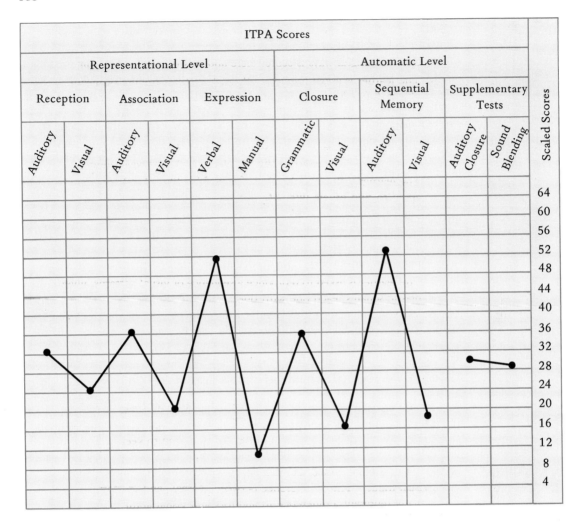

Figure 4–10. *Profile of scale scores for a child with specific learning disabilities. Notice that high scores are in auditory and verbal categories of behavior, while his low scores are in visual and motor (manual) categories. The fact that the visual and motor scores often occur together, i.e., both low or both high, is often taken to imply that they are closely related. Thus you hear people talk about "visual-motor problems." The same kind of occurrences lead to people talking about "auditory-verbal" problems. The major thing to note here, however, is that the child's abilities are quite different from test to test, and that he has some specific difficulties with manual expression. (Reprinted by permission of the University of Illinois Press.)*

Bypassing.   A learner with a disability is like a person with a sore finger or a wounded foot: he favors the injured part, and tries to avoid using it as much as possible.   To ask him to drill on the "sore spot" to make it stronger may be too much at first, so you look for ways to get around it.   If the learner has an auditory perceptual problem, you arrange to have all input given visually (as far as possible, anyway).   If there is a motor problem, you find ways of getting necessary things done without calling on the skill that is lacking.   If a learner has trouble learning addition or multiplication tables, you tape the tables to his desk or let him use a small electronic calculator.   Generally, you arrange things so that progress can be made in spite of, and without the use of, the ability that is weak or lacking.

Programming.   Programming is a term that has many meanings; we will use it here in a special way to mean developing a sequence of tasks which call on the weak or missing ability, but which start with such simple tasks that it is possible for the learner to do them.   Then, little by little, the difficulty of the tasks is increased. At each level of difficulty, you present a variety of tasks so that the "drill" does not become too monotonous.   Also, at each point where you increase the difficulty, you may want to use guidance or prompting, which is described next.   The essence of programming, then, is (a) a carefully sequenced series of tasks going from very simple to more complex or difficult, and (b) a variety of tasks at each level of difficulty to bring overlearning without boredom.

Guiding or prompting.   The third technique is helping the learner respond to tasks by giving him (or her) guidance or prompting, at first, and then gradually *withdrawing this guidance* as he becomes able to handle the task on his own.   This withdrawal is sometimes called "fading the prompt."   In dealing with learning disabilities of the input type, this is frequently accomplished by using the strong channel to guide or prompt the weak one; for example, for a learner with an auditory disability, you would present a task that can be solved on the basis of the auditory information or input, but that also has visual information which will enable the learner to answer correctly.   Gradually you reduce the amount of visual information in subsequent tasks, and thereby require or encourage the learner to rely more and more on the auditory information.   As was mentioned in the previous section, this technique can be used in a programmed sequence where the difficulty level is raised; guidance is used initially, and gradually withdrawn, leaving the learner operating successfully at the new level without help.

An example of a combination of bypassing, programming, and guidance

Suppose a learner has a visual-perceptual disability, and it becomes obvious that remediation will be necessary if she is to continue successfully in school or at work or both.   Suppose she is unable to understand the meaning of pictures in story books, and also is unable to understand the meaning of drawings and illustrations designed to help her learn to draw or sew or do crafts.   Initially we might arrange for her to have more complete and detailed directions given either on a tape-recorder (if she also can't read very well) or in writing, but without pictures.   This would be by-passing, and the purpose would be to enable her to function adequately in spite of the difficulty.   Then we would arrange relatively brief practice sessions each day—perhaps two or three a day, perhaps one—designed to improve her ability to interpret pictorial material and make the bypassing less necessary.   To do this, we might begin with extremely simple line drawings of very familiar and meaningful objects (the role of meaningfulness in learning will be discussed further in Chapter 9), perhaps of dogs and horses and other animals if she likes animals, or of cars or buildings or other things she shows an interest in.   While she is viewing the simple drawings, we tell her what they are orally, i.e., we guide or prompt her through auditory input, her strong channel.   Gradually we use less and less of this verbal prompting and keep practicing until she is able to identify the drawings easily without error.   Incidentally, this does not mean that you would practice contin-ually until success is achieved; rather, you would schedule practice sessions in such a way that she would not become too bored, and you would increase their length gradually as she became able to tolerate longer ones.   As you will find in Chapter 9, such distribution of practice also makes the learning more resistant to forgetting.

      After achieving success with these simple line drawings, we would begin at an-other level of picture complexity, and would use auditory guidance at first and grad-ually withdraw it until she was able to handle the interpretations on her own.   This general procedure would be repeated at successive levels of difficulty until she was able to interpret the types of pictures that are necessary in her schoolwork and/or vocation.

LEARNING DISABILITIES—COLLEGE STYLE

One study of college students' cognitive style found, through use of sophisticated statistical techniques, that their responses to test items in psychology indicated three distinctly different styles.   These were labelled "synthesis" (re-lated to divergent thinking), "analysis," and "knowledge-computation" (convergent) (For-syth, 1976).   Through further processing of test data three groups of students were identi-fied, each group being particularly low in one of these three abilities or skills.   You can regard these as learning disabilities of a more sophisti-cated kind.   Given this view, what would you do to help any of these groups of students, for instance, the group which was very low in abil-ity to synthesize material (i.e., to put facts together in a number of different ways, or to suggest a number of possible solutions to a problem).   Some of the suggestions for teaching problem solving might be relevant to this, don't you think?   (See Chapter 10.)

Summary outline with key concepts

☞ *Learning disabilities* include problems of auditory understanding, visual understanding, inability to concentrate, inability to learn to read, inability to express oneself verbally or physically / Learning disabilities do not include retardation, physical handicaps, emotional disturbance, or paralysis / Many apparent learning disabilities are the result of failing to learn basic skills at the proper time, rather than any of the above / Disabilities in learning are classified as input, processing, or output; processing involves cognition, including association and conceptualization.

☞ *Auditory perceptual* disabilities do not involve hearing difficulties, but inability to comprehend what is heard clearly / Tests of auditory abilities involve recognition of similarities and differences in sounds, and reacting to oral instructions correctly /Visual perceptual disabilities do not involve vision difficulties, but inability to comprehend what is seen clearly / Tests of visual perceptual abilities include position in space, form constancy, and visual-motor coordination tasks.

☞ *Visual dyslexia* is difficulty translating written letters into sound; auditory dyslexia is difficulty translating sounds into meaning / A visual dyslexic has difficulty learning to read whole words and pronouncing letters / An auditory dyslexic has difficulty learning to put sounds together phonetically and getting meaning out of the result / Some theorists find the basic problem to be one of poor automatic responding, as compared with good conceptualization; basic automatic abilities are weak / Other theorists see dyslexia as a delay in maturation of the brain which results in failure to develop basic central nervous system responses necessary to reading.

☞ *Overloading means* input in several channels at once, or a variety of input into one channel; learning disabled children have difficulty with both / Cross-modal problems involve such things as relating what you feel to what you see or hear, or what you see to what you hear, or translating what is seen into sound or what is heard into visual patterns associated with it.   Disabled learners are apt to have difficulty with such tasks / Figure-ground tasks require perceiving a pattern against a background, either visually or auditorially; disabled learners often have difficulty with such tasks.

☞ *Some otherwise* able learners have motor coordination problems, e.g., catching a ball, running, skipping / Motor problems affect adjustment, and indirectly, learning / Motor problems affect learning directly when the learning task involves motor expression or coordination (e.g., sensorimotor learning, Chapter 1) / Kinesthetic responses or feedback are important in motor learning / Gross motor abilities underlie most fine motor abilities / There are common symptoms of motor difficulty observable in classrooms, including winging, moving the whole body with the head, inability to cross midline, poor posture / Laterality and directionality are basic to much cognitive learning / Apraxias show the complexity of motor control and interaction of the two hemispheres.

☞ *Some learners* have behavior disabilities that prevent them from making friends or learning / Teachers often react negatively to such learners, and don't recognize the nature of their problem / Hyperactivity is one symptom; others are distractibility, impulsiveness, social negativeness, disinhibition / Hypoglycemia is related to behavior disabilities in some cases; it is controlled through a special diet / Hyperkinetic impulse disorder, or minimal brain disfunction (MBD), is a syndrome; a given learner will have several but not all of the symptoms; there is no test for it; there is no recognizable brain damage / Remediation for hyperkinetic impulse disorder or MBD includes (a) sensory deprivation, (b) drug therapy, (c) behavior modification, (d) vitamin therapy / Alcoholism and other drugs are an increasing problem for learners, particularly adolescents, and result in learning disabilities. Allergic reactions are another important source of learning and behavior disabilities / Megavitamin therapy is being used for MBD, hyperactivity, alcoholism, and schizophrenia; all of these are being treated increasingly as biochemical disorders.

☞ *Learning disabilities* tests have been developed to identify basic inabilities which affect learning in more than one area; their success is still being debated / The ITPA exemplifies learning disabilities tests which differentiate between channels and between input and output / The WISC is being used increasingly for diagnostic purposes, through combining subtests in certain ways / The usefulness of learning disabilities tests continues to be debated; some reject them, others use them regularly and effectively.

☞ *Helping learning* disabled people involves bypassing, programming, and guidance/prompting / These approaches are usually combined in one overall program of remediation.

Glossary

Aphasia: Usually refers to expressive aphasia, inability to formulate thoughts into words or gestures (receptive language problems are sometimes called "receptive aphasia").

Apraxia: Inability to give a motor response that most people can give, e.g., inability to raise your left hand when asked to do so, even though you can raise your right hand when asked.

Association: In learning disabilities literature often refers to cognitive processing generally, as in "the associative level" compared with "automatic level."

Auditory Dyslexia: Reading disability based on difficulty translating sounds into meaning.

Autism: Lack of ability to relate to others, lack of social behavior and feeling.

Automatic Response: Responses which don't require much thought, but which still require mental processing.

Bypassing: Helping a disabled learner by providing ways to operate without calling on the weak skill.

Cerebral Palsy: Condition marked by inability to control one or several physical responses or to maintain conventional posture.

Cross-modal: Relating input from different channels, i.e., relating visual and auditory stimuli, as in the sound made by an automobile; also, relating images in different channels.

Decoding: Translating incoming sensory information (visual, auditory) into meaning, e.g., understanding a word, or recognizing a picture or an object.

Directionality: Being able to tell which way to turn a screwdriver or to look for oncoming traffic; knowledge of direction.

Disinhibition: Lack of inhibiting responses, resulting in deviant behavior such as walking around a classroom instead of sitting in your seat.

Distractibility: Inability to concentrate; disposition to attend to background or incidental events.

Dyslexia: Inability to read, coupled with average or better ability to do other things.

Emotional Disturbance: Deviant behavior or inability to achieve which is caused by emotional problems such as hostile and punitive parents, high general anxiety, guilt over traumatic events.

Encoding: Translating thoughts into a form which enables you to put them into action, e.g., speak them, or act them out.

Epilepsy: Central nervous system condition resulting in occasional seizures in which the patient loses consciousness; loss varies in duration from seconds to minutes.

Figure-ground: Perceiving a pattern against a background of other stimuli, e.g., seeing a deer hiding in a clump of bushes.

Fine Motor Responses: Activities such as writing, playing piano, turning a knob.

Form Constancy: Recognition of a shape when it is shown in different sizes and among other shapes (*see* Sensorimotor Period, Chapter 1).

Frostig: Marianne Frostig, an internationally known figure in the field of learning disabilities; also a test of perceptual and perceptual-motor abilities which she published and which goes by her name.

Gross Motor Responses: Activities such as lifting, running, turning one's trunk, using big muscles.

Guiding: Presenting cues or prompts or guidelines to assist a learner to respond.

Hyperactivity: Means excess activity, but has come to be used for the syndrome defined here as "hyperkinetic impulse disorder" or "MBD."

Hyperkinetic Impulse Disorder: A syndrome of symptoms involving distractibility, disorganized activity, hyperactivity, lack of control; sometimes called minimal brain disfunction.

Hypoglycemia: A condition where intake of sugar results in a lower-than-normal sugar level in the blood, resulting in lack of energy.

Imagery: Mental recreation of past experiences, whether sounds, sights, feelings, or combinations of them.

Input Problems: Perceptual or sensory comprehension difficulties.

ITPA: Illinois Test of Psycholinguistic Abilities.

Kinesthetic Response: Stimuli coming from the body which indicate the position and state of motion of parts of the body.

Laterality: Being able to tell which hand is which, which foot to put a shoe on.

Learning Disability: Inability to learn in a specific area, coupled with generally average or high ability otherwise.

Mainstreaming: Bringing retarded or handicapped learners into regular classrooms.

MBD, Minimal Brain Disfunction: A syndrome of symptoms better described as hyperkinetic impulse disorder, involving distractibility, hyperactivity, disorganized activity, general lack of control.

Megavitamin Therapy: Treatment which involves high doses of certain vitamins in the B and C classes.

Output Problems: Problems expressing yourself verbally or physically.

Overloading: Too many stimuli coming in through the same channel (visual or auditory), or stimuli coming in through too many channels (visual and auditory, or auditory and kinesthetic, etc.).

Perceptual-motor Tasks or Responses: Tasks or responses which require coordination of perception and motor response; visual-motor or auditory-motor tasks (e.g., clapping your hands when you hear a certain signal).

Position in Space: Recognition of figures which have the same spatial orientation; one of the perceptual constancies (*see* Sensorimotor Period, Chapter 1).

Programming: Presenting a sequence of tasks which begin with very simple ones and progress very gradually to more complex ones.

Reauditorization: Creating a mental image of a sound that has been heard before, as in thinking of the sound associated with a letter that one sees.

Resource Room: A room with resources for working on various types of learning disabilities, i.e., tape-slide sequences, flash cards, remedial reading kits, and the like; usually supervised by a learning disabilities specialist.

Revisualization: Creating a mental image of a visual stimulus that one has seen previously, as in visualizing the letter that goes with a sound.

Sequential Memory: Memory for a sequence of things, like a set of directions.

Spatial Ability: Ability to recognize and deal with spatial relations, like avoiding obstacles, getting through openings without bumping or scraping, fitting parts of a puzzle or a shape together, putting together a model.

Visual Closure: Recognizing a shape or picture when only part of it is shown, i.e., recognizing a dog when only its head or its back end shows in the picture.

Visual Dyslexia: Reading disability based on difficulty translating visual symbols into sound.

Visual-motor Coordination: Coordination of visual perception and motor activity in tasks such as copying, reaching and grasping things, playing darts, and such.

Auditory Closure: Completing a word when you hear only part of it.

Questions for thought and discussion

1. Which is more serious, an input problem, an output problem, or a processing/cognition problem?
2. How do auditory and visual perception disabilities differ from poor hearing or vision? How do they differ from inability to think, i.e., cognitive disabilities?
3. What are some of the symptoms of auditory perceptual disability?
4. What are some of the symptoms of visual perceptual disability?
5. What are some of the symptoms of motor disability?

6. How does a perceptual-motor task differ from a purely motor task? From a purely perceptual task?
7. How important to learning are laterality and directionality?
8. How would you treat an auditory dyslexic as compared with a visual dyslexic?
9. What are some of the characteristics of behavioral disabilities?
10. What is "minimal brain disfunction?" How does one test for it?
11. Give an example of bypassing; of programming; of guiding or prompting.

Situations calling for applications of facts and concepts

1. Mary is a student in your fourth-grade class: she seems to be having difficulty keeping up with her work, and in adjusting to the class. She often seems to be unaware of what she is supposed to do, particularly when you give directions to the whole class; however, she is prepared when she has a reading assignment. What would you suspect to be her disability, and what kind of a test task might you give her to check this? How would you arrange things to begin to help her?
2. Bobby is a first grader who is somewhat uncoordinated. He can't catch a ball when at play, and he seems to have difficulty recognizing differences between such letters as b and d. If you ask him to shake hands, he will often give you the wrong hand. He is also having some difficulty reading. What would you suspect concerning disabilities, how would you go about checking up on your suspicions, and what remedial processes would you initiate if your suspicions were confirmed?
3. Ronald is a tenth-grade student who had difficulty understanding pictures and graphs; he reads very slowly, and has trouble with trigonometry although his other math grades are good. How might you bypass Ronald's problem; how would you check to see what his specific problem is; and how might you begin to help him?

Suggested activities

1. Contact your local school system, preferably at the elementary level, and ask whether the staff needs any help with learning disabled students. You might be able to work under the direction of a specialist, giving individual attention to one or more learners as the specialist directs.

2. Observe a learning disabilities program in your local school system, and relate the procedures (testing and teaching) to the concepts in this chapter.

3. Discuss with your colleagues your personal learning disabilities, and test each other to see whether your suspicions about yourselves are correct. You will have to adapt some of the evaluation tasks to your own levels, of course.

4. Give one of your friends the ITPA if you can get one to give, for the practice of giving it; determine from the directions how you would score the various tests, and discuss problems of scoring reliably and accurately. Also discuss the relationships between the various subtests and school learning requirements.

Suggested readings

There are many books on learning disabilities; one early one, still a classic, is by Johnson and Mylkebust. Another comprehensive one is by Lerner, and other popular works are by Gearhart, Hallahan, and Kauffman, Bryan and Bryan, and Johnson and Morasky. There are also journals, the earliest of which was the *Journal of Learning Disabilities*. *The Journal of Academic Therapy* carries articles that are practical as well as theoretical, and the Academic Therapy Press publishes many short books and pamphlets about learning disabilities that are worth reading.

PART

II

TEACHERS, GROUPS, AND MOTIVATION

5

Characteristics of
Good Teachers

CONTENTS

ABOUT CHAPTER 5

How this chapter will benefit you

Assuming that you want to be successful (or more successful) in some form of teaching—whether in schools, special institutions, groups like scouts or Sunday School, or with your own children—you can compare some of the characteristics of good teachers found here to your own. With the help of suggestions here and in Part IV, you can bring out your positive attributes and strengthen weak ones. You can also increase your understanding of teaching generally, as a critic and observer, and even analyze teachers' personalities and styles and identify what contributes to and detracts from their effectiveness. Since many of the characteristics of good teachers are those of effective and popular people generally, this will help your personal-social development as well.

What might make this difficult to study and learn

If you feel that good teachers are born, not made, then there isn't much point to analyzing good teaching except as a matter of curiosity. However, there is evidence that you can improve your teaching whether you are a good, mediocre, or poor teacher now. Another problem is that you might have some strong preconceptions about what makes good teachers, and you might find them contradicted or at least deemphasized here. Some feel that if a teacher reaches out to students and shows them how concerned and interested he or she is, and develops good rapport, then all will be well, but this is not always the case. You might be upset to learn that warmth and praise and empathy are not the primary characteristics of successful teachers, although they are very important qualities. However, if you look beyond some of these surprises, you will find many things that confirm your intuitions.

Reasons for studying teachers

Equally important to an understanding of the nature of the learner is an understanding of the characteristics of teachers, particularly "good" teachers. You may also benefit from information about the emotional and cognitive "climates" that teachers create, and how they relate to what students learn. Good teachers, of course, are found everywhere: as parents, club leaders, coaches, counselors, and learning specialists, as well as in the classroom. Therefore good teaching is more important than just school-teaching: it has to do with many facets of your life.

176

Assuring successful learning

You will have to tolerate a certain amount of confusion at first. This results from presenting many sides of the picture and several types of studies of teachers, before some of the fundamental attributes and important aspects of good teaching begin to come through. You should also assume that at least some of the attributes of good teaching are common to many grade levels, although others change from level to level. If you read the chapter through fairly quickly at first and then go back over it more thoroughly, it will help you to keep things straight and to relate early parts to later ones. Use of the summary outline in between readings will help also. You will find that good teachers have an internal locus of control and see themselves as responsible for their own successes and failures. One way for you to assure success here is to adopt such a view, if it isn't yours already. By taking responsibility for your own success here, through effort and careful thought, you will also be practicing behaviors that lead to success later on.

RATIONALE AND BACKGROUND OF CHAPTER 5

Teaching and educational psychology

Basically, educational psychology relates to teaching, and so the study of teachers and teaching is an important part of the field. This chapter deals with analyses of teachers and teaching, and some of their implications. Many studies of teachers have depended on reports of students, of other teachers, of administrators, and of the teachers themselves; more recently studies have concentrated on the actual behavior of the teacher in the classroom, through observations, and on the changes in learners which have resulted from this.

While this chapter addresses itself primarily to classroom teaching, it is nevertheless relevant to parenting and to helping others through therapy. Just as the characteristics of parents of effective (and ineffective) children relate to the characteristics of teachers and their students, so the characteristics of good teachers say something to parents and specialists who work with children.

Teaching and you

Since some of you have not had actual teaching experience, you may have only a vague concept of how a teacher feels and acts. Teachers' attitudes, like those of parents, leaders, and others who work with people, have an influence on learning and behavior. If you have a positive attitude toward other people, for example, you tend to assume that most of them are pleasant and interesting and that they will find you to be the same. If you have a negative attitude you tend to assume that other people are unpleasant and critical and not very likable; needless to say, this affects how you "come on" to other people, and how they react to you. If you become concerned about your own ability to reflect positive characteristics, remember that you are not the best judge of your own personality, and that you can bring about changes if necessary—and if you believe that it is possible.

ATTITUDES OF GOOD TEACHERS

Attitudes projected into stories

One thing worth knowing about good teachers is how their attitudes compare with those of other teachers.

In the 1960s there were reports of a study in which a large group of teachers was asked to write stories about some pictures they were shown (Burkard, 1962). The pictures illustrated various situations: e.g., a man looking down at a boy who is hanging his head. The teachers' stories were analyzed to determine their personality characteristics.

The investigators also asked each teacher's students to fill out a questionnaire indicating how he or she felt about the teacher; from these results, the teachers were given ratings of "good" or "poor."

Then the personality traits of the "good" teachers were compared with those of the "poor" teachers. There were differences.

Superior teachers, for example, seemed to expect success to be attained through effort and sacrifice, whereas the poor ones viewed success more as a matter of chance. Today we would say the good teachers had an internal locus of control, not an external one like the poor teachers. The better teachers felt that failure could be overcome by their own effort, whereas the poorer ones attributed failure to external factors and took little responsibility for it. For the better teachers, life was a matter of responsible ethical behavior; for the poorer ones, it was a matter of avoiding punishment and unpleasantness. Finally, the good teachers have a positive view of others, whereas the poor ones saw people as frustrating, unforgiving, and unhelpful.

These qualities of responsibility to the task and trust in others are themes that run through much of the literature on characteristics of good teachers—or of "good" people generally! Do you have these qualities? Perhaps others—your friends and advisors—can tell you something about this, if they will. Also, you can take personality tests, as well as interest and attitude tests. Scores on these will tell you something about yourself also. They can usually be taken at a counseling center, or with the help of a practicing psychologist.

How important are Burkard's results? How reliable are they? Does this study apply to teachers generally? Actually, this sample of teachers was not representative, since it used Catholic sisters in a Catholic school. This does not mean it was biased in a religious sense, but only that we cannot be sure what biases it might have, so other similar studies should be done with a broader range of teachers and schools. Another thing you do not know is the character of the questionnaire filled out by the students. Perhaps it was very biased, asking for responses about certain aspects of teaching, but not about others. In such a case, you would not know whether the "poor" teachers might not be strong in the unasked question

"Good" teachers often praise and encourage students.

areas or not. Also, you do not know much about the way the stories were analyzed. Maybe things are left out in that process, and perhaps certain traits are emphasized more than others. Perhaps you cannot tell about a person's personality
from analyzing stories! Therefore, before you make sweeping statements based on
these conclusions, you should look at other similar studies to see whether the results turn out the same.

Ryans' self-report characteristics

Another report in the 1960s was based on information on extensive research on
the characteristic of about 6,000 teachers in 1,700 high schools (Ryans, 1963).
The researcher identified superior teachers by collecting opinions about them from
students, supervisors, and administrators. Teachers also filled out self-report
forms. The teachers rated as "good" reported that they enjoyed pupil relationships
more, were more self-confident and cheerful, and had more hobbies and interests in
handicrafts. They said their childhoods had been happy, whereas the poorer

teachers indicated less-than-happy childhoods.   The less successful teachers were
evidently more restrictive and critical in their appraisal of others' behaviors and
motives; they tended to value exactness, orderliness, and practical matters more
than their successful colleagues, and they also appear to be less self-confident.
Overall, this study suggested that good teachers were more organized and responsible (supporting Burkard's findings), and more understanding, responsive, and stimulating.   They also evidenced greater ambition, more initiative, greater verbal
intelligence, and more participation in social groups.

Locus of control

In both studies the successful teachers saw themselves as responsible for their success or failure, and felt that it was up to them to cope with problems even though
they didn't cause the problems.   The concept of "locus of control" is related to this
feeling.   If you have an internal locus of control, you see yourself as responsible for
your own success; if you have an external locus, you attribute responsibility for
events (either success or failure) to others: the students, your own teachers or
parents, the community, society in general.   A recent study of teacher characteristics in the early grades (second and third) clearly revealed this viewpoint (Brophy
and Evertson, 1976):

> Perhaps the most pervasive and fundamental presage variable which appeared in our
> study was the teacher's basic role definition. . . . .   The less successful teachers were
> more likely to look upon teaching as "just a job" and to respond to problems and frus-
> trations by giving up and attributing failure to outside causes.   Instead of redoubling
> their efforts and searching for ways to solve problems, they tended to rationalize their
> failure in ways that allowed them to avoid assuming personal responsibility. . . . .

OBSERVING, RECORDING, AND
ANALYZING TEACHER BEHAVIORS

Controlling and facilitating

One way teachers
have been studied
is by observing and
recording what
they do while
teaching.

Marie Hughes (1962) investigated teaching behavior in elementary schools.   In
observing teachers, she focused on controlling (goal-setting, naming content),
content (dealing with subject matter), facilitation (classroom management functions), personal response (meeting individual requests, listening to students' interests), and positive and negative affectivity (praise and reproof).   Her data are summarized in Figure 5–1.   It seems evident that these teachers spent most of their
time controlling the children, and their next most frequent behavior was related to
content.   Incidentally, although this graph represents the average behavior of all
the teachers, individual teacher's graphs showed similar profiles, and most of them
had about the same distribution of behaviors.

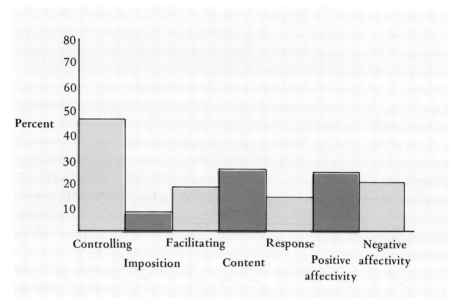

Figure 5–1. *Part of Marie Hughes' data on teacher behavior (Hughes, 1962).* (*Reprinted by permission of* Educational Leadership.)

Describing, designating, explaining, and directing

B. O. Smith and Milton Meux (1962) did a similar kind of study at the high school level. They reported frequencies of categories called "describing," "designating," "explaining," "directing classroom," "conditional inferring," and "stating"; the frequencies of these behaviors went from high to low in the order just given. However, there were great differences from subject to subject; for example, in biology the category "describing" had 110 out of 328 entries, whereas the same behavior in English had only 15 out of 348 entries. Obviously, "describing" was much more frequent and typical in biology classes than in English classes. There was also quite a bit of variation due to teacher personality, as you might expect.

The classroom game

The behavior of teachers is not very complex or varied, and is quite subject-centered (Bellack et al., 1966). The major things recorded in one survey were processes called "moves." For example, one move was "soliciting," where the teacher asked a question of the students; another was "responding," where the student answered (although sometimes the teacher responded to the student). "Structuring" was something the teacher did by setting up a situation, giving orders or directions, etc. (the "controlling" of Hughes' study and the "directing" of

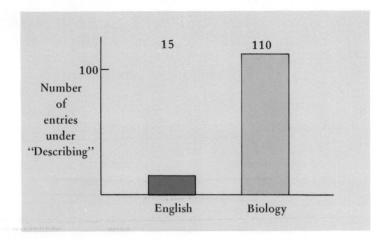

Figure 5–2. *Frequency of teacher behaviors.*

Smith's).   Another was "reacting," basically a teacher behavior.   Structuring accounted for about 6 percent of the discourse in classrooms Bellack and his colleagues observed, while soliciting, responding, and reacting accounted for approximately 30 percent each.   The general conclusion was that *the range of activities open to the student was very limited.*   They summarized as follows:

1. *Teacher dominated the verbal activities of the classrooms studied.*
2. *The pedagogical roles of the teacher and the pupil are clearly defined in terms of the frequency of behavior in each category of pedagogical moves. . . .   Only infrequently does the pupil solicit a response from the teacher or from another pupil. Seldom does the pupil spontaneously structure the discourse: when he uses a structuring move he frequently presents it as the fulfillment of a specific assignment made by the teacher, which usually involves a debate or a report.*

Interaction analysis

Another approach to research in teaching through observation is called "interaction analysis" (Amidon and Hough, 1967).   This uses a set of categories derived from nondirective counseling theories, which are discussed in Chapter 7.   There are two main categories, indirect and direct, with several behaviors in each.   Indirect behaviors include (1) "accepts feelings," (2) "praises or encourages," (3) "accepts or uses ideas of student," and (4) "asks questions with intent that a student answer."   Direct behaviors include (5) "lectures," (6) "gives directions," and (7) "criticizes or justifies authority."   Other behaviors not under either category are (8) "student talk in response to a question," (9) "student talk initiated by the student," and (10) "silence or confusion."   Obviously this analysis fits a conventional classroom with the teacher in front explaining and discussing better than

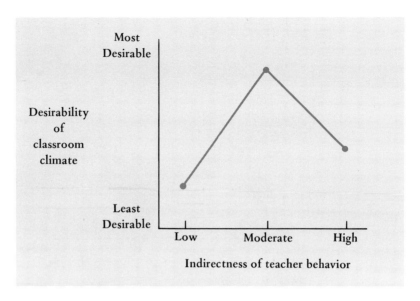

Figure 5–3. *Effects of different degrees of indirect teacher/class activity. Note that there is evidently an optimal amount of indirectness. (A composite graph adapted from Sandefur and Adams, 1976.)*

it does a group-oriented strategy, or laboratory approaches, or the like. However, as other studies have shown, the conventional theme fits a large proportion of classrooms.

Many research studies at different levels and in different subjects have been done to test the assumption that teaching which shows a greater proportion of indirect interactions is better. In general the results suggest that it leads to a greater diffusion of affect and better mental health, as discussed in Chapter 6, but it does not regularly lead to greater achievement. Evidently other variables are more important in regard to student achievement.

Focusing on thought processes

An important part
of what teachers
do is how they get
learners to think.

You may be wondering whether anyone has been concerned about how much the student learns in teaching situations, and how the teacher brings the student to grow cognitively. One system which concentrates on this subject classifies teaching according to four functions: focusing, extending thought on the same level, lifting thought to a higher level, and controlling thought (Taba and Elzy, 1964). An example of an interaction that is designed to "lift" thought is the following:

Child: They carried things in baskets on their heads.
Teacher: Explain why.
Child: I suppose they can carry more things that way.

Some teachers use the "duck hunter" technique.   They aim somewhere in the middle and hope for the best.

Both the teacher's question and the child's answer are classified as examples of "lifting."   Both "lifting" and "extending" are illustrated in the following exchange:

Child: They were working fast on the house.
Teacher: Why?
Child: They wanted to get the house done before the rain came.
Teacher: Why?
Child: Because unless it is finished the rain will destroy it.

Notice that one result of this emphasis on lifting is greater involvement and initiative by the learner, with the teacher providing a facilitating function rather than a directing or informing one.

In another project researchers classified intellectual processes in ways related to Guilford's model (Chapter 3):

1. *Cognitive Memory:* Simple reproduction of facts, formulae, and other items ("What are some of the main products of Brazil?").

2. *Convergent Thinking:* Analysis and integration of given or remembered data ("Sum up in one sentence what you think was the main idea or theme of Paton's novel *Cry, the Beloved Country*").

3. *Divergent Thinking:* Generation by the student of his or her own data within a "data-poor" situation, or taking a new direction or perspective on a given topic (often called "creative thinking").   For example:

Teacher: "Suppose Spain had not been defeated when the Armada attacked, but instead conquered England; what would the world be like?"
Students: "We would be speaking Spanish."
"We might have fought a revolution against Spain."
"We might have a state religion in this country."

4. *Evaluative Thinking:* Matters of judgment, value, and choice, as in the following exchange (Gallagher and Aschner, 1968):

Teacher: "What do you think of Captain Ahab as a heroic figure in *Moby Dick?*"
Student· "Well, he was sure brave, but I think he was kind of mean the way he drove the men. . . ."

These studies are important because they focus attention on the nature of the thought processes being taught over and above the nature of the content being learned, which is the preoccupation of most evaluations of school achievement.

ANXIETIES AND EXPECTANCIES

Are teachers anxious?

It may be surprising to know that what a teacher expects can affect what he or she gets—and that his or her anxiety can make students anxious.

Historically, the answer is yes; teachers have always reported being anxious about teaching (Coates and Thoresen, 1976).   "Anxiety" is usually measured by questionnaires.   In a number of studies the anxiety of the teacher was also reflected in the general anxiety of his or her students, as measured by special anxiety scales for children (Sarason et al., 1960).   In other studies, the *test* anxiety of students was higher when they had anxious teachers, but in still others, it was lower! The effect of teacher anxiety depended on the climate of the school; for example, in one type of school ("closed organizational climate") students of low-anxiety teachers had higher test anxiety, while in another ("open organizational climate") students of such teachers had lower test anxiety.

The anxiety of teachers has also been compared with the *behavior* of students. Generally, more anxious teachers are more concerned with behavioral problems and tend to pay more attention to them; they are also more concerned with grading, and give lower grades.

In addition to its effects on students, high anxiety makes teaching less enjoyable for the teacher.   Some of the concerns of beginning and experienced teachers are shown in Tables 5–1 and 5–2.

		Type of response opportunity			Type of question		Student answer				Teacher feedback					Sus
Student	Name	Call	Vol	N Vol	Book	NB	+	−	±	NR	++	——	Feed	Proc	Term	
5			✓			✓			✓		✓					

"5" means Student Number 5. "Checks" indicate that this is what took place. Time goes vertically, with first things at the top. The observer simply checks the appropriate columns for each interchange. For example, in the first row across, Student 5 volunteered an answer to a question that was not in the book; the answer was partly incorrect, and the teacher praised her for a good try.

Meanings of the abbreviations above

Name	Teacher calls on student before asking question.
Call	Student calls out answer without being called upon.
Vol	Student volunteers—raises hand or other signal.
N Vol	Teacher calls on student who doesn't have hand up.
Book	Question whose answer is in the book.
N Book	Question whose answer isn't in the book—assumedly calls for some thought.
+	correct answer
−	incorrect answer
±	partially correct answer
NR	no response
++	teacher praise
——	teacher criticism
Feed	Simple affirmation like "yes."
Proc	Teacher tells how to go about finding correct answer.
Term	Teacher ends the interaction by giving the answer, or calling on someone else.
Sus	Teacher continues the interaction by repeating question, or giving hint, or asking new question.

Figure 5–4. *A type of observation coding suggested by Good, Biddle, and Brophy, 1976, for analyzing the kinds of interactions that go on in class.* (From T. Good, B. Biddle, and J. Brophy, *Teachers make a difference,* New York: Holt, Rinehart and Winston, © 1976).

Table 5–1. *Sources of anxiety reported by beginning teachers (adapted from Coates and Thoresen's 1976 summary with permission of American Educational Research Association).*

- Handling problems of pupil control and discipline.
- Concerns with self—will I be well liked, will I be adequate, how will I be evaluated?
- Dealing with schedules, materials, records, grading, and such.
- Having enough material, getting the material across, keeping students motivated and interested.
- Getting along with supervising teacher (when beginning teacher is a student teacher).

Can interfering anxieties be reduced, thus improving your teaching performance? One project which gave experienced teachers extensive guidance in teaching a more varied, student-centered course in high school physics found that the self-concepts of the teachers involved were higher than those of a comparable control group (Smith, Poorman, and Schagrin, 1968). In another study two junior high school teachers who were high in anxiety were asked to study a self-instructional program designed to train them to use cue-controlled relaxation techniques; their anxieties began to decrease (Hendricks, Thoresen, and Coates, 1975). In still another study, systematic group desensitization techniques were used (these are discussed in Chapter 8); the anxieties of a group of elementary teachers in a low socioeconomic area were reduced. The conclusion seems to be that you can reduce anxiety by (a) showing teachers more effective teaching techniques, (b) changing teachers' focus from subject matter to student concerns, and (c) direct therapy for the problem.

The self-fulfilling prophecy

Teachers perceive competencies and potentials of individual students differently, and there is evidence that these expectancies are reflected in these learners' learning and their behavior patterns (Braun, 1976). One study involved the younger siblings of good students. In cases where the older sibling had been taught by the same teacher and the older sibling did *well,* the younger siblings performed

Table 5–2. *Sources of anxiety reported by experienced teachers (adapted from Coates and Thoresen, 1976 with permission of American Educational Research Association).*

- Barriers to teaching, including class interruptions, inadequacy of facilities, insufficient time for rest and preparation, incompatible relationships with supervisor, time for individual and remedial teaching.
- Concerns with pupils, including ability to understand their needs, problems of coping with behavior problems, problems of numbers of students, lack of motivation, interpersonal problems with individual students, inability to diagnose and prescribe for individual needs, "no-failure" ideal vs. "minimum essentials" ideal.
- Clerical activities, need for funds, inadequate salary.

better than students who were siblings of good students who had been taught by a *different* teacher. The opposite results were found when the older sibling was a *poor* student (Seaver, 1973). This study was done in a natural setting, and used naturally occurring relationships rather than producing them artificially, so it is quite convincing. (However, one reviewer has suggested that we can't be sure that it was the fact that the teacher had had the older sibling in class previously that produced the difference; other things could be involved, such as the effect of having an older sibling who is successful in school on the learner himself [Bronfenbrenner, 1976].) In another study, a similar effect was produced artificially in the laboratory. Researchers noticed here that the "self-fulfilling prophecy" effect was strongest when the teacher was unaware of the possibility that there might be such an effect (Smith and Luginbuhl, 1976).

The effect of teacher expectancies on learners was first demonstrated clearly by Rosenthal and Jacobson in 1966, in a study which stirred national interest. They notified a group of elementary teachers that some of their students were potentially better students than others, and noted that later on (end of first year for first and second grade, end of second grade for sixth grade) the children so identified were happier, more curious, more interesting, and had a better chance of being successful in later life—according to teachers! The "gimmick" was that these supposedly high-potential children were "drawn from a hat," i.e., chosen by a table of random numbers!

The concept of the self-fulfilling prophecy in teaching is involved in problems of poverty, race, and discrimination in schools and in society in general. Perhaps this is why one fascinating project received wide publicity and was eventually made into a book (Peters, 1971). This teacher announced one day to her elementary school class that research had shown that blue-eyed people were inferior to brown-eyed people, and divided her class into blue eyes and brown eyes for various activities. (She later reversed this by announcing that the research had been found to have its results wrong, and that brown-eyed people were actually inferior.) Her report of the results is striking; for example, this quotation:

> One lovely and brilliant blue-eyed girl, among the most popular children in the class, almost disintegrated under the pressure. She walked in a slouch, became suddenly awkward, tripped twice over things, did poorly in her work. . . . All of the (brown-eyed) children enjoyed being considered superior, and the feeling that they were had obviously pushed them to do better work than they had ever done before. But some of them took savage delight in keeping the members of the "inferior" group in their place. . . ." (quoted by Braun, 1976)

Cognitive dissonance

What is it about expectancies that result in the "prophecy" being fulfilled? From social psychology we can draw on "balance theories" for an explanation, especially one called "cognitive dissonance" (Festinger, 1957). This suggests that a learner will act in ways which he (or she) thinks are consistent with the way in which he sees himself; if he doesn't, a state of internal "cognitive dissonance" will result, which is undesirable and uncomfortable.   This leads him to take action to achieve a state of harmony consistent with the view that he has of himself.   (This self-concept is suggested to him by the way others treat him, including the teacher.) For example, one study found a boy in the 115–125 IQ range who failed mathematics and English, and attributed this failure to the fact (as he saw it) that he was not smart enough.   When he was informed of the empirical test evidence showing that he *was* smart enough, did his test grades improve?   No—he managed to score *lower* on the next intelligence test given to all students, and his IQ dropped to the 85–100 range (Felker, 1974).

It has probably occurred to you by now that expectations might well have an effect on *teachers* as well, in relation to their teaching success.   Perhaps the less

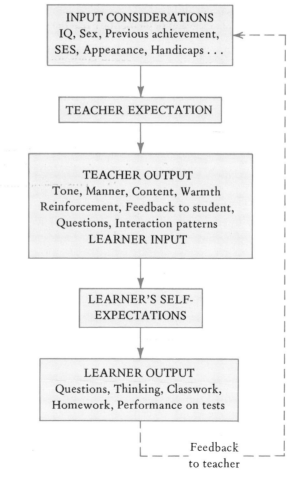

Figure 5–5. *A diagram showing some of the factors that affect what happens to a student (from Braun, 1976; copyright 1976, American Educational Research Association, Washington, D.C.)*

successful teachers in the studies reviewed previously were matching their performance to their own images of themselves!   One important element of teaching success is having a reasonably high expectation of your own ability to succeed as a
teacher.   This expectation may be based on your success with people in general,
your popularity, ability, and such, and in particular your success with learners of
the age group that you are planning to teach.   This would imply that someone who
has been very happy and successful in junior high, but less happy or successful in
senior high, might be better off teaching at the former level.

OTHER CHARACTERISTICS RELATING TO THE
CLIMATE OF THE LEARNING ENVIRONMENT

Warmth and acceptance

If you are warm
and accepting
toward learners,
will they learn
more, or just *feel*
better?

During the 1960s the concepts of warmth and acceptance of others became widely
supported as important attributes of personality.   This was especially true of college
age people who were concerned with the effects of big government and the impersonality of our society, especially in relation to the Vietnam war.   This was reflected in theories of teaching which placed heavy emphasis on these attributes as
important for good learning and good mental health.

"Warmth" is a general personal characteristic, of course.   "Acceptance" describes the way one reacts to others; in relation to teaching it means accepting students' feelings and also their contributions to class discussions regardless of correctness and the socioeconomic status, sex, or ability of the learner.

Research on the effects of these attributes has been somewhat biased by the
kind of commitment to them that was described above (Dunkin and Biddle, 1974).
When the research is examined objectively, some studies seem to bear out the expectations and others do not.   One study found that these attributes were associated with good teachers more often than with poor ones (Berliner and Tikunoff,
1976), but others found that less-warm and less-accepting teachers produced more
achievement (Henderer, 1971; Peck, 1976).   Given the emphasis on teacher
responsibility in the last section of this chapter, you might predict that these teachers had responsibility in spite of their personality faults or deficits.

Another study gives a different slant on this question.   These researchers
found that one of the common attributes of *un*successful teachers was a romanticized notion of the student as a "warm, wonderful, lovely, precious . . . person
who was a great pleasure just to be around . . . (Some of the) teachers who
painted this rosy picture had highly chaotic classrooms . . . which occasionally
became so out of control that the teacher exploded in anger and punitiveness in
spite of herself.   The more successful teachers were also successful classroom
managers . . . so that such explosions seldom were necessary" (Brophy and
Evertson, 1976).   Of course, we cannot tell from this report whether or not these
unsuccessful teachers were actually warm and accepting—perhaps they began that
way, and then became otherwise!

This may remind you of the characteristics of parents that influenced the personalities of their children, discussed in Chapter 3. Warmth and acceptance were important but ineffective without behavioral control; on the other hand, hostility and rejection worsened the bad effects of both over-control (leading to personality disorder) and under-control (leading to conduct disorder).

HARRY, JIMMY, AND JOE

Harry, Jimmy, and Joe are three new teachers in the high school. Harry, teaching government, has had more graduate work than any of the others; Joe has been a commercial artist and is teaching art without much college preparation; Jimmy is a football player who is coaching and teaching mathematics. Harry has a great deal of difficulty bringing his teaching down to the students' level at first, and does not communicate with them very well. He is very concerned that they learn a good portion of what he is presenting, and he becomes quite upset when they do not show more interest and motivation. As a result, the students become somewhat negative toward him and feel that he does not like them. Jimmy takes his teaching duties fairly lightly; he uses a medium-difficulty text, gives and collects assignments regularly, goes over them in class, gives students extra help when he can, but mainly plays the role of coach and counselor. The students seem quite pleased with this arrangement and enjoy having him in class because he is relaxed, cracks a lot of jokes, and does not worry about whether they are becoming "brains" or not. Joe becomes a general school favorite because he is so involved in his profession and so able to help students at any level in almost any form of art they are interested in, and because he lives his job, putting in long hours after school on special projects.

Although he occasionally blows up at some students who are not quite as interested as he, and is sometimes rather gruff, the students hang around him, work with him, and go to him for help in almost everything.

Harry is probably doing a good job of teaching, but his relations with the students are standing in the way and making it difficult for both him and them. He could relax a little, enjoy them more, and still get across much information. He is also probably more conscious of what he *does not* know than the others are. Jimmy is obviously successful with the students, but it is not entirely clear whether he is giving them all he can in the mathematics classroom. It might be that they could be motivated to do more, and that his approach to mathematics might be a little more modern and concept-oriented than he is making it. However, since most of them abhor mathematics, few if any are going to complain about it! Joe obviously is doing the ideal job, and both of the others could emulate some of his involvement and enthusiasm in terms of changes in the students and their interest in the work. Harry may be as interested, but he is not getting the students as involved—perhaps partly because he is not willing to put in the extra time. Jimmy puts in the time—but not in relation to mathematics.

Withitness

In a series of studies of teacher behavior which began in the 1950s researchers focused initially on how teachers respond to "deviant" behaviors of students in their classes. The purpose was to identify how more successful teachers handled this kind of thing as compared with less successful ones (Kounin, 1970; Kounin, Gump,

There are some
teacher behavior
patterns that deter-
mine whether
learners will work
or misbehave in
class.

Ryan, 1963).   Some differences were found, although the general picture was somewhat confusing.   For example, observers noted that te chers who used a rough tone
of voice to get students to desist seemed to generate trouble, rather than reduce it.
Teachers who did not have such a rough tone, but who were very *clear* about their
expectations (verbally) seemed to achieve more order and productivity.

Not being satisfied with the initial results, these investigators persisted in the
analysis of well-managed and poorly managed (occasionally chaotic) classrooms
through observations of videotapes, much as football coaches replay games to find
out where the defense or offense has broken down.   They finally succeeded in identifying characteristics that related to good classroom control.   Unlike the original
findings, however, these were not *reactive* processes, but *proactive*; they had to do
with *how* the teacher *anticipated* difficulties and avoided them.   One of the most
important ones had to do with the personality of the teacher and with classroom
management (Part IV).   This was dubbed "withitness" by the principal investigator in this research (Kounin, 1970).

Teachers who had "withitness" were aware of, and constantly monitoring,
events going on in all parts of the room, regardless of what they might be doing at
the moment.   They were able to spot potentially disruptive problems in the early
stages and nip them in the bud to prevent them from spreading (i.e., blocking the
"ripple effect," as these investigators called it).   When something did happen, the
"withit" teacher was more likely to handle the problem calmly and effectively and
was less likely to blow up.

This research concentrated on the behaviors of the students in the classrooms,
not on their achievement gains or on their expressions of liking or disliking of the
teacher, as in other studies we have reviewed.   However, other studies of teacher
and student behavior carried out since, some of which have used achievement criteria, have expressed basic agreement with the validity and importance of these dimensions of the teacher's behavior (Brophy and Evertson, 1976).

How can you evaluate your own teaching?

A good teacher
will want to know
how well he or she
is doing.

Whether you are teaching a class, leading a group, or tutoring students individually, there are several ways you can diagnose your own teaching and management
processes, and turn your weaknesses into strengths.   First, you need some information, and there are two main ways to obtain it: by objective observation of your
teaching behaviors (by professors or by other teachers or prospective teachers), and
by student evaluation of your teaching.   Given information, you can diagnose
some of your strengths and weaknesses.   Then you can set out to improve your
teaching by taking fuller advantage of your strengths and improving your weak
points.

To help students evaluate your teaching, you need a questionnaire that brings
out various sides of the teaching process, and also allows students to volunteer information on details of your teaching performance.   You should be careful not to

Ms. Eames seems to have eyes in the back of her head.

bias the questionnaire by stressing the things on which you think you do well and leaving out things that the students may want to comment on. (This is another reason for having some open-ended questions in addition to objective ones that can be processed statistically.)

Once you have identified your weak points, you might figure out some ways to get feedback on your subsequent teaching so you can practice improvements. Videotapes may help, but an observer who can comment immediately afterward, or by signals while you are teaching, would be even more helpful. You might also set up a system of rewards for yourself when you increase some particular behavior (like asking questions of the students) beyond your previous level; this may sound a bit childish, but it can be very effective in helping you improve. You might also reward yourself by congratulating yourself when you improve, and telling yourself how much better you are—a good self-concept is important in teaching! Hopefully, you will also get positive feedback from students that will further encourage you. (It may be that the feedback is in the form of less griping and less negative reactions; this kind of improvement gives what is called negative reinforcement.)

After several weeks of trying to improve, you probably should readminister the student evaluation form, or certain parts of it, and have another observation to see whether you are making any progress.

Before leaving this topic, here are some questions that you might ask yourself about your classroom experiences and how you can improve:

- Do my low- and high-achievement students indicate that I have equal interest in them?
- Do students report that I listen to them?
- When I ask questions, what percentage of the time do the students respond with correct answers?
- How long do I wait for students to respond? More for high- than low-achieving students?
- What percentage of my day is spent in instructional activities? (rather than meetings, other things?)
- Are there some students who need help but rarely seek me out?
- How much time do I spend with individual students?
- How do my classes compare with other teachers' classes in achievement?
- Do students work productively during independent work periods?
- How much time do they spend on homework?
- How much time do they study for tests?
- How do they study—what skills are they lacking, if any?
- How interesting do they find various lessons or topics?
- Are there students who never talk during small-group work? (Adapted from Good, Biddle, and Brophy, 1975)

TEACHER BEHAVIOR AND STUDENT ACHIEVEMENT

Does research look at what students learn?

Strangely enough, most of the early research on teachers ignored what or how much students learned!

Has it bothered you to find that few of the studies described so far said anything about what the students learned, or how much? For the parent, teacher, and counselor—but particularly for anyone interested in prospective teachers—it is important to know how good teachers act, and which actions and styles produce more learning and/or better feelings.

A review of studies of achievement vis a vis teacher behavior

A comprehensive review of achievement in the early 1970s (Rosenshine, 1971) included studies from nursery schools to college classes, covering a multitude of topics. There were differences in results from the various levels, and the picture that emerges is very complex, but worth examining. The studies reviewed did *not* show a strong relationship between teacher praise of achievement and the resulting achievement on tests. This seems surprising, but one conclusion is that approval

Teacher feedback can be crucial to performance in some grades and subjects.

probably has to be given very *selectively* to be effective. (Of course, this did not examine the effect of approval on feelings and attitudes of the learner, which may be a more significant one.)

Seven of the nine investigators who studied criticism by the teacher, or disapproval, found it to be a significant negative correlate of achievement, i.e., teachers high in criticism and control had students who achieved less on the various criteria used. (This refers to strong, consistent criticism and disapproval; mild criticism had no negative effects, and in two studies it yielded *higher* achievement.) Thus, although you need not worry about telling students they are wrong or about giving them directions, if you use a good deal of strong criticism and/or disapproval, you will have students who achieve less than they should.

In some studies in the primary grades, asking more questions yielded greater achievement. In higher grades, this was a more complex matter; there were some indications that there was a best frequency and a best type of question, but these "bests" depended partly on the subject matter. There was one study where "open-ended" questions resulted in *lower* achievement. One study suggested that the *variety of techniques* was important, not the number of questions. Another analyzed divergent and convergent questions (i.e., several answers and one answer), showing that a balance of the two was best for achievement. Obviously, then, questioning is related to achievement, but although there are probably optimal amounts, moderation and variation are both important. More research on this subject is obviously needed.

Highlighting the differences between concepts and pointing out their salient features proved effective in one of the studies, as well as giving correct labels and relating them to aspects of the learner's life. Using short statements to introduce or provide a focus for teacher-pupil interchanges also yielded higher achievement. Several studies in the primary grades indicated that giving practice on skills was an important aspect of bringing about achievement.

One recent study had doctoral candidates in anthropology and sociology observe reading and mathematics lessons in forty elementary classrooms. Their records of observations (called "protocols") were analyzed for elements that discriminated between classrooms and teachers, and these in turn were related to the success of the teachers in bringing their students to understand certain standardized experimental units (Berliner and Tikunoff, 1976). The observers came up with about sixty different variables, each related to success in reading and mathematics at second and fifth grades. Some of these dimensions, grouped in clusters of similar meanings, are as follows (a minus sign indicates something detrimental to achievement):

Cluster One

Abruptness (−), flexibility, pacing, waiting.
(These seem related to the "smoothness" dimension proposed by Kounin.)

Cluster Two

Openness, accepting, attending, complimenting, ignoring (−), praising, sarcasm (−).
(These seem related to indirectness, warmth, and acceptance.)

Cluster Three

Awareness levels, democracy, equity, individualizing, monitoring, learning, oneness (−), open questioning, peer teaching.
(These seem related to planning and managing.)

Determining what behaviors bring about achievement is not easy, however.

A general conclusion can be drawn that skill in managing the learning situation is related to student achievement, but so also are indirectness and warmth on the one hand, and an open, democratic, personalized organization of learning processes on the other.

In another set of studies observers found different results from different types of teacher interactions. For example, in teaching reading in second grade things like a variety of instructional material, instructing in groups, and monitoring individual performance with corrective feedback were positively related to pupil performance

(McDonald, 1976). This seems to imply that direct instruction is crucial. In second-grade mathematics, on the other hand, the amount of instructional content was critical, perhaps because teachers spent relatively little time on it so those who did more showed a big difference; also, individual help seemed more necessary than in reading.

Variety of instructional materials was a "no-no" at the fifth grade in reading: continuous reading in more complex materials that required thinking and under-standing seemed called for, and the teacher needed to spend time discussing, ex-plaining, questioning, and generally stimulating cognitive processes (a la Taba, no doubt). This also implies more class discussions and less individual or small-group work. For mathematics in grade five the critical things seemed to be group instruc-tion and a wider range of content covered. Independent work was ineffective, perhaps because the students' work has to be carefully monitored. The more these students covered, the more they learned.

A review of research on a number of major programs across the country in-volving low SES first and third graders drew some very suggestive conclusions con-cerning the relationships between learning outcomes and overall teaching em-phases (Stallings, 1976). Programs in which students spent more time in reading and mathematics activities and which had a high rate of drill, practice, and praise contributed to high reading and mathematics achievement of the children in-volved. Programs with more open and flexible instructional approaches and with a wider variety of activities and materials and more independence in their activities produced *less* achievement in reading and mathematics, but resulted in higher scores for children on nonverbal, problem-solving tests of reasoning. There were more absences from the structured and intense programs (described first), than from the open and flexible ones. One interesting difference came out in the feelings of children about responsibility for success and failure: the children from the first type of program indicated that they took responsibility for their failures, but not for their successes, while the children from the second type showed the opposite pattern. This poses a real question regarding the best attitudes for citizenship in a democracy (neither seems adequate!). You might want to try to relate this back to ego devel-opment and moral development in Chapter 1. In relation to social development, the more open and flexible programs also encouraged more work in groups, and their children showed a greater tendency to work in such task-oriented groups, as you might expect.

In studies on teaching low SES students in primary grades there is agreement that an optimal pattern allows a great deal of time spent on academic activities, with a predominance of seatwork using structured materials. Teacher and work-book questions are narrow and direct, and immediate feedback is provided along with praise and acknowledgment of student answers. Students work in groups su-pervised by the teacher, with little free time or unsupervised activity; this results in less off-task student behavior (Rosenshine, 1976).

The kind of teacher questioning seems to be an important dimension of stu-dent success according to many studies (e.g., Taba, earlier in this chapter). A re-

This may sound a little negative . . .

cent study shows that the amount of this kind of questioning has some surprising effects (Ward and Tikunoff, 1976). The graph in Figure 5–6 is a composite which shows the pattern of results found in this study, conducted in the sixth grade and involving the subject of ecology. It suggests that there is a level of questioning that either confuses or demotivates learners.

CHARACTERISTICS OF GOOD COLLEGE AND UNIVERSITY TEACHERS

How studies of college teaching differ from other research on teaching

Studies of college teachers differ from other teacher studies, but reveal some interesting relationships.

Generally, studies at elementary and secondary levels have not relied on the learners themselves to assess the teaching directly: classrooms are generally open to observation and analysis by the investigators. College professors and college classes, on the other hand, have traditionally been closed to people other than professors and administrators. Partly because of this, and partly as an outgrowth of student activism in the 1960s, research on teaching at the college level has emphasized gathering opinions about teaching from *students*, via student evaluation ques-

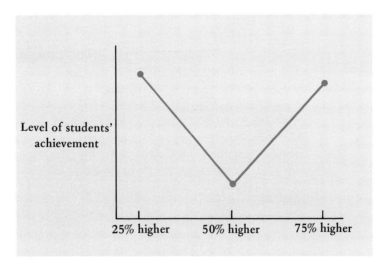

Figure 5 6. *Relative conceptual level of questions asked by teacher. (Adapted from B. A. Ward and W. J. Tikunoff, The effective teacher education problem: Application of selected research results and methodology to teaching,* Journal of Teacher Education, *Spring 1976, 27 (1), 48–52.)*

tionnaires.   Observations of college teaching, and analyses using various observational schemes, have not been as prevalent as at lower levels.   The recent trend toward using achievement tests as criteria for teaching has not been followed at the college level extensively either.   Therefore, unlike the research at lower levels, most of the knowledge about college teaching comes primarily from analyses of student opinions.   (Certain exceptions will be noted, however.)

The questionnaires used to evaluate teachers emphasize characteristics of teaching that loom large in the opinions and feelings of students; they do not place great emphasis on students' opinion of how much they are learning, nor do they assess the amount of effort that students put into their own learning.   For the most part, they are designed to apply to traditional lecture and lecture-discussion courses.

Analyses of student evaluations

Some interesting and suggestive research has been done using these questionnaires, however, partly by applying sophisticated statistical analyses called "factor analyses" to the data.   In several studies these factors have turned out to be as follows:

- Skill: Professional maturity, professional impression, instructor competence, communication, energy vs. lethargy, exciting-humorous-stimulating, overall evaluation, teacher's presentation.

This is an example of a student evaluation questionnaire that might be used to give a teacher feedback on how students are reacting to him or her. It would be a good idea to use such a questionnaire several times during the early part of a course, rather than waiting until very late in the course when it is hard to make changes.

DIRECTIONS

In each case, circle the number which best describes the teacher in relation to the activity or attitude which is given on the left. For example, the following rating was given by a student for a teacher who mumbled and was difficult to understand:

	Always or definitely		Sometimes or somewhat	Never, or definitely not
Speaks quite distinctly	5	4	3	② 1
Explains clearly	5	4	3	2 1
Is well prepared	5	4	3	2 1
Has a genuine interest in students	5	4	3	2 1
Makes the subject seem interesting	5	4	3	2 1
Accepts students' ideas and encourages them to contribute	5	4	3	2 1
Relates the subject to real life	5	4	3	2 1
Manages the class well	5	4	3	2 1
Gets me to do my best and put out my best effort	5	4	3	2 1
Provides variety in activities and approaches to the subject	5	4	3	2 1
. . . .	5	4	3	2 1
. . . .	5	4	3	2 1

You can write in your own dimensions for such a questionnaire. To be most useful, they should be short and cover a number of aspects of teaching.

Figure 5–7. *Questionnarie for evaluation of the teacher by students.*

- Rapport: Empathy, rapport, instructor empathy, friendly-democratic, lecturing versus student participation, approachable-warm-cheerful, affective merit, interaction, accessibility.
- Structure: Organization, control versus permissiveness, penetrating-clear-focused, planning.
- Overload: Academic emphasis, prepared-probing-demanding, stress, difficulty, workload.*

These research results imply that teaching "skill" is an important characteristic in college teaching, and involves verbal fluency, expressiveness, and enthusaism. It also relates to the ability to communicate, clarify, simplify, and to make students feel that the subject is both interesting and well enough organized so that they can master it. As the authors of the review conclude, "the highly rated teacher is verbally fluent and strikes his peers as cultured and sophisticated. He is expressive and enthusiastic. Items describing such an effective communicator are prominent in the evaluative scales of every rating form. . . " (Kulik and McKeachie, 1975).

Lecturing and achievement

If one type of teaching has been criticized and figuratively "run out of town" it is lecturing. Yet lecturing is still the backbone of teaching at the college level and is widely used in high schools as well. Another early seventies study explored various aspects of lecturing to isolate the good and bad features of this form of teaching (Gage et al., 1971). The researchers had a variety of teachers give two fifteen-minute lectures, based on common material for comparison's sake. Students rated the lectures according to a number of categories suggested and they also gave free opinions. Tests were also given to determine how much the students learned. "Good" teachers were those whose students achieved the most on these tests. They were characterized by the following student opinions:

1. Is organized and plans well.
2. Speaks at an appropriate conceptual level.
3. Is serious, does not openly display a sense of humor.
4. Has and uses an outline effectively.
5. Has a good introduction, in that it states objectives clearly and provides adequate background information.

---

* Adapted from Table 1 of J. A. Kulik and W. J. McKeachie, The evaluation of teachers in higher education, F. Kerlinger and F. E. Peacock (Eds.), *Review of Research in Education*, 1975, 3, 210–240, copyright 1975, American Educational Research Association, Washington, D.C.

Lecturing is still the backbone of college teaching.

Other aspects of the behavior of the "good" teachers were:

1. They gestured and moved more.
2. They used more rules and examples.
3. They used more "explaining links," i.e., more words and phrases such as "because," "in order to," "if . . . then."

Student evaluations compared with student achievement

Student evaluations of teaching: personality contests, grade-raisers, or valuable aids in the campaign for better college teaching?

Elements of teacher competence should be regarded as part of the "lore" of college teaching, inasmuch as they represent characteristics that students consider to be good and effective teaching.   There have been studies relating student evaluations to student achievement, but outcomes have been contradictory and controversial. Several studies have found that teachers whose students achieve more (on tests) show up *less* well on student evaluations (Rodin, 1973).   On the other hand, some studies have shown a positive relationship: college teachers who are rated higher on student evaluations also have students who achieve *more*.   These contradictory results occur in studies involving limited numbers of teachers and students; with larger numbers, the results suggest a low positive correlation (i.e., in courses where students rate their teachers higher, they tend to achieve *somewhat* more).

At present we must conclude that there are qualities or characteristics of teaching other than those reported by students which, when taken as a group, are more important in determining student achievement (Kulik and McKeachie, 1975). A recent study which supports this general conclusion also suggests that achievement is most closely related to *overall* student rating of a teacher's effectiveness in particular, i.e., response to "how does this teacher compare with all other teachers?" (Centra and Rose, 1976) Another recent study found that when the grading scale was varied for different groups taking the same course with the same examinations (without the students being aware that they were given grades according to different scales) evaluations of the teaching by students who received the higher grades were higher than those of the lower graded group (Vasta and Sarmiento, 1976). When compared on the same final examination, there were no differences in achievement.

The mysterious Dr. Fox

It would not do to conclude this discussion of college teaching effectiveness without describing a notorious study which, while it did not involve conventional college teaching, has interesting implications. In this study the "class" was a group of psychiatrists, psychologists, social workers, educators and administrators who had gathered to hear a lecture on a topic of common interest (certainly a potentially critical student body!). The "teacher" was introduced as an authority on the subject, and proceeded to give a very colorful, even charismatic lecture on the topic. However, the lecture itself had no substance or content of any merit, and was given by a professional actor who had been instructed to teach "charismatically and nonsubstantially." As you may have guessed, all fifty-five "students" rated the lecture and lecturer quite favorably. The initiators of the hoax concluded in their report that the ratings of teachers may be more influenced by the *style* of the teacher than by the substance of the presentation—a finding that would support previous observations that the better teacher is very verbal but not necessarily more able or intelligent (Naftulin, Ware and Donnelly, 1973). Incidentally, the lecturer in this study was called "Dr. Fox," and the impact of personality on ratings has often been referred to since as the "Dr. Fox effect." Perhaps researchers who found a negative correlation between student evaluations and achievement had a larger percentage of "Dr. Foxes." Also, in one study which concluded that the correlation was positive, there was still one teacher whose students achieved significantly less than the evaluations would have predicted; perhaps he was another "Dr. Fox" (Centra and Rose, 1976).

Table 5–3. *Summary of determinants of variation in student ratings of instruction.*

I. Student Variables. The student's general disposition toward instructors and instruction is the most important influence on within-class differences in ratings. Sex, age, grades, and major are of trivial importance.

II. Teaching Conditions. Factors that influence class ratings include class size, elected vs. required status of course, and discipline or department of course. While subject matter differences in class ratings within departments have not been demonstrated, this is a likely further source of variation in class ratings. For example, the teacher of the modern novel may enjoy an advantage over the medievalist.

III. Teacher Characteristics. There is probably a weak positive correlation between experience or academic rank and student ratings, although the size and direction of this relation may differ at different types of schools. Research productivity shows a similar weak positive relation to student ratings. To both peers and students, highly rated instructors seem to be cultured and sophisticated and especially articulate in classroom presentations.

IV. Interaction Effects. If the instructor teaches for the bright students, he will be approved by them and there will be a positive correlation between ratings and grades; if he teaches for the weaker students, he will be disapproved by the bright students and a negative coefficient will be obtained. There is some evidence that college students with different personality traits respond differently to highly structured and less structured teaching styles.

THE FRUSTRATED TA

Fred Smith was a TA (Teacher's Assistant) in psychology. He taught small sections of the Introduction to Psychology course at a large university. Occasionally, he was asked to do a lecture on some topic related to his thesis. He was a third-year graduate student, working in physiological psychology, experimenting with the effects of nutritional changes on maze learning in rats. Fred was very concerned about college teaching; he planned to be a college professor, and had always felt very negative about large-course lecture and discussion techniques and the impersonality and superficiality of introductory courses in psychology. Therefore, it was quite a shock to Fred when he received his first student evaluation results, since the students in his section indicated that he was not a very good discussion leader, that his lectures were hard to understand, and that while he was friendly and empathetic and very easy to get along with, he didn't seem to know whether students were understanding him or not.

Fred discussed this problem with the professor in charge of the course, and after some thought about the matter, concluded that he was overloading his students a bit, perhaps concentrating too much on the subject matter and too little on "getting it across." When he started greeting student questions with more concern, he began to see that they knew a lot less about the basics in the text and lectures than he had assumed. When he began to show more concern for what they knew and how they were feeling about it, they began to return the interest and concern, and he began to feel as if he were more accepted and respected by them. He still found himself dwelling at length on side issues and concentrating more on deeper meanings of the subject than the students' inability to understand, but gradually things improved in his sections, and he began to feel more confident that he was both "getting across" and gaining respect and support as well.

Summary outline with key concepts

☞ *Since educational* psychology relates to teaching, studies of teachers are relevant.

☞ *Superior teachers* expect to work hard and sacrifice in order to achieve success; poor teachers view success as a matter of chance / Superior teachers feel that failure can be overcome by personal effort; poor teachers see failure as due to external factors / Superior teachers have a positive view of others; poor ones see people as frustrating, unforgiving, unhelpful / Superior teachers enjoy pupil relationships, are self-confident and cheerful, have had happy childhoods; poor teachers are more restrictive and critical, value exactness and orderliness, appear less self confident / Feeling yourself to be responsible for success or failure, and for coping with problems, evidences an internal locus of control; attributing responsibility for events to others evidences an external locus of control / Less successful teachers rationalize failure in ways that allow them to avoid assuming personal responsibility; i.e., they have an external locus.

☞ *Elementary teachers* spend most of their time controlling learners, then dealing with content; secondary teachers spend most of their time describing and designating, then explaining and directing classrooms / The range of activities open to secondary students is limited; the teacher dominates the verbal activities of the "classroom game" / Indirect teaching behavior leads to better classroom climate, but not necessarily to better achievement; there may be an optimum level of indirectness / To extend and elevate thought processes, teachers focus, extend, lift, and steer thought / Teachers have been rated on emphasis on cognitive processes such as cognitive memory, convergent thinking, divergent thinking, and evaluative thinking.

☞ *Teacher anxiety* is prevalent, and depends in part on the climate of the school in which you teach / Teacher anxiety can be relieved by (a) teaching the teacher to cope more successfully, and (b) teaching the teacher to be more concerned about meeting learner needs, less about subject-matter needs / Relaxation techniques and desensitization have been used to allay teacher anxiety / The expectancy of a teacher for a group or an individual can influence the achievement of that group or individual / Teacher expectancy is more influential when the teacher is unaware of the possible influence it exerts (regarding negative expectancies) / Expectancy influences learner behavior by altering the self-concept of the learner, who then behaves in a way that fulfills this self-concept.

☞ *Warmth and* acceptance are associated more with good teachers than poor / Unsuccessful teachers often have romanticized notions about students / Successful classroom managers have "withitness," i.e., proactive strategies including ability to monitor all parts of the room, to spot potentially disruptive behaviors in early stages, and to handle problems calmly and effectively / Evaluation of your own teaching requires objective information, from students and from observers with professional expertise.

☞ *Only a* portion of the research examines what learners learn and relates it to how teachers teach / Criticism is negatively related to achievement / Variety in questioning is positively related to achievement / Moderate structure is positively related to achievement / Moderate rather than extensive drill is positively related to achievement / Encouragement of students in elaborating their answers is positively related to achievement / A variety of techniques appropriately used is the most general pattern producing achievement / Highlighting differences between concepts and pointing out their salient features is related to achievement / Giving clear labels to things and relating them to aspects of the learners' lives is positively related to achievement / Giving practice on skills is positively related to achievement / Evaluators of early elementary programs have found that achievement in specific areas (e.g., reading) depends on the amount of time spent each day in that area.

☞ *Teaching skill* (ability to put material across, stimulate curiosity, communicate expectations clearly) is the most important factor for success, according to college students / Important individual attributes are clear explanation, being well-prepared, giving lectures that are easy to take notes on, care and precision in answering questions, summarizing major points, stating objectives for each class, identifying what is important, encouraging discussion, showing genuine interest in students, and being enthusiastic / Attributes of college teachers important to their colleagues include doing recognized scholarly work, being well-read, being able to suggest reading in the field and giving advice on research, encouraging student dialogue and communication, interest in the work of colleagues / Generally, college teachers evaluated highly by students tend to get higher achievement from students, but the relationship is not a strong one and there are marked exceptions / The "Dr. Fox effect" demonstrated the degree to which charisma and presence can give the impression of scholarship and ability to communicate.

Glossary

Achievement Motivation: Desire to achieve for the sake of achieving.

Bias: Favoring of one view or type of learner or aspect of teaching over another.

Classroom Game: Bellack and Hughes's name for the common classroom interaction pattern.

Cognitive Dissonance: When an individual's actions are the opposite of how he or she feels or thinks, producing a feeling of conflict.

Controlling: Setting goals, determining content, directing activities.

Desensitization: A process for reducing anxiety, described in Chapter 8.

Dr. Fox effect: Positive effect of verbal fluency and charisma in convincing learners or audiences that a speaker is knowledgeable and that they are learning a great deal—whether they are or not.

Facilitating, managing the classroom to facilitate learning: Answering questions, furnishing materials, keeping things quiet.

Feedback: Information resulting from some act, which gives the person who acted information about its consequences.

Field independent: People who are not as swayed or influenced by surroundings.

Indirect teaching: Teaching characterized by accepting feelings, encouraging learner responding, and a high level of student-initiated talk.

Interaction analysis: A method of analyzing teacher-learner classroom interaction.

Lifting: Bringing thought to a higher level by encouraging the learner to enrich or augment his or her answer.

Locus of control: Position from which a person sees the control of his or her life, either from within or without.

Presage Variable: Something which you can use to predict something else.

Proactive: Acting in advance; anticipating or preventing disruption.

Self-fulfilling prophecy: An expectation or prediction which, having been adopted or made, influences an outcome in such a way as to make it come true.

Self-instructional program: A sequence of tasks which a learner can use to learn independently; answers are given, and error rate is low.

Skill: Pattern of activities and level of effectiveness in carrying them out that discriminates between good and poor teachers.

Spontaneity: Initiating activities rather than following schedules.

Questions for thought and discussion

1. How do successful teachers differ from others in relation to locus of control?
2. What are some of the effects of teacher anxiety on students?
3. How do teacher expectancies influence student behavior and achievement?
4. How important is teacher warmth?   acceptance?
5. How important is "indirectness" in teaching?
6. What behaviors characterize "withitness?"   How do "withit" teachers' classrooms differ from others?
7. Name some of the more important characteristics of good college teachers.
8. What characteristics of teaching have positive effects on achievement?
9. What is the "Dr. Fox effect?"
10. Is verbal communication ability any more important at one level than at another? Why?
11. In view of the concepts presented in this chapter, what are your personal views of the characteristics of good teachers?   Have they changed?

Situations calling for applications of facts and concepts

1. Mr. Brown is a principal of a middle school. He wants to reward good teaching by giving it attention and by showing everyone that he appreciates and respects it. He is told by the students and parents that Mrs. Johnson is an excellent teacher; they all love her and try to get into her classes. However, Mr. Brown finds that Mrs. Ames' students achieve more than other students, even though the students and their parents don't like Mrs. Ames. How would you go about rewarding good teaching, and which teacher would you reward?

2. Your friend Gary is teaching eleventh grade and really bombing out. His students are upset and say they aren't learning anything, and Gary is very defensive and says that the students are lazy and uncooperative and won't work. How would you go about helping Gary, assuming that he asked you for help? Give reasons for your strategies.

3. Mr. Waring is fifty, old-fashioned, rubs people the wrong way, talks slightingly of todays' students and is very sarcastic with them, complains about facilities and materials and classroom schedules and everything else. Students try to get into his classes, parents say he's the best thing that ever happened to the school, and you as the superintendent are asked by an influential schoolboard member to get rid of him somehow (probably because he offended that member, perhaps by flunking his son or daughter). How can you rationalize Mr. Waring's success in spite of all these negative characteristics, and what would you tell the school board about his positive traits? (What positive traits would he probably have?)

Suggested activities

1. Observe teachers at various levels and note their characteristics according to several of the observational systems described in this chapter. Decide for yourself which system best reflects good teaching or what combination of skills. Make up your own system, giving reasons for the categories you include.

2. If you are teaching in any kind of situation—pre-school, tutoring, Sunday School, or conventional classroom—have someone observe you and record some of the things that happen, using one or more of the approaches described here. Then discuss the results with your observer, and perhaps do it again later after you have had a chance to change some things that need attention. Also have the students evaluate you as well, according to one or more of the dimensions described: make your own evaluation questionnaire (short ones are often easiest to use).

3. Form small groups of three or more classmates and agree on some evaluation system, then take turns teaching each other and evaluating each other, to get some initial feedback in a small, nonthreatening situation, regarding your strengths and weaknesses.

Suggested readings

The study of teaching is an ongoing process, and you find new results and points of view every year. We suggest that you follow up on some of the references in the chapter, according to your particular interests, but that you also stay alert for forthcoming reports and books on the topic. *The American Educational Research Journal*, the *Journal of Educational Psychology*, and the *Review of Educational Research* are all apt to have research reports. Several of the reports mentioned here appeared in a special issue of the *Journal of Teacher Education*. Also keep an eye on subject-matter teaching journals, such as *The Mathematics Teachers*, *The English Teacher*, and the like. Some of the reports on college teaching appeared in *Science*.

6

Groups and
Individuals:
The Social Psychology
of Education

CONTENTS

ABOUT CHAPTER 6

What this chapter can do for you

All of you have had experience in dealing with groups, but not all of you have been group *leaders*. The contents of this chapter will give you some insights into your own experiences as a part of groups such as scouts, summer camp, teams, and committees, not to mention school classrooms. Knowing some of the principles of group processes should alert you to forces and reactions that you might not anticipate as a group leader, such as the "frustration-aggression reaction." The knowledge you derive will relate also to feelings between and among members of groups, and group "climates." You may become more sensitive to the feelings of others, and you will learn how to increase such sensitivity.

What might bother you about this material or make it difficult

Beginning teachers and some experienced teachers are often more concerned with putting knowledge across and dealing with individual learners than they are with the interrelationships of groups with which they are working. You may find these discussions somewhat irrelevant to your interests and concerns, and you may feel that they are not very significant. However, group forces can be very important to you in many ways, including matters involving groups with which you are working as a learner or a teacher. On the other hand, some aspects of this chapter are very humanistic in their orientation, and you may be one who feels that "nice guys always lose" and that sensitivity and related feelings are not your "cup of tea." Again, these may be concerns that are actually more important to *you* than to others who don't feel this way since they already accept the importance of such things.

Some reasons for studying this chapter

You deal with groups in many roles and tasks, but groups are made up of human beings, so it is important to be able to lead and motivate groups without forgetting to treat people as individuals as well. You have probably wondered if schools and classrooms couldn't be more pleasant places, or if it wasn't possible to increase learning by improving the climate of schools and classrooms. Many professional educators and critics have felt the same way, and they have suggested a variety of approaches.

Some have been more humanistic than others, and some have been more group-oriented than others, but all aim at an ideal condition where fear and threat are reduced and where enjoyment and security are part of learning. Not all such experiments have succeeded, partly because of the lack of understanding of the group processes and humanistic considerations involved.

Objectives

I want to introduce the social psychology of education, along with the recent developments in the study of individual sensitivity and interpersonal relations characteristic of sensitivity training and organizational behavior. I have tried to integrate these two approaches in one chapter because they seem to call for such treatment, in view of the fact that teachers and parents are continually struggling with the question of the demands of the group versus the demands of the individual.

BACKGROUND OF CHAPTER 6

Social psychology and education

Teachers work with groups, and so the study of groups is important.

The study of social psychology has been neglected in the study of educational psychology, yet its emphasis on groups and group dynamics, and on the patterns of interrelationships among people, are obviously quite relevant. Social learning, one outgrowth of this study, is becoming one of the most important and useful views of learning and has applications to motivation and the practice of teaching as well.

The individual and his or her environment

Is your personality and mine determined by our hereditary makeup or by our past experiences, as debated in the controversy over the determination of intelligence? Or is it possible that there is another factor at work: our present environment? Could it be that if you or I were put into a completely different environment, we would become different people, and take on different personalities? There is some reason to think that this is possible, to a larger degree than we might expect. Similarly, there is reason to think that "success" in leadership roles, including teaching, is determined by the nature of the organization as much as by the personal characteristics of the individual!

GROUP DYNAMICS

Climate as a determinant of behavior

Arrangements of the environment can have significant effects on the way groups behave, and thus on individuals in groups.

Climate usually refers to weather, but here it describes the emotional and attitudinal characteristics of a group or a learning situation.   One of the earliest studies dealing with this question (Lewin, Lippitt and White, 1939) involved extracurricular clubs for young boys, in which researchers studied the effects of three styles of leadership: authoritarian, laissez-faire, and democratic.   The leaders played different roles: authoritarian with one club, laissez-faire with another, democratic with the third.   Each club had several leaders, one playing one role for two weeks, then another playing another.   Despite the role playing and frequent changes, observers could discern common characteristics of group behavior and feeling that resulted from a given style.   For example, the authoritarian role brought better discipline, less confusion, and more production; but it also was marked by aggressiveness, when the proceedings of the club were interrupted, scapegoating, and a breakdown in order when the leader was absent.   The democratic role resulted in less order and productivity generally, but also less aggressiveness and scapegoating, and better order and productivity when the leader was absent than in the authoritarian club.

Although replications of this study have not always resulted in such clear-cut outcomes, and although the ability of individuals to play roles consistently has been questioned, this study suggested a large number of similar studies dealing with the reactions of people in groups of different environments and leadership styles.   It demonstrated that children, and also adults, change their behavioral characteristics both as groups and as individuals when their environments are changed radically.   It also suggests to educators that the behavior of learners in group settings is as much a result of the nature of the environment as of the personalities and characteristics of the learners themselves.

Another example of how group feelings can be affected by arrangement of the environment

In the 1960s a group of social psychologists conducted an experiment in group feelings which shed light on processes for dealing with hostility and aggression between individuals and groups, and also showed how individual feelings and attitudes can be manipulated through group dynamics (Sherif, 1956; Sherif et al., 1961).   A group of theorists and experimenters created an artificial conflict between groups of boys in an experimental summer camp.   The boys were mostly eleven years old, came from middle-class homes, were relatively well adjusted, and thus were representative of boys this age generally.   The camp leaders set out to transform them into two hostile, destructive groups; then, after they succeeded, they changed them from this extreme back into cooperative, constructive workers and friends who were concerned about each other and ready to make sacrifices for each other.

Learners react differently to the group experience.

To produce friction between groups, after dividing the boys into two distinct teams, the researchers arranged a tournament of games: baseball, touch football, tug-of-war, and treasure hunts. The tournament started in a spirit of good sportsmanship, but as it progressed, good feelings disappeared and the members of each group began to call their rivals names like "stinkers," "sneaks," and such. They began to refuse to have anything more to do with individuals in the opposing group. Some boys turned against other boys whom they had chosen as "best friends" when they first came to camp. Most of the boys gave very negative ratings to boys in the other group. The groups made threatening posters and planned raids, and one group burned a banner left behind by the other group which had defeated them in a tournament game. The next day, the second group seized the first group's flag, and the boys began to throw paper and food at each other at meals.

It might appear at this point that while this "experimental treatment" had been all too successful in creating hostility between the groups (as well as a certain amount of camaraderie and cohesion within each group), it would be impossible to turn it around as planned to produce a larger community of considerate, concerned boys. These researchers set out to do just that, but at first it looked as if they had created something they couldn't undo. They brought the groups together for social events such as movies, but this only served as an opportunity for the rival gangs to attack each other verbally. Finally, however, they hit upon a better plan; it was based on the fact that water was brought to the camp from a water tank about a mile away, through water pipes. They arranged to interrupt the water flow, and then they called the gangs together to inform them of the crisis. Both groups volunteered to search for the trouble; in searching, they worked together harmoniously, and before long they had located the trouble and fixed it. This gave the experimenters further ideas, and so on another occasion, just when all were hungry and the camp truck was about to go to town for food, it turned out that the engine wouldn't start. Both groups had to cooperate in pulling the truck to get it started. Thus through approaches which the experimenters labeled "setting of superordinate goals" they were able to achieve harmony among the groups and cooperation among groups and individuals.

This experiment was carried out under relatively isolated conditions, and therefore you have to consider applications to more typical situations with care (Bronfenbrenner, 1976). It is a little like the fictional situation depicted in the now-classic novel *Lord of the Flies*, where a group of boys of about this same age were marooned on a tropical island (after a plane crash) and by the time they were rescued they divided into warring factions, resulting in active combat and death.*

It may seem rather farfetched to apply such concepts to classroom teaching, but in a real sense the classroom is an "island" in the middle of the school for a certain period of time each day, and it is possible to generate "superordinate goals" for the class as well. For example, a superordinate goal for a Spanish class would be to prepare the group for a mythical journey to Spain, in which the students would cooperate in planning the itinerary, helping each other learn to speak the language, and working together during the trip to see to it that everyone has ample accommodations and food and enjoys his or her favorite or most hoped-for experiences. Of course, in doing this, you might find that you create an "in-group" which rejects outsiders through use of a different language and group activities. The experiment involving blue- and brown-eyed children, described in Chapter 5, is another case of the effects of environmental and social differences on individuals.

Some more recent studies of effects of environment on climate

Do large classes have different effects from small classes?

A series of studies of the learning environment in conventional classes, most of them physics classes, are interesting because of the kinds of group feelings that were investigated. Using a questionnaire called a "learning environment inventory,"

---

* Kohlberg's "conformist" stage of moral development has been called a "Lord of the Flies" kind of thinking. Eleven is about the right age for this; it seems likely that Loevinger's "conforming" stage of ego development would apply also.

researchers studied such factors as cohesiveness (members of the class are personal friends), diversity (the class divides its efforts among several purposes), formality (students are asked to follow a complicated set of rules), friction (certain students are considered uncooperative), and cliqueness (certain students work only with their close friends) in respect to environmental variables such as class size and experience of the teacher, preparation of the teacher, and organization of the class activities.   In this case, the greater the class size, the lower was the cohesiveness of the class as a group.   Group satisfaction also suffers, and formality tends to increase; the tendency of the teacher to dominate also increases (Anderson and Walberg, 1971; Walberg, 1969).   It is interesting to note in relation to these outcomes that other research reviews have concluded that the amount learned does not vary greatly with class size; however, that research was done mostly at the college level (McKeachie, 1963).

Some basic principles of group dynamics

How does membership in a certain group change an individual? How do group norms affect individuals in the group?   In discussing applications of the study called "group dynamics," another theorist has suggested that our major concern must be with how we can change group members without restricting their freedom or potential (Cartwright, 1951).   He accurately observes that society is more willing to have us "educate" than it is to have us "change" students, which would imply that education is desirable as long as it does not threaten to become too effective in changing those who are being "educated"!

You all know what a powerful influence groups exercise over your lives, in terms of dress, behavior, choice of a car, or choice of a party.   Cartwright set out to examine how groups can be exploited to bring about *desirable* changes in individuals.   He set down his guidelines as principles of groups to be kept in mind when teaching or leading groups of various kinds.

In his first principle Cartwright stated that the teacher and the learners should feel that they are members of one group in respect to their values and objectives. Since teachers are often of a different social status than their students, as well as different in age, they often do things that make students feel that they have very little in common, even though they do this without intending to create such a gap. Thus a teacher should emphasize the values that he or she has in common with the students to narrow the gap.

The second principle is that a group that satisfies the *needs* of its members will be more attractive and will exert greater influence.   Emphasizing the attractiveness of members of a class, of the teacher, or of the subject matter can have positive effects on the influence of the class and the teacher on individual students.

Cartwright's third principle is that the more relevant the group is to the needs of its members, the more the norms of the group will influence individuals.   Thus, if content is relevant, or if the teacher makes it *seem* relevant and meaningful in

*When the leader fails to satisfy group needs, the dynamics of the
group can work against him.*

terms of the student's present situation or future aspirations, the class will have a
stronger influence on him or her.

(4) The fourth principle indicates that the prestige of the group leader influences
members, as does the prestige of other members who subscribe to the group objectives. Thus a teacher who has prestige in athletics will have more influence, even
though he or she is teaching mathematics where there is no direct relationship.

(5) In the fifth principle Cartwright asserts that any teacher using a method that
produces behaviors incompatible with the accepted norms of the group will have a
hard time. The classic case is teaching romantic poetry to athletes, which calls for
careful and diplomatic behavior by the teacher. With such consideration, the task
is by no means impossible.

(6) According to the sixth principle, some time spent early in the course bringing
participants to see a need for such a course and the teaching processes to be used
will be beneficial later. (7) The seventh principle indicates that clarity of communication about objectives and rationale must be maintained for good functioning. (8) The eighth principle states that group processes inevitably cause strains
among participants, and a leader needs to attend to them to maintain the group
process.

USING GROUP DYNAMICS IN A SPECIAL CLASS

Mrs. Shepherd has been asked to take a special education class in the upper elementary grades (four, five, and six). She realizes that it is an important job, and that the school is trying to incorporate special education students (i.e., mentally retarded students) into regular classes as much as possible without hurting either the special students or the students in the average classes. She knows that morale is low in the special education class, which is understandable, of course, but that does not make her feel much better about it. She has, however, been reading about some effects of group dynamics in raising morale and motivation, and she decides she will try some of them. There does not seem to be anything to lose.

Her first move is to try to establish rapport with the students so they will view her as someone who has similar interests, problems, needs, and attitudes. Since in fact many of her characteristics are quite different, partly due to the difference in age and partly to her higher level of natural ability both intellectually and socially, she has to make a strong attempt to emphasize the things they have in common. She shows interest in things they are interested in, talks with them about things they want to talk about in a way that indicates those things are important to her, plays some games with them, and generally tries to make them all feel part of one group. She also tries to find common interests and values among the various students, and stresses their similarities rather than their differences. She also stresses the similarities between their views and interests and those of other students in the school, to narrow that gap as well.

At the same time, she orients group learning activities to satisfy needs that are common to all the students, as far as possible.

She also brings out aspects of students and of herself that are interesting and attractive, to build the image of the group indirectly as well. She plans activities that focus on the basic abilities that the children lack—social abilities in particular, so that they can build their ability to become part of other groups in school without sticking out. They work out the locations of classrooms, lavatories, the auditorium, and the cafeteria, since these children have some difficulty finding them; they work out the meanings of various signs and bells, and learn the schedules of the school and how to estimate time; they work on social skills involving verbal communication; and they deal with facial expressions and the like to improve their ability to function as members of a normal group.

Mrs. Shepherd brings to their attention, indirectly and subtly, the fact that she has been the advisor to some of the prestigious clubs in school, and also that she used to coach field hockey. This prestige adds to the cohesiveness and strength of the group. She also spends a good deal of time discussing and, indirectly, "selling" the objectives of school activities and of the special class. Finally, she devotes attention to "spreading oil on troubled waters" when the students get into difficulties with each other and with her, seeing these as natural aspects of the group process and pressures brought to bear on individuals by the group. She also allows time for individual, nongroup activities and counseling, so that the pressures do not become unbearable for any one student.

Mrs. Shepherd is pleased to see that these approaches result in a better class spirit and in cooperative behavior patterns that are far beyond any she had been led to expect in these students.

The dynamics of leadership

Are leaders born, or made? Does the nature of the organization determine who is a good leader?

Since teaching individuals is a time-comsuming and costly approach to education, most teaching involves groups of learners.   One theorist has analyzed the task of the leader of a task-oriented group and found two main functions: getting the job done, and keeping personal relations in good working order (Miles, 1961).   Teachers and other group leaders (scouts, Little League, and such) have the same two problems: to get something learned, and to keep the group functioning well at the same time.   Miles identified a number of leadership styles that are used to accomplish these goals, and he said that the effectiveness of a particular style is determined by the nature of the situation; the concept of a born leader has not been a very useful one for predicting the success of different leaders.   By the same token, we can conclude that the concept of a born teacher may not be a valuable one either, and it is worth noting what kinds of teaching styles are most suited to different situations.

Miles also went further in his analysis of the functions of a leader, noting that they included (1) helping each group member satisfy his or her needs, (2) helping the group do a job rapidly and well, (3) improving internal working relationships, and (4) performing leadership acts that help members grow in their knowledge and ability to contribute to the group.   These functions are relevant to teaching, especially in schools where a significant portion of the learning activities is carried out in small groups (in addition to teacher-centered large-group work and independent study).

Another theorist has classified leadership types according to task orientation and socioemotional guidance (Bales, 1969).   The leader needs to keep the group goals clearly in mind, to organize the group internally, to keep it moving on the right track.   At the same time he or she must be sensitive to tensions and frictions between group members and to the needs of individuals.   Sometimes one leader performs both functions, but leaders who do both well are relatively rare.   The driving personality who makes a good task leader does not always have the personal warmth that makes a good socioemotional leader.

Still another theorist says that *leader-member personal relationships* are **most** important because they are the only things completely under the control of the leader himself or herself (Fiedler, 1967).   The task structure of the situation and the power of the leader's position are both determined by the organization in which the leader and the group work.   In a traditional school where the school board rules with a conservative iron hand, a teacher may not be able to choose his (or her) own structure, for example, in respect to grades, testing, or using "questionable" books with references to controversial topics.   He must keep his "position power" in place below that of the principal and other senior teachers, to avoid conflict.   However, he *can* structure his relations with the students according to his own desires and personality, rather than by the school and its climate.   A task-oriented leader (as differing from a person-oriented one) performs best in two quite opposite organizational climates: where he has a great deal of power, and where he has practically no power at all.   In organizations where the power of the leader or teacher is medium in extent—neither absolute nor nonexistent—the person-oriented teacher functions best; this probably applies to most schools.

The success of a given leader, therefore, is determined partly by the climate of the organization, in our case the school. (This repeats what Miles said in a previous section). Thus, a person who is unsuccessful in one situation may be quite successful in another where the organizational structure, emphasis, and climate are different. The school determines in part what kind of teaching will be most effective, and a given teacher will be most successful if he or she chooses a situation where his or her style is compatible with the climate.

Teacher in the middle

If you view the classroom as a social system, the teacher is seen as caught between the demands of the institution (for discipline and achievement by the students) and the needs of the students themselves (for recognition and for help with individual problems) (Getzels and Thelen, 1960). There is also frequent conflict between cultural values outside the classroom and expectations within the classroom, e.g., community objections to readings with references to sex, or the debate over teaching evolution in some areas of the country. The teacher is usually viewed by learners as a representative of the institution, unless he or she disassociates himself from that view.

Another major problem is dealing with the eternal conflict between the demands of the subject matter and achievement on the one hand, and the needs of the individual learners and the group for motivation and variety and individual help and generally for personal attention. Traditionally, some subjects emphasize subject matter (e.g., science) while others emphasize the individual (e.g., art), but new curricula and teaching methods are changing this picture.

TASK ORIENTATION VERSUS PERSON ORIENTATION: TWO VERSIONS

Rob Moore was teaching Spanish to sophomores and juniors in high school. His course was very well organized, with plenty of variety, using explanations, discussions, language laboratory assignments, text assignments, conversations, and role playing in Spanish, among other things. This was balanced with a consistent routine that helped the students organize their work. He was involved in his teaching and wanted very much to have his students learn—so much so that he did a little too much for them, and did not let them do enough things on their own.

Yet when student evaluation questionnaires were filled out, the students showed that they found the subject dull and uninteresting, irrelevant, and felt that the teacher was not interested in either the subject or them. Rob asked another teacher to observe him and record data on his classes. By noting, every five seconds, which of several categories best described the behavior of the class, the other teacher took down a running picture of Rob's performance. The data, when analyzed, showed that Rob was highly directive, and weak in such areas as "accepting student's comments and ideas," "encouraging students to contribute to classroom processes," "showing enthusiasm for the subject," and "showing interest in individual students." The observer noted that the class was quite affiliation-oriented, whereas Rob was very achievement-oriented. Rob began to pay more attention to the people in the class—and he began to enjoy his teaching more.

Jessy Wilson was teaching English, and from the beginning she was very popular with the students as well as other teachers. She had an excellent personality, was very outgoing, and seemed to understand what the students needed in the way of support, approval, and general climate of the classroom. Students fought to get into her classes. She was asked to lead clubs and chaperone dances and trips. She seemed to know and like her subject, also. Although she occasionally introduced topics that were a little beyond the students and not typical of other English courses, the students did not mind too much and assumed that it was doing them some good. Also since she did not penalize them for not doing homework (actually she did not pay too much attention to the homework they did),

they were quite happy with things as they were. However, as the year went on, some of the more motivated students, particularly seniors preparing for college, began to ask for time and help from other, older teachers, after school and during free periods. They were preparing for college boards in some cases, and were beginning to be a little concerned that Mrs. Wilson was not pushing them quite enough or preparing them adequately. They noticed that she tended to exclude some of the traditional topics from her course and to go lightly on topics that students generally did not enjoy as much—including grammar and some of the more difficult literature. She did not push them to read on their own or do extra work in the course as other teachers did. Although she understood her subject generally, she was not always prepared to explain thoroughly each particular topic as they came to it, and acted as if it would somehow be absorbed through osmosis. Although she remained popular with the students, some of the early euphoria wore off, and teachers who had been seen as rather stiff and uninterested in students began to look as if they cared after all.

Teaching by using small groups

One strategy of teaching is to divide large groups into smaller ones of five to eight students. This encourages a greater level of participation and social responsibility on the part of the learner than in more traditional classroom procedures. For best results, each group should have a democratic leader who will assure a hearing for all viewpoints, who will distribute participation relatively evenly, and who will keep the group "on course." Teacher aides or students have to act as leaders since one teacher cannot fulfill these functions for several groups at once, and thus the success of small-group learning often rests on the training given to the group leaders and their effectiveness in leading the groups. Success also depends on how much experience the learners have with such processes: you can't just convert a conventional class into small-group learning without a period of training and adjustment.

Small-group learning presupposes a different approach to learning: students have to uncover and discover knowledge, as well as have the teacher "cover" it. Thus, just as the classroom observational systems described in Chapter 5 presupposed a traditional large-group approach to classroom learning, so small-group ap-

Teachers mediate between the classroom and the community.

proaches presuppose a problem-oriented, less teacher-directed approach. Different teachers and subject matters will lend themselves to this process in different ways. Well-known systems of teaching at various levels have utilized the small-group learning process successfully (some of these will be described in more detail in Chapter 13).   The management of such learning procedures also involves approaches and strategies discussed in Chapter 11.

RON BREAKS THE CLASS DOWN TO SIZE

Ron Adams was a teaching assistant in economics at the state university. He was a reasonably good lecturer, but he felt a bit uncomfortable giving lectures regularly because he remembered how thoroughly fed up with lectures he was in college—even with the good ones! Therefore, he looked for some other way of getting the material across and decided to try small-group learning. He had heard that this required fairly well-informed leadership in each group, so he asked the five best students in his class to meet with him and discuss the process. He told them how he wanted to proceed, and asked them to help him out by acting as group discussion leaders, to which they agreed. He told them what their assignments would be, and later gave them a set of questions for the groups to focus on and to stimulate the discussion. He had the leaders read the material in advance and meet with him initially to iron out any misunderstandings or questions they might have. Then he divided the class into five groups, told them that they would have student leaders, gave them the suggested questions for discussion, and let them go.

At first, it was rather quiet in the various rooms and corners that the groups had chosen for meeting. However, as the first class hour went on, most of the groups seemed to be getting into the process very well. A couple seemed to be dominated by one or two students, while one of the others was evidently getting a lecture from the group leader rather than having a discussion. Ron decided to meet with the leaders again and talk about discussion-leading techniques before the next class.

This meeting with the leaders proved very informative and helpful. They brought out a number of questions which had come up in the groups but which had never been brought up when Ron led the discussion in a large group.

Ron had a chance to discuss processes by which the discussion could be encouraged and kept going, and by which the leaders could prevent one or two people from dominating. He also described some of the tensions and anxieties that might arise from the fact that they were learning in a new way, and might be concerned about how well this would prepare them for tests.

The next two classes went even better, with the discussion groups working very well by all appearances. At the end of the unit, Ron gave a multiple-choice examination and was surprised by the level of the results. The class as a whole did much better than a similar class had done the previous year. One or two students who usually did very well did not do as well; there were also several who usually did poorly but who scored high on this test.

MENTAL HEALTH AND GROUPS

There are ways of making the members of a group friendlier with each other, and less "clique-ish."

One group of social psychologists has developed several postulates about student feelings in classrooms. These emphasize the need for attention to the "mental health" side of the classroom climate (Fox, Luski, and Schmuck, 1966). The first postulate has to do with the attitudes of a learner toward himself (or herself): if he feels that he is liked, valued, and accepted by his classmates, and if he describes himself in favorable terms, then he has what is called "mental health." This concept is discussed in other chapters as "need for esteem" or "good self-concept."

The second postulate is that a pupil's perceptions of reality should be free of distortions. These include feeling that everyone is against you or doesn't like you; feeling that you can't possibly succeed at anything and that failure is inevitable; or feeling that you will always be right and that you don't have to worry about others' feelings toward you, since all are positive. Some extreme distortions were discussed in Chapter 4 in relation to extreme hyperactivity and childhood schizophrenia.

The third postulate is that the learner should adequately meet school requirements for learning, and he or she should also try to establish adequate positive relationships with other students. (While this is a single postulate, you can see that it involves two rather major concerns. To make the learner adequate in meeting school requirements is not an easy thing, and much of Parts III and IV of this book are devoted to that problem, as well as Chapter 4, which you have probably read already. Furthermore, helping the learner establish positive relationships with other students is not a trivial task either, in some cases.)

The final postulate emphasizes the importance of processes whereby the student actualizes his (or her) own potential; it is presumed that if he does not use his potential or abilities well, he must have interference from excessive anxiety, worry, and hostile feelings. This is the traditional point of view of non-behavioristic and non-learning disability approaches to dealing with learners who are having difficulties. "Guidance centers" and counseling personnel in the schools approach school learning problems from this angle. It relates to the types of disorders known as "psychogenic." (These were listed in Chapter 4 as the things that were *not* implied by the term "learning disabilities.") They are also referred to as "emotional disorders" or "emotional disturbances," and professionals usually presume that they are individual problems which must be handled through special services, including counseling in the school, referral to child guidance centers, or referral to various kinds of therapists in private practice.

How to promote self-esteem and self-actualization

In this theory of mental health, difficulties such as interference are attributed to the impersonality and tension of classroom and school learning. Fox, Luski, and Schmuck state some basic assumptions about the effects of the traditional learning environment, which are summarized below.

First, the more diffusely structured the class, the more likely the students are to evaluate themselves highly as people. "Diffuse structure" implies a wide spread of affection among the learners in the classroom, rather than the more typical case where affection is concentrated on a few "stars" and most of the learners are "isolates" or "semi-isolates" (see Figure 6–1). One way for teachers to increase diffusion of affect and thus to improve each learner's self-concept is to downplay concepts of popularity and unpopularity, who is better, who are leaders, who is "no fun" or "dumb" and "nice" or "not nice," and to try to increase the social interaction among students in a way that relieves anxiety about their popularity and social competence.

Their second assumption is that the more highly a learner values himself (or herself), the more he will realize his own potential. This implies that he will study harder and learn more, regardless of the subject matter and his interest in it. Another way to put this is that the learner will find the subject more interesting and have more "free energy" to invest in studying and other activities related to schoolwork, i.e., he will be more motivated. Thus part of the teacher's role is to bring the learner to value himself highly, both through diffuse affect in the environment, and by helping the learner acquire realistic aspiration levels which enable him to succeed and thus maintain a good self-image. (This matter of aspiration levels will be discussed further in Chapter 7 on Motivation.)

The third assumption is that a lack of congruence between a pupil's own attitudes and those he (or she) attributes to the teacher is accompanied by low attraction to the class. Low attraction to the class will be accompanied by low actualization of potential, i.e., low achievement, despite any positive self-image the

A teacher can help a learner to value himself and his achievements.

learner has. This assumption is very similar to one of the principles of group dynamics discussed previously, involving the relationships between school norms and objectives on one hand, and the norms of the group with which the learner identifies. If they are quite different, then the pressure of the group norm acts against the school objectives.

One way to make the class more attractive as a group, and thus to bring the class norms closer to those of the learners and their non-class groups, is to play up the various points of congruence (similarity) between the teacher's and students' attitudes and opinions and to deemphasize the differences. To do this, the teacher needs accurate information concerning things that learners in his or her class like and need, and should plan activities and give rewards in such a way as to improve cooperation and good feelings among the learners. For example, the teacher might gradually work low-status children into roles that are viewed as having higher status.

Another strategy is the formation of a steering committee on which all pupils serve at some time during the year. Fox, Luski, and Schmuck also recommend discussion with students about the nature of individual differences, to increase their tolerance and acceptance of "inequalities." They suggest that the teacher also "model" desired behaviors and attitudes, accepting each student as an individual.

Still another way to deal with student concerns and to diffuse affect in the classroom is through a "Magic Circle." This is a sensitivity-like training approach in which the students sit in a circle, and each student shares with the others some of her or his interests and likes and dislikes. This is done at an early age, when the learners can more easily be trained to accept the interests and feelings of other learners and not to make fun of them. It is related to sensitivity training approaches for adults, discussed in the next section. Generally it reflects an increasing interest in education in teaching learners to accept others for what they are, and to be interested in them as individuals rather than as symbols for status and social power and success.*

How to check diffusion of affect

Figure 6–1 simulates a sociogram that was developed by asking children to list their first three choices of other children to "be with" or "play with." An arrow from one child to another means that the first child chose the second. Arrows both ways then mean they chose each other. A child who has arrows going *only* outward is sometimes termed an "isolate," whereas one who has many arrows coming into him or her is called a "star," and is obviously very popular. The sociogram is typical of those based on actual data and demonstrates the "sociodynamic" law that only a few children are very popular, whereas the majority are less popular than the overall average.

Here Judy is an "isolate," Alice is a "star." This imbalance is less likely to happen, or will be less frequent, if the concepts and attitudes of liking everybody and general equality are encouraged, and if the concepts of being better, or nicer, or winning are not brought up and are ignored when they occur.

Frustration and aggression

Many situations that involve discipline and control problems are the result of covert or overt aggression of one learner against another or several learners against a teacher. A general theory, called the "frustration-aggression hypothesis," holds that aggression is caused mainly by frustration (Horwitz, 1963). If you are frustrated by another person, you see that other person as giving your concerns, wishes, or needs very little consideration or "weight." A teacher may give students' desires

---

* In some school systems parents have objected strongly to "Magic Circle" sessions in which children have disclosed family information that was not for public consumption.

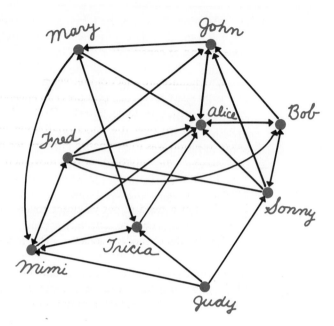

Figure 6–1. *A sociogram of children's playmate choices. Alice is a star; Judy is an isolate.*

either high or low "weight," i.e. consideration. A permissive or egalitarian teacher would probably give high weight to student's needs, whereas an authoritarian one would give them less weight or would give weight to other needs of the student that are perhaps not as immediate to the student himself. Horwitz's theory suggests that aggression occurs in school when the teacher's behavior implies that he (or she) has *reduced* the consideration or "weight" he is according to the students, as compared with what he showed earlier. If you follow this theory to its logical conclusion, you get a surprising outcome, because it predicts that the teacher who stands the greatest chance of experiencing (bringing on) aggression is the one who is most considerate of the students. That is, if you give students' needs and desires high "weight," then you are more likely to run into a situation where you have to reduce that weight, i.e., get tougher, which brings on frustration and aggression. If you are more authoritarian, i.e., give the students' needs and desires less weight initially, then there is less likelihood that you will have to reduce it—you might even be able to increase it later, after you have established control and order. What this implies is that a teacher must be relatively consistent in his or her treatment of students, and that you have to be careful not to establish precedents that you cannot maintain. If you begin by being more considerate in your rules and requirements of students' needs and concerns than other teachers, then you may experience pressure from the other teachers or the administration to change. But if you *do* have to change, you may expect student frustration and probably some aggressive behavior (certainly hostility) as a result.

SENSITIVITY TRAINING

Background of sensitivity groups

There are techniques for teaching people how to be more sensitive to each other's feelings.

Group dynamics are a fact of life, yet people have become concerned with the loss of individuality that group pressures can engender (e.g., Erikson's concern with diffusion of identity in adolescence). During the 1960s and early 1970s there arose a general concern over the impersonalization of our modern society, and a subsequent reaction was to emphasize concern for others and sensitivity to their wants and needs. One outgrowth of this movement was the "sensitivity group," which was based on group therapy processes used with emotionally disturbed people, applied instead to people who were adequately adjusted by conventional definitions but who felt a need to get in closer touch with their own feelings and those of others. These groups became very popular, and constituted a kind of general therapy for the ills of modern society. The processes varied, but some of those frequently used are given below. They are useful for bringing out one side of human interaction, particularly for task-oriented leaders, including teachers, who are less likely to be concerned with such matters. They might also be useful for groups (classes) where the internal friction is high and where diffusion of affect is very low.

"Getting acquainted with empathy"

Form pairs and spend ten or fifteen minutes getting to know the other person in your pair. Then make a circle and introduce yourself to the others, describing yourself in such a way that they understand your likes and dislikes, your strong and weak points, so they get to know you. There is a catch, however; you do not really introduce yourself, but you play the part of the other person in the pair. You introduce the other person, but you do it as if he or she were you—you "role play" that person.

"Sensitivity session in a goldfish bowl"

Form a circle if there are many people, form a smaller inner circle, and a larger outside circle of observers. If numbers permit, in the inner-outer situation, have each person in the outside circle select a person in the inside circle to observe, someone facing them across the circle, with the expectation that they will take that person's place in the discussion later on, and represent his or her role or attitudes at that time. Now set up the following rules for discussion: (1) nothing in the past or the future is to be discussed; (2) the main topic is feelings, i.e., how you feel, and how others feel; (3) you can guess how others feel from what they say and the way they say it, and share it with the whole group. This is the way the conversation gets going, i.e., a person's verbalization of feeling is based either on his own subjective experience right now, or on what he thinks someone else feels according to what he just said or did.   If you have a trained leader for this kind of exercise, he can facilitate the process by getting things started and by setting an example of deducing the feelings of others from what they say and the way they say it (even though the words that he or she uses do not relate to the feeling that others conclude that he or she has).

A CONFLICT OF STYLES

Sue Brown had some very deeply felt principles for dealing with elementary children in school, and when she started teaching in West Herford she began to put them into practice.   The school had a large number of children from families who were less than well-to-do; school was not the children's favorite place, and the general climate of the school was punitive and restrictive. Sue deemphasized the punitiveness and restrictiveness, emphasized relations with the students, tried to get them to do their best and realize their own abilities, and gave them a tremendous amount of consideration, attention, and time. The other teachers very soon let her know that she was on the wrong track, and that the children were to be kept in line and not allowed to talk out of turn or have such a great measure of freedom and autonomy.   The students in her own classes took advantage of the relaxation of tight restrictions more often than

not, although they also responded to her interest and concern.   Sue had a very trying time of it, what with the tremendous problems that many students had, the lack of time to help them sufficiently, the negative reactions of the other teachers, and the rather cold, critical posture of the administration.   She did not give up and was rewarded eventually by having many of her children respond and begin to improve and take more interest in learning.   In some cases she failed, and in some cases she suffered because the children could not handle the process and got out of hand.   At the end of the year she added it all up and found that she had made a difference, and that other teachers in the school were paying her the tribute of trying some of her approaches.   However, she also found that she was "burnt out," and she quit teaching to become an airline hostess.

FREEDOM VS. CONTROL

The school as an extension of society

There is an ongoing debate over how much weight to give to the needs of the individual, and how much to give to the needs of the group—or of society.

So far we have discussed a number of topics borrowed from social psychology, a discipline whose main subject is society in general.   Some of the theories of classroom management and structure have reflected general theories of social management and structure.   One important matter in discussing the structure of society, and thus the structure of schools, is the freedom and autonomy of individuals in relation to the requirements of society upon them and their responsibility to society.   Our political processes deals with this situation all of the time, with Republicans emphasizing the responsibility of the individual to society and Democrats emphasizing the responsibility of society to the individual.

A recurrent theme in debates about education is the degree of freedom—or lack of freedom—of students in our schools.   You can view the learner as someone who is too young to have and use freedom and independence, and justify rather restrictive institutional organization, or you can take the view that the learner should be learning how to function in a democracy, and thus the school should teach democratic processes and foster independence and responsibility by giving the learner as much freedom as he or she can productively use.   Of course, part of the hitch here is how much learners can use "productively" and what "productive" means.

These questions relate to teaching processes and attitudes, to the structure of the classroom and the use of groups and individualized processes, to the diffusion of structure and affect, and to many other matters that we have touched upon.   They also relate to behavioristic techniques of teaching, which will be presented in Chapter 8.   Some of the essentials of this general question and debate are embodied in views of schools and freedom and learning espoused by two internationally recognized psychologists, Carl Rogers and Frederick (or "B. F.") Skinner.

How much freedom to learn?

When you think about whether or not a learner should be free to learn, you will probably conclude that the crucial question is one of relative amounts of freedom and of structure.   Learners should be free to learn, but they should be shown how to learn and be guided in that learning.   Learning experiences should be well-organized but at the same time afford learners enough freedom to make the most of them.   In his very powerful book, *Freedom to Learn* (1969), Carl Rogers described this precarious balance:

> *A part of modern living is to face the paradox that, viewed from one perspective, man is a complex machine.   We are every day moving toward a more precise understanding and a more precise control of this objective mechanism which we call man.   On the other hand, in another significant dimension of his existence man is subjectively free; his personal choice and responsibility account for the shape of his life; he is in fact the architect of himself.   A truly crucial part of his existence is the discovery of his own meaningful commitment to life with all of his being.   If in response to this you say "But these views cannot both be true," my answer is "This is a deep paradox with which we must learn to live."* (p. 775)

One technique that Rogers recommends is building learning processes upon problems that the learner perceives as "real."   He refers to this as "self-initiated learning" that comes about when the individual comes in contact with a problem that he (or she) perceives as the real problem for *him*.   Thus Rogers recommends that teachers, parents, or counselors try to discover what problems or issues are real for learners and relevant to the course at hand, whether they are as simple as the credits to graduate, or *genuine interest* in some aspect of the subject. This view resembles Piaget's assimilation-accommodation theory and foreshadows certain theories of motivation.

The concept of freedom in learning and its application can result in paradoxes. Jonathan Kozol (1972) has described some of these problems in his recent book *Free Schools*. Although he believes in child-centered, open-structured, individualized, unoppressive education, he still has the practical experience and objective vision to say that there is a question about the way in which some people seek to *force* freedom on learners. They can be, as he says, incredibly dogmatic and even manipulative in their determination to coerce the parents of poor children to accept their notions about noncoercive education. Kozol describes two basic but opposite errors that are often made in subscribing to freedom in learning. One is to assume that learning is *never* the result of conscious teaching. (Carl Rogers' statements about teaching have sometimes been taken to imply that this is so, for example.) The other is to assume that learning is *always* the result of conscious teaching. Where conscious teaching is not necessary, Kozol maintains it is ill-advised to teach. When it *is* necessary, but where "in the name of joy and Freedom it is not undertaken," then parents of the children who fail to read as a result have good reason to be angry at the school and teachers who let them down.

Kozol goes on to point out that children emerge from conventional school experiences with a fear of learning, in many cases, and will do everything they can to avoid it. On the other hand, someone who believes that a child will seek to learn to read when he is "ready" or when he "senses his own organic need" can mess up such children badly. These children will need intense help in getting over the fears conditioned by conventional education, and then they will need intense help in learning to read so they can live in our society. Kozol concludes:

> There must be a million unusual, non-manipulative but highly conscious ways of going about the task of freeing children from this kind of misery. There is only one thing that is unpardonable. This is to sit and smile in some sort of cloud of mystical, wide-eyed, non-directive and inscrutable meditation—and do nothing.

This kind of criticism is leveled at practices that are often perversions or misrepresentations of approaches to child rearing espoused by A. S. Neill (1960) and exemplified by the conduct of his famous school "Summerhill." There, learners of various ages are allowed to choose what they wish to learn and how they wish to learn it, or, if they wish, they can choose not to learn at all. Summerhill has sparked great interest and enthusiasm, and much debate. Neill has written a book about the school, and a sequel to it called *Summerhill: For and Against* (Hart, 1970) has also been published. Investigations into the later lives of its students have indicated that the graduates often experience some difficulties adjusting to life, and few of them have found professions other than artistic or creative ones. On the other hand, some of them have evidenced contentment with themselves and "self-actualization" that convince many observers the experiment has been worthwhile.

A. S. Neill at the Summerhill School. (Photo by John Walmsley.)

Is the concept of freedom obsolete?

In an age of free schools and freedom in learning, one philosopher says that freedom is obsolete!

The concepts of "freedom" and "dignity" may be obsolete; that is, the very philosophy that holds these ideals to be basic and essential ingredients of our society may be standing in the way of changes that could solve the population explosion, nuclear holocaust, and world pollution. Can this be so? How can the liberalism that inspires movements to save the world from aggression and pollution at the same time lead to these unwanted ends?

Some solutions to problems are what are called *counterintuitive;* that is, an approach that previous training and experience suggest may actually make the problem worse, or lead one *away* from the solution, whereas an approach that seems ridiculous or dangerous may actually turn out to solve the problem. B. F. Skinner (1971), in his controversial book *Beyond Freedom and Dignity,* maintained that until we develop a technology of human behavior based on scientific principles of control, rather than on obsolete concepts such as freedom and dignity, we are doomed to repeat the mistakes of the past—perhaps leading to our own annihilation. This solution is counterintuitive, in that the way to freedom is seen as one of careful behavior control—but it may be a powerful one. What Professor Skinner proposes is a society in which people are brought to be cooperative and productive, without aggression and war, through carefully designed systems that use rewards rather than punishment.

This is done by arranging things so that productive and desirable behavior leads to rewards, while contrary behavior leads to no rewards. At present it seems evident that many behaviors that are dangerous to the human species are actually *rewarded* by society. Businesses that pollute the environment or produce weapons are profitable; people who disregard the rights and needs of others are rewarded through higher salaries and many privileges. (Of course, this is done in the name of the company, or team, or social class.) Attempts to limit this kind of behavior are dismissed on the grounds that they violate individual freedoms. Thinking that is "humanistic"—that considers the needs of others and stresses "freedom"—leads to a noncompetitive laissez-faire approach that is neither effective in combatting these problems, nor productive in terms of positive outcomes.

What is needed, according to Skinner, is a carefully designed, complex society where actions that benefit all members of society are rewarded and those that are inimical to society are eliminated by being ignored, or, where necessary, meriting punishment in nonharmful ways.

One example relates to the population problem. A government does not actually grant true freedom to reproduce or not to reproduce simply by refraining from restrictions on contraception or on abortion, although it and the people assume that it does. In fact, since it requires both time and money to purchase contraceptives and to pay for abortions, people who are impoverished do not have complete freedom to use these means of population control. They *would* have this freedom if the government compensated them for the time and money. Then whether they used them or not would depend on other factors.

Suppose, however, that a government not only reimbursed people for the time and money used, but also provided *rewards* for using them. One conclusion you might draw is that there would actually be *less* freedom, since people who are in need are not entirely "free" to refuse rewards; they are not as free as they would have been if there were no reward, but only fair compensation.

PROSOCIAL BEHAVIOR, RESPONSIBILITY, AND REALITY THERAPY

The concept of prosocial behavior

Social psychology is concerned with the effects of the group and the environment on the individual, as you have seen in preceding discussions in this chapter; it is also concerned with the relationship of the individual to groups and to society, as

The promotion of socialized behavior, and trying to change antisocial tendencies, lead to a number of theories and therapies.

you have noted in the preceding discussion of freedom. Another approach to these relationships has been taken in the study of moral behavior generally, since moral behavior involves relating one's actions to those of others and to the needs and rights of others. One relevant line of theory and research involves what is called "prosocial behavior" (Staub, 1975). This includes sharing, helping, cooperation, and other behaviors that benefit other people and usually demand self-sacrifice on the part of the person showing the behavior; the sacrifice may be of time, material possessions, the extension of effort or energy, or other things. Needless to say this relates to such classic stories as that of the Good Samaritan, which itself has many of the elements of the conflict involved in such behavior, i.e., the desire to help versus the selfish desire to complete what one is doing or get where one is going. Some early work in relation to cheating behavior (Hatshorne and May, 1928) suggested that there is very little consistency to such behavior (in this case, not cheating would be prosocial), but research since then and a reanalysis of the early data indicates that the consistency does exist and that such behavior can be identified and its precursors analyzed (Staub, 1975). Staub has reviewed research which indicates that responsibility assignment in early life may be important in enhancing prosocial behavior. Young children who are asked to "take charge" are more likely to respond to sounds of distress by another child in an adjoining room; in cultures where children have responsibilities that contribute to the maintenance of the family (tending of animals, care of brothers and sisters) they are also more helpful in other ways than children from cultures where fewer such responsibilities are assigned. Older siblings tend to initiate more helping behavior in response to sounds of other children's distress (even though older siblings appear less sure of themselves in other types of social situations). In terms of group dynamics, it may be that such children are taught a different norm from that learned by children not given responsibility. It is interesting that two children in the same family and society may be treated differently in such a respect, and thus they may learn a different norm of behavior even though they exist in the same family and societal group!

Children also learn social mores by observation; indeed, learning by observation has become identified by the title "social learning." Thus we can explain some of the relationships discussed in Chapter 3 on parental styles and children's personalities, and in Chapter 5 related to teacher characteristics and those of their pupils. Such learning will be referred to in Chapter 8 as "modeling," one of three basic approaches to what is called "behavior modification." However, prosocial learning has also been shown to take place because a child *taught* prosocial behavior to other children (i.e., the child-teacher learned it better), and through participation in group experiences in which prosocial behavior was paramount (some of this related to group dynamics, then, and some to imitation of others). Staub has concluded that parental teaching of such behavior must be accompanied by doing, as well. As he puts it,

> . . . participation in prosocial behavior of sufficient intensity and duration may itself enhance later prosocial behavior, and . . . . induction or verbalization to children may only be effective when it accompanies "doing."

The term "induction" refers to the process in which parents or other adults point out to children the consequences of their behavior on others, including its effect on the adult. The implication is that children need to be controlled to the extent that they are brought to participate in prosocial behavior, in addition to being taught about and observing it.

Maslow's needs hierarchy

One theory of human behavior which puts group processes and influences in some perspective is advanced by Abraham Maslow, who asserted that our behavior is directed and thus motivated by different needs, some of them more basic than others. According to Maslow, the most basic needs must be satisfied before other needs higher in the ladder will become effective, or will determine what we do. Learning for the sake of learning (which many feel is the best kind) cannot motivate us until the many needs lower on the ladder are satisfied. This may explain why we so seldom indulge in learning for itself alone! In respect to groups, one of the

Table 6–1. *Hierarchy of needs according to Abraham Maslow.*

Most basic, must be satisfied before next level motivates behavior:	SURVIVAL NEEDS: Eating, drinking, staying warm, staying alive.
Next most basic, must be taken care of before following level motivates behavior:	SECURITY NEEDS: Knowing where next meal comes from, free from threat.
If the physiological and fear-anxiety aspects of living are taken care of, then the next two levels motivate behavior:	BELONGING NEEDS: Being part of a group or tribe, feeling that others are concerned for your existence.
	ESTEEM NEEDS: Having others concerned for you beyond just existence, desire your company for your own unique qualities.
Only when the two socially oriented needs above have been satisfied do the next two levels become activated, first one, then the other:	NEED FOR KNOWLEDGE: Wanting to gain information, to know about things and how to do things, to understand the meanings of things.
	NEED FOR UNDERSTANDING: Wanting to understand relationships and systems and procedures that are described abstractly; wanting to know how things fit together.
The highest level is activated only when all the preceding levels have been satisfied, including those relating to achievement and intellectuality:	AESTHETIC NEEDS: Need to appreciate and enjoy the environment as it is, to see the beauty in it.

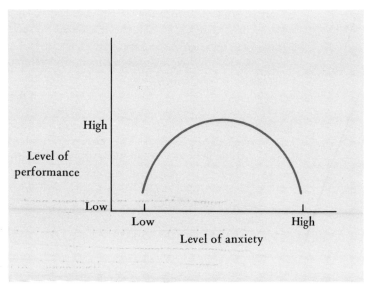

Figure 6–2. *A general view of the interrelationship of anxiety and performance that implies an optimal level of anxiety for best performance.*

more basic (but not most basic) needs is for belongingness, which of course involves others, and provides one explanation for the power of groups and the force of group pressures.   The hierarchy of needs is given in Table 6–1, and it forms a link between some of the discussions in previous chapters concerning individual differences and developmental differences, and discussions of motivation and of theories of learning (Chapters 7, 8, 9, and 10).

Reality therapy, responsibility, and dealing with social behavior

In discussing the theory of Freud, in Chapter One, I pointed out that a neurotic person is assumedly one whose superego is dominant; he or she is inhibited, anxious, and cannot express basic desires, i.e., can't "let go."   Neurosis is by far the most prevalent kind of problem that people experience, although psychosis (domination by the id, or selfish/pleasure/survival forces) is equally serious, and more threatening to society in many cases.   In either situation, the task of the ego is to balance the two forces and achieve a kind of resolution which results in the person achieving what he or she wants without violating society's constraints. Traditionally, as you will see from the discussion in Chapter 7, those who try to help individuals who are maladjusted have assumed that their problems stem from overconstraining superegos or from childhood traumas (bad experiences) which leave them unable to express their own desires and needs; as one commentator has put it, they have been too "good," not bad. Post-Freudian theories have been more socially oriented, in that they have stressed such needs as belongingness and security over and above the basic biological ones (cf., Maslow's hierarchy). One recent approach to helping people which places emphasis on the individual's relationships with others (and thus with his society and group) is called "reality therapy" (Glasser, 1975). Here, instead of freeing a person from inhibitions which stand in the way of normal gratification (as in traditional approaches), the individual is encouraged to improve his or her *social* functioning and thus to win greater love and respect from others. This, of course, emphasizes the "belonging" and "esteem" needs in Maslow's hierarchy, and assumes that the basic physiological needs are generally met adequately in our modern, affluent, permissive society.

Since in Glasser's approach all problems are reduced to ones involving social responsibilities and performance of social behaviors, neuroses and psychoses are treated the same basic way, although the details differ with each case. First, you become closely involved personally with the learner who has problems, so that the learner feels a sense of belonging and concern by others, thus satisfying this basic need. Then you present the realities of the situation to the learner in such a way that it is clear what kind of behavior is needed in order for him or her to achieve the esteem of others, whether it involves giving up alcohol, ceasing to steal, becoming more assertive and less inhibited, or other changes. This matter of esteem is presented as one of responsibility as well, i.e., in order to win others' esteem or respect you have to live up to your responsibilities to others; you cannot satisfy your own needs at the expense of making others unable to satisfy theirs. This also brings in concepts of what is right and wrong, based on the idea that right and wrong are determined by the effects of behaviors on others. This in turn relates back to the problems Kohlberg poses in the process of bringing learners to higher moral levels; these problems might also present a means of bringing about greater learning of "prosocial" behaviors in the manner suggested by Staub.

CARING, RESPONSIBILITY, AND HELEN KELLER

In his book *Reality Therapy* William Glasser uses the example of the initial problems faced by Ann Sullivan in teaching the deaf, dumb, and blind girl Helen Keller. Helen behaved very badly, was terribly spoiled, and as a result, was unteachable. When Ann would make attempts to help her, Helen would run to her parents to gain sympathy and avoid responsibilities. Ultimately Ann had to convince her parents that it would be necessary to keep Helen alone for two weeks in a small house on the farm. During those weeks Ann succeeded in establishing a warm relationship and then bringing Helen to confront her responsibilities. It was done with considerable conflict and frustration and upset, of course, but only through this process was it possible to forge a relationship which would then sustain Helen as she confronted the realities of her situation and tried to do something about them. Glasser suggests that this extreme example of a teaching problem suggests that similar approaches will be successful with problem learners generally: establishing a caring relationship with the learner must then lead to teaching the learner responsibility, and then to bringing the learner to improve his or her social behavior and learning behavior to the point where he or she can win personal esteem and the regard of peers and parents. That this can be done in a group situation, with a difficult class rather than one difficult individual, is the subject of a book and subsequent film entitled "To Sir With Love," in which a young male teacher wins the love and changes the attitudes and behavior of a group of London delinquents through caring and teaching responsibility.

Summary outline with key concepts

☞ *The social* psychology of education is an important but neglected subject / It deals with problems of the needs of the individual versus those of society / It has to do with group processes and forces and influences.

☞ *The nature* of the environment determines individual behavior and personality / One classic study showed how different leader types brought out different group behaviors and feelings / Another classic study showed how group attitudes could be manipulated from very negative (toward each other) to very positive.

☞ *There are* accepted principles of group dynamics, i.e., the nature of the influences of groups on individuals / Teachers should emphasize values in common with students to make the class a group / To be attractive the group must satisfy the needs of its members / To be influential the group must be relevant to the needs of its members / To be influential the leader and group members need prestige / Behaviors incompatible with group norms will be resisted by members / The ways in which the group satisfies needs should be communicated by the leader, also objectives and rationale, if the leader wishes to build solidarity / Group processes cause strains among members; a good leader deals with them / Teaching and learning can be accomplished by forming small groups in the classroom / This calls for planning and structure and a problem-oriented approach to learning / Small-group learning requires good leadership in each small group.

☞ *The teacher* represents requirements of subject matter, needs of students, needs and responsibilities of the school system; these are not always compatible elements / Leaders, including teachers, need to attend to achievement of goals, and also to maintaining group functions / Leaders who combine task-orientation and person-orientation are rare / The nature of the organization determines, to a large degree, the kind of leadership (and thus the kind of teaching) that will be successful.

☞ *Mental health* implies being liked and valued by others and having self-esteem / Mental health implies an undistorted view of reality / Mental health requires success in meeting obligations, including school requirements for quantity and quality of work / Mental health implies the actualization of a learner's potential / Diffusely structured classes and diffusion of affect promote mental health / The teacher should promote the learner's self-esteem / Congruence between teacher and learner attitudes is important for mental health / Diffusion of affect can be evaluated through a sociogram / Reduction of consideration or "weight" given learners leads to frustration and subsequently to aggression.

☞ *Sensitivity training* is an extension of group therapy with disturbed adults; it applies to normal adults, increases sensitivity to the feelings of others / Several exercises or techniques were described, including "getting acquainted," and, "sensitivity in a goldfish bowl."

☞ *Some modern* theorists, including Rogers, feel that learners should be more free to learn, free of structures and schedules and other constraints, and that a person can learn only by discovering things himself—nobody can "teach" him / Kozol points out some of the shortcomings of some "free" approaches to teaching and learning / Skinner asserts that freedom and dignity are obsolete concepts / Neill asserts that the constraints of traditional school are undesirable and unnecessary; children will learn when they are ready.

☞ *Prosocial behavior* can be taught and is a function of altruistic tendencies modified by selfish needs and goals / Prosocial behavior is learned by observation, participation, and "induction" / Social learning has certain characteristics of interest to educators / Maslow's hierarchy of needs begins with basic physiological ones and ends with very abstract, higher-level concerns / Glasser's reality therapy emphasizes our needs for caring/love/belongingness, and for esteem and respect / In reality therapy one becomes involved with a learner (giving her some of the caring she needs) and brings her to face reality and responsibility (thus giving her the respect she needs from others and herself)

Glossary

Congruence: Acting in a way that is compatible with how you feel, i.e., if you are angry, showing it.

Democratic Leader: Leader who seeks the input of members of the group in making decisions.

Diffusion of Affect: Situation where there is relatively little unbalance of liking, where everyone likes most everyone else, not a small group which is very popular.

Empathy: The ability to share others' feelings, to put yourself in another's place.

Free Energy: Energy available to get things done, not tied up in worrying or defending.

Group Dynamics: Ways in which groups exert pressures on individuals, and factors which determine how much force groups exert.

Induction: Learning by having the consequences of some act pointed out.

Magic Circle: A process used in elementary schools to bring out feelings and anxieties and concerns of children, somewhat in the manner of sensitivity training.

Mental Health: A state of balance between id and superego brought about by a strong and effective ego; self-esteem, liking by others, productiveness apply.

Needs: Things which are necessary or important to a person.

Position Power: The power and influence that a person uses or indicates he or she has available to use.

Prosocial Behavior: Helping, sharing, cooperating, benefiting others at some sacrifice to yourself.

Rapport: A feeling of friendliness and ability to communicate that you have for another or for a group, and which is reciprocated.

Scapegoating: Picking on one member of a group as an outlet for frustration or hostility against some outside person or group.

Self-actualization: The realization and putting into operation of your potential and abilities, as compared with hiding them or not using them for various reasons, including being inhibited against using them.

Social Learning: Learning social behaviors, usually by observation.

Socioemotional Concerns: Matters of relationships between people which involve emotions (fear, hope, love, and such).

Weight: The consideration you give another or others; the degree to which their needs influence decisions about procedures and policies concerning them.

Questions for thought and discussion

1. What are the two main functions of a leader in a task-oriented group, including the teacher as leader?
2. What are some principles of group dynamics that can be used to bring about changes in individual members of a group?
3. What provisions would you have to make in order to make small-group learning effective in a class?
4. Are leaders born or made? How are they made, according to information on leadership styles and functions?
5. There is an old saying in teaching, "Never smile until Christmas." Does this relate in any way to the operation of the frustration-aggression phenomenon?
6. What are the basic requirements in a group for producing mental health in its members?
7. How does one bring about more diffuse structure in a classroom?
8. What is a "sensitivity group"? Describe some techniques used in such groups.
9. What is the paradox of modern living, according to Rogers?
10. What fault does Kozol find with free schools?
11. Why is freedom obsolete, according to Skinner?
12. What are the characteristics of prosocial behavior?
13. According to Maslow's hierarchy what is necessary before a person will learn for the sake of learning?
14. What are the two basic needs of every person, according to Glasser?
15. How do caring and responsibility relate to each other in reality therapy?

Situations calling for applications of facts and concepts

1. Suppose you are conducting a Sunday School class, and the children, mostly sixth and seventh graders, are becoming disinterested. You want to build up group co-

hesion and attractiveness. How might you use principles of (a) group dynamics and (b) diffusion of affect to do this? What leadership style(s) would you stress?

2. You have a tenth-grade class that is made up of learners from a variety of backgrounds, and there is very little friendliness and a lot of hostility among the members of the class. Are there any aspects of sensitivity training that might be utilized here to bring about more understanding and friendliness? Any aspects of group dynamics, or of the diffusion of affect?

3. You are dealing with a group of seniors who are very turned off toward school, often hostile, occasionally aggressive. How might you apply some of the basic assumptions of reality therapy to bringing about greater responsibility and support? Any aspects of social learning that could be applied? Approaches to prosocial behavior?

Suggested activities

1. Experiment with some of the approaches to sensitivity groups with other students in the course. Don't go too deeply into feelings, however, because you are dealing with very basic and powerful aspects of personality. If possible, have a professional "trainer" lead the group.

2. If you have access to some younger group, administer a sociogram and discuss the results with the group leader.

3. Form a class or group for the purpose of experimentation, and take turns leading the group in some activity; do it according to different leadership styles: authoritarian, democratic, laissez faire. Note differences in your personal reactions to these styles, and in the reactions of others.

4. Form an experimental group and set about to assure diffusion of affect in this group through the processes suggested in the book. Note how this works out, whether or not you have trouble doing some of the things required, and whether everyone feels that this is worthwhile.

Suggested readings

One good compendium of readings in the social psychology of education is a book edited by Miles and Charters entitled *Learning in social settings*. Another helpful short book is Miles' *Learning to work in groups*. You may also want to follow up a number of the references given in the chapter.

7

Theories of Motivation

CONTENTS

ABOUT CHAPTER 7

How this chapter can benefit you

Success in motivating comes from having a number of techniques and knowing when to apply them. This chapter will give you a number of ways to motivate learners. It will also give you the ability to recognize a number of types of existing motivation, so that you can take advantage of all possibilities. It may also give you some ideas as to how to motivate yourself to higher achievement.

What might make this difficult to learn

Strangely enough, the study of motivation is not the most motivating thing in the course, in spite of the fact that it is so important and useful. This is sometimes because people have their own well-formed idea about how to motivate students, sometimes because those who haven't tried to teach unmotivated learners assume that motivating is not a problem. Experienced teachers know, however, that it is *the* problem, but they often reject alternate approaches because they conflict with their personal philosophy or they don't resemble ways of teaching that they have tried or experienced. We suggest that you keep a very open mind on motivation. Some of these approaches may come in very handy someday, with students or your own children or in other special situations.

Reasons for studying motivation

Some of the reasons have been listed above. Motivation is often the major problem in teaching: if students won't try to learn, all the planning and clarity and preparation and support you give won't make much difference. Another reason is that the more approaches to motivation you use, the better chance you have of succeeding.

Objectives for this chapter

I want to give you some tools for getting learners to invest effort in learning, to want to learn, and to be interested. To do this, I have to present a number of different points of view. I want you to know about these positions so that you can utilize them over the years ahead, even though you don't apply them all immediately.

BACKGROUND AND RATIONALE OF CHAPTER 6

Why study motivation?

You can lead a horse to water, as the old saying goes, but you can't make him drink. This chapter deals with getting learners to "drink." When you set out to teach someone you often assume he or she wants to learn, but "it ain't necessarily so." One psychologist who set out to find what prevented poor learners from learning (what they couldn't do, what their learning disabilities were) found instead that they were trying to avoid learning, even though they were perfectly capable of it: they didn't want to be ostracized by their friends or looked upon as different by their parents! Thus, the study of motivation is important because it gives suggestions for bringing learners to be interested in learning and to want to learn and to invest effort in learning.

What is motivation?

Q₁

If Johnny studies, then we assume he is "motivated" to do so—motivation is a hypothetical construct of our minds to explain what he actually did. Johnny may have desired to pass, to avoid flunking, to learn about the subject, to please his parents; he may have had to overcome a desire to fall asleep, watch TV, listen to the radio, go out with friends; he may have had to overcome a fear of failing, or not being able to understand, of having his foot fall asleep, or of missing something good on the tube. Behaviorally, motivation is the same as doing something: doing

You may learn something about motivation by pairing the proper caption
to each of the drawings above.
1.   *"Who wants to leave early?"*
2.   *"Who brought a pencil?"*

evidences motivation.   Cognitively, motivation is a cluster of ideas that give direction to behavior, e.g., "It's important to study to get ahead," or "If I flunk Dad won't come through with my allowance."   Emotionally, motivation is likes and dislikes and wants and fears.   Socially, motivation is a desire to approach some things and to avoid others, or it is aspirations to goals where some things are more desirable than others.   Let's look at some theories of the origins of motives.

Genetic pattern theories

One view is that motivation is built into everyone through heredity, as the result of evolution.   The love motive, for example, is a necessary one for survival of the species, because we are very aggressive and we need some protection against killing our own families and friends (Lorenz, 1965).   Unaggressive animals such as sheep do not show "love," while lions do.

Homeostasis and motivation

If your body becomes too hot, you sweat; the evaporation of the sweat from your skin uses energy, thus cooling your body.   If your body is cold, you feel like rubbing yourself and moving; this process converts food and body fat into energy, which warms your body.   These are homeostatic mechanisms; that is, mechanisms designed to regulate your body temperature and keep it static, or unchanged.   There are similar homeostatic mechanisms related to the nervous system, social behavior, and motivation (Hebb, 1949).   For example, a group of college students was paid to undergo a stimulus deprivation experiment in which they were shielded from all incoming stimuli—visual, auditory, etc.—and did nothing but lie on a comfortable bed with optimal constant temperature.   After a while they were so bored they found market reports on the radio quite fascinating.   (Aside from research, stimulus deprivation has been found to have positive effects on certain neuroses and psychoses, and is being used as therapy.)   In terms of cognitive balance, Piaget's view of equilibrium is homeostatic, i.e., he asserts that a learner faced with an optimal discrepancy (one he cannot quite assimilate) will accommodate through changes and syntheses in cognitive schema, and will arrive at a new equilibrium

Drives

Motivation can be ascribed to basic "drives," hypothetical conditions that result in activity.   Some are primary, such as hunger, thirst, and sex, while others are secondary, i.e., built on primary ones, and substitutes for them.   For example, art is a redirecting or "sublimation" of sexual drives (Freud, 1949).   Instead of pursuing sexual objects, an artist might paint them or some abstract representation of his emotions instead.   Your behavior is the result of a balance between selfish, survival-oriented drives and inhibitions which avoid uncomfortable or painful outcomes experienced in the past (Chapter 1). There are other drives, not all biological ones, that have been proposed as well; sometimes they are posed as "needs." The basic idea is that when a drive or need is satisfied, the learner comes to expect that kind of resolution again, and this expectation becomes a "motive."

Secondary drives are conditions or situations that have become associated with primary drives, and thus have become motives themselves. Becoming associated also implies becoming substituted, so that where a primary drive cannot be fulfilled (such as a desire to dominate others for one's own selfish purposes) then a secondary one associated with it takes its place (e.g., forming social relationships of various types where one achieves goals through reciprocal arrangements such as teams and unions, "going steady" and such).

Socially based theories

As was mentioned in Chapter 1 and again in Chapter 6, early emphases on biological needs and drives have given way to emphasis on social concerns and needs. Murray's list of needs has been described in Chapter 3, and Maslow's hierarchy of needs in Chapter 6. Such needs have been called "psychogenic" to differentiate them from biological needs. From a teacher's practical point of view it opens up questions of how to deal with learners who have a strong need for affiliation, power, or achievement. In one study, for example, researchers found that in a ninth-grade group of boys with above average intelligence those who were academically successful were higher in need to achieve while those who were unsuccessful were higher in need for affiliation (Ringness, 1965). Two other studies have also shown that students with high need to achieve are more likely to attempt to succeed at learning tasks, and particularly at discovery learning (this is described in Chapter 13) (Wendt, 1955; Evans, 1967).

Educators of Maslow's persuasion are committed to self-motivated activity and learning achieved by satisfying higher-level needs (need to know, and to actualize one's potential) instead of basic needs (security, food, avoid danger, and such). Unfortunately, many parents and teachers emphasize avoidance (flunking, for example) and dwell on the dangers of life and minimize its attractions (this may apply to warm, restrictive parents as discussed in Chapter 3). Maslow points out that people act to get rid of deficiency needs, but *seek* the pleasure of "growth" needs. The satisfaction of deficiencies leads to a sense of relief and satiation, according to him, but the satisfying of growth needs leads to pleasure and a desire for further fulfillment. (Growth needs include learning and understanding, aesthetic needs, and self-actualization.) According to this theory deficit-motivated people are dependent on others, while growth-motivated people are independent and problem-centered.

There is another "need" theory which also rejects the notion that motivation must be attributed to basic biological drives. Consider early behaviors like visual exploration, crawling, and attending; these aren't motivated by hunger or thirst, but by the fact that they enable us to interact effectively with the environment. The term "competence" has been used to describe what these behaviors have in common. Competence is based on playful and exploratory activities that have direction and persistence, although they aren't directed toward satisfying some "deficit" (White, 1959). A similar point of view is that curiosity and exploration are basic needs of the human learner (Berlyne, 1966). The last two theories suggest that one motivates learning by presenting things to master and explore that excite the need to be competent and things that arouse curiosity or enable one to explore. Maslow's theory suggests that one motivates higher processes by satisfying the lower needs. These are not incompatible theories, of course; perhaps one needs to satisfy the basic needs, then present situations that lead to mastery or exploration.

The motivation engendered through competition is related to competence motivation. Most of us are spurred to greater achievement when we see others getting ahead of us; participating in an individual sport such as tennis or golf releases or spurs great effort during the game and when practicing for it ahead of time. Team sports combine this motivation of competition with group dynamics: the individual tries harder in order not to let the team down as well as to succeed or win for himself. The use of competition in teaching has good and bad sides. It is one

Table 7–1. *Satisfying deficiency needs.*

- Make sure the learners are not hungry, that they don't have to sit too long, that the room temperature is conducive to learning.
- Be sure that the room is safe and the learners feel safe in it.
- See to it that classes afford students an opportunity to participate actively, but that recitation is not threatening; don't force participation in activities until the students are ready.
- Be sure there is no humiliation or embarassment; some students may be recovering from past experiences of this kind and need an extra promise of security.
- Make learners feel as if they belong by learning and using names as fast as you can.
- Keep records for individual pupils and refer to specific accomplishments, so that children feel that their work is recognized individually.
- Enhance the attractions and minimize the dangers of learning.
- Don't penalize guessing on examinations; don't impose restrictions or conditions on assignments if they will hurt the learner's enthusiasm and effort.
- Demonstrate the values of learning and the disadvantages of not learning, without emphasizing the negative or punishing effects of not learning.
- Plan direct learning experiences so that they bring feelings of success.
- Failure is subjective; make it clear to a learner that he or she has succeeded even though his or her level is not as high as that of other students.
- Encourage learners to improve on their previous performance, without setting up unrealistic aspirations.
- Encourage development of the desire to achieve and use of it where it exists.

From R. Biehler, *Psychology applied to teaching,* 2nd ed., Boston: Houghton Mifflin, 1974.

way to bring learners to try harder, but on the other hand cognitive learning does not always lend itself easily to a game format. Sometimes the game is pursued at the expense of real knowledge or understanding.

Early environment antecedents of motivation

If you raise monkeys with surrogate mothers they often show more fearful and neurotic behavior and are less motivated to explore and to socialize and to learn (Harlow, 1959). If you raise young rats and handle them frequently, they will have higher activity scores as adults than rats who have not been handled (Dennenberg, 1963). Motivation is a function of how you are raised. Different kinds of parent treatment make a difference in personality and motivation, as discussed in Chapter 3. So some motivation is "built in" by the time the learner is ready to learn in school, and part of the parent or teacher's task is to bring out what is there. This calls for variations in techniques.

Self-actualizing teaching

In a very interesting and useful book designed to help teachers grow themselves, Angelo Boy and Gerald Pine (1971) made some suggestions for what they call "self-actualizing teaching" designed to improve mental health. They observe that to "actualize" his or her own potential, a teacher, counselor, or learning specialist needs to become an "expanded person." Such a person thinks well of himself, is honest with himself and with others, thinks well of others, and is concerned with the welfare and enhancement of others. He sees the value of mistakes and is not afraid to move forward; he trusts his own feelings and intuitions, and he is therefore more creative than someone who just reacts to his environment. As a result of these characteristics, when he becomes involved in some teaching relationship he is able to develop effective communication with one or more students. This happens partly because he is able to listen to the students and deal with their needs and concerns. He sees them as unique individuals with their own potentials and understandings. He provides a learning atmosphere which is free of ridicule, attack, or moralization, and which enables the student to be himself and to express his ideas, concerns, and doubts. Such treatment of students encourages them to assume responsibility, motivates them, involves them in their own growth process, and makes them feel understood. It also promotes both self-discipline and an ability to engage in problem solving without feeling anxious or threatened.

These characteristics appear to reflect the characteristics of good teachers described in Chapter 5 and the person-oriented aspects of leadership described in Chapter 6.

A self-actualizing teacher is involved and encouraging.

MOTIVATING BY REMOVING EMOTIONAL BARRIERS TO LEARNING

Rationale for dealing with emotional barriers

One source of difficulty in learning is found in emotions and feelings which can weigh a learner down, distract him, make him feel incompetent, and generally provide barriers to the effective use of his learning abilities. Some approaches to dealing with these problems by spreading positive affect and increasing sensitivity are discussed in Chapter 6. The traditional approach to dealing with emotional disabilities that prevent learning is psychoanalysis or psychotherapy; a more recent outgrowth of these approaches is what is called "nondirective therapy," also "reality therapy." It is important for educators to understand the basic concepts on which these helping techniques are based, because they will often be involved with

Like a satellite in space, you will keep going if there isn't anything to slow you down; so to motivate, eliminate the resistance.

learners who have emotional problems and need help, or who are in the process of receiving such help.   Parents and teachers can deal with such problems, when not extreme, through a number of approaches, including reality therapy (Chapter 6), nondirective conferences (described below), behavior modification and behavior therapy approaches (Chapter 8) and the Dreikur's approach (Chapter 8).   In serious cases, of course, parents and teachers and other in-school specialists will only render "first aid," and they will refer the learner to an appropriate clinical specialist.

Analytic psychotherapy

In analytic psychotherapy the therapist attempts to help his (or her) patient retrieve experiences from his (or her) subconscious memories that are troubling him and may be affecting his current behavior.   The patient has to expend considerable "psychic energy" to keep these memories repressed in his subconscious mind, and this detracts from his ability to function adequately in his job or in school.   If the basic causes are not confronted and recognized, according to the underlying theory, then maladaptive behaviors will occur and continue.   The therapist attempts to bring these memories to the conscious level, enabling the patient to confront them, and thus to release the psychic energy used to suppress them.   When the therapist probes the subconscious of the patient, however, he risks having the patient transfer some of his suppressed aggressions and resentments (i.e., some of his blocked basic urges, or "id" forces) to the therapist himself.   Indeed, this "transference" is part of the therapy process, and is expected and allowed.   Ultimately, however, the therapist attempts to put the patient on his own by bringing him to a state of confidence in his own ability to handle his problems.

Psychoanalysis

Freud discovered that if a patient simply let his (or her) mind roam and then reported the associations that emerged, patterns would be revealed that he would not have discovered any other way.   Free association and dreams became means by which the patient's unconscious thoughts were discovered.   The psychoanalyst interprets these associations and dreams.   He (or she) does not confront the patient with them until the patient is ready, however, and usually brings the patient to confront them himself.   However, the patient has inner barriers to these confrontations to avoid the pain that will result from confrontation.   For example, he may talk about trivial things at some length to avoid confronting significant ones.   People who use terms like "honestly" and "really and truly" a great deal may be avoiding being honest and true with themselves.

Psychotherapy, chemotherapy, group therapy

Psychotherapists differ from analysts in several respects—they may prescribe drugs, among other things. They concentrate a bit less on giving insight and more on giving guidance and support than psychoanalysts do. Chemotherapists use drugs primarily, and they do not deal with insight or guidance. Antidepressants are one type of drug used extensively. They enable patients who are depressed and who cannot function adequately to resume their jobs and lives generally. Group therapy is a treatment where a patient is also a therapist to his fellow patients. Under supervision, a group will discuss troubles and both give and get support.

Nondirective therapy

Nondirective therapy emphasizes the function of the therapist as a mirror of the patient's mind. The therapist provides an accepting, nonpunitive, warm atmosphere for the patient, and the effect is gradual improvement of the patient's self-concept and the patient's discovery of the nature of his own difficulties. It is assumed that this improvement in self-concept and self-understanding is reflected also in the more adaptive behavior of the patient in everyday life.

An important factor in nondirective counseling is the behavior of the therapist. He (or she) is continually trying to provide an accepting audience for the patient and at the same time trying to avoid acting like a "phony" by pretending that the thoughts of his patient do not affect him emotionally. This leads to a search for what Carl Rogers (1969), the founder of this approach, has called *congruence*, i.e., behavior that is simultaneously accepting of the patient as a human being, yet representative of the therapist's honest reactions to the patient.

NONDIRECTIVE THERAPY/BEHAVIOR THERAPY: EITHER-OR, OR BOTH?

A nondirective approach. Mary is very anxious about her ability to deal with social groups: she gets very upset when at a gathering—at a party, or during intermission at a concert, or such. She decides to seek help, and she goes to a therapist at the counseling center. The therapist—a woman—asks her to talk about the problem and listens very attentively and sympathetically. Occasionally she nods, and once in a while she rephrases something Mary has said about what she is afraid of or what makes her happy or unhappy. Mary feels very warm toward the therapist, although she doesn't have a feeling of learning anything or "getting any-

where" during the first session, and she promises to come back. During the second session, she begins to tell more of her feelings and thoughts about other people. The therapist encourages her to go on talking, again reflecting back to her some of the thoughts that seem relevant to the problem. Mary begins to realize that she is actually causing a lot of the anxiety herself; when she hears herself describing the problem, it begins to come into better perspective. The therapist also helps her focus on important aspects of her anxieties and concerns, by rephrasing more of her verbal descriptions, and by going even further to suggest an alternate meaning to what she has said. As Mary continues to examine her own feelings, with the therapist's help, she begins to feel some release from anxiety. At one point she has tears in her eyes as she tells the therapist that her fears and anxieties are not that real and that she is obviously putting herself down without reason by feeling inadequate. After this session, she feels much better about herself. This feeling lasts for a couple of days, but soon she feels a need to repeat the experience and regain the good feelings that she had about herself. As time goes on, however, Mary is able to maintain a good concept of herself over longer periods of time, and she loses some of the fear of being with others.

A behavior-therapy approach. Mary is quite anxious about her ability to deal with social groups. She gets very upset when at a gathering—at a party, or during intermission at a concert, or such. She decides to seek help, and she goes to a therapist at the counseling center. The therapist—a woman—asks her to describe her problem, and listens very attentively and sympathetically. Occasionally she nods, and once in a while she asks a question about some particular situation that makes Mary very tense. Then, after Mary has told the therapist most of what she can remember about the problem, she asks whether help is possible. The therapist asks her to come back the next day, after she has had time to work out an approach to Mary's problem.

The next day she returns, and the therapist brings in two or three other people, and hands Mary a script. This looks like a play: it has parts for Mary and for the other people, and it portrays a scene at a cocktail party in which Mary is talking to one stranger, discusses a few unimportant things with that stranger (in a dialogue, the stranger taking part), then excuses herself to "see someone she hasn't seen for a long time," and goes on to another stranger and introduces herself. At first, Mary has a hard time reading her lines, because they seem so foreign to her own natural inclinations. However, the therapist praises her for reading some parts well, and ignores her hesitation in other lines. The people acting the other parts are very warm and seem very interested in her also. After they come to the end of the scene, the therapist again praises Mary for getting through it, gives her a few moments to catch her breath, tells her of some of the things she needs to keep in mind (mainly an air of confidence) and then has her play the part again. Praise is a bit more frequent this time, but as Mary does this several more times, the therapist begins to reward (praise) only the best of Mary's lines, and ignore some of the others which she would have praised during the first phase of training. Gradually, then, Mary becomes able to carry on extended meaningless cocktail-party conversations, and she is able to leave one person and go on to another without feeling apologetic or guilty—and without actually becoming involved in any of the people she talks to. She is obviously better adapted!?

CHANGING A PERSON'S MOTIVATION

Some motivating processes derived from research

Twelve practical methods for getting people to do things, based on many different kinds of research.

David McClelland has identified a number of possible ways by which people may be motivated to change (McClelland, 1962). These processes are potentially useful to anyone who wishes to bring about changes in people, whether young students or adult businessmen. Here are his methods, or "propositions," with some of the reasons based on his review of the research.

Goal setting.   McClelland's first proposition is that the more reasons a person has to believe that he or she can, will, or should do or become something, the more likely he or she is to bring about such a change.   He notes that this is supported by research on the effectiveness of prestige and suggestions on attitudes, the "hello-goodbye" effect where patients who make one visit to a prestigious doctor or therapist are cured without any actual treatment, and the effects of parents who set high standards on the achievement motivation of their children.

Reasoning.   The second proposition is that the more an individual perceives that developing a motive is consistent with the demands of reality and reason, the more likely you are to change him or her.   Supporting facts are that national arguments help change attitudes, that knowledge of legal realities or presence of detaining forces does modify racial biases, and that the recognition of reality is a dominant aspect of human thought and the last to "go" in psychosis.

Conceptual clusters.   The third proposition is that the more thoroughly an individual develops and clearly conceptualizes the network of mental associations (relationships, meanings, comparisons, thought processes) that make up a motive, the more likely that individual is to develop the motive itself.   People will do things they wouldn't ordinarily if you tell them "this is a game" or "this is an experiment"; this is referred to as "mental set."   We change our behavior if we adopt a new role (i.e., mental set), as when you become a parent or a teacher or a policeman.   In traditional psychotherapy a patient is taught to produce mental associations that may be threatening to him, e.g., to recognize his difficulty as related to the Oedipus complex, and to "work it through" in a way that establishes a new set of associations and meanings for his memories and experiences.   McClelland suggests that this explains the effectiveness of nondirective therapy, because *directive* therapy merely teaches new labels while nondirective therapy brings the patient to form new networks of associated ideas and relationships with the area which is causing concern.

Relating thoughts to actions.   In proposition four McClelland asserts that the more a person can link new networks of associations and ideas to related actions (i.e., to the behaviors that express them and by which others recognize the presence of the new motive), the more likely both thoughts and actions are to occur and the longer they will endure.   Research in human learning shows that recitation is important to verbal learning and social-psychological research shows that overt commitment to participation in actions related to attitudes makes for changes in attitudes.   Case study approaches to learning have proved very effective in business schools where new attitudes are put into practice and subjected to the test of real business pressures after graduation.

Relating associations to life.   According to proposition five, the more an individual is able to link the network of associations (which constitute the cognitive aspect of the motive) to events in the everyday life of that individual, the more likely the

Group participation and dynamics can motivate the learner.

complex of thoughts is to influence his or her thoughts and actions *beyond* the environment or situation in which he or she is learning them.   Part of the conventional psychotherapy involves working through and clarifying new meanings and relationships in relation to old memories, recent events, dreams, and hopes of the future.

Seeing change as an improvement.   Proposition six points out that the more the individual can perceive and experience newly conceptualized motives as an improvement in his or her self-image, the more the motive is likely to influence his or her future thoughts and actions.   For example, hypnotists can get a person to do things which are a bit "far out" if they can make those things seem consistent with the person's self-image or values.

Seeing change as an improvement on the existing culture.   The more an individual perceives a change as an improvement on prevailing cultural values, the more likely he or she is to change (proposition seven).   Church associations, ethnic ties and standards, and peer group influences all may conflict with the concepts and associa-

tions which come with the new motive; these potential conflicts need to be resolved so that they won't weaken the motive later on.

Getting a commitment.   If a person commits himself (or herself) overtly through
some action to the goals or outcomes which the motive implies, then he is more
likely to follow through on the change (proposition eight).   Salesmen know that if
they can get you to pledge something or sign something or take the first of a series,
you are more likely to follow through on a purchase.

Keeping a record of progress.   If a person keeps a record of progress toward a goal,
i.e., toward the adoption or change to some new motive, then he or she will be
more likely to complete the change (proposition nine).   Research in learning demonstrates the importance of concrete feedback or knowledge of results.

Warmth and support.   Proposition ten says that a change in an individual's motives
and attitudes is more likely if the environment is characterized by warmth, honesty,
support, and respect for that individual.   Research in attitude changes suggests that
the less manipulation that is attributed to the experimenters, the more likely they
are to get changes (Hovland et al., 1953); nondirective counseling and therapy
places great emphasis on this kind of climate as conducive to successful changes in

"Actually, it's an effective motivator, and the retention hasn't been
all that bad."

the individual (Rogers, 1961); the lower the anxiety, the better the achievement and performance for certain types of people (Sarason et al., 1960).

Arranging the environment.   The more the setting dramatizes the importance of self-study and lifts the study out of the everyday routine, the more likely changes are to take place (proposition eleven).   Most modern therapy and change programs take place in retreats; there is less likelihood of interference from other concerns and ideas, and more support from the people involved if they are alone.

Using group dynamics.   Proposition twelve suggests that the more the new motive is established as a sign of membership in a new reference group, the more likely it is to be maintained and have effect.   The establishment of "cells" is a traditional approach to organizing parties (communism) and spreading religions; the importance of the reference group in maintaining motives and attitudes is generally well established.

Using the twelve propositions to motivate learners

It is one thing to know a theory, and another to utilize it in teaching, parenting, or in special helping professions.   Here is a list of applications that could be made based on these propositions; some others that have been used experimentally (based on propositions three and four) are given later.

Creating confidence.   Bring to bear prestige based on previously successful teaching, therapy, testimonials from former students or clients.   Describe concrete goals that learners will achieve, such as "you will be able to read a French newspaper" or "you will be able to cope with _____."

Giving reasons.   Point out that the course is required (if it is,) or that it is important to know the content in order to do something else that is worthwhile, or because it is fundamental to living generally, or that the therapy process has rational and experimental support.

Teaching thoughts that motivate.   Discover the mental associations that differentiate between good learners and poor learners, then teach those associations or thoughts to the poor learners; e.g. "Drive and determination lead to success," or "It's important for future success to do well in English," or "Knowing about your own body is very important."

Linking thoughts to action.   Show learners what motivation means in terms of actual behaviors: hours of studying, taking an interest in certain kinds of things, finding material in the library, showing interest in others.

Relate the course to life.   Point out how the local countryside reflects geology; how existing vocabularies use Latin or Greek; how you use mathematics every day, including the typical thought processes; how learning goes on beyond school.

Improvement in self-image.   Show students that knowing Subject X will improve them in their ability to get along, to relate to others, to make an impression, to look intelligent, etc.; utilize the social status of attractive members of the class; show how improvement will make them more attractive.

Make improvement a cultural advance.   If the local rotary club or coaches' group or trade union should endorse your course as important, or if a relative of a student indicates that the subject is important to the goals of the ethnic or socio-economic group, it will take on new importance.

Get commitment from the learners.   Get them to start on something, studying, practicing, or whatever; get some verbal commitment to a level of excellence or an amount of work in a given time, or both (possibly by a contract;) get a commitment to being more effective or less impulsive.

Demonstrate progress.   Keep charts on individual students, so that they can see how they are progressing; use other methods to emphasize the progress of the class and the individual (note: this doesn't mean give lots of quizzes).

Give warmth, honesty, and support.   This has been dealt with in Chapters 5 and 6.

Make the classroom a retreat.   If you are teaching French, make your classroom seem a part of France, and have French things up on the walls, have a French routine for beginning and ending class, etc.; if you move from classroom to classroom, or from individual student to individual student, bring your "props" along; run therapy sessions at someone's home or summer cottage, over a weekend.

Deal with cultural values.   Know your learner(s) well enough to know when you are treading on thin ice with ethnic or cultural values, and turn them to a positive use by avoiding clashes and emphasizing those which are most compatible with your needs; show how outcomes are compatible with peer group norms or religious values.

EVERYTHING BUT THE KITCHEN SINK

Mr. Anderson has been doing some research on theories and applications in motivation, and he decides to see what he can do to increase motivation in his classes in psychology. So, for a unit on learning, in which he intends to discuss different theories of learning and some of the research done on learning, he "goes for broke," and incorporates every motivational process he can think of.

First, he spends a couple of class periods

previewing the subject, and trying to make clear to the students what it will be like to have learned this material: how it will make them understand certain things better, what kind of problems they will be able to solve using it, how it might relate to their future careers, and how it will help them "hold their own" in a conversation about human behavior. Then, after this, he gives them a breakdown of the unit in terms of possible goals and objectives within the larger goal that he has set, and he asks them to choose some of these subgoals. They are set up in terms of level of difficulty, amount of work to be done, and grades that can be earned by certain combinations of amount of work and level of difficulty. For example, a student can see that if he does one paper and a project satisfactorily, plus passing an examination at the high difficulty level (i.e., with questions of high difficulty), he can earn an A; however, with another combination, he can earn a B, and so forth. The amount of time within which this is to be accomplished is given: students are encouraged to write up a contract stating how much and what level, and they are allowed to revise this contract if after a week they find they are not going to make it—or if they can do more than they thought. Then, on the principle that variety in experiences is motivating, Mr. Anderson schedules a variety of experiences for class meetings, including lectures, demonstrations, discussions, films, field trips, games, laboratory experiments, and visiting speakers. However, he has a backbone of regular experiences around which these events are built, i.e., the main process is a fairly regular classroom-homework assignment routine which the students can depend on and which gives them security and lets them know what to expect.

Having done some research on psychologists and students of psychology, Mr. Anderson has a list of typical thought patterns of motivated people in this subject. He gives the students a workbook that teaches them these thoughts by having them complete stories about people who think the thoughts. He also refers to them often in classwork in relation to topics that are being presented or discussed. One of

the thoughts, or thought patterns, for example, is related to interest in the causes of human behavior, and can be stated something like this: "The study of human behavior is important if the human species is to survive." Another is "The proper study of mankind is man."

Mr. Anderson also has studied the behavior patterns of psychologists, and he provides laboratory experiments and field-trip problems that are of the type which not only turn the students on, but which call for behaviors typical of psychologists. For example, he shows the students an experiment that compares the learning of rats in a maze who have been fed to rats that have not been fed. They do the experiment to try to find out whether the fed rats who explore the maze without paying much attention to the food at the end learn as much as those who are hungry and explore to find the food. Mr. Anderson sets up the experiment in such a way that the students succeed best by demonstrating the behavior patterns typical of psychologists—and he provides guidelines which make it apparent to the students how to succeed.

While Mr. Anderson is carrying out the various activities, including lectures and demonstrations, he models (makes himself an example of) interest in the subject matter, motivation to learn, and behaviors that are typical of motivated learners. He also provides a supportive atmosphere for learning and achievement, by permitting the students to learn independently and to become actively involved, and by warmly encouraging them in their learning experiences. He accepts them as people, while at the same time reacting honestly to their responses, pointing out both strengths and weaknesses in their ideas and their approaches to the subject. Occasionally, he cracks jokes or expresses displeasure over a student's lack of concentration or application.

At intervals during the unit, Mr. Anderson takes time out to discuss the goals again, making them clear, and he also discusses various problems about studying the subject that he has found students to have in the past—problems of personal hang-ups about studying human behavior, ways in which the study of behavior can threaten somebody (for example, studying learning could be threatening to someone who suspects he has a learning disability, although this could motivate interest also). He also takes some time to get the learners to express their feelings about the course and about him as a teacher, not only to get feedback on his own teaching, but to bring them to confront any concerns and feelings that may be inhibiting them and making it difficult for them to learn in the course. He often finds that some of the potentially best students have the strongest hang-ups about certain parts of the course. One type of difficulty he tries to bring out, in case it is present, is moral and ethical problems related to such topics as reinforcement theory and behaviorism in the study of learning. Some students have trouble learning reinforcement processes and conditioning as a form of learning because their religion or ethical training causes them to reject such approaches to human characteristics. Occasionally he has individual conferences with students who have this kind of problem, and sometimes it turns out best to have them change courses if they feel strongly enough, but this does not happen often. Mr. Anderson tries to make the class become a group, with its own norms and functions, through emphasis on field trips and meetings outside of school time, as well as through unique procedures and topics discussed in class. Sometimes he has the students as a group study the behavior of other students, or other teachers, without advertising the fact that this is going on. This gives an in-group

feeling. On the other hand, where topics or points of view clash with other groups' norms that are very strong, such as norms that view massed practice (cramming) as a valid and desirable approach to studying for exams, he takes it very easy and presents both points of view so as not to make it difficult for them to handle the accompanying attitudes or necessary to reject the class in favor of the other group. Mr. Anderson also pays homage to other important groups and activities in the school, being aware of them and knowledgeable about them, as well as knowing individuals in the class by name and something about each of them as well. He does not try to be one of the students; rather, he tries to be knowledgeable in his profession, which includes students as well as subject matter.

In matters of discipline, Mr. Anderson encourages a positive view by commenting on productive behavior—primarily in terms of the behavior rather than the person doing it—and ignoring unproductive or disrupting behavior as far as possible. He tolerates a certain amount of noise and confusion as long as it is productive, but firmly restricts unproductive or counterproductive behavior and talk. He grants freedom for good behavior fairly often, by giving students a chance to talk freely at random toward the end of the period if things have gone well. If things are not going well, or the class is disruptive or noisy, he does not reinforce the behavior by letting them go, but insists on order being restored before the class is dismissed.

An example of applied research related to proposition three

Proposition three states that you can change (increase) motivation by having the learner acquire new or additional thoughts and concepts associated with the motive. An example of how this can be done is found in a method developed by Alschuler and his colleagues to teach people how to "think achievement."

In this research, examination of data from projective tests identified ten thoughts which characterized achievement-oriented persons. Once the ten thoughts were identified, special stories were made up which used the ten thoughts

Here are two ex-
amples from a
teaching method
designed to make
learners want to
accomplish more,
i.e., to raise their
motivation.

in consistent order.   Then students were given these stories to read.   After they had read several complete stories, the remaining stories were left incomplete.   The students completed the stories, using the thoughts themselves in a carefully planned context.   Students completed more and more of each successive different story, so ultimately they were writing a complete achievement-need story themselves.   Writing such a story demonstrated their knowledge of the ten thoughts.

The ten thoughts to be learned (i.e., the associative network that constitutes the need-achievement motive) are as follows:

- NEED—Person expresses a need that is unfulfilled
- PO—The person identifies some personal problem or obstacle that prevents him or her from fulfilling that need (personal obstacle)
- WO—The person writes of an obstacle which comes from outside himself or herself (world obstacle)
- FOF—The person expresses some fear of failure (fear of failure)
- FaF—The person recalls how he or she felt when failure occurred in the past (failure feeling)
- ACT—The person visualizes some action that can be taken (Action)
- HELP—The person conceives of help coming from source to get him going or to get him over one of the obstacles
- HOS—The person expresses some hope for success (hope of success)
- SuF—The person anticipates how it will feel to be successful (success feeling)
- AIM—The person imagines how it will be to have succeeded (achievement imagery)

Here is one of the stories.

GREG*

SuF represents the thoughts a high achiever has after he has succeeded. HOPE OF SUCCESS (HOS) is the feeling and the thoughts a person has about the possibility of success in the future. HOS sometimes involves the person in very detailed ideas of what his achievement will be like and how it will feel. Fill in the sentences for HOS, SuF, and AIm in the story of Greg.

Maybe it was foolish, Greg thought, but making a good set of walnut bookends had come to represent the most important goal he'd ever had in his life. (NEED) He'd have to call his life completely happy—good school marks, good parents, good home, lots of good friends—if it weren't for his unbelievable clumsiness. (PO) His gym teacher called him "Tanglefoot" and his shop teacher called him "Thumbs." (WO) None of it bothered him much until he started as a volunteer at the Brawley Street

* From *Ten Thoughts,* an element of the *Achievement motivation series* by Alfred Alschuler, Diane Tabor, and James McIntyre. Middletown, Conn.: Education Ventures, Inc., 1970. Reprinted by permission.

Youth Center, praying each day he wouldn't fall apart in front of the little kids who needed someone to look up to. (FOF)   Then he managed to butcher a woodworking project where it hurt most; right before the eyes of Tommy, a pathetic kid who was always trying to cover up his fear and hunger by mocking everyone around him. (FaF)   Greg talked fast: "Tommy, I'm going to make you a beautiful set of bookends, and then we'll get you some books of your very own." (ACT)   Because Tommy believed him, Greg arranged a crash course in woodworking with old Andy Svensen, a master craftsman. (HELP) _____

_____

_____ (HOS)

_____ (SuF)

_____ (Alm)

Since students have completed several other stories previously, they are able to complete this one as well, showing that they have "mastered" or "learned" these last three thoughts well enough to utilize them in a new situation.

An example of applied research related to proposition four

You have read about the thoughts of achievement-oriented people.   There are also *behavior* patterns typical of people high in this type of motivation.   The most important of these behaviors are:

(a) Prefers to have responsibility in the choice of goals, i.e., to choose goals themselves rather than have others set them for them.
(b) Bases aspirations on past performance.
(c) Likes frequent clear information on progress, i.e., feedback on how she or he is doing.

As part of the training process designed to increase the achievement motivation of students in junior high schools and high schools, Alschuler and his colleagues devised games which simulated certain aspects of business achievement.   They designed the rules in such a way that there was the highest pay-off or best chance of winning if you behaved according to the characteristics listed above, i.e., the games were "rigged" so that achievement-need types of behavior would "pay off." For example, in one of these games the learners participate as if they are manufacturing a certain type of spaceship for the government   The spaceships are made by folding paper, much as you make a paper airplane.   Participants in the game are shown how to make the ship, and then given a chance to make another one while being timed.   In this way they get information about their capabilities in making these ships.   Then they are shown a table of figures indicating how much they have to pay for raw materials for the ships (i.e., pieces of paper to fold), how much they will get for each ship they make (up to a number which they later specify in a contract they sign), and of course the profit they will make on each one.   By playing this game many times, with slight variations in the kind of thing made, students learn to write contracts to produce things on the basis of their initial performance in trial runs.   Thus they learn to have realistic aspiration levels.   Since they are choosing the goals themselves, they become accustomed to this process as well, and they learn to expect immediate information on how they are doing.   Thus, by playing this game many times, they learn to behave like achievement-oriented people: this means that they are more likely to behave this way in other situations of the same type.   Since they are more like people who are achievement-oriented, they have *become* more achievement oriented.   Thus, we can say that their basic motivational structures or patterns have been altered!

Motivating isn't just being warm and supportive, or just being organized, or just recognizing individual differences: it is applying a number of strategies simultaneously.

Motivating through thoughts, or behaviors: Which?

McClelland's answer to this question is "both"—you motivate people by affecting their thought processes *and* by changing their behaviors.   Neither is sufficient without the other.   When you come to study behavior modification and behavior therapy in Chapter 8, then, remember that it is one important side of dealing with learners, but not the only one.

MOTIVATING—OR DEMOTIVATING—THROUGH GRADES

It is very easy to criticize grades and to find a number of reasons why they should not be used.   However, few theorists or practitioners have developed successful systems to take their place.   This may be partly because grades are so well established in our educational system, and parents and teachers and administrators are accustomed to using them and dealing with them.   It may also be because motivational systems which do not use grades have failed.   What are some of the pros and cons?

Grades come much too late to have effects on the important behavior, which is studying for the next day's class or studying for a quiz or an examination.   On the other hand, as long-range threats and/or rewards grades show who can work for delayed gratification (older learners, higher SES learners, learners who have been trained to work for delayed rewards).   Grades are often awarded on the basis of systems that require some of learners to be unsuccessful (curves, distributions): this guarantees failure and thus frustration for some.   The author had a friend who labored mightily with a class of unmotivated and low-ability eighth graders with unusual success (compared with previous teachers).   His motivation to go on

Grades seem to be here to stay, but they aren't the motivators some teachers assume they are.

teaching and their motivation to go on learning was severely impaired, however, when at the end of the first grading period he learned that he could not give anyone in the class a grade higher than C−, because the whole school was on a "curve" and that class had low-ability students!   (We will talk about "curving" in Chapter 15.)   On the other hand, if everyone is graded for effort, then an A or a B does not represent knowledge of the subject, since two students may put in the same effort and learn quite different amounts.   We can go on with the pros and cons for hours: what does research say about grades?

There is a short book by Kirschenbaum, Simon, and Napier which discusses the grading problem in an interesting fashion and gives a complete annotated bibliography.   Kirschenbaum and his colleagues quote research which suggests that the better students are motivated by grades (i.e., success) while poorer ones are apt to have lower aspiration levels as a result of their low grades or occasionally, unrealistically high ones (Kirschenbaum, Simon, and Napier, 1971).   The famous eight-year study of high school students who were free of the usual requirements of college entrance (grade levels, courses, etc.) showed that they did as well in college as a matched group which had traditional high school requirements, but this doesn't mean that the experimental group received no grades at all (Chamberlin et al., 1942).   Past grades predict future grades, but the one-third portion of the variance they explain is still low.   Grades seem to have little relationship to job or professional success.   As one investigator has put it, considering the importance of grading for both students and instructors, it is regrettable that there is so little empirical research on it (McKeachie, 1963).

THE EFFECTS OF FAILURE AND SUCCESS ON MOTIVATION

There has been a fair amount of research on the effects of success and failure on motivation.   Generally, researchers have concluded that success and failure affect learners differently according to their previous success and failure.   If a learner has been successful regularly, then failure is liable to spur him or her to greater effort, just as you found that a challenging approach to teaching is more effective with higher SES (and higher ability) learners (Chapter 5).   On the other hand, if a learner has failed repeatedly, failure will decrease his or her motivation, just as a challenging or a traditional approach to teaching was found to be ineffective with low SES learners (Chapter 5).

One effect of repeated failure is to warp a person's aspirations: the effect can be either of two extremes.   Either the person aspires to an impossible goal (thus opening up an excuse for further failure, and protecting self-esteem), or the person aspires to a very easy goal that is a "sure thing" (again protecting the learner's self-esteem) (Atkinson, 1958).   Achievement-oriented people aspire to goals within their reach, as determined by their own past performance; they protect their self-esteem by picking out a reasonable and fairly sure goal (Alschuler, Tabor, and McIntyre, 1972).   These facts imply that you can recognize a person who has failed repeatedly by his or her aspiration levels (too high or too low), and that you can teach a person to succeed (and motivate him or her thereby) through teaching him or her to aspire to goals that are reasonable for the individual in relation to past performance.

Failure, and fear of failure, are more often demotivating than motivating.

Learners avoid failure by a number of strategies.   One is to avoid evaluating oneself: if you don't look at the results, you can't find out you have failed.   Another way is to associate with other people whose abilities are lower than yours, so that you are always above the standard of the group.   Still another way is to choose only very easy or very difficult tasks: very difficult tasks make failure more likely, so you aren't so obvious or exposed if you fail.   Still another way is to avoid participating in things where you might fail, and finally, you can reject responsibility for failure (rationalizing by blaming fatigue, bad luck, etc.).   If a learner can't avoid a failure situation, however, he or she may become resigned and apathetic; children who have been punished regardless of what they do show this tendency, and sometimes come to a state of autism where they withdraw from any social contact with others. Most learners, however, are caught up in a circle of events where they fail if they participate, but not participating leaves them out and is something to be avoided as well.

Teachers can reduce failure by avoiding situations where learners are held to a common standard, by having them compete against their own best efforts in the past, for example.   They can also reduce stress on success in competitive games, emphasizing the teamwork that is necessary and the value of every participant to the team, even making up rules which enhance the value of participation.

MALCOLM AND FAILURE

Malcolm had some difficulty learning in the first grade. His problem was due to poor eyesight, but this was not discovered until later. He became identified as a poor learner, and didn't get much encouragement from his teacher. In the next grade he was put in a special group for low achievers. The teacher was rather negative toward the students because she didn't like having a slow group; however, she tried to help him and the others. The result was that the only reward for trying was the end of the session or the end of school. Malcolm gradually became completely turned off to school, because it was associated with failure and negativeness. His parents amplified this problem by putting more and more pressure on him to do well in school, and this increased the fear until he couldn't bring himself to do anything about it, even when he was given a special tutor who tried to "bring him around" and make him enjoy learning.

Motivation as a topic in other chapters

Motivation is a broad subject: entire books have been written on it. This chapter introduces it, but it is not the only place in the book you will find related concepts and theories.   For example, the concept of presenting an optimal discrepancy introduced by Piaget is a motivating process.   Giving learners problems appropriate to their cognitive stage is also.   Theories of moral and social development have implications for the kinds of treatment and settings that learners will find motivating. Allowing for individual differences in anxiety, creativity, and learning style will have effects on motivation.   Teaching in ways that bypass learning disabilities, and simultaneously working to strengthen such weaknesses, will improve motivation. The characteristics of a good teacher, discussed in Chapter 5, can be viewed as the characteristics of a motivating teacher.   Spreading affect, reducing cliqueness, and utilizing group dynamics generally are methods of motivating groups described in Chapter 6.

In subsequent chapters you will study various aspects of behavior modification; those are motivating processes as well.   There is a chapter on problem solving, and posing problems can be a motivating strategy.   Then, in Chapter 11, many aspects of the management of teaching/learning situations are reviewed, all related to motivation, and "motivation" as a topic is reviewed also.   In Chapter 12 the various operations which constitute "teaching" are reviewed, and these relate to motivation as well.   The use of media and systems to improve and give variety to teaching is discussed in Chapter 12, and this has its motivating aspects.   Finally, in Chapter 13, types of tests are discussed: you know, in some ways unfortunately, that one of the basic motivators for learning in schools is the challenge—or threat—of tests.

Summary outline with key concepts

☞ *Motivation is* important in teaching and learning / If someone learns, or does something else, you can say he or she was motivated / One theory is that motivation is inherited / Another theory is that we are motivated to preserve accustomed levels / Another theory attributes motivation to basic drives / Socially-based theorists see motivation resulting from social needs / Some theorists view motivation as representing a need for competence; others see motivation as resulting from early experiences / Teachers' motivations are important: some are motivated by a need to actualize their own potential.

☞ *Emotional problems* provide barriers to learning; removing them is motivating / Psychotherapy and psychoanalysis are traditional approaches to dealing with emotional problems / Nondirective therapy is another approach to use for emotional problems.

☞*According to* one theory basic motivation can be increased; other theorists disagree / There are a number of ways of bringing individuals to change, and thus of motivating them: setting goals, giving reasons, teaching new thought networks, linking thoughts to action, relating thoughts to everyday life, seeing change as an improvement in oneself, seeing change as an improvement on cultural values, getting a commitment to change, keeping a record of progress, providing warmth and support, providing a retreat setting free of interference with change, invoking group dynamics.

☞ *There are* practical ways of applying the ways listed above, including creating confidence, giving reasons for change, teaching new thoughts, teaching new behaviors, relating change to life, improving the learner's self-image, relating change to cultural advancement, getting commitments from the learner, demonstrating progress to the learner, giving warmth and support, making the classroom a special retreat setting, and relating the course to cultural values in a positive way / There are examples of methods for changing thoughts and behaviors.

☞ *Grades are* motivators, but not as motivating as some would assume, and they have some demotivating effects.

☞ *Failure and* success affect motivation, but the effect depends partly on the individual's past record of failure or success / Learners who fail repeatedly need support and help and success; failure discourages them / Learners who succeed regularly need a challenge; failure spurs them on / Learners who fail repeatedly choose unrealistic goals, either too difficult, or too easy / One way to change failure to success is to teach the learner to aspire to goals that are realistic in terms of his or her previous performance.

Glossary

Achievement Motivation: Motivation to achieve, not for power or for money or for respect, but for the sake of achieving itself.

Behavior Therapy: Therapy for emotional and behavioral disabilities which uses conditioning processes, not insight into past experiences.

Competence: The state of being competent; a need or psychogenic drive that leads to efforts toward mastery.

Congruence: Behaving in a way that is compatible with one's feelings and convictions.

Curve, Curving: Ranking scores from highest to lowest and then assigning grades according to percentages, e.g., top 7 percent gets an A, etc.

Drive: Condition leading to activity or effort, i.e., which motivates; some are biological, some are psychological.

Homeostasis: Condition in which mechanisms act to maintain a certain level or state, as when the body reacts to maintain a consistent internal temperature.

Insight Therapies: Therapies that place emphasis on the importance of cognitive understanding of the past events and current situations which cause the problem.

Need: A psychogenic drive or motivator, e.g. the need to be loved.

Nondirective Therapy: Therapy in which the patient discusses his or her own problems, encouraged and assisted by the therapist, and as a result comes to solutions to his or her own problems.

Psychogenic: Things that are psychological or cognitive in nature, rather than biological or behavioral; e.g., anxiety.

Retreat: Environment free of interference from everyday concerns.

Questions for thought and discussion

1. Give several ways of defining motivation.
2. Give several basic theories of motivation.
3. How does the concept of "homeostasis" apply to motivation?
4. What is a "drive"? A "secondary drive?" Give examples.
5. What is a "need?" How does it differ from a "drive?"
6. What are some of the needs common to all learners? (review Chapter 6)
7. What do "competence" and "curiosity" theories have in common?
8. Are there any drawbacks to using competition for motivating learners?
9. Give some examples of early environment antecedents of motivation.
10. Describe "self-actualizing" teaching.
11. How do emotional disabilities relate to motivation?
12. What do psychoanalysis, psychotherapy, and nondirective therapy have in common?
13. Describe at least five approaches to changing people.
14. Which tactic would you use to motivate, changing idea clusters or changing behavior patterns? Why?
15. Do quizzes and examinations demonstrate progress, and thus act as motivators?
16. Were group dynamics mentioned in relation to motivation? How? Does this resemble the treatment of groups in Chapter 6?
17. What do HOS and FOF mean? How are they related to motivation?
18. What is the point of filling in stories like the one about Greg?
19. What are the disadvantages or weaknesses of grades as motivators?
20. Does failure result in increased effort, and under what conditions?
21. How does repeated failure affect aspiration level?

Situations calling for applications of facts and concepts

1. Select a grade level and subject matter for teaching, and describe how you would incorporate the following motivating strategies into that teaching process: competence, removing emotional barriers, giving hope of success, teaching thought clusters, teaching behaviors. Point out where any one of these strategies might be incompatible with any of the others, if this occurs.
2. Select a grade level and subject matter for teaching, and describe how you would incorporate the following motivating strategies (all in the same general process:) curiosity, goal setting, record of progress, warmth and support, retreat setting.
3. Select a grade level and subject matter for teaching and describe how you would incorporate the following motivating strategies (all in the same general process): creating confidence, giving reasons, optimal discrepancy (Chapter 2); nondirective therapy for emotional barriers; showing how learning will improve the learners' self-images.

Suggested activities

1. Observe a course at some level in some subject, and identify motivating methods used; also describe some that could be used but were not.

2. Work with someone who is teaching, and advise him or her on ways to improve motivation, then observe to see whether the methods you suggest (possibly several of them) work.

3. Offer a mini-course in some subject that is usually considered not very interesting, and incorporate a number of the motivating processes given in this chapter. See whether you can make the material interesting.

4. Apply the strategies and theories of this chapter to some way-out situation like getting people to give blood, or to recycle paper, or to practice birth control.

Suggested readings

A historical review of four theories of motivation is found in *Theories of motivation* by Weiner, published in 1973. There are other books on motivation which you can find in a card catalogue. Perhaps because motivation is such a broad and inclusive subject (and concept) it is difficult to suggest particular readings related to it, other than those referenced in the chapter. Almost every topic in learning and teaching relates to motivation in some way.

PART

III

LEARNING
AND
INSTRUCTION

8

Theories of
Behavior Modification

CONTENTS

ABOUT CHAPTER 8

What this chapter can do for you

Studying this chapter will provide you with the means to give learners new feelings and attitudes or to remove fears and anxieties; it will show you how to teach learners new behaviors, how to reshape old ones, or how to get rid of them; it will show you how to teach behaviors and feelings simply by exemplifying them, and how to avoid teaching things that you don't want them to learn. Then you will have the means of motivating learners by modifying their behaviors, their emotions, and to some degree their thoughts. The processes you will learn have been referred to in earlier chapters, but not discussed in detail. You will also acquire some insight into possible ways of changing society beyond the limits of education.

What might make this chapter difficult to learn

This chapter represents a scientific approach to teaching and learning; this may be contrary to your view of teaching as a humanistic, helping profession. It deals with the control of human behavior; this may cause you some anxiety or make you want to avoid it. It takes a deterministic view of human behavior, i.e., that behavior is determined and that one can find the causes and control them. This leaves out willpower and responsibility and freedom, as was mentioned in Chapter 6. You may object to such a point of view, and you might argue that what I have said in previous chapters about locus of control and responsibility in respect to good teaching contradicts this view (Chapters 3 and 5, also 6). This chapter will deal with methods of discipline and classroom management based on "reinforcers"; many people see these as equivalent to bribes and feel they are out of place in schools, while others fear that their use may ultimately kill motivation (although it increases it in the short run).

Some reasons for studying behavior modification

The processes described in this chapter work, and that is a good reason for understanding them and being able to use them. They have some negative implications or dangers for society, and it is best to understand those dangers and to be ready to cope with them, rather than hiding your head in the sand. They have some positive implications not only for schools but for society generally. Finally, they are modern expressions of some age-old, well-known ways of dealing with human behavior. Every teacher would know how to use these processes, then decide individually when and where to apply them.

Objectives

To introduce learning processes as a basis for understanding teaching and therapy, and for recognizing them when used, and so that you may utilize them to improve teaching, parent/child relations, and various kinds of therapy.

RATIONALE AND BACKGROUND OF CHAPTER 8

Rationale

Behaviors are indicators that learning has taken place. You can't go inside the learner's head to see what has happened. you have to observe him or her learning indirectly through responses to questions and approaches to solving tasks just as Piaget did in analyzing cognitive development (described in Chapters 1 and 2). In order to deal effectively with behaviors, you have to notice what goes in (input, stimuli) and what comes out (responses, behavior). Then you have to deduce from these facts how you can go about changing behavior in a predictable, desirable way. This is a scientific approach to human behavior and to teaching.

Learning and teaching defined

What is "learning?" It is a change in the way a person perceives his environment or in the way he responds to it, or both. Learning is not achievement, or ability: it is a *change* in ability. It is recognized by a change in the way a person does something or accomplishes some task.

What is "teaching?" It is any process whereby you change or arrange the environment of a learner so that learning is more probable than it would be otherwise. You can arrange both the antecedents to a response (the environment) and the consequences (what happens as a result of it). Presenting problems, lecturing, showing a film, and taking a field trip are all "arrangements" of the environment. So is giving a learner a piece of candy or patting him on the back for a correct response.

The learner's environment includes both external and internal things: a classroom, hunger, a warm bath, a headache. (The internal aspects are often overlooked in teaching.) Considering the external environment, you have to focus on specific parts which are often referred to as "stimuli." Actually, stimuli are occurrences that affect the learner's senses: sights, sounds, smells, and the like. Physical stimuli are therefore sensory inputs to the learner from the environment, like sounds, light rays, pains (internal in some cases), and smells. There are also psychological stimuli (patterns of physical stimuli that a learner perceives as a whole), like a chair, a horse, a musical chord, a melody, a shape. For a long time, for instance, investigators of child development have assumed that babies perceive only confusion in their early days. It is becoming evident, however, that they actually perceive features of their environment more accurately and clearly than we thought. Thus, there seem to be some patterns (psychological stimuli) that we have the capability of perceiving very early, whereas others (like shapes, faces, objects) have to be learned through experience.

Another important word is "behavior." Behavior involves stimuli from a particular person; when we perceive or hear a person, our interpretation of what he is doing is his "behavior." A response is some part of a person's behavior, such as his saying, "How are you" when we say "Hello" to him.

Responses defined

There are three general types of responses. The first has several names: operant, psychomotor, enactive, physical, or voluntary. Examples are waving, pushing, kicking, looking around, speaking, running, and throwing. The second type of response is called classical, or emotional, respondent, affective, involuntary, or reflexive. Examples are love, fear, anxiety, and the action of involuntary reflexes such as an eye-blink or knee-jerk. The third type of response is not observable but is inferred from patterns of the other two types. Its names include cognitive, thinking, mediating, associating, and mental. Examples are picturing a horse when someone is talking about one, hearing a word in your mind when you read it silently, calculating an arithmetic problem in your head, making mental notes of something, or thinking ahead to what you are going to do next.

Acknowledgment of contributions

The theories explained here are in a large part the result of the thought and experimentation of two men: Ivan Pavlov, in classical conditioning, and B. F. Skinner, in operant conditioning. The recent contributions of Albert Bandura in relation to vicarious conditioning ("modeling") should also be acknowledged. If the references in this chapter seem somewhat thin as compared with others, it is because these areas of research and theory are part of the very foundations of modern psychology. To reference and acknowledge each individual contribution to the theoretical structure would be impractical, just as it would be inappropriate to reference and acknowledge every contribution to mathematics in a basic text on that subject.

CLASSICAL CONDITIONING AND ITS APPLICATIONS

Classical conditioning theory

When you receive an electric shock, you feel pain; you cringe or react in some way that is involuntary and unlearned, and you also experience involuntary internal reactions. Suppose someone were to flash a light and then shock you. If he did this several times, you would come to feel an anticipation of the pain when the light flashed, before the shock. You would feel anticipation even if the shock were not given. This is a classically conditioned response: it is involuntary, emotional, reflexive, or respondent (to mention a few titles). The conditioning involved the simultaneous occurrence of the shock (an unconditioned stimulus) and the flash (a conditioned stimulus after the pairing, but neutral before it occurred). This is the way we learn fears, hopes, likes, and dislikes, emotionally speaking, by having previously neutral stimuli paired with ones that provoke those reactions naturally.

This is about how you learn and unlearn fears and how you learn to like things also.

Classical conditioning was first demonstrated by Ivan Pavlov in the 1920s. He experimented with a hungry dog; the unconditioned stimulus was food powder placed in the dog's mouth, and the unconditioned (involuntary) response was salivation. The conditioned stimulus (initially neutral) was a buzzer. By pairing the buzzer and the food powder a number of times, Pavlov found that he could get the dog to salivate in response to the buzzer alone.

If you use the conditioned stimulus (buzzer) without the unconditioned one (food) frequently, the response will decrease in strength. This is called "extinction." To prevent extinction from happening, you have to bring back the unconditioned stimulus every so often. Bringing it back to maintain the response to the conditioned stimulus is called "reinforcing the conditioned stimulus."

Teaching an emotional response

To bring someone to respond emotionally in a certain way in a certain situation, first find another situation or stimulus that already elicits that emotional response. Then arrange things so that the situation (the unconditioned stimulus) follows or accompanies the stimulus you want to elicit the response. Do this a number of times, then withdraw the one that already brought the response, i.e., present the new one without the old, and note whether or not the response occurs.

An example of this is teaching a child to fear fire. If he sees the fire and then touches it, he will experience pain; the next time he sees the fire he will experience a facsimile of that pain as he begins to reach for it. Contact with the fire is the unconditioned stimulus, and sight of the fire and reaching for it is the conditioned stimulus. Pain is the unconditioned response, and anticipation of pain is the conditioned response.

This diagram is designed to give you an understanding of the temporal relationships involved in classical conditioning. In this experiment a dog is placed in a harness (to keep it from running away) and then a shock is administered to some part of its body. Just before the shock is administered, a buzzer is sounded. After this happens several times, the dog begins to show reactions to the buzzer (trying to get out of the harness, whining, and such) which are similar to those that it has to the actual shock. We assume that there is an internal reaction or "response" to the shock that sets off this behavior, and this internal reaction is a "classical" or unconditioned or involuntary response. The lines below show the sequential occurrence of the buzzer, the shock, and the internal reflex response to the shock in the initial phase of the experiment.

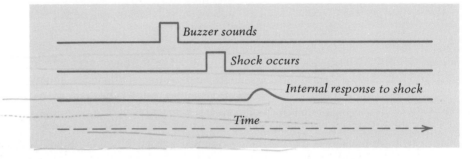

The next diagram shows the same buzzer, but without the shock occurring (the dotted lines show where the shock did occur before); notice that the internal response has changed in position, and now it occurs immediately after the buzzer. It is a "conditioned response" now, since it has been "learned;" the buzzer is now a "conditioned stimulus," where previously it was neutral in its relationship to the internal response. Since the internal response is an anticipation of the shock and its effects, we might call it "fear of shock," or "anxiety over shock."

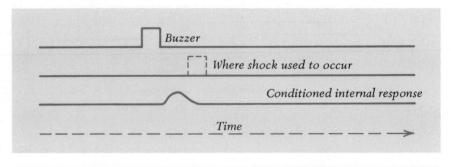

Figure 8–1. *Time-line diagram of classical conditioning.*

As another example, suppose you shout at a child when she is reaching for a toy, and scare her. The next time she sees the toy, she will experience an anticipation of that fear. Unfortunately, since you also shouted, she may also experience fear when she sees you again.

CLASSICAL CONDITIONING AND MADISON AVENUE

Semi-precious stones are relatively neutral as far as inspiring emotional responses goes, at least for some people. However, when a page of pictures shows nearly nude men and women wearing nothing but amethyst jewelry—and engaging in passionate embraces of near-pornographic connotations—then some of the emotional reaction engendered by those poses becomes associated with the jewelry. Amethyst becomes, at least temporarily, a sex symbol! Associating (pairing) cigarettes with the open country of the West is another example of this use of conditioning. Advertisers use classical conditioning broadly and directly. Its power is evidenced by the results, which in turn are attested to by the money spent on the advertising!

Advertising's use of classical conditioning (photo by Elizabeth Hamlin).

Getting rid of emotional responses by extinction

To get rid of an emotional response, arrange for the situation that elicits the response to occur a number of times without the stimulus that originally brought the response, i.e., the original unconditioned stimulus. For example, if a student fears a learning situation, say a mathematics class, because failure or punishment has occurred in that kind of class in the past, then arrange things so that he experiences it without failure or punishment. As another example, suppose a child fears lightning because of the crash of thunder that follows it. On a warm summer night let her see far-off lightning without hearing thunder, or a film of lightning without sound; her fear of lightning will decrease after this happens several times.

Extinction through successive approximations

To eliminate an emotional response that does not yield to simple extinction, as above, develop a list of situations that begins with some events that are only slightly similar to, or very weak forms of, the feared one, and that get closer and closer to the feared one as you go up the list. Extinguish the fear to the one which is least like it, then to the next, approximating the problem situation more closely as you go through the list, and extinguishing it at each stage. For example, if a student fears hour-long exams but is only slightly bothered by quizzes, then expose him to short quizzes, then longer ones, and so forth, without failure or unpleasantness.

Counterconditioning

Another way to reduce an emotional response is to accompany the painful situation with a stimulus that gives a response opposite to the one to be reduced. For example, if a learner is very fearful in a situation where a specialist is trying to help her with a learning disability, the specialist might try involving her with toys or games that she likes, or playing music that she likes, or both, to counter the negative emotional reaction.

Desensitization

Emotional responses are classical or involuntary responses. One of the most common classical responses that you deal with in teaching—and that you experience yourself—is the emotion of fear. If you are afraid of something, it is probably because you have been conditioned to be afraid of it. However, you don't necessarily remember how this came about. If you were conditioned to fear many things early in your life, then these have probably generalized to a fear of almost everything; this is called "general anxiety." When a person fears some particular thing or situation, in contrast to being generally anxious, then it is not an easy matter to reduce this fear; however, the fear may be causing the person a great deal of distress and inconvenience, and sometimes such fears threaten the effectiveness of a person in his or her job, or as a parent or husband or wife.

If you are afraid of something, you can't talk yourself out of it; you have to be counter-conditioned or de-sensitized.

One technique that has been found to be effective in such cases is called "de-sensitization." It uses the imagination of the learner to bring him or her into "contact" with the feared situation, and it does this in very carefully planned steps rather than dealing with the situation all at once. Here is how it works.

The patient (the person with the fear) and the therapist first discuss the fear, but they also discuss other things that the patient fears, particularly ones that are in some way similar to the primary thing. The therapist looks for ways by which he or she can help the patient develop a hierarchy of feared things with things that cause only slight fear at the beginning or bottom, and things that cause the most fear at the top. There are two basic ways of developing such a hierarchy: one way is to deal with the feared situation but at a distance, either physical or temporal. For example, if you are afraid of snakes, you might put the thought of "a small snake one hundred feet away" at the bottom of the hierarchy, and "a large snake right next to you" at the top of the hierarchy. The other approach is to deal with things similar to the feared situation first; for example, you might start with thoughts of "a small worm" at the bottom, with the thought of "a make-believe snake" in the middle, and "a real snake" at the top of the hierarchy. Naturally, you can combine these tactics, having things slightly similar and at a distance, and things very similar and closer at hand.

Once you have determined a hierarchy that seems to have possibilities of success, you get the patient to relax. This usually involves a comfortable reclining chair, perhaps some soft music in the background, and relaxation exercises. These exercises have been developed to teach people to relax on command, and ultimately to relax when *they* tell themselves to relax. They consist of muscle control exercises in which the person tenses certain muscles as much as possible and then relaxes them (i.e., "Make a fist, and squeeze just as hard as you can and hold that tension until I say 'relax'; hold it; hold it . . . now relax."). Through these techniques the therapist gets the patient quite relaxed, and then asks the patient to imagine certain things. He (or she) begins to describe some of the situations that have been put at the bottom of the hierarchy. He tells the patient to lift a finger if he feels any anxiety due to the imagined scene; if the patient lifts a finger, showing that the imagined scene makes him anxious, the therapist changes the subject, and gradually works back to it again later, meanwhile making sure that the patient becomes relaxed again first. When the patient is able to imagine the lowest scene on the list without anxiety, the therapist introduces the next, and so on.

This seems like a long process, but in comparison with more traditional kinds of therapy for such fears and compulsions (see Chapter 7) it is relatively short and generally quite effective. After being able to imagine without anxiety the situation which was feared initially, the patient is sometimes able to deal with the actual situation without becoming upset. In other cases, it helps to introduce the real world gradually, through a series of approximations in reality rather than in imagination.

CURING JEANNIE'S FEAR OF TESTS

Jeannie is an eighth grader who has somehow acquired a very bad case of "test anxiety." Whenever she takes a test, she "blocks" on everything she knows. Fortunately, or perhaps naturally, there are not many tests in her courses. Science stresses laboratory work, mostly using a discovery-oriented technique, and language arts calls mostly for writing, reading, and reporting in various ways, with very little grammar. However, in social studies she has a teacher, Mrs. Jones, who used to be a history teacher at the high school and feels that it is her mission and contribution to the junior high to "get these kids ready" for high school—which is not a bad idea in itself, but since she gives a lot of stiff tests, it is killing Jeannie.

The counselor talks with Jeannie at some length and tries to find out what originally conditioned this fear. Jeannie cannot remember ever *not* being afraid of tests, but thinks it might have had something to do with the time when she went to school feeling slightly ill in the sixth grade, and threw up in class during a test in social studies. It was only a short test, but after that Jeannie said she did not do well on tests and this failure made her problem worse. The counselor discussed these concerns with her, and then spoke to her teachers, asking them if they could arrange for Jeannie to be tutored some other way.

Since the other teachers were generally pretty well-organized and gave few tests anyway, some of them were able to stretch the process a little. However, Mrs. Jones was not too happy about this idea, and although she tried to help Jeannie by giving her easier quizzes more frequently, so she could "get used to" tests, Jeannie's fear continued unrelieved.

Jeannie's parents finally decide to take her to a behavior therapist, partly because her problem is not very "deep," partly because this process is quicker and less expensive than traditional psychotherapy, and partly because they have a negative feeling about the implications of psychotherapy in relation to Jeannie—a rather unfortunate view, but somewhat prevalent. The behavior therapist talks with Jeannie for some time, asking her about her schoolwork, her friends, and her home life. They get pretty well-acquainted, and as they talk, the therapist begins to get a feel for the kinds of things related to tests of which Jeannie is afraid. He does not ask her what caused the fear, or probe into her past, or into her "subconscious" as a psychotherapist would, however; he deals primarily with the present.

Finally, he writes down a list of situations that cause Jeannie fear, from what he has gathered in their conversations, and checks it with her. She thinks it is about right, in that the lowest things on the list do not bother her very much, while the top things do. Some of the lowest things are "A ten-minute quiz one week away" and "The teacher asks questions in class about the homework," while some of the really threatening ones are "You are about to go into social studies for a mid-term test" and "You are about to take a standardized achievement test for English which lasts two hours."

Then Mr. Smith, the therapist, asks Jeannie to relax in a comfortable chair, and he talks to her for a while in a very soothing tone of voice, telling her that she will feel very pleasant and easy, and not to think of anything that bothers her. Rather, she should think of good things she likes to do, like watch television, eat snacks, go bicycling with a friend, or listen to some cool music. When she is quite relaxed, he then asks her to visualize or imagine a situation from the bottom of the list, like "Imagine that you are in class and the teacher is about to ask for an answer that you know, but she does not look as if she is going to call on you. Does that make you at all anxious or worried? Just lift your index finger if it does." Jeannie does not make any response, signifying that this scene does not bother her. Then the therapist says "Now stop thinking about that situation, and think about something you like to do for a few minutes. . . . Now let's imagine another scene." This time he picks the next scene up the list, and goes through the same process. If Jeannie can tolerate that, he will keep going in this way. If she becomes anxious, he will "back off," talk about other things, perhaps introduce one of the less-worrisome scenes again, and so forth, finally coming back to this one later. Ultimately, he and Jeannie work all the way through the hierarchy, in the course of several sessions. As the sessions go on, Jeannie finds herself becoming less and less worried about social studies and the tests, until after a while she finds that she can remember things during the tests and get down what she knows. She does not get A's on them, but she *does* them, and furthermore she realizes that she *can* take tests now!

Some facts about fear

Fear is a classical response: it is irrational, illogical, and unpredictable. For example, most of us are much more afraid of being murdered in a dark alley than of being killed in an auto accident—we clutch when we pass a dark alley and not when we get in a car—yet the automobile accident rate is about three times that of the murder rate (Scarf, 1974).

Fear is learned: in relation to theories of "drives" (Chapter 7), it is an acquired drive. Once a fear is learned, a person or an animal is unlikely to return voluntarily to the situation where the event occurred that conditioned it. This is why one has to use "desensitization" to get rid of fears through imagination, rather than bringing the person into the actual situation and having the fear extinguished. A rat that has been shocked in a compartment painted white will always thereafter struggle to get out of such a compartment into a black compartment next door; it will even learn to solve puzzles to get out, or it will run for hours on a treadmill in order to get a door to open so it can get out. So humans will avoid or escape from a compartment in which they have been punished repeatedly, even when that punishment involves repeated cognitive failure rather than physical beating—the analogy to school is obvious.

Dogs trained to fear a compartment in a similar manner jumped over a barrier hundreds of times in order to escape long after the shocking mechanism that conditioned their fear was turned off. Actually, they never stopped jumping, and while

Teachers may have to "desensitize" some learners to anxiety.

they jumped, their jumping style improved considerably. When, later on, they were shocked on the *other* side, do you think that they stopped jumping? No—they improved even more! So like humans, who though punished for a maladaptive behavior learned years ago, continue to use the behavior nevertheless!

We learn to fear things that we are genetically programmed to fear: open spaces, specific animals, heights, insects, closed-in spaces, strangers, foreigners. Many other things which are objectively no more or less threatening we do not learn to fear so easily. We don't have pajama phobias, hammer phobias, or electric outlet phobias! Unpredictable pain arouses more fear than predictable pain. The effects of living with chronic fear and constant mobilization of our defense responses (secretion of adrenalin, blood sugar, increased breathing and heart rate) are fatigue, depression, slowdown of mental processes, slowdown of body movements, restlessness, bursts of aggression and irritability, loss of appetite, tendency to startle, insomnia and nightmares. Headaches, ulcers, high blood pressure and asthma have fear foundations as well.

OPERANT CONDITIONING

Classical responses, which have just been discussed, are involuntary; you can't control them by willpower or by wanting to, and the conditioning process occurs whether you want it to or not. We will now discuss responses that are more subject to voluntary control, although not entirely, as you will see. These are called "operant responses." They "operate" on the environment. They are sometimes called "psychomotor," which implies that they are physical but also governed by mental processes. Examples of operant responses are running, talking, turning, throwing, and the like; there are different degrees of cognitive involvement in these actions. (You went through these distinctions between cognitive and motor responses back in the first chapter, in relation to the sensorimotor stage of development.)

Increasing operant behaviors by reinforcing them

The key to modifying voluntary behaviors lies in altering the *consequences* of those behaviors, as well as the antecedents.

Classical responses were "conditioned" by pairing a stimulus that already elicited them with one that didn't at first, but was successful after several pairings. This process, called "stimulus substitution," also works with operant responses if you know what stimulus will bring on the operant response initially. Often, however, you do not. For example, if you want a learner to make a certain kind of movement in a certain situation, but he doesn't do that now, then you may not know how to get that movement in the first place, i.e., you don't know what already evokes it.

Therefore, you wait for the movement to happen, then "reinforce" it. Immediately after it occurs you present some stimulus that makes it more likely to occur again. For example, if you give a hungry animal a pellet of food immediately after

Q

it does something that you want it to do more often, then it will do it more often; if you keep presenting food immediately after the response, the response will increase in frequency.   This is called "reinforcing" the response.   As an example of the use of reinforcement with people, suppose you want someone to smile more; then you wait until she smiles (or half-smiles, if it's a real tough case), and then you smile back, or act particularly friendly, or offer her a reward.   You will find that she smiles more often.   You have "reinforced" smiling.   Incidentally, the person may not realize that you are doing this with such an objective; to that extent, the smile is not "voluntary."   On the other hand, it isn't involuntary either, although it may be a strong habit under certain circumstances.   If you told her not to smile, she probably wouldn't, while if you told someone not to be *afraid* of something (fear is a classical response), he or she would still be afraid of it.

Why not do it the easy way and say "you ought to smile more often?"   Because this doesn't work; she may smile more for a while, but she will forget.   On the other hand, if you reinforce smiling in a number of different kinds of situations, then the frequency of smiling will increase generally.

Let's review this process.   In order to condition an operant response, i.e., to make it more frequent, you reinforce it.   A reinforcer is a stimulus that you present immediately after the response.   Whatever works, i.e., whatever makes the response more frequent, is called a "reinforcer," by definition—a circular definition, admittedly.   For example, if a group of kindergarten children won't sit still, but continually run around and yell, you might say, "If you sit still for five seconds, I'll let you run around and yell."   If they sit still for five seconds, then you say, "OK, run around and yell"; next time you say "sit still," they are able to sit still for longer, and they do it more promptly than they ever had before.   Again, you wait five or maybe six or seven seconds, and then say, "OK, run around and yell."   Next time they will sit still immediately on command and keep sitting even longer.   You are reinforcing "sitting still" by "running around and yelling."   You have used running around and yelling as a reinforcer!   Moral: Reinforcers are where you find them!

Suppose you want a learner to pay attention more frequently in class.   You notice or pat him on the back every time he is paying attention, or you give him a piece of candy, or you give him a slip of paper which he can trade in later for candy or something else he wants.   If you do this every time he pays attention, he will probably begin paying attention more regularly.   You will have increased this desired response by "reinforcing" it when it occurs.   However, if he doesn't do it more often, use some other consequence and note the frequency again.

Prompting, or cueing

There is a way to shorten the process of waiting for the response to occur naturally.   This is to "cue" the response, or to "prompt" it, i.e., to do something that makes the response more likely, even though that something is not part of the final rela-

This diagram is designed to show the temporal relationship between occurrence of a desired response (in this case, increased concentration on schoolwork while sitting at one's desk in class) and occurrence of a positive reinforcer (in this case, increased level of rock music being played over the classroom intercom speaker). The reinforcing stimulus (increase of music level) occurs immediately after the desired response (increased concentration). The teacher might have waited until this increased concentration occurred naturally, and then turned up the volume of the music; however, this might have meant a rather long wait. As an alternative, the teacher can prompt the increased concentration by saying something like "Let's get busy," then reinforce the resulting behavior by turning up the volume.

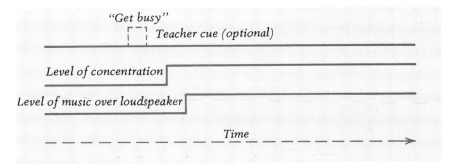

This does not necessarily work: if the concentration level, or frequency of concentration at that level, doesn't increase as a result of this kind of treatment, then the teacher should conclude that the increase of music level is *not* a reinforcing stimulus, and try something else. Perhaps the teacher can give out tokens each time he or she catches a learner concentrating harder, or perhaps he or she will want to punish "goofing off" by turning the music off when too many students are not working. Practical approaches are discussed in more detail in Chapter 11.

Figure 8–2. *Time diagram of positive reinforcement.*

tionship you want to establish.   For example, you might say "smile" and then reinforce the smile when it occurs.   Or you might smile yourself more often, and hope that the person imitates you; then you reinforce the smiling.   (This is called "modeling" the behavior.)   Later on, you would withdraw the cues and reinforce smiling when it occurs in natural circumstances.   You may have noticed that we assumed, in introducing prompting, that some known stimulus (the "prompt") evoked the operant response; the example given was saying "smile" to get a person to smile. This works for people, when it is a response which has a known command, but it doesn't work for animals since they can't understand most language, and it doesn't work for people when the response is something for which they have no recognized command.   You can't prompt a person to execute a parallel turn in skiing by saying, "do a parallel turn" unless he or she has already learned that skill; therefore, in order to prompt aspects of the skill you may have to use other things, and maybe you won't be able to prompt it, you may have to "shape" it instead.   So, prompts are useful when you can find one to use, but often they aren't available for helping with a given response or behavior.

Whatever the situation, if you use a prompt to get a response in order to have another stimulus control that response, you have to remember that the prompt is a temporary helper.   You give it, and also have the other stimulus occur, and then you gradually withdraw the prompt by making it smaller and smaller or quieter or less perceptible in some other way.   This leaves the learner responding to the new stimulus alone.   Removing the prompt gradually in this way is called "fading."

JERI DEFUSSES HER SON

Jeri is a married college student with a 1½ year old son who fusses at meals.   He won't eat on his own; he refuses bites of food offered by parents or grandparents; he squawks, cries, upsets his food, and generally doesn't eat even when he is hungry.   Jeri is taking a course in behavior modification, and as a project she decides to reduce this fussiness if she can.   Since it is a continuous behavior rather than something that happens once and then again and so forth, she uses an interval method of recording the behavior.   Since meals range in length from 15 to 30 minutes and recording is difficult while trying to feed him or to eat herself while her husband feeds him, she observes his behavior for a minute only; however, she does this several times during each meal.

Jeri takes a baseline count over ten days without trying to change anything; she finds the fussiness ranges from 80 to 20 percent of the intervals, with an average of about 70 percent. (The fact that the amount varies so much is even more irritating, since she never knows whether a meal is going to go badly or not, and her anxiety communicates itself to her son, who is more likely to be fussy as a result.)   Earlier in the course Jeri had tried extinguishing the fussiness, i.e., getting rid of it by ignoring it, but her son would either play in his food, play with a toy on his tray, or fuss louder to get attention. It was very difficult to ignore this for a long

period of time because of the whining and crying, and because her son's endurance was greater than her tolerance limits.   She also tried punishing him through a "time out," by putting him in his crib; in a few seconds he would stop and play, or call "Mama" or "Dada" to get him out.   However, on returning to the meal he didn't behave any better.   Jeri concluded that he couldn't remember well enough or generalize well enough at this age for this kind of punishment to work.

Spanking or slapping or withdrawal of toys were equally ineffective, for the same reason. He simply didn't remember well enough to apply the experience to the next situation.   However, Jeri noted that he did understand what she told him, including when she told him not to play with his food or gurgle in his drink: he would either stop, or continue in a way that made it evident that he was being defiant.

Jeri decided to use reinforcement.   Since Donnie liked lemonade and would ask for it morning, noon, and night, she began by giving him lemonade after every bite of food.   After a few days, she and her husband changed this to an intermittent schedule, trying to get Donnie to have as many bites as possible before giving him lemonade (i.e., before reinforcing him).   She noticed that the reinforcer also acted as a stimulus for more eating, i.e., eating, drinking lemonade, eating, drinking lemonade became a chain of responses, each part of the chain rein-forcing the previous part and stimulating the next. At first, and occasionally later, Jeri had to prompt Donnie by showing him the reinforce-ment (the lemonade) and saying, "Take a bite," or "Stop playing and eat." She also applied the Premack* principle by saying "If you take a bite of food, then you can have a drink of lemon-ade." (The high frequency behavior was drinking lemonade, the low frequency behavior was eating.)

As days went on Jeri and her husband found that they had to prompt the behavior and reinforce it less and less. By the sixth day the presence of the lemonade on his high-chair tray was enough to prompt Donnie to take a bite, or often several bites, before he took (or was given) a drink. Two days later they moved the drink from his tray to the table in front of his chair; they "faded" the prompt. For two days after that this did not work: Donnie insisted that the lemonade glass be kept on his tray. But by the tenth day of the experiment the cup could be left on the table. Furthermore they were able to

give the lemonade for reinforcement on a variable-ratio schedule, i.e., every so many bites on the average. The ratio was planned in ad-vance, but resulted from two things: (a) how long Donnie would eat before demanding lem-onade, and (b) Jeri's refusal to give lemonade for anything less than two bites, and her attempt to hold out for more.

Over fifteen days Donnie's fussiness went from about 50 percent to about 8 percent of the time during eating. There were many ups and downs, particularly up to about day eight, and then the progress was quite steady. Toward the end Jeri began to try to substitute milk for lem-onade, and this fading of the prompt and changing of the schedule and intensity of rein-forcement proceeded gradually. She and her husband also began to rely more on social rein-forcement, making their praise more enthusi-astic, and associating it with the lemonade while gradually withdrawing the lemonade. During a twenty-minute meal there will still be one or two spells of fussiness, but a verbal or visual prompt, or some praise, makes them very brief. Meals are less a chore and more enjoyable. Jeri and her husband feel better psychologically because Donnie has eaten a good meal, and their stom-achs are relieved from the nervous indigestion caused by anxiety during the meal.

---

* This principle states that a highly frequent be-havior can be used as a reinforcer for a less fre-quent one.

Skinner boxes

Reinforcement processes were developed originally through experiments with an-imals, including rats and pigeons. The classic experiment is done in what is called a "Skinner box," which is a cage with a mechanism for vending small food pellets. A bar in the cage activates the food mechanism; if the animal presses the bar (or pecks at a disc) a pellet of food drops into the feeding tray. Various conditions can be arranged in the box; for example, it can be wired electronically so that pressing the bar dispenses food only if a light above the mechanism is on, or only when the light is red but not green. When this is done, the pigeon (or rat) learns to peck (or presses) the bar only when the red light is on, and not to the green. This is called "discrimination learning," and the red light is called the "discriminative stimulus." However, you can do it the other way too; once the animal responds to the red light only, you can reinforce it for responding to an orange light as well; initially it

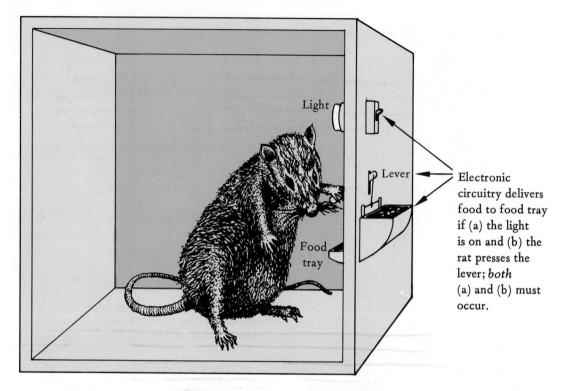

Light

Lever ◄——

Electronic
circuitry delivers
food to food tray
if (a) the light
is on and (b) the
rat presses the
lever; *both*
(a) and (b) must
occur.

Food
tray

Figure 8–3. *Diagram of a Skinner Box.*

will respond less frequently to the orange, but it will respond.   This is called "stimulus generalization," i.e., bringing the animal to respond to a broad range of similar stimuli, or teaching it not to discriminate.

Secondary reinforcers

Reinforcing stimuli, i.e., things you present to the learner immediately following a response that you want to increase in frequency, are often things that the learner likes or associates with something positive: a compliment, a pat on the back, some free time to read an interesting book or work with an ongoing experiment in the science center in another part of the room, a piece of candy, or a token which can be used to purchase one or more of these things.   You can compare reinforcing stimuli to the stimuli involved in classical conditioning; that is, they are stimuli that elicit a positive response internally.   Now, you may remember that in classical conditioning you could pair a neutral stimulus with one that already elicited a response (a classical, involuntary response), and the neutral stimulus would come to elicit the same response by itself.   It is then no longer neutral but a "conditioned

Time to read can be a secondary reinforcer.

stimulus." So it is with reinforcing stimuli; if you have a stimulus that acts as a reinforcer (that is, it is effective in making the response that it follows occur more frequently in the future), then you can pair some neutral stimulus with it a number of times, and that neutral stimulus will come to be a "reinforcer" also.

For example, in training animals, the most effective reinforcer initially is food; this is made more effective by not feeding the animal. However, giving an animal a food pellet or morsel when the animal is in the middle of a chain of new responses is sometimes a bit difficult. One way around this is to have a clicker or a buzzer that you can sound any time you want; you pair this with the presentation of food immediately following a number of different responses that you are teaching. After a while, the clicker can be used as a reinforcer by itself, without the food. It is of course much more convenient because you can reinforce the animal at a distance, and you can sound the clicker immediately following some particular response where feeding takes a bit of time. The clicker is called a "secondary" or "conditioned" reinforcer; it gets its "reinforcing power," if you will, from being associated with "primary" reinforcers.

Just as a neutral stimulus becomes a conditioned stimulus when paired with an unconditioned one (classical conditioning) so a neutral stimulus becomes a conditioned reinforcer when paired with something that is reinforcing.

DRUGS—AN EXAMPLE OF REINFORCEMENT POWER

Drugs have physiological effects, one of which is a decrease in anxiety about the future, about immediate problems, and about life in general. This decrease reinforces the chain of behaviors that leads up to it: getting drugs, preparing them, and taking them by whatever means. (This applies to alcohol, coffee, and cigarettes as well as to marihuana, heroin, and LSD.) This releasing effect is built into our physiological makeup—unfortunately so, since it is a very powerful effect with which it is hard to compete. You can reinforce other responses that are incompatible with taking drugs, but it is difficult to find reinforcers that are as effective. Furthermore, when a person takes drugs for a time, his or her body becomes accustomed to them and objects to a cessation of drug-taking; thus, not only are you reinforced for taking the drug, but you are punished for the opposite behavior. This punishment, which we call "withdrawal symptoms," may be physically painful in some cases; in other cases, it may not be painful, but may simply remind you of what you are missing.

One way to compete with this system is to mix something into the drug that punishes you for taking it, that is, something which makes you sick. However, the fear and anxiety which this conditions as a response to the drug-taking will usually not be sufficient to keep you from trying again later. And if you do not get sick later (i.e., after you have been "treated" and have gone back to your regular existence) then the fear extinguishes and the original reinforcing reactions bring the response back to full force in a short time.

Another way to "kick a habit" is by using willpower. This is not something that is easy to analyze from a reinforcement point of view, but it does work in some cases. Perhaps you can look upon it as an application of mental reinforcers and punishers to not-taking and taking drugs, respectively. However, even though a person succeeds in "kicking" the habit through willpower, the old responses that lead to taking the drug (like taking out a cigarette and smoking it) are still in some force and still occur in situations where "taking" was frequent. Again, the effect of the mental reinforcers and punishers will wear off once the person involved begins to concentrate on other things, and he often finds that he soon wants very badly to take the drug again—the response is still very strong. Once he does so, the reinforcers reestablish it in full strength—perhaps even stronger, since the anti-taking responses have been weakened.

Extinction of operant responses

Suppose you have increased the frequency of some operant response by reinforcing it when it occurs. Then, if you stop reinforcing it, the frequency will decrease; that is, the response will extinguish. Therefore, if you want to reduce or eliminate some operant response, you can arrange things so that it is not reinforced. For example, if you want a learner to stop talking in class, you make sure that you do not react to his talking in any way (you might be reinforcing it by criticizing or scolding!); you also make sure that no other learners are reinforcing it, i.e., through approval or through snickers when he talks. As another example you may have noticed that conversation will lag when certain people begin to participate; one explanation is that the person does not listen to what other people are saying, and

Table 8–1. *Table of classical and operant conditioning processes.*

Classical conditioning
Associate neutral stimulus with unconditioned stimulus; neutral stimulus comes to elicit the same response.

Operant conditioning
Present a stimulus *after* the response, one which has the effect of making the response more probable in the future; it's called a "reinforcer."
NOTE: Classical conditioning deals with involuntary responses—fear, love, liking, and such—also knee jerk and other reflexes. Operant conditioning deals with voluntary responses.

Extinction
Classical: Stop giving the unconditioned stimulus with the conditioned (formerly neutral) one.
Operant: Stop reinforcing the response.

Stimulus control (*Operant*)
Reinforce the response *only* when it follows a particular stimulus, and that stimulus will come to "control" or "evoke" the response.

Stimulus substitution (Operant and Classical)
When a stimulus has been conditioned so that it controls a response, you can get another stimulus to do the same by making it *contiguous* with the first, i.e., by having it occur with or just before the original.

thus he extinguishes their conversation (does not reinforce it by being attentive). Teachers often extinguish student-initiated discussions and questions in the same way, even though they say they want to encourage such participation. Parents extinguish many desirable behaviors in their own children by this process, and they may later criticize those same children for not having or showing the behaviors that they, without knowing it, extinguished long before.

Intermittent reinforcement

In order to strengthen a response so that it will be given in the future without reinforcement and will not extinguish as a result of lack of reinforcement, gradually change from reinforcing it every time to reinforcing it either every "n" times, or every "t" minutes. For example, suppose you have helped an adult to stay in shape by arranging things so that she is reinforced every time she refuses a piece of candy or rich food. In order to have this response maintained after the "training" period, you will begin to reinforce it every other time instead, then every three times, and so forth. Of course, you will mix it up, so that she cannot anticipate exactly which time it will be reinforced.

This is called "ratio" reinforcement, or a "ratio" schedule; you might instead arrange to have the reinforcement occur every fifteen minutes if she has not taken any candy in the interim, and then you can stretch the time interval to twenty minutes, forty, an hour, etc.   This is called "interval" reinforcement.   The trouble with regular interval reinforcement is the learner responds heavily just before it's given—like students cramming for a Friday quiz Thursday night.   By using variable ratios, on the other hand, you can get a high response rate using only a few reinforcers—like giving out approval for good work only every once in a while, rather than every time it occurs.   (When a learner does very little good work, it may be necessary to reinforce it each time until it becomes more frequent, then to use a variable ratio.)

Applied operant conditioning—an example

Suppose you have an autistic child, one who does not relate to others, does not speak, and does not communicate or interact with other people in any way, except to reach for a piece of candy.   Then you use the sight of the candy as the present controlling stimulus, and pair it with some suggestion like "take it," and reinforce the reaching with the candy.   Gradually, you can vary the situation by substituting other things, i.e., pairing other things to reach for with the candy, and reinforce reaching for them with the candy.   Eventually, you can hide the candy, and present some toy, and say "take it."   Then, when the child reaches for it you can reinforce it by candy.   Along with the candy, in each case, you give a social reinforcer, i.e., saying "good boy" or giving a hug; these become conditioned reinforcers, and can be used to reinforce other behaviors.   However, their "power" may extinguish if they are not accompanied by the primary reinforcer, candy, occasionally.

NANCY GETS IT TOGETHER

Nancy procrastinates. Whenever there is a free hour in her day (she is a college student), she sits around, talks to friends, or listens to the radio rather than starting her assignments. She is so used to being behind that actually starting to catch up is a threatening idea. However, as part of her teacher education requirements she has elected a half-course ("module") on behavior modification, and as a project she decides to use a token system to get herself to work. She awards herself one token each time she works "on-task" for 15 minutes. The quality of work done is important, but first she wants to get the initiative to settle down to work whenever there are free periods in the day.

First she defines her target behavior: any reading, writing, or studying material for a course, copying over notes, research in the library, or practicing voice or flute or French horn (she is a music major). She chooses the 15-minute interval because she can study without feeling as if she has to work for a whole hour, and she can record on-task behavior more easily at that interval. It is more convenient to complete a 15-minute study period and then take a break or something to eat or drink, than to complete an hour period.

To account for her time, she keeps a daily log. At the end of each day she establishes free time by counting the number of hours she is awake, subtracting classtime, meals, getting ready in the morning and at night (washing up, dreaming), travelling to and from campus, meetings, appointments, and anything else she was required to do that took time from her schedule. Taking the total time spent studying, she got a percentage of free time that she did schoolwork. For the first seven days she just kept track of how she spent her time. She didn't add up the numbers or anything because she didn't want the baseline readings to be affected by her knowledge of the results. However, from these records she was able to draw up a chart listing activities and food that could be exchanged for tokens. She wanted activities that were more beneficial to her (anything that would further her musical development) to be "less expensive" than leisure activities (watching television, crocheting, etc.). She set it up so that five tokens were worth 10 minutes of leisure activities, or 15 minutes of an enjoyable but beneficial activity. Time exchanged for tokens was not counted as free time that day, in order not to have her feel guilty about not working.

Tokens were tiny mint candies: any time she completed a 15-minute interval she would make a check mark on a piece of paper (which she carried around with her) and these would be changed into tokens (mint candies) when she got home. These would be put into a jar. When she wanted something on her food or activity list, she would record what she spent for it, and would take that many candies out of the jar. The candies served as visual reminders of the time she used to study, so they showed her progress as well as acting as tokens for reinforcing things for which they could be traded. She found that if the jar got low, she wanted to work to earn more candies, although she didn't have a particular activity in mind to exchange them for. Because she knew she really could do anything she wanted *without* the tokens (after all, it was *her* system) their buying power wasn't the major factor in modifying her behavior. The practice of writing everything down made her conscious of the amount of time she wasted. Thinking in terms of time slots when she could do school work added more structure to her days. She found herself planning studying periods ahead of time, not just whenever she felt like it. She was also motivated to keep working once started, since 15 minutes is a short amount of time, and the check marks accumulated significantly. Overall, she found that her percentage of free time spent on school work increased from 34.9 during the baseline observation period to 50.7 percent for the overall period of receiving tokens and back-up reinforcement.

Classroom contingency management

The instructional processes covered so far have been applied to a general approach to classroom management that has come to be called "classroom contingency management." Although it has a new ring to it and has been given some modern trappings, it is also as old as the hills. It involves careful diagnosis of classroom problems, accurate measurement of the frequency of those problems (whether something to increase or decrease in frequency), and the application of operant conditioning processes to deal with those problems.

One of the basic aspects of this approach to classroom handling is the idea that one "accentuates the positive and eliminates the negative," to use words from an old tune by Johnny Mercer. The teacher is taught to ignore behavior that he or she does not want, and to notice and reward behavior he or she does want. This seems logical and even obvious, but if you observe teachers, you find that they often do the opposite!

Ignoring wrong behavior and praising right behavior is an effective classroom technique (?).

Classroom contigency management is an application of the basic processes already discussed here. It will be described in more detail in Chapter 11.

STIMULUS GENERALIZATION AND DISCRIMINATION

Generalization

In classical conditioning, if you condition a fear response to a musical tone, a musical tone that is somewhat different will still elicit the response, although the response may be slightly weaker. This is called "stimulus generalization." In operant conditioning, if you harness an operant response to one situation, then another similar situation will bring that same response, although it may be less frequent, less probable, or weaker than the original. This too is called "stimulus generalization." Since no two events or situations are exactly alike in every way, this is an important characteristic of learning. It makes a learning process effective beyond the precise training situation.

Stimulus analysis

It is natural to generalize: if you want to understand a person's behavior, you need to observe and determine just how he or she generalizes.

To bring about a response that you have seen a learner give before, observe it on more than one occasion and identify the elements common to the situation that precede and accompany the response. Then reproduce this common set of stimuli in order to evoke the response.

An example of this is found in the case of a child with a writing problem. His writing became progressively smaller as he went along, until it finally disappeared. Careful analysis of the words preceding each place where it became smaller showed that the child had a habit of making all of his As like capital letters, even in the middle of a word (i.e., he generalized "capital A" to *all* As). Then, he would make the next letters smaller than the capital A, as you would after any capital letter (another generalization). Thus, he would make the capital A in the middle of a word, but he would make it the same size as the small letters that preceded it. Then he would make the next letter smaller still, since they came after a capital!

This analysis enabled the teacher to identify what was bringing about the response. Then her problem was to change the response, to teach the learner not to make a capital "A" when the letter "a" occurred in the middle of a word. Once this was accomplished, through practice and through checking the student's papers and catching errors, the disappearing writing ceased to disappear!

Another example of the use of stimulus analysis is found in teaching a learner to serve in tennis. Since the serve is a complex stroke, you would like to find some occurrence of a similar response in the learner's own repertoire of skills. One way to do this is to give him a ball and have him throw it: if he throws well, then you have it made. All you have to do is give him the tennis racquet and have him throw it straight up in the air, without letting go of it at the end of the throw. The stroke that results is very close to the serve stroke, and you can shape it from there. Of course, coordinating this stroke with tossing the ball is another major hurdle.

Stimulus discrimination

Sometimes you want to avoid generalization, or to get rid of it, because it leads to an incorrect response. For example, suppose you want a learner to take cover when a light of a given color flashes. You teach him to do this, but you find that he takes cover when a light of another color flashes also—a color that indicates no danger or is a sign for some other behavior. Then you want the learner to *discriminate* between the two, responding differently to one than to the other. To do this, you reinforce the response (whether operant or classical) when the desired stimulus is involved, and not when the other one is involved. (Remember, "reinforce" means different processes in the two types of conditioning.)

Of course, the capacity of the learner to discriminate between similar stimuli is limited. Pavlov, for example, used a circle as a stimulus for a classical response—a response which was involuntary—and an ellipse for another. The animal involved was able to discriminate between the two even as the ellipse was made more and more like a circle.   Finally, it came to a certain point where the discrimination was beyond the capability of the animal's perception; at that point, the animal had a "nervous breakdown."   It struggled to get away, whined, cringed, and acted generally as though it were being punished severely—even though no punishment had been administered.   (One wonders sometimes whether children in certain school situations are not reacting in a similar fashion because the cognitive tasks presented are beyond their immediate ability to cope.)

Teaching stimulus discrimination

To bring a learner to respond to one stimulus but not another similar one, reinforce the response when the desired stimulus is involved, and do not reinforce it (that is, extinguish it) when other stimuli are involved.   For example, suppose you want a group of children to be afraid when they see a poisonous mushroom, but not when they see an edible one; then you arrange to present a fear-producing stimulus (such as saying "That will kill you") with the poisonous one, but not with the edible one. (Note that this would also involve forming the concept of a poisonous mushroom, but concept teaching is discussed in a later chapter.)

As another example, suppose you want a group of adults to attend carefully to one type of material, say that involving numbers and calculations, and to ignore another, say abstract discussions of relationships.   Then you reinforce responses based on the first type (perhaps by saying "That's right on," or "That's what we're looking for," or "That will be on the test") while extinguishing (not reinforcing) responses based on the other type.

MS. JONES GUARDS AGAINST CRISES

Ms. Jones wants a happy, warm class, but she also wants her second graders to respond quickly to orders when it is important to get things organized or when there is an emergency. On the other hand, when an emergency comes she does not want to have the class get panicky. Therefore, she wants to teach them to discriminate between her tone when something is serious and has to be done, and her tone when no exceptional weight has to be attached to her words, although she does not want to teach a fear reaction to the serious tone.   Therefore, she cultivates a particular tone of voice, somewhat stern but not too rough and still quite clear, when she wants something done immedi-

ately without question.   For example, she may say "Let's quiet down, please" or "Clear your desks" in her regular, less-serious tone and continue to reinforce questions, comments, and general conversation even though the children do not immediately conform.   She may reiterate the request a few times in order to make it clear, but she does not make it top priority.   On the other hand, another time she may say the same thing ("Let's quiet down, please") in her more stern, serious voice, again very clearly and without implying the children are "bad."   This time she does not reinforce subsequent behaviors that are other than those requested, and she very pointedly reinforces behaviors that she *does* expect under this condition. Initially she may also deprive one or two children of some privilege when they fail to respond to that tone of voice, later giving them the opportunity to earn the privileges back by responding correctly. The "emergency" tone gradually comes to exert very complete but not threatening control.

Transfer of training

In teaching or therapy, you need to determine what you want the learner to transfer training to (to generalize to) and what you don't want transferred (what you want discriminated).

If you condition a child to say "thank you" or some other appreciative remark when someone does something for her, by reinforcing her for expressing appreciation under such conditions in the home, then assumedly this behavior will occur when a similar thing happens at a neighbor's house, or in a doctor's office, or in school. The "thank you" response generalizes to other appreciative responses, and the stimulus (someone helping her at home) generalizes to other helping stimuli both at home and outside the home. This process is called "transfer" or "transfer of training." Of course, it is not limited to operant conditioning situations, but is an aspect of all learning. If you condition a child to fear a neighbor's dog which is apt to nip, or if this happens naturally because the child gets bitten, then the child will generalize this fear to other dogs. You may be able to teach the child to discriminate between different dogs in terms of knowing their names and kinds, but the fear may still transfer to all or some of them. You may have to desensitize the child of fear of dogs, as a result, or at least extinguish the fear of other dogs by getting the child to pat other ones and thus find out that they won't bite. Verbal prompting will help get the child to do this, but the actual experience of having other dogs behave in a friendly fashion is necessary to extinguish the fear (i.e., you can't "talk him out of it").

Transfer is a general objective in teaching and learning, of course, and it will be discussed in other sections as well, and in Chapter 10 when you study verbal learning and concept learning.

NON-TRANSFER AND MIS-TRANSFER

The author once ran into a problem of generalization that was quite unexpected, but quite clear and quantitative. I taught my algebra class that

$$a(b + c)$$

was equal to

$$ab + ac$$

and really drilled the students on this principle.

Then I taught them another, different process, namely

$$(x + y) + z = x + (y + z)$$

Then on a quiz I gave the following problem

$$x(y + z) = \underline{\hspace{1cm}}$$

The students answered as follows:

$$(x + y) + z$$

They had failed to transfer (generalize) from "a(b + c)" to "x(y + z)," and they had generalized *incorrectly* from "(x + y) + z" to "x(y + z)." It wasn't because they hadn't learned their lessons, however! Almost all students in the class did the following problem correctly:

$$a(b + c) = \underline{\hspace{1cm}}$$

The moral of the story? Use greater variety of examples in teaching the process, so the learners won't be "thrown" by such changes!

SHAPING OPERANT BEHAVIOR

Response shaping

Sometimes what you want to bring out in a learner is not there to begin with, except in a very crude, undeveloped form. Then the problem is to teach a new behavior, beginning where he or she "is at" and working gradually toward the kind of behavior you want.

In order to bring a learner to give a response that he cannot give already, find some response that he does give, and that resembles the desired one in some way, no matter how small. Then reinforce that response, and build it in frequency. After that, pick out those versions of the response that are closest to what you want, and teach the learner to discriminate by reinforcing the better versions and not the others. Through a series of such steps, each approximating the target behavior more closely, you will finally achieve the goal.

Shaping changes behaviors through successive approximations, just as desensitization changed feelings through successive approximations; both begin where the learner is.

For example, suppose a child writes very poorly, almost illegibly. Pick out the best aspects of the existing writing, and comment positively on them, and perhaps even give rewards. As the writing improves slightly, become slightly more discriminating, but always reward the positive and extinguish the negative (but do not punish). Gradually, through a series of steps, the writing will begin to approximate the desired quality.

As another example, suppose that an adult has difficulty in participating in group discussions. Observe him, and reward (reinforce) immediately those behaviors that resemble in some small way what you (and he) are after. As these increase slightly in frequency, become more discriminating, and always extinguish (ignore) undesirable behaviors. Gradually the person will improve. This will be particularly true if other members of the group have been coached to help the shaping process.

Environmental shaping

To bring a learner to give a response under certain conditions, you can alter the conditions initially in such a way that the response occurs, and then reinforce it,

Table 8–2. *Steps in the shaping process (Becker et al., 1975a).*

1. Define the target behavior.
2. Decide what existing behavior is enough like the target behavior that you can use it to begin with.
3. Establish some reinforcer: tokens, points on a card, back-up reinforcers.
4. Outline the program of steps to get to the target behavior.
5. Start training with the first step, i.e., the first reinforcement criterion level.
6. Decide when to shift to a new criterion for reinforcement.
7. If the learner can't meet the criterion at a given step, return to the earlier step, or add a new step in between it and the previous one.

gradually changing the conditions back toward the desired ones, always reinforcing the response.

A good example of this process is the "GLM" or "Graduated Length Method" of teaching skiing. A learner is started out on very short skis, so that the basic responses come very easily. Then he is given longer and longer skis, until he is executing these same responses with skis of normal length. The correct technique is reinforced throughout.

SHAPING BASKET-SHOOTING

Billy was a first grader in a school where basketball was very popular. He spent most of his gym periods shooting baskets, but he only made two or three baskets all fall. The physical education teacher finally decided that his persistence should be rewarded, so he switched him from a basketball to a volleyball, and he lowered the basket from ten feet to seven feet. Billy began to make baskets, and he improved so much that the teacher changed him back to a basketball after a week, then a few weeks later raised the basket back up. Billy was then able to make the baskets the regular way (adapted from Becker et. al., 1975). Of course, this is environmental shaping, rather than shaping the response itself.

SHAPING AN ASTRO-MONK

Early in the space program, monkeys were sent up in satellites rather than risking human lives. In one case the monkey was to press a certain button within one second after a warning tone sounded, in order to correct some difficulty. He was trained to do this, and at one point in the training he was making the response in four seconds on the average. The trainers then proceeded to shape this response by reinforcing responses of four seconds or less, not reinforcing responses of *more* than four seconds delay. Then, when most of the responses were occurring in less than four seconds, they upped the requirement for reinforcement to three seconds or less. When this was met on most trials, they shifted to two seconds, later to one and a half, and so on, until the monkey was responding in less than a second regularly (reinforcers were bits of banana).

MODELING

Rationale for modeling

Classical condi-
tioning and coun-
ter-conditioning,
or operant con-
ditioning and
shaping, are too
personalized and
slow to account
for for all human
learning: vicarious
conditioning better
explains the
amount and speed
of social learning.

Operant and classical conditioning both assume that the learner will respond personally; in operant conditioning, he or she will then be reinforced or punished,
while in classical conditioning a neutral stimulus will be presented along with the
stimulus that causes the response.   Some theorists have pointed out that conditioning processes, particularly those involved in operant conditioning, do not explain the remarkable speed and complexity of human learning.   For example, children acquire language in a way that cannot be adequately explained by concepts of
reinforcement and shaping and extinction.   There must be other mechanisms by
which they add words and sentences to their repertoires, and by which they create
new sentences that they have never heard (see Chapter 2).   Some theorists explain
this by saying there is an innate mechanism which matures to enable the learner to
create language to communicate.   Other theorists point out that children imitate
adults, and that much of their language can be explained by this imitation.   No
one group of theorists is entirely correct; together their theories begin to explain
some of the complexities of human learning.   In this section we will examine what
is often called "social learning," or learning by imitation.   From a teaching point of
view, this can be called "modeling," or teaching by setting an example.   It is a very
important and powerful approach to teaching, as well as an important part of
learning.

Shaping a response "from scratch" is a useful teaching process, but it can be
very slow.   You can sometimes speed up the response by "prompting" certain aspects of the response, or the whole response, through some verbal cue, but this assumes that the person has already learned the response and just needs a particular
prompt to bring it out.   Modeling can save a great deal of time, and can be less
frustrating to the learner as well.   You simply exemplify or demonstrate the
response, and ask the learner to imitate you.   Most learners have learned to imitate; if they haven't, then an important learning skill is missing, and they should be
taught to imitate.   Of course, all of us could increase our imitating ability; a professional mime, for example, could teach us a great deal about imitating through gestures and facial expressions.

One example of modeling is found in teaching a would-be-skier to side-slip.
You would demonstrate the side-slip, and have the learner imitate you.   Then you
would begin from the learner's best imitation, and shape his behavior from there
until he had it right.   You might also combine ordinary shaping (reinforcing his
best attempts, and raising the criterion gradually) with environmental shaping
(starting with short skis, working up to longer ones).   Modeling a complex skill in
stages, shaping each stage before modeling the next, would be called "graduated
modeling."

Conditions for modeling

Learners imitate and thus learn from models. Research indicates that this occurs under very specific conditions, however, and there are three kinds of learning that can be brought about this way (Bandura, 1969). Before describing the three types of learning, I will describe the conditions under which modeling takes place most productively and efficiently. These conditions are: (1) that the model has influence on the learner, either as a prestige figure or someone with whom the learner identifies; (2) that the model achieves some goal or is reinforced or rewarded for the observed behavior. Given these conditions, the three types of learning which can be brought about through modeling are:

1. Acquisition of new responses;
2. Increase of strength of old responses;
3. Inhibition of existing responses.

An example of (1) would be the previously mentioned learning to side-slip in skiing. An example of (2) comes from research on the effects of television programs on children's aggression: after watching sequences that featured aggressive acts, children were found to demonstrate a higher frequency of aggressive acts in their play (Bandura, 1969). An example of (3) comes from research on classroom management and the "ripple effect"; it was found that if a teacher uses some technique to get a learner to desist from some misbehavior, and if the learner actually does desist, then the subsequent behavior of the whole class is better, and the teacher is regarded by the class as being better able to manage a classroom (Kounin and Gump, 1962). The effects of this process, by the way, were greater when the student involved had higher status with other students, thus demonstrating the importance of the prestige of the model. One implication of this research is that whatever a teacher does before a group has multiple effects; i.e., a teacher herself, and in interactions with students, models the kinds of behaviors and learning (including motivation, you remember) that the learners will adopt. If the teacher permits unproductive behavior in one or several learners, other learners will imitate this to a degree; if the teacher encourages one student to actualize his or her potential, then other learners will be more likely to do the same.

One interesting example of the use of modeling is found in a project designed to increase the amount of reading done by middle-school learners. Individual conferences were held once a week, conducted by an adult volunteer; when the learner entered the conference room, the adult would be seated in a chair in a comfortable position, reading a book. The adult would act quite interested in the book, but would obviously break off from reading and greet the learner warmly, and say something about what she or he was reading and how interesting it was. After the conference (in which the reading done by the learner was discussed and the learner-

A classmate can model a desired behavior.

selected goals were set up for the coming week with the encouragement and support of the adult), the adult would say goodbye to the learner, and then return to the reading with obvious pleasure (Klausmeier, 1976). This project was successful in bringing the learners to increase their amount of reading significantly.

MR. BROWN LEARNS SPANISH CONVERSATION

Mr. Brown is being assigned to an office in Spain for his company, which partly comes from the fact that he was a Spanish major in college and his boss feels that he may be able to "brush up" enough on his conversation to improve relations with Spanish suppliers. However, his language major was primarily in literature. He never did develop good pronunciation and was unable to take the foreign study trip because he was working and playing soccer. Therefore he engages a Spanish-speaking person to help him, and asks for advice from a professor who spent time with the Peace Corps training people for positions in various foreign countries. They work out a system that involves both modeling and shaping. They arrange situations that call for standard conversational give-and-take, such as introducing oneself or eating in a restaurant. Then the tutor, Miss Gray, models the conversation, taking both parts and "acting it out." Then

Mr. Brown takes one of the parts—usually without a script, since the parts are short, but sometimes with a script to prompt him. He tries to imitate Miss Gray's model in pronunciation and intonation. At first she accepts his imitation and reinforces it, as he becomes accustomed to the overall conversation. Then she picks out one aspect—perhaps a word or phrase—and begins to shape his conversation by reinforcing his best efforts in that respect, and not responding in any particular way to his poorer efforts. Thus she focuses on certain aspects of the task, and when they begin to become acceptable, shifts her focus to other aspects. Things she accepts in one session she does not let pass later. The particular things she works on generalize to other aspects of the conversation, of course, so that Mr. Brown is improving overall, as well as in the particulars. By the time he leaves, he is ready to handle quite a number of situations that he will meet, although, of course, he is not a complete conversationalist by any means.

PSYCHOMOTOR LEARNING

Research in basic motor abilities and skills

Operant responses are the building blocks for complex chains or sequences that are often referred to as "skills" or "abilities." These have been usually taught as part of physical education. Some recent research sheds light on the fundamental units that one can expect to deal with in such teaching (Fleishman, 1964; Singer, 1975). These researchers differentiate between "ability" and "skill," viewing abilities as the inherited and learned traits that an individual brings with him when he begins to learn a new task. One example is the ability to visualize spatial relationships, which is related to *skills* involved in aerial navigation, blueprint reading, and dentistry.

Fleishman set out to isolate or identify abilities that are basic to a great number of tasks. By investigating more than two hundred different tasks administered to thousands of subjects, he identified the following psychomotor ones ("psychomotor" is essentially the same as "operant," for our purposes):

- Precision of control over muscles.
- Ability to coordinate a number of limbs simultaneously.
- Ability to select and correct movements in respect to a changing stimulus.
- The speed with which an individual can respond to a stimulus, i.e., "reaction time."
- The speed with which an individual can make a gross, discreet arm movement (not reaction time).
- Ability to make continuous anticipatory motor adjustments relative to change in speed and direction of a moving target.
- Manual dexterity.
- Finger dexterity.

- Arm and hand steadiness.
- Wrist-finger speed.
- Ability to rapidly place dots in very small circles ("aiming").

He also identified basic physical proficiency abilities that do not involve mind-muscle interactions:

- Ability to flex or stretch the trunk and back muscles.
- Ability to make repeated rapid flexing movements.
- Ability to expend a maximum of energy in one or a series of explosive acts.
- The maximum force which a subject can exert, for a brief period, continuously at that maximum.
- The ability to exert muscular force repeatedly or continuously over time (endurance, resistance to fatigue).
- The strength of trunk muscles, particularly the abdominal muscle.
- Ability to coordinate simultaneous actions of different parts of the body.
- Ability to maintain equilibrium despite forces pulling one off-balance.
- Capacity to continue maximum efforts, requiring prolonged exertion over time (stamina).

A good case can be made for incorporating the learning of basic motor skills into the elementary public school curriculum.

Fleishman and his associates have found that as practice at a task continues, changes occur in the particular combinations of abilities that contribute to performance. Abilities that are most important *early* in the learning of a particular skill (or set of skills) became less important *later*. Then other abilities which did not affect the early performance come to be more important. Thus, a person with early aptitude in ballet or football or tennis may lose ground to someone else who has a greater measure of those abilities that become important in the later stages of development of the skill.

One more finding of Fleishman's and his associates that is surprising is that there was virtually no loss in skills found over time, regardless of the length of the interval between original learning and relearning or evaluation. The most powerful predictor of retention was the level of the original learning, i.e., how well the skill was learned in the first place. For all intervals, even up to two years, individual differences at the end of the learning correlated in the .80s and .90s, with subsequent performance after periods of no practice. This is interesting particularly when you realize that there have been similar results found in research in verbal learning (discussed in the next chapter) where the amount retained was primarily related to how well the material was learned originally and was not related significantly to various conditions of practice or the meaningfulness of the material learned. Generally, this consistency implies that if you want students to retain either knowledge or skills, the best way to ensure retention is to have them learn well in the first place.

In terms of individual differences and learning disabilities, Fleishman points out that many potential engineers are lost for lack of spatial orientation, and many students have difficulty in dental school because of poor manual dexterity. According to Fleishman, this implies that schools need to develop programs for training all students in basic physical and psychomotor abilities, and there is a need for research on the use of motor-ability assessment in predicting school achievement generally.

Building chains of responses

To teach a sequence of two responses so that the second response occurs automatically after the first, you must condition the second response so that the first one is a stimulus for it; then the first response evokes the second. The steps are as follows:

1. Evoke the second response with some prompt (or stimulus) that gets the learner to give the second response;
2. Evoke the first response to whatever stimulus will initiate the chain when the chain is complete;
3. Substitute the first response for the prompt for the second response, i.e., make the *prompt* for the second response contiguous with (come just after) the first response.

TEACHING BILLY A CHAIN IN REVERSE

Billy is a retarded boy who has trouble putting on his clothes. His special teacher wants to help him learn to put on his shorts. She puts them on for him until they are almost up to his waist, and then she tells him to pull them up the rest of the way. When he does so, she rewards him with an M&M candy. Then they take them off and try again. She puts them on almost all the way, stopping only slightly short of the point where she stopped before. He again completes the task, pulling them up to his waist, and is reinforced. Next time, she leaves a little too much for him to do, so she realizes her error and pulls them a little farther, then asks him

again to pull them up. Gradually, by this reverse process, Billy finishes a larger and larger portion of the task, until eventually he is doing the whole thing from the beginning.

Shoe-tying and other such tasks are sometimes taught this reverse way. It has been called "backward shaping," but it is really "backward chaining," although the process of successive approximations is present in both. (Note that successive approximations is a basic approach in a number of instructional processes, including desensitization, as discussed under classical conditioning.)

Guidelines for teaching skills

(a) Analyze the skill to be taught and break it down into subskills; check to see whether the learner has all the subskills.

(b) Teach the parts or subskills that are missing and review the others before putting them together.

(c) Build new skills, or the integrated skill, through graduated modeling and shaping, giving intermittent reinforcement in the process.

(d) Extinguish old competing responses that interfere, through practice of those responses without reinforcement, partly as a means of bringing them under voluntary control.

(e) Have the student overlearn new skills; that means practicing them to the point where they are automatic and where they are not overcome by old competing responses.

(f) Allow time for practice immediately after the teaching session, but not too much time if the practice is without immediate feedback (old incorrect responses may revive).

(g) Maintain new skills by incorporating them into other, more complex skills, so that they will be supported by the other skills involved and also reinforced in the same combinations and sequences.

(h) Where a plateau is reached, encourage the learner to keep practicing, and tell him or her that this is a natural part of the process.

(i) Take advantage of initial interest and enthusiasm, but do not overuse it; distribute practice sessions so that the learner doesn't build up a negative reaction to the learning, and try to make drill and practice fun as well.

Replacing old habits with better ones in
athletics

In sports one is often hampered by old responses or habits that don't stand up in competition, for example, a poor swing in golf or an inability to do anything but slice a backhand in tennis. The problem is partly one of learning a new response, or response chain, i.e., a new stroke or other skill. It is also partly one of practicing the new skill so that it competes with the old one: after a week or so of using the new one, the old one is liable to come back—perhaps even sooner than a week. The author, for example, learned to hit a backhand in tennis with a topspin, which is more reliable and forceful in most cases than a slice backhand due to the way the ball spins. I learned the new stroke by backward chaining, starting with the racquet very close to the ball (i.e., to where it would come at the top of the bounce), and then bringing the racquet further and further back as I mastered the stroke. However, it would very often happen that at the last minute, if I lost concentration or tried to start too far back with the racquet too soon, the old response would come back, and the racquet would turn (seemingly involuntarily) in a way that gave a slice instead of a topspin. Thirty years of slicing could not be denied that easily! Unfortunately, it meant that the ball, instead of heading for the backboard at moderate height, would fly over it, necessitating frequent retrievals, and making the author look a bit silly. (However, it didn't come immediately enough to serve as a punisher.) Constant practice over a period of a year and a half was necessary before the new stroke began to be reliable, and the old one ceased to interfere regularly. However, in moments of stress in a match, the old stroke still returns unbidden and often at the wrong time. Perhaps this is the true meaning of the saying "you can't teach an old dog new tricks!"

Learning curves and plateaus

When you learn, do you acquire much initially and taper off, or learn more and more? When you forget, do you forget a lot at first, or more and more as time goes by?

Generally when you learn a skill (or a particular cognitive ability), your learning begins very slowly—there is a starting period when not much happens—and then your ability picks up quite rapidly. Ultimately, for various reasons, you begin to level off: you have either approached a condition where you can't improve much more, or there's not much more to learn, and each increase comes a little harder. When you plot this on a graph, it looks like this:

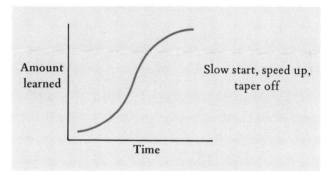

Figure 8–4. *Learning curve.*

This is generally called the "S-shaped curve of learning." Now when you are learning something which incorporates a number of previously learned things, there often occur periods where no noticeable progress is made. Things are happening internally, however, because after such a period, progress begins again. These "flat" periods are called "plateaus." When graphed, they look something like this:

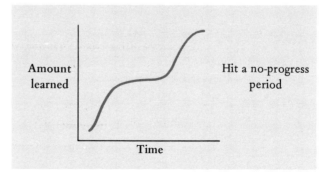

Figure 8–5. *Learning plateaus.*

Some things interact with each other in such a way that the more you learn, the more you *can* learn: this involves long-term learning, as in a mathematics course or in learning French, over weeks or months or a whole school year.   This, when graphed, looks as follows:

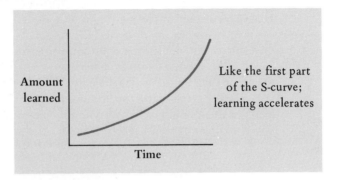

Figure 8–6. *Long-term cumulative learning.*

Finally, there is forgetting: when you have learned something, forgetting occurs over time something like this, i.e., you forget the most right away, and less and less as time goes on:

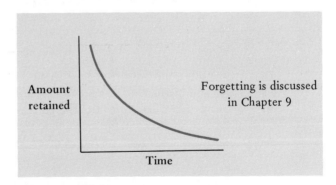

Figure 8–7. *Long-term forgetting.*

REDUCING OR ELIMINATING OPERANT RESPONSES

Using extinction

Part of teaching is building new skills and understandings; another part is eliminating old skills, reducing their probability, or putting them in new contexts.   Eliminating

or reducing the frequency of undesirable behaviors is one of the most obvious problems that teachers face, yet one of the most difficult and perhaps the least well-handled.   Behavior that upsets the class, responses that compete with effective skills, and other such problems "bug" teachers and learners alike.   As was pointed out in Chapter 5 the best way to handle them is organize and manage in a way that prevents them (Kounin, 1970).   However, in this imperfect world, there will always be some behaviors that have to be dealt with.   Then your option is to use one of the following recommendations or a combination of them:

1. Extinguish the response (see operant and classical conditioning discussions).
2. Teach another response to the same stimulus, preferably a response that is incompatible with the undesirable response, i.e., which cannot be given simultaneously; do this by shaping or modeling or a combination of approaches.
3. Arrange for the response to be followed by something unpleasant to the learner, such as loss of a privilege, or the threat of something he or she does not like or fears, or actual physical punishment like a shock or a blow.
4. If possible, see to it that the stimulus which brings the undesirable response does not occur.

The use of punishment

Is punishment
an effective tool
in teaching and
therapy? Can it
be used without
bad side effects?
Is it ethical?

If you punish a response, i.e., if you present an unpleasant stimulus immediately after the response occurs, then a learner will usually avoid giving that response again in the same situation. Since punishing something usually makes it stop immediately the teacher is reinforced for punishing (because the undesirable behavior ceases). As you know, reinforcement makes the behavior more probable, so the teacher is more likely to punish again next time in the same situation. Thus punishment can unfortunately become a conditioned response, or a habit.

If the learner avoids the behavior, that does not mean that the learner has un-learned the behavior. If the threat of punishment ceases, the behavior may reappear. So, if you punish, you have to keep the threat of punishment alive in order to maintain the avoidance conditioning. This can be quite a burden in some cases. However, this does not mean punishment is ineffective or should never be used: it simply means that it has some undesirable side effects.

If a teacher punishes frequently, she or he is modeling aggressive behavior. Other learners who observe this will learn to behave aggressiv ly. This is why hostile, aggressive parents who punish hostile aggressive behavior still end up with hostile aggressive children! As you found in Chapter 3, if the children are afraid to take out their resentment on their parents, then they will take it out on some other adults or other children, including teachers and classmates.

Therefore you should use punishment that does not model hostility and aggression, and that does not become a habit for the teacher because it is so easy to do. One way to do this is to take away some privilege the learner has. If you do this, it is important also to set up an agreement as to the kind of behavior the learner has to demonstrate in order to get the privilege back. Another type of punishment is a "time out," where you simply remove the learner from the ongoing class activities, thus depriving him or her of the opportunity to participate, to be reinforced for participating, and to earn back privileges previously lost.

Another thing to remember is that punishment is usually most effective if given the first time an undesirable behavior occurs. Furthermore, if you find that the behavior recurs, even though you keep punishing it, then stop punishing because it isn't working: somehow you seem to be reinforcing the behavior, even though you didn't intend to.

Some teachers have difficulty administering punishment because it goes against their philosophy of education, or because they associate punishment with unfortunate experiences in their past, or because they feel guilty when they do it. Often teachers who are shown how to punish effectively will do it, and feel guilty about it even though it works and even though they find that their relationships with students are the better for it. This is a difficult thing to handle, but usually the teacher will become adjusted to the necessity and will be able to deal with it reasonably.

Sometimes, on the other hand, teachers use punishment to vent their own latent hostility, and justify it by saying that it is necessary for keeping discipline and that it is good for the learners. Punishment should be used only infrequently, and then not regularly for any behavior (as mentioned above). Positive approaches to motivation are far more effective in the long run in most cases, and so extinction of the undesirable behavior plus reinforcement of alternate desirable ones is the best general strategy.

CONSTRUCTIVE USE OF PUNISHMENT

Jimmy Allen tends to be aggressive in the fourth grade, and his behavior often reaches a point where it endangers other children. Reasoning does not help, nor does ignoring it and reinforcing other children for cooperation. Jimmy does not seem to be susceptible to such treatment—or maybe he cannot break his habitual outbursts, which seem to release some pent-up emotions or help him solve some basic social problem. The teacher, Mr. Trent, decides that the only way to handle Jimmy is through consistent punishment for aggression. He does not want to set an example of aggression while doing this, however, since that could result in more of the same. Therefore he looks for some neutral stimulus which is aversive and which he can apply to Jimmy conveniently whenever Jimmy starts to go after one of the other kids. He decides to try an old approach where he grasps Jimmy by the back of the neck with his thumb and third finger and squeezes rather hard—enough to really hurt, but not enough to do any permanent damage. He does it in a way which is nonaggressive, and which does not in any way indicate that he is terribly angry or upset, or that he dislikes Jimmy personally. He simply does it every time Jimmy is aggressive and continues it as he steers Jimmy in some other direction. He follows it up with a short period of isolation; he puts Jimmy in a partly enclosed space in the classroom and has him stay there for about five minutes, after which he tells him he can come out again.

Before he starts this punishment program, he observes Jimmy over a period of about five days, and makes a note each time Jimmy behaves in the manner that is causing the problem. He gets an average, or a "baseline," and then continues to count after he institutes punishment. He finds that the frequency decreases steadily over the next few days. When he stops the punishment, the frequency increases again, although not up to the former level.

Avoidance teaching

One type of learning contingency, or set of contingencies, combines both classical and operant conditioning, and is a very prevalent and important process to understand. This is "avoidance learning." In this type of learning, a learner changes his behavior in a situation where he anticipates some averse outcome, or punishment. When certain stimuli indicate that a certain behavior is likely to be punished, the learner substitutes some other behavior to avoid the punishment.

To bring someone to do something in a certain situation, arrange things so that the situation makes him or her anticipate punishment, so that the thing you want him or her to do has the effect of avoiding that punishment. For example, if you want a student to study hard, than arrange her schedule so that she expects a quiz the next day, which she is afraid of flunking. She will study in order to relieve her anxiety over flunking and to avoid actually flunking.

Note that since avoidance teaching is based on the threat of punishment, the behavior taught this way may become a conditioned stimulus for the same fear or anxiety that was used to make it occur. If a student crams in order to pass, out of fear of flunking, the anxiety and fear become associated with the subject matter, the place of study, and studying generally. This also increases the likelihood of future avoidance of the subject matter, and of studying generally.

A solution to this problem would involve emphasizing hope of success, desirability of studying the subject, its inherent interest, and using other positive approaches to motivating it that are outlined in Chapter 7. Also the incorporation into teaching of behaviors and characteristics described in Chapter 5 and in Chapters 11 and 12 will help avoid the necessity for emphasis or reliance on punishment.

CONDITIONING AND COGNITION

Should we deal with thoughts or behaviors?

Recent innovations in teaching and therapy cross the boundaries between feeling, behaving, and thinking.

For many years there has been a debate between those who emphasize the behavior of people and animals and how it is shaped by conditioning, and those who emphasize that humans are primarily thinking beings who do not conform to conditioning procedures in their learning and lifestyles generally. This debate has often obscured the similarities between the views and has made it difficult to see conditioning as a basic characteristic of human behavior, along with more complex and sophisticated behaviors, traits, and thinking processes. Among the severest critics of behavioristic approaches to analyzing human development are the linguists, who point out that humans learn complex verbal processes without going through slow conditioning processes, and that animals (who *can* be conditioned) cannot learn to speak a language. Those who have analyzed the development of verbal behavior from a behavioristic (conditioning) point of view have been held up to ridicule. As in the heredity-environment debate and other similar dilemmas, however, it is probably most productive and best for learners if a parent, teacher, or counselor assumes that both views and approaches have their place, and that they can exist side-by-side.

Can chimpanzees learn to talk?

To illustrate the possibility that there is a continuum of behavioral levels and that highly sophisticated behaviors can be explained either way, some information about a project in which a chimpanzee was taught to "speak" may be appropriate. This was reported by David Premack (1970) in an article entitled "The Education of Sarah" in *Psychology Today*. Premack and his colleagues, in teaching a chimpanzee named Sarah to speak, used what they called a "functional" approach. They listed some functions that Sarah's behaviors had to fulfill in order to say that she was "speaking," and then they listed strict training procedures to produce these functions. Four of the functions were "word," "sentence," "question," and "metalinguistics." (The latter means the use of language to teach more language, as in "M is the name of X.")

Since speech as we know it is physically impossible for a chimpanzee because of the formation of its mouth and tongue, Sarah was given "words" in the form of plastic shapes that varied in shape, size, color, and texture. These adhered to a magnetic language board by their metal backs. To write a sentence, Sarah placed the "words" in sequence, vertically from top to bottom.

To teach Sarah, the trainers would place something on the table—say a banana—and observe as she took it and ate it. Then, one day, the trainer would introduce a particular plastic shape that was to stand for "banana"; it would be placed where she could reach it easily, while the banana was placed out of reach. When Sarah placed it on the language board, she would be reinforced with the banana itself. Sarah quickly learned to play this game. Then new fruits were introduced, and new words for them. After playing this many times correctly, Sarah was given two "words" and one fruit; she would get the fruit only if she took the correct "word."

Later, the person who presented the fruit was varied. When Mary was present, for example, Sarah would have to place the word for "Mary" on the board ahead of "apple" to get Mary to give her the apple. Ultimately, Sarah learned to say "Mary give apple Sarah," and more complex sentences as well, through chaining and shaping processes.

These techniques, interestingly enough, have been adapted to teach severely retarded learners to speak. Success has been achieved in bringing these learners to communicate where they have never communicated before, and some of them have begun to vocalize spontaneously after first learning to talk through the medium of concrete word forms. This program is called "non-slip" for "non-speech language initiation program" (Anders, 1975).

Biofeedback: Where cognition fails and two types of conditioning merge

Biofeedback involves wiring a person to an electronic system that measures changes in stress, body temperature, blood pressure, and other reactions. With practice, a person can learn thought processes or relaxation techniques that induce calm and return the electronic indicators to normal when they show that the person is getting tense. Achieving relaxation in this way, before stressful situations actually occur, is a method being used to increase people's effectiveness in such situations. The "feedback" is reminiscent of the "reinforcement" of operant conditioning, but the reactions being dealt with are the supposedly "involuntary" responses of classical conditioning. When a person begins to feel tense about an impending event (a test, a performance, or even having sexual relations) the feedback from the electronic system shows the tension in the form of increased blood pressure, faster heartbeat and so forth; this comes to the person himself or herself as an audible or visual signal. By using relaxation techniques learned previously, or simply by trial and error, the person becomes able to control these symptoms and to bring them back to normal. Thus what was once considered "involuntary" now has become, in this sense and to this degree, voluntary. We might even say that in reducing heart rate or blood pressure, the person is "reinforced" for his or her relaxation behavior (in operant conditioning terms). However, another time the same situation is likely to occasion less anxiety, and therefore he or she has been "deconditioned" in a classical conditioning sense. The cognitive aspects of the process may lie in the kinds of thoughts the person thinks in order to get himself to relax, or in the verbal instructions he gives himself; however, it is obviously not the kind of thinking that is usually considered in studies of problem solving and conceptualizing.

How might this information be used? One example is an experiment where hyperactive learners had electrodes taped to their heads to record their brain waves. It turned out that they had few if any alpha waves, the kind of brain waves which indicate a calm, relaxed state. These learners were given training in which they were reinforced for producing more alpha waves. They were able to learn to do this when the alpha waves were translated into signals which they could perceive, and for which they could be reinforced. This demonstrated that such children could actually learn to control their brainwave output. The effects on their behavior were not as clear, however; some of the experimental group showed significant improvement (they were able to sleep better, read better, write more legibly, attend better, and were more relaxed). The number of such learners was small, and the results were not conclusive regarding the effectiveness of such training on classroom behavior.

Biofeedback training is in its early stages of development, and while it has promise, you will want to follow future experiments in this field to see whether that promise is realized.

Summary outline with key concepts

☞ *Learning is* shown through behaviors, or responses / To analyze learning and behavior, you have to observe both input and output / Theories of mental processing are developed from observations of input and output / Learning is a change in the way a person perceives his or her environment and responds to it / Teaching is a process of changing the environment so that learning is more probable / The environment includes things inside the learner as well as outside / Stimuli are occurrences in the environment / Behavior is what you observe coming from a learner, i.e., a pattern of responses / Operant responses are physical or motor ones; they "operate" on the environment / Cognitive responses involve thinking, relating, associating, and such / Stimulus-response analyses of behavior are not un-human, but represent a method of analyzing human behavior and what determines it / The theories in this chapter are largely attributable to I. Pavlov and B. F. Skinner.

☞ *In classical* conditioning a neutral stimulus comes to elicit a classical response on its own, by being paired with or just preceding an unconditioned stimulus which already elicits the response / To condition an emotional response to some stimulus, associate that stimulus with something which already elicits that emotion / To reduce or eliminate a classically-conditioned response, extinguish it / To reduce or eliminate a classically-conditioned response, present with the conditioned stimulus another stimulus which elicits an opposing response / To desensitize a classical response (e.g., fear) present a series of closer and closer approximations to the conditioned stimulus, either in imagination or reality, along with stimuli which elicit an opposing response.

☞ *Operant responses* are voluntary, where classical are involuntary / Operant responses operate on the environment; they are psychomotor / If you reinforce an operant response, it increases in frequency / In order to get an operant response to occur, prompt it / When you prompt, you later have to withdraw the prompt / A secondary reinforcer is one which was associated with a primary reinforcer / To extinguish an operant response, withhold reinforcement / To develop stimulus control, reinforce the response only when the desired stimulus precedes it.

☞ *A response* which has been conditioned to one stimulus will be evoked by another similar stimulus—this is stimulus generalization / A response which has been conditioned to one stimulus will not be evoked by another which is different—this is stimulus discrimination / You can teach discrimination between two stimuli which evoke the same response, by reinforcing the response when one precedes it, and not when the other does / If a person learns to do something in one environment or situation, and then does it in another similar one (without additional teaching), then he or she has learned to "transfer" the learning to a new situation.

☞ *In shaping* you start with the best the learner can do; reinforce that; then begin to reinforce only better performance, gradually raising your criteria for reinforcement until the learner gives the response you want / In environmental shaping you alter the environment gradually while keeping the response the same, rather than reinforcing increasingly adequate responses.

☞ *Both types* of conditioning can be accomplished vicariously through modeling / Graduated modeling is used when the learner cannot imitate the full response right away / Modeling can teach new responses, and strengthen and weaken old ones.

☞ *Psychomotor abilities* are basic to many different skills; a number of them have been identified / Purely motor abilities include such things as flexing or stretching the trunk or back, and others / Abilities important in the early phases of learning a skill may not be important (or as important) as other abilities during later phases / There is virtually no loss of well-learned skills over time / There is a need for programs which train learners in basic physical and psychomotor abilities in the early grades / Building chains of responses involves associating a cue for one response with another response which precedes it, i.e., using stimulus substitution / Sometimes it is most effective to build a chain of responses from back to front / Guidelines for teaching skills include extinction of old competing skills, building the new skill through graduated modeling and shaping, having the learner overlearn the skill, and incorporating the skill into other skills / The learning curve is S-shaped except when there are plateaus /

Long-term learning of related things or concepts results in acceleration of learning: the more you learn, the more you *can* learn / Guidelines for learning and teaching skills can be and are given.

☞ *To reduce* or eliminate operant behavior, either extinguish the response, or punish it and reinforce another response in its place / Punishment can be effective, but it can become a habit / Some kinds of punishment model aggressive behavior / Punishment does not eliminate a response, but suppresses it; when the threat of punishment ceases, the response will return / Avoidance teaching means getting learners to do things to avoid punishment.

☞ *Conditioning of* behavior is held by some to be inferior to teaching through insight, or to teaching concepts and ideas / Language learning has been a case in point: behaviorists have succeeded in teaching languate to lower animals (chimpanzees) through operant conditioning processes.

Glossary

Avoidance Teaching: Teaching something by invoking threat, so the learner learns to avoid punishment.

Backward Chaining: Teaching a response chain from back to front.

Biofeedback: Electronic systems which give audible or visible evidence of internal involuntary responses, such as heartbeat, blood pressure.

Chain, or Response Chain: Sequence of responses integrated into a unitary sequence, as in reaching for a piece of bread, or tying one's shoe.

Classical Response: Involuntary reflex behavior, involving the sympathetic and autonomic nervous systems; fear, hope, love, as well as certain reflexes such as the knee jerk or eye blink.

Cognitive Response: Response which is internal, unobservable, and involves the brain: associating, relating, remembering, thinking.

Conditioned Response: Response which was originally given to an unconditioned stimulus, but through conditioning is now given to a conditioned stimulus, i.e., a stimulus which was formerly neutral (classical conditioning).

Conditioned Stimulus: Stimulus which was formerly neutral but which, through conditioning, has come to elicit a response (classical conditioning).

Contingency: Relationship where something happens only if something else happens.

Counter-conditioning: Invoking stimuli which compete with a particular stimulus in classical conditioning, i.e., which elicit responses incompatible with the one elicited by the other stimulus.

Cue: Same as prompt.

Desensitization: Reducing or eliminating emotional responses through a series of imaginary experiences (or real experiences) which approach gradually the target situation.

Discrimination: Differentiating between two situations that vary slightly by responding differently to them.

Extinction: In operant conditioning, withholding the reinforcer; in classical conditioning, withholding the unconditioned stimulus.

Fading: Gradually removing a prompt or cue.

Generalization: Demonstrating learning in a new situation similar to the one in which the learning occurred originally.

Graduated Modeling: Modeling in successive stages, instead of all at once.

Intermittent Reinforcement: Reinforcing every second or third or fifth time, or in some other ratio; reinforcing every three or ten minutes or every hour, instead of every time the response is given (ratio and interval reinforcement).

Interval Reinforcement: Intermittent reinforcement according to time interval.

Modeling: Teaching by setting an example, or demonstrating; conditioning learner A (operant or classical) by having her observe the conditioning of learner B, i.e., vicarious conditioning.

Operant Response: Response which operates on the environment—walking, reaching, etc.

Pavlov, I.: Russian psychologist whose experimental work led to the identification and analysis of classical conditioning.

Plateau: Period in learning a skill when little progress is made.

Premack Principle: The principle that any behavior that is frequent can be used to reinforce a behavior that is less frequent.

Prompting: Presenting a stimulus which evokes a response, in order to reinforce the response, or in order to substitute another stimulus for it.

Psychomotor Response: Motor response with some cognitive involvement.

Punishment, Punisher: An aversive stimulus, one which the learner will avoid.

Ratio Reinforcement: Intermittent reinforcement according to a ratio, e.g., every n times the response is given.

Reinforcer: A stimulus which, when presented immediately following a response, makes the response more frequent in the future (operant reinforcement).

Response: An observable behavior of a learner.

Secondary Reinforcer: A stimulus which acquires reinforcing capabilities by being associated with a primary reinforcer.

Shaping: Teaching some behavior by beginning with an existing response and reinforcing aspects of the response most like the desired one, through a series of successive approximations to the target behavior.

Skinner, B. F.: American psychologist whose experimental work led to the identification and analysis of operant reinforcement and related effects.

Skinner Box: A special experimental cage or box with an automatic food-vending mechanism which operates in response to some action of an animal within, e.g., pecking at a bar.

Social Reinforcer: A reinforcing stimulus given verbally or physically by one person to another, e.g., a word of praise.

Stimulus: An event in the environment which affects a learner, i.e., which the learner receives, or perceives through his or her senses.

Stimulus Substitution: One stimulus comes to elicit a response originally evoked by another stimulus, by being contiguous with it (i.e., coming just before or at the same time).

Transfer: Learning demonstrated in a situation different from the one in which it was acquired.

Variable Reinforcement: Ratio or interval reinforcement where the number of responses or the time intervals vary from reinforcement to reinforcement, e.g., every five times on the average but actually after one, then seven, then three, etc.

Questions for thought and discussion

1. What is meant by operant conditioning?   What is "reinforcement?"
2. What is classical conditioning?   What is a "conditioned stimulus?"
3. How do operant and classical conditioning differ?   How are they alike?
4. Describe extinction, in relation to both types of conditioning.
5. What is a "prompt?"   How do you "fade" a prompt, and why?
6. What is meant by "desensitization?"   Why is it necessary for getting rid of fears?
7. What is "shaping?"   When should it *not* be used?
8. What is "modeling?"   How do you go about it?   What kinds of teaching can you do with it?
9. How do you condition a chain of responses?
10. As you continue to learn an extensive body of related skills or concepts, does learning increase in speed (i.e., do you learn faster and faster, or slower and slower)?
11. Is punishment effective?   Under what conditions?   What are some of its bad side effects?
12. What is "biofeedback?"   Is it anything like "desensitization?"

Situations calling for applications of facts and concepts

1. How would you condition a tenth-grade girl to like homework?
2. How would you increase the amount of attention given in class by a sixth-grade boy?
3. How would you desensitize a thirty-year-old woman who is afraid of being in church?
4. How would you reduce the number of times a high school junior (boy) talks out of turn in class?
5. How would you teach a class of very hostile teenagers to be less hostile and aggressive, through modeling?   Through other behavior-modification approaches?

6. How would you teach a chain of responses where a basketball player is supposed to fake to the left, then to the right, then drive to the left and make a lay-up?

7. How would you teach someone to relax during a test, through biofeedback?

8. How would you use punishment to stop a seventh-grade girl from picking on another girl?

9. How would you reduce the acting-out and increase the organization of a hyperactive seven-year-old boy?

Suggested activities

1. Observe a friend who is having difficulty in managing his or her class, and analyze how he or she may be reinforcing undesirable behaviors and/or extinguishing (or even punishing) desirable ones.

2. Get together as a class and agree on a strategy for shaping the instructor's behavior in some way, through varying your attention during lectures or through some other process involving reinforcement and extinction.

3. Try to desensitize a friend of some fear.

4. Help a friend (or yourself) to increase some behavior which is desirable (like smiling more, responding more to other people) or to decrease some undesirable behavior (like smoking, or talking too much, or using bad language). Start by recording the behavior and drawing a baseline, then reinforce and extinguish (or punish) as appropriate.

Suggested readings

A very practical text which is partly self-instructional is *Teaching 1: Classroom management*, by Becker, Engelmann and Thomas. A thorough, programmed approach is *Analysis of behavior*, by Holland and Skinner; this is the progenitor of all programmed texts. You may want to read Skinner's *Walden Two*, a novel that demonstrates applied behavioristic principles, or his *Beyond freedom and dignity*, which discusses implications of those principles for the future of society. Albert Bandura's *Principles of behavior modification* gives a thorough explanation of modeling and its relationships to conditioning processes. Journals which carry research in these areas are the *Journal of Applied Behavioral Analysis* and the *Journal of the Experimental Analysis of Behavior*.

Teaching Verbal
Responses and
Concepts

CONTENTS

What this chapter can mean to you

This chapter will prepare you to deal with forgetting and remembering. Memorization is a basic aspect of learning, and some things are easier to commit to memory than to look up continually—a prime example is vocabulary, whether related to geology, Spanish, or economics. You will gain an understanding of the reasons for and uses of review questions. You will also acquire a method and rationale for teaching concepts, which are the foundation of all learning from the sensorimotor stage through advanced graduate study. They vary in complexity and sophistication and depth, but concepts are the mainstay of learning. With this knowledge you may be better prepared to handle some of the learning tasks you are faced with as a student as well. You will also begin to see how people can study for months or years yet feel they cannot remember anything (although they can) and cannot use what they remember (which is often the case). You should also be able to formulate some teaching strategies which prevent this from happening.

What might make this chapter difficult

This chapter begins with a discussion of rote verbal learning; you may feel that rote learning is unrelated to the kind of meaningful learning that can and should go on in schools or in special education. However, processes that emerge from this kind of research apply to all learning, and no learning is entirely without meaning. The chapter also deals with memorizing, and you may believe that this is either an innate capacity (you have a good memory or you don't) or that memorization is another thing to be strictly avoided in teaching. However, memorization has its place, and there are ways of teaching learners to remember better—one of them is by making things more meaningful! Finally, you may feel that concept learning is a matter of reflection and higher thought, and that the strategies for teaching concepts here are not necessary for motivated and interested students; we hope that you will reconsider this stand because teachers generally fall very short in their attempts to teach concepts well, and this failure is felt by most learners who try to apply what they learned later on.

Reasons for studying the teaching of verbal responses and concepts

There are two basic problems to be surmounted in teaching in addition to motivation; one is to get learners to remember what they have learned (i.e., retention), and the other is to get them to apply it beyond the classroom and textbook (i.e., transfer). This chapter deals with basic characteristics of verbal and conceptual learning that determine retention and transfer, and is thus fundamental and important in the study of teaching. No teacher or administrator should fail to comprehend the facts, concepts, and processes covered here.

Objectives

Verbal learning and concept teaching are important parts of the education of anyone interested in teaching, in whatever context it is done. I want you to be aware of the important processes, relationships, and strategies which these topics involve and suggest.

BACKGROUND AND RATIONALE OF CHAPTER 9

The meaningfulness of rote verbal learning

Research in the learning of lists of nonsense syllables, discussed in the first part of this chapter, is research in learning generally; as one of the leading investigators in this field has explained, even rote learning is meaningful to some degree. Meaning implies relationships and associations, and we perceive nothing without these factors, partly because we perceive in terms of previous experience (Underwood, 1964). As you will see, objective, relatively scientific strategies for studying verbal learning have yielded some rather surprising and suggestive results in relation to teaching generally. However, many regard such research as irrelevant to meaningful human learning.

The background of concept learning research and its relevance to other chapters

Rote verbal learning is not meaningless: concept learning is fundamental to our thinking processes.

Jerome Bruner's early book *A study of thinking* was among the first to emphasize the importance of concept learning in understanding learning generally. Bruner later applied many of the ideas generated by this kind of research to theories of teaching (see *Toward a theory of instruction*). In the first book Bruner and his colleagues examined the strategies of thinking used by students who were attempting to identify complex concepts shown them, for example, on cards; the subjects were not given the names or descriptions of the concepts but were forced to acquire them by discovering the relationships themselves. This research led ultimately to the guidelines that you will find for concept teaching, later in this chapter. Such learning is quite practical, by the way: it is a little like the task you face in social learning, where you have to decide what is important and unimportant in the behavior of someone whose success in life you admire and want to emulate. It is also a little like language learning, where the child observes and imitates, but also "picks up" the meanings of phrases and the uses of grammatical constructions by seeing them in action.   It is also a bit like the approach to learning taken by Piaget, as interpreted by Kohlberg when he commented on the importance of viewing the child as a philosopher who was trying to solve problems posed by his or her environment and society.   Obviously you can also regard it as a problem-solving process, and thus relate it to the discussions you will come to in Chapter 10.   You will also find, in reading about verbal learning research in the first part of this chapter, that when people recite lists of syllables, words, or names (without trying to get them in any particular order), they produce clusters with similar meanings or sounds.   It turns out that the mind stores or remembers things in terms of common attributes and relationships of various types, and this is part of concept learning also, since concepts are categories of things with something(s) in common.   Finally, in setting the stage for this chapter, you may remember that during the sensorimotor stage of development the learner forms "schema"; these were the fundamental building blocks of learning, combinations of visual and auditory and tactual and kinesthetic experiences integrated into these early, probably rather crude mental patterns. These schema can be viewed as concepts as well, or as an early precursor to what we call "concepts" in adult thought.

Cognitive learning

For some years now "cognitive learning" has been a field of exploration that has been differentiated sharply from such lower forms of study as "rote learning" or "behavioristic learning" or "trial and error learning."   Yet all of the types and levels discussed so far, whether Piagetian, behavioristic, factual, or social, have involved cognition.   In studying learning disabilities, we discriminated between automatic and representational (or associational) learning, as on the ITPA; however, it was pointed out at the time that the very basic process of recognizing a chair, while considered an "input" or "decoding" process, has an element of cognition. Between this exercise and abstract theorizing may be many levels of increasingly "cognitive" processing.   Of course, Piaget and Bruner have pointed out that the older the child, the more abstract or "cognitive" his or her thinking.   Yet we have just talked about the meaningfulness (or cognitive nature) of rote verbal learning, and the concrete operational stage involved quite complex relationships and strategies of solving problems.   The moral, ego, and psychosocial levels described in Chapter 1 interacted with growth in thinking ability, as you remember: they become, then, increasingly "cognitive."   In studying motivation, we addressed the question of the influence of thinking over behavior, i.e., whether knowing the thought processes of a certain type of personality would lead to behaving that way. You also saw that traditional psychotherapies relied on insight or the intellectual appreciation of the source of problems: this is a cognitive theory of emotion.

So you have been dealing with cognitive learning in various forms throughout this book; you will be dealing with it again here, and in another form in the next

You have studied "cognition" before, and you will be reading more about it later as well.

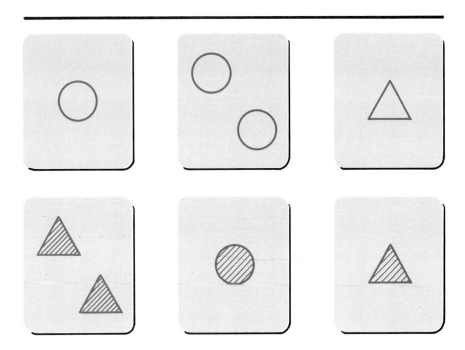

Here you see cards that have two different shapes, and each shape comes either singly or in pairs; there are also shaded and unshaded versions. Thus three attributes can be presented, and there are two "levels" of each; i.e., one attribute is shape, and there are two shapes; another attribute is number, and there are two numbers (one circle or two circles), etc. If we only have the three attributes and the two levels of each attribute, how many different cards do we need to make a complete set?

One concept that might be learned from these cards is "shaded circle." In a typical research approach, all cards with shaded circles would be considered "positive exemplars"; all others would be "negative exemplars." As the experimenter, you would either present cards one at a time and have the learner guess which it is (positive or negative), or you would lay out all the cards and let the learner select one, make a guess, and then give him or her information about the answer (whether correct or incorrect). The first process is called a "reception" strategy, the second a "selection" strategy.

Figure 9–1. *Simple versions of Bruner's concept learning cards.*

chapter. In the final part of the book, you will also deal with it again in terms of the various kinds of knowledge that can be evaluated by tests, and the effects of different types of testing on the kinds and amounts of thinking done by learners.

VERBAL LEARNING RESEARCH

Serial learning

A student sits in front of a device that reveals one syllable every two seconds from a list of syllables whose order is kept the same each time the device presents the list to the learner. The first syllable might be something like BOK, for example, and the second RIV, and the third NOX, etc. (These are called "nonsense syllables.") The student is to anticipate RIV when he sees BOK, and NOX when he sees RIV, and so forth. As he goes through the list a number of times he begins to anticipate each syllable. He will learn the first part of the list quickly, then the last part, then the middle. This is evidently due to the fact that learning one syllable interferes somewhat with learning another, so those in the middle suffer this interference from both sides, as it were. This results in what is called the "serial position effect" shown in Figure 9–2.

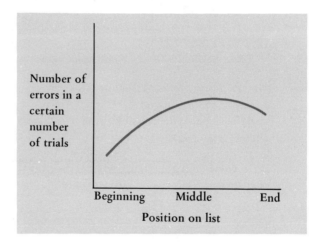

Figure 9–2. *The serial position effect.*

Forgetting in serial learning

If there are two groups of students, one of which learns more slowly (on the average) than the other, and if both groups learn the list to the same degree—say, to two times through without an error—then their retention of the list over a period of time will be about the same; neither will forget more than the other. This suggests that the speed of learning does not determine retention; rather, the degree to which you learn something determines how well you remember it. This was found in research on motor learning as well, as was reported in Chapter 8.

Forgetting occurs mainly in the period immediately following learning, as shown in Figure 9–3. Current theories of forgetting attribute it to interference

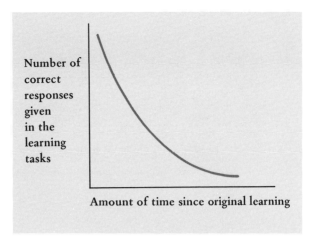

Figure 9–3. *Pattern of forgetting, called "proactive inhibition."*

Things to re-
member often
come in sequences:
you learn the first
parts first, the last
parts next, the
middle last.

from other learning, particularly from things learned before.   This kind of interference is called "proactive inhibition."   In the words of the old jingle, then:

Why study at all?
The more you study, the more you learn,
The more you learn, the more you forget,
The more you forget, the less you know,
So why study at all?

Forgetting due to interference from things learned later on is called "retroactive inhibition"; for example, where learning French interferes with your memory of the
Spanish you studied before.

Teaching serial lists

To teach lists of things, arrange for items in the list to be presented one by one, and
ask the learner to recall the next one each time.   Then present the next one, and
repeat the process.
    One example is the learning of a poem.   Since the learner can hold phrases or
whole lines in his (or her) mind, you have him learn it line by line.   He says one
line, then tries to think of the next; after he has thought, show it to him, and have
him think of the next, etc.   The essential thing is to withhold the next item (word
or phrase) in the list until the learner has attempted to anticipate it.   Of course,
the learner can do this for himself, by hiding the next one, and this is something he
should be taught to do if he does not do it intuitively.   If a sequence of facts is to be
learned in the same order as given, then enough repetitions are needed so those in
the middle of the sequence are learned, due to the serial position effect.

Teaching unordered lists

If the order of a list is not important, then assist the learning (1) by grouping items according to some common attribute—kind of things, common names, common sounds, or common meanings; (2) by incorporating the members of the list into a story, so the meaning of the story helps recall the various parts; (3) by relating each member of the list to a previously memorized set of things through visual images of some connection or situation involving both of them; and (4) by choosing the items in the list so they are very meaningful to the learner.

An example of (1) would be grouping members of the following list:

cat, field, banana, tree, cow, avocado, tulip

as follows:

cat, cow   field, tree, tulip   avocado, banana

An example of (2) would be making up a story such as the following:

In the field under the avocado tree stood a cow peeling a banana, while between the horns of the cow sat a cat holding a tulip.

An example of (3) would be a case where a person had memorized a list of very odd, vivid, personal things—such as blood, hat-rack, genitals, scream, etc. Then the person would relate each item in the list to these already memorized items through some unique vivid, relationships, ideally a visual one—for example, relating "cat" to "blood" by imagining a cat being dissected in an anatomy class and blood running over the table, and then imagining a hat-rack standing all by itself in the middle of a large field with silk hats hanging from it, and so forth.

An example of (4) would be teaching reading to a poor reader by teaching her words that are personally meaningful: family names, verbs related to things she likes to do, and so forth. Then you would have her read simple stories with words in them: the meaningfulness of these words to her would make them easy to learn and to read in another context (Ashton-Warner, 1963).

Paired-associate Learning

Serial learning resembles conventional learning in some respects, but there is another kind which is somewhat more sophisticated and which resembles other aspects of school learning. It is called "paired-associate" learning. Suppose you are shown the stimulus BAV, a nonsense syllable. Then you are shown the stimulus ROS, as follows:

First show BAV   Then show BAV-ROS

You are asked to anticipate the second syllable of the pair before it is shown to you. Then you are given another, say MUX, followed by MUX-SIM. Thus, given the first of each pair, you have to anticipate (say) the second. There might be twenty or more pairs in the list (as in French vocabulary assignments, for example). Then the list of pairs is shuffled so that, although the same second syllable follows the first in each case, the order of the pairs has changed.

To "learn" the list you have to anticipate correctly each second syllable, and give the correct response. Sometimes you are required to do this twice or three times through the list without error, to demonstrate "learning."

Suppose you were asked to learn *two* paired-associate lists, one after the other, as below:

A-B	A-C
fos-rel	fos-siv
gav-gox	gav-mub
etc.	etc.

Note the relationship between the first syllables (they are the same in the two lists). This is called the "A-B, A-C" paradigm. The second syllables are quite different. You could have a list where the second syllables were similar, like "fos-ril" and "gav-gus"—this would be called "A-B'." Learning A-B has an effect on the

Another frequent learning task involves names of things or foreign language word equivalents; these involve paired associate learning.

learning of A-B' and on A-C. In A-B', since the first syllables are the same and the second ones similar, you might expect A-B' to be easier if A-B were learned first than if it were not. This is ordinarily the case, and is called "proactive facilitation" or "positive transfer." On the other hand, learning A-B might interfere with learning A-C; this would be called "proactive inhibition," or "negative transfer." Thus, what you have learned before, and what you will learn later, affects what you are learning now.

Teaching names

To bring about the learning of names for things, pictures, or words that go with other words (as in learning vocabulary), present the things, pictures, or initial words one at a time, and require the learner to furnish the name or equivalent without seeing the answer; then show the answer. After doing this for all the things involved, allow a short time to intervene, then do it again but in a different order. Continue this until all are learned.

An example is learning the names of different birds, animals, or both: you show a bird, or a picture of it, and ask for the name; after a few seconds, you give the name. Then show another bird or another picture, and so on. After doing all the birds this way, take a short break, then start over again, but present them in a different order.

Another example is learning vocabulary. Suppose the words are: table—la fenêtre; chair—la chaise; book—le livre; and so forth. Present "table" and ask the learner to give the French equivalent, telling him (or her) the answer, or indicating that he is right; then present "chair," and so forth. After going through the whole list, start over, but present it in a different order—perhaps "book" first, then "table," then "chair," and so forth.

Mediation

Consider two lists of paired associates, the first being like this:

> soldier - pipe
> dog   - leaf
> hatter - pot

and the second like this:

> arm   - then
> just   - hold
> organ - tan

Would there be any difference in the speed of learning the two? Soldier is related to "sailor" and that in turn to "hornpipe," and thus to "pipe." "Dog" relates through "tree" to "leaf," and "hatter" through "tea party" to "pot." Although not every learner would be conscious of these relationships, the fact that they exist would probably mean that the first list would be learned more quickly. (Of course, this assumes that there are not comparable verbal bridges between the terms in the second list; you might find some that are just as effective.) These mental bridges are called "mediators."

This is a useful tool not only for learning vocabulary in languages, but also for learning names, either of things or people. If you can think of some type of mediator between the name and the thing named, it helps you recall it. For example, if Mr. Moon has a very round face, or if the name of a tower in India is Qutar Minar and you remember that a minaret is a tall slender tower but that this one is quite the opposite of "cute." Teachers can help students remember key facts by inventing mediators for them—sometimes in the form of rhymes, like "i before e except after c," sometimes in the form of relationships with directions and everyday things as when you tell a learner that the letter "b" has the loop to the right side just as the *bus* goes on the right side of the street, while "d" has the loop on the left just as the *driver* sits on the left side of the bus. A visual mediator can help also, as when you act out the saying "spring forward, fall back" for helping people to remember which ways to set their watches when time changes from standard to daylight savings or vice versa.

Distribution of practice

When two groups learn the same list to the same degree, but one group learns it all at one sitting whereas the other has practice sessions distributed over a longer time (each one shorter than the mass practice of the first group), then the groups show different resistance to proactive and retroactive inhibition, that is, to interference from other learning. Generally the distributed practice group has less trouble with such interference, and thus retains the material better if there is other material of a similar nature that has to be learned as well.

This implies that in teaching skills or facts you should have short practice sessions and frequent ones, with other activities (including other learning activities) in between. However, this is not enough of a science as yet that we can say *how* long or *how* many or *how* much material to have in between. Another form of distribution of practice, of course, is review. You ought to plan to go back and review things learned earlier, and do this quite often.

OTHER TEACHING TECHNIQUES SUGGESTED BY VERBAL LEARNING RESEARCH

Review

In order to ensure future use of any learning when it is needed (i.e., to provide for retention and recall), returning to the material intermittently is an important process. This return can either be passive (a presentation of earlier material, in

Distribution of practice, review, and overlearning are important teaching techniques for verbal learning and other learning.

original or reduced form) or active (requiring the learner to respond to tasks based on the material). Generally speaking, review should occur after a small amount of additional material has been introduced, then again after more material has been introduced, and then at increasingly larger intervals.

It is often possible to provide for the review function by designing the learning process so that the learner must use previous knowledge in acquiring new knowledge. This keeps the old material fresh in mind and relates it to new material at the same time. This also makes it unnecessary to have formal, independent review sessions.

Overlearning

You read earlier that the degree to which something is learned determines how well it will be remembered: you probably don't believe this! You have heard, no doubt, that the more meaningful and relevant the material, the better you will retain it. Indirectly this is true, since you learn meaningful material better, or to a higher degree, in a given time. However, if you spend enough time on nonmeaningful material you can learn it to the same degree, and you will retain it as well.

Practically speaking this means that there are two basic ways of assuring retention, or combatting forgetting. One is to make the material studied more relevant and meaningful by relating it to things that are familiar and important to the learners and to other things they have learned, and by using mediators. The other basic way of assuring retention is by overlearning, by practicing, drilling, repeating beyond the point where something is "learned" in the usual sense, so that the learning is brought to a higher degree. (Admittedly, we don't know exactly what "higher degree" means in all situations, but additional practice does seem to work in this way.)

In learning physics or languages or tennis, it is not always possible or convenient to make everything that needs to be learned "meaningful" and "relevant" to the learners; there just isn't time to do this and still cover the basic facts and concepts. So the alternative is to overlearn, to practice and drill on the fundamental facts and concepts, preferably through distributed practice sessions, until they are so well learned they become almost automatic. Of course, the practice or drill can be varied and can take the form of simple games or routines that are fun, in many cases; furthermore, students become accustomed to drill when it is regular and consistent. They don't resent drilling as long as they see a reason for it, if others are doing it, and if it is done consistently and not for too long.

Advance organizers

"Advance organizers" are reading passages designed to facilitate learning the reading passages that come after them (Ausubel, 1968). For example, if a subject requires the reading and understanding of some complex material, say a series of

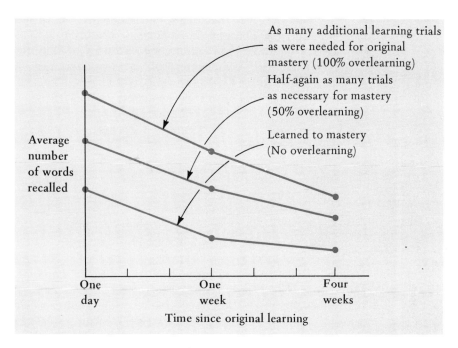

Figure 9–4. *How overlearning improves recall (from an experiment by Krueger in 1929, adapted by Gage and Berliner, 1975, readapted here).*

crucial events in history or a deep philosophical essay, you might first use a reading assignment that introduces some of the general concepts involved. This preliminary assignment may not cover the same facts, but it may present the kinds of ideas and concepts that are treated, and thus "organize" the thinking of the learner in advance. Thus it would "transfer" to the more complicated reading, and make it more possible for students to comprehend it.

In a larger sense, the first part of any well-structured course is usually an advance organizer for the later parts, and introductory courses are advance organizers for more advanced courses. In a more technical sense (in anticipation of the discussion of concept learning and teaching in the next section), advance organizers may ultimately take the form of more powerful basic concepts; that is, just as the "schema" of the sensorimotor period provide the foundation for later learning (Chapter 1), so the learning of more powerful all-encompassing concepts in the early grades would make it possible for students in the future to learn more and more easily than you and I did. Jerome Bruner has referred to this as an "implosion" of knowledge to counteract the knowledge "explosion" of recent decades.

Ausubel, the originator of this idea, has recommended its use early in a lecture to provide a foundation of ideas to help students understand facts and more complex concepts which are presented later. He also recommends that teachers ask questions about what the students already know about a subject, then use their prior knowledge as "advance organizers" where it relates.   This also has the effect of making the subject more meaningful and relevant to the learners personally, of course, and thus blends with recommendations given in the sections above.

There has been some research on advance organizers, and not all of it has shown them to be effective; however, enough experiments have been supportive to conclude that they are a useful strategy in teaching (Frase, 1969; Merrill and Stolurow, 1966).

An information-processing view of verbal learning

In discussing language acquisition in Chapter 2, the differences between input and output functions were emphasized; in discussing learning disabilities, input and output were again differentiated from cognition, although there was no easily identified dividing line.   In discussing problem solving (Chapter 10) this information-processing view will be expanded.   However, since language and learning disabilities involve verbal learning, and since verbal learning is involved in thinking generally, some reference to the information processing model is appropriate here as well.   Furthermore, it affords a logical opportunity to discuss a basic element of learning that has been only alluded to previously, namely, memory.

The input—cognition—output model for information processing is relevant to verbal learning also.

In the information-processing model, "input" in the form of sensory stimuli is "decoded" by some kind of first stage of processing.   This involves holding the input in temporary storage; for example, if you are listening to a sentence, you have to "store" the first part in some kind of short-term memory (STM) while you receive the last part, before you can decode the whole message.   Given this short-term memory, there are two functions which require a long-term storage, or long-term memory (LTM) as well.   First, you have to compare past experience with the present, in order to understand present experience.   Second, you will want to store some of your current information in long-term storage, or memory, in order to use it later.   Research in memory suggests that the transfer of information from STM to LTM requires either (a) encoding of the information in terms of prior learning, i.e., relating it to material that is already in memory storage, or (b) repetition in short-term memory for some period of time (probably about 30 seconds) until it gets stored in LTM even without obvious relationships or associations. This, of course, sounds a little bit like the previous discussion of memorizing either by meaningfulness or overlearning (repetition).   Beyond this, however, not much is really known about the processes by which we store information, other than the fact that it takes longer to store material in LTM (i.e., 5 to 10 seconds per unit memorized) than to retrieve or "read out" ($1/2$ second to 1 second) (Newell and Simon, 1972).   Most of the literature on memorizing deals with strategies for making material "meaningful" or "relevant," i.e., for encoding it in terms of previously stored information.

In this information-processing model, "thinking" about verbal information, or "understanding" it, is the process of matching incoming information with stored information, and of choosing or selecting relationships that seem most useful.

This is why two people with the same information may behave quite differently: they may have different information in storage to which to relate the information (thus they "see it" differently), and/or they may select different relationships as being most important in that particular situation.

This whole discussion, incidentally, can be regarded as a kind of advance organizer for the coming discussions of concept learning (in this chapter) and of problem solving (in the next chapter).

TEACHING THE FACTS OF BRIDGE

Mr. Jones formed a bridge club for older people as part of a recreation program for a retirement community. This included a number of people who had never played before, so he decided to teach that group the basics as quickly and efficiently as he could. He warned them that there would be some memorization involved, but some of them told him that memorization was the way they had learned to learn when they were in school! With that encouragement, Mr. Jones went ahead. To teach the bidding system, he had to teach values for individual cards and for combinations; therefore, he made up some "flash cards" that represented single-card values and combination values. They were large facsimiles of playing cards, so everyone in the group could see them at once. He put the value of the particular card or combination on the back, e.g., four for Ace, three for King, seven for Ace-King, and so forth. He also had a card labeled "void" and another labeled "six-card suit" and so forth, to cover counts for different distributions. He shuffled all of these and showed them one at a time to the group; after they looked at each one for a couple of seconds, he turned it over and showed them the value. Then he went on to the next. After going through all of them, he would shuffle them and start over. It was not long before the whole group could give the values without hesitation. Some of them came easier than others, because they were simpler or more vivid. In order to make it go faster, Mr. Jones gave some stories to go with some of them, like "the King has three crowns, one gold, one silver, and one platinum" or "the Queen has two French poodles," so they

could carry a visual image in their minds that reminded them of the number associated with the card. He made these mediating images as vivid and emotional as possible.

After going through these facts enough times so that everyone was getting the answers easily, without error, Mr. Jones gave the group a break and promised to come back to this learning problem later. Meanwhile, he went on to the general process of playing bridge, and to other club matters. Then he had another practice session on the values of the cards, before the end of the meeting. He tried to get in three or four of these, with rest in between, during each club meeting; this distributed the practice, and made the resulting learning more dependable and less subject to forgetting, i.e., to interference from other learning. Of course, the practice sessions became shorter as they became more proficient, so they really were review sessions after a while. Meanwhile, more and more other learning material was introduced, and was also reviewed in these sessions as it became well-learned. For example, Mr. Jones worked up another set of cards that had the bid, overtricks, and under-tricks written on them, with the suit, and the related score on the back. Of course, he found some errors made on this task resulting from confusion with the other cards, and he learned that this new task resulted in an increase of errors when reviewing the other cards also.

In order to increase retention, Mr. Jones had the group practice beyond the point where they were getting them right in each session. This overlearning decreased the time it took them to think of the right score when they were playing, and also increased their accuracy. He also began to give them simplified simulations of a real game of bridge, to avoid the negative results of overdoing the drills and the frustration of not having a chance to actually play. As they became more able to utilize the connections with ease and in the face of other distracting considerations, i.e., the rules and procedures of the game, the conversation, and so forth, he would give them more and more realistic situations to cope with, until they were eventually playing the full game, albeit somewhat slowly at first.

TEACHING AND LEARNING CONCEPTS

What are "concepts?"

A concept is a combination of things. First of all, it is the synthesis of many examples or things that exemplify the concept. For example, the concept "dog" is made up of many examples of dogs—poodles, hounds, bulldogs, retrievers, and so forth.

Second, a concept involves rules or descriptions (although some concepts do not have convenient rules or definitions). For example, the book you are reading is one example of the concept "book"; you could define the concept by saying, "A book is a set of pages bound within two covers" or something like that. It is obvious that such definitions use other concepts (in this case, "page" is one), and therefore definitions are only useful if the concepts they use are understood.

Concepts also have titles: the title of the concept "dog" is the word "dog"; however, another title is "canine," and in France the title would be "le chien." Not all concepts have titles—some that we use do not have convenient names. Sometimes a concept has a name in one language but not in another: bilingual people sometimes find that there are things they can express in one language that they cannot express well or precisely in another.

Inductive and deductive learning

Types of concept learning and teaching are basic to all education; consider them carefully.

You can learn a concept by seeing examples, or you can learn from rules. In either case, a teacher can supplement the information with hints and verbal assistance, and can arrange the presentation in a way that makes it easier or more difficult. Learning from examples, and forming generalizations from them, is often referred to as "inductive" learning, while learning from a rule is often referred to as "deductive." However, these traditional classifications do not specify what kind of understanding is to be reached. In either case, the test of understanding may be to identify examples and nonexamples, or it may be to give the rule or definition in different words, or it may be to apply the concept to learning some other concept or to solving some problem.

Concepts can be learned from examples as well as from rules.

Guidance versus discovery in concept learning

Similarly, if the student learns without hints or special help from the teacher he or she is said to learn by "discovery," while help from the teacher is called "guidance." However, inductive learning is often referred to as "discovery" learning as well. If the student learns only from examples, without verbal hints from the teacher, then it is "pure" discovery, whereas if he or she learns with some help of this kind, it is called "guided discovery." Part of the difficulty experienced in interpreting research and theory in education is the lack of agreement as to the specific meanings of such terms.

Teaching concepts deductively

You can teach a concept deductively by having the student read and learn to use the rule if the learner already understands the concepts that the rule or definition uses, and if the learner understands the relationships between these concepts that the rule or definition describes. For example, if someone describes a "hairy underfed cross between a seal and an alleycat" then you might be able to identify examples and nonexamples of such a creature—but again you might not. This would depend on your ability to combine your images of "hairy," "underfed," "seal," and "alleycat" according to the generic process implied by the word "cross." Since a "cross" can yield a number of possible combinations according to the rules of genetics, this definition might well be ambiguous, that is, you might well be able to come to several conclusions or "images" other than the correct one. (This assumes you are at the formal operational stage, as in Chapter 2.) As a result, you might not successfully identify examples and nonexamples (assuming there are such things, of course).

On the other hand, suppose you were told that a "witzuf" is a kitchen chair with one leg fatter than the other three: you would probably then be able to discriminate between witzufs and non-witzufs without much trouble. This is because the concepts "chair," "fat," and "leg" are pretty well-understood by most people, and thus there is not much ambiguity. However, a young child or a person just learning the language might not be able to do this quite as effectively or accurately.

Most concept teaching and learning come about through a combination of rules and examples, i.e., a combination of deductive and inductive learning. The important questions about concept teaching and learning, therefore, involve how you combine rules and examples, and how you present examples. Most of what you read in this chapter will deal with such questions. One interesting combination of deductive and inductive teaching using this approach involved the concept "noun"; this was viewed on the TV program *Electric Company,* and went something like this:

The NOUN ran through the NOUN,
and as the NOUN began to catch up with him
he threw a NOUN at it.

The action was described through cartoons that accompanied the writing, and had the effect of pointing out the common properties of nouns while also giving visual examples.

Teaching concepts by example

Both examples and nonexamples of concepts can and should be used in teaching a concept. To begin, suppose you present a learner with the triangle below and say, "This is an example of the concept," or "This is a triangle."

Then suppose you show him another example, such as the one below, and say, "This is also a triangle," or "This is another example."

Then suppose you show him another example, and say, "This is not a triangle."

Now you could switch to a questioning approach, and show him the example below, and say, "Is this a triangle?" or "Is this a positive exemplar?" or "Is this an example or a nonexample?"

You can teach concepts without explaining them or defining them first; in some cases it is better that way.

It might be that he would say "No" or "It is a nonexample." Then, if you reviewed what you had showed him, you could see that there is a logical reason, namely that the first two examples were shaded in and the third was not; therefore, you taught him that "triangle" meant "shaded." Another way to express this is that you taught him (implicitly) that shadedness was relevant, where it actually was not. Another possibility would be that you present this example and ask him whether it is or is not a triangle, or whether it is an example or a nonexample:

For the same reason, he might say, "Yes, it is." Or, you might present him with this shape:

Here he might say yes for the wrong reason, that it is shaded, or he might say no for the wrong reason, namely because it did not have equal sides and equal angles (notice the first two examples did have equal sides).

What this amounts to is that, in order to teach a concept, you need to present a number of examples, and you have to make sure that the irrelevant attributes (such as shadedness, equality of sides) are varied, and that the relevant ones stay the same. For example, in teaching the concept "triangle," you should use some or all of the following, where + indicates that it *is* an example, or is a positive exemplar, and where − indicates that it is a nonexample, *not* an example, or a negative exemplar.

Overgeneralization and Undergeneralization

Understanding of a concept implies, among other things, the ability to identify examples and nonexamples of it. To understand the concept "dog" you should be able to identify a Cocker and an Irish Setter as dogs, and a cat and a bear cub as nondogs. Someone who is in the process of learning this concept might identify a Pekingese or a Chihuahua as a nondog because of its size; similarly, he or she might identify a Great Dane as "not a dog" because it is so large, where the others were so small. This would be an example of undergeneralization: the person would not generalize sufficiently from the first examples identified to others that vary one way or another from those.

On the other hand, someone in the process of learning the concept "dog" might call a very small pony a "dog," particularly if he had just made the error of saying that a Great Dane is not a dog, and was corrected. This would be an example of overgeneralization: the learner would have generalized too broadly from the examples he or she had been exposed to before.

Sometimes learners both overgeneralize and undergeneralize in respect to the same concept. For example, someone might identify most houses correctly, but also call a small church a "house" (overgeneralization) and call a very modern dwelling something else, or say it is *not* a house (undergeneralization). This situation where both over and undergeneralization occur is sometimes referred to as a "misconception."

Allowing for overgeneralization and undergeneralization in teaching

In teaching a concept by example, or by a combination of rules and examples, it is important to present two types of examples that establish the boundaries of the concept: (1) examples which lead the learner to think they are nonexamples, i.e., which lead him or her to undergeneralize the concept; and (2) nonexamples which

Over- or undergeneralization?

lead the learner to think they are examples, i.e., which lead him or her to overgeneralize. The two types must be close enough to examples or nonexamples, respectively, that they represent likely errors. You might think of this as a process of "inoculating" the learner against likely errors.

For example, if you are teaching the concept "red," you will want to present oranges and purples which are close to red, but which are not to be called "red"; also you want to present extremes of red which the learner might be tempted to call "not red." Thus you are establishing the limits of the concept.

SOME ADDED GUIDELINES
FOR TEACHING CONCEPTS

Amount of variation versus amount of repetition

In teaching concepts through examples, there are often a large number of possible examples from which to draw. You seldom have the option of using all of them,

Teaching for generalization (transfer), considering the amount of variation in examples, and going from simple to complex and from concrete to abstract—all are important guidelines for teaching generally.

but you do have to decide how many different ones to use. This choice is affected partly by considerations discussed in other instructional processes, but generally speaking, there seems to be an optimal amount of variation (and conversely, of repetition). That means that you can show too few examples, but you can also show too many. Too few makes it difficult to identify the critical attributes, even though they are repeated several times, but too many also makes learning difficult, partly because there is too much information for the learner to handle.

For example, in teaching the concept "three" inductively to a young child, different examples of groups or sets of three things should be used. It seems likely that although there should be several sets with different things in each set, there should also be some repetition, i.e., they should be given the same set to use that they had before, after having some other sets in between. (The task might be counting the members of the set, or comparing them with another set in a one-to-one correspondence, or some other variation that brings out the concept of number.) Of course, as suggested in other precepts, there should also be nonexamples, in this case sets with more than three or less than three, to which the learners can respond.

Proceeding from simple to complex examples

To make a concept easier to learn, begin by reducing the number of dimensions or attributes, both relevant and irrelevant. As teaching progresses, increase them. This can be stated more simply as: go from simple to complex as learning progresses.

For example, if you are teaching biology students about the heart, it is more effective to begin with a line drawing and then to progress to more complicated drawings and to photographs. (The photograph would have too many relevant and irrelevant dimensions to use at the beginning.)

Proceeding from concrete to abstract

Generally, other things being equal, it is advisable to begin with concrete examples and move toward more abstract examples as learning progresses. (Note that within one level of abstractness it is also possible to move from simple to complex.) For example, in teaching the concept "slope" in analytic geometry, it is a good idea to give examples that are concrete and three-dimensional, such as a model of an inclined plane where the rise and the run can be pointed out and measured, and where the incline can be changed and the changing ratio can be derived experimentally by the learner. Then one could move to the "iconic" level, that is, to diagrammatic representations of the inclined plane, with similar measurements being carried out. Then you could make the diagrammatic representation more abstract, by taking out some of the features that add realism, and make it more and more symbolic, approaching a straight line graph. Finally, you could present it en-

This is an .0625
compacted graphite marking instrument
encased in the exact center
of a wood fiber handle,
with a metal-bonded,
aft-mounted synthetic rubber tip.

Wouldn't it be terrible if people had to identify things, or companies,
with a complete description of all their components or activities?

We'd have to call our company the Northern Natural Gas and Butane
and Ethane and Propane and Ethylene Glycol and Hydrocarbons
and Energy Systems and Plastic Coloration and Anti-Freeze and Fabric
Softener, Detergent and Germicide Ingredient Company.

Northern
Natural Gas
Company
Home Office: Omaha, Nebraska

The gas company that's something else.

Figure 9–5. *What if you had to learn concepts by such rules or definitions as this? What does this rule presuppose? Would it perhaps be easier to learn the concept in the concrete or iconic mode than in the symbolic?* (© 1971 by The New York Times Company. Used by permission.)

tirely symbolically, with words and mathematical symbols, not using a diagram at all.   At any stage, concrete or iconic, you could make the initial examples quite simple and go to more complex ones, before going on to the next stage of abstractness.   (Enactive/concrete, iconic, and symbolic levels were discussed in Chapter 2 in relation to cognitive development.)

Varying irrelevant dimensions

In teaching concepts by examples and nonexamples, irrelevant dimensions of the concept should be varied from one example to another, so that the relevant dimensions, those common to the examples, may be identified more easily.

For example, in a picture of a certain kind of rock, or in a concrete example of it, the size of the sample is irrelevant.   Thus the examples should vary in size. Also, depending on the nature of the rock involved, the color may be relevant or irrelevant.   If it is irrelevant, then color should be varied, and if color is relevant, the shades of color should be varied to correspond to the variations one finds in nature.   Another way to describe relevant dimensions is by calling them the "critical attributes," i.e., attributes that make one thing an example and another thing not an example.

Teaching by a selection strategy

To teach through examples and nonexamples, you can present them in an order that you select yourself, in each case asking learners to say whether each item is an example or not, and giving them feedback as to whether they are correct.   This is called a "reception" strategy.   On the other hand, you might present a number of examples and nonexamples at the same time, and have learners select one and respond to it, then tell them if they are right.   This is a "selection" strategy.

For instance, in teaching the concept "acceleration" in physics, a teacher can present examples of acceleration in a sequence that he thinks makes it clear, including both true examples and examples which are not acceleration but which have some things in common with it.   He can ask students in each case whether the example represents acceleration or not, and can explain to them why they are right or wrong—or ask them to explain why and comment on their answers, or have other students comment on their answers.   However, another possibility is also open to him.   Given the appropriate facilities and equipment, he can make it possible for each student, or small groups of students, to select one or another example of acceleration, demonstrate it for themselves, and form a hypothesis as to whether it is an example or a nonexample.   Then the teacher can arrange for each individual or group to receive feedback on their reasoning, either by discussing it with them, making explanations available, or having them discuss it among themselves.   Although this process is more difficult to arrange and calls for independent learning skills on the part of the students, it can be very effective and satisfying, and encourages students to take more responsibility for the learning process.   It is also a form of problem solving, which is discussed more extensively in the next chapter.

ROCKS—IN THE HEAD?

A new instructor is preparing his geology class for a field trip. He wants his students to recognize various types of rocks and formations. Therefore, he makes up a display which shows a colored picture of each type of rock that they will encounter (about twelve), and has his class memorize them. Then he gives a test using the same pictures, in mixed order of course, and asks that they be able to pass it with a score of 100 percent before the upcoming field trip. Finally, after several retests, everyone does so. The instructor is dismayed to find that once on the mountain the students are unable to recognize any of the rocks in their natural habitat, except maybe granite. He begins to think of the students as "granite heads" in his complete frustration.

After he has cooled off, one of the teaching assistants who is taking a course in educational psychology asks the instructor if she can help the class to recognize the rocks. When given the go-ahead, she asks for all the pictures the instructor has of different types of rocks, and also for all the specimens he has available. Then the TA arranges a display so that there are at least three examples (either pictures or speci-

mens) of each type of rock, and so that at least one of the examples has enough other things in it or around it to make it seem like something else. Then she arranges these in the display in a complete mixed fashion, and gives each example a number. Then she lists all the types of rocks and assigns a letter to each, i.e., A for granite, B for gneiss, and so forth. She then provides two rows of buttons, one with letters and one with numbers, and wires the display so that if a student pushes a number and a letter simultaneously, a red light flashes if he is wrong and a green light flashes if he is correct; for example, if the student pushes the button for example 2 (which is quartz) and the button for A (granite), he gets a red light. By this selection strategy, each student individually can learn each of the concepts, with several examples of each, and of course the other specimens function as nonexamples. The next field trip is a success, because the students have prepared using more than one example, and they have had to formulate their own rules or descriptions for the various specimens. Thus they can generalize to the field examples more readily.

Guidance versus discovery–again

Varying dimensions, allowing for discovery, providing feedback—these emphasize that how you organize content makes a difference!

Researchers who have investigated the effects of different amounts of guidance, as compared with discovery of concepts and solutions to problems, have concluded generally that some amount of guidance is helpful. This can be given through verbal directions, by giving the answers at first and then letting the student figure them out, or carefully making the initial examples or tasks so simple that it is very difficult to avoid giving the correct answer. This guidance is an integral part of all teaching. However, it is often misused, because teachers do not reduce or withdraw the guidance as learning progresses. This leaves the student in an incomplete state of learning so that he or she is not able to handle the task independently.

For example, suppose you are teaching the concept "commutativity" in mathematics. Then you give concrete examples of it, i.e., situations that are analogous to commutativity. For example, if you have these two activities, "Put on your shoes" and "Put on your socks," are they the same—do they give the same result—no matter in which order you do them? Obviously not, so this is a nonexample of commutativity.   An example would be the two actions "Drink your milk" and "Eat your potatoes"—at least, we do not know of any significant difference in the result when you alter the order.   Then you might go on to less concrete, perhaps diagrammatic examples.   You might show pictures of things and ask if the order in which they are done makes any difference.   You might give addition problems like "7 + 2" and ask whether the operation of adding can be done in either order, i.e., 7 first or 2 first.   As you went to more complex examples, from other operations and other fields, you would use as much guidance as was necessary to get started and then withdraw it.

Providing feedback

The word "feedback" refers to the information you receive as the result of some response; some of this feedback or information comes from your own nervous system and some of it from the effects of the response of the environment.   For example, when you reach for something, you can feel yourself reaching for it and you can see your hand approaching it.   This feeling and this visual image are part of your feedback.   You might also get feedback from someone who says, "You're getting close to it!" or "You're almost touching it!"

Feedback, or knowledge of results, facilitates understanding.

Suppose a student is learning the concept "chair" by selecting examples from an array of pictures (a "selection" process). Each time he makes a selection, you can assume that he has some hypothesis about what a chair is, and that he is testing that hypothesis by that selection. Then he needs "feedback" or information about his choice, whether it is or is not an example. This could be printed on the back of the picture, or you could give it to him on request.

Feedback can be either intrinsic or extrinsic. Intrinsic feedback is what the learner gains by interpreting the outcomes of his own responses, say in solving a problem. He tries a solution, observes the result, and interprets it in the light of his objectives. Thus the system that he is working with gives the feedback.

On the other hand, he could also receive extrinsic feedback. An instructor or assistant could observe his solution process and give him some idea as to whether he is on the right track or not. This might be necessary or at least helpful in places where the results of the solution process don't make it clear whether progress is being made or not.

Ideally, learning environments should be arranged so that intrinsic feedback is available, and learners should be taught to use such feedback. However, extrinsic feedback is important and necessary in most cases.

Inductive learning and the "intuitive leap"

In his seminal book, A *study of thinking*, Bruner noted that learners presented with examples and nonexamples of a concept and asked to learn to identify them without the help of a rule (i.e., inductively, or through discovery) would begin to demonstrate understanding before they could verbalize the understanding. They would begin to make correct identifications—"that is an example; that is *not*," etc.—and only later, after identifying many of them correctly, would they describe the correct attributes and relationships *verbally*. You could describe this as an intuitive or nonverbal "leap," or a nonverbal "insight." Teachers and parents should realize, then, that learners *can* understand things without being able to describe them.

CONCEPTUAL HIERARCHIES

Examples of hierarchies

Suppose you wanted to teach someone the concept "red square." Suppose that person had not formed the concept "red" or the concept "square." Could you teach her the concept "red square" without first teaching the concepts "red" or "square"? The simple logical answer would be "Of course not." Some research indicates that if you teach subconcepts first, then the "super" concept is learned more easily. However, it has not been demonstrated convincingly that you cannot teach the superconcept first, and thereby teach the subconcepts as well. For example, if you gave many, many examples of red squares and red nonsquares, you might enable a learner to understand (i.e., to come to identify which are which in complex situations) without first teaching her "red" and "square." As a matter of fact, she would learn something about what "red" is and what "square" is also in the process, although her understanding of these would obviously be incomplete. However, there is reason to believe that this would be the hard way of teaching it; you could make better progress overall if you taught "red" and "square" first.

Concept types

Suppose again you want to teach the concept "red square", i.e., the relationship where a positive example must have *both* redness *and* squareness. An alternative relationship is "red *or* square *or both*," or "red *or* square *but not* both." If you were to try out all these types on a given group of learners, you would find that they would learn the "and" concept more easily than the "or"; nobody is completely sure why this is so, but it demonstrates an important thing about concept learning, to wit, some *kinds* of concepts are harder to learn than others, even though they are presented in the same manner.

This is an example
of "shaded circle,"
also of "shaded
or circle or both."

This is a nonexample
of "shaded circle," but
an example of "shaded
or circle or both."

Teaching concept hierarchies: Gagne's approach

To teach a concept you need to make sure that learners understand other concepts that are subsets of or support the one you wish to teach. For example, if you want to teach the concept "dappled gray mare" by using a verbal description, your students will need to know what "dappled," "gray," and "mare" mean. They would also have to understand the implied relationship; examples of the concept would have to have all three properties, not just one or two of them. Now there are some who feel that it is impossible to learn such a concept unless you know all the sub-concepts that make it up; this is a hierarchical view of concept formation. As another example, suppose you want to teach the concept of a "strike" in baseball. To do this verbally, you would expect learners to know what "plate," "swing," "foul," and "strike zone" were, or you would expect to teach them first. One learning theorist and experimenter has extended this kind of analysis past concept learning to learning generally, and to problem solving (Gagne, 1970). The classic example, of course, is that of animals as differentiated from plants: animals are defined in terms of movement, sensory organs, nerve organs, and such subconcepts; classification hierarchies are an important part of subjects such as zoology. In one of his experiments Gagne broke the general study of sets and the intersection of sets in mathematics down into subconcepts such as intersection, and then into types of intersections (line, triangles with lines, curves and lines), and those into triangles and lines and curves themselves, and those into the parts of those figures (lines, angles, etc.), until he came to the most basic concepts such as the identification of a point and the ability to discriminate between individual entities and to form them into groups.

In order to demonstrate the practicality and validity of this approach, Gagne conducted studies to test learners "down through" the hierarchies, and to teach them step-by-step "up through" them. He was able to demonstrate that in most cases learners needed to have command of the subconcepts before they were able to learn the higher concepts based on them: they had to master one level before proceeding successfully up to the next. However, there were exceptions to this, and these exceptions give some credence to the theory of learning from whole to parts, which is discussed in the next section.

Whether to teach the parts first, or to start with the whole and break it down—this has been a continuing debate.

Teaching concepts whole-to-part: Ausubel's approach

If a concept is made up of several subconcepts, and if some of the subconcepts are not understood, then you can sometimes teach the subconcepts by teaching the whole concept first. This is obviously in opposition to the approach just described. For example, in the "dappled gray mare" example given earlier, if a learner understood "grey" and "mare," he might formulate the concept "dappled" through a teaching process that combined verbal descriptions with examples (actual horses, or pictures). It is even conceivable that a bright learner might learn what both "dappled" and "grey" meant through such a process, if given sufficient verbal guidance and enough examples and nonexamples. As another example of such whole-to-part learning, you might teach the elective process in social studies by teaching the concept of democracy, where most or all of the examples would involve an elective process. Again, the concept of "nucleus" might be taught first by teaching the concept of "cell," then by identifying the common element (the nucleus) in the examples.

Ausubel has recommended this whole-to-part approach as a basic and general strategy for teaching (1968). His version is to present the most general statements or ideas first and have the learners master them, then to move to statements and ideas of lesser generality, and finally to specific details. He calls this "progressive differentiation," and the approach resembles analyses of learning processes made years ago by Gestalt psychologists (that topic is discussed in the next chapter).

This also relates to Ausubel's interest in "advance organizers," discussed earlier in this chapter.

MR. BROWN TEACHES "DEMOCRACY"

Larry Brown is a government teacher who has just completed a workshop on concept learning and teaching. The idea of teaching concepts by presenting students with examples and nonexamples, and letting them learn inductively by trying to identify which are and which are not, has really excited him. He sees this as a way out of the endless routine of lectures, readings, and discussions of the conventional mode that seem to lead inevitably to memorization of facts, no matter how much he tries to emphasize broad concepts and understandings. He decides to do a unit on "democracy" using what he calls the "concept teaching approach."

As he sets out to identify and organize examples and nonexamples, however, he runs into difficulty. It is not easy to find examples of a democracy, other than the United States at various periods in its history, and even then there are many confusing attributes, or attributes that are undemocratic. Also, he finds some difficulty in presenting "an example" because whatever he wants to use requires quite a bit of reading and lecturing to make it clear and comprehensive to the students; the presentation of "an example" is not a trivial task like the presentation of "triangle" or something of that order in the workshop. Furthermore, if he wants to proceed from simple examples to more complex ones, then actual democracies will not do at first. He is forced to consider simpler examples—perhaps clubs, or other relatively simple organizations that can be run democratically or otherwise. He has some difficulty identifying such things. Obviously athletic teams are not entirely democratic, and he has some doubts about the organization of the school where he is teaching, since his impression is that it is more of a dictatorship. Finally, he decides to design and try out a concrete enactive example of a democracy, by creating a

simple governmental structure in the classroom itself. He writes out descriptions of various roles in the government, forms a constitution, and then has the students act it out and draft legislation and amendments to the constitution. He also designs alternative systems which are similar in ways, but which are not democratic. In doing this, he is forced to make many decisions about what is, and what is not, democratic—and he is not sure that his historian colleagues would agree with all of them, which makes him feel a little uncomfortable about what he is teaching.

Then he goes on to identify readings which describe various governments throughout the world, present and past, and in rereading these himself to refresh his memory, he makes a decision as to whether they are or are not democracies. He makes these readings available in a small "library" in the back of the room, and checks the various examples and nonexamples in and out himself so that they do not get lost. He has some problems making enough of them available so that individual students do not have to wait, and finally he has to insist that all of them be present during class (i.e., the examples and nonexamples) so that they can be used in school. He also asks that nobody take them home more than one night. He has a key which explains whether or not each one is an example of democracy and why. This is kept in the room, and he will give the answer to students who report they have read the appropriate reading and want to get feedback on their decisions. When he has time he asks them to explain their decision personally before giving the prepared answer so he can be sure that they are really giving it some thought instead of guessing to get the answer and get on with it.

As the examples become more complex, they take more and more time to read. He finds himself presenting some of them through lectures, so that each student does not have to read that particular one (since there is only one copy sometimes). He also finds himself using the text occasionally, where it describes an example well enough so that it can be visualized by the students and they can make a decision on it.

As the learning progresses, Larry begins to ask them for verbalizations regarding the concepts, encouraging them to generalize what they have found in verbal terms as well as identifying new examples and nonexamples. He realizes he has not carefully provided examples that will tend to make them overgeneralize, or others that tend to make them undergeneralize, to "inoculate" them against these kinds of errors, but he just has not had time to organize the material that well as yet.

As a final test, he gives them two new cases, one an example and one not, and asks them to identify which is which and to explain why in terms of rules or definitions that have been generally agreed on in class. Ultimately, Larry feels that the class knows more about democracy, and has a more usable kind of knowledge, than any of his classes ever did before. But then, he also feels that *he* knows more than he did also, through the analytic process that this approach required. He also notes that his students have begun to acquire a new learning strategy, i.e., to extend their ability to learn in different ways. He also knows, however, how much work this approach involves, and although he does not have to do it all over again for this module, we can imagine that he may think twice before he undertakes to do this with another topic, or that he might decide that conventional lecturing is the easier approach after all.

MORE COMPLEX CONCEPTS

Processes

A process is a sequential concept, a pattern involving a sequence of events rather than simultaneous stimuli; a forehand in tennis is a process, while a racquet is a concept. Learning of processes is brought about in the same way as the learning of concepts. However, the presentation of examples is more complicated in some ways, and requires modeling either by the teacher or through films (16mm. or 8mm.) or simulation through sequences of pictures or diagrams. Thus the presentation of positive and negative exemplars is less conveniently accomplished, since the production of each exemplar is more difficult. Process learning is not identical with learning chains of responses, but it is related, since chains are taught in part by modeling also.

Principles

Principles are relationships between concepts; the relationships themselves are also concepts or processes, such as the relationship "or," as in "black or circle or both," and the relationship "if-then," as in "if it is raining, we will get wet." Of course, "is" and "get" are also concepts and relationships, "is" being an equivalence relationship and "get" a process.

To teach principles, the following guidelines are helpful:

1. Model the principle by demonstrating the relationship (equivalence or implication or the like); if possible, model both positive and negative exemplars as in simple concept learning, including probable over- and undergeneralizations;

2. If learners have difficulty identifying the principle or using it, teach the relationship on which the principle is built, that is, give other exemplars of the kind of relationship, e.g., equivalence or implication, until the learners can identify that type of relationship; this is an example of hierarchical concept learning, where a concept or process basic to the new concept has not been acquired sufficiently strongly;

3. Have the learners put the principle into their own words, with feedback (knowledge of results, correction, guidance);

4. Have the learners apply the principle, i.e., use it in some problem or to form some new principle, or complete an example or demonstration of it, or a simulated demonstration (pictorial representation or word description).

SUMMARY OF CONCEPT-TEACHING PROCESSES

Inductive

1. Present an example of the concept and identify it by the title or by signifying that it *is* an example of the concept;

2. Present another example that is *not* an example of the concept, and identify the dimensions that are relevant, i.e., that make it a nonexemplar;

3. Present several examples and nonexamples where the irrelevant attributes or dimensions are varied and the relevant ones stay the same; this can be done one at a time, or all at once; the learner may respond to examples as presented by the teacher (reception), or he may select examples himself and receive information as to whether they are positive or negative (selection);

4. Examples should be given which tempt the learner to generalize beyond the limits of the concepts, i.e., which appear to be examples but are not, also ones which appear not to be, but are (i.e., which tempt the learner to undergeneralize);

5. Initially examples should have few irrelevant dimensions, and may even represent only part of the possible set of examples with that number of dimensions (redundancy);

6. Initially one or more irrelevant dimensions may be presented with positive exemplars and not with negative ones, to serve as cues for the correct answer;

7. As the learning progresses, the cues in (6) above will be withdrawn (or the additional exemplars introduced), and additional irrelevant dimensions will be added to the exemplars, so as to make the presentation more similar to the target or criterion set of examples (reducing redundancy);

8. As identification of new exemplars becomes accurate, suggest that the learners form a verbal description (rule, definition) of the concept if this is appropriate, i.e., if there are words convenient for describing it;

9. Ask learners to create new exemplars of the concept themselves;

10. Ultimately, arrange a situation that involves learning another concept which is built in part on the one just learned.

Deductive

1. Identify the concept by presenting a rule, i.e., a verbal chain that employs other concepts which together describe the concept in question, and which describes the relationship between these other concepts, e.g., "The concept is all things which are both red and circular—red circles"; "Parallel lines are lines that never meet, and are therefore always the same distance apart"; "A strike is a pitched ball which both (a) passes the batter at a level above his knees and beneath his shoulders, and (b) passes over the 'plate,' *or* a pitched ball which the batter swings at and misses, *or* a pitched ball which the batter hits foul if the batter does not already have two strikes on him."

2. Present examples for identification by the learner as in the steps under "inductive" above.

Summary outline and key concepts

☞ *All learning* is meaningful—even learning nonsense syllables / Concept learning is also cognitive learning / Concept learning was implicit in cognitive development covered earlier, in relation to "schema," and to social learning and modeling / Cognitive learning has been dealt with previously in learning disabilities, language learning, motivation, and cognitive development.

☞ *Serial learning* research reveals the serial position effect / Serial learning research reveals proactive inhibition and retroactive inhibition, both involving interference from other learning / Forgetting is due to interference (inhibition) / Learning unordered lists reveals conceptual clustering in memory / To teach lists, utilize grouping, stories, and vivid and meaningful associations / Paired associate learning also reveals inhibition from other learning / Paired associate learning involves mediation or mental "bridges" between terms / Mediators are helpful in teaching names and vocabulary / Distribution of practice facilitates retention by combatting interference.

☞ *Active response* by the learner is an important teaching technique / Frequent cumulative review is important for increasing retention / Overlearning is another important strategy for insuring retention / Advance organizers are sophisticated applications of proactive facilitation / Information processing involves short-term memory (STM) and long-term memory (LTM) and transferring information from one to the other.

☞ *Concepts have* examples, rules, and titles / Understanding concepts involves giving the rule, or identifying examples, or using the concept to learn another concept, or using it to solve a problem / Inductive learning is learning through examples; deductive, through rules / Guidance implies help from a teacher or other source; discovery implies learning without such help; both relate to the inductive-deductive dichotomy / There are certain techniques and problems associated with deductive teaching / Teaching inductively, by examples and nonexamples, also involves certain techniques / Concept teaching must allow for over- and undergeneralization by the learner.

☞ *Variation and* repetition of examples must be balanced / Teaching should proceed from simple (few irrelevant dimensions) to complex / Teaching should generally proceed from concrete examples to abstract ones / Irrelevant dimensions should be varied in examples / A selection strategy (related to discovery learning) calls for more active hypothesis formation by the learner: the learner selects which example to have feedback about / Research suggests that a balance of guidance and discovery is most effective / Providing feedback, or knowledge of results, is an important requirement / Learners often make "intuitive leaps" and come to a functional understanding before arriving at a verbal understanding.

☞ *Concepts exist* in hierarchies; each concept is based on other concepts / There are different types of relationships which synthesize attributes into concepts; some are more difficult to learn inductively than others / One approach, identified with Gagne, is to teach from bottom to top in the hierarchy / Another approach, identified with Ausubel and also with Gestalt psychologists, is to teach from top to bottom, or from whole to part, through analysis of the whole concept initially / A "process" is a sequential pattern, i.e., a concept that exists in time / Principles are relationships between concepts; the relationships are themselves concepts or processes.

Glossary

Advance Organizer: Reading passage or learning experience designed to make a later, more complex passage or experience more understandable, although it doesn't necessarily cover the same content.

Clustering: Where learners reciting a list give terms that are similar in some way, i.e., similar terms come out together, although they were not learned one after the other.

Cognition: Thinking, problem solving: an approach to learning that emphasizes the problem-solving abilities and propensities of learners, in contrast to behavioral approaches or strategies involving memorization or highly guided learning processes.

Conjunctive Concept: A concept which is a combination involving an "and" relation, e.g., "red table" (i.e., red and table, both).

Decoding: Translating incoming stimuli into a form useful for thinking.

Deductive Learning: Learning from rules, or from abstract descriptions.

Disjunctive Concept: A concept where subconcepts are related with an "or" type relationship, e.g., an allergy involving household dust or eggs or both.

Encoding: Putting the results of thoughts into a form suitable for activating an overt response (talking, action).

Exemplar: Example.

Feedback: Information about results of a response or behavior, either resulting from the behavior itself (intrinsic feedback) or given by someone else (extrinsic).

Inductive Learning: Learning from examples, facts, or observations.

Inhibition: Interference with learning, from things learned before or after.

Insight: The point where the learner arrives at an intuitive or behavioral understanding, i.e., begins to identify examples correctly but can't describe them.

Irrelevant Dimension: Dimension or attribute that is not important for identifying the concept, e.g. the color of a car in identifying automobiles.

Mediation: Mental associations between terms of a pair, e.g., you could associate "king" with "pie" by thinking "King George" and then thinking "Georgie-porgie puddin 'n pie" (of course this assumes that both of these are part of your past learning).

Negative Exemplar: A nonexample of the concept, something which is not an example of the concept.

Nonsense Syllable: A syllable like GOX or BIV, used in lists for memorizing.

Overgeneralization: Identifying something as an example of a concept when it is not.

Overlearning: Learning beyond the point of mastery.

Paired Associates: Two-term pairs used for research in verbal learning, e.g., dap-cug.

Positive Exemplar: An example of the concept.

Principle: A relationship between concepts that applies to or explains something, e.g., "weight times distance equals weight times distance" on a balance

Proactive Inhibition: Interference (forgetting) due to previous learning.

Process: Sequential concept or pattern; e.g., finesse in bridge.

Reception Strategy: Teaching by presenting examples and nonexamples one after another; the order of presentation is determined by the instructor.

Rote Learning: Learning or memorizing without relating to meaningful things.

Selection Strategy: Teaching by presenting examples and nonexamples and allowing the learner to select the one or ones he or she feels represent the concept, then giving information about his or her choice.

Serial Position Effect: In a serial list, the middle things are learned last.

Undergeneralization: Identifying something as not an example of a concept when it actually *is* an example.

Questions for thought and discussion

1. You can teach a concept by presenting examples and nonexamples; you can also teach it by describing and defining it. Since the latter takes less effort and preparation, why would you bother to do the former?

2. Is there concept learning involved in social learning? In behavior modification processes? In language acquisition? In verbal learning?

3. How would you take into account the serial position effect in planning a lecture which covered quite a few facts? How would you take proactive inhibition into account?

4. Assuming that the research in verbal learning applies to broad learning situations like courses, what would be the pros and cons of learning French and Spanish during the same semester versus learning them in successive semesters? (Consider distribution of practice, proactive and retroactive inhibition/facilitation, advance organizers, etc.)

5. The jingle "why study at all" was quoted, somewhat facetiously, in the chapter; however, considering proactive inhibition as well as retroactive, how would you convince someone that it *is* worth studying in spite of them?

6. A major debate during the 1960s was related to the effectiveness of guidance as compared with discovery, as modes of teaching and learning. What would you conclude about this? How would you recommend teachers teach, through discovery learning or using guidance?

Situations calling for applications of facts and concepts

1. Describe how you would teach the concept "love" through examples and nonexamples, using a selection strategy. Could you allow for over- and undergeneralization?

2. Show how you would teach the concept "metal" through examples and nonexamples, using a *selection* strategy. Could you allow for over- and undergeneralization in this process?

3. Describe how you would teach the names of a large number of different trees or plants in a botany course, using the various facts about paired associate learning described in this chapter.

4. A student is having difficulty learning Russian vocabulary. He comes to you for help. What kinds of suggestions might you make, based on verbal learning research?

5. You are teaching a language, in a situation where the major objective is to enable the person to use a limited vocabulary very fluently, without hesitation. How would you structure the training for this purpose?

Suggested activities

1. Choose a concept in some subject of particular interest to you, and try to teach it by a combination of inductive and deductive processes, or by guidance and discovery. This means planning how you would do it, and then trying it out.

2. Discuss with a professor in your major subject how an important concept in that subject is taught. Are examples used? Nonexamples? Reception or selection? Feedback? What criterion for "understanding" is used? How could you devise a better system for teaching that concept? Discuss the pros and cons of such a system with the professor.

3. Observe the teaching of one or more concepts by one or more teachers in your major subject or some area of your interest, at some other level than college. Note which if any of the guidelines for concept teaching are used. Observe other teachers in the same area (subject) and see whether your observations seem valid.

4. Conduct an experiment in forgetting and interference, using a list of some kind, or some other learning task. Design the experiment so that proactive inhibition will show up; also retroactive.

Suggested readings

Markle and Tiemann's *Really understanding concepts* is a worthwhile learning experience. You can get a lot out of the workbooks even though you don't have the slides and the tapes, but it is better in complete form. Becker, Engleman, and Thomas's *Teaching 2* is another semiprogrammed text on this topic.

10

Teaching
Problem Solving

CONTENTS

363

ABOUT CHAPTER 10

What this chapter can do for you

When you have completed this chapter you will be able to teach students how to solve problems, as an alternative to teaching facts and concepts. You will also be able to use problems as a teaching strategy by presenting learners with problems to solve. You may also gain some insight into your own problem-solving skills, and find some procedures which help in your own learning.

What might make this difficult

Unfortunately learners do not always gain experience or skills in solving problems, either in particular subject matters, or generally. This may be true of you as well: much of your learning has probably been of the "rote" kind, where you master facts and some concepts, but don't spend much time solving problems. As a result you might find this subject uninteresting or irrelevant because it isn't a part of teaching and learning as you know it. On the other hand, you may feel that problem solving is important, but that the kinds of problems dealt with here are unimportant and a waste of time. You should realize, if this is the case, that problem solving is a general skill, and the particular problems used to demonstrate that skill are not important in themselves, only as they represent that basic ability.

Reasons for studying problem solving, and teaching through problem solving

We are solving problems much of the time outside of school, and yet it is one of the things the average person does very poorly. In school, many students come to grief on examinations because they aren't able to apply simple problem-solving techniques that would enable them to demonstrate their learning in applied situations. Attention to these skills, then, may well pay off beyond the value of a similar amount of time spent on conventional subject matter information.

Objectives

I want you to be aware of the possibility of using problem solving as a strategy of teaching, and of the possibility of teaching learners how to solve problems. I also want you to see teaching itself as a problem solving activity. If you can also regard the learner as a problem solver, at least potentially, I feel that you will take a step toward a better philosophy of teaching and learning.

RATIONALE AND BACKGROUND OF CHAPTER 10

What is a problem?

We all have problems, and solving them is a basic part of living. It is also a goal of learning to be able to solve problems, whether they occur in mathematics (as equations), French (ordering what you want in a restaurant), or economics (predicting whether prices will rise or fall). One extensive treatise on human problem solving has defined a problem as a situation where you want something and don't know immediately what series of actions to take to get it (Newell and Simon, 1972). The thing you want may be tangible (something to eat) or abstract (the solution of an equation). The things you have to do may be psychomotor or purely cognitive. All problem solving calls for mental manipulation of symbols that stand for the parts of the problem in the real world; this symbolic manipulation is required whether the problem is to get an apple hanging on a tree, or to find the best plan for winning a battle.

Problem solving at various levels and in various forms has been a part of psychology and of research in learning for many years. The following descriptions of some of these experimental approaches will help you form a concept of the variety and the common factors in such research.

Insight

An ape is shown a pipe about a foot in diameter and longer than twice his arm reach. He observes an experimenter place food in the middle of the pipe through a door in its side, which is then closed. There is a pole in the vicinity that can be inserted into the pipe. The ape tries to reach the food with his hands several times but the door is locked and the pipe is too long. He then loses interest, plays with the pole, rolls it along the pipe, then tries to reach the food with his arm again, and then plays with the pole some more. By chance the pole becomes lined up with the pipe. The behavior of the ape now centers on shoving the pole into the pipe, ejecting the food from the other end. Thus the ape solves the problem after some unsuccessful trials, and with the help of the accidental hint in the lining up of the pole with the pipe. There is an observable change in the quality of the behavior just prior to the solution, which is often termed *insight* (Kohler, 1925).

Experiments of this kind were designed to show that learning does not come about through trial and error, but through the use of higher mental faculties. Kohler was a member of the "Gestalt" school of psychology, which will be discussed later in this chapter.

Learning sets

Some of the early
investigations of
problem solving
involved animals;
however, the
basic processes
relate to human
problem solving.

A group of monkeys is confronted (individually) with a sequence of problems of the type described just above. If one of these problems is given to another group of monkeys, which have not been through the same sequence of problems, they will have more difficulty solving the problem than those who have had such experience (Harlow, 1949).

Since the animals with more extensive experience in problem solving show greater ability to solve new problems, many researchers conclude that they have *learned* something about problem solving in general. They have "learned to learn." Another way to say the same thing is that they have developed a "set for problem solving" or a "problem-solving set," where "set" is used to mean an attitude of a cognitive nature that leads them to expect certain strategies to work (as well as the possession of those strategies, or memory of them).

This type of experiment led to concepts of teaching that stressed the importance of teaching learners how to learn, i.e., giving them learning sets that would improve their abilities in handling later, more complex learning. We have alluded previously to Bruner's idea of teaching more powerful basic concepts, for the same purpose (Chapter 9); both approaches have the same objective.

Insight and learning sets combined

Retarded learners were taught to choose the larger of two stimulus objects, regardless of changes in the way they were presented (including the absolute size of the objects) and the nature of the objects. These learners had difficulty with this problem, and it took them a long time to learn to do it without error. Eventually, however, they developed a learning set; they came to a point where they could do this problem fairly quickly.* Interestingly enough, the manner in which they solved the problems after they had attained the learning set reminded the experimenters of insight-learning experiments with animals; they would seem to consider the problem and then have a "flash of insight" in which they came to the solution (Harlow, 1959). The investigator's conclusion was that the amount of previous experience a learner has had with a type of problem is what determines whether his or her solution process seems to be a trial-and-error one (little previous experience) or insightful (much previous experience, learning to the development of a learning set, or "learning how to learn"). Average or above-average ability students, therefore, will be more likely to demonstrate "insight" learning in problem situations, because they will have had previous experience with a variety of problems and they will be able to recall these experiences and apply them to a much greater degree than the animals or retarded learners described above. However, in situations that

---

* This kind of problem has often been referred to as concept learning in the past: this emphasizes the relationship between concept-learning processes, dealt with in the last chapter, and problem solving, which is the subject here.

are both new and complex, *all* learners will show aspects of trial-and-error learning as well, and retarded learners do have the capacity for insightful learning.

Cognitive development and problem solving

In discussing cognitive development in Chapters 1 and 2, I described Piaget's problem-oriented research technique and presented some of his conclusions about cognitive stages.

Piaget used problems which were not common to the education of the learners involved, so one would expect some trial-and-error behaviors according to the discussion in last section above.

RESEARCH RELATED TO PROBLEM SOLVING

Guidance and/or discovery

Guidance in concept teaching was discussed in Chapter 9. It is also important in teaching learners to solve problems. One study of the comparative effectiveness of guidance and discovery used a series of problems of the following type: "Fill in the missing numbers: 0, 1, 1, 2, 3, 5, __ __*." Three modes of learning were used to bring about understanding of the process for completing such a series. In one, the learner was given the principle and asked to apply it to an example; in another he (or she) was given examples and asked to discover the principle; in the third he was given examples and provided hints to help him discover the principle (this was called *guided discovery*). In a test in which he was required to transfer this knowledge to other series of the same type, but new to him, the student who had been exposed to the guided-discovery approach performed more effectively than those in either the discovery approach or the guidance (given principle) approach (Gagne and Paradise, 1961).

It is appropriate to underline that the guidance-discovery question is one of *degrees* of guidance. Obviously, in the discovery approach, the nature of the series used for the learning tasks, their sequential relationship to each other, and the difficulty of the rule and the size of the numbers used all affected the "learnability" of the exemplars. The discovery sequence could have been tried, revised, and tried out again several times until it was so organized that students would learn more easily from it than from the guided-discovery sequence.

Some of the processes involved in concept learning are also important in problem solving: concept learning is, after all, a kind of problem solving.

Guidance by feedback

The concept of "feedback" was also introduced in the last chapter, and is important here as well; actually, feedback is a form of guidance. In another study, learners

---

* Missing numbers are 8, 13.

Feedback can be a form of guidance for learners.

were exposed to a concept-learning task similar to those described in the preceding chapter.   In one treatment the subject was told the correct answer immediately if he gave an incorrect response; in the other the subject was told to keep trying until he "discovered" the correct answer.   Comparisons of outcomes indicated that there were no significant differences in the number of concepts named correctly or in the number of presentations required to name them correctly, but that the discovery group learned to recall and recognize significantly more definitions of concepts, and also learned to recall definitions of a greater percentage of the concepts that they had learned to name correctly (Gagne, 1964).   In another study, however, two groups were compared in their ability to decode unfamiliar cryptograms. One group derived the coding principles from examples, whereas the other had the principles given to them (both groups had the same learning tasks and the same criterion tasks).   There seemed to be no consistent difference between the "deriving" and the "given" groups on either immediate or delayed post-tests (Haselrud. 1974).

In still another comparison of discovery and nondiscovery learning groups in mathematics researchers concluded that the discovery approach resulted in better retention of concepts and better application to new situations; some of the advantages, however, showed up only when a post-test was given after some months had elapsed (Worthen, 1968). In a small study of different types of guidance in learning concepts inductively I also found this kind of unexpected outcome: the differences between the treatments I used did not show up on an immediate post-test, but were evident on a delayed post-test, three months later, i.e., with a summer vacation in between (Smith, 1970). Obviously, there are things to be learned about various forms of guidance and discovery in learning and we do not have a thorough understanding of all the factors at the present time. One fascinating possibility is that "understanding" (as measured by transfer to other problems or tasks) is something which can happen *after* the initial observable learning process; if so, how long does it go on, and how long after learning does it come to fruition? You often hear complaints from people who say they have forgotten everything they ever learned in high school or college; maybe they are still learning and don't know it!

Previous experience and problem solving

The examples given in relation to the guidance-discovery problem concentrate on the interaction of students' and teachers' efforts to reach problem-solving solutions. Another type of research in problem solving sheds some light on factors that affect difficulty in relation to the interaction of previous experience. The following is a classic example.

Two strings hang from a ceiling, and the problem is to tie them together. They are so far apart that you cannot grab them simultaneously. However, if you tie something to one and set it swinging, then you can hold on to the other and grasp the first when it swings your way. This requires you to use some object as a weight for the pendulum, often an object that you have recently used for some other thing. For example, there may be an ashtray, provided for you since you smoke. However, the experimenter has provided it also as a possible weight for the pendulum, but has not told you about it. Another approach is to have the learner try to fasten something to a wall with a screwdriver (before the experiment), and then leave the screwdriver there as a possible weight (Duncker, 1945).

In one variation of this experiment the learners were previously given another problem in which they had to use either a switch or a relay (two types of electronic components) to complete an electric circuit. One group used the switch, the other used the relay. When they came to the rope problem, both a switch and a relay were made available to each of them; of course, they were not told what they were for. The question was, would the learner solve the problem using the switch or the relay? Data from this experiment, when tabulated, appeared roughly as in Table 10–1 (these are not original data, but chosen to simulate the results) (Birch and Rabinowitz, 1951).

Obviously, the group that had previously used the switch to complete the electric circuit tended to use the relay as a weight, and vice versa. Neither was inherently more adaptable, since the group having no previous problem chose them

One helpful approach to solving problems is to try to view familiar situations in a new or different way.

Table 10–1. *Results of switch and relay experiment.*

	Used Switch	Used Relay
Group previously using switch	2	7
Group previously using relay	10	0
Group having no previous problem	3	4

about fifty-fifty. What does this say about problem solving and previous experience?

The two-rope problem solved—almost.

One way this effect has been described is by the term "functional fixedness." Those who used the switch in the circuit tended to see it as a switch, not as a weight. Thus, its "switch-ness" interfered with its potential for other uses. Another way to refer to this would be as an example of "proactive inhibition," i.e.,

Previous experience and problem solving.

interference from previous learning. It could also be seen as an example of the effect of an unhelpful "learning set." Still another view of it would be related to creativity—more creative people would be more likely to use the switch for something different than its previous use. Practically speaking, from a teaching point of view, no matter what you call it, it is obvious that part of teaching learners to solve problems is getting them to see old things in new ways, and getting them to try things that are not entirely conventional. This also has to do with the idea of "brainstorming."

Another example of interference

Consider the problem below—the object is to draw four connected straight lines that intersect all nine points, without taking your pencil off the paper. The solution is difficult because you have an interfering learning set.

```
●   ●   ●

●   ●   ●

●   ●   ●
```

If you allow one of the lines to go outside the boundaries implied by the dots (but not stated as a constraint), you won't have much trouble. But previous experience leads you to stay within the lines.

TWO THEORIES OF PROBLEM SOLVING

Gestalt psychology and problem solving

In the early 1900s a "school" of psychology developed which emphasized experiments with perceptual phenomena and related them to problem solving and cognition generally. This approach, called Gestalt, emphasized the ability of the mind to perceive patterns and to analyze wholes into parts (we have already referred to this in Chapter 9 in discussing part-to-whole and whole-to-part learning of concepts). It also emphasized the importance of the phenomenon of "insight" in problem solving, asserting that while animals usually learned by trial and error, humans depend on something more complex, a higher order thought process which leads up to insight. We have given examples of this process, and of the relationship between trial-and-error and insight learning, earlier in this chapter. While the experimental foundations for Gestalt theory were never developed as extensively as in other theories, Gestalt concepts of learning have been very influential ever since.

In addition to the insight concept, Gestalt psychologists asserted several other postulates (assumptions) about learning. One was that the whole is greater than the sum of its parts; this implied that you could not explain or teach something by a part-to-whole process, since the whole was more than the parts, and had to be analyzed itself. They would demonstrate this by examples showing that the parts in themselves were meaningless until put together in certain configurations; e.g., the letter A has straight line segments as its parts but they are meaningless by themselves. Gestalt experiments with visual perception phenomena also led to such concepts as "closure," which is the tendency we have to complete some figure that is incomplete: if you see a circle with a piece of the circumference missing, you are likely to perceive it and/or remember it as a complete circle. This concept was reflected in discussions of learning disabilities, in Chapter 4, where "closure" was one of the types of test tasks used in both the ITPA and the WISC (Picture Completion).

The Gestalt emphasis on learning through analysis of the whole rather than starting with the parts has been reflected in Chapter 9 in the whole–part discussion and in the concept of "discovery" learning. Obviously, approaching a problem by analyzing the whole involves discovery of relationships and patterns; however, it is not discovery in the sense of being without guidance, since you could give guidance to a learner in a whole-to-part process just as in a part-to-whole. On the other hand, since the natural tendency of teachers is to give guidance in a part-to-whole format, discovery learning and whole-to-part learning are often thought of as synonymous.

If you were to classify the problem-oriented research of Piaget, you would probably conclude that it is similar to the Gestalt approach also, by emphasizing whole-to-part, since in Piagetian tasks (designed to analyze thinking, not to teach it, incidentally) the problem is presented and the learner is left to solve it independently.

In their book on human problem solving, Newell and Simon (1972) present a basic structure that is involved in problem-solving behavior: they call it an "information processing system," or "IPS." The receiving systems of the problem solver (or receptors, i.e., nerve endings and the pathways by which senses travel to the brain) are connected to a processor, which in turn utilizes a memory. The memory also feeds information into the processor as well, which in turn feeds information to the effectors, i.e., motor processes that carry out decisions in the problem-solving process. The diagram* given by Newell and Simon is shown below:

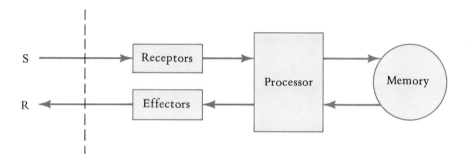

They give as an example an IPS for sending and receiving Morse code. The receptors perceive the dots and dashes, which are symbols. These symbols are processed by the processor, and a message regarding them is sent to short-term memory. Inside the STM some kinds of units that correspond to these symbols are activated; these symbols would be communicated to the long-term memory, where the equivalent letter would be stored. This would be fed back to the short-term memory and to the effectors, which would write (or think) that letter.

Figure 10–1. *The information processing system.*

* From Allen Newell and Herbert A. Simon, *Human Problem Solving* © 1972.   Reprinted by permission of Prentice-Hall, Inc., Englewood Cliffs, New Jersey.

Theorists' methods of information processing

Ultimately research such as Newell and Simon's will lead to models of the working of the human mind and will explain how we solve problems. This in turn will suggest better ways of teaching poeple how to solve problems and better ways of solving the major problems that confront our society. At present, these investigators are using models derived from the design and workings of computers. Through these models, and through observation of individuals solving complex problems, they are trying to deduce how the human information-processing system works. This is not easy to do: you can't always tell what is inside a box by shaking it or weighing it or other experiments with it, short of opening it up, and obviously, we can't open up the human mind as you can a box (although some of the research in physiological psychology, like putting electrodes inside the brain, is approaching this).

One type of problem that Newell and Simon have used for doing this research is called "Cryptarithmetic." Here is an example of such a problem:

$$\begin{array}{r} \text{SEND} \\ + \text{ MORE} \\ \hline \text{MONEY} \end{array}$$

Each letter stands for a different digit; of course, M stands for the same digit wherever it appears. Your task is to figure out what digits the letters stand for: when you get the answer, then the number corresponding to "SEND," and that corresponding to "MORE," will add up to the number corresponding to "MONEY." The investigators record everything you say about how you are going at it, and from this information they attempt to put together a theory of how your mind solves the problem.

An important feature of the theory is the concept of "problem space," the internal representation of the relevant considerations that are to be used in solving the problem. One example of a problem space is given in the anecdote below. The problem is described first (i.e., the game of "Number Scrabble"), then a particular "problem space" is also described, the visual representation that Mr. Smart uses to win.

MR. SMART SWITCHES SPACES: AN EXAMPLE OF A "PROBLEM SPACE"

Some of Mr. Smart's students in mathematics have been playing a game, and they decide to challenge Mr. Smart to see if he is as smart as his name suggests. The game is called "Number Scrabble." It is played with a set of nine square pieces with the numbers from one to nine on them; one piece with "1" and one piece with "2," etc. Two people play; they draw one piece at a time, taking turns. The first player who holds up any set of three pieces that add up to the number 15 wins the game. For example, if

John has the numbers 5 and 7 and he draws a 3, then he wins; however, if his opponent Sarah anticipates this and draws the 3 before he does, he can't use the 5–7 combination to win, but must get some other combination, for example 7, 2, and 6. Meanwhile, Sarah may have reached 15 first.

Anyway, they challenge Mr. Smart, and he plays with them and beats them every time! They can't figure out how he does it—he doesn't even seem to have to think about it—he anticipates all their moves, and always seems to know when they are about to score on him. They ask him if there is any trick, and he tells them that there is: he uses a different problem space than they do! They can't figure this out, so he shows them. He draws a tic-tac-toe game, and fills numbers in as follows:

2	7	6
9	5	1
4	3	8

Each of the verticals, horizontals, and the one diagonal adds up to fifteen; when they draw a number, he mentally fills in a zero, and when he draws one he mentally fills in an X, in the correct space. Then he has a visual record of where they are threatening to complete a set of fifteen (i.e., a vertical or horizontal line or a diagonal). He explains that you have to memorize the tic-tac-toe diagram with the numbers, and that you have to have a good visual memory for the Xs and the Os, but then, it's quite easy. You have to pick a problem space that suits your particular talents!

"Problem space" is one of those concepts that is hard to define. Obviously, it is a strategy of representing the relevant facts in a convenient way. The general characteristics of a problem space, as presented abstractly by Newell and Simon, include the following:

1. Symbolic representations of knowledge about the task.
2. Operators that produce new states of knowledge from existing ones.
3. Initial knowledge about the task.
4. An objective or goal, which compared with the initial knowledge defines the nature of the problem.
5. A storage of previously acquired relevant knowledge.

Empirical approaches for representing knowledge, operating upon it, changing representations, and keeping track of past operations are given in guidelines for problem solving later in this chapter.

Implications of these two theories for teaching problem solving

The implications of these two theories of problem solving, Gestalt and information processing, are general rather than specific, and not everyone agrees on them. Gestalt psychology suggests a whole-to-part, discovery-oriented approach, where the ability of the learner to analyze and compare and decipher new situations in terms of the old are brought to bear. This is similar to Ausubel's approach described in Chapter 9.

The information-processing view of problem solving suggest that adult problem solvers use strategies that can't be described as simply "whole-to-part" or "part-to-whole." We can infer certain conclusions about ways of teaching a system, although such inferences are a bit premature.

Inference 1.   Because of the limited capacity of STM and the time it takes to store information in LTM, it is helpful to have an "external memory" available for solving problems, i.e., a pad of paper on which to write and record steps and conclusions, or a computer to store them for you until you need them.   Another reason for having this is that the human information processor can only handle one operation at a time; therefore, it is necessary to record the results of one operation before attempting another.

Inference 2.   Humans solve problems according to a systematic approach that is like a "production system."   This is a list of "if-then" statements which direct the learner in operating upon the problem, one operation at a time, and deciding what operation to accomplish next.   Newell and Simon give the following example of an imaginary internal system of directions that could produce the kind of behavior you observe in people:

Production system for crossing the street at a traffic light (one with a separate red and green light for pedestrians):

Traffic-light red $\longrightarrow$ Stop
Traffic-light green $\longrightarrow$ Move
Move and left-foot-on-pavement $\longrightarrow$ Step-with-right-foot
Move and right-foot-on-pavement $\longrightarrow$ Step-with-left-foot

---

The computer within you follows these instructions in order: if the light is green, it ignores the first direction and goes to the next; then, at the command "move," it determines which foot is on the pavement, and moves the other, repeating this as necessary.   Not given here are the parts of the system which instruct the computer when to start this routine, and when to stop it.

One implication for teaching is that you should consider the implicit production system for solving the type of problem you wish to teach, and devote some time to presenting that system.   This might emerge, incidentally, as an "advance organizer" in the manner of Ausubel (Chapter 9).

Inference 3.   Human behavior, including problem-solving behavior, is goal-oriented.   In the information processing system, this means that there are symbol-structures (concepts) which include (a) a test to determine whether the goal has been attained, and (b) some means of bringing about relevant behaviors, i.e., which are related to the goal and thus help attain it.   Thus part of teaching problem solving is teaching the learner how to set up his or her goals and how to recognize when he or she has attained them.

TEACHING LEARNERS TO SOLVE PROBLEMS

Problem solving as behavior modification and as
concept teaching

A problem is a task of getting from some beginning situation to some goal. The learner knows the solution, or can recognize it, and has a number of strategies—or behavior chains—for getting there. He or she needs to select a strategy, try it out, evaluate the progress made, and either continue with that strategy or change it. This may also mean changing the internal representation of the problem, or the "problem space," that has been used.

The solution process can be viewed as a chain of behaviors, which has been conditioned or learned previously, and is applied to this problem because aspects of the situation are similar to those of previous situations where that chain was effective; the learner generalizes from previous situations to this one. One thing that the learner must do is follow the chain correctly and accurately; e.g., in doing long division, the method may be correct but the learner may add or subtract wrong and get the wrong answer. Another thing to do is to recognize when the chain is not producing positive results—when you aren't getting closer to the objective—so it can be changed.

The problem can be viewed as a concept or as one of a type or class of problems. If you can recognize the problem as belonging to that class, then you can utilize a solution process that was successful previously.

The solution process itself, while also a chain of behaviors, is a process and thus a concept, i.e., a sequential pattern. This means that there are two aspects of solving problems: first, recognizing or identifying the solution process (as a concept); and second, producing it as a chain of behaviors.

Teaching problem solving, then, involves (a) teaching the type of problem as a concept, (b) teaching processes which represent solutions to that type of problem, and (c) teaching the behavior chain necessary for carrying out each solution process. Since identification of the *type* of problem is not a simple matter, errors will be made; the feedback you get that relates an error is usually the fact that the solution process doesn't work. Then you have to be able to restructure your thinking and treat it as another type of problem, which means identifying it as another concept. This is similar to identifying a nonexample as an example, in concept learning (i.e., an overgeneralization), but with delayed feedback about your decision. Such things are frustrating to learners who are used to simpler concept identification problems and to immediate feedback; therefore, persistence in the face of this frustration is one of the behaviors you need to shape.

For a given problem type (a concept) there are sometimes several possible solution processes. Again, it is a matter of selecting one and trying it, then returning and beginning over if it doesn't work out. In the early stages of learning to solve problems, guidance from the teacher can be helpful in avoiding blind alleys, but

Teaching someone
to solve problems
involves kinds of
learning and
teaching you have
already studied,
but the details
are unique.

ultimately the guidance should concentrate on helping students interpret results themselves, with support and encouragement to persist in their efforts and not to give up when frustrated by an ineffective solution process.

An instructional system for teaching problem solving

Instructional systems are specially developed programs for helping to teach certain skills or understandings. They are tried out on learners, and revised according to the problems those learners have with them, then tried out again, until they work well for a reasonable variety of learner types and abilities. This systems development process will be described in more detail in Chapter 13. One fairly extensive and effective instructional system has been developed for teaching learners to solve problems (Covington et al., 1972). The Covington system is based in part on research in creative problem solving conducted during the 1960s (Covington and Crutchfield, 1965; Olton and Crutchfield, 1969). It is published in the form of about fifteen booklets in sequence. Each booklet uses a cartoon-like format, and develops stories about how learners solve simple problems, and then later on more complex problems. Some examples of the format are given in Figures 10–2, 10–3, and 10–4.

Problem-solving skills taught by the Covington system

The Covington booklets begin with simple problems, and the characters in the story (who are representatives of the learners themselves, in a sense) are given plenty of help in solving the problems. As the booklets procede, the boy and the girl who are the main characters gradually solve more and more complex problems, and do so more and more independently. The stories stress (by example) various aspects of problem-solving skills, and these are summarized at the end of the booklets as follows:

A. *Getting started on a problem:*
Take time out to reflect on a problem; decide what you are trying to solve (goal setting).
Get all the facts of the problem clearly in mind.
Work on the problem in a planful way.
Keep an open mind. Don't jump to conclusions about the answer to a problem.

(NOTE: each of these may be considered a concept or a process, for each of which the various stories in the booklets give several examples.)

B. *Thinking of ideas:*

Think of many ideas; don't stop with just a few.

Try to think of unusual ideas.

As a way of getting ideas, pick out important objects and persons and consider each carefully.

Think of several general possibilities for a solution, then think of several ideas for each.

As you search for ideas, let your mind freely explore things around you: almost anything can suggest solutions.

C. *Evaluating ideas:*

Always check each idea with the facts to decide how likely that idea is

D. *Getting unstuck:*

If you get stuck, keep thinking; don't be discouraged or give up.

When you run out of ideas, try looking at the problem in a new and different way.

Go back and review all the facts of the problem to make sure that you haven't missed something important.

Start with an unlikely idea; just suppose that it is possible, and figure out how it could be.

E. *Explaining puzzling things:*

Be on the lookout for odd and puzzling facts in a problem.

Explaining them can lead to new ideas for solutions.

When there are several different puzzling things in a problem, try to explain them with a single idea that will connect them all together.

Dewey on problem solving

John Dewey, a famous educational philosopher and practitioner and the main force behind what was called "progressive education" in the 1930s, placed great emphasis on the importance of problem-solving skills. His analysis of the process of discovery, which is related to problem-solving and which was the foundation of his project-centered educational theory, went something like this:

- Preparation—Acquiring knowledge, recognizing problems, seeing how things relate.
- Incubation—Sorting out the ideas, sometimes subconsciously, putting things together in various ways, playing with patterns and combinations.
- Illumination—The insight experience, when things fall into place, the solution becomes clear.
- Verification—Testing the solution against facts and requirements on the solution, and then checking it. (Dewey, 1910)

"Yes. That mystery about Carlos and Mike's water disappearing from the can was great," Jim agrees. "Thinking can be fun! Gee, imagine *me* saying that."

"I found out something, too," Lila says. "I had to stand up in class and give a report today. Nobody laughed at my ideas. They seemed to like them! Imagine *me* saying that!"

"I'm not surprised at all," Uncle John replies. "I've noticed that just in this short time both of you seem more willing to try to think. I believe both of you have improved."

Many people feel this way. Perhaps even you do.

Figure 10–2. *The Covington system for problem solving: A mystery. (Reprinted by permission of the Charles E. Merrill Publishing Co., publisher of* The Productive Thinking Program: A Course in Learning to Think, *by Covington, Crutchfield, Davies, and Olton.)*

Figure 10–3. *The Covington system for problem solving: Aquanaut options. (Reprinted by permission of the Charles E. Merrill Co., publisher of* The Productive Thinking Program: A Course in Learning to Think, *by Covington, Crutchfield, Davies, and Olton.)*

While Lila is doing this, turn to your Reply Booklet and do the same thing.

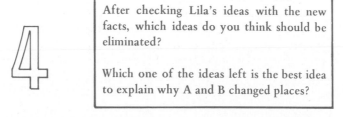

Figure 10–4. *The Covington system for problem solving: Eliminating ideas. (Reprinted by permission of the Charles E. Merrill Publishing Co., publisher of* The Productive Thinking Program: A Course in Learning to Think, *by Covington, Crutchfield, Davies, and Olton.)*

USING PROBLEM SOLVING AS A MEANS OF TEACHING

Problem posing

To teach through problem solving, you present a situation that calls for some solution process, and that makes it evident what the solution is like. For example, to teach the solution of an equation by problem solving, you need to present an equation initially that is understandable to the learner, and you also need to make it clear to him or her what conditions the correct answer will satisfy (i.e., it will be a number which, when you put it in place of the unknown, will make a "true statement").

What number can you put in the box to make this a true statement?

$$2 \times \boxed{} \times \boxed{} + \boxed{} = 21$$

Of course, this is a quadratic equation. However, you could lead up to it by presenting simpler problems like this:

$$3 \times \boxed{} \times \boxed{} = 12$$

or, earlier,

$$\boxed{} + 2 = 9.$$

Just as concepts can be taught without verbal explanation, so various topics can be taught by presenting students with a problem to solve.

For a nonexample, consider a teacher who presents an equation, asks the learners to watch while he solves it, and explains how the answer makes a "true statement." The only problem for the learner would be to pay attention while the teacher goes through it.

For another nonexample, consider a teacher who teaches a student to identify pronouns by saying "Find the pronoun in this sentence" and then saying either "You are right" or "You are wrong" when the learner identifies a word. To be involved in a problem-solving process, the student would have to have some way of knowing when he (or she) had found it himself, i.e., he would have to have some way of recognizing whether he had the answer after he made his decision, some way *other* than being told. As Newell and Simon put it, "A problem is *well-defined* if a test exists, performable by the system, that will determine whether an object proposed as a solution is in fact a solution. By *performable* we mean performable with a relatively small amount of processing effort." (To understand this statement, you will have to substitute the word "learner" for "system.")

Presenting an optimal discrepancy

To use problem-solving processes to teach something, you have to arrange things so the problem is within the ability of the learner to solve with reasonable effort—not too difficult, and yet difficult enough to challenge him (or her) and make him want to solve it.   This is what is meant by an "optimal discrepancy."   (See Chapter 2).

For example, in teaching the concept of "sonnet" you might pose a problem to a student that consists of writing a sonnet, given a rhyme scheme and other relevant characteristics.   This could be too difficult, in which case she would give up; or it might be about right, in which case she would create a sonnet from the guidelines.

The secret to motivating by posing problems is to make the discrepancy optimal.

MR. ROSS USES A PROBLEM TO TEACH

Mr. Ross wants to teach his social studies class the processes by which a need of society is translated into law through the legislative procedures that enable people to carry this out democratically.   Rather than have his class read about law making in the text, or do research on it and write a paper, he is looking for an approach that will dramatize this and get his students involved, so that they will understand it better and remember it longer.

He invents a case study, i.e., a simulation of this process, which involves the recognition of a problem by citizens, a series of meetings in which the idea of passing a law occurs, then a process whereby the problem or need is translated into legislation, brought up before the legislature, and eventually passed. Since there are several phases to this, and since he wants the class to be familiar with each phase, he presents this in stages.

First he creates a dramatization situation where he asks the class to develop a scenario, extemporaneously, in which there is a town meeting to discuss a very difficult problem. He asks members of the class to play the roles of different members of the community, each with his own goals, interests, and opinions about the problem. Then he has them make up their lines as they go along, to see how the thing develops. Fortunately, after quite a bit of beating around the bush, they get to the point where they want to do something about it. He then has one of the characters suggest presenting it to the state legislature for being made into a law.

In the next stage, he presents information in writing about the makeup of the legislature, the necessary steps for writing and presenting a bill, and so forth. He divides the class into several groups, each group having a description of several roles to be played, and each group also having access to the information they need in drawing up the bill and going through the various steps in presenting it. This is done so that each individual in the class will have a closer involvement in the process.

He circulates from group to group, helping them out of difficult situations and guiding them to next steps, helping them organize the process and divide up the responsibilities. He also directs them to reference sources for information they need, and occasionally supplies some advice on how to proceed when they are bogged down. He also does a lot of encouraging and urging so that they will not give up, since they are not accustomed to learning through problem solving.

After the individual groups have prepared the bill, representatives of the groups discuss the various versions with the others looking on. They ultimately agree on one version of it. Then the class is assigned roles in simulating a session of the legislature at which the bill is introduced and voted upon.

Through this process, the sequence of events is learned, and information is gained about committees of the legislature, the involvement of personalities in the democratic process, and the procedures for voting. These are acquired through active involvement with a definite goal in mind, rather than through a more conventional reading-discussion-test-taking process.

Berlyne's approaches to "optimal discrepancy"

Daniel Berlyne (1965) has offered a number of strategies for motivating learning through curiosity and inquiry. For example, he suggests using "surprisingness" by presenting things that contradict the expectations of students, and following it by the rewarding experience of adapting to the surprise. Another is the stimulation of doubt, by presenting a general principle which may or may not be valid. Doubt is relieved as the accumulation of instances convinces the pupil of the validity of the principle. This might be completed by some kind of proof as well. Berlyne also suggests setting up a problem with several different answers; uncertainty is relieved by selecting one of the suggested answers as probably the best, and by checking it in some way to see whether it will work. Berlyne also suggests problem solving generally, or "problem posing" as it has been presented earlier, as a means of motivating. The problem is resolved by the student's own efforts or by help from the teacher (guided discovery). Finally, in this same line, he suggests showing the student contradictions, or apparent ones, as in the famous paradox of Zeno where Achilles can never catch the tortoise. (Achilles runs ten times as fast as the tortoise, and the tortoise goes ten feet as Achilles runs one hundred. If Achilles is one foot behind, the tortoise covers one-tenth of a foot as Achilles covers the foot. When Achilles covers that tenth of a foot, the tortoise is still one-hundredth of a foot ahead, etc.)

It is interesting to note that Berlyne treats the solution of the problem or resolution of the paradox or difficulty as if it were a reinforcer. That is, he sees one aspect of this process as similar to intrinsic reinforcement. If you consider the anxiety of "not knowing" as aversive, then you could even look on it as negative reinforcement, but the positive aspects of successful solutions are usually emphasized here. If you look at problem solving this way, it is a combination of behavior modification (Chapter 8), motivation (Chapter 7), and encouragement of cognitive development through use of optimal discrepancies (Chapter 2).

Are two or three or more heads better than one?

If you want to solve a problem, should you get help, or do it by yourself? Small-group learning processes have advantages that are discussed in Chapter 6; however, not much is said there about problem solving per se. A general conclusion from a number of studies of group and individual problem solving is that small groups do better most of the time (Klausmeier et al., 1964). However, the best individual problem solvers do better than groups (Duncan, 1959). Therefore, in deciding which process to use, you have to consider the following questions:

1. Which is more important to teach, group problem solving processes or individual ones?
2. Do group processes prepare each individual to solve problems independently as well, and do individuals improve more in problem solving through working with groups or by themselves?

It seems likely that both types of objectives, i.e., group processes and individual strategies, are desirable; thus, if you are trying to teach learners how to learn, both types of experiences—individual and group—are important. Perhaps one way to work this out would be to have small-group problem solving at first, with able problem solvers in each group to show the way and model the processes; you could also give guidelines for problem solving to the groups, and have them evaluate their procedures after they had completed the task. Then you could give similar problems to the class for individual problem solving, either in class or as homework. (Of course, not all homework is done individually, is it!)

Small-group problem solving can prepare learners for later independent work.

LEARNING A STRATEGY OF LEARNING

Mr. Hunter uses a lot of problems in the earth science class. He seems to some of the students to be wasting a lot of time having them look for answers when he could just tell them and be done with it. They sort of resent the fact that they have to take each problem given and analyze it into what is given and what is to be found, solved, or proved, i.e., what the outcome is. He also has them list all the procedures they can think of which might help solve the problem given, in each case. This is pretty monotonous after a while, and they envy other students who have Mrs. Benchley in earth science because she always keeps the class going in a lively fashion, asking questions about the reading and the homework, telling jokes, and giving occasional quizzes to see whether or not they are "on their toes." All Mr. Hunter does is make them do all the work themselves, and solve problem after problem related to topsoils, what is needed for various types of crops, what might have caused a given formation, and such. On field trips, instead of telling them about what they see, he asks them if they can figure out what it is they are passing—some old mound or something, which he seems to think has some significance regarding the course. Some of the students complain that this course is ruining their social lives. Every time they are with a group and something happens or they see something dif-ferent, they start analyzing it and trying to fig-ure out what caused it or how it could have hap-pened, instead of cracking a couple of good jokes about it and going back to their conversations and fun. Some of the kids who had Mr. Brown and then went on to other science courses say that it helped them a lot to study on their own and figure things out—but they were good students anyway, probably, and so it does not seem that this is going to do much good—it certainly is going to be a drag until the course is over!

Moral: Promoting cognitive growth doesn't always make you a hero!

Brainstorming

"Brainstorming" is a group problem-solving process that emphasizes creativity. It assumes that the major obstacle to good problem solving is a lack of creative hypotheses or alternate solutions or different ways of going at the problem. Therefore, in brainstorming all criticism of ideas is suspended; the objective is simply to produce ideas, not to critique them once they are produced. (This is similar to sensitivity group approaches where all reference to past or future is ruled out, and only feelings are allowed to be expressed, except in this case the focus is on creative ideas instead of feelings.)

One outcome of brainstorming is that the number of good ideas increases, but so also does the number of bad ones (Torrance, 1961; Guilford, 1962). Research on the effectiveness of brainstorming as a means of bringing about good problem solving is mixed in its implications, with some indications again that individuals do as well as groups (Taylor et al., 1968; Dunette et al., 1963). Brainstorming is probably best viewed as a technique for increasing the production of creative possibilities or hypotheses where individuals or groups are limited in this respect.

Summary outline with key concepts

☞ A *problem* is a situation where you want something and don't know immediately what series of actions to take to get it / Problem solving has been part of educational research and theory for many years; a variety of types of problems have been addressed / Some important concepts in problem-solving research and theory are insight, learning sets, and cognitive stage.

☞ *Other matters* involved in problem-solving research are guidance and discovery, functional fixedness, and interfering learning sets / Feedback can be considered a form of guidance / Interference from learning sets needs to be allowed for in teaching problem solving.

☞ *Gestalt psychologists* emphasized a whole-to-part approach to teaching / They also emphasized the importance of "insight" / An information-processing theory of problem solving views the mind as similar to a computer / One aspect of the information-processing theory is the concept of "problem space" / Gestalt theory suggests teaching learners to analyze problems by analyzing the whole, rather than parts / Information processing theory suggests teaching learners to use external memory aids, determining the nature of the production system needed and teaching it, and teaching learners to identify goals and how to recognize solutions.

☞ *Problem solving* can be taught as a skill by strategies adapted from concept teaching and from behavior modification / There are instuctional systems which teach learners how to solve problems / The guidelines from one system include getting started, thinking of ideas, evaluating ideas, getting unstuck, and explaining puzzling things / Dewey suggested a number of steps in problem solving generally, including preparation, incubation, illumination, and verification.

☞ *Problem solving* is also a means of teaching / To teach by problem solving, pose problems that represent optimal discrepancies / Berlyne's approach to teaching by problems illustrates the similarity of problem solving to motivation, cognitive development, and behavior modification / Group problem solving has elements that are different from individual processes / Brainstorming is an approach to increasing learners' creativity and openness for problem solving.

Glossary

Brainstorming: Allowing ideas to be voiced without criticism, to get more ideas out for future consideration and analysis (*see* Chapter 3).

Discovery Learning: Learning by finding relationships and solutions and associations and similarities, with minimal or no assistance or guidance from others; also implies a problem-posing approach to teaching.

Feedback: Information concerning the effectiveness or correctness of a response or series of responses; guides future problem-solving activities.

Functional Fixedness: Inability to adopt different points of view or attitudes, due to previous learning or habit; e.g. inability to view a hammer as a possible weight to tie to a string, because you see it as used for nails.

Gestalt: "Pattern"; refers to a theory of psychology which emphasizes that we perceive according to patterns or "Gestalts."

Guidance: Assistance during learning or problem solving, through hints or verbal directions or other interventions.

Hippocampus: Part of the brain where electrical activity occurs during learning.

Incubation: Stage in problem solving proposed by Dewey.

Information Processing: A view of how the human mind works in dealing with everyday information, based on how computers work; emphasizes involvement of short- and long-term memory, processors, receptors, and effectors.

Illumination: Stage of problem solving, according to Dewey.

Insight: Behavior just preceding the solution of a problem which indicates that the solution comes "all at once" rather than little by little.

Learning Set: Learning or concept formation shown by the fact that a learner solves problems of a certain type more easily after having solved others of the same type.

LTM: Long-term memory, where past experience is stored for future use.

Optimal Discrepancy (see Chapter 2):   A discrepancy or unusual situation which causes the learner to try to "figure it out" because it is not too different and yet different enough to motivate such thought.

Problem Space: The information or organizational system which the learner uses in solving a problem.

STM (Short-term Memory):   Where the human mind holds information that it is currently dealing with; humans have a small STM compared with a computer.

Verification: Stage of problem solving, according to Dewey.

Questions for thought and discussion

1. Using the definition of problem solving given in the chapter, would you say that concept learning is problem solving? If not, why not? Is it paired associate learning? Social learning (modeling)?

2. Do you suppose you could teach the ape described in the anecdote about insight to solve problems better? Would you use the Covington guidelines, or try to teach a learning set, or what? Does this relate to teaching chimpanzees to communicate as described in Chapter 8?

3. How many types of guidance can you identify for use in teaching problem solving in such subjects as mathematics or social studies? There would be a number of kinds of verbal prompts or cues, and there would be feedback types, but what other subtle methods might you use as well?

4. Is it possible to use problem posing as a method for teaching languages? Literature? History? Home economics? (Don't give up without trying to find a way.)

5. Can you give an example of the whole of something being more than the sum of its parts? Then can you identify a process by which a learner could come to understand it by analyzing the whole rather than putting together the parts?

6. Are there any similarities between Covington's guidelines and Dewey's? Do these relate to the inferences drawn from information-processing theory? To teaching concepts?

Situations calling for applications of facts and concepts

1. Find an Agatha Christie or Dorothy Sayers or Ellery Queen mystery, and try to solve it, using the guidelines given by Covington et al.

2. Get a group of fellow students together and play "Clue" or some such game which

involves problems; identify some of your processes as you go.

3. Try to invent a problem which is easy to solve, and yet which people will find difficult because of previous learning sets or "functional fixedness." Test it on your fellow students to see if it works the way you expect.

4. Select a subject matter and topic of interest to you, and devise a problem to pose which will help teach it, i.e., a problem which learners are able to solve (optimal discrepancy) and yet which will result in learning as they go about solving it. Specify what it is they will learn, and then seek some other way to check whether or not they actually learned it through this process.

5. Select some problem and then determine how you would teach learners to solve it by (a) a whole-to-part method and (b) a part-to-whole method. Don't be surprised to find that they aren't all that different—it happens in some cases.

6. Select a problem and determine how you would teach learners to solve it using (a) Covington's guidelines, (b) Dewey's guidelines, and (c) the inferences drawn from information-processing theory.

Suggested activities

1. Observe classes in some subject at some level, or observe individual tutoring (e.g., for learning disabilities); note whether any problems are posed or selected, explicitly or implicitly, and whether the student learns to learn in any sense (as differentiated from learning facts or concepts or skills).

2. Observe or participate in some experimental work in problem solving, where such variables as discovery, guidance, or amount of feedback are examined; you may want to design such an experiment yourself.

Suggested readings

One interesting and short book on problem solving is Polya's *How to solve it*, written in 1965. The Crutchfield series would be interesting to read also, if there is a set available. The Newell and Simon book *Human problem solving* is tough reading, but rewarding if you can stay with it. Dewey's books relate to problem solving within the context of a social learning objectives approach, i.e., his objectives were to produce learners who could function as good citizens in a democratic society, rather than achievement in the subject matter per se.

PART

IV

APPLICATIONS
OF
THEORY
TO
TEACHING

11

Managing and Motivating

CONTENTS

ABOUT CHAPTER 11

What this chapter can do for you

This chapter will combine a number of theories and strategies discussed previously and present a general overview of approaches to managing learning situations, including classrooms, and to motivating learners, including groups of learners and classes. You should have more options and techniques for handling a variety of learning situations when you have finished. You will also have reviewed a number of principles and concepts related to teaching which were discussed previously, and thus have them more firmly in mind.

Possible psychological difficulties to watch for

If you have no experience in teaching it may be difficult to envision some of the applied processes described here. If you do have experience, you may find some of the implications of theories are strange and seemingly un-useful. You will need to keep an open mind, and to visualize the applications and processes described; most have been used successfully. Finally, you may have skipped some of the processes or concepts, and thus some discussions may be difficult to understand. Selective reading should be sufficient to clear this up.

Reasons for studying this chapter

This chapter discusses implications for and applications to teaching from the theories and processes discussed previously. In the process, it also reviews these theories. After meeting so many new ideas, and experiencing so much proactive and retroactive inhibition, these are powerful reasons for studying this chapter and the next one. "Repetition is the mother of learning," an old saying goes, and so some repetition is appropriate. However, this will not be entirely repetition: I will introduce some new concepts and processes and some new relationships between those that you have already met.

Objectives

The purpose of this chapter is to present the elements of teaching theory, as distinct from learning theory, in a readable and understandable manner; the next chapter also carries out this purpose. It is also designed to pull together a number of threads from previous presentations to integrate them in a meaningful way.

This should contribute not only to your comprehension of teaching and ability to accommodate to a variety of teaching/learning situations, but also should contribute to the development of the theory of teaching in the long run.

RATIONALE AND BACKGROUND OF CHAPTER 11

Relation to previous chapters

The rationale for this chapter has been discussed in the previous section. The background of this chapter is the material in previous chapters. The organization of the chapter stresses two basic functions of teaching, namely, managing (particularly in group situations) and motivating. Teaching processes themselves are described in Chapter 12.

What "management" involves

Management involves scheduling activities and dealing with behavior problems; the latter include behaviors that are undesirable and need to be reduced, and behaviors that are weak or missing and need to be increased. Management is necessary in one-to-one tutoring just as in a classroom situation, but the need isn't as pressing or obvious in the former case. Another part of management is the programing of learning itself: decisions regarding the scheduling of practice or drill or problem solving; the amount of time to be spent in laboratory experiences or listening to lectures or viewing films; working out field trips and other experiential situations. Some of these decisions are based on theories of learning and teaching; some are based on considerations related to motivation; and some relate to needs of individual learners and groups. Most teaching methods, however, were not derived originally from theory, but have been handed down from generation to generation of teachers. For a short history of teaching method, by the way, you may want to read *Exemplars of Teaching Method*, by Broudy and Palmer.

MANAGING BY PLANNING AND SCHEDULING

Options for organizing group (classroom) learning

This is not a chapter on methods as they apply to particular subjects or concepts or topics. However, it does present a number of basic approaches to the management of teaching that can apply to all subjects at all levels, some more than others. Since this is not a methods chapter, it will not attempt to deal with all the possible arrangements of groups for learning. However, it may be appropriate to list them here, so that you may have in mind the breadth and range of strategies and structures that are possible. This is done in Table 11–1.

Table 11–1. *Some options for organizing classes and presenting information.*

Large-group methods
> Lecture, and lecture/discussion.
> Oral reports to the class by individuals or groups.
> Films, slides, and overhead transparencies, with or without accompanying comments.
> Television or radio programs (also applies to small groups or individuals).
> Field trips.
> Laboratory exercises.

Small-group methods (five to eight learners in each group)
> Small-group discussions.
> Role playing sessions.
> Project-development planning and discussion.
> Discussions of questions raised by teacher or text, prior to whole-class discussions.
> Discussions of tests and quizzes.

Large-small group
> Goldfish bowl discussions, with inner group discussing and outer group looking on (Chapter 6).

Individual instruction
> Individual study and/or problem solving in class.
> Individual project work in class, with passes to visit library.
> Individual use of learning aids—films, programmed texts, slide-tape-text systems, computer-based instruction.
> Individual solution of a problem prior to either small-group discussion or large-group discussion.

Previous discussions of planning and scheduling activities

A number of innovative approaches to planning and scheduling will be discussed in Chapter 13 in relation to instructional systems development. Small-group approaches to classroom management were discussed previously in Chapter 6. Some approaches to management were also described and/or implied in discussions of the characteristics of good teachers in Chapter 5, and in discussion of leadership styles in Chapter 6. Some approaches to individual instruction and tutoring are suggested in discussions of the management of learning disabilities, later in this chapter.

An example of planning and scheduling

The scheduling of classroom activities involving such common teaching processes as lectures, small-group discussions, laboratory experiences, films, and the like, not to mention assignment of homework and independent study, can be a very complex matter itself. The possible combinations are practically infinite, as you can imagine. To show you one approach to combining the various possibilities we have

The pattern of scheduling and the variety of approaches in this example could be adapted to many subjects and levels.

presented a schedule for a unit in physics at the high school level, in Table 11–2. This unit was designed during one summer by a group of physicists and teachers, and tried out during that summer on a few students in order to check the timing of the various components and to see whether the material was "going over." Then revisions were made, and it was field-tested in selected physics classes across the country, with very positive reactions from both students and teachers. These reactions seemed to reflect the variety of experiences built into it, the emphasis it placed on student activity, the appropriate pacing and scheduling resulting from summer trials, and allowance for student needs in terms of clarity and integration of class and homework activities. The program was designed to illustrate the variety that could be built into such an experience, and how experienced traditional teachers could adjust to a more student-centered approach to teaching than they were accustomed to. I present it here as one example of how a number of different strategies and processes can be integrated in a traditional educational setting.

Table 11–2. *Example of a carefully prepared unit plan allowing for multimedia presentations, extensive student involvement in the learning process, and using the teacher as a guide and resource more than as a presentor and information source (lectures, however, are included, as you can see). Homework assignments are given between days, slightly below the other information. What cannot be shown here is the careful preparation and trial-and-error process which guaranteed that the assignments were appropriate, that the timing of each activity was practicable, and that assignments and other student input paid off in terms of subsequent discussions and use in additional concepts and processes.*

Day (1)	Day (2)	Day (3)	Day (4)
Film: Frames of reference; small-group discussions (SGD) on film	Pretest 1	Lab stations 1 Uniform motion	Pretest 2
Text; reader	*Text; programmed sequence*	*Text*	*Quiz*

Day (5)	Day (6)	Day (7)	Day (8)
Lab stations 2 Accelerated motion Quiz	Film: Straight line kinetics; Small-group discussions (SGD)	Experiments: Orbit of sun; Naked eye astronomy Quiz	17th century experiment
Text; programmed sequence	*Quiz; programmed sequence*	*Programmed sequence Text*	*Text; reader*

Day (9)	Day (10)	Day (11)	Day (12)
Programmed instruction Velocity and acceleration	Small-group problem solving	SGD on reader	Teacher presentation: Galileo quiz
Text; lab writeup	*Reader articles*	*Quiz*	

Day (13) Computer-assisted type problem	Day (14) Lab stations 3	Day (15) Lab stations 4	Day (16) Film: Inertia Programmed sequence: Proportions
Text; Orbit of Sun	*Text*	*Text; programmed sequence; Naked Eye Astronomy*	*Text; programmed sequence*
Day (17) Small-group problem solving	Day (18) Film: Frames of reference Demonstrations: Galilean relativity	Days (19) (20) Lab stations 5 Projectile, circular, and simple harmonic motions	Day (21) Student presentations on lab outcomes
	Programmed sequence	*Text*	*Reader*
Day (22) Review	Day (23) Unit one test	Day (24) Discussion of Unit 1 outcomes and observations for Unit 2	
	Study for test.		

The management of homework

The more you study the more you learn. However, there is no simple relationship between homework and learning. One review found that of nine studies comparing the effects of homework with no homework, six reported no significant differences while three reported that homework did make a difference (Alper et al., 1973). Another study found that occasional homework was preferable, and that it was important to evaluate it quickly (give feedback) and to give hints (prompts, guidance) about the problems assigned (Lash, quoted in Gage and Berliner, 1975). The explanation of these paradoxical outcomes may lie in learners' motivation to study (whether they actually do study), or in their understanding of skills which enable them to study on their own effectively, or in the degree to which the teacher structures assignments and teaches them how to study.

One analysis of attitudes and behaviors that are typical of students who *do* study is found in a questionnaire designed to determine the study habits and attitudes of high school students (Brown and Holtzman, 1968). Some behaviors and attitudes which are important according to this questionnaire are:

- Stick with difficult or long assignments.
- Make certain you clearly understand what is wanted before beginning work.

Ⓠ ②

Learners don't acquire the ability to work independently by magic—it calls for planning and guidance.

- Don't skip over figures, graphs, and tables.
- Be interested in most school subjects.
- Don't object to lack of freedom in selecting topics (reminiscent of characteristics of achievement-motivated students, who *would* object to such lack of freedom).

Some guidelines for giving homework and seeing to it that it is done, therefore, are the following:

- Teach the students to work on their own, partly by devoting class time initially to such work, and by guiding them in the use of the time.
- Make the assignments clear, with guides and hints as to methods (processes) and answers; teach students how to check the work they do as well.
- Make "doing homework" pay off; have it handed in promptly and return papers promptly; incorporate aspects of the homework into class discussions; occasionally give quizzes which call for an understanding of the homework; have small-group discussions and question-answer sessions based on homework.

Homework needs management to be beneficial.

- Ascertain the amount of time students are spending on homework; make sure that assignments are reasonable both in respect to what other teachers give, and in respect to how much total work the students have to do.
- Allow for interfering events: night games, dances, weekends, and such; reward faithfulness in doing homework with frequent "nights off."
- Have discussions of strategies for doing homework, bringing out ways of helping make homework feasible and interesting at the same time.
- Do not take homework for granted, or ignore it; guide it, prompt it, program it and reinforce it.

Managing independent study

Independent study is not the same as homework, but is the assignment of more long-range projects of various types, done either by individuals or small groups. Independent study has been considered a good way to provide for individual differences, to encourage individual approaches and interests, and to teach learners to be autonomous and self-sufficient.   Unfortunately, it has often amounted to a routine assignment of long-range projects that are poorly done and have little meaning to the student except as a chore.   Even when well and thoroughly done, these projects often do not receive the recognition that such a successful performance calls for.

Research in self-directed study in *higher* education has found that self-directed study is more successful in advanced courses, where students have previously studied the material.   This study also found that students in courses which used self-directed study rather than lectures were more attentive to the few lectures given than students in courses with traditional, regular lectures.   Such students also showed more curiosity and interest in the subject when examined some months after the courses were finished.   However, in spite of these positive outcomes, students didn't *like* self-directed study courses in general, even though they showed more favorable attitudes toward opportunities for intellectual independence as a result (Gruber and Weitman, 1962).

Extensive research on independent study was done at Antioch College in the 1960s.   The report on this experimental work laid down some guidelines for writing contracts for such independent study (Baskin, 1961).   These should include:

1. What is to be learned.
2. The way in which the student will demonstrate achievement.
3. The resources to be used by the student in carrying out the contract.
4. The steps or tasks to be carried out.
5. The intermediate points at which progress can be judged.
6. The time schedule to be met.

This kind of structure, if handled carefully and with fairly frequent personal contact between the student and the advisor, could avoid some of the negative effects discussed above. The major advantages of such study lies in the increased ability of the student to use his or her own resources for learning.

MANAGING LEARNING

Here are some examples of good and poor management of teaching and learning from notes taken at a crafts fair by a student in educational psychology:

Crewel Workshop: Went around the group to determine the extent of everyone's experience. We were also to identify ourselves as teachers, leaders, or just interested, to decide in what context we'd be using the skills, and the extent she would go into detail. Handing out stitch charts, she went over all fifty of them to see which ones we could eliminate because we already knew them. She examined the tools we brought, explained the pros and cons and uses for all, then issued the necessary equipment to those who had inappropriate equipment. Passing out samples, she explained the uses of various materials, weaves, and yarns and their relationships. Sending everything around to be handled, she exhibited finished products as examples of how her concepts fit together. She also included three nonexamples of poor applications of the principles. Our materials were passed out in individual packages for speed. When everyone had what was necessary, she explained the basic steps to set them up. While this is at the beginners' level, people wanted to be sure they had the right techniques. Since we had time to look everything over, she asked us which ones we'd like to learn while indicating which ones seem to be the most important in terms of use. We all agreed on what we wished to learn and set up our goal. She began with the simplest stitch beyond which we already knew and demonstrated it several times, describing it as she went. Then we tried it while she watched us. If someone couldn't do it, she'd go over it with her, guiding her needle and hands while the

others continued to practice. She watched each person doing it, encouraging and commenting to everyone intermittently. That type of guidance gave reassurance that she wouldn't let us go astray while making us feel that we were fully capable of asking for help. The occasional compliment acted as a reinforcement. As time went on, people began to tire and not attend as well. Two hours is a long time to sit still and concentrate. At this point she asked if we'd like to reconsider our goal since we were running out of time anyway. No one wanted to and interest and attention improved immediately. I think this was because we were responsible for our own learning, we'd invested a long travel time, family time, money, and our pride and didn't want to leave without getting full return on the investment. We managed to accomplish all we'd set out to do, but we probably wouldn't have if the teacher's personal characteristics weren't such that she controlled the situation.

Crewel instructor's guidelines.

- Always find out what they know first or they'll accuse you of wasting their time and money and will be bored.
- Briefly review basic skills they claim to have to be sure you understand their level.
- Start simple and progress to complex.
- Have people work along with you to be sure that they understand. Repeat instructions many times.
- Point out their own work to use as good examples, but you produce the bad examples.
- Set goals and stick to them. They'll criticize you for allowing them to digress—so don't allow it to go too far.

IMPLICATIONS OF DEVELOPMENT CONCEPTS FOR
MANAGEMENT

Preschool

Theories of social and moral development, discussed in Chapters 1 and 2, have implications for techniques and objectives in managing learning. For example, kindergarten children are working out problems of autonomy versus doubt and initiative versus guilt (Erikson). Management should therefore be geared toward structured autonomy and encouragement of a reasonable amount of initiative. This is also the preconventional stage of moral development (Kohlberg), and so rules should be clear and consistently enforced. The teacher should not spend a great deal of time moralizing about rules, or talking about guilt and responsibility. A similar conclusion comes from ego development (Loevinger), since the children are either at the impulsive stage or the "opportunistic" ("self-protective") stage; "good" and "bad" have concrete rather than abstract meanings.

> The study of development and developmental stages isn't just for your greater information—it has implications for teaching both individuals and groups.

Cognitively, preschool learners are in the preoperational stage, thus are stimulus-bound and unable to conserve easily or to reverse (Piaget). They can accumulate much concrete knowledge, but relationships and principles (many of which involve reversibility and conservation) will not emerge easily as they do at later stages. You shouldn't expect broad generalizations. Management should take into account these childrens' need for concrete experiences and for ways to practice psychomotor abilities as a basis for cognitive development. The more that cognitive and social and affective learning can be integrated into a variety of activities, the better.

Primary grades

Management of primary grades should take into account the fact that although concepts of right and wrong are emerging, with the early conventional stage of Kohlberg and the self-protective stage of Loevinger, rules are still followed because they are there. There is no shame experienced for being wrong or doing the wrong thing, only the upset due to error being known. Socially this is the age of development of industry as compared with a feeling of inferiority; management should provide contexts for the exercise of this industry and encourage productive activities, while integrating cognitive and psychomotor tasks into them. Since failure is subjective, the teacher or parent should manage to avoid having the child feel that he or she has failed. Since the learners are emerging from the preoperational into the concrete operational, concrete experiences for cognitive learning should be integrated into the projects and tasks which are designed to develop the feeling of industry and competence. Since learners are fairly eager and compliant at this age, there should not be major barriers (other than the teachers' time and effort and creativity) to creating and involving students in activities. However, low ability and low SES learners will require more attention to such things as "off-task" behavior and fighting.

Late elementary

During the later elementary grades there will be a continuation of the need for developing industry and competence. Morally, the learners will be approaching a period of conformity where they internalize rules and identify with authority. They begin to feel shame over doing wrong; the Golden Rule is paramount; good behavior is what is approved by others, and intentions are also taken into account. Management may want to take cliques and group dynamics into account by designing small-group work and projects on which more than one learner works. Cognitively these children will be entering the concrete operational stage, and learning experiences should be designed to encourage them to deal with relationships and abstractions, even though they are still stimulus-bound.

Middle school

In the middle school or junior high years both girls and boys are entering adolescence. Management should take into account early and late development characteristics of individuals. Due to their increased ability with formal cognitive operations, they will be questioning a number of things accepted previously, and management may do well to "bring them into the act" by having them plan and choose objectives and activities as much as possible without interfering with cognitive and social progress. They will still be at the conformist stage, but some of them may begin to express concerns and questions related to Loevinger's "conscientious" stage, and Kohlberg's "social contract." Their thinking will begin to show the greater flexibility of early formal operations. This means striking a balance between considerations of order, structure, pace, and the need to meet objectives, on one hand, and the need of the learners at this age to explore beyond the subject matter on the other. If their creativity and abstracting abilities and interest in questions are stifled at this stage, they may not be easy to reawaken later on. Their psychosocial concerns are beginning to turn to matters of their own identity, also, which further motivates discussions as to the meaning of things and their relevance to each individual and to the age-group. These explorations are of course supported by their gradual development of abstracting abilities, characteristic of the formal operational stage.

MODERN THIRD GRADE MANAGEMENT

Sharon is a student in educational psychology, and she has chosen to observe a third-grade class. She hasn't visited elementary school since her own school days, and she has visions of children being forced to sit quietly and straight in their chairs while the teacher writes on the blackboard. What she finds surprises her. She sees a large and relatively uncluttered room, with five groups of children (both boys and girls) at small tables, five or six to a table. The learners are working on their own. Their work is kept neatly in buckets on the left side of the room, where there are also many shelves, bookcases, and cabinets, all within easy reach of even the smallest child. There is also a kitchen area inside the classroom. Most tables are integrated sexually, but two tables have only boys and only girls; the children made decisions to sit where they please and no one is forced to sit somewhere else permanently. The students are working on self-instructional mathematics materials. Sharon finds that the teacher talks to the whole class very infrequently, except to introduce new concepts from time to time. After such an introduction the learning process is individualized. Students come up to the teacher's desk to check answer keys and to have certain problems explained to them. Sharon had helped the teacher (before class) design a small donkey cart on paper that the children could cut

out, color, and put together; they enjoyed this, and they competed to see who could make the best one.

The teacher told Sharon that the most important thing in this kind of classroom was for the teacher always to be organized: it is necessary to keep a steady pace of work going in the class (she said) so that the students have fun but don't get bored. There is a certain amount of structure, in that the students are usually working on the same topic, but they always work at their own levels. The teacher, with the help of a teacher's aide, spends as much time as possible moving from table to table, getting as much one-to-one contact as possible. When things got a bit noisy, she just dimmed the lights a bit to let them know she was waiting for them to be more quiet.

High school

Management in high school involves dealing with a host of the same types of problems and levels of development, but in more mature form and to a large degree reflecting the coming emergence of the students into society. The fact that the search for identity is paramount at this stage implies that high school teachers should seek strategies that foster a sense of individuality and autonomy, without an accompanying threat of loss of status or peer approval. This may imply a need for a halfway stage of autonomous work, where small groups or pairs work together. It may also imply a moderate approach to students' control over their own learning processes, backed up by a carefully prepared structure that makes it all work.

When you are struggling with the management of homework and quizzes and other learning processes, you need to remember that the learners are preoccupied with matters other than concepts, principles, and problem solving. This implies a need for appropriate supporting aids, including clear assignments, frequent reminders of due dates, advance notice of tests and projects, deadlines that don't conflict with key social occasions, and the like. On the other hand, these students have plenty of time and energy available for good work if the standards are reasonably high, the requirements regular and consistent, the skill of the teacher adequate to the needs and interests of the students, and if the teacher takes the trouble to try to motivate them in a number of the ways described in Chapter 7.

Management at this level should also take into account students' need for guidance in becoming more self-sufficient, more mature in the organization of their lives and in taking responsibilities, and more sophisticated in their problem-solving

High school management calls for a balance of guidance and encouragement.

processes. These should be part of the teacher's "agenda" regardless of the subject, and whether or not the teacher or specialist or parent makes them explicit. However, there is some reason for saying that these should be made explicit to the students, and perhaps evaluated and taken into account in the grading process as well, since this would formalize weighing them as significant objectives.

Management of high school students should also take into account that they are capable of "social contract" moral thought, formal operations, and "conscientious" ego functioning. That means treating them accordingly in relation to self-control and group discipline, but expecting and allowing for occasional regression to earlier stages.

Parents and teachers and specialists should all be aware of the continual threat of alcohol and other drugs, and of their cost in terms of motivation, clarity of thought, and social ability; these are the more serious, long-lasting losses incurred in using drugs, although problems with the law and lack of academic preparation are the more obvious and immediate symptoms. If you notice unusual memory gaps, uncharacteristic clumsiness, inability to reason, and high levels of defensiveness and the inclination to be quarrelsome and aggressive, you should consider these danger signs in relation to alcohol and other drugs, as well as evidence of certain types of parental treatment, rather than as personal attacks on yourself or on the adult world.   These drugs alter personality as well as cognition through their cumulative effects on the learner, and these alterations add greatly to the burdens of managing learners and learning at the high school level.

MANAGING CLASSROOMS

Helping versus challenging

There are many
techniques for
dealing with
classroom
problems; a few
are described here.

As you go up the educational ladder, the skills required for managing a class change somewhat in their balance and emphasis.   At lower levels management is usually oriented toward dealing with individual needs, while at higher levels it tends to deal more with groups and concentrate on the content of what is taught.   That of course does not mean that individuals are forgotten at higher levels, or that content is ignored in the early grades.   As was observed in Chapter 3, the helping relationship and emphasis are also more in demand when dealing with low SES and minority groups than with other groups, whatever the level.   On the other hand, one of the frequent complaints that good students have about homogeneous grouping is that they are continually placed in the toughest competition and have to work harder to hold their own in respect to grades.   This competition sometimes takes away from the intrinsic interest of the subject, and from the enjoyment of less convergent approaches such as "discovery learning," described in Chapter 12.

Kounin, in Chapter 5, suggested that the effective teacher was one who knew what was going on around the room even though not directly involved in every activity, who could identify students who were misbehaving and step in at the right time, who was able to handle more than one problem at the same time without getting confused, and who could maintain classroom momentum and pace and thus prevent slowdowns which invite deviant behavior.   Other techniques for accomplishing this include calling on nonparticipating students occasionally, calling attention to important points, asking questions that make the whole group think, and maintaining some suspense about the answers to problems.   Such teachers also hold students accountable for paying attention, generate enthusiasm, and provide a variety of work assignments and class activities (Good, Biddle, and Brophy, 1975).

In Chapter 5 you also read about research implying that better teachers vary their approaches and activities more than poorer ones.   This variation or flexibility also seems to bring about higher student achievement.   More effective teachers not only have a larger repertoire of techniques, but they are also more adept in suiting the technique to the particular situation or to the climate of the classroom at a given time (Rosenshine, 1971).   Also important are the clarity with which the teacher explains, and the teacher's enthusiasm, task-orientedness, and willingness to communicate on a number of different levels (Rosenshine and Furst, 1973).

Another source has listed some specific strategies for dealing with individuals or groups (Redl and Wattenberg, 1951):

- *Supporting self-control:* Clear your throat or stare at a student who is misbehaving, shaking your head, or saying "someone is making it hard for the rest to concentrate."
- *Proximity control:* Place yourself close to the troublemaker, even place a hand on his or her shoulder.
- *Interest boosting:* Examine some work the student is doing, reinforce some positive behavior, point out some good aspect of his or her work.
- *Humor:* If you can react to some minor misbehavior with humor, you avoid a negative reaction; this is another way of saying that roughness of tone and manner breed greater rather than less disruption.
- *Support from routines:* Establish set patterns for starting and stopping, getting ready for regular events, taking roll and such, to avoid horseplay and other deviant behavior that often crops up between activities.
- *Nonpunitive exile:* If some student gets carried away by anger or some other uncontrollable behavior, ask him or her to leave the room until it has passed.
- *Removing seductive objects:* An example would be a nearby waste basket that a seventh grader can't resist trying to hit with waste paper, or a window that is hard not to look out of.
- *Defining limits:* Make rules and limits clear, and enforce them firmly particularly in the beginning. If it is a serious matter, invoke punishment the first time the rule is broken so that it will not happen again. (Punishment will be discussed further under behavior modification.)
- *Conferences with individuals:* It is often most effective to ignore a behavior as much as possible in class, and to talk with the individual about it after class.
- *Interpreting group feelings:* Sometimes you can make it clear that you understand how the group feels—getting tired, it's a bad day, or it's a good day and they want to get outside—and this makes you less the target of their resentment over being cooped up.
- *Appeal to outside authority* (getting self off the hook): Under such conditions one can make it clear that the necessity for undergoing some undesirable experience or for routines that are disliked has been dictated by a higher source—that you the teacher find it difficult to take also.

How different teaching strategies relate to student involvement

The degree of student involvement in learning tasks depends in part on the kind of learning experience or teaching strategy that is being used. Involvement accounts for 20 to 30 percent of the variation in classroom achievement (Dunkin and

Biddle, 1974). A recent study explored the nature of differences in involvement in relation to the kind of learning experience. It surveyed ninth- through twelfth-grade students in one classroom in a suburban high school. Presentation strategies (lectures, audiovisual presentations) brought involvement by only the high IQ students, not others; "seat work alone" involved only students who thought of themselves as "good students." "Seat-work with others" was the least conducive to involvement in learning. "Classroom discourse" (discussion, not lecturing) was best for average and low-IQ students; they became more involved in learning in that mode than in others (Scott and Anderson, 1976). This study suggests that one-way communication types of environments maximize the differences between levels of IQ, while participatory exercises like classroom discussion *minimize* these variations. Given that involvement implies achievement, the implications for classroom management are clear.

Classroom contingency management

Some teachers reject the use of contingency management on ethical grounds, but all recognize its effectiveness in certain types of situations.

You have studied reinforcement theory in Chapter 8, and know that responses which are reinforced increase, and those which are not reinforced decrease (extinguish). Many teachers habitually take notice of behaviors they do not want, and ignore those that they do want; this is sometimes called the "criticism trap." There is also the "helping trap," where teachers reinforce dependent behavior in certain learners by giving them help whenever they call for it, although they could manage on their own if they had to. One example of this is the case of a teacher who was using a small-group approach to reading, i.e., "reading groups" of different ability. In this approach the teacher works with one group while the other groups engage in learning activities the teacher has previously organized, but without the teacher's continued presence. In this case, the noise level for the classroom was very high, and the students were running around the room, talking to other students, hitting each other when lining up for recess, and generally being very unproductive. The teacher would occasionally threaten them with punishment if they didn't quiet down, and they would do so, but the disruption would begin again, greater than before. Two boys were picked out for special observation in this case because they were among the worst behaved: one was distractible, had poor work habits, never finished assignments, and would wander about the room or twist and turn in his seat. The other was nervous and "hyperactive," cried or threw tantrums if criticized, and was described as having "minimal brain dysfunction."

The teacher was taught how to change her management methods. She was given three general instructions, with a signal from the consultant for each one. If the consultant held up one finger, she was to stop all activities and explain the rules of behavior, describing precisely what it was she wanted the students to be doing in general and in each particular group. If the consultant held up two fingers the teacher was to ignore undesirable behavior that was going on and if possible find some learner who was doing the right thing and call attention to him or her, e.g., by saying "Laura, I'm glad to see you are working on your workbook." If the consultant held up three fingers the teacher was to reinforce some behavior which showed improvement on the part of one of the students or on the part of one of the reading groups. By this change in procedure, reinforcing rather than criticizing or threatening, the general behavior of the class was improved and the measured behavior of the two worst students was also found to improve significantly. Furthermore, the behavior of the teacher changed from mostly negative acts to mostly positive ones; this made the teacher feel much better about herself as well. Most important, the behavior of two particular individuals was shown to change as a result of a general approach to management for the whole group—without particular attention to their cases, although initially they were the kind of student which is often referred to as "hyperactive" or "disturbed" or "brain damaged" or some such label (adapted from Becker et al., 1975a).

MRS. JOHNSON USES SMALL-GROUP CONTINGENCIES

Mrs. Johnson was teaching an open classroom with the help of an aide, but she was not doing well. The children were leaving the centers to which their groups were assigned and wandering about, also interrupting when she or the aid demonstrated something. Very little was being accomplished, and Mrs. J. was on the verge of going back to a traditional approach, when she thought of trying contingency management. First she and the aide observed and recorded baseline frequencies for the various desirable and undesirable behaviors; this went on for about five days. Then they informed the members of each group at each center that if there were no infractions of the rules for working in their respective learning centers, all members of the group would be awarded 15 minutes of special activity time. Each infraction by a group member would result in subtracting 3 minutes of activity time. Each group spent one period at each center: the periods were kept short at first. At the end of the four periods (there were four centers) a token was presented each group with no infractions, and time was deducted from the free period of each group where there was an infraction. Behavior improved, infractions decreased, and Mrs. Johnson and her aide were able to spend much more time explaining activities, guiding, giving directions, and in other helpful acts. Before, they had spent most of their time redirecting students and disapproving of their behavior.

Managing through token systems

As mentioned in Chapter 8, one effective approach to reinforcing desired behaviors is giving tokens for responses or behaviors. These can be plastic chips, pieces of paper like play money, or simply check marks on a chart. In starting a token system you should make out a "menu" of things that a learner can "buy" with his or her tokens. There are two things you have to determine initially in order to make this system function well. One is how much behavior is necessary to earn a token, or how many tokens a learner can get for a certain behavior: this is sometimes called "wages." The other thing to work out is the "prices" of rewards, i.e., how much each reward on the "menu" will cost. For concrete objects such as toys or food this cost is usually set in respect to customary costs of that article. However, for activity-reinforcers used as rewards (e.g., using a tape recorder for 15 minutes or spending 10 minutes in the game area) you have to estimate a reasonable price and see whether it seems to work out well, possibly changing it if it is unsuccessful.

A menu for a token system can list several types of reinforcers. There are edibles (candy, milkshakes), toys (model airplanes, dolls), and privileges and activities (running errands, taking care of class pets, choosing where to sit, having a lesson outdoors). For older students the tokens can be exchangeable for tickets for skating or bowling or athletic events, for privileges and rewards at home (worked out with the parents), for food at the cafeteria, or even for grades.

In institutions for the mentally ill, token systems have been used as part of the therapy in order to get patients to show more normal behaviors. Attendants pass out chips, award points, or use some other method to present tokens. One approach used successfully with mentally retarded and psychotic adults and with juvenile offenders (each in separate cases), has been to deprive the inmates of all but the barest necessities of life, then to make it possible to earn certain amenities through tokens: such things as use of a private shower, a more comfortable mattress, a screen around one's bed or a small private room, cigarettes and other articles at the store. These systems have brought improvements in inmates who had previously been antisocial and unwilling to take care of themselves or to deal reasonably with other people or to begin to learn basics such as reading. However, in a few cases the patients have hired lawyers to challenge the right of the institution to deprive them in this way, resulting in court decisions guaranteeing the civil rights of patients to the amenities that these systems have deprived them of (Wexler, 1973). Now some of the legal restrictions make it difficult to use these effective methods of therapy. One solution will be to find other token systems built on different types of reinforcers, such as the reinforcement that comes from living up to the norms of one's group, or maintaining group standards so that others (as well as oneself) can gain certain privileges above and beyond the normal level. Such systems have been found to work well in some cases.

MS. ARNOLD RAISES THE ANTE

Ms. Arnold has scheduled her son Billy for a study period every evening, in order to get him to catch up on some subjects where he is behind. She finds that he can't concentrate for more than 25 percent of the time that he is "studying." (She observes him every 10 minutes to get an initial idea of how he is working.) So she has Billy study where she can watch him, and she tells him he will get points for each 30-second interval that he pays attention to his work. She tells him each time he gets a point. After he completes about twenty of these 30-second intervals, she changes the criterion to one point for each 60-second interval. Then, gradually, she works up to one point for every 600 seconds of attentive behavior. Billy is saving the points in order to get a model airplane that he has chosen as his "back-up reward." By adding up the points for each level (30-second intervals, then 60, and so forth), he finds that he accumulates the necessary number of points when he completes two final 10-minute (600-second) intervals of concentrated work (adapted from Becker et al., 1975).

Dealing with individuals in a class setting

It is possible to help individual learners in the context of classroom teaching, although this must be limited and the teacher must learn to carry on group activities at the same time. Experience suggests you should try it first with only one student, in addition to regular class processes. If a teacher's aide or learning specialist can help, it is of course simpler. Fundamental to the process is pinpointing the behavior you want to change by identifying, observing, counting, and recording its frequency and nature. For example, you may focus on the amount of time the learner pays attention, or on the number of correct spellings out of twenty spelling words, on how many times the learner pronounces letter combinations in reverse, or on the portion of class time he or she spends paying attention and not paying attention. You have to decide what behavior you want to change, and note carefully what it is like to begin with, before you attempt to change it. In order to do this in the regular classroom, you have to sample the behavior, that is, observe it every so often rather than continuously, so that you can do other things too. One method is to observe the behavior at timed intervals and record whether or not it is happening; you might observe a particular learner every five minutes and note whether or not he is paying attention or working productively. Keep a card on your desk and put a "+" on it if he is paying attention and a "0" if he is not. Another way is to have a stopwatch and start it each time you observe him beginning to work, and stop it when he stops; then start it again when he starts again, and so forth, noting the accumulated time at the end of the period or day. Still another way to do this is simply to count the times you notice him not working: make a tally mark for each one, and count the tallies at the end of the designated period.

However you record the behavior, do so for three to five days, and plot the results on a graph. Then average them. For example, Jimmy was observed in order to count the number of times he got out of his seat at the wrong time each day. The numbers for each of the first five days is shown on the graph in Figure 11–1 with the average given underneath. (This kind of measurement can be done for the number of problems correct in arithmetic, for the number of correct papers handed in for language arts, for the average score on quizzes in French, for the number of times a learner is observed paying attention (or not paying attention) in physics, or for any other facet of learning behavior that needs to be changed.)

After a baseline has been recorded, you need to identify some helping processes to use to change the behavior. For classroom teachers, it must be a process enabling them to deal with the class as a whole at the same time they are helping the individual learner, or one which they can use after school or during free periods, or during periods of the day when the learners are working on their own. Many of the kinds of treatments which have been used in programs which emphasize baseline measurement and deal with individual learners in the context of the classroom have been "behavioral" in nature. They emphasize the use of reinforcers as explained in Chapter 8. They "program" the process in short steps, reinforcing these short steps with small amounts or small reinforcers, both to help the learner succeed, and to make the available reinforcers go further. For example,

Contingency management can be used with groups as well as individuals, and with individuals in a group setting.

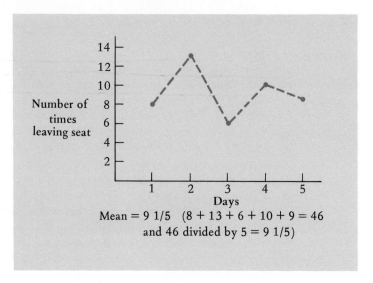

Figure 11–1. *Chart recording five-day observation of a student's behavior.*

suppose you want to deal with Jimmy's work habits in class, and you have taken a baseline measure.   You might then tell him that you are going to check him every fifteen minutes, and each time he is working when you check him, you are going to give him a poker chip.   This chip will signify that you approve of his behavior. Then you might arrange for him to have some free time to work on some project that he likes, if he accumulates ten of these tokens, or twenty, or whichever turns out to be appropriate.   (Sometimes you have to adjust the numbers on the basis of experience with the particular learner.)   You keep noting +s and 0s as before, and watch to see whether the number of +s increases as a result of this arrangement. You need to do this over a period of five days or more, however, because human behavior fluctuates in these situations, and you need to concentrate on average number of behaviors or +s in order to determine whether progress is being made. A typical graph of the results would look something like Figure 11–2.

Pinpointing and charting

Behavior modification and contingency management usually emphasize the use of reinforcers, sometimes token ones as you have seen.   However, Ogden Lindsley (1972) has demonstrated the effectiveness of an approach which emphasizes counting and charting behaviors and which deemphasizes the role of reinforcers. This approach also stresses the importance of the autonomy of the person involved in the treatment by having that person choose what he or she wishes to change in terms of personal behavior.   For example, suppose you are concerned about your weight, and you wish to reduce it.   Then you would discuss your eating behavior

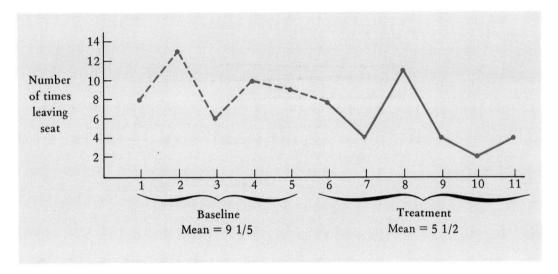

Figure 11-2. *Chart recording results of classroom treatment.*

with a therapist, and you would decide on some behavior related to eating for purposes of charting. This would be *your* choice, not the therapist's. Then you would figure out some way of keeping count of this behavior—say it was snacking between meals—and you would record it on a chart daily. After a number of days of this charting, in which your snacking would probably go up and down in frequency, you would notice that the average amount of snacking was decreasing. Meanwhile, you would probably begin to understand better the nature of your own eating behavior, and you might decide to chart some other behavior, either in place of this, or in addition to it. You might even decide that the occurrence of a *craving* for food (an internal event, not something another person could observe) was important, and then begin charting these occurrences as well. It would be interesting to compare cravings with snackings (i.e., "giving in"). You would also decide on some level of snacking that you would be willing to accept as reasonable, rather than striving for complete elimination—none of us is perfect!

This approach emphasizes the intrinsic reinforcement of making progress toward some goal. It also avoids some of the most obvious elements of outside control of behavior that anti-behaviorists object to.

An "Adlerian" or "Dreikurs" approach to managing behavior

Another approach to dealing with misbehavior is an outgrowth of the psychology of Alfred Adler (a personality theorist) which has been developed into an effective and widely used method (Dreikurs, Brunwald, and Pepper, 1971). It is based on the assumption that any learner who misbehaves has one of four goals:

1. To get attention.
2. To get power.
3. To get revenge.
4. To convince others that he (the one who misbehaves) has a deficiency (stupidity, lack of skill) so others will leave him alone.

An example of a modern technique of management that combines elements of contingency management and of nondirective counseling.

Useful behavior is classified as either active-constructive (leading to the "model" child or "teacher's pet") or passive-constructive (the "cute" child admired for what he or she is, not does). Not-useful behavior is classified as either active-destructive (a pest, a disobedient rebel, or a bully) or passive-destructive (shy-dependent, stubborn, negative, or very withdrawn). The objective of the method is to bring the learner to impose discipline upon himself (or herself) and on his peers. The process involves getting the learner to be accepted by others and, as a consequence, to accept and approve of himself or herself. Thus it is based in part on group pressures, discussed in Chapter 6.

The procedure is to recognize the goal of the learner, then either to confront him or her with that knowledge, or to use the consequences of the behavior as punishment, or both. First you ask a learner why she misbehaves: the learner will probably say she doesn't know, or will rationalize her behavior in some way. Then the teacher says "Do you want to know what I think?" If the learner agrees, the teacher says something like "Could it be that you want my attention?" or "I think you want to beat me by not doing what I have asked" or "I think you want to get back at me because someone was mean to you recently" or "You want to be left alone because you can't do anything very well." The learner considers the analysis and, if it is correct, probably begins to smile as she understands her own goals. This recognition is usually the preliminary to a better discussion and some resolution of the problem. With adolescents, the goals are more complex than those listed, and include defiance of adult demands, showing independence, seeking anti-adult excitement (as through drugs), and such.

Another basic strategy is to make it clear to the learner that you expect positive things, and that he or she can do worthwhile things. This means (a) planned ignoring of a certain amount of bad behavior (extinguishing it), (b) not allowing yourself to be pulled into a power struggle where the students seeks power through bad behavior (avoiding the criticism trap), (c) drawing the line on aggressive behavior that seeks revenge (thus not reinforcing such behavior), and (d) not allowing the learner to pretend that he or she is unable to do anything or is handicapped in some way that makes productive work impossible (thus not reinforcing the avoidance behavior). Another similarity to behavior modification lies in the emphasis on natural and logical consequences, which would be called "intrinsic reinforcers" or "intrinsic punishers." "Going hungry if you don't eat" is one *natural* consequence, while "cleaning up if you spill" is a *logical* one. Some disturbed learners will not submit to a request for obeying logical consequences, but all will react to natural ones.

One example of a natural consequence is found in the case of a third grader who was apt to be late in getting ready in the morning; her mother constantly pushed her to get to her bus on time.   Finally, the mother let her miss the bus, and made her walk to school: she asked an older brother to walk with her, to make sure she made it and was protected.   The practical problem in such cases is that some parents and some teachers cannot bring themselves to allow natural consequences to work, and of course it requires some judgment to discriminate between cases where you can allow them to happen and those where you can't.

The proponents of this system say that such logical consequences, and natural consequences, are preferable to the use of rewards for good behavior.   They maintain that if good behavior is rewarded each time it occurs, then it will disappear when rewards cease (i.e., it will extinguish).   This suggests that you should use intermittent reinforcement to maintain the behavior, and gradually remove the reinforcers entirely.   However, the Dreikurs strategy is to encourage good behavior by commenting on its outcomes, thus emphasizing the intrinsic reinforcers rather than relying on extrinsic ones.   Therefore Dreikurs recommends using *natural* consequences to reward and punish.

Dreikurs' recommendations extend to general classroom management as well. Here are some of his guidelines:

- Give clear-cut directions for expected actions of the learner.
- Don't remind a learner of how he or she used to be or act.
- If a learner misbehaves, present alternatives of remaining without disturbing others, or leaving the class.
- Discuss a learner's problems at a time when neither of you is emotionally charged.
- Use natural consequences instead of traditional rewards and punishment.
- Use natural consequences that have a direct relationship to the behavior, and be sure the relationship is understood by the learner.
- Let children assume responsibility for their own behavior and learning; a teacher who is afraid to leave the room prevents children from taking responsibility; be prepared for them to act up at first, since such training takes time.

Managing to avoid cheating

Cheating can be a drag on a teacher's motivation and involvement, and can affect the impact of teaching processes on learners.   However, cheating has always been a source of confusion and puzzlement to educators; nobody knows quite how to handle it.   Some research has been done on this matter, and the results have some interesting implications.   The research has indicated that cheating is not related to how motivated the learner is to achieve, although it is related to how well the learners have prepared for the class or examination (Fakouri, 1972; Corey, 1937). External pressures which raise anxiety increase cheating, and cheaters often attribute their acts to such outside forces, including the teacher's failures (Diensther and Munter, 1971; Knowlton and Hamerhynck, 1967).   One study concluded that students cheat in order to hide their ignorance from their friends, not from teachers or parents (Taylor, 1966).   This suggests that social acceptance is one objective, not getting good grades per se.   It also suggests that you can reduce cheating if you make test-taking more private, rather than in classroom group settings.   It also suggests that if you teach students to prepare for tests, and organize the schedule and system so that such preparation is built in, you will have less cheating.   Since cheaters tend to blame teachers, you can also minimize cheating by making tests appropriate in both content and difficulty.   Try to avoid making them seem so impossible to the slower students that cheating is the only solution.

MANAGING LEARNING DISABILITIES

Diagnosing and treating en masse

Individual treatment for learning disabilities was discussed in Chapter 4.   It is possible to diagnose learning problems collectively in a regular classroom, then treat them the same way.   Suppose, for example, that you have a class of twenty-five or thirty learners at the third-grade level and you suspect that a significant number of them are experiencing difficulty in blending letter sounds into words.   It would not be difficult to give the entire class a test in which the students listen to letter sounds given in sequence (b . . . a . . . t), then circle one of several pictures that might represent the word (a shovel, a bat, and a cat).   If you find that five or ten students are having great difficulty with this task, then you can make up a number of exercises, or a game, which involves sound blending, starting with very simple tasks and going to more difficult ones.   You can have the entire class play these games or do these exercises, once or twice a day for several weeks.   Then you can give the test again and note whether there has been improvement in those learners who were weakest and in others who were stronger, but not solid.

Another strategy that a teacher can use to adapt regular classroom processes to the needs of disabled learners involves general arrangements of materials and equipment.   For example, if there are hyperactive learners in the class you might arrange the room so that there are fewer distractions.   Materials could be put away in closed cupboards; bulletin boards could be put in order and have minimum material on them; there might be fewer pictures on the walls; and distractible learners might be seated away from windows and doors and other sources of visual and auditory distraction.   A small room, or part of the room, could be set off by cardboard partitions and used for "time out."   A learner would go there to "gather himself together" when he begins to have difficulty maintaining his concentration.   If possible, carpets and acoustic tiles could be used to cut down noise.   The available space can be kept ordered and neat, with desks having only what is needed on them for the current activity.

A well-structured and consistent program will help disabled learners, though other learners might function adequately with less structure.   If a teacher lists daily activities according to the order in which they are to be performed, and follows difficult tasks (such as reading) with easier ones (games, free time), he or she will be helping those with learning problems. If the learning activities can be short, with some chance to move around occasionally, that too will help.

Evaluation of the whole class in relation to preferred channels (visual, auditory) might reveal that one group does better with emphasis on auditory input, while another functions better with visual. The teacher might emphasize the better channel at first, and then place greater and greater emphasis on the other channel through the year, just as with an individual learner with such difficulty. This grouping would hold for only a part of the day in most cases.

Emphasis on active participation in learning will be helpful also, particularly on giving concrete experience with concepts and processes before proceeding to the abstract. This holds equally for preschoolers learning the concept of numbers and graduate students in literature who are taking an elective in physical science. Where visual presentations are to be made, it may be better to use an overhead projector and magnify the writing and diagrams; this intensifies the image and improves visual reception. When writing on the board, be sure to make letters and numbers large and readable. When oral presentations are made or directions are given, a clear communication (with reiterations using other words) can help those who find auditory reception difficult. In both visual and auditory presentations, the amount of background noise (visual and auditory) is an important factor: if there is a constant buzz of conversation, or if things are going on which distract visual concentration, or both, then the proportion of learners who receive the communication (i.e., understand it) will be reduced. Finally, where possible, it is worthwhile to rotate teachers occasionally to provide some variety in the pattern and style of presentation.

In recent years classroom teachers have become more versatile and flexible. They are determining the needs of learners both collectively and individually. They are increasing the variety of activities and procedures by which learners can attain skills and knowledge, and they are trying to fit learning activities to the individual learner's characteristics. They are using large-group, small-group, one-to-one, and independent learning activities where formerly there were only teacher-led classes. They are employing peer teaching, learning centers, teaching aides, team teaching, and specialists in the classroom. Finally, there is a general move toward placing learning-disabled and educable-retarded learners in the most advanced and normal environments possible, rather than referring them to special classes or special teachers. This is sometimes referred to as using the "least restrictive environment," and means that the general objective is to move learning disabled and handicapped learners *toward* normal classrooms *from* special classes and special environments, rather than *to* special classes and environments and *out* of normal classrooms. Furthermore, referrals from regular to special arrangements (whether tutoring, part-time involvement in a learning center, or special class) are made increasingly on the basis of demonstrated learning performance in a school situation, not on the basis of psychometric data such as intelligence or aptitude tests or learning disabilities tests.

SANDY OBSERVES A SPECIAL EDUCATION CLASS

Sandy is taking an educational psychology course and is interested in special education. As a project for the course she observes and reports on a special education class conducted in a neighboring town. She notes that one method used in the classroom is behavior modification: good behavior is rewarded with pretzels and plastic chips, bad behavior is ignored. The teacher tells Sandy that he is gradually eliminating the pretzels and going completely to the token economy (i.e., plastic chips). The class begins with a "news session": each day one child is leader and tells the class something that has happened to him or her, or brings something to show. When the leader-for-the-day is finished he chooses someone else to tell her "news." Rewards during this session go to those who are sitting quietly in their chairs. Then the children go to the back of the room and form a circle for a speech lesson: the teacher uses a puppet, and the puppet asks the children questions and they answer. Large cards with pictures on them are also used; some of the questions relate to these pictures. Responding when spoken to, sitting in one's chair, answering in complete sentences, and pronouncing words correctly are all rewarded during this session. After this the children work on mathematics at their seats. They are learning to count, and the worksheets have boxes which have objects: the children count them and circle the proper number. They work alone, raising their hands for help, and they receive help only after they have tried to do the assignment on their own (to avoid the "helping trap," reinforcing dependent behavior unnecessarily). A chip is given each child who finishes the worksheet before recess. The teacher tells Sandy that these learners spend a part of their day with the other learners in the school, but that this isn't enough to enable them to be accepted; the teacher has noticed that on the playground they spend very little time with the other children in play.

Obtaining assistance from a specialist

A number of specialists may be available for helping teachers deal with specific disabilities. They will usually examine the teacher's description of the problem, then recommend additional diagnostic procedures. With the results of the additional tests, they prescribe approaches to remediation and help work out arrangements for accomplishing this remedial teaching. Sometimes the specialist will demonstrate the remedial process in the classroom or with the learner alone, so that the teacher or an aide can learn how to go about it. In some cases, the specialist is also in charge of the learning center, or works in the center, and thus uses the facilities of the center and may have the learner attend there part time.

    The following functions describe the typical role of the specialist and his or her relationship with the teacher and the learner or learners:

1. Referral: The classroom teacher submits a written referral—a simple one-page form—of the child; it is anecdotal and summarizes the teacher's procedures so far.

2. Observations: The specialist observes the learner(s) in the regular classroom.
3. Referral Conference: The specialist confers with the teacher to update information, clarify their respective roles and responsibilities, and arrange times and places for the learner to have special help.
4. Diagnostic Teaching: The specialist conducts informal and/or formal evaluation and remediation, observes results, determines potentially successful approaches.
5. Educational Prescription: A written report is prepared which recommends techniques and materials for helping the learner in the classroom, describes their use in detail, and makes suggestions for a home program as well.
6. Prescription Conference: The specialist and the teacher meet and go over prescription.
7. Demonstration: The specialist demonstrates the process in the context of the teacher's class, acting the role of the teacher.
8. Immediate Follow-up: The specialist follows up the prescription to see whether this process is having a positive impact.
9. Evaluation: The teacher completes a single-page evaluation form on the effectiveness of the procedures.
10. Long-Term Follow-up: The specialist continues periodic checks with the teacher until both feel that the process has been established and progress is assured.

Regular classroom teachers are usually responsible for the progress of their students; they should work with the specialist to help the child but at the same time observe the results to make sure that the child is being helped.

Mainstreaming handicapped learners

Learning disabled children are not retarded or handicapped. However, modern programs for children who *are* retarded or have other handicaps avoid traditional labels and attempt to deal with learners in terms of their difficulties in school learning, rather than in terms of their scores on intelligence tests. Therefore, although learners who would formerly have been called "retarded" have more general learning deficits than the "learning disabled," all learners are becoming part of the same overall system. Thus some of the things that are being done in the name of "retarded" or "handicapped" learners, or in the name of "special education," are relevant to this discussion of instructional strategies for the learning disabled.

One of these is the general policy called "mainstreaming." This is based on the principle that most children should be educated in regular classrooms, and that special education should be provided on the basis of learning needs, rather than categories of handicaps. In mainstreaming, children with learning problems receive expert help without being labeled or excluded from association with other children of the same age or grade.   Regular and special teachers share their skills and knowledge with each other, and regular education and "special education" are synthesized into one overall system.   By this means, a wide range of individualized services can be provided for all children according to their learning needs, and all children benefit rather than a few.   Of course, learners differ in their ability to profit from regular classroom education.   Therefore, the objective is to keep them in regular classes for as much of the school day as is productive for them, whether this means all but an hour, or only an hour.

In a typical mainstreaming program, the educable retarded child is assigned to a regular class homeroom.   He or she leaves class to go to the resource room only for essential small-group instruction, individual tutoring, educational assessment, or to pick up and deliver assignments that may be prepared by the resource teacher but are completed by the child in the regular classroom.   The resource teacher, a specialist in teaching retarded pupils, works out an individual schedule for each pupil's use of the resource center; involvement ranges from a few minutes to several hours, but is usually less than the majority of the school day.   The regular classroom teachers and the resource teacher share responsibility for the retarded pupil's achievement progress, and both instruct the child.   The regular class teachers have opportunities to send other pupils from their classes for help from the resource teacher also.   These youngsters often have learning problems arising from conditions other than mental retardation, i.e., specific learning disabilities.   The resource teacher contributes assessment and instructional services for such children.   He or she also shares instructional know-how with the regular class teacher, who reciprocates in kind.   Thus mainstreaming is a carefully designed, balanced, and individualized quid pro quo teaching arrangement beneficial to children with a variety of kinds of school problems (Birch, 1974).

MOTIVATING LEARNERS

Motivating compared with managing

Managing is important: it sets the stage for teaching and learning and works out logistics.   A well-managed classroom is more motivating than a poorly managed one.   There have been many discussions in earlier chapters about elements relevant to motivation: teacher effectiveness, learning disabilities, and behavior modification, to mention a few.   These have had management aspects and implications as well.

Expectancy of success and fear of failure

It is important for the teacher, parent, or specialist to convey an expectancy of success by encouraging good work and deemphasizing failure possibilities.   This can be done, for example, by saying such things as "It's a good thing to get that problem solved: the experience will help you solve others;" this acknowledges productive behavior and encourages more of it.   Not every student can be highly successful, but some teachers are overcome with the gloomy assumption that many learners cannot be successful and teachers can't do anything about it.   However, the teacher, parent, or specialist *determines* what is successful, i.e., he or she labels the learner's attempts as success or failure, and therefore holds the key to success.   You can define success in terms of the change in the individual, rather than entirely in terms of absolute standards.   It is not just a rationalization to say "Mary, you made a C, and that may not be what you hoped for, but it represents real progress over your starting level."   If you can document this by using examples of the learner's earlier work to show much progress has been made, this may be more effective. Generally, the secret is to act as if every student can succeed, and as far as possible see to it that they all have a really good chance to do so.

It's not just how well you manage learning, but the tone and manner in which you do it, that communicate a sense of confidence and potential success.

The other side of this coin is avoiding fear of failure.   Teachers often communicate a fear of failure by the tone of voice and manner that they adopt in talking about tests.   This practice often reveals a teacher's fear of failure, in regard to both personal success as a teacher or in life generally, and in regard to the potential of the students to do well.   Communication of anxieties from teacher to students was discussed in Chapter 5.   As a teacher or parent, you should become aware of your own fears, and learn somehow to avoid communicating them to students.

An example of how to establish a nonthreatening atmosphere is found in a set of guidelines from Greenspan et al. (1975) for employing *games* to improve communication.   They suggest that teachers try to tailor the games to the cognitive levels of the individual participants, by starting out with relatively easy ones, then moving to progressively more difficult ones.   The optimal situation is to use games sufficiently within the child's current skill repertoire so that they are enjoyable, but still require sufficient stretching to be of interest.   This "one step ahead" approach has been successfully used in training children in making moral judgments (Turiel, 1966).   However, occasional use of excessively difficult games need not be catastrophic.   Potentially negative effects of possible failure are ameliorated if the teacher adheres to a policy of friendly nonevaluation.   Since cognitively egocentric children tend to be somewhat lacking in self-analytic ability, and particularly tend to think that their own perspectives are the only possible ones, responsibility for failures in the communication process are usually ascribed by the child to the other participant in that process, whether that other participant is the communicator or listener.   Unless the experimenter or participating peers overreact to the child's failures, therefore, it is likely that they will be perceived not so much as failures, but rather as interesting occurrences that require further thought.

Ironically it is when a child has made marked improvement in his or her referential communication performance and is on the verge of achieving real competence that failures are more likely to be experienced; then minimal failures are sometimes taken more personally than more glaring ones.   So it is essential that the adult leaders of such games allow participants to draw their own conclusions from these games and actively intervene only when participants are making negative comments about their own or another's performance.

MRS. DANVERS MAKES IT INTERESTING

Mrs. Danvers is a high school science teacher. She projects an attitude of positive expectation that includes every student, male or female, bright and motivated, or just tolerating the course as a necessity. She has a great fund of information about the world including what is immediate: geology, chemistry, physics, astronomy. She uses her knowledge. She has an attitude that teaching is a calling and a privilege but also a challenge and a responsibility: every student is worth devoting effort to; every student regardless of reputed aptitude or behavior or interest can and will learn if a good model is set and it she or he is expected to do the best. She is continually illustrating points by giving examples from the local area or the region. She organizes field trips frequently and fills them with interesting observations and anecdotes. Girls who have always hated science surprise their parents by telling them about things they observe while riding in an automobile or just looking out the window at dinnertime. Boys spend extra hours exploring or working on projects where previously they were interested only in athletics or clubs. Somehow if you ask them about grades, they act as if they hadn't thought about them: and it seems as if they actually had not—they hadn't had time. Yet they exert unusual effort in completing their assignments, and they pay attention in class. One thing they do say is that there is always something to do, and that things seem to be organized so that you can actually get somewhere and learn something. Other teachers sometimes seem to get in the way of learning, but not Mrs. Danvers. There is also an attitude on her part that the learners need to be made responsible for their own learning, and that they don't have to have every last assignment or quiz or exam or project spelled out in fine detail, or have every task made due on a certain particular date or demerits for misbehavior or that sort of thing. She models the kind of attention and interest and involvement that she expects them to show, and most of them show it. If someone misbehaves, it seems out of place, partly because nobody is frustrated or hostile or upset—they are just obviously there to learn and that is what everyone does! Student teachers who are assigned to Mrs. Danvers come to realize after a while that a great deal of thought, planning, organization, and hard preparation go into this. Mrs. Danvers is energetic and persistent and never wants to go into class without being thoroughly prepared, and she worries some about classes that don't seem to go well or when a number of students show signs of losing interest or concentration. They also find that there are actually reasonably rigorous standards. Mrs. Danvers takes this for granted and the students learn it through hearsay and by having quizzes and papers turned back with positive suggestions for improvement as well as praise for whatever they did well.

Motivating through modeling

One of the most powerful motivators, perhaps second only to the impact of your expectancy level, will be the example of motivation that you set for the learners, whether in first grade or fifteenth grade! Evaluations of good college teachers always feature such characteristics as "enthusiastic," "makes you want to know more," "interested in subject," "makes me interested in it." As you found in Chapter 8, modeling is a very effective teaching and conditioning process, and here we are talking about modeling motivation to learn. One reason for a lack of interest in learning in students generally and particularly junior high school students is the lack of interest in learning shown by parents and teachers. How often do parents demonstrate an interest in learning for themselves, and model a learning process (as compared with a process they already have learned, or past achievement)? How often does a teacher actually engage in learning in front of a class or even with a single student as audience? Students see teachers as task masters, rather than models of learning processes, because that is primarily the way they (the teachers) behave. Model learning yourself: even though you know something, go through the process of learning it over again, including verbalization of the internal process. But whether you do that or not, you should model an interest and enthusiasm for the subject matter. As the cliche goes, "Enthusiasm is never taught—it's always caught."

Motivating by presenting optimal discrepancies (problems) and sparking curiosity

How you present the material to be learned makes a difference. One way to motivate involvement in the subject matter is to present it as a problem that is easy enough to solve but not so easy that it is obvious. It should be designed in such a way that the student will learn something in solving it, or, in some cases, will practice some skill while solving it. The problem or situation may be abstract or concrete, and it may be drawn from any subject area, or several combined. (This was discussed in Chapter 2 and again in Chapter 10.) For example, if you wish to teach the concept of "reinforcement" or reinforcing stimulus, you might start out with the following case:

> An important part of motivation is managing the content and presentation so that they present just the right degree of challenge.

A pigeon who has not eaten for some time is placed in a cage which has on one side a mechanism that delivers a pellet of food to a tray inside the cage every thirty seconds. The pigeon is left in the cage for several hours. At the end of this time, the pigeon is observed to have very odd behavior of some kind–it may turn in circles continuously, or it may bow and scrape regularly like an eighteenth-century courtier, or it may show some other bizarre behavior. How could it have possibly come to this state, i.e., acquired this behavior pattern?

This is an intriguing problem that might bring a number of learners to discover or reason out or guess at the concept of operant reinforcement.* For those students this would be an optimal discrepancy, and a good motivator as well as a good

---

* The food pellets occur right after some (unpredictable) response of the pigeon, which as a result increases in frequency, so that it is more likely to be reinforced again (by chance) later.

teacher. On the other hand, this problem might be too difficult for some, who would struggle with it a while and then give up, in which case it would not be optimal, and not a good motivator. For a few it might be so obvious that it wouldn't motivate; they might have had prior knowledge, or related experience.

You don't have to pose a problem or discrepant situation in order to excite curiosity. All you have to do is come into class with a paper bag with something in it that moves, or tell the students that you are going to show them something they never saw before, or tell them about an incident that puzzles them, or present them with some dilemma, or show them a gadget that does interesting things, or demonstrate something in science. There are many ways to excite curiosity. It adds a great deal to the learning situation and makes it more intriguing, even if the outcome is not that exciting after all. A well-known lecturer on chemistry who attracted crowds wherever he went was not above putting two large jars filled with colored water and some dry ice on the ends of the lecture table before he began—they had nothing to do with the lecture, and most everyone knew that it was dry ice that was causing the vapor and bubbling—but it added to the interest and suspense of the situation nevertheless.

THE UNWILLING PROBLEM SOLVER

Bob Morse has been tutoring a boy who is two grades behind him, in grammar. The boy has been having a great deal of difficulty in his language arts courses, and Bob's teacher figures that Bob will learn quite a bit about the subject by helping someone else with it. (Bob has not been a star in grammar himself!)

Bob has been going over the rules for agreement of verb and subject and such for some time, but somehow they do not stick with the younger boy, whose name is Will. Will just cannot seem to turn the definitions or rules into accurate responses. Bob decides to try a problem-solving approach. He sets up a paragraph and tells Will that there are ten cases of grammatical errors in it, somewhere, and his problem is to find all ten. This somehow turns Will on; he is evidently naturally competitive,

no matter what the game. Will then attacks the paragraph and comes up with two cases almost immediately. Bob congratulates Will—and also himself for his great idea! Then Will identifies another grammatical error, but it turns out not to be an error. Will is crestfallen, and really turned off, but Bob talks him into trying again. Will gets another one wrong and gives up completely. Bob cannot talk him back into it, and Will says it is a dumb game anyway. Bob begins to realize that Will is so sensitized to making errors, and being punished one way or another for errors, that he cannot see corrections as "feedback" or information, and finds it threatening to risk a response that might be wrong. What was an optimal discrepancy initially is changed by his anxiety and fear of failure. Some desensitization seems to be in order!

Dealing with emotional barriers

In Chapter 7 some attention was given to emotional barriers. To allow for the existence of such barriers, and to prevent them from impeding learning, a teacher

Small-group discussions may help students overcome emotional barriers.

or leader can arrange therapeutic situations involving individuals, small groups, or large groups; in these situations, inner psychological barriers are explored, identified, and dealt with. For example, suppose a group of learners is concerned about quizzes. Individuals can talk about their anxieties in small-group discussions and find that other learners have the same concerns. Erroneous ideas about quizzes may be identified, and the function and need for them discussed. The teacher or counselor's acceptance of the learners' feelings will also help, as well as assurances that the quizzes are not that difficult, that they are not used in a punitive way, and that they can be mastered with some preparation and study of techniques for dealing with them. In extreme cases, desensitization, either individual or with a group, will be in order.

Tests do not necessarily cause all of the negative emotional reactions that interfere with good learning processes. In the subject of educational psychology, for example, some learners are found to have negative feelings about behavioral control and the study of operant conditioning and classical conditioning; in some cases, this reaction interferes with learning so severely that the students involved cannot pass an objective examination or write a competent essay about the subject. This calls for individual therapy, as with nondirective counseling or desensitization or both. However, some attention to this problem by the instructor when presenting the material to a group or class may help ameliorate some of the feelings, and will reduce the general negative reaction.

Motivating by matching the process to needs

It seems likely that an approach which motivates one part of the class may leave another part cold.

Another way to motivate learners relates to such desires as the need to achieve, but does not involve changing the learner's basic motivation. To illustrate this, let's assume that you are teaching a class in which about one-third of the learners are high need-achievers. This third of the class is not likely to be highly motivated by traditional teaching approaches, because they don't offer learners an opportunity to choose their own goals, to get frequent information on their progress toward those goals, nor to take responsibility for their own learning. We can assume that another third of the class is reacting reasonably well to the methods used and still another third reacts somewhat neutrally.

Suppose now we train the teacher to use a different approach in which the needs of the achievement-oriented learners are met, through choice of goals, frequent information about their progress toward those goals, and so forth. Then the achievement-motivated third of the class might suddenly "become motivated." The other two-thirds might react in various ways: some would be turned off by this approach, others would be neutral toward it.

Obviously, the ideal would be to know what kind of teaching/learning strategies are best designed to "turn on" *each* personality type (or motivational type, if you will), then to teach each subgroup in a way that is most meaningful and motivating to them.

At present we have evidence that anxious learners need more structure and a stronger helping relationship with the teacher. This seems to include both low SES students and low ability students, as you read in Chapter 3. We know that achievement-oriented learners respond to the kind of course structure described above: more choice of goals, autonomy, frequent feedback regarding their progress. They like to feel that they are in charge of their lives and their activities. We can presume that learners high in need for affiliation might respond better to a warm, accepting classroom where a high proportion of group work and activities enable them to go about learning in the company of, and with the support of, their friends; projects that are done in groups, student government activities which involve committees, language clubs and mathematics clubs. As Coleman pointed out in his research on adolescents some years ago, many affiliation-oriented activities (teams, clubs, cliques) have norms and interests that *compete* with academic interests. In many schools it is very difficult to get the more able learners to be motivated to learn any more than they have to in order to get by; in such situations the level of achievement is relatively low since the students with status tend to set the example and only the teacher with a martyr complex can hold out for higher achievement (relative to other schools) by withholding As and Bs from the whole class. When a teacher *does* hold out for higher standards, it usually reflects badly on the teacher rather than the students, since the teacher is so far out of line in his or her grading that there is pressure from other teachers and administrators, as well as from students, to bring the "curve" within reasonable limits.

Group norms, management, and motivation

A learner will be more likely to learn if the norms and behaviors of the learning group and the processes used are congruent with those of groups to which he relates and belongs, i.e., if nonlearning behavior implies a deviation from group norms. For example, if a boy from a social class that expects children to go to college fails to study during the crucial college-preparatory phase of his education, he may feel some pressure from his parents, but also he may feel some pressure from the group of students to which he belongs, since they are "in the same boat." On the other hand, if his peer group has rejected this goal of college preparation, then his group's norms will support nonstudying, and the teacher's objectives will be counter to the group norms and will meet resistance. Thus it will be difficult for the teacher to motivate the class. On the other hand, if the class is an attractive one, with attractive members, then it will compete more effectively against groups having other norms, and thus it might be competitive enough (along with other college-oriented pressures) to get the learner to study for it—even though somewhat halfheartedly! Group pressures and their effects were discussed in Chapter 6 and in Chapter 7.

Orchestrating management and motivational processes

Whether you are dealing with one learner or many, preparation and planning and the execution of those plans calls for "orchestration" of many different strategies. If you are dealing with one learner the temptation is greater to "take things as they come," and indeed many teachers do this in classroom situations also. However, when you review some of the important considerations such a laissez-faire approach looks less attractive. From the first two chapters you would want to incorporate approaches to discipline that are compatible with the moral and ego development of the learners and provide tasks and challenges appropriate to the cognitive level as well. You will want to foster social development by arranging for experiences which help learners cope successfully with their psychosocial stage. From Chapters 3 and 4 you will want to take suggestions for identifying individual and group differences in such things as socioeconomic status, intelligence, anxiety, auditory and visual perceptual weaknesses, motor and perceptual-motor problems, and expressive difficulties. Chapter 5 will give you some guidelines concerning the characteristics of good teachers that you will want to emulate, and you will want to incorporate some of the processes which harness group dynamics effectively from

Chapter 6. Then there are a number of motivational strategies which you will want to incorporate from both Chapter 7 and this chapter; they are not mutually exclusive, and some overlap.

The conditioning processes in Chapter 8 and verbal learning and concept teaching processes in Chapter 9 are basic, of course, as are the approaches suggested by research in problem solving in Chapter 10; the applications of such matters are considered in more detail in the next chapter. They too will be orchestrated into a smoothly working system. The possible combinations are numerous, obviously, and their applications to different levels and subjects and teaching environments are even more numerous. Many examples of applied strategies have been given throughout the book, but the integration and synthesis of all of these theories and concepts calls for an advanced course in the subject. As one example of the possibility of combining approaches to teaching, one which is not worked out in detail but simply sketched in a superficial manner, consider the following description of an imaginary course in writing.

The course begins with sensitivity-training-type sessions designed to bring out the interests of the learners and their concerns about writing. These are subsequently converted into creative writing projects for individuals, based on those interests and concerns. The course would incorporate goal setting as discussed in Chapter 7, and would teach the learners the kinds of thoughts that motivated writers to think, as well. It would also create simulated writing situations of a game-like nature which would provide practice in the kinds of behaviors that are typical of creative writers or journalists or technical writers—whichever turned out to be the most compatible with the goals of the group of learners involved, or subgroups of them. These simulations would also utilize group dynamics for motivation. The organization of the course would include a variety of strategies besides this, from full-group presentations and discussions to small-group problem solving to individual project work. The projects would be of graded difficulty so that the learners would acquire independent study skills as they went along. For anxious learners there would be greater structure. For learners with auditory perceptual problems there would be alternate ways of acquiring concepts originally presented verbally. For less creative learners there would be brainstorming sessions to bring out their ability to formulate alternate interpretations and views, and to desensitize them of emotional blocks to unique or fluent responses. Individual conferences would be held to deal with psychological barriers to the writing process as well as with particular technical difficulties of individual learners. The teacher would be especially supportive with learners from low SES backgrounds, and perhaps assign high-ability learners to help them with the fundamentals of writing. The teacher would conduct sessions in which he (or she) would model the writing process himself, and also model the enthusiasm and interest that the learners should acquire. Definite guidelines and rules would be established for behavior during class, and for procedures to observe while writing: these would be consistently and firmly enforced, but at the same time the teacher would stress the likelihood of success and how it is contingent on effort and a positive attitude toward writing. The course would be problem-oriented, using optimal challenges, and would deal initially with concrete processes and situations. It would be programmed to assure success for each learner in building some kind of literary product that would satisfy his or her personal need. The learner's attempts would be received in a way that would bolster his or her ego but in a realistic manner as well, and which would avoid feelings of inferiority and powerlessness.

This is a large order, and only uses some of the approaches that have been presented previously. Some of them might turn out to be contradictory and incompatible, but certainly not a majority of them. You can see, however, that planning and orchestrating are not trivial tasks.

Summary outline with key concepts

☞ *This chapter* is based on previous chapters / It stresses two basic functions of teaching: management and motivation / Management involves programming learning, organizing group processes, and dealing with individual needs.

☞ *There are* many possible organizational formats for group learning / Planning and scheduling of group learning activities are important functions / Preparation does not guarantee good teaching, but it helps / Homework assignments must be incorporated into the overall plan so that they are seen as important and as contributing to learning / Independent study has not always lived up to expectations; this is due to insufficient planning and preparation of the learners for engaging in this kind of learning.

☞ *Development concepts* applying to different levels have implications for management / Implications are summarized for various levels.

At *lower levels classroom management traditionally emphasizes helping*, while at higher levels it tends to emphasize information and challenge to learners / To be successful, teachers need to fulfill a number of different roles and functions / Controlling the class can be done many different ways / One basic strategy for controlling is to organize and conduct activities in a way that makes difficulties less likely to happen / Certain teaching processes or strategies bring more learner involvement than others; those emphasizing student participation in discussion bring the most / Behavior modification techniques are effective in controlling and managing classrooms / A modern application of behavior modification involves token systems; these are effective, but in some institutions they have been challenged in the courts / Another recent approach to behavior management is the "Dreikurs" approach, which assumes that students seek either attention, power, revenge, or isolation / Research on cheating suggests strategies for minimizing it.

☞ *Learning disabilities* can be managed in a classroom setting / One approach is diagnosing and treating en masse / Another approach is forming smaller groups to learn different things / One can also deal with the individual in a class setting / There are a number of roles or modes of assistance open to specialists working with teachers / Teachers have the primary responsibility for students' learning and should not pass it on to specialists / There are a number of types of specialists and services / Mainstreaming presents teachers with an opportunity to understand learning disabilities.

☞ *Good management* contributes to motivation / Modeling and communicating expectancy of success increase motivation, as does avoiding fear of failure / Presenting optimal discrepancies, sparking curiosity, and involving the competence motive are another interrelated group of strategies / Removing internal barriers to release energy for learning is motivating; this involves both cognitive and emotional barriers / Sometimes a change in the requirements and format of a course will release unsuspected sources of motivation from parts of the class; however, such a change may also demotivate another part of the class / A general objective in motivating learners is to orchestrate strategies and processes, i.e., to integrate and synthesize a number of motivational strategies into a given teaching process or unit or course.

Glossary

Backup Reinforcers: Rewards given in return for tokens.

Channel: Avenue or way of receiving information, i.e., visual, auditory, etc.

Cognitive Barriers: Difficulties stemming from the complexity or unfamiliarity of learning tasks.

Dreikurs Approach: A theory of managing behavior derived from Adler's psychology.

Emotional Barriers: Conditioned negative responses and attitudes that have been formed in the past and generalize to whatever is being learned.

Extrinsic Reinforcer or Punisher: A consequence presented by a teacher or parent, not a natural outcome of the learner's behavior.

Homogeneous Grouping: A method of assigning learners to classes on the basis of their abilities, so that you have fast and slow classes.

Independent Study: Carrying on learning independently, without a teacher, or with minimal guidance.

Intrinsic Reinforcer or Punisher: A consequence caused by a response of the learner, not one presented by a parent or teacher or specialist.

Learning Disabilities: Specific learning problem encountered by a learner who is otherwise of average or above average ability; see also Chapter 4.

Mainstreaming: Teaching handicapped learners (intellectually or physically handicapped) in regular classes, rather than in special classes.

Mean: An average of scores, obtained by adding the scores and dividing by the number of scores (see Chapter 15).

Menu: A list of rewards of various types, usually given with the price of each, as part of a token system.

Multimedia System: A plan for teaching which integrates many media and modes.

Orchestrating: Integrating and synthesizing a number of different teaching techniques or strategies or processes into one overall system.

Price: The number of tokens required to obtain a given reward on the menu of a token system; e.g., five tokens are needed to earn fifteen minutes of free time.

Wages: The amount of behavior or number of responses required to earn a token, or the number of tokens given for a certain behavior or accomplishment.

Questions for thought and discussion

1. Compare the Dreikurs approach, control through behavioristic techniques, and the "reality therapy" approach presented in Chapter 6: Do they have methods in common? How do they differ?

2. What elements of classroom management by planning and scheduling would be most applicable to the problem of dealing with individual learning disabilities in a classroom setting?

3. What elements of management and motivation in this chapter apply most directly to teaching individual learners in a tutoring situation? In the home?

4. Do any of the classroom management techniques contradict any others? Could you apply them simultaneously?

5. Could you carry on a token system and still motivate through optimal discrepancies and sparking curiosity? Why, or why not?

Situations calling for applications of facts and concepts

1. Given the implications of development concepts for management, select one of the levels covered in that section of this chapter and show how you would incorporate motivational processes and classroom management processes into ideal learning experiences (give examples, but don't describe every last detail).

2. Suppose you have a tenth grade which is giving you a "hard time," because they have been allowed to "get away with murder" by the previous teacher. Select a control method, a motivational process, and a scheduling approach that you would integrate to handle the problem, and show how you would synthesize them.

3. Devise a method by which you could deal with a behavior problem through the Dreikurs approach and at the same time remove inner emotional barriers to learning which are causing problems (e.g., suppose the learner has been taught to reject the value of learning good grammar).

4. Johnny is hyperactive and has an auditory sequential memory problem. How would you manage a third-grade class, and Johnny individually, in order to help him?

Suggested activities

1. Get a group of fellow students together and set up a simulated class at some level and a topic to be taught. Then role-play various learner types, and work out a man-

agement and motivational plan for handling that topic with that type of class (you may be surprised at how adept you are at playing various student roles.)

2. Observe classroom procedures at some level and analyze them for management and motivational techniques. List those that are not covered here, as well as those that are. Ideally the exercise should be done with one or more other students in the course, so that you can compare notes and discuss your conclusions.

3. Observe a tutoring or learning-disability remedial process (individual) and analyze the management and motivational techniques used; also identify some that could have been used but weren't. Again, it helps to have someone else observing also, for comparing notes. Note: Both (2) and (3) could be done using videotapes instead.

4. Develop a multimedia system for teaching a topic at some level, incorporating management and motivational techniques into it. Possibly you might even try it out in a simulation situation like the one described in (1) above,, or bring in some volunteer students to try it out as was done in the system described in this chapter.

Suggested readings

For readings relevant to this chapter you should consult journals that deal with methods in various subject matters, and analyze those methods according to the concepts and principles reviewed here.

12

Modifying Knowledge,
Behavior,
and Feelings

CONTENTS

ABOUT CHAPTER 12

What this chapter can do for you

In previous chapters I have emphasized applications of concepts and theories which *suggest* ways of teaching. In this chapter I will review some of these suggestions and give you a set of guidelines for teaching, i.e., for modifying knowledge and behavior and feelings. These guidelines apply to different levels, subjects, and situations, and they can be used in situations ranging from classroom teaching to clinical teaching to teaching your own children at home.

What might make this chapter difficult

If you are a prospective teacher you will have to contend with your own inexperience and try to visualize situations in which these approaches might be used. If you are an experienced teacher you will find some approaches quite different from those that you have used in the past or been taught in "methods" courses; they are more basic and less tied to particular levels, subjects, or skills. Thus you may have some difficulty imagining how they might be adapted to your own situation.

Rationale for studying this chapter

As an extension of previous chapters this one will be useful in reviewing and integrating different concepts and processes. These processes should be common knowledge for anyone involved in education. Since they comprise the fundamentals of a theory of teaching, they are basic to any long-range objectives for improving teaching.

BACKGROUND AND RATIONALE OF CHAPTER 12

Relationship of this chapter to the previous chapter

Good management and effective motivation are basically means to an end, which is change in the learner, or modification. Too often administrators and school boards—and even teachers—are content with good management and motivation, without paying primary attention to the most important function, to bring about changes. Everyone assumes that "teaching" is an art and a science that is well understood and thoroughly mastered; you, as students as well as educators, probably realize that this is not the case!

I have chosen the term "modification" to represent functions which are designed to bring about changes in the learner directly; I treat them as "operators" in the theory of teaching, the change-agents that act directly on the learner to bring about significant and desirable differences which would not occur otherwise, or would not occur as frequently or dependably. These operators will be labeled actively—for instance, "concepting" will refer to teaching concepts—to emphasize that they are things that teachers do with learners in order to bring about change.

A theory of teaching

There are a number of theories of learning, but few if any theories of teaching; teachers are usually expected to translate learning theory into teaching practice themselves. In *Toward a theory of instruction* Jerome Bruner discussed the need for such a theory, and some of the attributes it would have; in *Conditions of learning* Robert Gagne developed a partial theory. This chapter continues that tradition, without stating its principles in terms of postulates or theorems. My objective is to lay down fundamental principles of how one goes about changing knowledge, behavior, and feelings. Some of the principles may seem so fundamental that they are trivial, but that is what happens in any theory when you begin at the beginning.

PREPARING TO TEACH

Baseline measures

In Chapter 11 you saw examples of observing and recording the learner's initial state before instituting any treatment. This is a good strategy for *any* teaching process, whether in a class, a learning center, or an individual tutoring context. For example, if a girl is described as "hyperactive," it is important to observe her over several days and record the nature of the "hyperactivity," its frequency, and the conditions under which it is most likely to occur. You might find, for instance, that this hyperactivity consists of jumping up to investigate sounds (an auditory reception problem, perhaps) or sharpening her pencil and talking when a quiz is announced (avoidance behavior), or picking on other children when they are busy following instructions in their workbooks (visual comprehension difficulty?). You might also find, when you come to count the occurrences of this behavior, that it is much less frequent than the teacher says it is (a hyperanxious teacher?), or that it really involves clumsiness on her part, like knocking things over unintentionally (a gross motor problem?), and her teacher is very "up tight" about such things. If you

The kinds of preparation described here are not always followed in practice, and don't guarantee good teaching, but they would improve it.

are the teacher, then such objective observation and recording will protect you against your own biases and hangups, as well as provide a record of initial behavior to which you can refer later as you institute some kind of teaching treatment.   A similar need for careful observation is found when a learner is having problems with mathematics or reading or social studies: it is just as important to analyze the nature and frequency of the problem before initiating any helping process.   In a classroom this can be done through a diagnostic pretest and ongoing formative evaluation (see Chapter 14).

Focusing on operational objectives

One way to certain frustration in helping learners is to try to do too much; another is to be vague about what you are trying to accomplish.   You need to focus on one or a few kinds of responses, and to try to increase or decrease these, or change the quality of them, in a way that makes it possible to succeed over a relatively short period of time, like several weeks or months.   One way to make sure that you do these things is to state your objectives for the learner in "operational" terms that can be observed and measured, so that there is no doubt whether or not you and the learner have succeeded.

These terms are often called "behavioral objectives," but we are talking about cognitive and affective outcomes as well.   Setting realistic *operational objectives* will help the student learn to make his or her aspirations realistic.   This applies to groups as well as to individuals; for example, you can pick out realistic goals for groups or classes by referring to their collective performance in the past and making estimates based on those results.   As you know, this is one strategy for motivating learners.

Stating objectives operationally means that you should avoid such words as "understand" or "appreciate" in describing objectives.   You need to be specific about the nature of the task(s) that will be used to evaluate their learning.   For example, you might say that a given learner will be able to spell nine out of ten words correctly on each of three samples, each drawn randomly from a list of a hundred words (or five hundred, or a thousand).   If you are setting objectives for a group, you might say that 80 percent of the class will attain such a level as that just described, or perhaps 90 percent.   An example of this is the reading specialist who obtains a graded list of words to be recognized (i.e., lists of words which a third grader should recognize, another that a fourth grader should recognize, and so forth), then tries them out on a girl who is having problems in reading.   She finds the level at which the girl gets all of them correct, then goes ahead in the lists to a level where the girl only gets three out of ten correct.   Then the specialist teaches the words at that level until the girl is able to get nine out of ten correct on several different samples taken from the lists for that level.   This is defined as success, and constitutes an *operational objective*: getting a certain portion correct at a certain level of difficulty.

"Programming" learning experiences — *designing a sequence of learning activities to meet each individual*

When you have determined where the learner(s) will begin, and the objectives (or, ideally, worked these out with the learner(s)) then it will help to lay out a series of learning activities or tasks that seem to be appropriate for bringing the learner(s) to the target behaviors. A rough plan or sequence will help you anticipate the major problems that will arise in relation to the subject matter or skill itself. Learners will find one portion more difficult than another, of course, and you often have to revise on the spot, or extemporize. There may be hierarchies of abilities that have to be learned in a certain order, or the concepts or relationships may form a network that is *not* hierarchial, so you could start anywhere and end anywhere. The previous experience of the learner will help determine the best place for him to start or the best direction for her to go.

Another consideration is whether to begin with concrete processes or examples, and this relates to the learner's previous experience and to his or her cognitive stage of development. A good rule to follow is to introduce concrete experiences first, then proceed to more abstract ones. Related to this is the general strategy of beginning with simple things and going to the more complex. Another important guideline is to begin with plenty of guidance or cuing and to withdraw that support as you proceed. Another consideration is the pace or speed with which you cover the material. Some students can progress in large leaps, i.e., they can handle tasks that involve several components of the learning at once, while others need to take these one factor at a time and then put them together gradually. If a student is ready and able to take big jumps, it is not fair to require her to follow a small-step sequence, and it may even be bad for her development of learning strategies. Of course, such a situation is not as obvious as one where the student is unable to handle the size of the step involved. However, giving too large a step is really no more a disservice to the student than giving one that is too small.

BASIC MODIFIERS

Associating and memorizing

The most basic modifier, or process, for teaching a learner involves presenting one thing to the learner and having him or her try to respond with something to be associated with it. Naming is a common example; another is learning foreign word equivalents such as "face–le visage." Naming a person, a street, or a mountain is also an example. This is also called "memorizing," sometimes "rote memorizing," in terms of what the learner does, although memorizing lists ("serializing") is another form of it.

The primary process here is presenting the first term (whether it is a word, picture, diagram, or a concrete object) and signifying to the learner that he or she is to give the second term (which can also be a word or a signal or some action).

What is it that
you do in order to
bring someone to
learn? What do
you show the
learner, or tell her,
or how do you
arrange the learning
situation?

Having done this, you present the second term or say "that's right" or "that's wrong" as the case may be, then either present other associates in a similar manner, or wait for a time, and present this one again ("review;" also distribution of practice). Assumedly mediators will facilitate the learning; one "advance organizer" for this type of task would be to teach the use of mediators generally, by using other associates and pointing out the possible mediating bridges.

Prompting, or cuing

Another aid that is helpful when used correctly is giving cues or prompts. There are many ways to do this. In some cases the cue is intrinsic to the learning, as when you suggest cognitive mediators that come from previous study in the subject; for example, you suggest processes for beginning to solve an equation based on previous theorems in mathematics. Other cues are not as relevant, but build upon past associations, as in suggesting mediating links for associating a Russian word with an English one. Still other cues are related to superficial characteristics of the response; for example, you might sound the first letter or syllable of the correct response, or you might say "The answer rhymes with _____."

The major error made in using cuing (often referred to as "prompting"), is the teacher's failure to remove the aid as the learner progresses. This removal process, when done gradually, is called "fading." For example, if you are teaching phonetics and you have all vowels and vowel combinations that have the same sound printed in the same color, you could gradually "fade" that color (have it become less brilliant, and gradually become more like ordinary black print).

There are no rules for how fast you should "fade" prompts. Prompts are a form of guidance, of course, and this was discussed in Chapter 9 in respect to concept teaching.

Serializing

Lists are a part of our lives since we frequently need to learn things in some order, like lists of things to check before you leave the house, directions to follow to get somewhere, or a recipe. Remembering the contents of a lecture is related also. There are two basic strategies for teaching a list. One is to give the whole list (if it is not too long) and have the learner try to repeat it, then keep presenting it and having it repeated until the learner can give it all (a variant is to have the learner repeat it just after you, word by word, instead of waiting until you finish). The other is to give the first thing and have the learner try to give the second, then give the second and have the learner try to give the third, and so forth, as in serial learning in Chapter 9. (You probably would go through the whole list once first, in this method.) To assist in the learning, you can cue the next word each time (with a "hint" or by giving the first letter), or just cue the ones that come harder

Table 12-1. *Teaching learners to memorize.*

1. Teach them to rehearse things over and over "in their heads," as in rehearsing a telephone number silently between the time you look it up and the time you dial it.
2. Teach them to classify information in whatever way is possible: putting all plants or all animals together, or all things to do with clothes, or all things that are to play with.
3. Teach them to group things in threes or fours, especially lists of numbers or letters.
4. Teach them to visualize items to be remembered as being in certain locations: the first one in the hall, the second on the closet floor, etc.
5. Teach them to visualize things as parts of a silly picture, like an elephant wearing a coat and tie and sitting on a barber chair (to remember that your coat and tie are on the chair).
6. Teach them to put unrelated things into a sentence or story.
7. Teach them to look for common attributes of things to be remembered.

NOTE: You can regard these as different techniques for making information "meaningful."

than others. Another way to assist is by giving mediators that connect one word and another on the list. Still another strategy is to make a story out of the list, making it easier to remember.

Sometimes prompting is helpful in memorization tasks.

Distributing practice or reviewing

As you found in Chapter 9, distributing practice on anything means that it is less subject to interference, thus better recalled. If you distribute practice on something, and put other, somewhat related learning in between—as in studying a chapter in a book, where you follow one paragraph with another—then distributed practice becomes review. If you teach paragraph A, then paragraph B; then review A, and review B, then teach C; then review A; then review B; then review C, and so forth—you are actually distributing the practice, but the second and third time are seen as "review." The main implication is that you need to break up learning anything, particular where it involves drill and overlearning; the secondary implication is that where you are learning a series of things which are related but which don't necessarily build or support each other, then you need to review frequently in order to retain the material. Therefore, if you cover the science of the Renaissance, in one or several days, and then go on to cover the art for several days, you should expect to review the science (ideally along with the art) afterward. The more you can embed review in ongoing learning, the better; for example, when you study some aspect of the art, relate it (historically, aesthetically, or conceptually) to aspects of the science already studied. By this means you can avoid some of the interference between the two, and bring them to facilitate and support each other instead. However, don't depend on this to avoid interference entirely; cumulative review will still be needed (overlearning is effective for retention, or "repetition is the mother of learning").

Discriminating and generalizing

Discrimination and generalization are inherent in the teaching of associations. We usually assume that a learner can tell the difference between different objects, words, pictures or sounds. Therefore, when he associates object A with word X, he doesn't make an error another time and associate object B with word X because B has something in common with A; also he doesn't associate object A with sound Y because X and Y sound a bit alike. If, however, the learner fails to discriminate, or if he fails to generalize in other cases, discrimination and generalization can be taught as well. You can teach someone to discriminate between two colors by teaching him to associate one color with one thing (an object, sound, or response) and the other with another. This can be done in various ways. One way is through classical conditioning: you could teach a person to fear one sound, but not to fear another similar to it by pairing a painful shock with one and not the other. Another way is through operant conditioning: you could reinforce a response when it is given to one sound, but not when it is given another similar sound.

You can do the same with generalization. For example, suppose a person naturally discriminates between two sounds because she likes one and not the other. You can arrange for something pleasant to happen each time you show her either or both, and she will come to like them both. This means you have taught her to generalize.

Knowing when to discriminate and when to generalize are important aspects of learning. This includes social learning, as the eighteenth-century courtier would find if he snubbed a powerful person or paid court to a lady who was out of favor, or as corporations found in the 1970s when they failed to generalize laws governing hiring practices from men to women and were sued as a result. In basic associations, it amounts to teaching that "les chevaux" is one French word (horses) and "les cheveux" quite another (hair); sometimes, novice conversationalists have said some embarrassing things in confusing one with the other, such as saying to a lady, "I would love to run my fingers through your horses."

Shaping

Shaping is a topic usually discussed in relation to behavior modification and applied primarily to motor or psychomotor activities. In shaping you start with a response that resembles the target response that you want the learner to be able to furnish ultimately. You reinforce that response so that its frequency increases; then, when its frequency is sufficiently high (i.e., when it occurs reasonably often in the teaching/learning context), you begin to reinforce only versions of the response that most closely resemble the target response. (We could talk about "behavior" instead of "responses"; it all depends on how complex and sophisticated the response pattern is. With older learners you begin with more sophisticated behaviors but you are also aiming at even *more* sophisticated and complex behaviors.)

Reinforcing only certain versions of a response, and not others, is called "differential reinforcement." Also, it is a version of discrimination learning (or discrimination teaching, if you wish); this was just discussed in the previous section.

When the learner's responses regularly show the new level of complexity or sophistication, then you begin to reinforce only responses that come even closer to the target behavior. Of course, you have to exercise judgment about how much you require at each step in order to get reinforced, and experience is needed in this regard if you are working with a particular type of learner (e.g., retarded or handicapped) or one who is very anxious.

Modeling

Modeling is another very important modifier borrowed from behavior modification techniques. It is important not to overlook this; for example, it would be too bad to put in a great deal of time shaping creative responses, as in the last section, if you could get all or part of the same results by simply setting an example of creative behavior so regularly that the learners begin to imitate it naturally.

You may remember that in previous discussions I pointed out that many behaviors are taught *unconsciously* by parents and teachers: punitive parents teach aggression and hostility; anxious teachers teach anxiety; teachers with an internal locus of control teach responsibility; and teachers who are interested in their subject model motivation. However, you may also remember that learners are more likely to imitate (modeling is more effective) if the learners identify with the teacher and see him or her as someone who is achieving something worthwhile, and if they see the teacher reward the kinds of behavior that are desirable. Thus, a teacher who wishes students to enjoy learning must enjoy it himself or herself, and a teacher who wants students to use their heads must model such behavior. The teacher who wants a quiet and well-behaved class must be a quiet, well-mannered person. Extreme levels of enthusiasm and impulsiveness breed similar behavior in the classroom; while they are not all bad, the teacher with that type of personality should expect that kind of response. Of course, the ability to imitate behavior depends partly on being able to discriminate between one behavior and another similar to it and to generalize from one situation where the behavior occurs to another. It also requires concept learning because when you try to imitate someone who is successful at something, you will have more success if you can identify and imitate the most important attributes of his or her general behavior, and ignore the unimportant attributes. For example, if you watch a champion bowler who demonstrates a habit of snapping his fingers just before the ball hits the pins, you might mistakenly identify that fingersnap as an important attribute of his game, and imitate it (without much effect on your bowling, of course). Obviously, the essential behavior that should be imitated (one that may not be apparent, however) is the four hours of practice he put in every day for the last two years, or the concentration that he gives to the sport when he is doing it, or the way he approaches the release of the ball, or some other element of his game.

Concepting

The most basic way to teach concepts, and the most powerful, is to present a series of different examples and nonexamples of the concept, first identifying for the learner(s) which are which, and then asking them to do so. If it is done so without such guidance, it may be viewed as discovery learning. There are many who feel that such discovery learning is the ideal, because it requires the learner to formulate his or her own mediators, descriptions, and definitions, and, thus, to relate the concept more closely to his or her personal learning history.

Another way to teach concepts is to present verbal descriptions of the crucial attributes of the examples which are mapped onto the title, for example, "we are going to study the concept of a triangle, which is a closed figure with three straight sides." This approach is often referred to as "deductive" or "guided" learning.

The kinds of thought processes involved in learning from examples (inductive, or discovery) and learning from rules or definitions (deductive, or guided) are not necessarily different.   Most learners find the inductive or discovery approach more difficult, but this is partly because they have become accustomed to learning primarily from rules.   Social learning, however, is primarily inductive, although you get guiding rules and definitions from parents, siblings, and friends.

Research on concept learning indicates that a combination of the two approaches, sometimes called "guided discovery," is usually more efficient than either strategy in its pure form.   While this approach is often followed intuitively by good teachers, other aspects of good concept teaching are generally overlooked.   One is presenting a number of different examples, in which the unimportant attributes of the examples vary while the important ones (technically called the "relevant" or "critical" ones) stay the same.   Another is presenting nonexamples that might be mistaken for the concept.   One source refers to these as "close-in" nonexamples (Markle and Thiemann, 1974).   To balance this, of course, you should also present examples that are far out, i.e., things which are examples but which might be called nonexamples by the learner.

Yet another neglected aspect of concept teaching is student responding.   Initially you might present examples and nonexamples and label them, yourself, but soon you would want to have the students make the identification, saying whether each thing presented is an example or a nonexample, and perhaps stating why so you can guide them to the relevant attributes as they proceed.   (This is similar to Piaget's insistence that learners *justify* their decisions in the process of solving problems.)   You might use a "selection" strategy, in which you would simultaneously present quite a few examples and nonexamples mixed together, and let them select any one, identify it, and find out whether they are correct or not.   This activity encourages students to form hypotheses and to check them out, and it makes concept learning more of a problem-solving experience than if the teacher selects the order of presentation.   Of course, the teacher makes feedback available in any case; he or she gives learners information about whether their choices are correct, and may or may not guide them with advice as to the crucial attributes.

One final concern in teaching concepts is assuring transfer to other examples or situations; this is often neglected in planning to teach.   Here are some principles to remember in teaching for transfer and retention:

1. Maximize the similarity between teaching and the ultimate criterion or testing situation by moving from simple examples and rules to complex ones like "real life."

2. Provide adequate experience with the task through plenty of practice.   The first time you do something, even though you get it right, you don't master it; as you do similar tasks many times, you learn more and more about the details, and this learning pays off in transfer later on.

3. Provide for a variety of examples and nonexamples when teaching concepts and principles; the best amount of variety is not too much.   With greater amounts of variety, you may need to give more experience with or practice on the task.   (Don't forget to include far-out examples and close-in nonexamples.)

Ⓠ₃

The matter of transfer is crucial: going from concrete to abstract and simple to complex help, also using guided discovery.

4. Label or identify important features of a task to help students distinguish important features and structure in their minds.

5. Give enough practice and experience and variety so that general principles become clear, ideally by having the learner form the general principles himself or herself (from examples and nonexamples), perhaps with some guidance or prompting.

TEACHING READING AND LANGUAGE TO SLOW LEARNERS

Learners who do not learn to read, and some who cannot speak, bring out the best in those who would design teaching processes to help them. Here are three relatively recent approaches, the first dealing with the lowest 5 percent of reading ability in the schools, the second with retarded learners, the third with such severely retarded that they cannot even communicate orally.

Donald Durrell teaches lowest ability readers to identify the sounds of letters through "letter name sounds" like the "p" in the word "peanut" and the "f" in the word "effort." Only after they are able to do this does he begin to teach them to recognize regular phonemes: the "i" sound in "sit" or the "t" sound in "top!" He also finds it useful to teach them the names of the letters. Then he gets them to write the letters when they are dictated orally, and finally, to match words they hear spoken with words on a printed page. He finds that at this point they are ready to learn to read by conventional means, along with other learners.

Renee Fuller teaches retarded learners to read by the "ball-stick-bird" method. She uses three basic forms, as follows:

$\bigcirc$ ball | stick $\vee$ bird

She teaches them to put these forms together to form letters, and then teaches them the sounds of those letters:

$\vee$ as in "VROOM" $\bigcirc$ as in "DEAD"

Then the learner forms words, starting with two-letter words, and stories begin when he or she has four letters. Thus the learners find that symbols have meaning. She has found that severely retarded children learn to read rather complicated stories this way. They also learn longer words more easily than short ones, in some cases.

Joseph Carrier has created the "non-SLIP" method for teaching severely retarded, nonverbal boys to speak and ultimately to read. He uses concrete shapes made out of Masonite. They stand for *words*, not for letters, so he doesn't have to go through the phonetic process immediately. The boys learn to associate the shapes ("words") with actual things that they refer to, then to build sentences using the words. For example, they say "Robert eats apple" by putting the three corresponding shapes in the correct sequence. The sequence is taught by having them memorize a sequence of colors, then making the various parts of speech different colors so that when they put them in the correct sequence, they have the correct grammatical structure. The boys learn nouns first; after learning a couple of them, they pick them up quite quickly. Verbs take a long time to learn; the concept of a symbol standing for action is evidently more difficult. After about a year they become able to converse with the concrete shapes, and they often begin to try to vocalize as well. They learn to read directions and other communications as well as to form them.

Giving knowledge of results or "feedback"

In all the processes described so far the learner is assumed to make an active response as part of the learning process. In modeling and shaping he (or she) responds by imitating, then by practicing the response while the teacher reinforces him for the best tries. In drilling and practicing and memorizing, the learner responds to each stimulus by giving the response that is to be associated with it, as in giving the sound of a letter. In teaching concepts the learner identifies things as examples or nonexamples, and by doing so demonstrates his or her understanding of the concept. All of these assume a reaction by the teacher to the learner's response, i.e., the teacher should give the learner information as to whether he or she is correct or not. This may be in the form of "you are right"; it may be in the form of the correct answer itself, leaving the learner to compare his or her answer with it; it may be in the form of an exhortation to continue and seek the correct response or to continue to follow a solution process; or it may be in the form of some hint which helps the learner adapt his or her thinking and make a better attempt. You will recall that cuing or prompting is given before the response; on the other hand, feedback or knowledge of results is given afterward. . Both are forms of guidance. In the case of exampling and nonexampling, where many examples are given and the response is essentially "yes" or "no," then the feedback given to one response also acts as a guide or cue for the next.

Some forms of feedback used in working with learning disabilities are:

1. Pointing out reversals in writing to the learner as he (or she) makes them.
2. Recording a learner's reading, and having him listen to himself read.
3. Tracing letters (involves cuing also, of course, since the learner is following the lines).
4. Learner expresses orally what he is thinking about as he solves a problem: this is feedback for the teacher as well as the learner; the teacher can give the learner additional feedback on how productive his thinking is apt to be, as well as guidance (prompting) on productive next steps.
5. Correction of poor articulation by the teacher, or teaching the learner to discriminate between good and poor articulation so he can hear his own errors.

Facts, concepts, and principles

Facts involve associations between concepts. For example, the fact "rain is wet" involves the concepts "rain" and "wetness," plus the relationship signified by the word "is." These are all concepts which are learned early in life, and are quite well formed. Therefore the "rain is wet" has little ambiguity.

Principles are associations of concepts, just as facts are. They are a bit more sophisticated or complex, perhaps, but the basic teaching processes are the same.

Concepts build on other concepts: facts are relationships between concepts: principles are relationships between facts. But relationships are concepts too!

Let us take as an example the principle "prices are determined by a combination of supply and demand; if the supply is low and/or the demand high, prices rise; if the supply is high and/or the demand low, prices fall." First, of course, the teacher must be sure that the concepts (terms) in the definition are understood: prices, supply, demand, combination, determined. Then the teacher may or may not assume that the learners have some prior experience which relates to this information, i.e., assume that they have observed prices in stores, and read the papers or seen on TV announcements about the fruit crop being ruined in Florida or the coffee crop in Brazil, and how that will make prices of fruit or coffee higher next year. Such experiences can be brought out and used as examples; some that the students offer will be nonexamples and will be labeled as such by the teacher or other students.

Another way to teach this principle or set of relationships is to treat it as a multiple association, and have the students learn it as such: learn the association "if demand is high, prices tend to go up" (or shortened to "demand up, price up"), then the association "if supply is high, prices tend to go down." Some mediators might be applied: "Demand high, everyone wants it, there's competition, so the seller sees that everyone is eager to buy, and will pay a higher price, so the seller raises the price"; and "Supply high, every store has some, all are trying to get rid of them, so they put them on sale so people will buy them at that store—then the other stores put them on sale, too, in order to compete and get them sold." Another mediator might be "Supply low, can't get them, some people want them badly enough to pay more to be sure to get them, then everyone ups their prices." Obviously, teaching the principle through examples and nonexamples of how it works is similar to teaching more basic concepts. You might want to start by presenting the rule: if supply goes up, or if demand goes down, prices fall, and if supply goes down, or demand goes up, prices go up. Then give a case where supply goes up and prices go up and ask, "Is this an example of the principle?" Then give one where demand goes up and prices go up and ask "Is this an example of the principle?" and so on, until all learners—or most—are answering the question correctly no matter which case you use (and you would want to have ten or fifteen cases, some examples and some nonexamples of the way the principle works).

TEACHING PREPOSITIONS À LA MONTESSORI

The concept of "preposition" in grammar, and the processes by which one uses the concept in forming sentences, was beautifully worked out in a teaching strategy by Dr. Maria Montessori in the early 1900s. Her teaching process consisted of three main parts: analyses, permutations, and lessons and commands. In the *analytic* part, young learners compose sentences using colored cards with words on them: red cards have verbs, black ones nouns, brown ones adjectives, tan ones articles, and violet ones prepositions. There are also some white cards with sentences printed on them. The child chooses a sentence card and then constructs the same sentence from the colored word cards. The following series of such sentences is taken from Montessori's book entitled *The Montessori elementary material* (1973):

Take the box *with* the colored beads.
Take the box *without* the colored beads.
Take the box *together with* the colored beads.

The child builds the first sentence with his (or her) cards, and then reproduces the second and third by simply changing the preposition cards. In this way he sees how the position of objects relative to each other is determined by the use of the preposition. This is part of his concept-formation process.

To give the child the concept of the normal position of prepositions, a series of *permutations* may be made leaving the preposition and its object in their normal positions:

Stretch a string from the door to the window.
From the door to the window stretch a string.
Stretch from the door a string to the window.
From the door to the window a string stretch.
From the door stretch to the window a string.

The child will recognize that the right sentence is the simplest and clearest.

Finally, the teacher may take groups of children and give them short *lessons* on the preposition to explain the meaning, selecting if possible two or three antonyms or synonyms each time. This lesson should be full of action. For example, the teacher or one of the students gives *commands* for the others to follow, such as, "One of you boys stand in the middle of the room. Now you others go and stand *near* him. One of you stand *next* to him. Now all go *far away* from him." In such a lesson involving commands, the child responds in a way that indicates his understanding or lack of understanding of the particular relational concepts involved, as well as broadening his understanding of the main concept, "preposition." Here, then, understanding is expressed through use of the concept in dealing with new behaviors, tasks, and concepts.

Questioning as a teaching process

One recent paper on the use of questioning in teaching lists the following rules for the process, with some examples (Collins, 1976):

Teaching through questioning and teaching through discovery learning are similar in nature to teaching through problem solving, discussed in Chapter 10, and to learning concepts inductively, as described in Chapter 9.

Rule 1: Ask about known cases; "Do they grow rice in China?" This brings out well-known facts the student is familiar with.

Rule 2: Ask for related things; if the student says they do grow rice in China, ask why—this brings out causal factors.

Rule 3: Ask for intermediate considerations; "Why do monsoons make it possible to grow rice in China?" This insures understanding of the steps in a causal chain.

Rule 4: Ask for preceding factors; if a student mentions water as a need, ask "How do they get enough water?" This again insures understanding of causes.

Rule 5: Form a general rule for insufficient reasons; "Do you think any place with enough water can grow rice?" This requires learners to consider other influences.

Rule 6: Pose a counter-example; pick a place where there is enough water and ask "Do they grow rice there?" This also insures consideration of all possible influences.

Learning through questioning, discovery, and problem solving are similar experiences.

Rule 7: Form a general rule for unnecessary factors; "Do you think it is necessary to have heavy rainfall to grow rice?"

Rule 8: Pick counter-examples for unnecessary factors; "Why do they grow rice in Egypt when they don't have much rain?"

Rule 9: Pick a case with an extreme wrong value; "Why don't they grow rice in Alaska?"

Rule 10: Pose a misleading question; "Do you suppose they grow rice in Egypt?" (assuming the student feels that rainfall is necessary).

As you have probably noticed, this question-asking process is similar to the problem of giving examples and nonexamples of a concept. Some of these questions can be regarded as "close-in examples" while others can be seen as "way-out nonexamples," in the language of concept teaching. The process is also related to teaching by discovery, to be discussed next.

Teaching by discovery learning

Discovery learning was introduced in Chapter 10. As it has been applied to classroom teaching, however, discovery learning is not primarily an approach to solving a particular problem (achieving some previously determined end result), but a method of exploring the environment and learning by experimentation and careful observation of outcomes. An example is found in a hypothetical plan for teaching a girl how to make a pudding (Cronbach, L., in Shulman and Keislar, 1966).

> *Although recipes can be discovered or invented, I would start by giving experience in following recipes along with reasons for measuring exactly and following directions. . . Around, perhaps, age 12, my class would experiment. The most elementary experiments might be to vary the amount of water added to one cup of pancake flour and observe the product under standard baking conditions. Trivial as this is, it can float profound enough notions in its wake; optimization, control of experimental conditions, interaction of variables, variations in criterion with the purpose or artistic taste of the judge, etc. While these simple experiments would initiate new thinking about recipes and cooking, I'd guess that six such parametric inquiries could teach nearly as much as six dozen. We might well shift back to prescription and demonstration when we teach the girl to make pie crust. Once she has some experimental background she should not*

There are certain risks inherent in discovery learning.

have any difficulty in accepting the teacher's statement about what chilling the crust before rolling does to the texture, particularly if the teacher supports the statement with photographs and samples. We had her make discoveries to establish an attitude. This attitude, once established, can be sustained to subsequent didactic teaching. Later exposition can and should continually hold in view the experimental base of recipes, the legitimacy of adapting them to fit personal criteria, and other such concepts. From time to time there will need to be further experimentation, in inventing recipes, for example. When I propose that some small fraction of the course use discovery methods, I am not saying and let the rest of the course remain as it was. On the contrary, I want didactic teaching modified to capitalize on the meanings and attitudes that were established through discovery.

Now there may be those who argue that a girl simply cannot fully understand the technique for making a pie crust if she is told how to do it. Then what is the right experiment to determine how much discovery is needed? No short-term treatment can provide any evidence. Instead, we need experiments lasting at least a semester, and ultimately extending into studies of long term growth.

Another proponent of discovery learning relates the following incident as an example of the kind of thinking and acting that experience in discovery learning is designed to avoid (Davis, R., in Shulman and Keislar, 1966).

A few years ago in a hospital nursery . . . the formula for new-born babies was made with salt instead of sugar. By the time the error was discovered, a dozen or so babies had either died or suffered severe and irreparable brain damage.

Now, who or what was at fault? Many babies—indeed, virtually all of them—simultaneously developed feeding problems. Some of the mothers—but none of the nurses!—tasted the formula and complained that it was unusually salty.

No nurse heeded either clue. The nurses had been trained to soothe a new mother's anxieties, lest they be passed on to the infant and create feeding problems.

. . . [The state] responded by passing a new law . . . which . . . makes it illegal to store salt in a room in which nursery formulas are prepared.

This is a significant step in the wrong direction.

Everytime we attempt to bypass human resourcefulness—by laws, rote training, or otherwise—we move toward, and not away from, the unintelligent behavior of the nurses who were trained but not educated. The response of the mothers was more appropriate . . . but the nonadaptive blind weight of authority decided the outcome in favor of the "trained" nurses.

I think it important for every teacher always to remember that he [or she], the teacher does not know the right answer or the right response—he can only hope that, when the time comes, his former students will respond appropriately.

The present emphasis on creativity and divergent thinking would never have occurred—and never should have occurred—but for the fact that we had gone all too far down the road labeled training, and had, surprisingly, lost sight of education.

These two quotations have something in common to say about discovery learning, and indirectly, about other innovative approaches to teaching. They suggest that such innovations or strategies should be integrated into the curriculum and learning experiences of the student so as to give the learner a different way of going about things, a more complete strategy for coping with difficulties, problems, and objectives generally.

COACHING AS TEACHING

Coaching: A complex teaching (and management) process

Some of the most effective managing, motivating, and modifying in educational institutions takes place on athletic fields. While the management of football or basketball or hockey teams is beyond the scope of this book, the teaching aspects of sports are quite relevant. There have not been many analyses of coaching from an educational-psychological point of view, but one of some interest was done involving a famous basketball coach, John Wooden of the University of California at Los Angeles (Tharp and Gallimore, 1975). The breakdown of his coaching activities with proportion of time spent on each was:

Verbal statements about what to do or how to do it (directive, as compared with nondirective teaching)	50%
Verbal statements to activate or intensify previously instructed behavior (motivation and reinforcing)	13%
Demonstrations of how to perform or how not to perform (modeling of response chains)	5%
Verbal compliments and encouragements (social reinforcers, praise)	7%
Verbal reprimands, statements of displeasure (social punishment)	7%
Nonverbal compliments or encouragements (social reinforcers)	1%
Scowls, gestures of despair, temporary removal of player from scrimmage to shoot freethrows by himself (social punishment; deprivation of privilege; isolation)	rare
A clear scold referring to a particular act, *plus* a reminder of a previously instructed behavior e.g. "How many times do I have to tell you to . . ." (special combination of social punishment/feedback and cuing/prompting, with a background of high expectation)	8%

The investigators found the last category of coaching behavior to be quite different from behavior they had observed in classroom teachers (they began by using their standard classroom observation categories); it was so unique, as a matter of fact, that they dubbed this "scold-reinstruct" process a "Wooden."

Some aspects of successful coaching apply to successful teaching.

Using the "Wooden"

Some of the best teaching, in the form of coaching, takes place on our athletic fields.

Tharp and Gallimore assert that they have used the "Wooden" with success in teaching elementary school children standard (cognitive) subjects as well; however, you should note that the total of reprimands (scolds, plus Woodens) is greater than the total of praise episodes.   One very noticeable aspect of the coaching process in this case was the intensity and careful planning and management of the session; this, of course, is partly the result of the tremendous pressure on college coaches and teams to win each game.   Similar intensity is found in the teaching of drama, dance, and music.   Perhaps this is partly because the results of the teaching are on display, and so much more apparent than the results of cognitive learning. Would it improve teaching in our schools if we found ways in which to make cognitive outcomes more apparent, perhaps even competitive?   Or would this be incompatible with the objectives of cognitive learning itself? The authors assert that the preparation of Ph.D. candidates for oral examinations has a similar intensity and performance objective, and that this tuning of the mind is important for survival in the intense competition of the academic world. Others say that this view of higher learning is counterproductive, and such intense preparation might interfere with, rather than facilitate, thorough and deep knowledge of the subject.

CLINICAL TEACHING

What is "clinical teaching?"

What would happen if dentists took care of patients the way teachers take care of students? Or if doctors diagnosed and prescribed as teachers do? They would take twenty-five or thirty patients at once, and try to help their individual problems on a mass basis. Perhaps the same treatment would be prescribed for all of them: those who did not improve would be dismissed—or sent to a counselor for help with their emotional problems.

With the advent of greater interest in learning disabilities, a type of individualized, diagnostic/remedial teaching has developed that is coming to be called "clinical teaching." As open classrooms and individualized instruction gain recognition, "clinical teaching" is beginning to find its way out of the learning disability clinic and into schools themselves.

The basic elements of clinical teaching are:

1. Diagnosis of the abilities and disabilities of the learner, both through special tests and through observation and recording of his or her in-school learning behavior and independent study processes.
2. Selection of potentially helpful remedial learning experiences and teaching strategies.
3. Trial of the remedial processes, and assessment of their effectiveness, through careful monitoring and recording of progress.
4. Revision of the strategies or techniques, and retrial of the modified strategies.

Bypassing

Sometimes specific learning disabilities are so severe or resistant to teaching that it is necessary to work around them, either permanently or while they are being strengthened. Sometimes a learner is so conscious of a disability and so sensitive about it that to try to help her only makes things worse, and results in her avoiding it and avoiding the person trying to help. Here too it is important to find some way around the difficulty initially, to enable the learner to cope while the problem is dealt with carefully and sensitively. A learner who can't learn arithmetic tables might have them taped to his desk so they are available to help him do arithmetic problems. A learner who can't read well enough to take a test might be given a chance to do it orally. Learners who have difficulty writing can be given an opportunity to make reports orally. If a learner has poor visual reception the teacher can seat her at the front of the room and describe visual materials as they are presented; if on the other hand, the learner has poor auditory reception the teacher might concentrate on visual presentations or on discussing readings, rather than describing things orally. Learners who have poor fine motor control might be given extra-large pencils and crayons, and encouraged to write in large letters, or to write on the blackboard in letters a foot high.

Programming

Programming was discussed at the beginning of this chapter; in the present case, it would consist of combining bypassing with a sequence of remedial experiences (clinical teaching) taking the learner from his (or her) initial state to one where he is better able to learn. The sequence of remedial experiences would incorporate the basic modifiers covered previously, and deal with the disability itself, directly.

Guiding, prompting, cuing

Somewhere between bypassing the inability and programming remedial exercises to strengthen it is the process of prompting or cuing the response; this was discussed earlier in the chapter. However, in respect to learning disabilities, the guidance (i.e., prompting or cuing) is often given through the stronger "channel," i.e., it is given visually if the learner has an auditory problem, and vice versa. These three processes—bypassing, programming, and prompting—are basic to the remedial processes of clinical teaching.

TEACHING FOR PERCEPTUAL DISABILITIES

Classroom practices for auditory perception disabilities

The "first line of defense" in learning disabilities is the classroom, and some general approaches to classroom teaching can reduce the difficulties that auditory receptive disabilities create. These can be carried out without interfering with the ongoing teaching. One such strategy, for example, is to alternate auditory and nonauditory activities frequently. Learners with auditory difficulties tire more easily, and may give up, if they have to struggle with listening tasks continuously. Unfortunately, many of us assume that everything can be explained verbally, and so teachers are apt to go on and on with oral descriptions and explanations.

Another general strategy is to reduce verbalization and emphasize demonstrations, examples, pictures, and models. Talking or writing about something is often easier and more efficient than bringing things into class to show or than working on a demonstration of something, but the showing and demonstrating are both more motivating and more informative in many cases. Bringing the learners to participate in the process is even better.

Still another general strategy for classroom teaching is to try to reduce extraneous background noises like traffic, playground, and other-class noises as much as possible. Also the teacher can try to face a learner whenever she is saying something he needs to hear. Particular learners can be seated toward the front, and reminded occasionally when their attention begins to wander. Behavior modification and contingency management techniques can be employed for such problems.

In teaching a class with students who have auditory problems, you should try to avoid speaking in a monotone. Changes in pitch and tone quality make it easier to concentrate or may call attention to an oral message. A learner with a severe auditory receptive disorder may be able to detect inflections and rhythmic patterns and respond to them, but may not be able to comprehend the individual words of a communication. One way to deal with such problems is to use basic commands in very consistent ways, and to say them with distinctive melodic patterns and accompany them with visual cues as well. For example, the teacher may say "lunch time" at the appropriate time, with a distinctive melodic pattern, and accompany it with gestures imitating eating, or rubbing his or her stomach, or something of that sort. After this is done consistently for some weeks, the melodic pattern and the visual accompaniment may be withdrawn little by little to see whether the learner can respond to the sentence without these cues. Repetition is also a key to treatment. Another is teaching language in small units like words and phrases, then putting them into increasingly complex contexts. It helps to use words that are meaningful to the individual learner as well, to give many examples of each word (not just one) and to associate experiences with the words (not just single objects or pictures). For example, "apple" may be associated with a trip to an apple orchard, rather than just an apple on the teacher's desk, also with bobbing for apples and the smell of apple pie.

Some other things to keep in mind when dealing with auditory problems in the classroom include cuing the child when he or she should be listening, and giving opportunities for the whole class (and thus the child) to practice remembering oral directions or sequences of oral communications (lists of numbers, letters, things).

Clinical teaching for auditory perceptual
disabilities

An important part of the remediation process is beginning with simple basic abilities and working up to more complex ones. If you are dealing with a single learner, it is easier to go back to "where it is" (where he or she began to fail) than if you have a class. However, even with a class you can go back some distance in terms of auditory abilities, and give some practice in those basic skills. There will be some who don't seem to need such help but who are having a hard time with hearing and putting in extra effort to compensate; added drill will help them. Some will have acquired the skills very recently, and need practice to "fix" them or put them in long-term memory. Others who have the skills in hand will be over-learning them, which contributes to their retention and use of them, making them more "automatic." It is a little like leading a group of young people on a mountain hike. The trip goes better if you keep the pace down to where all the hikers can handle it, and take frequent rests; you shouldn't let the faster and stronger hikers push the weaker ones so that they give up. Of course, just as you can start hiking at a pace that is too slow for everyone, so the first steps in remediation may be too elementary. In reading about various types and levels of remediation below, then, you should keep this in mind, and begin prescribing at a level that seems appropriate for the individual learner.

Teaching basic auditory discrimination

Step 1:   Teach the learner to discriminate between sound and no sound. To do this, have the learner respond physically in some way when he hears a sound, for example, by tapping the table with a pencil when a bell rings, or raising his hand when he hears something.

Step 2:   Localization.   Have the learner follow a sound as it changes position, and identify the source when the emitter is hidden (an alarm clock, for example).

Step 3:   Discrimination.   Have the learner say whether two sounds are the same or different; have him or her identify which of several sounds is the same as the one given first. Use such sounds as telephone versus doorbell, knock on the door versus tramp of feet on the floor, and voices of different people in the class.

Step 4:   Memory.   Bounce a ball and ask how many times it bounced; if the learner has difficulty, have him (or her) watch at first, then try it with his eyes shut; clap your hands a number of times and have the learner imitate you.

Step 5:   Figure-Ground.   All of the exercises so far can be done with varying degrees of background noise, so that the learner has to separate the important sound(s) from the background sound(s).

Step 6:   Attaching meaning to sounds.   Teach appropriate behavior in relation to meaningful sounds, and use such sounds consistently where it is convenient. For example, teach learners to respond to the school bell at the end of recess or lunch.

Teach them to respond quickly to words and tone of voice that indicate danger. Teach them consistent responses to the sounds of automobiles, trains, fire trucks, telephones, doorbells, signals in games (whistle in football), air raid warnings, fire whistles for their particular locality, and such. Associate the sound with the function, by having the sound occur along with the sight of the associated objects or events or actions, as well as with the appropriate activities on their part.

Step 7: Teach *appropriate responses to words,* rather than sounds. There is a significant difference between knowing the meaning of the *sound* of a train, and the meaning of the *word* "train." The sound of the word has no relationship to the sound of the train itself, of course. Similarly, the word "chair" has little resemblance to the sight of a chair, and the word "loud" may be spoken very softly regardless of its meaning. The difference we are talking about here has been described by a variety of terms, including "abstractness," "symbolic thought," and "secondary language" or "secondary system." Of course, meanings can be taught directly, but if there is a problem in teaching them thus, one can return to one of the earlier stages as in 7-a below:

(a) *Recognizing letter sounds:* The teacher says "ssss" then the learner says "ssssss." The teacher says "raise your hand when you hear 'sssss'." Then she says "mmmmmmmtttttttssssssssttttttttbbbbbbbbssssssssnnnnnnnn . . . etc." When the learner can do this, she then uses more difficult combinations like "ssssfffffshshshshshvvvvvvvvssssssss . . . , etc.

(b) *Discrimination of vowel sounds and consonant sounds:* The teacher asks whether a pair of sounds is alike or not. Pairs like "p-s" or "k-r" are used, then more difficult ones like "s-z." Then vowels are used, asking for discrimination between ay, eee, eye, oh, and ou (these sounds, that is). First they pick them out of a group, as with consonants, then they say whether pairs are the same or different. Start with long vowels, i.e., "a" as in "late," then go to short ones, i.e., "a" as in "bat." Work up to discriminating between pairs of nonsense syllables like "ab-eb" and "ib-ob."

(c) *Encoding sounds without giving them "meaning":* Give the learner a number of wooden blocks, several of each color. Have the child represent visually sequences of sounds, using the blocks. For example, give two or three sounds that are the same, and have her represent this with three blocks of the same color. Then two or three which are different, and have her represent this with three blocks of different colors.

(d) *Recognizing words:* The recognition and understanding of words given orally is more than just an auditory process: it involves conceptualization, since each word we use refers to a number of different experiences which belong to the same class.

Some additional individual and group techniques for auditory problems are:

1. In teaching nouns, avoid using parts of the body initially as the learner may have body image problems. Use dolls or pictures for this.

2. Say a word and have the learner clap his or her hands or sound a buzzer when the word is heard again, either in pairs of words, or in connected discourse.

3. Tell a short story, then ask some questions that can be answered "yes" or "no."

4. Play games where the learner carries out directions. Give the directions only once, and at a level appropriate for the learner: "Bring me a chair," or "Go get a pencil."

5. Give the learner(s) practice in repeating a sequence of digits or letters, to exercise their short-term auditory memory.

6. Tell stories with things left out or wrong; let learners detect the errors.

7. Teacher begins by saying, "I went to the store to buy some butter," and then asks "What did I buy?" The child responds, "Butter." The teacher then says "I went to the store to buy some butter and eggs. What did I buy?" Child responds, "Butter and eggs," etc.

Classroom and clinical teaching for visual perceptual disabilities

Just as you should alternate auditory tasks with visual ones for learners with auditory difficulties, so you should alternate them for those with visual difficulties. You should also make the visualization as simple and free from background interference as possible. Where it is possible, you should give auditory cues to the meanings of visual presentations. Where possible, you should enable each learner to have visual material at his or her seat, rather than showing it on the blackboard or on a projector, although projecting it on a screen and pointing to the important parts and talking about it might be preferable in certain cases because of the greater auditory (verbal) cuing and guidance that this makes possible. Here are some steps for dealing with visual disabilities.

Step 1. Have the learners respond to visual presentations in appropriate ways. For example, teach them the meanings of modern traffic signs that use iconic symbols to get their messages across. You could have them play at being automobiles and follow the directions as they move on "streets" around the room.

Have them match pictures to other pictures, and put a series of pictures (representing different phases of some activity) in correct order.

Exercises in visual "reception" and "association" like those on the ITPA would be in order; as a matter of fact, most of the test tasks described previously can be employed as learning tasks, merely by starting with the very simple ones and giving feedback. Of course, successive approximations, auditory cuing in the early stages, reward for trying, and reward for increasingly adequate performance are general guidelines.

Step 2. Here are special secondary responses to visuals, which do not involve symbolic interpretation:

(a) *Discrimination:* Present tasks that require the learner to match an item to a sample; i.e., present a sample—a shape, a color—and then two or more choices from which to choose. These can be concrete initially, then abstract (diagrams, pictures). Alternatives can differ in configuration, in position, in size; there are obviously many dimensions for this. Letters can be used also, but at this stage they are not to be translated into sounds.

(b) *Figure-ground:* Things (shapes, objects, animals) can be picked out from a background of other things, either in reality (which is what one does in identifying objects) or in pictures and diagrams. Some of the test tasks mentioned previously are relevant here. In a somewhat trivial sense, of course, identifying letters and words involves seeing them against the background of the page.

(c) *Constancy of Form and Shape:* This is a special case of matching in which something is recognized even though it changes orientation or size. In the three-dimensional world, it involves seeing an automobile as such, even though the actual image on the retina is small; i.e., an automobile remains an automobile as it goes into the distance. Also, it involves seeing a table top as such from different angles; if you drew it in two dimensions, it would actually be a nonrectangular figure (view it from just above its end).

(d) *Visual Memory:* Present a number of visual things—concrete or abstract—and then have some way for the learner to reproduce them without naming them (since at this stage we aren't dealing with giving the names or translating visual things into meaning). For instance, show a sequence of blocks in a row (different colors or designs); then scramble them up and have the learner reproduce the original pattern from memory.

Step 3. Have the learners interpret more complex visual situations, both concrete and figure-ground.

(a) Play a detective game, where the learner sees a room (or picture of one) with three or four people doing different things and certain objects lying around; then take him out of the room (or remove the picture) and ask him to name who was there, what he or she was doing, what was on the table, etc.

(b) Practice noting and describing the attributes of objects (soft, thin, red, many pages, heavy, and so forth). This obviously involves verbal expression and fluency as well, but the verbal expression must be based on the ability to interpret visual images.

(c) Label and discuss what the learner sees and how it functions; a bus takes people places, a saw cuts wood, etc.

(d) Allow the learner to make up stories about pictures or explain them to others.

(e) Have the learner match actions to pictures, or select pictures to match actions.

(f) Have learners practice interpreting facial expressions in pictures or as put on by teacher or other learners.

(g) Play charades; this is practice in expression for the one who is interpreting something, but also practice in visual interpretation for those trying to guess what it is.

Step 4.   Have the learners attribute meaning to abstract symbols, including letters and words.   The exercise in Step 1 in which the learners were taught the meanings of nonverbal traffic signs is one step in this direction, since it means translating a semiabstract visual presentation into meaning.   Another common ability related to this, but not the same, is naming things one sees, and then pictures of things one sees—things which are present, rather than things that have to be imagined.   This deals with the ability to translate familiar visual objects into words (to find the verbal title for them), which itself may involve auditory mechanisms as well, i.e., "reauditorization," or hearing something in one's imagination.

The basic approach to this step can be translating letters into their sounds, translating words into their sounds, or translating syllables into their sounds. There is a great deal of debate going on concerning these three approaches, and I will not take a position in this debate here.   As a matter of fact, it seems likely that all three have a place in the process: learning certain frequently used words by sight, learning letter sounds and how to blend them, and learning syllable sounds and how to blend them.   They probably interact and support each other in the ultimate development of the ability to read.   The development of these abilities, of course, belongs primarily in the field of reading instruction.

Step 5.   Practice visual-motor abilities and integration.   Have the learner draw between lines, do dot-to-dots, copy simple figures, go through obstacle courses which involve avoiding objects, crawling through things, opening things, lifting things, and such.

Step 6.   Practice revisualization and visual memory. Show something, then hide it, and have the learner draw it or pick it out from several alternatives, or describe it—whatever requires the learner to carry the image in his mind.   (The detective game in Step 3 is like this also.)

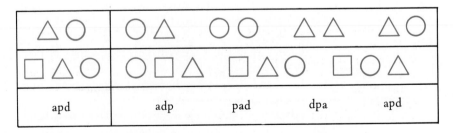

Figure 12–1. *Exercise for visual sequencing.*

Figure 12–2. *Exercise for perception of detail.*

APPLICATION OF MULTIPLE ASSOCIATING, REPETITION, DISTRIBUTION OF PRACTICE, AND SERIALIZING, IN CLINICAL TEACHING

Most clinical teaching processes have been derived empirically, through trial and error, not in reference to basic instructional theory. Here is an example of a practice that incorporates a number of basic modifiers from the first part of this chapter.

A teacher uses flash cards with three different symbols on them:

$$+ \quad - \quad 0$$

She teaches learning disabled children to associate the "+" with clapping their hands, the "−" with stamping their feet, and the "0" with a pause. Then she shows a card with a sequence of these symbols, for example,

$$+ \quad 0 \quad - \quad -$$

Then she removes the card, and the learners are expected to give the sequence through actions: a clap, a pause, and two stamps in a row.

Here associating and serial memory are used as a tool to get at visual sequential memory improvement through practice. There is also a motor-response element which might or might not be a weakness of the particular learners.

We might assume that the teacher would use repetition, distributed practice, and perhaps occasional cuing at first until students learned the "code" well.

CLINICAL TEACHING FOR MOTOR DISABILITIES

General techniques for psychomotor responses

In Chapter 8 some basic strategies for teaching operant behaviors were described. One was modeling, in which you demonstrate the skill and have the learner imitate it. Another was shaping, where the learner practices his (or her) best approximation of the skill, and you reward him for the best attempts, gradually raising your criteria as he improves. Another way is "molding," where you guide the learner physically through the process, then gradually reduce this guidance as he improves (this is a special case of prompting and fading the prompt). Then there is chaining, in which you teach a sequence of motor responses, often working backward through the chain. Finally there is giving verbal directions or guidance; this is used frequently, and sometimes abused, but verbal cues and guides can assist in the motor processes.

Conventional remedial approaches emphasize general exercises that can be done individually or in groups. Among the exercises and games which are often used are running, jumping, hopping, skipping, throwing, walking on raised things like curbs or balance beams, and gymnastic exercises (somersaults, cartwheels, and such). If these can be incorporated into games, so much the better; for example, you can invent a playground game which requires the learners to run to one goal, then skip to another, then throw something through a hole, etc. Points can be given for each part of the routine, and learners can practice with the objective of raising their point totals.

Exercises for balance and movement include jumping rope, leap frog, calisthenics (toe touching, knee bends), hopping on one foot and then the other, standing on one foot with eyes closed, learning dance steps, and again, gymnastic exercises and movements such as hand-stands.

Exercises for body image and awareness, in addition to those listed previously, include imitating the poses of others, pantomiming, charades, and making clay models.

Exercises for laterality and directionality include following directions having to do with right and left parts of the body, "Simon Says" kinds of games calling for actions of the right and left sides, and imagining which side familiar things are on without seeing them (the door, etc.).

Exercises for fine motor skills include weaving, tracing, sorting, paper folding, buttoning, using tools, and many games that involve hands and fingers and finger movements.

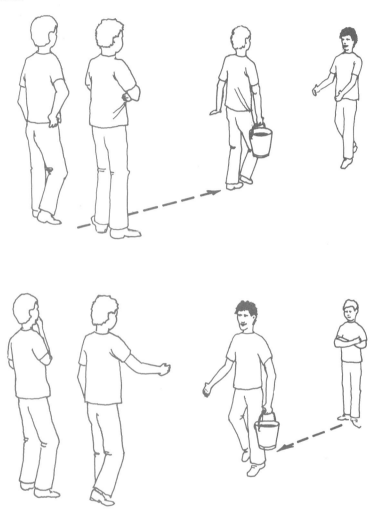

Figure 12–3. *Example of a game used for motor training.*

THE CASE OF DEBBY

Debby was a four year old who had difficulty climbing stairs, could not hop or skip, and had some difficulty running and grasping things. She babbled to herself, used nonsense syllables, and on a standardized test was found to be behind in both verbal and visual-motor performances. The specialist who dealt with Debby started out by trying to get her to ask for and name things; he used pictures and objects to do this. He also used fingerplays to get Debby to respond verbally. They played "Simon Says" in order to get Debby to identify body parts ("Simon says point to your nose"). They also did marching and rolling and crawling games, and set up obstacle courses on which Debby had to move over and under and around objects. The specialist had Debby do role-playing exercises ("Make believe you're the mother and you are taking care of your baby," and such); also simple pantomimes ("Make believe you are drinking a glass of milk"). Since Debby liked music, the specialist used it, too; he had acting records that required Debby to translate the words into motor responses ("Put your finger in the air"). After about four months, Debby's improvement was obvious: she was moving up and down stairs, running races, hopping, and speaking in two- and three-word sentences. Her score on the standardized test went up about fifteen points.

Sensory integration treatment

In recent years, occupational therapists have become involved in helping uncoordinated learners through "sensory integration," described in Chapter 4 (Ayers, 1972). Where a learner shows tactile defensiveness and/or a lack of dizziness when spun round and round in a hammock, simple stimulation (rubbing the skin with a cloth) and spinning in the hammock are used frequently (this is called "vestibular stimulation"). Where basic motor responses are involved, one remedial approach involves a skateboard. The learner lies on her stomach on the skateboard, then rolls down a very slight incline; to do this, of course, she has to keep her head, arms, and legs off the floor. (The skateboard is only about a foot or so in diameter.) This task meets the basic requirements for sensory integration; it requires putting together several things that the learner can do, but in a new (integrated) configuration, and gives a pleasant, concrete objective to accomplish which motivates practice. Thus, the general term for this kind of treatment or therapy, "sensory integration."

In addition to skateboarding, occupational therapists recommend a number of other exercises for improving sensory integration. In one, the child lies on a large ball—one almost as big as he is—and is rocked back and forth; this has the effect of relaxing the child, as well as offering a situation where body stabilization systems can react in a noncrucial situation (i.e., without a resulting accident). For a child who has trouble lifting up her head from a supine position, the therapist picks up her head for her, and then allows the child to let it go back to the floor slowly. Another exercise that is sometimes used is called the "wheelbarrow"; here the therapist holds the child's feet, and the child "walks" on his hands while the therapist moves the child around the room like a wheelbarrow. Another exercise is to have a learner walk along a line, putting her right foot on the left side of the line and the left foot on the right; then, when this is not a challenge, doing it backward.

Movigenics

In recent years an approach to physical education that emphasizes the development of efficiency of movement has gained wide acceptance. This is done through exercises in which the learner is asked to discover ways to solve a problem involving his or her body and some kind of space. For example, the learner may be asked to discover three different ways he can move from the floor to a table and back. Such problems lead the learner to explore movements and situations that call for most of the capacities of the human body. Each task is performed in a variety of settings and contexts, and is done slowly, rapidly, forward, backward, and in other variations. Each learner develops his own limitations in movement efficiency. Stress is placed on planning the movement, rather than just doing it "ex tempore." Thus, the approach combines elements of gymnastics, ballet, and athletics, but in a broad and generalized form.

An extension of this concept of posing spatial/movement problems is the design of a playground which encourages the teachers of learning disabled and retarded learners to teach movement and bodily control (Cratty, 1969). One objective of this development is to influence memory and persistence and other abilities that are important in academic learning; it is not clear whether such training does have positive-effects on cognitive learning, and if they do, why this is so.

Eliminating old responses

In Chapter 8 I described teaching new skills. However, one of the most difficult problems any person has to overcome, whether handicapped or not, is competition from responses that were learned previously and interfere with new ones. Consider, for example, a better-than-average athlete who wishes to improve his tennis game by learning to hit a topspin backhand. He has always hit a slice backhand, but since the trajectory of a sliced drive is very flat, and since the ball slows down and "sits up" for his opponent, it is not a strong shot in most cases. However, having played for some years, this tennis player has overlearned the slice to the point where it is automatic. When he goes to the backboard to practice swinging the racquet up through the ball (from below the ball), with the face closed (aimed slightly down toward the ground), he finds that at the last split second before contact with the ball the racquet face opens up on him (points upward slightly instead) as it has always done in slicing the ball.

Slice   Topspin

As a result, he hits ball after ball over the backboard, even though he is consciously directing his arm and wrist muscles to keep the racquet face closed. He finds that he can go through the swing correctly when there is no ball to hit, but as soon as he bounces the ball and focuses his eyes on it, the chain of responses that he has learned so well takes over, and even though he starts the racquet from a low position in respect to the ball (instead of a high one as in the slice), his wrist betrays him at the last minute and the ball sails over the backboard. This is no "handicapped" or "uncoordinated" learner, yet he has real difficulty controlling his muscles. He finds, for example, that the only way he can control this situation well is to start toward the end of the swing, then work backward. First he holds the racquet two inches in back of where the ball will bounce, and swings from there; then, after practicing that on the bouncing ball about five times, he starts back a few inches more in the swing, and so forth. This way he consistently hits the ball the way he wants, but every once in a while his concentration slackens, and up and over it goes!

MODIFYING FEELINGS

How feelings are involved in teaching

Most teachers try to change their students' attitudes toward various things in the process of teaching: you often hear such objectives as "I want them to appreciate good music" or "I want them to have a feel for what a good mathematician does," or the like. These attitudes are based on feelings or emotions. They are basically classical responses, and were dealt with thoroughly in Chapter 8. Here we will review some of the processes by which you change those emotions, and relate them to what we usually call "attitudes."

Teaching feelings directly: Associating

As was described in Chapter 8, you teach new feelings (or "condition" new emotional or affective responses) by associating the thing which you want the feeling related to with something that already evokes that feeling. Examples included associating cigarettes with open country and horses, with attractive women, or with whatever will evoke the kind of positive response that the manufacturer wants the cigarettes to evoke. To condition a positive response or attitude toward the content of some course, a teacher associates that content with whatever evokes such a response: popular music, good times, laughter, food, aspirations toward a successful future, attractive students, teachers, and community figures, and anything else that serves the purpose. The association may be made verbally or concretely.

Reducing or eliminating negative feelings

Many times student have already formed emotional responses to aspects of learning or school, and the task is to reduce these as well as to teach positive ones. To change a negative feeling you can follow a process like that used in "desensitization," where someone gradually loses a negative response to something through a hierarchy of imagined situations. This is done in a very positive setting, and with relaxation of the person to compete with the tension that negative feelings involve. The basic operating process, however, is the successive approximations to the situation that evokes the feeling, and maintaining a positive environment.

In case this process seems unnecessarily complicated, you should remember that feelings and emotions, the foundations of attitudes, are involuntary and cannot be controlled through "will power" or reinforced or extinguished as operant responses can. Therefore, in order to change them, you must teach (or condition) a different response and reduce the existing one at the same time. This cannot be done by ordinary lecturing, exhortation, or encouragement: it must be done gradually, through counterconditioning (see Chapter 8).

Modeling feelings

Probably the most effective and general operator or tool that a parent or teacher has for instilling certain feelings and combatting others is his or her own behavior, as a model. If you want a child or a class to be optimistic, be optimistic; if you want them to be interested in a subject, be interested. If you want them to feel that they have a good chance to be successful, treat them in such a way that they get the feeling that you expect that they will be successful.

On the other hand, if you want them to be anxious, be anxious. If you want them to fear failure, behave in such a way that they can see you fear that they will fail. If you want them to dislike school or fear aspects of it, then show that you feel that way. A teacher can instill more anxiety over grades by lecturing to students about not worrying about grades, if he does it in the wrong way, than he can by simply not talking about grades at all!

LEARNING NOT TO DRINK (UNLEARNING AN OLD RESPONSE)

Alcoholism affects about 5 percent of the population over fifteen years of age. Even when an alcoholic recognizes his or her problem, it is another thing to stop. Helping alcoholics to quit is risky: the success rate is low. Alcoholics Anonymous (AA) has as good a batting average as any similar organization. One problem is that alcoholics who quit drinking become disappointed and resentful because their families and friends don't show appreciation and gratitude. The family has been through this before, and they aren't quick to be convinced that the alcoholic *has* quit. But resentment against this hesitation can serve as the alcoholic's excuse to drink again!

Another problem is that the family or boss expects the alcoholic to function at full capacity, even to make up for time lost because of the problem. Actually gradual recovery is the best he or she can do, and not drinking must come ahead of everything else, including work and friends. The most difficult problem, however, is this: giving up drinking does not solve the combination of conditions which led to drinking in the first place, and it adds one problem—the physiological effects of being deprived of alcohol. The causes of drinking are not known: they are a combination of personality, environmental, and biochemical reasons, each to different degrees in different individuals. The effects of quitting are for the most part desirable, but this doesn't mean that the alcoholic can appreciate them fully. Feeling better is fine, but is also reminds alcoholics that they haven't had a drink, and they miss drinking even though they feel better. Also, the personality and social and physiological problems that brought about excessive drinking are still pushing alcoholics to drink again. On the other hand, alcoholics drink for the same reasons that other people drink, but something (or things) about the alcoholic make him or her more likely to drink more and to drink more often. Finally, defense mechanisms come into play heavily: "I was never that bad," "That job I have would make anybody an alcoholic," "A little wine with dinner won't hurt," and such (Weinberg, 1973).

What *does* work? A combination of approaches has the best chance. The alcoholic should be warned of attacks of irritability, tension, and depression which occur about five weeks after quitting, and again in the fifth month and again in the twelfth month: these seem to be physiological in nature, and pass in a few days. She (or he) should also be warned that once in a while she will feel some of the things she felt when drinking: a hangover after a party, or other things typical of when she was drinking. She should be advised to guard against two dangerous attitudes: a feeling of not being able to succeed and of low self-esteem and unworthiness, and a feeling of being on top of everything and able to give up and being past the worst of it—either of these can lead to drinking again. She should also be advised not to take her own ethical and moral resolves lightly, but to live up to her own values religiously. She should be particularly honest about things, and she should not be at all permissive about nonmarital sex relations: in both cases, this is to avoid subsequent guilt feelings which can in turn lead to a relapse into drinking to get rid of them. Finally, if such a relapse occurs, you must be careful not to feel betrayed and not to reject her and refuse further help: most alcoholics have relapses, and they can be brought back to nondrinking if their lapses are handled carefully and without a holier-than-thou attitude.

Summary outline with key concepts

☞ *Management and* motivation set the stage, but teaching processes produce learning / Basic teaching processes for all levels and subjects lead ultimately to a theory of teaching.

☞ *Before teaching,* record the initial state of the learner / Before teaching, state objectives operationally ("behavioral objectives") / Program the learning task into steps or sequences of learning subtasks.

☞ *Associating things* and memorizing names involves mediators, rehearsal, clustering, and visualization / Use cues (prompts) to assist learning, then fade them / Teaching ordered lists involves item-by-item rehearsing, or modeling the whole list (or a segment) for imitation / Distributing practice assures retention; it is related to review / Discrimination is taught by reinforcing the response to one stimulus and not to another similar stimulus, or by teaching an association to one stimulus and a different association to another; generalization involves reinforcing the same response to both / Shaping involves successive approximations to the target behavior, raising the criterion of reinforcement gradually, step by step / Concept teaching is not well done in most cases because not enough examples and nonexamples are used, also because instructors don't start with simple concrete examples and go to complex abstract ones / Feedback, or knowledge of results, is often omitted from teaching.

☞ *Facts—associations* between concepts—can be taught verbally, or through concrete examples, or both; the association is itself a concept / Relationships and principles, like facts, are associations between concepts: the teaching processes are the same as for facts, and thus the same as concepts / Questioning is a valid and helpful technique: it is sometimes similar to teaching concepts by example and nonexample / Teaching by discovery learning emphasizes exploration, curiosity, and learning through experience rather than just verbally.

☞ *Coaching is* a teaching process in part / For one coach the combination of a reprimand followed by a review of previous learning was a frequent and effective strategy.

☞ *Clinical teaching* involves a combination of diagnosis and remediation / Bypassing means finding ways around a disability / Programming means focusing on the weakness by moving from very simple tasks through short steps to more difficult / Prompting means giving guidance through a strong channel, then removing the guidance / Clinical teaching for auditory disabilities involves a series of steps from simple to difficult, and in increasing abstractness / Clinical teaching for visual difficulties involves a similar series of steps.

☞ *Clinical teaching* for motor disabilities involves conditioning of operant behaviors / Standard remedial activities are common physical tasks done in groups: running, skipping, and such / There are exercises for balance, for body awareness, for laterality and directionality, and for fine motor skills / Sensory integration treatment is used for very basic motor disabilities such as posture, body stabilization, lifting head and feet when prone, and such / Getting rid of bad motor habits is a common teaching problem / Movigenics involves a discovery-learning approach to efficient movement.

☞ *Teachers* try to change feelings and attitudes as well as teach knowledge / Teaching feelings involves classical conditioning / Reducing or eliminating negative feelings involves desensitization or other related processes / One basic way to teach feelings is to model them.

Glossary

Associating: Teaching paired associates; more generally, arranging things so that one thing evokes the memory of another.

Baseline: Measure of number of responses and/or quality of responses, taken before teaching begins.

Clinical Teaching: Teaching involving diagnosis, programming of learning, teaching (usually one-on-one), frequent evaluation of progress.

Concepting: Teaching concepts.

Cuing: Giving a hint or prompt in order to get the right response.

Fact: Relation between concepts.

Feedback: Knowledge of results; information resulting from a response.

Modifier: Some process which changes behavior, cognition, or feelings.

Operational Objective: An objective stated in terms of observable behaviors, rather than abstract terms.

Principle: A more complex association between concepts, involving relationships.

Programming: Developing sequences of instructional experiences or tasks that bring the learner from where he or she is toward the goal of teaching.

Serializing: Teaching lists or sequences.

Transfer: Using learning in a new situation where it is appropriate.

Wooden: A combination of a "scold" plus a reminder of previously instructed behavior.

Questions for thought and discussion

1. Analyze the teaching of addition to primary grade children in terms of basic teaching processes, and combinations of them.
2. Consider how history is taught, through your own experience with it: Does it emphasize the teaching of concepts? If not, what modifiers does it use, primarily?
3. Is it possible to combine associating, discriminating, shaping, and concepting in a teaching process, or are they all independent and incompatible?
4. Does sensory-integration treatment utilize any of the basic modifiers mentioned in the chapter? Which ones?
5. How would you coordinate the teaching of feelings, input and output responses (abilities), and concepting in the teaching of some aspect of grammar; for example, the use of the subjunctive?

Situations calling for application of facts and concepts

1. Describe how you would teach a learner with poor auditory sequential memory to follow directions, using basic modifiers and combinations.

2. Alice has trouble remembering the rules in basketball: she is always doing the wrong thing, and can't answer when asked by the coach to say what it is that she did wrong. How would you help her, using basic modifiers and combinations?

3. Bill is having difficulty learning to form the correct sentence structure in French, although he can remember the word-equivalents and the verb endings and such. How would you help him?

4. How would you program learning experiences to help an eight-year-old girl learn multiplication tables?

Suggested activities

1. Observe some clinical teaching and analyze it in terms of basic modifiers.

2. Observe some coaching and analyze it in terms of coaching processes described in the chapter, and in terms of basic modifiers.

3. Assist some learning disabled person through processes suggested in the chapter, and in Chapter 4.

4. Design a teaching process for some teaching problem of interest to you, according to the requirements outlined in the chapter. Then try it out and note weak points as well as ideas for general improvements.

Suggested readings

Gagne's *Conditions of learning* develops a general approach to teaching that parallels the guidelines in this chapter and goes into more detail. Bruner's *Toward a theory of instruction* outlines the requirements for a substantial theory of teaching, which this chapter is designed to lay some foundations for. Becker, Englemann, and Thomas have published two softcover books with excellent guidelines for both behavior modification and for the teaching of concepts; they are called *Teaching I* and *Teaching II*. You may want to refer also to books on learning disabilities, many of which were referenced in Chapter 4.

13

Media,
Teaching Strategies,
and Systems

CONTENTS

ABOUT CHAPTER 13

What this chapter will do for you

After studying this chapter, you should have a wider range of options and techniques for bringing about learning, whether in the classroom, home, or elsewhere, and you should also be more aware of the applications of basic concepts and processes covered earlier. You will also have a better understanding of the advantages of well-developed instructional systems and the kinds of considerations that are taken into account as they are put together and tried out.

Difficulties you might experience

You might consider this more of a "methods" chapter than basic educational psychology; however, effective educational psychology eventually reaches the point of applications. You might have some biases about educational media, or about certain types of presentations; for example, some people feel that lectures are the bane of education, and they would object to the amount of space devoted to analyzing them and giving guidelines for their use. An analogy would be the situation of a doctor who must study physiology and anatomy, even though she might find those subjects unpleasant, or a lawyer who studies corporation law even though he feels that large corporations are dominating our government and society and that laws favoring them should be repealed.

Reasons for studying this chapter

The "tools of the trade" of teaching are presented here. Most of them are familiar to you, but some of the possible uses and combinations may not be. In addition, you will find out about techniques for designing and developing systems that utilize the "tools" in new ways—perhaps more effective ways—of teaching. There is a futuristic aspect to this idea, of course, but in another sense it is very old-fashioned: it deals with the engineering of teaching, just as civil engineering applies basic theories of physics to building bridges and buildings that work and don't fall down. At present people are comparing new types of systems with old-fashioned teaching, and noting that the new systems are not doing any better. Obviously, they forget that in earlier days the automobile just about broke even with horses; harness makers were soon out of work, however.

478

RATIONALE AND BACKGROUND OF CHAPTER 13

Some historical notes on theory and technology

John Dewey (1963), in a significant book entitled *Experience and Education*, written late in his illustrious career as an educator, observed that when you begin to teach in new ways you feel a need for some kind of philosophy of teaching. Traditional teaching does not create such a need. Dewey wrote his book in retrospect, looking back on many years of educational innovation patterned on his theories, called "progressive" education. Much of educational innovation today takes its principles from that movement.

Maria Montessori (1973), in a book describing materials used in her elementary schools, made this telling discrimination between educational philosophies:

> In preparing this material we have worked for her [i.e., the teacher]; we have acted as the workmen who produce the various objects necessary to life; she has but to "live" and "make live." This will show still more clearly how far from truth is the modern conception of pedagogy which attempts to realize its desire for freedom in the school by saying to the teacher, "Try to respond to the needs of the pupils without being conscious of your authority over them." When we ask a teacher to respond to the needs of the inner life of man, we are asking a great deal of her. She will never be able to accomplish it, unless we have first done something for her by giving her all that is necessary to that end.

Dr. Montessori not only prepared materials, but also carefully programmed teachers' guidelines for using them to bring about more involving and enjoyable learning.

Jerome Bruner (1966), in a more recent book entitled *Toward a theory of instruction*, has also argued for a theory. The title implies that there is none as yet, but that there will be one—or more—soon. Bruner points out that such a theory would be a tool whereby we could increase our understanding of people and how they are "shaped" by others. More than that, it would be very practical for guiding teaching, the process of passing on the knowledge, skills, and viewpoints of a culture. Bruner proposed four major aspects that should be included in such a theory. First, he said, it should address the factors that bring a learner to learn (motivation). Second, it should concern itself with the way knowledge is structured and presented to the learner. In this respect, Brunner feels that certain basic concepts in each subject are the most powerful in supporting learning, and that these concepts should be identified and used. Third, Bruner feels that a theory should deal with the sequencing of experiences for learning (how teaching progresses from initial stages to final stages). Finally, he feels that a theory should address the questions of reward and punishment and arranging successes and failures.

Jean Piaget, the Swiss scientist who has spent a lifetime studying the cognitive development of children, has also recognized the need for a science of pedagogy.

His view is reminiscent of Dewey's, and is revealed most recently in his book *Science of education and the psychology of the child* (1971). To Piaget, pedagogy is a science comparable with other sciences, and a difficult one at that. He points out that medicine both employs other sciences that are themselves advanced, and collaborates in the development of other disciplines that come in between those and the practice of medicine. Pedagogy, however, receives only modest aid from its mother sciences, such as psychology and sociology. Thus it is faced with the task of developing intermediary disciplines by itself, with little help; furthermore, it has to do this using basic disciplines that are not themselves as well-ordered as those underlying medicine.

Another man who has contributed greatly to an understanding of the processes involved in teaching is B. F. Skinner. Although he objects to the concept of a "theory" of education, he has developed from his basic principles of behavior an approach to teaching, as well as an approach to organizing society, which he terms a "technology" of behavior. At present, he says, we lack a behavioral technology that is comparable in power and precision to physical and biological technology. He feels that unless we develop it, we will not be able to prevent the catastrophes toward which the world seems to be moving, including nuclear holocaust, overpopulation, and excessive pollution. He emphasizes the low level of our present understanding by pointing out that although Aristotle would not understand one page of modern physics or biology, Socrates would have little trouble following the most current discussions of human behavior.

INSTRUCTIONAL SYSTEMS AND THEIR DEVELOPMENT

Background of instructional systems

Systems development, used widely in industry and by the military, has been applied to education as well.

"Systems development" is an organized approach to preparing to accomplish some regular, ongoing task or job. It has been used extensively in industry and applied to teaching as well. One theorist has described the requirements for designing an instructional system as follows:

1. Analysis of what is to be achieved: the competence or state of knowledge or skill (or combination of these).
2. Description of the initial state of the learner(s).
3. Review of the "modifiers" that can be applied: the conditions or arrangements that can be used to bring about a change from the initial state (2 above) to the final state or goal (1 above).
4. Identify assessment procedures for determining the immediate and long-range outcomes of the processes reviewed in 3 above (adapted from Glaser, 1976).

These four steps will now be related to concepts you have studied previously.

Analysis of outcomes or goals

This process of identifying the nature of the objectives or goals is tied in with the process of assessing outcomes, which is the fourth item on the list. It is also discussed previously in Chapter 12 on "Preparing to teach," and in relation to operational objectives, Chapter 14.

Learner diagnosis

Identification of the learner's beginning characteristics, including individual differences and learning abilities and disabilities, relates back to Chapters 1 through 4, as well as to the section in Chapter 12 on preparing to teach. It is difficult to determine learners' entering abilities exactly, since it is difficult to pose questions in a way that is relevant to their previous experience. For example, a learner may have studied equations in mathematics, but may have done so through a concrete discovery process involving a balance beam or some such analogue; therefore, if you test that learner on written equations you may not find much understanding, but the basic concepts and relationships have been learned nevertheless. However, it is still worthwhile to assess learners' competencies before you begin to teach them, and some of the considerations from the past chapters mentioned above would be:

1. The cognitive stage: preoperational, concrete operational, or formal operational. Remember that older students may be at the concrete or preoperational stages in respect to some subjects or concepts, while they are at higher levels in others (see Chapter 2).

2. The previous strategies that have been learned, i.e., whether they have learned to learn by rote, by taking notes, by imitation, by discovery, by listening or by watching, by projects, by independent study, by watching films, by laboratory exercises, and so forth. This will relate to the strategy to be used in the class, and the type of criterion tasks to be used to determine whether or not they have learned (see Chapter 12).

3. The personalities of the learners, individually and as a group. Are they impulsive or reflective, achievement-oriented or affiliation-oriented, anxious or relaxed, questioning or silent? (see Chapter 3)

4. The readiness of the learners in terms of learning disabilities, as measured by such tests as the Frostig, Bender, and the ITPA. Will the learning tasks require learning by ear or by eye? (The learner may be a visual or auditory dyslexic.) Will it require psychomotor (visual-motor, perceptual-motor) skills that he does not possess? Does it require speed of response, or careful consideration of alternatives? Does it favor an impulsive or a reflective learner? Does it involve too much tension for high-anxiety students, or too little for low ones? (see Chapters 3 and 4)

Review of teaching strategies or "modifiers" and
programming learning tasks

The purpose of Chapter 12 was to present the various ways in which you can teach;
Chapter 12 in turn reviewed "modifiers" from several earlier chapters.

Assessment or evaluation of outcomes

This is the function of Chapter 14, and it is involved also with determining objectives or goals.   When you use operational objectives (what are often called "behavioral objectives") you specify not only the kinds of behaviors that you expect to
emerge from the teaching process, but also the nature of the tasks that you would
use to determine whether or not the learners have achieved these goals, both before and after teaching.

MS. STEVENS CREATES OPERATIONAL OBJECTIVES

Ms. Stevens is teaching eighth grade reading and she has been to a workshop on behavioral objectives and is all fired up to institute these in her teaching processes.   She takes time to make a list of areas in which she wants to create such objectives, and then starts on one of the first areas: reading a paragraph.   She first specifies the nature of the audience or students who are to achieve whatever learning is involved.   She writes, "Students will be able to . . ." and then realizes that this is not very specific, so she says "Eight grade students will be able to . . ." but then she realizes there are other eighth grade students than hers, so she writes "Eighth grade students in periods 4 and 5 under Ms. Stevens will be able to. . . ."   That sounds better, so she goes on to what it is they are to do, i.e., what she wants to observe: "Able to answer correctly questions on a paragraph after having read it."   Then she realizes that she has not specified the nature of the question, or the nature of the para-

graphs to be involved—she has not described the environment or situation.   So she says, "Able to answer a set of questions which have been created to cover information in certain paragraphs; these paragraphs and the questions associated with them are given below."   That seems to specify about as closely as is possible the nature of the situation or problem to which the learner has to respond.   Then she says "These answers will have to be correct . . . ," but she realizes that "correct" is a very subjec-tive term, so she says "The answer to each ques-tion will have to include at least three-fourths of the major points, reasons, or facts which are listed below after each question."   Initially this seems to do it, but then she realizes that there is one more loophole, and writes "And the learner will have to meet this criterion for three-fourths of the questions on the test."   Then she gives each paragraph, with questions and answers, for reference.

SOME COMPREHENSIVE INSTRUCTIONAL SYSTEMS ("MACRO-SYSTEMS")

The impact of systems development

Thoroughly planned and implemented systems development is relatively rare in education. In the past educational systems have been planned with a bit less organization and modern attention to detail. However, it is interesting to examine some of these older approaches and note their strengths and weaknesses.

Herbart's system: Part of instructional history

Broad strategies or theories of teaching, when worked out in some detail, can be regarded as systems: "macro-systems" is a term for such broad systems.

Instructional systems are as old as the hills; teachers have systematized instruction for years. A book by Broudy and Palmer (1965) entitled *Exemplars of teaching method* will give you an excellent historical view. One early set of systematic guidelines for teaching was promulgated by Johann Friedrich Herbart, a lecturer in philosophy at Königsberg in Germany in the early 1800s. His system was divided into five steps called "preparation," "presentation," "association," "systematization," and "application."

For Herbart, preparation involved recall of materials similar to those in the learning task, analogous or opposite to it, antecedent to it, a result of it, or in some other way related to the learning of it. This is similar to processes for dealing with interference from other learning, discussed in an earlier chapter. Presentation meant calling the students' attention to the relevant dimensions of a concept or process. Association and systematization called for the learner to compare and contrast instances of phenomena being studied, something reminiscent of concept learning and teaching. The third step represented a break with the current philosophy of Herbart's day, in a way similar to that in which behaviorism contrasts with maturational approaches to learning today. Herbart maintained that teaching was a systematic exploration of the best way to cluster elements of experiences both for storage and retrieval; i.e., as Broudy and Palmer put it, some schemes of classification can handle large amounts of information well, while others cannot.

The last step was "application," where exercises were given in which the pupil had to generalize, give new examples, or do problems. Although all of this is similar to concept learning and teaching as presented in Part III, Herbart placed more faith in the power of ideas in determining behavior than in behavior itself—reflecting the "brainwashing" approach to motivation discussed in Chapter 7. His view of learning was that a new "idea cluster" would replace an old "idea cluster," and that, as a result, the person would change his way of doing things as well as his thinking. Partly because of this abstract approach, without concrete processes to follow or imitate to carry it out, Herbart's system did not inspire the creation of workbooks, practice exercises, and teacher's guides that could bring teachers generally to follow his precepts. Thus, although his system influenced educational procedures for many years, it was not as well applied by teachers as it might have been.

The project method

Another historically important prescription for teaching, or "instructional system," was the "project method," which was introduced by William H. Kilpatrick as an application of John Dewey's educational theories. In his book *A sourcebook in the philosophy of education*, Kilpatrick (1934) described it thus:

> *The aim and process of teaching as now best conceived differs significantly from what formerly prevailed and, as we have seen, still largely prevails in high school and college. . . . In the newer outlook the emphasis is on helping develop desirable, inclusive character and personality, with especial regard to the dynamic quality of such a character. Does the person being taught grow as a total personality? Does he grow, as a result of the teaching, more sensitive to possibilities inherent in life around him so as to seize upon those fruitfully? Is he disposed to take hold effectively to bring things to pass? . . .*

The project method involves the student in many kinds of learning.

Kilpatrick went on to mention other objectives, the last among them being "knowledge." The technique of attaining these objectives is very simple in theory, and thus the technology is simple also. It consists of arranging for the learner to be wholeheartedly involved in purposeful projects. Some projects would embody an idea, as in presenting a play or building a boat, whereas others would involve the enjoyment of a story or a musical work, and another would be to solve a problem or acquire some skill or knowledge. The role of the teacher in this system is to help the learner (or help learners in small groups) plan and initiate activities to accomplish some purpose, to carry out the activity to some conclusion, to evaluate their own progress during and after the activity, to think up and note new leads, to formulate the new leads by writing them down for later recall, to keep pupils critical of their own thinking en route to the solution, and to draw conclusions at the end so as to emphasize certain kinds of lessons and help the learners synthesize their experiences into useful generalizations and rules for the future.

Individually prescribed instruction (IPI)

not widely used
Teacher has to write a learning prescription for each learner

Here is an example of one early but well-developed system for individualizing instruction:

"IPI" was one of the first thoroughly developed macrosystems in our educational history, however, you can look back to Montessori for an early precursor system.

> Oakleaf Elementary School, located in a blue-collar suburb of Pittsburgh, has been operating an individually prescribed instruction program (IPI) since 1963. Research and development for the IPI curriculum originated in the federally funded R&D Center located at the University of Pittsburgh. The purpose of IPI is to enable each student to go through the curriculum at his own speed, working independently much of the time. Courses thus programmed are math, science, reading, and writing. At Oakleaf, the system is learner-centered and the role of the teacher has been sharply redefined. Little of the teacher's time is spent in lecturing to a group. Much of the information transmission takes place independently of the live teacher through the media of booklets and worksheets and, in science, audiotape cartridges and three-dimensional manipulative equipment. The teacher's main tasks are evaluating individual pupils' progress, preparing daily learning prescriptions for each child, and tutoring children on a one-to-one or small-group basis (Commission, 1970).

Q5

As mentioned above, IPI places a great deal of reliance on programmed instruction. This means that learners need to adapt to the requirements of programming, both in terms of individual progress and in terms of the types of responses that programs require. The tests for IPI are criterion-referenced, and when a learner completes a programmed unit, he can ask for the progress test for that unit and attempt to pass it. He then either goes on to the next unit or gets remedial work designed to teach him what he has missed. The role of the teacher in this system is primarily that of academic guide and counselor. Teachers find it necessary to adjust to this role, which may not always be as satisfying as that which gives

IPI encourages independence and emphasizes the learner's progress.

the teacher a central function in the learning process and which places him in charge of a large number of students. IPI students have no problem related to non-promotion, since they are "promoted" in short-unit steps according to their own speed. There are few problems in the IPI school with teacher absences and the shortcomings of substitute teachers, since there are fewer absences of teachers and the task of "covering" for the teacher is simpler.

IPI students seem to "hold their own" in the junior high school to which they graduate, where those junior high schools are traditional in format, even though the IPI students are, on the average, younger, due to the fact that none have been "held back" (approximately one out of every five children has been "held back" somewhere in traditional elementary schools). Teachers find these children some-what more inquisitive and independent than children from conventional schools, which in most, but not all, cases, leads to a positive reaction by the teacher.

An audio-tutorial system

A freshman botany course at Purdue University has been totally restructured with the aim of defining clearly all objectives. Students, teaching assistants, and academic and *research colleagues have been consulted extensively, and all identifiable "busy work" has been eliminated. <u>Most of the factual information is acquired through independent study in a specially designed learning center containing thirty booths.</u> Each is equipped with a tape player, an 8mm movie projector, a microscope, live plants, test tubes, diagrams, and other materials pertinent to the week's study. Learning activities may include listening to short lectures, performing experiments, reading from texts and journals, studying demonstrations, viewing short films, dissection of specimens, and any other study activity deemed helpful by the senior instructor or the student. Since the independent study is unscheduled, experiments do not have to be designed to fit into a three-hour time interval, and some experiments can take the form of miniature research projects (Commission on Instructional Technology, 1970).*

One major achievement in the Purdue project was spreading out available laboratory time over days and weeks, so that more students could be served by fewer duplications of the same laboratory experimental setup. It also integrated laboratory work, lectures, and text reading with viewing films and slides. Of course, if you individualize instruction in this way, you also individualize conferences and other guidance and counseling functions of the professor or teacher. This is ideal in one sense, but in terms of sheer time required of the professor it is more costly, because he is giving of himself on a one-to-one basis rather than one-to-many. This can be done either with an open-office approach or by appointments.

JENNY MEETS A SYSTEM

Jennifer is a student from a "disadvantaged" background. She has been recommended to college by her high school principal and guidance counselor on the grounds that she seems to have the native intelligence to handle college work. She was ranked high in her graduating class, but her high school is not in the top-ranked schools in the state. She is apprehensive about college.

When Jennifer gets to college, she finds that she is scheduled to take four introductory courses: psychology, English literature and composition, college math, and biology. (For purposes of illustration, we shall consider only psychology, although the same principles could be applied to all.) During "Orientation Week" she takes an examination that covers the objectives she is expected to know when the work on the course is completed. She finds that there are one or two areas where common sense helps

her to put down what she thinks are the right answers, but there are many answers that she simply does not know. She meets with a counselor from the department, who has a digest of her test results in front of him. He explains to her what the course is about and gives her printed material that spells out specifically what she is supposed to learn and also clearly states the ways in which she can learn it.

For example, she finds that she is responsible for a number of units of work that are related. She finds that she can hear lectures either in person or by television tape. These are scheduled at a number of different hours throughout the day, and are repeated at other times throughout the school year. She is given a copy of this schedule. She also finds that she can go to the learning laboratory, where a series of lessons have been prepared for use in a multimedia carrel. She can see and hear the lessons as many times as necessary. She also finds that the counselor has office hours which are extended beyond normal hours so that he is available to her for discussion. There are seminar discussion groups scheduled for a regular period several times during the week, and the subject for discussion at these is left open enough that questions can be answered either by peers or by the discussion group leader.

The values of these options to the student are manifold:

1. She can seek out the kind of learning situation in which she feels the most comfortable.

2. She has access to the professor of the course through personal conferences and through the seminar small-group sessions.

3. When she is ready to take an exam, it is administered to her in a testing center in the department, and she is not graded in competition with others in the course, but on the basis of how well she had demonstrated proficiency with the instructional objectives of the unit of the course.

4. She is not singled out as a disadvantaged student who needs extra help, but she has been able to compete with other students from other backgrounds all of whom have exercised the option of choice of learning method, as she did (Sanders, 1969).

An elaborate elementary system

At one elementary school for Indian children a highly elaborate teaching system was set up under the direction of a private company. Daily tests were administered on the concepts that had been taught in each subject area. Tests results were processed by a computer and a printout of the conceptual areas in which each child was deficient was given to teachers before the beginning of school the next day. At the same time, several hundred films had been catalogued according to the concepts they presented. The computer searched out the films which corresponded to the areas in which most of the students appeared deficient. The relevant films were transmitted by closed-circuit TV throughout the school. Teachers could make the choice as to whether they wished their class to view a film, which film, and when (Commission, 1970).

Before continuing to read this description, you should consider your reaction to it as an example of an instructional system. As described so far, it is not too different from many which have already been described, and which by implication have functioned quite successfully. Now let us examine the results:

The elaborate program was discontinued the next year, much to the relief of students and teachers. The term "concept" had not been sufficiently defined; many of the films which were to teach specific concepts actually were irrelevant to the teachers' purposes; the film took much too long to achieve what the teacher could do alone in a matter of minutes. Observers reported that toward the end of the school year most teachers left their TV receivers turned off all day long (Commission, 1970).

This is included here to make it clear that elaborate systems do not always work well in practice.

A LESS ELABORATE SYSTEM THAT WORKS

Mr. Andrews has it made this period. Most of his students have been sent to the learning resource center to work on learning activities packages while he attends to problems of some of the slower students with the earth science course. Billy Williams, for example, has picked out of the file of topics one which says "Earth Formations Which May Be Indian Mounds—Or May Not Be" and has gone to the resource center to get the box, which has an introduction, directions for using the materials, a short text, pictures, and references for further reading (references to books that are catalogued in the library). Since Billy has been checked out on finding books by their catalogue numbers, and since Billy has used other LAP's* before, Mr. Andrews knows that he will be using his time profitably for the next period at least. He is not so sure that Monte Childs would use it as well—but Monte is one of those to whom he is

giving special help, so that does not pose any problem. He will be right there, working away. John Dunn, however, is another story: he is very bright and interested, but also he gets involved in other things—such as causing a little trouble occasionally when he is not being watched that closely. Mr. Andrews picks up the phone and buzzes the LRC (learning resource center) and asks them to let him know if John Dunn either does not show up or leaves prematurely. Mary Brown will be working on her project on conditions of the environment which encourage animal populations to increase, while Janet Smith will be working on an LAP related to the effects of nuclear power plants on life in the sea, into whose water they discharge waste products. Generally, Mr. Andrews feels, the period should be smooth and productive for all concerned. He makes a note to ask for a report of progress from each one the next day, however, so they will feel that they are not working in a vacuum.

* Learning Activity Package.

MODES AND MEDIA FOR TEACHING ("MICRO-SYSTEMS")

Relationship to systems

Traditional teaching methods can be viewed as systems, and developed accordingly.

Systems use a variety of modes and methods of teaching. By taking a new look at some old methods, such as lectures and discussions, you may be able to see them in new ways.

Lecturing

The lecture is one of the oldest teaching techniques; it is useful for presenting information, integrating ideas, clarifying and elaborating on a text, anticipating questions that are likely to be asked, and for motivating. The convenience, versatility, and effectiveness of the instructor as communicator and presenter via lecture should not be underestimated, even though lecturing is often a highly overworked strategy in colleges and high schools. When integrated with films and discussions and laboratory experiences, lecturing is even more effective. When learners are taught to take notes at lectures and study from them, the experience can be most productive.

Lecturing can be appropriate at many levels, from college down through middle school. Generally, the lower the educational level, the briefer the lecture should be and the more extensive the discussion of it which follows. As was pointed out in Chapter 11, presentation modes are among the least involving for low- and average-ability learners.

Among the strong points of the lecture are flexibility, adaptability to student response, auditory rather than visual communication (a benefit for learners who are auditory-inclined), and the capability of presenting new materials without waiting for them to be published. Among the disadvantages are the fact that learners have to take notes and thus have to be taught to do so, the fact that lectures are used too much and students become satiated with this mode, the problem of reviewing things that don't "get across," and the fact that speaking and listening constitute a much slower communication process than reading a text. In spite of these draw-backs, students will often profit greatly from well-designed and well-presented lectures, and they will continue to prefer an instructor's live presentation to reading the text and other activities that are available.

Elements of a good lecture

1. Introduction: The introduction to the lecture should accomplish two purposes: (a) Gain the attention of the audience and set it at ease; (b) Give a preview of the subject matter and objectives of the lecture. Both are sometimes accomplished by a title and descriptions of the topic which are intriguing, have some surprise value, and at the same time relax the audience in expectation of a presentation that is both informative and enjoyable. Some information on the potential impact or on value to the audience may also increase motivation. Note: Ordinarily, the students will know in advance what is expected of them in the way of note-taking and the importance of the lecture in relation to other aspects of the course [text, outside reading, tests, and so forth]; while it is wise to be clear about these matters in early lectures, it is more important to be consistent in the treatment of the information (i.e., if it is never used in discussions or required on tests or papers, then students will pay less attention.)

2. Setting the stage, previewing: An introductory section of the lecture which outlines the subject matter in a way that "sets the stage" and outlines major concepts which apply to it—perhaps giving an anecdote or two which covers the reason for the lecture and its function in relation to other topics—will often be helpful. One theory implies that such "advance organizers" make the material more easily understood (Ausubel, 1968; Bertou, Clasen and Lampert, 1972; also see Chapter 9 in this regard).

Lecturing is still a valued and potentially exciting teaching technique.

3. Present information through both definitions/descriptions and examples/nonexamples. (Where needed, use audiovisual aids to present the examples, rather than describing them in words.) Be sure to include a complete set of examples and nonexamples, i.e., use far-out examples and close in nonexamples.

4. Review previous knowledge which is relevant to the subject in such a way that the students' previous experience and learning are made relevant and they have a set for applying that knowledge as you proceed.

5. Where the content involves a sequence of facts, allow for the serial position effect by (a) relating the various facts to each other, pointing out similarities and differences and ways in which they depend on or are built on each other, (b) reviewing facts or concepts, i.e., review Fact A after discussing B, and A and B after discussing C (Rothkopf and Johnson, 1971), (c) giving extra time to the review and discussion of material in the middle of the lecture as compared with that at the beginning and end (serial position, Chapter 9). Also take care that the overall organization is logical and clear (Thompson, 1961).

6. Provide intermittent reinforcement for attention, either through jokes, praise for attending, allusions to positive aspects of the audience and facilities (e.g., things for which they are noted, such as high ability, interest in

good causes, good athletic teams, competitive spirit, interest in scholastic matters), or occasional light shifts of subject to things that are somewhat irrelevant such as "a funny thing happened to me on the way to school this morning."

7. Keep the content limited and integrated and have a recognizable ending as well as a beginning, i.e., have a planned wind-up and exit that leave your listeners wanting a little more, and ideally sum things up with a finishing touch. The author is reminded in this respect of a chemistry lecture on gases in which the lecturer filled a couple of balloons at the beginning and they floated up to the ceiling—his timing was so perfect that as he finished discussing the diffusion of gases through a membrane and how it explained (among other things) how balloons eventually lost their contents and came back to the ground, he held up both hands and the two balloons floated down into them, right on schedule.

8. Provide for structure, particularly when notes are to be taken, by giving transitional guides from one topic to another and from subtopic to subtopic; more important, provide verbal descriptors which guide the learner in the relationships between individual thoughts and sentences (e.g., "however," "therefore," "this makes it clear that," "this takes into account the previous fact, etc.) (Gage et al., 1971).

MR. MURPHY TEACHES NOTE-TAKING AND STUDYING

Mr. Murphy is teaching high school history, U.S. Government, to be exact. He has been increasingly concerned over reports of former students that they have trouble taking notes and studying for tests in college, so he decides to do something about it. He plans at least two short lectures a week, about 20 minutes apiece. He requires students to take notes on the lectures, and has them hand in their rough notes along with whatever additional work they do in order to learn what is in the lectures. This is so that they will not feel they have to put the notes in smooth form (which they would not do in college), and also to require them to reprocess the notes somehow before passing them in (in college they would study them for a test, of course). He finds, to his amazement, that only about two out of every twenty students are able to take good notes, and that they do very poorly on an examination that he gives on the lectures without in-class discussion and explanation by him. He decides to teach them a strategy for studying in college. Instead of asking students to take notes on his lectures, or on their text readings, he asks them to make up test questions on various aspects of the lecture or text, along with suggested answers. At first they have a great deal of difficulty doing this. Some of the questions are pretty ridiculous, and where the questions are reasonable, the answers are often incomplete, as they would be if he were giving a quiz. As a result, he continues to emphasize this method of studying, with the assumption that when they learn to do this, they will have a valuable tool for studying in college, where the lecture is an even more important part of the teaching/learning system.

Table 13–1. *Sample data on presentation modes from multimedia research. Note that students rated lectures first in effectiveness!*

	Response to Media from Semantic Differential Questionnaires		
Rank	Preference[a]	Easiness[b]	Effectiveness[b]
1	3	3	1
2	4	4	7
3	7	2	5
4	6	7	4
5	1	6	12
6	2	11	10
7	5	1	6
8	8	12	3
9	10	5	2
10	12	8	8
11	11	10	11

Key to numbers in last three columns:

1 Lecture	7 Films
2 Teacher Demonstration	8 Overhead Transparencies
3 Laboratory Experiment	9 Programmed Instruction
4 Laboratory Stations	10 Small-group Discussions
5 Text	11 Eight Millimeter Loops
6 Reader	12 Text Problems

[a] Preferences refers to the students preferences of media.
[b] Easiness and Effectiveness similarly refer to the ease or effectiveness of the specific medium.
From M.D. Smith, G. Poorman, and M. Schagrin, Multi-media systems: A review and report of a pilot project, *School Science and Mathematics*, February 1968, 68 (2), 96–102.

Text presentation

Use of lectures, textbooks, and demonstrations are the backbone of secondary and higher education, along with large- and small-group discussions. They are also involved— in adapted forms— in elementary and middle schools.

A textbook can be self-instructional to a degree, and motivating in the sense of a good lecture as well. It also presents questions, examples of applications, and suggestions for additional activities and readings. It is available as a reference. The equivalent of "taking notes" is underlining portions of the text for later review. However, there is too much in any text for any student to master or comprehend entirely, so it has to be cut down to size and the highlights emphasized by the instructor. If the text is relied upon by the instructor, then lectures, discussions, activities, and examinations can be based upon it, and the whole course moves at a faster pace. However, it is often important to help the student discriminate between important and unimportant aspects and to recognize places where the text may be unclear or misleading.

The advantages of a text include its convenience, its reference capabilities, the use of its index, and most basically its provision of a common source of information for all learners in a course. Its disadvantages include superficial coverage of any given topic (since it must cover all topics) and its tendency to be obsolete in some respects due to the lag between writing and publication.

Demonstrations

While difficult to prepare and thus requiring extra time, demonstrations of concepts, principles, and processes can add tremendously to the interest of a lecture or a discussion period. Many of the concepts in this book are difficult to demonstrate, but a little creativity can do wonders. Instructors often underestimate the impact of even the simplest demonstration as clarification, as concrete evidence of what is otherwise verbal and abstract, and as a change of pace from the continuous stream of verbalization. Of course, well-developed films are one vehicle for demonstrating things that cannot be easily demonstrated otherwise: a good example of this is a film on Piaget's concept of conservation, where the action shows children trying the tasks and showing the characteristics of different cognitive stages, with a minimum of verbal guidance or comment.

Among the advantages of demonstrations are their clarity, their inherent interest, and their concreteness. Disadvantages include the difficulty of preparing and presenting a good demonstration, the time required, and the impossibility of demonstrating everything that would lend itself to demonstration.

Elements of a good demonstration

1. The relationship of the demonstration to the current subject matter should be clear, either before you begin, or (in a discovery-oriented or punch-line type of presentation) by the end or outcome of the demonstration. If you want to demonstrate the great tendency of sodium to combine with other elements by putting a small piece in a pail of water, you might not want to predict the outcome ahead of time; however, after the surprise has occurred, you should explain how this relates to the periodic table and such.

2. The demonstration should be visible, and it should proceed slowly enough that all can follow.

3. The verbal accompaniment should contribute and clarify, but it should not distract or detract (some demonstrators talk too much; others don't say enough; allow for possible visual receptive problems).

4. The sequence of events should be reviewed afterwards to make sure that all important aspects were perceived and related to the result or to the principle that is being demonstrated (serial position effect).

5. Ideally, where a principle is involved, several demonstrations should be presented, differing in irrelevant attributes, and also at least one which demonstrates another principle, but which might be mistaken for the one at hand (examples and nonexamples, a la concept teaching).

6. There should be follow-up to the demonstration built into the schedule, i.e., the teacher should discuss it with the students and both ask and answer questions, or there should be small-group discussions with leading questions provided to guide them, or there should be homework or independent study assigned relevant to the demonstration.

The fact than an instructional system is innovative or uses media does not guarantee its acceptance.

Films

Films are seldom designed as systems, but they could be, as well as being used as parts of larger systems. They are one of the most widely used—and abused—methods (or media) in teaching.

The strongest use of films is to demonstrate processes and behaviors and examples of concepts that cannot be presented otherwise, particularly those having to do with historical events.   They can also present famous personalities, and preserve views and scenes that are otherwise lost to us.   When used to present lectures and discussions, there is some question as to their effectiveness.

There is some research to indicate that showing a film twice to the same group rather than once is an effective strategy for learning.   There have also been experiments in which the film has been stopped, with questions asked and discussed before continuing.   In a recent film-based course, the professor ensured learning by

Q ①

giving carefully designed tests before the film was viewed as well as after. These tests alerted students to concepts and processes that they were expected to "watch for," and the outcomes confirmed the value of this approach.

MR. BROWN AND MR. ALLEN SHOW FILMS

Mr. Brown is a heavy user of audiovisual aids in his sociology course, particularly of films. He shows at least one film a week, when he can get one, and he does not always insist that it be on the precise topic being covered. He sits the class down in the projection amphitheater—which he has reserved regularly so that there is no problem in getting it—and after a brief introduction mainly concerned with not making too much noise, he signals for the film to be projected and leaves. The students know pretty well where he is going—to the faculty room for a smoke, although sometimes he drives downtown for a cup of coffee and a donut. Although many of the films are interesting and relevant, and although they are a good break from the regular routine of Mr. Brown's lectures and weak jokes, the class at times wonders whether they are worth it—since the subject matter of the films seldom is discussed in class or referred to on tests. However, the course is not too difficult, Mr. Brown isn't a bad guy, and you have to take something, don't you?

Mr. Allen uses films occasionally in his United States history course. He previews them a day ahead, and then gives a series of questions to be answered from viewing the film, mentions some of the especially interesting or important points or scenes in the film, and relates it to text readings and class discussions. Occasionally, when a film is particularly significant and full of information, he will have the class view it twice. They notice that they see a lot of things the second time that they missed the first. Mr. Allen shows the film with the lights turned partly up so that the students can take notes on various aspects, and then he reviews the film later. Test items are partly based on the films.

Programmed self-instruction

Programmed self-instruction was one of the most promising innovations of the sixties. It is still widely underrated and misunderstood.

Programmed self-instruction is a teaching tool that combines a number of modifiers and motivators: it analyzes what is to be learned into short steps and thus proceeds by successive approximations, as is done in shaping and desensitization (Chapter 8). It requires frequent response by the learner (Chapters 9 and 12), and gives him or her feedback concerning the correctness of that response (Chapter 9). It is developed by trial and error, using one student at a time, and changing tasks that are too difficult or unclear adding steps where progress becomes slow; the altered sequence is tried on another, then revised again, and tried on still another learner. Then it is field tested on groups of learners. Through this process the author makes sure that the level of difficulty is appropriate, and that most if not all learners will be successful in learning if they use it. An example of a programmed sequence is given in Figure 13–1.

Some observers have said that programmed instruction is ideally suited to teaching facts, but it is not appropriate for dealing with concepts or more complex learning. Actually, the opposite is true: programmed instruction lends itself more to teaching concepts and principles and relationships than to basic facts; on the other hand, since facts are relationships between concepts, this statement is somewhat contradictory.

There are several advantages to programmed instruction: learners can move at a pace that reflects their level of understanding and learning speed; the materials are carefully developed so there isn't much confusion; and the teacher is not a necessary adjunct, except at intervals. Disadvantages include negative reactions to programmed materials by students, partly due to the degree of intense concentration that is maintained, partly due to the seemingly oversimplified presentation as compared with conventional textbooks.

$A \cap B = \phi$ states that A and B have nothing (no mass) in common; their intersection is the empty set.

$A \cup B = X$ states that X is the set of all things in both A and B; X is the union of A and B.

2

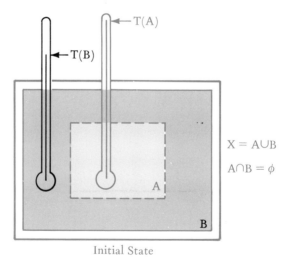

Initial State

The temperature of A is T(A). The temperature of B is ____

T(B)

---

3 How does T(A) compare with T(B) in the initial state pictured above? (use the symbols =, <, or >)

T(A) > T(B) ("$>$" means "is greater than")

---

4 If you observe T(A) at a later time, you will find that it has changed, and thus that System A has changed (since temperature is one aspect or variable related to System A). Can you predict anything else about the data recorded later?

You may have predicted that T(B) changes also, and you are correct if you did.

---

5 You may also have guessed that T(B) will have increased: we agree, but we are not going to discuss the direction of changes yet: for the present, the important thing is that a change in A is accompanied by a change in its surroundings. This implies that changes occur:
(a) one at a time
(b) more than one at a time

(b) more than one at a time—of course we cannot make a general rule from one example, so let us look at other examples where changes occur.

Figure 13–1. *An example of a programmed sequence of tasks designed for use in a chemistry course, as part of an introduction to energy. The learner is supposed to use an opaque sheet of paper or cardboard, and hide the answer from himself (below the statement) until he has completed it. This is not as convenient a method as putting the answer on the next page, as many programmed texts do, but it is much easier and more economical to prepare and publish such a programmed format for groups of learners in a given school or system.*

Computer-assisted instruction

Programmed instruction can be given via computer. Computers can also monitor more complex problem-solving approaches to learning, which were described above. Computers can be programmed to "branch" students to more difficult or easier sequences according to their performance on early parts of the lesson. Computers can also store data on the students' progress and teachers can read this out at any time to determine how individuals or groups are progressing.

There are several models of how the computer can be used to assist instruction. In one the learner is given the computer language to use and is asked to program the computer to solve a simple type of problem. In teaching the computer, i.e., programming it to solve the problem, the learner teaches himself or herself the basic properties of that kind of problem, and comes to understand it more fully. In another mode, the computer presents programmed instruction, as discussed; these programs can be of various types and complexity. In still another mode, the computer is used for drill and practice in basic cognitive skills, i.e., presenting problems, then giving the correct answer.

Among the advantages of computers as teaching tools are the capability of storing information that might be needed by the learner, and the ability to present things sequentially at a controlled pace (controlled by the learner in many instances); they can also furnish a learner with reactions to his or her responses, although these are limited by the ability of programmers to anticipate such reactions and allow for them. Disadvantages include the cost of computer time, the difficulty in making it available to reasonable numbers of students, and the lack of well-developed teaching programs ("software") for the computer. One thing that is sometimes a disadvantage can also be an advantage: the fact that the learner is interacting with a machine may represent a lack of human interaction, but with some emotionally disturbed learners for whom human interaction is a threat, the computer can be a preferable mode of learning.

You might assume that the computer would be limited to teaching basic facts and concepts because of the relative inflexibility of its programming. However, there has been some progress in programming computers to teach problem-solving skills (this process was discussed in Chapter 10). One program, for example, presents a problem in chemical analysis, and then presents data from certain tests that might be made. Although the learner does not actually do the tests in the laboratory, he or she must use the information to reach conclusions concerning the tests and concerning other tests that might or should be done. The answers given by the learner to the computer can be interpreted according to previous experience with this problem, and the computer can suggest to the student that he (or she) is on the right track, or that he is going in the wrong direction, or that he has failed to take one factor into consideration, or some such hint. Thus, the computer can be programmed to guide the problem-solving process; once programmed, it is perhaps less likely than human tutors to give the learner more help than is intended (something which often prevents the learner from deriving as much as he should from the solution process), partly because the computer is more patient.

Computers can present programmed instruction in a more sophisticated, flexible way than texts can. They can also carry on interactive learning processes in a simulated tutorial mode and help manage individualized instruction.

Television

A general comment on the use of television as a teaching medium in schools was made by Frederick Breitenfeld, Jr., in the Commission Report (1970) as follows:

> With few exceptions, television is usually simply imposed on long-established curricula and administrative systems. As such, television becomes an addendum, an adjunct and ultimately an insignificant line item in the school budget. Solid attempts to use the medium effectively for instructional purposes are few.

Television has potential, as do films, for presenting examples of things that cannot be otherwise seen during or in school. It can bring current events into the classroom, and it can bring great teachers into contact with millions of students. As in the case of the program *Sesame Street*, it can develop instructional systems that are sophisticated, appealing, and effective with special groups of children, par-

Television is part of the learning strategy in this chemistry course.

Does television act to decrease the level of education of learners, because they watch it so much, or to increase the level because they see so much more? Is such passive learning effective, or do students need to interact with materials to learn?

ticularly where the many channels available through educational broadcasting and cable-television education allowances make such variety more possible than through commercial television. Also under development are satellite-relayed television programs which, as with cable TV, make possible the production and broadcasting of programs for special audiences rather than large general audiences as with commercial broadcasting.

The advantages and disadvantages of television are much the same as those given for the use of films in teaching. However, the capability of television for live coverage and immediate reporting is obviously somewhat greater. Another application of this facet is to the use of "immediate replays" for teaching athletic skills: showing the learner exactly what he or she is doing immediately following a performance.

Most of the research in television has been concerned with its effects on knowledge, attitudes, and behavior; the indirect influences on the child through the modification of patterns of family life have scarcely been mentioned, let alone investigated.

A field survey found that 78 percent of the respondents indicated that no conversation occurred during TV viewing, except at specified times such as commercials, and 60 percent reported that no activity was engaged in while watching (Maccoby, 1951). Maccoby concluded:

The television atmosphere in most households is one of quiet absorption on the part of family members who are present. The nature of the family social life during a program could be described as "parallel" rather than interactive, and the set does seem quite clearly to dominate family life when it is on (Maccoby, 1951, p. 428).

One criticism of television teaching is that the learner cannot interact. A recent experimental study of learning from TV concluded that older children learned an enumeration task as effectively by simply observing as by performing and receiving corrective feedback. Such was not the case with the younger children, who were only able to perform on the enumeration tasks if they had experienced directed participation as well as vicarious instruction (Swanson and Henderson, 1976).

Since television is primarily a "presentation mode" of teaching, you might also expect that involvement in television teaching/learning processes would be greatest for the learner of high ability, as discussed in Chapter 11. Assuming that older children are more intelligent than younger children, this would be supported by the evidence presented in the paragraph above, also. We need much more research on the actual and potential effects of television on learning, both direct and indirect.

Instructional media can show examples of processes to be learned, but active involvement is also important.

Language laboratories

The history of the language-laboratory movement illustrates the general problem of technology in education, and is given as found in the Commission Report:

> *Language laboratories began to appear at some of the larger universities in the early 1950s. After 1958, when the passage of the National Defense Education Act provided matching funds for the purchase of such equipment, thousands of schools and colleges in every part of the country began to install it. However, there was a serious lack of software. The assumption was that the classroom teacher could write the script in her spare time and record the tapes that would be needed. "The results were sometimes disastrous," Elton Hocking, Professor of Modern Language Education at Purdue University, told the Commission. "Lacking the facilities and techniques for successful recording, the high school teacher produced a soundtrack that was amateurish at best. More important, the materials were often copied from the textbook which never was intended for such use." After a few years . . . the early enthusiasm for language laboratories declined. Interest was reawakened only after the arrival on the market of commercially produced integrated materials which included films and filmstrips along with tapes and textbooks. Although these packages promised to be effective, they were expensive, and many school boards therefore purchased just the book and tape combinations, foregoing the films and filmstrips . . . the teachers . . . found themselves . . . cataloging, book-keeping, ordering supplies, arranging for repairs required as the result of breakdowns or vandalism. Today, after nearly a dozen years of intensive experience, it is clear that language laboratories have realized only a fraction of their educational potential. Moreover, their success is likely to depend to a large extent on comprehensive reforms in the method of teaching languages. The traditional grammar-based method is likely to be changed only over a considerable period of time (Commission, 1970, p. 33).*

You should not conclude that language "lab" approaches are ineffective or without potential, however: only that they have not always been used well.

Games and simulations

Games are involving and motivating, and they also expose the participants to attitudes and feelings related to the simulated situations. The learning of more conventional cognitive relationships from such games has not been very well investigated or documented, and recent evidence suggests that the effects of simulation games on intellectual skills are only moderate at best (Reiser and Gerlach, 1976).

On the other hand, it seems likely that there are types of learning outcomes that can best be brought about through games which involve the learner in situations that are unlike any that he meets in his day-to-day life or in the classroom. One example of such games is called "Diplomacy," where each participant takes the part of a European country in the 1800s, and is given tokens representing military power and economic goods to use in acquiring political power. The object is to gain control of Europe, and the game is played on a map of Europe of that era. The rules of the game are complex, as are the playing processes, and take some time to learn. Once learned, the game teaches players the attitudes of diplomats in positions of power, the problems of diplomacy and power politics, and the problems of strategy in making treaties and the like. Some players have observed (and some complained) that they learned how people in power can come to disregard individual human lives in the pursuit of their objectives. There is also some evidence that players learn concepts of the geography and politics of Europe which carry over into better understanding of the politics of the present, as well as better ability to visualize the various countries of Europe in respect to each other.

While the possibilities for games and simulations are impressive and their potential for teaching effectiveness seems logical, results have not always borne out their promise. One review concluded that "the results of the research conducted with simulation games in education are, for the most part, not very positive. This is especially true with regard to the effects of simulation games in the cognitive domain. Results indicate that [they] rarely have a significant effect on the acquisition of knowledge, and usually do not have a significant effect on intellectual skills. The intellectual skill most likely to be affected by game participation is the ability to play the game. In the affective domain, there is no apparent pattern to the effects simulation games have on feelings of efficacy and attitudes toward the subject matter represented in a game. Studies also have indicated that students are interested in participating in simulation games, but that the simulation games do not necessarily arouse student interest in the subject matter the games represent" (Reiser and Gerlach, 1976).

The teacher as an instructional system

The teacher is a most versatile and adaptable system. Here are some of the roles the teacher can fulfill:

1. Presenter of information
2. Information source for use by students
3. Guide for discussion processes
4. Arranger of learning problems
5. Evaluator of student learning behavior, directly or through design and production of evaluation instruments
6. Guide for independent study
7. Model of interest and enthusiasm
8. Model of inquiry and discovery processes
9. Model of interpersonal processes

10. Model of learning and analytic strategies
11. Producer of instructional systems that have been designed by someone else (carrying out directions, arranging things, etc.)
12. Designer of own instructional systems
13. Tutor in problem-solving processes
14. Guide in respect to remediation for learning disabilities
15. Interpreter of text or other readings
16. Inquisitor regarding understanding of homework and reading assignments
17. Leader of discussion groups
18. Participant in discussion groups
19. Presenter of demonstrations
20. Guide on field trips
21. Diagnostician relevant to learning abilities and disabilities

With the help of auxiliaries, the teacher is beginning to take on the roles of instructional guide and consultant for the individual learner. He (or she) is also being called upon increasingly to implement sophisticated instructional systems, and to have deeper understanding of the structure of his subject so that he can avoid teaching meaningless relationships.

MR. ENRIGHT TEACHES ENERGY

Mr. Enright, the physics teacher, wants to get across to his students the concept of energy in a general way. He realizes that he will have to give them specific examples of energy in order for them to understand the general concept, so he begins to analyze different phenomena from this point of view. One demonstration which he plans has to do with an engine, perhaps an automobile engine; he wants to show how the energy in gasoline is transferred into energy of motion and energy of heat. In order to do this, however, he first wants the students to know about computing the energy of motion—and this requires an understanding of velocity. This in turn involves an understanding of rates, as well as the measurement of time and distance. On the other hand, he wants the students to have some idea of the measurement of temperature and how heat passes from one container or object to another, so he feels that he needs to first demonstrate something about the transfer of heat. Another demonstration he would like to use has to do with the difference between potential energy and kinetic energy, which means he needs to talk about acceleration of some object due to gravity, which in turn means discussing acceleration and gravity. Another thing he wants to show is that if you drop a ball from a height into water or onto something solid, the energy is transferred into the water or solid object in the form of heat—at least, part of it is. He would also like to demonstrate the experiment done originally to measure energy, by turning paddles inside an insulated water-filled container and measuring the increase of temperature. Again some knowledge of temperature, heat, and insulation are needed. Mr. Enright is going to have to decide which concepts to teach or review first, and which next. He is going to have to make a decision as to how much preparatory work to do with the learners before showing demonstrations of energy. He might, for example, give the demonstrations and have them discuss and analyze them afterward, teaching them things they do not already know as it becomes evident they do not know them. On the other hand, he might do a carefully sequenced series of review or prelearning sessions, where he takes up each subconcept in turn—velocity, temperature and heat, acceleration, gravity, and so forth. Then of course he will have to consider which examples of energy (i.e., examples of situations that are made more understandable by the hypothetical construct called "energy") are best given, and whether to present a lot of them at random to be selected and observed by the learners or whether to present them according to a carefully prearranged sequence. He also considers the problem of nonexamples, i.e., situations that do not involve energy or energy transfer. This causes him some puzzlement, because he never thought before of what is *not* energy, and when he starts to consider it, he begins to wonder just what a "nonexample" of energy woud be! (And yet he cannot help but feel that there must *be* such nonexamples, since not everything is energy!)

As he considers these problems, Mr. Enright realizes that there is not much he can go on to help make a decision. On the other hand, he also realizes that in considering these problems and finding some tentative teaching approach (i.e., sequence of learning experiences), he is probably anticipating more of the problems that students will have with the concept than if he had not thought of these problems and tried to solve them at all.

SOME SPECIAL STRATEGIES (SYSTEMS) FOR TEACHING

Mastery learning

Whatever you pick as an evaluation strategy—whether multiple-choice, essay, or take-home exam, paper or project—the task can be done on a mastery basis. This means that the student has the option of taking whatever grade he (or she) receives on his first try, or retaking the exam or rewriting the paper until he does better; perhaps until he gets an A.

Through this mastery approach you can reward effort and maintain standards at the same time. It is possible to achieve understanding and still be graded competetively. The teacher can give high grades without inflating the credit and becoming a "gut" course. However, there is a great deal of work in reevaluating papers or making out and reevaluating new exams.

Individualized, self-paced learning

It is possible, although not always easy to arrange, to have each student proceeding at an individual pace through the use of a variety of materials and sources, i.e., partly independent study. Sometimes this approach stresses the use of programmed self-instruction texts, which are described below. Such an approach

Individualization of instruction, one of the greater goods in education in the 1960s and 1970s, requires careful preparation (as in systems development), greater input of effort, and more complex teaching skills than traditional teaching; it is often more expensive as well.

often implies a need for progress tests that can be given when the individual is ready for them.   These are usually handled on a mastery-basis, as described above.

This approach tailors the course to the individual in terms of pace (though not necessarily in terms of type and difficulty of content); it encourages individual motivation and independence in planning a study program; it allows students to take the time they need for learning each part of the course or unit, and at the same time it allows faster students to go ahead and learn up to their capacities.

Such a self-paced approach is time consuming since it calls for a great deal of preparation and organization on the part of the teacher in order to make the necessary materials and tests available on an individual basis; it also calls for learning skills on the part of the student which may not be developed, and may be hard to learn; it requires additional versions of the tests or frequent reevaluation of papers as in mastery learning; it makes it difficult to use lectures, films, and other group processes, since the students are at different points in the unit or course.

The personalized system of instruction ("PSI") or "Keller Method"

This is a system which combines mastery learning and self-paced learning.   The course material is broken into independent units, each with detailed objectives and study questions.   Each student takes each test when ready; if he (or she) fails, he restudies and retakes the test.   Interaction is between the student and a proctor; the proctor is often a student aide who previously completed the course.   The proctor tutors, and also administers progress tests. Lectures are infrequent and optional.

There is a Center for Personalized Instruction at Georgetown University in Washington, D.C., funded by several foundations.   A how-to-do-it manual by Born is available from College Bookstore, 200 University St., Salt Lake City, Utah.

Contract learning–College level

A student and an advisor draw up a document that specifies what the student will learn in a given period of time, and how.   The contract is distinct from traditional course credits or semester equivalents, and it is evaluated but not graded.   Such contracts may involve learning through a community service (such as experience in a museum) or a social service agency, study at one or more campuses of the University, correspondence study by mail, study in an urban setting with a recognized writer or artist, or other such experiences.   The success of the student in completing his or her contract may be determined by the advisor alone, or by one or more review committees.   Sometimes the contract is broken down into subcategories: among these might be program goals, student objectives, lists of learning experiences, documentation, and a student narrative in which he or she brings together a variety of learning experiences into one statement to give the review board an overall view.

One of the chief problems of contract learning is the evaluation of what the student has learned. In most higher education systems where such nontraditional approaches are used, there is an ongoing debate concerning standards and methods of evaluation. There is also some problem in translating contract learning into credits for admission to graduate schools.

Peer teaching–College level

Peer teaching involves interaction between people with equivalent roles in a system, as compared with the traditional, one-way expert-to-learner communication. Some or all of the students in a peer teaching situation will play the role of teachers. In playing this role the student "learns how to learn," since he or she must analyze the basic structure of a subject and the development of the teaching steps so that he or she can teach it. Taking the teacher role is not easy for many students and they often find themselves imitating negative as well as positive behaviors of their former teachers.

Peer teaching puts great emphasis on communication skills. Students may need special training for it. The "proctor" system of the PSI approach is one version. Students who have previously taken and done well in the course are put in the teacher role. This permits repeated testing, immediate scoring, almost unavoidable tutoring, and a marked enhancement of the personal/social aspect of the educational process. Also in PSI every student goes through the material at a different rate: to complete each unit the student must give evidence of his (or her) mastery in a formal, ten-minute interview. The first student to finish is interviewed by the instructor: each of the other students is interviewed by one of his classmates who has already completed the unit. Before a student can *receive* an interview, he is required to *give* an interview to another student on a unit he has previously completed. The interviewer acts as listener, evaluator, and summarizer. If he rejects an interview as inadequate, he provides suggestions for further study.

An example of the integration of many strategies:
Individually guided education (IGE)

A very sophisticated, large-scale system or model of teaching and learning that is instituted in entire schools (both elementary and middle schools) is called Individually Guided Education, or "IGE." I will not discuss the managerial and administrative aspects of this program, which affect the role of the principal and of individual teachers and give increased responsibility to teachers for dealing with a variety of functions and needs in the school. I will instead focus on the system as it deals with teaching and learning processes, because it is another example of an approach

IGE combines many of the management, motivation, and teaching processes that have been presented previously. Administrative and organizational aspects support these innovations.

that integrates a great number of theories and concepts in its process and relates to management and motivation (Chapter 11) and modifying (Chapter 12). The learning program has many facets, which are summarized in the categories and subcategories below.

1. Learner Outcomes: The skills, understandings, and factual knowledge which pupils will learn are stated in a way that will make it easy to measure student mastery.

2. Assessment of students: (a) Initial placement of each pupil in general level of instruction; (b) Use of pretests to assess student skills to determine specific skills to be mastered; (c) Knowledge of "how" each pupil better learns (which diversified activity?); (d) Post-tests, work samples, and performance as assessment techniques along with usual tests.

3. Diversified learning environment: (a) Varied learning materials: textbooks, workbooks, programmed materials and kits; commercial and/or teacher made audiotapes; overhead projections, filmstrips, 35mm slides, movies; learning centers for interest or skill development relates to learner objective; (b) Modes of learning: large group—balance of teacher and/or pupil led; small-group (3-8) for different purposes; one-to-one tutorial learning; independent; (c) Various learning environments: formal 5 x 5 (rows and chairs); informal arrangements of small groups; exciting atmosphere displays and learning centers; use available areas other than classroom; resource library-media center; community resource, people and places.

4. Grouping and regrouping of pupils: Multi-aged grouping; sharing movement of children between team members; initial placement of pupils based on assessment; schedule of the time that groups will spend on specific activities; regrouping based on continual assessment as appropriate for each individual learner; interest grouping (based on child's interest).

5. Changing role of teacher: Balance between teacher and pupil directedness; skillful as observer in assessing individual learners; regroups frequently after assessment; tries new ideas for instructional techniques that better motivate learners.

6. Individual record-keeping system: Kept for each child on a frequent basis and simple for teacher to manage; based on mastery of learner objectives in curriculum area being individualized; used as a way to report to parents.

7. Pupil outcomes and working together: Analysis of all pupils' achievement in the class of objectives of unit taught; student comments on their reactions to the learning program and how they learned best; information on how the new ideas tried worked out; how the team worked together; sharing ideas—strengths and weaknesses.

In this system, teachers—or teams of teachers—are expected to prepare each day and week of instruction with great care and to incorporate many of the different teaching strategies outlined above.   This preparation is done by carrying out the following steps, which are similar to the fundamental approaches to systems development described previously:

1. State the educational objectives to be attained by the student population of the building in terms of level of achievement and values and action patterns.

2. Estimate the range of objectives that may be attainable for subgroups of the student population.

3. Assess the level of achievement, learning style, and motivation level of each student by use of criterion-referenced tests, observation schedules, or work samples with appropriately-sized subgroups.

4. Set instructional objectives for each child to attain over a short period of time.

5. Plan and implement an instructional program suitable for each student in a preplanned program.   Vary (a) the amount of attention and guidance by the teacher, (b) the amount of time spent in interaction among students, (c) the use of printed materials, audiovisual materials, and direct experiencing of phenomena, (d) the use of space and equipment (media), and (e) the amount of time spent by each student in one-to-one interactions with the teacher or media, independent study, adult- or student-led small group activities, and adult-led group activities.

6. Assess students for attainment of initial objectives.

7. If a student does not attain the objectives, take that student back to the beginning of the sequence above; if he or she does attain them, implement the next sequence in the program.

The system described above is an example of the ways in which various approaches to teaching and learning can be integrated into an overall structure with significant success.   IGE is the outgrowth of applications of theory to practice initiated and directed by Herbert Klausmeier of the University of Wisconsin, an educational psychologist.

MR. O'NEIL OBSERVES OPEN LEARNING, ENGLISH STYLE

Mr. O'Neil is an elementary school principal who has decided to take an educational tour to Great Britain to see what this "open education" is really all about, because he has been asked to provide something of this kind at home. He takes notes as he observes in several schools which use this organizational pattern. His notes look something like this after two or three schools:

- They don't have their own seats—they go from one activity area to another, or from one small group to another, as they choose. Mrs. Rawlins would have a fit!

- There are different corners or tables for sand play, number work, water play, science, music, art. . . .

- In this one the kids can use the whole

school, visit other classes, work and play outdoors when the weather's good; I can see some of our kids going downtown and getting in trouble (or would they?).

- They're talking all the time with each other, and the teacher only comes in when they have questions or when they are obviously confused or getting nowhere.
- These teachers seem to have eyes in the backs of their heads, but then, our good ones do too!
- I wonder if we could get our teachers to leave it up to the child what he or she wants to study or do or participate in, what kind of work—wouldn't they all avoid arithmetic—we'd really get it in the neck from the cooperative achievement tests if they did!
- These teachers will take over and teach directly when necessary, but they hold back most of the time. . . .
- Wow, does this call for a variety of materials and processes—it's tough!

Teaching at a distance

To teach adult learners in their homes and communities, a group of higher educators has put together a system with the following components:

1. A schedule for reading the text (e.g., for covering the four chapters in Part One of this book, if the unit were on "Personal-Social Development").

2. TV broadcasts related to each unit. These broadcasts would go over cable or educational TV, and would consist of demonstrations of certain phenomena or processes described in the chapters, either through existing films and TV programs or through programs that have been produced specifically for that unit.

3. Broadcast notes, giving stills from the film, reviewing it and giving additional relevant information.

4. Possibly some radio broadcasts involving discussions of topics in the unit by practicioners or theorists or other well-known people in the fields.

5. Laboratory-type kits with the necessary equipment and materials for experiments or observations by the learner. For example, there might be equipment and materials (forms, questionnaires, directions) for observing certain types of behavior, or for diagnosing certain types of personality traits, or learning disabilities.

6. Multiple-choice quizzes that the student completes and sends to an evaluation center or to the teacher. These are graded and returned to the students, perhaps with previously prepared (standard) explanations of the questions.

7. Essay-type questions that the student answers and sends in to the teacher or a part-time tutor hired for the purpose, who evaluates them carefully, grades them, puts on extensive helpful comments, and returns them.

The Open University, or the "university of the second chance," was the Labor government's way of helping to make up for years of lack of opportunity for higher education for the people of Great Britain.

The Open University allows for much individualization . . .

8. In some courses a one-week, all day summer session is held in some central
   location, where the students meet and have an intensive residential experience involving discussions, lectures, demonstrations, laboratories, and tutoring.
9. Final examinations which the students take at the end of the course, given in
   some location central to the geographic region for a given group of students.

This approach had been used successfully by the Open University of Great
Britain, and could be adapted to other levels, since some learners would prefer not
to have a residential experience but would rather live and learn at home. Also, some
learners get more out of an independent approach to teaching and learning than
from a traditional lecture-attending and/or discussion mode.

Another example of teaching at a distance is found at Empire State College,
which uses conceptual and cultural frameworks to aid the student in planning his or
her own program, working with an advisor or "mentor." These frameworks or
basic categories of learning include vocational/professional, disciplinary,
problem-oriented, and holistic/thematic. They constitute an innovative classification scheme for human learning and knowledge, and open the way for a more
flexible and relevant organization of the cirriculum. A student is not required to

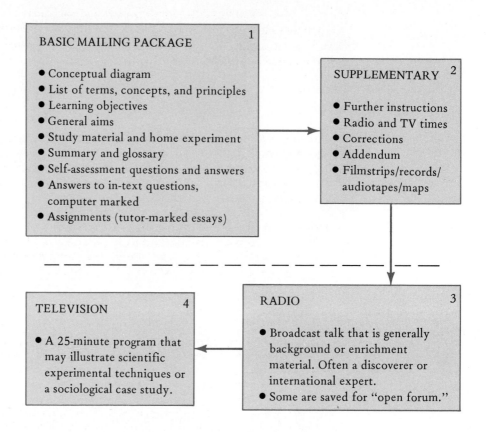

The essence of freedom here is that the open university is *space-free* (nonresidential) and *time-free* (students can complete at their own rates, do not have to conform to on-campus semester and examination schedules).

Important note: Behind the success of the open-university approach is a very carefully designed and carried out instructional-systems development process.

Figure 13–2. *Teaching-at-a-distance as it is organized by the Open University of Great Britain.* (*Reprinted by permission of Dr. George McKiel.*)

satisfy criteria in all of these categories: he or she submits an initial prospectus, which answers a series of questions that require some careful thought to clarify the kind of program that he or she needs personally. Then the student and a "mentor" develop a plan of study which takes into account his or her background, interests, and capabilities. Learning contracts are then developed, typically for two to three months each, with evaluation following each contract, until the student fulfills his or her program.   One feature is awarding credit for past experience relevant to the program; for example, a man who had learned to construct harpsichords as a hobby might be given credit for this toward a degree in music, if a panel of music faculty and professional musicians decided that was appropriate.

Summary outline with key concepts

☞ *Instructional systems* development is an application of systems development used in industry / Analysis of outcomes is the first step / Learner diagnosis is the second step / Reviewing teaching strategies and programming the learning tasks constitute the third step / Assessment/evaluation of outcomes is the final step; when outcomes are stated operationally, however, this is related to the initial step.

☞ *Careful and* thorough systems development is rare in education / Herbart's system is of historical interest / Dewey and Kilpatrick's project method is also part of educational history / Individually prescribed instruction is one of the first modern systems to have thorough development and testing / Some large-scale systems don't work.

☞ *Lecturing is* a traditional but still effective mode of teaching / There are guidelines for the construction of a good lecture / Text presentations will continue to be a basic approach to teaching / Demonstrations are valuable, and there are guidelines for them / Films are valuable but have been abused in teaching / Small-group discussions are an effective strategy for teaching / Programmed instruction teaches concepts and processes well, is less effective in teaching facts / Computer-assisted instruction has valuable uses in teaching / Television has been highly touted for teaching and has had some impact; some of its weaknesses have been overlooked, however / Language laboratories have potential for instruction that has not been exploited / Games and simulations have stirred great interest as teaching processes, but their results have not been well-assessed and their impact is not clear / The teacher is a relatively untapped resource in that she or he is heavily used but not well-used.

☞ *Many strategies* for teaching are not widely used; they include mastery learning, self-pacing, diagnostic-prescriptive teaching (clinical teaching), audio-tutorial approach, personalized instruction (Keller method, or PSI), contract learning, peer teaching, IGE, and teaching at a distance / "Individually-guided education" is the title of a large-scale, complex system primarily for middle schools (or junior high schools) / The Open University of Great Britain is an example of large-scale system development which incorporates traditional textbook production, television teaching, and correspondence learning, in what is being called "teaching at a distance."

Glossary

Advance Organizer: Text passage that prepares learner for more complex reading.

Computer-managed Instruction: Management of individualized instruction by computer.

Hardware: Equipment, machinery, as compared with programs and educational materials (software).

Language Laboratory: Room where large numbers of tape-deck systems are available for students to hear conversations and practice them by recording their own voices and listening to themselves.

Mastery Learning: Learner takes a progress test when ready; if he fails, he restudies and takes it again; also applies to rewriting papers.

Operational Objective: Objective stated in operational terms ("behavioral").

Programmed Instruction: Sequence of learning tasks requiring frequent student response and giving information to the student about the correctness of response.

Proctor System: Peer teaching by students who have just completed the content themselves (and passed a progress test or an oral by an instructor).

PSI: Personalized system of instruction, or "Keller method."

Software: Programs, written learning sequences, directions which make computers operate.

Systems Development: Designing a system, trying it out, revising it, then field-testing it.

Teaching at a Distance: Teaching by correspondence and television and radio, where students learn at home or at work, without attending classes.

Technology: (A) The engineering of teaching, applying theories of learning and instruction to instructional systems; (B) the hardware or machinery of teaching, including film projectors, overhead projectors, tape recorders and such.

Questions for thought and discussion

1. Suppose you want to present some information and teach some concepts; what are the pros and cons of using a lecture, a text presentation, a film, or a demonstration? What combination of approaches would be ideal? Why?

2. How does development of an instructional system differ from regular teaching?

3. Could you use computer-assisted instruction and games and simulations in a diagnostic-prescriptive approach to teaching?

4. Does Herbart's system have anything in common with IGE?

5. Does the project method relate to modern open education? to IPI? to small-group discussions?

6. How would you adapt lecture guidelines for use in fourth grade?

Situations calling for applications of facts and concepts

1. Suppose you are a principal of a middle school, and you want to improve the instructional procedures in that school and bring about more learning and a happier climate as well. What kinds of techniques or systems would you select to introduce or encourage in your school, and how would you get your teachers to support your changes?

2. Suppose you are a parent and you are concerned because your son in Grade Two and your daughter in Grade Seven are not learning as well as you think they ought, considering their abilities. You feel that the teachers are not demanding high enough quality, and that they are trying to go too many directions at once, which results in unprofessional and ill-planned teaching methods. What kinds of teaching strategies and systems would you suggest, and how would you bring them to the attention of other parents and to the principal and the teachers?

3. You are a traditional teacher at the eighth-grade level, and you are asked to adopt a new multimedia instructional system. What reasons would you have for objecting to this proposal? Can you see any reasons for adopting it, considering the extra work that it would entail? What conditions would you set for using it? What might convince you to try it? (Cf. Chapter 12.)

Suggested activites

1. Develop a self-instructional programmed system involving both words and diagrams; follow the steps of instructional development in the process. When you have a trial version ready, try it out on one student, observing her responses, but not interfering except where absolutely necessary. Take notes on difficulties she experiences, for future use in revising the program. Revise it and try it on another learner, and so forth, until you feel it is ready for field trials; then try it on a whole class.

2. Simulate a multimedia system in some subject, for example, government or English literature. Use the schedule given in Chapter 12 as a model, but be creative also. Show it to other students or your instructor and get their reactions as to its practicability.

3. Find a computer-assisted or computer-guided instructional program, learn to use the computer, and then try learning with the use of the program.

4. Find a computer-based simulation game and make arrangements to participate when it is being used; then try designing your own game (without actually programming it) which would utilize the computer in the same way.

5. Consider teaching some topic that you know well, and first state your teaching objectives in operational terms ("behavioral objectives"). State these objectives in such a way that they cover the three domains: affective, behavioral, and cognitive. Then consider your teaching strategies in relation to these objectives; consider how you would teach to achieve the affective and behavioral objectives as well as the traditional cognitive ones.

6. Consider some films in a topic that is familiar to you. Observe the film, then ask yourself how you would use it in a teaching process. What objectives would it achieve? How would it relate to lectures, texts, discussions, and such? How would you determine whether or not they learned anything from it? How would you maximize the benefit from having the film?

Suggested readings

For a traditional overview of media capabilities and techniques as well as some information on instructional development, see Wittich and Schuller, *Instructional technol-*

ogy: Its nature and use (Harper & Row, 1973).   For an approach to systems development of curriculum, see Drumheller, *Handbook of curriculum design for individualized instruction* (Educational Technology Publications, 1971).   For systems development applied to vocational and technical training, see Butler, F. C., *Instructional systems development for vocational and technical training* (Educational Technology Publications, 1972).   For a collection of readings on instructional development, see Merrill, M. David, *Instructional design: Readings* (Prentice-Hall, 1971).   For a treatise on the use of instructional development in industry, see Baker and Schutz, *Instructional product development* (Van Nostrand-Reinhold, 1971).

PART

V

EVALUATION
AND
MEASUREMENT

14

Uses of
Evaluation and
Types of Tests

CONTENTS

ABOUT CHAPTER 14

What this chapter can do for you

You will be familiar with a greater number of types of tests and formats for testing when you have studied this chapter. You will know some of the things to watch out for in developing your own tests, and you will have some basis for reviewing and criticizing published tests. You won't necessarily have changed your opinion of testing and evaluation, but you will have better grounds for using it or not using it, and you will be apt to design or use better tests when you do evaluate. You will have some guidelines for assessing the state of students' learning at any given time, without exposing them to an exhaustive battery of tests. You will also be better able to understand and interpret information about individual students that is made available to you in the form of scores from different kinds of tests: aptitude, intelligence, achievement, personality, creativity, learning disabilities, attitudes, and motivation.

What you may find difficult

You probably don't care too much for testing and evaluation: you have had too much of it in your school experiences. Therefore, you may not want to get into the topic at all. You may have some strong biases about certain kinds of tests, e.g., intelligence tests or personality tests or others. The author has seen otherwise acute and objective students become radical evangelists when writing about intelligence tests. The topic brings out deep emotional reactions that get in the way of clear and convincing arguments. You may then find this topic hard to swallow. On the other hand, you may think it is trivial and not really an important part of teaching; this is worse than being very emotional about it.

Reasons for studying evaluation and testing

Evaluation and testing are in the opinion of the author the most important factors in determining the kind and extent of learning in our schools today: yet they are usually treated as relatively mechanistic necessities of secondary importance to the teacher's knowledge and personality and the learner's motivation. However, your studying behavior and your learning sets and the focus of your efforts are all affected, if not largely determined, by the nature of the quizzes and tests that you are given in a course or area. This may be overestimating the case, although I do not believe so. Nevertheless, there is a significant effect of testing, as you know, and it is important that teachers face this fact and handle their evaluation processes accordingly.

Objectives for this chapter

This chapter is designed to present you with an overview of the uses of tests, the variety of types of tests, and how they function in the general educational scheme. In this way you will begin to see what testing, evaluation, and assessment mean in education, so that you can begin to form your own ideas as to how they can best be used. Hopefully, you will begin to consider the relationships between testing and teaching, and to see testing as an integral part of the teaching process, both short-range and long-range. This may result in less use of tests for the sake of testing, and greater emphasis on tests as a functional part of a learner's process of acquiring knowledge and skills.

TYPES OF EVALUATION

How students regard tests

Students tend to see tests as instruments that are used to classify them and to determine whether or not they have passed or failed. They see testing as a "gate-keeping" function in a society that has too many people for its relatively few positions of prestige, status, and power. Thus, an economy and philosophy of scarcity seems all too often reflected in our use of evaluation. This interferes with instruction, whatever its general importance to society; but it also motivates learning, albeit through avoidance or deficit motives, and this is a continuing paradox.

Students also note that little use is made of the information gathered on tests. In this sense they see them as a form of "intellectualization" on the part of teachers and administrators, i.e., they see that those people act as though labeling a person by a test takes care of the problems that the test reveals. What *are* the valid uses of tests, and how do they relate to teaching?

Evaluation for placement

There are many uses for tests, and test development and sales make up a large industry.

You all have heard of "College Boards" and "Graduate Records," and their relationship to the admission process. You also may have experience with "standardized tests" and their implications for being assigned to different tracks, groups, or levels within a given subject, not to mention their placement in your records. Placement in a "track" or "homogeneous group" is based on the assumption that achievement on a test can predict how well a person will do in the future.

Exams affect students differently.

"Placing" a student in a fast class or in a slow class involves a decision as to whether the student is "suited to" or "prepared for" or "a good risk for" a given class, course, program, or institution.   What it boils down to is a prediction based on available information, of which there are two main kinds: the learner's past achievement (grade-point average, or GPA) and his or her scores on tests.   Generally speaking, past achievement is as good a predictor of success as tests are, if the past achievement is relevant to the future task, e.g., general grade average in high school predicts general grade average in college as well as aptitude tests or achievement tests.

Evaluation for diagnosis

Another use of tests is in diagnosing and prescribing for learning abilities and disabilities.   This was quite common in schools several decades ago, but has fallen out of fashion except in relation to the area of "learning disabilities," which is discussed in Chapters 4 and 12.   Teachers do not use tests for diagnosing individual or class problems as much as they used to.   They tend to use them more now as indications of the general level that their classes are achieving.   It is not uncommon for administrators, as well as parents, to insist on these tests to check on the effectiveness of the teaching process and the school as a whole.   There has also been pressure for using such measures as the basis for salary increases to determine "merit pay."

However, in relation to the teaching process, the use of the information from tests to identify areas where a student or class is ahead or behind (in order to make decisions about teaching) is the most valid and desirable process.

Formative and summative evaluation

When evaluation is used in the process of teaching to identify places where the instructional process is not effective (not to identify which students are failing), then it is called "formative" (Bloom, Hastings, and Madhaus, 1971). When evaluation is used to determine whether or not the learners have achieved the ultimate objectives that have been set up in advance, then it is "summative." Formative evaluation can be used as a basis of remediation of the learners as well, but its main intent is to evaluate the teaching process, not the student. Similarly, summative evaluation indicates the success of the system, not the success of the learner, although again the desirability of reteaching the student can be deduced also. Summative evaluation can be used for predicting future success and for placement, as well as for diagnosis of the system and remediation of individual students. One implication of the use of these two terms is that instructional developers and teachers both should employ evaluation along the way ("formative" evaluation) more frequently than they do, and they should make better use of the information gained, both in respect to helping the student and in respect to revising the system.

Norm-referencing and criterion-referencing

Tests result in scores, but such scores are meaningless until they are compared or "referenced" with other scores. For example, suppose you give a spelling test and Mary gets nine out of ten items correct. You might conclude that she deserves an A because her score is 90 percent; however, if Mary is in high school and the words on the test include such toughies as "but," "the," and "for," then perhaps she should be flunked for missing one of them! Her score of nine is only meaningful if you compare it with scores of other high school and elementary students. Suppose a group of sixth graders score nine, on the average; then you could say that Mary is at the sixth-grade level in spelling. However, that wouldn't be fair either, because the test doesn't allow Mary to show what she is capable of. A group of high school students would probably average nine also; their mistakes might be due to careless errors or poor penmanship.

It is not good to "teach to the test," but it is equally poor organization to test things that you don't teach; referencing criteria to teaching helps with this problem.

Comparing a learner's score on a test to the average score for other learners at various levels (or of various ages instead) is called "norm-referencing." A norm is an average for a certain group; the "norm" for ninth graders would be the average score for a representative sample of ninth-grade learners. (You will find more about this in Chapter 15.)

Now consider a different kind of comparison. Suppose each word on the spelling test was an example of a different kind of spelling problem; for example, one word might be "yield," which would represent the group of words that can be spelled by using the rule, "i before e except after c"; another word might be "fought," which represents a group of words ending in "ought" that are not spelled like "cot" or "hot." This would be a "criterion-referenced test," where each item (or group of items) on the test is designed to evaluate the learner's achievement in relation to a specific objective of teaching. Each objective can be represented by an operational criterion such as "spells correctly words in which i precedes e, such as "yield" and "field." A similar criterion in French might be "translates English sentences correctly using the subjunctive." In physics, it might be "solves problems in which acceleration and time are given, and distance is to be computed."

Thus norm-referenced tests report scores as they relate to some average, and criterion-referenced test scores are related to the goals of teaching.

Validation

In validation, the final level of the learners after teaching is given by using two figures, one for the percentage of tasks completed correctly on the test, and the other for the percentage of students who have reached that level. For example, "80/70" would mean that 80 percent of the learners attained a score of 70 percent or better on the test. Another related concept is that of the "gain score," which involves the change in score from pretest to posttest, and thus the learning attained. If a learner gets thirty on a pretest and ninety in the same test used as a posttest, then his gain score is sixty.

Evaluation for assessment

In addition to using tests as part of teaching, and for selection and placement, there is another use which is often called "assessment."* This is designed to measure the overall outcomes of instruction in courses, programs, and schools, and to compare them with outcomes from other such courses, programs, or schools, and to establish levels of educational results for geographical areas and for the whole country. A battery of tests is agreed upon in advance, and then a sample of schools or courses is chosen which is representative of the area, or of the country as a whole. Parts of the battery are given to one school, and other parts to another, in a given area. Within the schools, part of the battery is given to one group of students and another part to another group; thus no one student has to take the entire battery, and no one school has to, either. When all the results have been collected, a composite score is made that represents overall achievement on all the tests of the battery.

You can assess educational outcomes without evaluating any one student or teacher or school; this is being done on a national basis.

---

* Assessment is also used generally to refer to testing and evaluation of a more conventional kind.

The Sphynx had only one quiz and devoured students who failed. When finally someone passed, she killed herself.

However, since no one individual or school has used the entire set of tests in the battery, no one person, school, or system can be singled out and pointed to as higher or lower than the others.

A national assessment of this kind has been in progress since 1969. Among the findings so far are the following:

- Most students are stronger in biological sciences than physical sciences.
- The percentage of rural students who could answer a typical science question increased in the second assessment. (There had been two assessments by 1976, when this information was reported.)
- Science knowledge among American students generally is declining!
- Science achievement in the south did not decline as much as it did in the rest of the nation for either black or white students. The science knowledge of nine-year-old southern black students actually improved!
- Essays written by three different age levels showed that the mechanics of writing did not decline but stayed at the same level during the four years between assessments.
- Overall writing scores declined somewhat; there was a movement toward writing styles used by newspapers, TV, and the advertising field.
- Functional literacy of in-school seventeen year olds improved, especially among students living in inner-city areas.
- Only 1 percent of seventeen year olds and 16 percent of adults could correctly balance a checkbook.

- At all ages, males do better than females on word problems in mathematics, while females tend to do better in "pure" math computation; males do better in exercises dealing with household and buying situations.
- Children whose parents have no high school education performed 8 to 13 percent below the national average.

The ten learning areas now being surveyed in the national assessment include art, career and occupational development, citizenship, literature, mathematics, music, reading, science, social studies, and writing. Further results are released as they are compiled (Forbes, 1976).

During the middle 1970s a trend in achievement test scores across the country elicited a great deal of discussion and debate. The trend was a decline in the scores of college bound high school seniors on the Scholastic Aptitude Tests and the American College Testing Program tests. Also, females fell below males on the verbal aptitude test for the first time. High school juniors showed a similar drop in scores on the Minnesota Scholastic Aptitude Test (MSAT) and the Iowa Tests of Education Development (ITED), although not on the Preliminary Scholastic Aptitude Test (PSAT). The Comprehensive Tests of Basic Skills (CTBS) and the Iowa Tests of Basic Skills (ITBS) showed declines for levels down to the fifth grade. The National Assessment (NAE) showed declines in science as was mentioned, but increases for reading and literacy. Finally, intelligence test scores of preschool children, ten year olds, and adolescents showed that in 1972 all three ages were higher than their counterparts in the early 1930s—but three years later, scores of children at these same age levels had declined an average of three points. One source has attributed the decline to a number of factors, among them:

1. Public reluctance to increase or maintain resource-flows into education in the face of diminished enrollments;
2. The so-called affluent society in which the pressure for grades and a college education has been reduced, particularly in the face of difficulties experienced by college graduates and advanced degree holders in getting jobs appropriate to their educational level (Harnischfeger and Wiley, 1976).

In the late 1970s there seems to be a reactionary movement toward increased emphasis on fundamentals—reading, writing, arithmetic—which may also tend to reverse this trend or at least stabilize achievement test levels.

COMPETENCY-BASED AND PERFORMANCE-BASED EDUCATION

Rationale for competency-based education

Education has been under fire for being irrelevant to modern society, for teaching in ways that do not result in retention of useful knowledge, and for teaching ab-

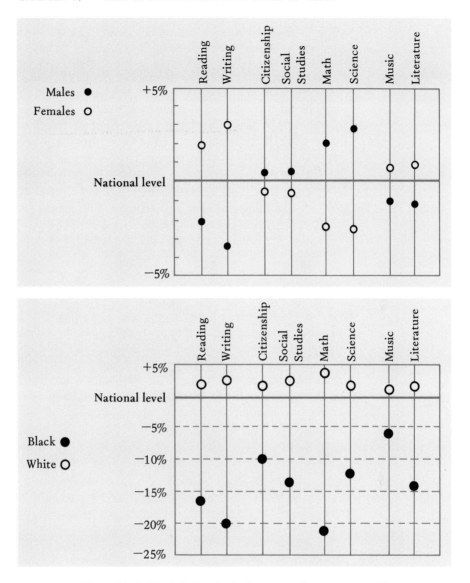

Figure 14–1. *Typical educational achievement of seventeen-year olds by sex and race. (Used with permission of the National Assessment of Educational Progress, a project of the Education Commission of the States.)*

stractions that cannot be translated into applications and actions. Some of this criticism reflects a lack of understanding of the role of education in our society, but some of it is much more valid than many educators like to admit. There seem to be three main roots to the problem: one is teaching things that are not relevant or applicable, another is failing to evaluate adequately or to make the teaching correspond to what is evaluated, and another is failing to translate abstractions into concrete realizations so that students learn to apply the theoretical structures that they learn.

One partial solution to this problem is what is being called "competency-based" or "performance-based" education; when applied to teaching, it sometimes takes on the name "criterion-referenced" teaching. The basic process here is one of specifying or identifying the outcomes of the teaching/learning process in terms of the tasks that learners are asked to do for showing they have learned, i.e., in terms of tests or evaluative processes.

By specifying the outcomes of teaching in terms of specific, observable tasks and behaviors of the learner, you avoid (or at least reduce) the amount of teaching that is unrelated to what the student is expected to be able to do. This has advantages and disadvantages. Its advantages lie in the greater efficiency of the learning process: the student does not spend a great deal of time reading and relating and solving and generally studying where that time does not pay off in actual required performance. Its disadvantages lie in the limitations this imposes on the teaching process; if the teaching is "tied" to the test, which can only cover so much, there is a danger that teachers will get the wrong idea, and teach only what is on the test. Now, the test is only a *sample* of what is to be learned. This approach to education implies that the sample should be valid—not that the sample should be the entire amount of what is taught.

Competency-based or performance-based teaching improves the relevance of the educational process indirectly, by making very apparent what is being taught and bringing it out in the open for inspection, discussion, and criticism. However, one can have a competency based on performance-based teaching system in how to kill crocodiles, and teach it to Eskimos!

Table 14–1. *Pros and cons of using objectives (adapted from Good, Biddle, and Brophy, 1975).*

Advantage of objectives

They increase the teacher's awareness of what the learner should be working toward, and result in better planning.
They provide a basis for assessing continuing progress.
Students have a better idea of what they are about, and learn more.
When used to facilitate individualized instruction, they help learners find time to work on their own projects (after reaching basic goals).

Disadvantages

Having objectives may result in greater teacher control, less student freedom in learning and less student control over goals and pace.
Objectives are likely to over emphasize things that are easy to measure, and neglect important abilities and knowledges that are hard to measure.
Once established, objectives tend to become rigid and constraining.
Teacher time used in creating objectives might be used better in other ways.

In practice, the competencies or performances are specified operationally in terms of the actual behaviors and skills and abilities that the learner is supposed to demonstrate after the learning. This relates to "operational objectives" or "behavioral objectives" discussed previously.

EVALUATING AFFECTIVE OUTCOMES: EMOTIONS AND ATTITUDES

Background

Every teacher has seen students solve a problem or write a good report on some topic and then say that they do not "understand" what they have done. Understanding is partly a feeling of familiarity and confidence with concepts, processes, or skills. The fact that a learner can carry out tasks or solve problems does not guarantee that he or she feels confident about doing so.

Another aspect of "understanding" is related to what is called "empathy," the ability to experience vicariously the feelings and behaviors of others. Thus if you "understand" how a person feels who has just had an operation, or just failed an examination, or just won an athletic trophy, it means you can "put yourself in the other's shoes," and feel as he or she feels.

Diagnosing or assessing such feelings involves unique problems of measurement. Most tests in this domain sample your responses to questionnaires, but some get you to write stories about certain situations and then analyze what you write ("projective" tests). It is somewhat risky to believe or take at face value someone's report of their feelings or attitudes. They may be too threatened to give an honest response, they may not be too sure what their feeling or attitude is, or their feelings may change tomorrow. People tend to respond generally in the manner that they feel the tester or evaluator wants, or in the way that they feel is proper. No one wants to look bad. This is especially true in any face-to-face kind of evaluation. It is also known that those who complete these affective scales or measures have a tendency to be set in their manner of responding; thus they may subconsciously check "agree" spaces, or they may habitually put an "x" on the right hand side of the scale. These are forms of what psychometricians (testing experts) call "response bias" or "set," and designers of such tests have to take this kind of responding into account as they develop the test for general use.

> We talk about objectives such as "appreciation" but we seldom test for them; however, attitudes and feelings *can* be measured.

Attitude, opinion and interest questionnaires

Certain tests are designed to sample peoples' attitudes, interests, and opinions by asking questions with different degrees of "face validity." This refers to the degree to which a test item looks as if it measures what it is supposed to measure. For example, an item with high face validity would be the following:

Engineering is a profession that is interesting and challenging.

Strongly Disagree   Disagree   Neutral   Agree   Strongly Agree

An item with lower face validity, also designed to test interest in engineering, might be as follows:

When one sees a bridge he is struck by the beauty of the form and at the same time the strength and practicality of the structure.

Strongly Disagree   Disagree   Neutral   Agree   Strongly Agree

The second is not as direct or obvious as the first; it might be just as appropriate on a test of interest in aesthetics, or it might not. What determines its validity is whether or not it has been found to discriminate between those who are interested in engineering and those who are not, which is only determined by trying the items out on both types of people and observing their comparative responses. The following item has no face validity in respect to engineering. However, it is conceivable that it might discriminate between engineers and nonengineers, nevertheless:

The sight of a rusted motor on a junk pile is a very terrible thing.

Strongly Disagree   Disagree   Neutral   Agree   Strongly Agree

One type of attitude or opinion that has not received much attention, but which is quite important in teaching, is the attitude of the teacher toward herself or himself. This is sometimes referred to as the teacher's "self-concept." A questionnaire can be used to determine this. A sample question that might be used is:

YOURSELF AS A TEACHER

Knows If Students Are Trying   Does Not Know Whether
                                                        Students Are Trying

5   4   3   2   1

There would, of course, be many other two-ended scales like this, dealing with such things as motivating the students, making students feel secure, making the class interesting, and the like. Of course, this differs from the teacher evaluation by students in that here the student's attitudes and the teacher's performance are judged by the teacher, in relation to himself or herself.

A similar type of questionnaire can be given to students to determine their attitudes toward college or high school, toward other students, toward teachers, and so forth.   An item from such a questionnaire could look like this:

MY SCHOOL

Rate your school on the basis of the following dimensions.

Authoritarian   5   4   3   2   1   *Democratic*

Under the same heading, and thus in respect to the same thing, namely, the school, would be many other scales (called "bipolar adjectives"), like warm-cold, interesting-dull, conservative-liberal.   Tests like these can be used to compare student attitudes in one school with those in another, or changes from one year to another.

Tests of anxiety

Another area related to emotions is anxiety.   This was discussed in Part One, in relation to interindividual differences.   An anxiety questionnaire might have items such as the following:

When I view a film, I wonder whether other students will understand it better than I, and this worries me:

Never   Sometimes   Always

Obviously if a learner or a group of learners has high anxiety, a teacher will want to do something about relieving it so that it does not interfere with productive learning experiences.

Creativity tests

In Chapter 3 creativity was defined, one type of test task for creativity was described, and comparisons were made between creativity and intelligence.   It was pointed out then that tests used in school, and school teaching and learning generally, have emphasized the kinds of thinking that are referred to as "convergent," i.e., they converge upon one or a few correct answers.   "Divergent" thinking, which comes up with alternative hypotheses and new ways of looking at things, has

"Divergent thinking" highlights learners' unique responses.

not been encouraged by traditional education to the same degree, and yet it is an important part of thinking and is crucial to problem solving and creating things. Tests have been developed to identify creativity, and one type of problem found on such tests is the following:

This is a brick.   Give as many possible uses for this brick as you can in the time given you. These uses must be appropriate, but at the same time uniqueness is desired.

The scoring is done on the basis of both uniqueness of the response and number of unusual responses given, as long as they are reasonably appropriate and not entirely ridiculous.

AN EXPERIMENT BACKFIRES

Mrs. Robinson is coordinating an experimental program for college freshmen in which the students are able to choose their areas of study and how they are to study them (they do not have to go to any classes if they do not want to), and which will show their ability to master these areas by passing a comprehensive examination when they feel they are ready for it. In order to know something about the motivations of the students who volunteer for this experimental program and to compare them with students in the "regular" program, she decides to administer a battery of tests to the students in both programs. One of these is a questionnaire that samples general opinions, attitudes, and interests. Another is a questionnaire that samples their feelings about themselves and such aspects of personality as anxiety, need for achievement, and need for affiliation. Still another test is a general survey of their level of being informed, i.e., a general knowledge test related to world events, cultural things, and salient aspects of society such as economy, history, and such. Another test, which is given later in the semester, has to do with their attitudes toward the college, toward other students, and toward the faculty and administration.

Some of the comparisons that emerge from the data from these tests are interesting and surprising. For one thing, the students who volunteer for this experimental program are somewhat above the average of the other students in their general information level, their college board scores, and their confidence in themselves. Their interests are somewhat more broad and altruistic, and less oriented toward specific professions; however, the variation among the experimental group is greater than among the others, so the experimental group has more extremes of interests and attitudes. One surprising and dismaying fact that also emerges from the data from the questionnaire on their attitudes toward the college and faculty, as well as on their anxieties, is evidently related to the effects of the experimental program, since it is from tests given after the semester is well underway. The experimental students are much more anxious than the others, have a more negative attitude toward faculty and administration, and feel that college is a less-secure and encouraging place than the other students do. This is most disturbing to Mrs. Robinson because the experimental program was designed to make the students more at home, more at ease with faculty and administration, and less anxious and more secure by giving them the freedom that they need to pursue their particular interests. It seems, however, that this freedom has only made them very "uptight," that they are working more hours than other students, attending more lectures, reading more books, and having less fun. It begins to appear that the conventional program protects students against these things, by structuring their learning for them—even though they generally object to the structure and rebel against it.

Instruments for studying personality in children

People who counsel children and their parents use instruments developed to give insight into the personalities of those children; however, you will not necessarily find direct relationships between current theories (such as those discussed in this chapter) and the aspects of development and personality reported by such tests.

For example, the *Children's Personality Questionnaire* of the Institute for Personality and Ability Testing is for children between the ages of eight and twelve. A sample item from the CPQ 1975 edition is given in Table 14-2 along with some of the personality "factors" on which the child is scored.

Table 14–2. *Sample personality factors.*

Reserved, detached, critical	vs.	Warmhearted, outgoing, easy-going.
Obedient, mild, accommodating	vs.	Assertive, aggressive, competitive
Uncontrolled, lax, follows own urges	vs.	Controlled, socially precise, follows self-image.

Sample Item

1. Would you rather read a book ☐ or ☐ play a game.
   If you would rather read a book, you would fill in the box to the left, next to that answer. If you would rather play a game, you would fill in the other box on the right side next to that answer. There is no right or wrong answer, because people like to do different things.

From the *Children's Personality Questionnaire*, 1975 edition, Institute for Personality and Ability Testing.

EVALUATING COGNITIVE OUTCOMES OF TEACHING

Knowledge

We seldom consider carefully the *kinds* of understanding that we want, or that we teach for—yet the way we test shapes the kind of learning we get!

Some items on a test, or even whole tests, evaluate the knowledge of the learner. Knowledge is a sophisticated form of paired-associate learning, in which either the stimulus, the response, or both are somewhat more extensive and complex than is typical in general paired-associate experiments. Yet the cognitive relationship is of the same order. The stimulus is aimed at "calling up" a specific response. For example, consider the following item:

Which of the choices below best represents an example of the concept of validity?

1. The test gives the same results each time it is given to the same group;
2. The test contains medium-difficulty items, which yield a normal curve;
3. The test has a representative sample of the concepts taught in the period covered.

Number 3 is correct, as you will find in Chapter 15. Thus, knowledge as we use it here relates to the ability to recall or bring forth factual material almost directly from memory due to earlier learned associations of the subject under consideration.

Interpretation and extrapolation

Interpretation and extrapolation involve starting with a certain amount of information and developing additional conclusions and implications. In a sense it is the recognition of an old, learned concept in a new setting, or the creating of exemplars of it. In another sense it involves following one or more logical chains or processes suggested by the information presented. The information represents an environment in which a number of different concepts can be assimilated by the learner, as in problem solving. To the extent that the learner takes a number of elements of the situation and synthesizes them into one conclusion, this is convergent thinking; to the extent that he or she sees a number of different possibilities, it is divergent or creative thinking.

Application

Application is a mediating process that resembles the interpreting and extrapolating process above, but that also requires the student to provide the data for that interpretation and extrapolation from his or her own information. Thus, he or she is not given much initial information. The information is assessed, obtained, or described through the title of a principle or generalization, i.e., the title of a concept or process that is based on experience with phenomena of a certain type. For example, you might be asked to apply the process of "shaping" to a behavior problem in an elementary school classroom, or to the problem of a retarded boy who cannot put on his shoes and socks. This would require you to describe the reinforcing process you would use, what initial responses you would reinforce, and how you would reinforce differentially as the learning progressed. An example of a multiple-choice question that requires extensive application of facts and concepts is given on page 546.

Analysis

This is a process in which examples of concepts, principles, or relationships are identified in the context of a situation or in a quotation. An example would be found where you are given the responses of a student to a series of examples and nonexamples of a concept, and you have to determine whether a learner understands the concept: whether she is generalizing correctly, whether she is undergeneralizing, overgeneralizing, or both. Take the examples given below, along with the responses of a mythical learner to them, and analyze her understanding.

Example	Learner's response
1. A baseball is pitched and passes over the plate andbetween the batter's knees and shoulders, without his swinging at it.	Strike

2. A baseball is pitched and it passes outside the plate; the batter   Strike
   swings and misses.
3. A baseball is pitched and goes outside the strike zone; the batter   Not a strike
   begins to swing but checks his swing before his wrists "break."
4. A baseball is pitched and the batter hits it to the left or third   Not a strike
   base.

Your analysis task is to determine whether the learner has the concept of "strike" or
not, and if not, what is wrong with his concept. In (1) he responds correctly, but
in (2) he undergeneralizes, in (3) he overgeneralizes, and in (4) he undergeneralizes again. If this were part of a multiple-choice question calling for analysis, you
would respond by checking the alternative which said that he did not understand
the concept, or that he only understood it partly. If one of the alternatives said it
was a misconception, you would check that instead, since this would be the technical term that applied best to his particular type of partial understanding.

Synthesis

Synthesis is a process in which the learner is asked to take a set of facts or relationships, or some body of information, and produce from it a unique point of view, a
plan, or a set of abstract relations. The example below is taken from a book by
Bloom, Hastings, and Madaus entitled *Handbook of formative and summative evaluation of student learning*:

> *The experiments described below have actually been performed, with the results which
> are given. They are basic to the theories which have been proposed to account for the
> manner in which cells accomplish chemical transformations which either do not occur
> spontaneously or which occur spontaneously at extremely slow rates.*
>
> *In answering the questions following these experiments, you are to use the evi-
> dence given by the experiments themselves, interpreting these as nearly as possible in the
> terms considered appropriate by cell physiologsts such as Potter and Dixon.*
>
> *To understand the methods employed in these experiments, you will need the follow-
> ing preliminary information.* *

> **Information:** *Methylene blue is a synthetic dye whose blue color disappears when
> its solution is treated with a mild reducing agent. Hydrogen gas itself does not decol-
> orize methylene blue solution. When reduced methylene blue solution is shaken with
> air or oxygen gas, the solution absorbs oxygen and becomes blue again. The absorbed
> oxygen has combined with hydrogen from the reduced methylene blue to form water.
> Thus, methylene blue can act as a hydrogen acceptor in some cases, and, after having
> received the hydrogen, can yield it to oxygen to form water.*

---

* From Bloom, Hastings, and Madaus, *Handbook on formative and summative evaluation of student
learning*, p. 203. Copyright © 1971. Used with permission of McGraw-Hill Book Company.

No 11: *Many of the necessary technical details in these experiments have been omitted from the descriptions. One such detail is that the mixtures for the experiments are made up with neutral buffer substances which keep the mixtures neutral even though an acid or a base is added in reasonable amounts.*

Experiment A: *Methylene blue solution was placed in a closed flask filled with helium, an inert gas. Lactic acid solution was added to the mixture without opening the flask. No color change was observed. Analysis of a sample showed that the lactic acid was still present.*

Experiment B: *A living frog was decapitated. One of its larger leg muscles was finely chopped, washed in several changes of physiological salt solution. The washed muscle was mixed with a methylene blue solution in helium gas as in A. No color change was observed.*

Experiment C: *The mixture from A was added to the flask in B. The blue color disappeared and analysis showed much less lactic acid than had been used in A.*

Experiment D: *When a similar muscle was heated to the boiling temperature before chopping, no change occurred and no lactic acid disappeared, in a test situation such as in C.*

1. *What kind of atoms were probably added to or removed from the lactic acid?*
2. *Use your knowledge of living tissues to invent an explanation for the difference between the results in A, B, C, and D.*

Evaluation as a form of cognitive understanding

Another form of relating existing concepts or principles to a body of information is called "evaluation." An example of an evaluative item is given below.

Write an essay on The Bewitched Mill *(1913), an oil painting by the 20th century German artist Franz Marc (1880–1916), in which you express your own critical evaluation of the picture, supporting your evaluation by specific discussion of the work. During the course of your essay indicate the criteria you have used in your judgments, and reveal the assumptions about art on which your views are based. You may, if you wish, refer to various authors whose works have been studied in the course: this should be undertaken only as a natural and connected part of your essay and should not appear as a parade of knowledge or authority. These references should not be a substitute for the exposition of your own views, since your essay must stand by itself.*

(Bloom, Hastings, and Madaus, Handbook 1971, p. 222. Used with permission of McGraw-Hill Book Company).

Relationship of these cognitive outcomes to learning and teaching processes

The categories of cognitive outcomes that have been described in this section are derived from a taxonomy of educational objectives that is not directly comparable or related to the kinds of learning and strategies of teaching described in previous chapters (Chapters 8 through 10, Chapters 11 and 12). These taxonomies (Bloom, 1956; Krathwohl et al., 1964) have been proposed as organizing structures for simplifying the language of education. The task of integrating these objectives' classifications with classifications of kinds of learning and kinds of "modifiers" mentioned previously, then, is one which remains to be accomplished. This is not presented as a criticism of the field, but rather a statement of our present condition. It is, however, somewhat confusing when you try to relate "problem solving" as discussed in Chapter 10 with the categories "interpretation/extrapolation," "analysis," and "synthesis" mentioned here; assumedly the last two are incorporated into the complex processes of the first. It would also be interesting to compare "interpretation/extrapolation" and "synthesis" here with the concept of "creativity" and the measurement of that ability, discussed in Chapter 3 and previously in this chapter; also to relate "analysis" to the area of concept identification and learning discussed in Chapter 9 and again in Chapter 12. You should not be surprised, however, by the fact that there is much in the way of analysis, synthesis, and application to be done in this field of educational psychology!

SOME SUGGESTIONS FOR MAKING YOUR OWN TEST

Guidelines

Of course it is not possible to show you how to make a test in a book such as this, but you can get some general ideas about the process to keep in mind. The following guidelines are based on a pamphlet entitled *Making the classroom test,* published by the Evaluation and Advisory Service of Educational Testing Service (1959a).

The kind of test you give determines what students learn to learn: it has to be valid (cover the material you taught), it has to be of reasonable difficulty, and it should be free of tricks and clues which give answers away.

1. Consider carefully what you want the test to do—assess how well your students have learned, rank them according to their achievement, or diagnose their strengths and weaknesses? These purposes do not determine completely different types of tests, but your content and type of question would differ somewhat from purpose to purpose.

2. Make a plan for your test questions, by listing the topics and subtopics that you have covered, and the important aspects of each that you wish to test for, and then be sure that you have items which relate to each of them, and that you do not write too many items for one topic and too few or none for another. Without such a plan, your test is very likely to be unbalanced.

3. If you want to diagnose strengths and weaknesses, and you have several topics or areas in which you want to make this diagnosis, you should have a good number of questions in each topic or area, rather than one or two, so that you get a good sample of what the learners know in these areas.

4. If you are trying to find out how well your students have learned a particular topic, area, or unit, you should be sure that the test touches on all aspects of it, and that the items are of medium difficulty so that each student can show what he has learned on the test.

5. If your purpose is to rank your students on their understanding of the topic or unit, then the questions should go beyond the medium-difficulty level, and should concentrate on critical aspects of the concepts and facts and should require applications of knowledge, reorganization of the data, and such advanced expressions of understanding.

Table 14-3 can guide you in constructing essay and objective tests. It compares the scope, abilities measured, ease of preparation, scoring, and what incentives are offered to pupils in the two formats. The grid in Figure 14-2 suggests ways to analyze subject-matter tasks.

Item Pools

One very helpful procedure for constructing valid and useful tests is the acquiring of a collection, or "pool," of test items. It helps to have a plan or blueprint for the test first that outlines the specifications for the questions to be collected. It will describe the objectives of the course or program to be evaluated. This may be done on a two-dimensional table, with one axis containing subject matter and the other containing behaviors to be evaluated. Each combination of subject matter and behaviors should then be given a "weight," which is a number that represents its relative importance in the overall set of objectives. This makes it possible for several teachers to cooperate in building a test, since they share the work, each filling several "cells" on the grid, i.e., intersections of objectives and behaviors. Once items are designed, they should be evaluated by each member of the group and rated as to their desirability. Each item can then be accepted or rejected, and if accepted can be given a code title indicating the subject matter, type of behavior, content topic, and perhaps also the textbook or unit for which it is designed.

Such item pools, if well-designed and coded for use, could be made available to school systems or regions or stored in a computer memory for access by various teachers and schools. Through such a scheme, the mechanical and electronic analysis of test data and items could be made very simply and quickly. The computer could score the tests thus made up and used, and return to the teacher and students individual student cards that indicate which items a student got right and which wrong, his score for each subtest and for the total test, information for the teacher about the difficulty of each item, a reliability score for the test based on data from these students, a standard error of measurement (to be described) and the mean and standard deviation and other descriptive statistics (also to be described).

Table 14–3. *Making the classroom test—a guide for teachers.*

	Essay	Objective
ABILITIES MEASURED	Requires the student to express himself in his own words, using information from his own background and knowledge. Can tap high levels of reasoning such as required in inference, organization of ideas, comparison and contrast. Does not measure purely factual information efficiently.	Requires the student to select correct answers from given options, or to supply an answer limited to one word or phrase. Can also tap high levels of reasoning such as required in inference, organization of ideas, comparison and contrast. Measures knowledge of facts efficiently.
SCOPE	Covers only a limited field of knowledge in any one test. Essay questions take so long to answer that relatively few can be answered in a given period of time. Also, the student who is especially fluent can often avoid discussing points of which he is unsure.	Covers a broad field of knowledge in one test. Since objective questions may be answered quickly, one test may contain many questions. A broad coverage helps provide reliable measurement.
INCENTIVE TO PUPILS	Encourages pupils to learn how to organize their own ideas and express them effectively.	Encourages pupils to build up a broad background of knowledge and abilities.
EASE OF PREPARATION	Requires writing only a few questions for a test. Tasks must be clearly defined, general enough to offer some leeway, specific enough to set limits.	Requires writing many questions for a test. Wording must avoid ambiguities and "giveaways." Distractors should embody most likely misconceptions.
SCORING	Usually very time-consuming to score. Permits teachers to comment directly on the reasoning processes of individual pupils. However, an answer may be scored differently by different teachers or by the same teacher at different times.	Can be scored quickly. Answer generally scored only right or wrong, but scoring is very accurate and consistent.

From *Making the classroom test: A guide for teachers.* Copyright © 1959 by Educational Testing Service. All rights reserved. Reprinted by permission.

NTE
Biology and general science
Item distribution

ABILITIES

SUBJECT MATTER

Subject Matter	Understanding of basic scientific concepts and principles	Ability to distinguish basic concepts from those which are irrelevant or inappropriate	Ability to anticipate and diagnose concepts likely to prove easy or difficult for students	Ability to select and devise appropriate demonstrations for effective teaching	Ability to recognize and utilize appropriate sources of information	Ability to give a lucid explanation of scientific concepts and principles	Ability to apply scientific concepts and principles to every-day experience	Ability to evaluate student learning	Ability to stimulate and guide the individual student	TOTAL
Chemistry										
Physics										
Astronomy										
Geology										
Meteorology										
Histology										
Botany										
Zoology										
Human anatomy and physiology										
Biology and human welfare										
Ecology										
Heredity and evolution										
TOTAL										

Figure 14–2. A grid for assisting in the development of a science test battery outlining things to be covered. (From Mult ple-choice questions: A close look. Copyright © 1959 by Educational Testing Service. All rights reserved. Reprinted by permission.)

TEST FORMATS AND TYPES

Objective versus subjective tests

Tests are sometimes classified as *objective* or *subjective* (nonobjective). Objective tests are designed so that the responses of the learners can be evaluated by someone who does not know anything about the content of the test, or by a machine. In a multiple-choice test, for example, the student circles one of four or five letters that represent the alternatives; a machine can be programmed to recognize the correct alternative by the letter that represents it. The advantages of this system are enormous when large numbers of students are involved. You cannot appreciate the advantages unless you have spent time correcting a test taken by thirty or more students, either multiple-choice, essay, or some other form.

Objective tests, if well-designed and tried out on a sample of students in advance, can be very informative, and can bring out a deep knowledge of subject matter. However, the questions that are most challenging and require the most complete understanding are often somewhat ambiguous and misleading as well; therefore, students are more likely to challenge such questions and argue about them. As a result, objective tests have come to be made up of questions of medium difficulty that do not require a deep understanding of the subject.

Another problem with such tests is that the answers can be discovered and stolen; a student who is given the correct answers in terms of the letters which stand for them (i.e., the key) can pass the test without knowing anything. The need for secrecy which results from this fact leads to security precautions surrounding the tests that are inimical to the objectives and best conditions for learning and teaching, and in the case of commercial standardized tests prevent teachers from having easy access to the tests that will be used to evaluate their students. This in turn can and sometimes does cover up invalid questions or poor coverage of subject matter.

Another drawback to objective tests is that they can be "psyched": students can learn to find cues to the correct answers (particularly on multiple-choice tests) and thus can achieve scores that do not reflect their understanding in relation to other students, but rather their superior test-taking skills. Also, if the test is a fairly long one, since there is one chance out of four or five of guessing the correct answer by chance, chance scores enter into the calculation of grades—i.e., a student can by chance score high enough to get a good grade even though he has not studied the material. This happens infrequently, as the laws of chance dictate, but when such a student spreads the word that he passed the tests by guessing, it has a bad effect on academic morale.

Essay tests

Essay tests must also be scored or corrected, and the correcting must be done by someone who understands the subject matter and the objectives of the course, usually the teacher.   It is difficult to evaluate essays written by different students on the same topic in a way that is fair and thorough.   One problem is boredom and fatigue on the part of the evaluator: after reading five or so, one's mind begins to wander.   It is also difficult to evaluate content rather than writing style and writing ability: some students write so well that they make very little knowledge appear to be much more, whereas others write so poorly that no matter how much they understand, it does not come through well.   Another problem is the "halo" effect whereby a teacher tends to evaluate the better student higher regardless of the contents.   (One way to combat this is by hiding the name of the student until the test is evaluated, but the handwriting often gives it away anyway.)   There have been a number of research studies showing that when several able teachers evaluate the same group of subjective tests, usually essay tests, they come up with radically different grades: one student might receive five different grades from five different teachers on the same test paper.   The reliability of grading by one teacher is also questionable: the same teacher might give a test paper an A on one reading, and a C on a later reading, if the teacher does not know it is the same paper.

Objective-subjective correlations

Test-making corporations often point out that when a group of students takes both a subjective and an objective test on the same subject, the correlation between the scores is high.   This means that those who are high on one tend to be high on the other, and those low on one low on the other.   They give this result as evidence that the objective test gives the same results, and thus is as good as the subjective.   However, this ignores the effect of the kind of test used on the kind of studying behavior and the kind and degree of learning that is required and therefore reached.   It is possible for the tests to correlate highly, but still represent different levels of understanding.   Since objective tests usually stress recognition rather than recall, and since they are less adapted to testing the ability to integrate information or the ability to relate facts and concepts and apply them, there is reason to believe that they are less apt to encourage these types and levels of learning than tests that *do* call for such responses.

Multiple-choice tests

Multiple-choice questions call for the selection of one correct answer from four or five alternatives, in most cases.   It is possible to have more than one alternative correct, but most test-scoring machines lack the capability for coping with such procedures, so usually multiple-choice tests feature one correct choice per item.   It is possible to make the selection process more difficult by including as one alternative such things as "all of the above are correct" or "none of the above are correct."   It is also possible to include possible answers which distract the student who is trying to guess, i.e., which look plausible to someone who is not familiar with the subject or who does not understand it thoroughly. On the other hand, there are many ways in which a student can guess the correct answer for the wrong reasons. For example, the person designing the test items may make a habit of writing questions where the correct answer has more words than the incorrect ones, or where it is usually one of the first two alternatives, or where the alternatives are silly, or where you can eliminate several or all of the alternatives for irrelevant reasons.

Multiple-choice questions can be designed so that they require thorough understanding, and so that the student must make creative judgments and solve fairly sophisticated problems in order to determine which of the responses is correct. One example of such a question is given in Figure 14–3. The difficulty with multiple-choice tests stems primarily from two sources. The first of these is determined by the need for tests which give "good" outcomes in terms of a smooth, normal curve, so that grading can be done easily. To get this kind of distribution in the scores, it helps to have test questions which are of medium difficulty and which cover a broad range of items. Therefore, test designers are tempted to make the questions mostly of intermediate difficulty; this means there are few very easy ones, and few very difficult ones. Students come to expect this and study accordingly.

The second difficulty stems from the problems that occur when one "goes over" a multiple-choice test in class, or hands it back to the students to inspect. Due to the nature of the test and the choice made, it is difficult to avoid ambiguities in the questions; furthermore, if you want the choices to be reasonably difficult, then some of them have to contain a "grain" of truth in them. When you try to design questions that really make the students think, then, it is difficult to avoid creating a situation where students object to your decision as to the right answer, and where they argue about it and feel that they are being cheated.

Some educators think that multiple-choice tests have ruined education. While they can be very well designed to test deep understanding, the fact is that they are often trivial and shallow: success is a matter of how much you put into the development of the questions.

Table 14–4. *Some suggestions for writing multiple-choice questions (adapted from Thorndike and Hagen, 1969).*

The introduction to the question, or the "stem," must present some kind of problem situation.

Most of the information should appear in the "stem"; the alternative answers should be quite short.

The stem itself should be as short as possible (the example of a multiple-choice item given elsewhere in this section is not a good example of this, obviously!).

Use negatives only infrequently in the stem, and when you do, underline the "not" so that students are sure to see it.

Use new material in the stem problems: don't just quote the text: attempt to measure applications rather than just straight facts.

Include only one correct or clearly best answer, yet try to make the options plausible.

Don't include clues to the answer in the stem; also avoid including clues to the answer in the choice of alternatives, i.e., don't make the correct alternative the longest or shortest, and don't include alternatives that can be eliminated on irrelevant grounds.

Question 4

In the following questions you are asked to make inferences from the data which are given you on the map of the imaginary country, Serendip. *The answers in most instances must be probabilities rather than certainties.* The relative size of towns and cities is not shown. To assist you in the location of the places mentioned in the questions, the map is divided into squares lettered vertically from A to E and numbered horizontally from 1 to 5.

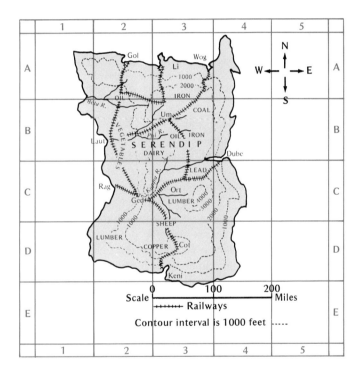

Which of the following cities would be the best location for a steel mill?
(A)   Li   (3 A)
(B)   Um   (3 B)
(C)   Cot   (3 D)
(D)   Dube   (4 B)

Figure 14–3. *A sample of the creative use of multiple-choice format. (From* Multiple-choice questions: A close look. *Copyright © 1963 by Educational Testing Service. All rights reserved. Reprinted by permission.)*

Statistical Analysis

| RESPONSES | STUDENTS CLASSIFIED BY TOTAL TEST SCORE | |
	LOWEST 27%	HIGHEST 27%
Omit	8	
A	10	2
*B	40	84
C	4	1
D	9	6
Total	71	93

Percent of total group of 370 students answering correctly: 75% Correlation between success on this question and total score on test: .43 (A somewhat different form of analysis was used for this test. Discrepancies in total numbers in each group are caused by drop-out of students not completing the test.)
* Correct answer

A map of an imaginary country, such as that shown in [Figure 17-2], offers numerous possibilities for questions which measure important understandings. One could ask several questions requiring an understanding of the symbols used on the map. To determine student comprehension of the meaning of contour lines, for example, one might ask which railroad has the steepest grades to climb. Similar questions can be developed which require knowledge of the factors influencing population distribution, economic activities, and so on.

The question reproduced beneath the map requires knowledge of the natural resources used in producing steel and an awareness of the importance of transportation facilities in bringing these resources together. It was part of a general achievement test given to high school seniors.

The student who knows that iron is the basic raw material of steel and that coal commonly provides the necessary source of heat would proceed to locate deposits of these resources in relation to the cities listed in the question. He would be able to eliminate Cot immediately, since there is no iron or coal in its vicinity, although Cot might be an attractive choice to students who mistakenly think that copper is a basic ingredient of steel. Both Li and Dube are located reasonably near supplies of iron, and therefore might be attractive choices. Um, however, is the more clearly "correct" response, because not only are deposits of iron and coal nearby, but they are more readily transportable by direct railroad routes.

Figure 14-4. *An example of the capabilities of the multiple-choice type question for testing understanding. The statistical analysis (i.e., "item analysis") shows how poor students (lowest 27 percent) and good students (highest 27 percent) answered each of the alternatives; the theory is that if good students do well and poor students do poorly, the item is "discriminating" and thus is a "good" item for that purpose. (From Multiple-choice questions: A close look. Copyright © 1963 by Educational Testing Service. All rights reserved. Reprinted by permission.)*

THE DON QUIXOTE OF TESTING

In the 1960s the physicist Banesh Hoffman became concerned about standardized tests and what they were doing to learning; he made one of his main targets the very successful and prestigious Educational Testing Service, one of the largest publishers of tests. In articles in *Harper's* and *The American scholar,* and in his book *The tyranny of testing* (1964), he set out to, in his own words, "dispel that awe [of the professionalism of the testers] by subjecting the testers to public examination." One of Hoffman's main contentions concerning objective tests, and the multiple-choice questions which they feature, is that they favor the shallow thinker over the deep thinker. He also observes that, in limiting the learner to a very narrow range of response, it also robs him of the opportunity to respond originally, thoroughly, and from his own frame of reference and fund of facts; he is forced to rely on the test, just as the students in most schools are forced to rely on the teacher.

MEASURING THE PRODUCT OF EDUCATION

The concept of an educational "product"

What did you get out of your four years of high school, or your college education so far? What are these educational institutions actually producing, beyond diplomas? Actually, we don't have a very good idea, do we?

We don't usually think of schools "producing" something: we usually see them as institutions that help people learn and prepare for life and absorb the many facts and concepts that make up our civilization. However, when schools and school budgets are under attack and the value of schooling is questioned in relation to its cost, educators often wish that there were some more direct way to demonstrate the nature of their product and convince "hard-nosed" businessmen and politicians that education is a good investment. On the other hand, it may be better to compare education and teachers to professions such as medicine and law, where the "product" is equally vague and undefined, although the need for the service is unquestioned; however, even in medicine and law people look for more evident outcomes: restoration to health, in the former, and staying out of jail, in the latter.

One approach to identifying the benefits of teaching

There have been a number of approaches to identifying and quantifying the outcomes of education in relation to the costs: one common term today is "cost-effectiveness," which implies such a comparison. We will present just one example of this analysis, in which the benefit of education is expressed in terms of a new unit called the "bentee" (Page and Breen, 1973). To set the stage for this, we quote the authors of this approach in some examples of the need for such a quantity or unit:

Recently, in a well-published study, a researcher gave low performers remedial work in mathematics. The students improved, somewhat reducing their lag in that one subject. Left unreported, however, was what happened to them in other subjects, from which the extra time was taken. Let us assume they suffered slightly in these others (as would surely be true in a well-run school). Then how would one decide whether the combination gain-and-loss is desirable?

A school board is considering possible allocations of teaching effort. One option is to give heavy emphasis to programs for the academically weak; another is to spread available resources more evenly across the board of talent; a third is to emphasize the gifted. How may we establish cost-effectiveness ratios for the three options, in order to compare them? If we define "effectiveness" for the weak students, the measures will not work for the gifted. How can the benefit to the total youth of the district be measured? Surely the choice should not be resolved purely at the level of politics or public relations.

A high school is swept up in a fashionable movement for student "freedom" in course selection. As a result, a large number choose no math, no hard science, no foreign language. One body of teachers argues that the students are developing

Can we measure the "product" of educational efforts?

"responsibility" and "creativity," and these values are more urgent than the purely academic considerations.   Is there any responsible technical procedure for balancing these claims, and for interrupting the confusing circle of warring opinion?

The method used to calculate the benefit of a given procedure or teaching strategy would be to have a group of judges allocate points to the outcomes in question, so that a subjective judgment can be translated into objective or quantitative terms. These judgments are then translated into standard scores (these are discussed in Chapter 15) that represent relative weights or values for the matters judged, whether they are outcomes, or methods of teaching, or the achievement profiles of different students.

The impact of assessment or evaluation on teaching

The approach to quantifying educational benefits described briefly in the previous section may not meet with your approval on philosophical grounds, but if you think of it you have to realize that we are already constrained and governed by measurements of outcomes that are less precise.   Grade point averages, scores on cooperative standardized tests, aptitude and achievement scores, and the like determine many of our decisions and aspirations in life.   Teachers generally and traditionally abhor the concept of "teaching to the test," yet to some degree all teachers shape their strategies and emphases according to such outcomes.   If your students don't show up well on a particular standardized test, or they don't do well on College Boards or the local equivalent, your talents as a teacher are suspect, regardless of the amount of appreciation, creativity, complex problem-solving ability, or concrete usefulness in your teaching outcomes.   In college teaching today, the value of an instructor's teaching (whether he or she is a full professor or a part-time-laboratory assistant) is often assessed through the kinds of student evaluation forms that were described in Chapter 5.   These forms seldom have reference to what the student learns.   Measuring the product of teaching may be a rather mechanical and undesirable facet of evaluation in your mind, then, but you should also consider the possibility that it may turn out to be an important part of the defense of good teaching and good education.   It should be done more thoroughly and carefully.

Summary outline with key concepts

☞ *Students regard* tests as evaluative and punitive / Placement is one function for "standardized" tests / Tests were once used for diagnosis more than they are now; attention to learning disabilities has partly reversed this trend / Formative evaluation assesses the instruction; summative evaluation assesses whether the learners have reached objectives / Norm-referenced tests relate a learner's score to those of other learners; criterion referenced tests relate subscores to teaching/learning objectives /

"Validation" refers to an arbitrary level of learner success set in advance and then compared with the final results; comparisons are made in relation to the proportion of students attaining a certain percentage on criterion test / "Assessment" has come to refer to a particular type of evaluation where emphasis is on the general level and quality of achievement, not on individual learners or classes or schools.

☞ *Competency-based education* evaluates outcomes in terms of observed abilities or competence; in cognitive areas this means applying concepts rather than giving facts / Performance-based education is competency-based in terms of some performance; e.g., teaching ability in a course on teaching. Behavioral outcomes are similar to competencies and performance criteria; they are objectives specified in terms of observable behaviors / Long-range outcomes such as appreciation, interest, and application of life are seldom assessed or evaluated; we don't know their nature and extent.

☞ *Intelligence tests* are fairly good predictors of future achievement, but they are limited in this respect / Aptitude tests are generally similar to intelligence tests, although some are designed for specific fields like law; their predictive ability is similar to that of intelligence tests / Achievement tests and general grade averages are also good predictors of future achievement, often as good as intelligence or aptitude tests / There are tests of attitudes and interests and motivation which predict future achievement about as well as intelligence tests and past achievement.

☞ *Evaluating feelings* and attitudes is done widely through tests, but such testing has not been accepted as a valid objective of conventional teaching / Attitudes, opinions, and interests are sampled by a variety of tests / Anxiety and creativity are also measured through questionnaires / There are instruments for studying the personalities of learners, including young learners.

☞ *Evaluating the* cognitive outcomes of teaching is a complex matter / Rote memory or rote learning have been rejected as outcomes of teaching, but aspects of these techniques are important / *Knowledge* is a general term, with a particular meaning in discussing evaluation / *Interpretation and extrapolation* are another level of cognitive outcome: they require developing additional conclusions and implications/ *Application* means using concepts and processes to deal with some problem / *Analysis* means identifying concepts and principles in new situations / *Synthesis* involves producing a unique point of view or plan from a set of independent facts / *Evaluation* means taking some situation and expressing a judgment or critique of it based on certain principles.

☞ *Guidelines are* given for consideration in making your own test: they include consideration of the goal, listing topics covered, devising several questions for each topic, controlling the difficulty level / A helpful procedure for constructing tests is to collect a pool of test items and store them according to some system.

☞ *Objective and* subjective tests give similar results in the sense that they correlate with each other, but they call for different abilities / Both types of tests call for certain skills, and some students do better than others on each type because they have developed these test-taking skills / Multiple-choice tests are widely used because of their convenience / Multiple-choice tests can evaluate a wide range of cognitive outcomes, but in practice they often fall short / Oral examinations are effective for certain types of evaluation, but they are time-consuming / Learners can be evaluated in the context of a group discussion, but this requires careful observation by the evaluator.

☞ The "product" of education is seldom discussed or referred to / One project has identified a new unit for expressing the benefits of teaching called the "bentee" / Evaluation and assessment have a great impact on what is taught and how; however, this impact is not adequately recognized.

Glossary

Analysis: Using facts and principles to determine the nature or state of some situation, i.e., to relate it to some theory or to classify it.

Applications: Using given facts and your own information to accomplish some objective or solve some problem.

Aptitude: Basic general ability, similar to "intelligence" but relating more closely to a specific area or field, e.g. "law aptitude."

Assessment: Technically refers to evaluation that does not single out individual learners, classes, or schools, and where no learner responds to the whole range of subtests.

Behavioral Outcomes or Objectives: Outcomes stated in terms of observable behaviors (relates to performance objectives also).

Bentee: A unit of measure of the benefit of an educational process.

Competence-based Education: Teaching and learning evaluated by the competences of the learners.

Correlation: A measure of the relatedness of two sets of scores which were made by the same group of learners (see Chapter 15).

Criterion-referenced Test: Test whose items are from a number of categories, where each category relates to some teaching objective.

Evaluation: As an outcome, means judging the quality and nature and desirability of some situation or object of art or system.

Formative Evaluation: Evaluation to determine the progress of learners during teaching and learning.

Intelligence: (A) learner's score on an intelligence test; (B) hypothetical innate ability to learn and/or achieve (see Chapter 3).

Interpretation and Extrapolation: Developing additional conclusions and implications from facts.

Item Pool: A collection of test questions classified according to subject matter and difficulty, and kept for making up tests.

Knowledge: Ability to recall facts or principles from memory.

Norm-referenced Test: Test on which scores are compared with some "norm," e.g., the mean of scores made by other learners (see Chapter 15).

Objective Test: A test that can be scored by someone who does not know the subject, but uses a "key."

Performance-based Education: Teaching and learning evaluated by the performance of the learners.

Reliability of a Test: Ability of the test to return the same score time after time for the same learner; degree to which it measures accurately (see Chapter 15).

Response Bias: Tendency of learners to respond in a certain way, or with a certain "set," on tests of attitudes and opinions.

Rote Learning: Memorization of unrelated facts or lists.

Subjective Test: A test that must be evaluated by an expert, i.e., where evaluation of the response calls for expert judgment.

Summative Evaluation: Evaluation to determine whether learners have reached a certain objective or set of objectives.

Synthesis: Producing a new relationship or point of view from a set of facts or relationships.

Tracking: Putting students in homogeneous groups.

Validation: Determining what percentage of the learners have reached some arbitrary level, e.g. 70 percent achieve 80 percent on a test.

Validity of a Test: Relation between the content of a test and some other measure, either another test, what was taught, or achievement in some subject (see Chapter 15).

Questions for thought and discussion

1. Could you have a competency-based or performance-based test to evaluate affective outcomes? What would it look like?

2. Are the examples of evaluation or analysis or synthesis also examples of competency-based tests? Would they be used for formative or summative evaluation (or both)?

3. Is the multiple-choice item in the section on that type of test also an example of "applications"? Would it belong in a competency-based test? In a performance-based test? Does it relate to creativity? to analysis? to synthesis?

4. What kind of studying would you do for an essay test that you would not do for a multiple-choice test? Which would foster the greater understanding?

5. Does an essay test necessarily test application? analysis? synthesis? extrapolation/interpretation? evaluation?

Suggested activities

1. Using a topic in some subject in which you are well informed, design test items to test the types of cognitive outcomes described in this chapter. Then design evaluation processes for formative evaluation, summative evaluation, diagnosis, and placement. Then describe some behavioral objectives and some performance objectives. Also consider long-range outcomes. Then plan to put all of these together into two types of test: norm-referenced and criterion-referenced. Then add to the items in

such a way that you have both an objective part and an essay part. Then plan how you might also give an oral examination on the same topic.

2. Consider the tests that are given in the courses that you are now taking, and classify them in as many ways as you can according to aspects of this chapter, as enumerated in (1) above.

3. Ask the testing center to let you examine various types of tests that they handle, and to discuss with you the uses to which different schools put tests.

4. Design a test of anxiety, or appreciation, or some other unusual or different ability or condition.

5. If you can obtain access to a standardized achievement test in some subject with which you are very familiar, perhaps your major, then analyze it in relation to various types of knowledge described in this chapter.

Suggested readings

Evaluation is a neglected subject in teacher education. An excellent source for general information, however, is the *Handbook on formative and summative evaluation of student learning* (New York: McGraw-Hill, 1971). A classic text in the field of measurement and evaluation that is still worth reading thoroughly is Robert Thorndike and Elizabeth Hagen's *Measurement and evaluation in psychology and education* (New York: Wiley, 1961), and a very helpful source of advice about testing and measurement is a kit published by Educational Testing Service's Evaluation and Advisory Service (Princeton, New Jersey 08540). A now-classic small paperback in the field of objectives in Robert Mager's *Preparing instructional objectives* (Belmont, California: Fearon Publishers, 1962). A more recent comprehensive treatment is Norman Gronlund's *Measurement and evaluation in teaching,* 2nd edition (New York: Macmillan, 1971).

15

Interpreting
Measurements
through Statistics

CONTENTS

ABOUT CHAPTER 15

What this chapter can do for you

Believe it or not, even if you are very poor at mathematics, this chapter can show you how to calculate simple statistical measures like the mean, the mode, the median, and the standard deviation. You will also learn to deal with the concept of "correlation," so that when someone says "intelligence is not correlated with achievement" or "intelligence *is* correlated with achievement" at least you know what he is trying to get across, even though you can't tell whether or not he is lying! (There is an interesting book out called *How to lie with statistics.*) You will also be able to discuss such fascinating topics as "distribution" and "variance" and "sampling" and "norms" at your next beer bust: this will make you the life of the party! You will also be able to interpret scores of your children or your students (or yourself); for example, you will know how to interpret a college board or SAT score of 600.

What might prove difficult

No topic in educational psychology is as generally disliked and avoided as statistics. Numbers may turn you off; using statistics to evaluate people may also. Using statistics to figure grades might seem like an anathema to you. But it can be done and it works very nicely—students are even happier with it that way, in some cases! Generally, what might turn you off is a basic antipathy for mixing mathematics with helping people learn: if this isn't the case for you, then you are lucky.

Reasons for studying Chapter 15

You live in a world of statistics: one good reason for understanding a little about them is to protect yourself. Another is that statistics are useful in reducing a lot of numbers to a very few. That is their danger also, of course, because as you reduce the number of figures you lose information and synthesize individuals into a collective, as it were. Another reason is that you should be able to translate statistical reports about your students or your children into meaningful statements, as with such statements as "Betsy is at the 61st percentile in math" or "Robert's standard score on the arithmetic achievement test was $-.8$" or "Sarah's stanine was 7" or "William is in the lowest quartile." Finally, you need to know what a statement such as this mean: "There was an inverse correlation between the number of teacher education courses and the positiveness of the classroom climate" or "The correlation between the two tests was .72." These are not difficult to understand, so you should take the trouble.

What this chapter does not do

This chapter does not prepare you to compute statistics for large groups, although you could figure out how to do it the long way from what is given here. This chapter does not teach you how to use statistical models to help interpret the results of research, or how to interpret research reports, except in the most simple reporting. There are, of course, books on these topics, and there are courses you can take. There are also programmed texts for self-instruction in case you want to learn some of these things on your own.

HOW DO YOU KNOW WHAT TESTS MEASURE?

Sampling and norms

It is not an easy thing to make sense out of information that you gather from measurement and evaluation. You have to "boil down" information and describe the data in simplified form. If you are to know whether the scores of learners obtained on a test are comparable to scores that would be obtained by other groups on the same test, you need to know something about the group that received the comparative scores published with the test. This means you have to understand "sampling," i.e., choosing a sample of trial students representative of those to whom you want to give the test. If Mary achieves a score of 127 out of a possible 205 on a reading test, you cannot tell whether she did well or not until you know what the average score on that test is for learners of Mary's age or grade. To get such an average, you have to select a sample of such learners that represents all learners of that grade or age, give them the test, and find their average on it. If a test is to be used nationally, then you need a random sample drawn from all parts of the country, and this should include urban, suburban, and rural areas, public and private schools, and learners from different socioeconomic levels, among other considerations.

What does a test score mean? Very little until it has been compared with some "norm" or standard.

Once the characteristics of the sample have been selected, a procedure must be designed that makes it possible to obtain a *random* sample. This means that the sample of the various schools, or of types of learners involved, must be taken. (Not *every* learner or school can be evaluated for the purpose of getting scores for comparative uses.) This sample must be chosen through some method that prevents the experimenter from allowing personal biases to affect the choice. It must also be chosen in such a way that the statistical treatments that will be used in handling the scores will be valid, i.e., so that the theories behind the statistical processes will apply to the sample. This means that the sample must be chosen by a chance process, such as drawing numbers from a hat, or from a mixing cage such as is used in lotteries, so everyone has an equal chance of being chosen.

For the teacher and parent, the sampling process and the nature of the sampling population are important because they determine the meaning of grades that learners receive on standardized tests. If a learner is given a grade or ranked according to a "percentile" on a test, but that test has been normed on a population of learners who are older or have had a better learning environment or have had teaching that emphasizes the material on the test more, then the grade or ranking is likely to be lower than it would be if the sample were representative or appropriate. By the same token, if the students in a certain school are very far above the norms for the country generally, then their grades (to be competitive) should perhaps be adjusted so they don't suffer from competition with each other.

How a test is "normed" or "standardized"

A test is "normed" or "standardized" by administering it to a large number of learners who fall into a certain classification. For example, suppose you have a test that requires the learner to identify well-known rock groups of the day by their sound. A series of excerpts from popular recordings are given, and the learner identifies the group from a set of alternatives given. You administer this test to five thousand preadolescents, say age fourteen, both male and female. You then take the scores and find the mean (i.e., the average, which is explained later). This score then becomes the "norm" on this test for fourteen year olds; if a given fourteen year old takes the test and achieves a score above that "norm," then he is "above average" in that ability or subject.

The particular norm may be something like 5.4, or 192, or 38—it depends on how many questions there are on the test, and how the average happened to turn out. Very often, test makers will translate these actual norms into what are called "standard scores"; this amounts to choosing a new set of numbers (often from one to one-hundred) and assigning each of the old scores to a new score in such a way that the mean (the "norm") comes out to be in the middle—say fifty. (College board scores for many years used such a scale with a mean of five-hundred.) Thus the norm for our test of rock groups may come out to be fifty on this new scale. Then a score of fifty-five will be above the mean or norm, while a score of forty will be below it.

Test validity

A test may be seen as a *sample* of the knowledge, behaviors, or feelings of the learner. From the responses of learners to this sample set of tasks, you make inferences about overall knowledge, behaviors, or feelings. The validity of the test has to do with how well it represents the range of things that the learner is supposed to

A test is "normed" by giving it to a large group of learners who fall into a certain classification.

People often say
something is or isn't
"valid": in testing,
this word has
several well-defined
meanings, and two
are given here.

have learned, i.e., how good a sample it is. For example, if a learner has been expected to learn to spell a hundred words and she is to be tested, you might draw a sample of ten words from the hundred. If the learner makes two errors, then you might assume that she would have made twenty errors if she had been given all one hundred words. If the sample was easier or harder than the average, however, the score she gets might not be representative, or *valid*. This type of validity is called *content validity*.

Another type of validity is *predictive validity*. This has to do with how well the test predicts what the learner will do on another test or in some other situation which is evaluated. In the spelling test, for example, predictive validity would relate to the ability of that test to predict how well the student would do in future spelling tests, or how well he would do on writing a story or on some other task that is more or less closely related to spelling. The predictive validity of an intelligence test in respect to mathematics, then, is its ability to predict how well a student will do in that subject—how close the relation is between how well people do on the test and how well they do in mathematics.

Test reliability

Another factor in testing should be kept in mind. This is "reliability," which is the ability of a test to produce the same results or measurements each time a learner or group of learners takes it. Suppose a learner took an intelligence test today and his IQ was determined to be 120. Imagine then that he took the same test again next week and his IQ was determined to be 90. This would normally be considered an unreliable instrument, because of the large difference in results. (Of course, with one learner there are many reasons why this might happen, so large groups of learners are used to check reliability, not one or two.)

If a test is not reliable, then it cannot be valid either. No matter what it measures, if the scores vary from one time to the next, you cannot be sure that it is measuring what the student knows, regardless of the content.

One regularly published reference work deals with reliability, validity, and other characteristics of the thousands of tests that are used in education and in other social science professions in this country. This test reference source is called "Buros," which refers to the name of the original author, Oscar Buros. The title is *Mental measurements yearbook.*

A VALIDITY GAP IN CALCULUS

Students in Mr. Alden's calculus section in the university fall into two categories—those who understand the game, and those who do not. Those who do not take voluminous notes, ask many questions, read the assignments, and do the homework religiously. Those who do understand the game, having been told by students who have had Mr. Alden before, and who have learned the hard way in some cases, do not pay a great deal of attention to homework and class sessions. They make a great deal out of Mr. Alden's presentations regarding the beauty of mathematics and his illustrations of same, and butter him up as best they can when there is a gap in the flow of brilliant comments which he spews forth. However, they also go to the library and look up the old examinations in his course and study them carefully, because they know that what Mr. Alden does in class is virtually unrelated to what they will find on these examinations. Sometimes, when there is a particular problem on the examinations that causes them difficulty, they will find a graduate student who knows how it is worked and will get help from him for a beer or some other appropriate consideration. Technically speaking, the examinations are not valid in respect to the work that goes on in class—or perhaps it should be put the other way around. However, students have found that the tests are reliable. That is, if they flunk the test the first time, and do not study for it, they will flunk the parallel form which is given for a makeup. This is small consolation to those who did not understand the system, however.

COMPARING DIFFERENT EDUCATIONAL TREATMENTS

How can you compare groups of learners?

When you have a large number of scores, say from a quiz or a test, and you want to summarize them in some way, to describe what they can tell you about the difficulty of the test or about how the class "did" on it, or how the group compares with other groups that took the test, then you have to have some system for boiling down the data to some representative figures.   You have known for a long time what the gen-

When you give a
test, you get a lot
of scores after it has
been evaluated. In
order to describe
the outcomes
briefly, you have
to "boil down"
those scores to one
or more descriptive
statistics.

eral meaning of the term "average" is: you know what an "average" student is, and how the temperature in a given winter may be below the "average" or "norm" for that date or month.   You know what "batting averages" are, or "earned run averages."   All of these are ways by which you cut a large amount of data down to size, so you can think about its meaning and compare it with other similar sets of figures.   In this part of this chapter, you will find a slightly more technical treatment of "averaging"—there are several types, and they are generally termed "measures of central tendency."   The most common one, and the one most people mean when they talk about an "average," is the "arithmetic mean," or just "the mean."

The mean

Suppose you have thirty test scores and wish to describe them collectively, according to the way they "tend to go."   You wish to use a single number to describe all thirty.   One measure that does this is the "mean."   It is a simple statistic to compute.   You merely add all the scores, and then divide by the number of scores (in this case, the number of learners taking the test).   For example, if you gave the test to five students, and their scores were 5, 7, 8, 3, and 9, then you would add these $(5 + 7 + 8 + 3 + 9)$ and divide by five.   This would yield the statistic 6.4.

A general formula for the mean can be stated simply as follows.   Call the first score x_1 and the second x_2 and so forth; let N represent the number of scores (in the case above, $N = 5$, $x_1 = 5$, $x_2 = 7$, $x_3 = 8$, and so on).   Then the formula for the mean (which is called x, or x-bar) is:

$$\bar{x} = \frac{x_1 + x_2 + x_3 + \cdots + x_N}{N}$$

Problem 1:   Find the mean of these scores:

24, 30, 40, 90

(The answer is at the end of the next section.)

The median

If you rank all the scores on a test in order from highest to lowest, the middle score of the ranking is called the *median*.   If there is an even number of scores, then the median is taken as a number midway between the two middle numbers.   Thus the median of the scores used in the previous section (5, 7, 8, 3, and 9) is found by ranking them (9, 8, 7, 5, 3) and then identifying the middle score (7).   What is the median of these scores?

$$12, \ 14, \ 21, \ 9, \ 3, \ 5$$

If you rank them, you get the following:

$$21, \ 14, \ 12, \ 9, \ 5, \ 3$$

The two middle scores are 12 and 9.   Midway between them is 10.5, so the median is 10.5.

Problem 2:   What is the median of the following scores?

$$45, \ 92, \ 81, \ 76, \ 5$$

The answer will be given at the end of the next section.

Answer to Problem 1:   The answer to the question in the previous section is:

$$\overline{x} = \frac{24 + 30 + 40 + 90}{4} = \frac{184}{4} = 46$$

The mode

One other statistic is often considered a measure of central tendency, even though it may indicate that a group of scores tends to have several centers.   Since it does not communicate too much about a group of scores, it is only used occasionally. This statistic is called the *mode*.   The mode is the score that appears most often in a set of scores.   In the distribution 5, 8, 9, 8, 16, 20, 8, 10, the number 8 is the mode because it appears three times, while the others appear only once.   In the distribution 6, 9, 10, 5, 12, 21, 12, 9, 32, 15, 15, 10, 13, 9, 15, 14, two numbers appear more than the others.   The numbers 9 and 15 appear three times each.   Since, if the scores were ranked, there would be other scores between these two (for example, 10, 12, and 13) we say that the distribution of scores has two modes, or two different scores that appear equally often in the set.   Another name for a distribution with two modes is a *bimodal* distribution.   As you can imagine, some sets of scores can have three, four, or many more modes.

Answer to Problem 2:   The answer to the problem in the previous section is 76, which is the middle number if you ranked them from highest to lowest.

*In statistical language, there are three measures of central tendency—
each useful in special circumstances.*

MEASURING HOW MUCH SCORES ARE SPREAD OUT AROUND THE MEAN

Why look at the "spread"?

Some groups will have scores that are widely distributed; for instance, these scores have a mean of seventy:

0   70   140

Other groups have scores that cluster together; these scores have a mean of seventy also:

$$69 \qquad 70 \qquad 71$$

If the only information you have is the mean, you don't know much about the range or "spread" of scores. (This is not the same use of the term "spread" as in gambling on football or basketball games.) The conventional measure of this quantity is the "standard deviation," which is calculated from the "variance."

Computing the variance of a set of scores

Consider this set of test scores:

$$8, 9, 10, 11, 12$$

Since this is a symmetric set of scores, you can probably guess the mean without bothering to compute it: it is 10. Now, what are the differences between the individual scores and the mean? Respectively, they are:

$$2, 1, 0, 1, 2$$

(I.e. 10-8, 10-9, 10-10, etc.; don't worry about signs.)
What are the squares of these differences?   4, 1, 0, 1, 4
What is the sum of the squares? $4 + 1 + 0 + 1 + 4 = 10$
If you divide this by the number of scores, 5, you get the "variance," which is 2. Therefore, to get the variance, you find the mean, then find the difference of each score from the mean, then square each of the differences, then add the squares, then divide that sum by the number of scores you had to begin with.

The standard deviation

There is one more statistic that is derived from this computational process. It is called the *standard deviation*. To obtain it, all you do is take the square root of the variance. Thus the standard deviation of the set of scores just used is the square root of the variance. Since the variance was 2, the SD (standard deviation) is about 1.41.

Problem 3: Compute the standard deviation of this distribution:

$$5, 6, 10, 14, 15$$

The answer will be given at the end of the next section.
The standard deviation is more than just the product of a calculation process, in many cases. If the scores on a test are distributed normally, and if you know the standard deviation and the mean, you can deduce some other things about any individual score.

THE NORMAL DISTRIBUTION AND THE NORMAL CURVE

What is a "normal" distribution?

If you measure the individual heights of thousands of individuals, you will find that they cluster about a central point. If you made a graph of thousands of people's heights, with different heights graphed along the horizontal axis and the frequency (or number of times) of each measurement plotted on the vertical axis, you would find that the graph had a bell-like shape. This shape is referred to as the "normal curve," or "normal distribution" and appears as in Figure 15–1.

Figure 15–1. *A normal curve or distribution.*

If you measure any natural phenomenon, you are apt to find that the cases cluster around a central point in the same way, forming bell-like curves; however, you have to have many, many cases before you get a smooth shape like that shown. These are called normal curves if they meet precise mathematical requirements as to shape, but we will not go into the details of this.

Some normal curves are spread out and low, and others are squeezed in and high, as shown in Figure 15–2. Each distribution which gives these curves has a

Figure 15–2. *Varieties of normal curves.*

mean, a variance, and a standard deviation. If the curve is symmetric (perfectly normal, so that the curve is exactly the same on both sides of the center), the mean will lie at the center or high point. Since the variance and standard deviation are measures of spread, the variance of the curve on the left above will be greater than that of the curve on the right.

Using the "SD" in a normal distribution

The usefulness of the standard deviation can now be explained: it relates to the nature of the normal curve. Whether you have a spread-out or squeezed-in normal curve, it happens to be a fact that about two-thirds of all the measurements (cases) cluster in between one standard deviation below the mean and one standard deviation above the mean. This is shown in Figure 15–3.

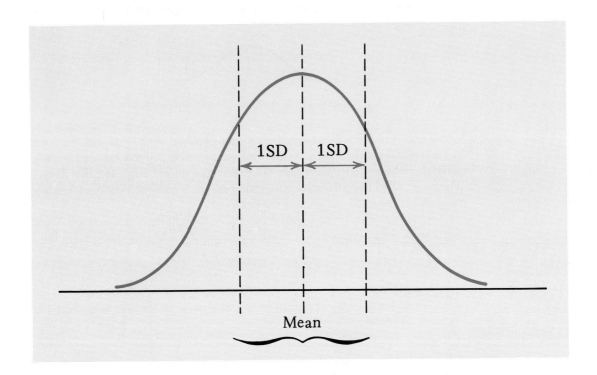

Figure 15–3. *Two-thirds of the scores lie between one SD below and one SD above the mean.*

Why is this such a useful fact? Suppose you know the mean and standard deviation of a test, i.e., of the scores of students who have taken the test in the past. Now suppose you also know your own score, and that it happens to lie one standard deviation above the mean. Then you know that your score is above fifty percent of the scores on the test; furthermore, you know it has one-third, or $33\frac{1}{3}$ percent, of the scores between it and the mean. From these facts you can calculate that your score is better than $50 + 33\frac{1}{3}$, or $83\frac{1}{3}$ percent of the scores that have been made on that test.   This is called the 83rd "percentile."

The normal curve is symmetric, and so the median and the mean are the same.   Beneath the median lies fifty percent of the scores.   Between the mean (since it is the median too) and the score one standard deviation above are one-third of the scores, as explained.   More than this, however, you can calculate what percentile *two* SDs represents, or three.   (There are tables that give you percentiles for such figures as 1.7 SDs.)

Problem 4:   Suppose the mean for a test is 46, and the standard deviation is 9, and your score is 37.   What is your percentile?   (The answer is at the end of next section.)

Answer to Problem 3:   The answer to the standard deviation problem in the previous section is 4.05.

Standard scores

The meaning of such things as means and standard deviations are based on the fact that most abilities have a chance or "normal" distribution.

Suppose you score 80 on a test that has a mean of 70 and a standard deviation of 5. Your score then differs from the mean by two standard deviations; it is two SD's above the mean.   Your standard score then would be $+2$, for it indicates how many standard deviations from the mean your score represents.   Let us imagine another score on the same test.   This one is 62, it is therefore 8 points below the mean.   It can then be said to be 8/5 or 1.6 standard deviations below the mean.   Therefore, the score of 62 is equivalent to a standard score of -1.6.   If we have the proper table, we can convert these standard scores into percentiles, which tell us what per-cent of the scores lie below yours.   This again is only possible, however, if the distribution of scores on the test is close to a normal one, because the table is based on facts about a normal curve.   These standard scores are also referred to as *z-scores*.

Answer to Problem 4:   Since one-third of the scores, or 33.3 percent, lie between the mean and one standard deviation below the mean, and since 50 percent lie entirely below the mean, then subtracting $(50 - 33.3)$ you can find that 16.7 percent of the scores lie below the score which is one standard deviation below the mean.   Since this is where the given score, 37, lies, it falls at roughly the 17th percentile (16.7th percentile).

BILL'S STANDARD SCORE

Bill Anderson has taken an entrance examination that is nationally normed; many different colleges use it, and it is administered by a private company.   He remembers there were about eighty questions on it, but other than that he cannot remember what it was about—he assumes it was some kind of aptitude test. He gets his score through the mail, and it is given as 572. This seems a bit confusing, and to make matters worse, the company seems to have forgotten to put any explanatory material with the report so that he can interpret it. He goes to see Mr. Adams at the high school. Mr. Adams teaches mathematics, and so Bill figures maybe he can help. Mr. Adams says he cannot help him, however, because he does not know which statistical system is being used by the company; it is some kind of standard score, he says, but he does not know the mean and standard deviation for it. He sends Bill to Mr. Williams who is the college placement advisor for the high school. Mr. Williams tells him that he has the necessary information. It seems that on this particular test, the mean is 500 and the standard deviation is 100. Bill says "Oh" and looks a little puzzled. Then he says, "How can the score be 500 when there were less than 100 questions—does each count five or ten or something?" Mr. Williams says that the actual score Bill got may be quite different, but that it has been translated into a standard scale, where the mean is 500 and so forth. This means that Bill's score of 572 is about .7 SDs above the mean. Mr. Williams says this is better than average, but not really great. He would guess it is about the 75th percentile, but he does not have his tables there to check his accuracy. (One SD above would be about the 83rd percentile.) Bill asks if this is good enough for the college he wants. Mr. Williams says that the college accepts scores in this area, but it will help if he has high grades also.

One example of a modern use of scores related to standard tests is the system of "scaled scores" used on the WISC (Chapter 3). For each subtest, the learner's score can be transformed into a scaled score by using a table for that age group. These scaled scores go from one to nineteen; the mean is ten, and the SD is three. Therefore, if a learner's scaled score is thirteen, she is one SD above the mean. Thus thirteen is quite good, but seven is quite poor; sixteen would be very superior (two SDs above the mean), and four would be very inferior. Scores in between give finer gradations.

WHAT DOES AN IQ SCORE MEAN?

An IQ of 100 does not mean that a learner has 100 units of intelligence, nor does it mean that the learner scored 100 points on the test. Rather, it means that the test score was the same as the average score made by a large number of other learners across the country—learners of the same age but from all walks of life, social classes, and geographic areas. These people made up the "sample" on which the test was "normed."

The number 100 was chosen to represent the norm for this group, i.e., the average or, "mean" of their scores. Other scores are translated into appropriate numbers relative to this average. Thus a score in the 90s (after being translated to this scale) is below average, whereas a score in the 100s is above average.

More on the normal curve

You very seldom, if ever, get a perfectly normal curve from any set of measurements, but many experimental results *approach* it.

Many comparisons between groups using different learning processes are made on the assumption that the scores of the groups are part of a normal distribution, so that if each group had been large enough, the scores *would* have been distributed normally. Intelligence test scores yield a normal curve if you have a large-enough group of learners taking the test. Achievement test scores do also if the items on the test are of medium difficulty and if they cover a wide range of topics. On the other hand, if you have an achievement test that does not cover many different things, but which has questions ranging from very easy to very difficult, you are liable to get something other than a normal curve. In teaching algebra on the secondary level, you might get a curve like the one in Figure 15–4.

Figure 15–4. *A flat curve.*

This is essentially a "flat curve," if you do not mind the contradiction that such a term involves. What hypotheses might you make from such a curve? What does it suggest about the test from which the scores were taken?

Grading "on the curve"

The concept of the normal curve is often inherent in grading practices. To illustrate this, let us look at some examples. On a test of arithmetic that you have given, the following test scores were made:

80, 78, 78, 65, 64, 63, 63, 63, 63, 61, 59, 58, 50, 49, 45, 31, 20, 10

"Curving" grades is a common practice, and has advantages and disadvantages.

You have a group of learners who are distributed normally according to their intelligence, aptitude, and standardized achievement scores. Therefore most of them are in the middle range of scores on those tests; some are, of course, higher and some lower. How will you grade the test scores above? One way you might do this is to make two assumptions: first, that if you gave the test to a thousand or so students, their results would be distributed according to a normal curve, and second, that *your* students are a representative sample from those imaginary thousand. In such a case, most of the scores from the larger group of a thousand or so would range around the middle. In fact, about two-thirds would fall within one standard deviation above or below the mean. Now you have to decide what grade you are going to assign to this *middle* group. You decide that the middle group should receive a C. Then the largest number of scores should receive C, with the others ranged on either side, perhaps as follows:

80 <u>78, 78</u> <u>65, 64, 63, 63, 63, 63, 61, 59, 58, 50, 49, 45</u> <u>31, 20</u> 10

 A   B   C   D   F

(Note: More often, Cs are given to scores from $\frac{1}{2}$ SD below to $\frac{1}{2}$ SD above.)

Suppose on the other hand that you had found that your students scored above the national averages on standardized intelligence, aptitude, and achievement tests. Perhaps you would feel that while the largest group should not necessarily receive a B, they might receive either $B-$ or $C+$ (this of course would entail using minuses and pluses all along). You might then assign the grades as follows:

80 <u>78, 78</u> <u>65, 64, 63, 63, 63, 63, 61, 59, 58, 50, 49, 45</u> <u>31, 20</u> 10

 A B+ & B   B$-$ & C+   C & C$-$ D

There are certain advantages to grading with the aid of the normal curve. For one thing, it provides some protection for the teacher (and students) when he or she makes out a test that is too difficult, in that it assures students of getting a reasonable grade nevertheless. It also provides some motivation for the student, in that he feels that he has a reasonable chance of doing well in competition with his peers. There are some disadvantages also. If you adhere rigidly to the normal curve, someone always has to flunk. However, if a student is trying at all over a number of different tests, he will usually get scores that average out above a flunking grade.

The student under glass.

On the other hand, with the use of the normal curve, not everyone can get an A, no matter how hard they try. This too can be a disadvantage. Some students "ride the curve," in that they know they are going to be higher than most of their colleagues and so are not challenged to do their best. There are ways of attaching conditions to the basic curve so that some of these disadvantages can be eliminated. For example, you can set an absolute value about which the curve will be formed, in advance, so that if the class does not hit this as a group, they will all get low scores. Also, the use of standardized tests with national norms will help the teacher determine his relative grading severity as well.

One last word about the normal curve and grading: a teacher should first make sure that she has a normal distribution of ability in her class before using the normal curve for grading. This might be done by graphing the results from some general diagnostic type of test and observing how the class is distributed. If she has a group of very-high-ability students, then it may be more fair to give a higher percentage of As and Bs than is usually suggested by the normal distribution; perhaps she may want her central point of the curve to be in the $B-$ or B category.

Again, the major point to be made here is that the teacher (or grader) determines the nature of the grades; they are not absolute values, but relative ones, and this fact should be faced in giving out comparative grades. You should not hide behind statistics.

Alternatives to traditional grading

Teachers, particularly beginning teachers, often feel constrained and frustrated by the necessity of giving traditional grades. There are alternatives that can be proposed, however, and the effectiveness of grades as motivators can be questioned on the basis of research.

A number of other evaluative possibilities have been considered and tried over the years. One of them is using written evaluations rather than grades. This allows the teacher to personalize the evaluation and mention strengths and weaknesses; however, it does not provide a comparative rating that schools and parents usually demand. Individual evaluations are also extremely time-consuming. Another possibility is self-evaluation and self-grading. Some teachers incorporate this into traditional grading by taking into account the opinion of the student as to the grade he or she deserves. Another solution is to give grades but keep them secret; the problems that might arise here are fairly obvious. Another alternative is a contract system, where the amount and quality of work needed for different grades is stated. The student contracts to produce work of a certain amount and quality and when he or she finishes receives the appropriate grade; however, this can amount to the same process of comparative grading if the student does not attain the quality desired, and this judgment is still up to the teacher. A mastery-approach can be used, where conceivably every student can get an A if he or she simply keeps at it, retaking examinations and rewriting papers; however, the time involved is very hard to determine and it takes extra time from both teacher and student. Also, not all students succeed in bringing themselves up to the level they aspire to, even with reruns, and this can be even more frustrating than the conventional system. Furthermore, some such systems (particularly the Keller system, or PSI, discussed in Chapter 13) find that they have more drop-outs because students put off progress-tests and then find themselves behind (this of course assumes that the material is self-paced as well).

These comments on alternatives are not designed to discourage their use, but only to point out that every grading system has its drawbacks, and changing to an alternative system does not solve every problem. One set of guidelines which seems quite useful and potentially valuable suggests some approaches to grading which makes the process more meaningful regardless of the particular system used (Kirschenbaum et al., 1971):

a. Copies of specific course objectives should be distributed to and discussed with students at the beginning of each course.
b. These objectives become the basis for evaluations, progress reports, and grades in each course.
c. Students will write self-evaluations based on the specific course objectives, as well as their own personal goals as they relate to the course. Teachers will read these and return them to the students with appropriate written comments.
d. Student-teacher conferences are encouraged when needed.
e. Reports to counselors and parents include these student-teacher evaluations.
f. These reports will be sent to counselors and parents every marking period. Additional reports may be sent as needed (eliminating the need for "warning letters").
g. These student-teacher evaluations should be kept on file in the guidance office to assist students, parents, and counselors in the process of college and vocational guidance. They should not under any circumstances be sent to colleges or employers.

THE CORRELATION COEFFICIENT

What does "correlation" mean?

One of the most widely used statistics is the correlation coefficient: it is also widely misinterpreted.

The correlation coefficient is a statistic that applies to situations where one group of learners takes two tests; you have two different sets of scores for the same group of people. For example, if you give the same group of learners a test and then later give them another test, you might want to know what the relationship is between the two tests—whether they seem to assess different things or the same things. If they correlate highly, you might assume that they measure similar things. You might want to know instead how the scores made on an aptitude test relate to scores or grades in a course in mathematics.

A correlation indicates the probability that a student who is high on one test will be high on another, or the probability that a student who is low on one is low on the other. You can get a better view of correlation from what is called a

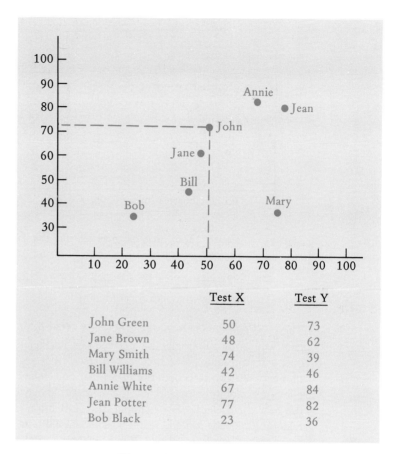

	Test X	Test Y
John Green	50	73
Jane Brown	48	62
Mary Smith	74	39
Bill Williams	42	46
Annie White	67	84
Jean Potter	77	82
Bob Black	23	36

Figure 15–5. *A scatter diagram.*

"scatter diagram." This is a plot of each student's scores on both tests, as an or-dered pair, i.e., one test on one axis and another on the other. The test results are shown plotted on the graph in Figure 15–5.

You will notice that the points in this scatter diagram tend to fall roughly in a line from lower left to upper right. Rather than describe it as a line, you might better describe the plot as forming an ellipse, with its left end lower than its right. This is a typical pattern for a *positive* correlation, i.e., a correlation in which the lower students on one test are also lower on the other, and higher students on one test have higher scores on the other. If it had been a *negative* correlation, the scores would have fallen in the pattern of an ellipse from upper left to lower right. (These general patterns are illustrated in Figure 15–6.) This would indicate that lower scorers on one test tend to be high on the other, whereas higher scorers tend to be lower on the second measure.

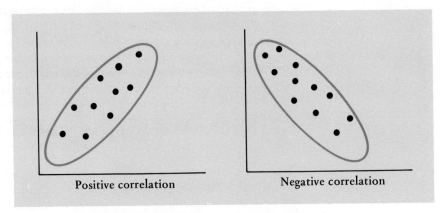

Figure 15–6. *Scatter-diagram patterns that indicate positive and negative correlations.*

Errors in using the correlation coefficient

There are two common mistakes to avoid when using the correlation coefficient. First, you cannot normally use a correlation coefficient with two different groups, only with the same group taking both tests. The second warning is that correlation between two tests does not mean that one causes the other in any way; it implies a common relationship, but the relationship may not be anything identified by the tests themselves. For example, the correlation between a certain numerical reasoning aptitude test and scores on standardized tests of achievement in English is about .81. This is very high. Obviously numerical reasoning ability is quite different from the abilities that are required in English, but the correlation is still there; there may be some connection—some common element that is not obvious. Another illustration of the fallacy of interpreting correlation as causation is the following. A woman wrote to an airline that she wished they would not let the pilots turn on the "Fasten Your Seat Belts" sign so often, because every time the sign went on, the ride got bumpy.

Summary outline with key concepts

☞ *When you* have a lot of scores, you have to reduce the amount of information they contain in order to handle them: this results in "averages" and "norms" / When you have averages and norms, you have to understand "sampling" in order to interpret them / A "sample" chooses people or schools at random, and gets scores from them in order to produce "norms" so that you can compare individual scores with them / "Standardized tests" are tests that have been "normed" in this way / Validity is a measure of the content of a test in relation to some other amount or score or content; there are several types of validity / Content validity involves a comparison with what has been taught / Predictive validity involves a comparison with a later score, e.g. grades / Reliability is a measure of the accuracy of the test, i.e., whether it gives the same measurement every time when given to the same person or people.

☞ *Statistical significance* and educational significance are not the same / To compare groups of learners you need to use "averages" / The most common "average" is the "mean"; you get it by adding the scores and then dividing the total by the number of scores / The median is another average: it is the middle score when all scores are ranked / The mode is another average: it is the score that occurs most often.

☞ *Two groups* may have the same mean on a test, but still be spread out differently / The variance is a measure of the spread of scores, i.e., how closely they cluster around the mean / The standard deviation is the square root of the variance, and also measures spread.

☞ *Scores on* tests and measures of natural characteristics generally have a "normal" distribution / If you know that the scores are distributed normally, and if you know the SD, then you can translate any one score into a percentile / Given the same conditions as above, you can report any one score in terms of the number of SDs above or below the mean; this is a "standard score" / Grading on a curve is a convenient way of adjusting one's standards so that they are neither too easy nor too hard / There are different bases for giving grades, some relatively fixed, others based on the ability of the learner / There are alternatives to conventional grading, including written evaluations, self-evaluation, keeping grades secret, using a contract system, using a mastery system, pass-fail, and credit-fail.

☞ *The correlation* coefficient reports the degree of relatedness between two sets of scores achieved by the same group of learners / If the same learners are high on both tests, and the same ones are low on both, then the correlation is positive / The fact that two things correlate does not mean that either causes the other; however, it is reasonable to suspect that there is a common cause for both.

Glossary

Concurrent Validity: How well a test correlates with success on tasks that logically relate to the test.

Construct Validity: Judgment of the content of a test based on non-test considerations such as what was taught, how it relates to curriculum, etc.

Mean: The sum of a group of scores divided by the number of scores.

Median: Middle score when all scores are ranked.

Mode: The score that occurs most often.

Norm: An average (usually mean) for a particular group of learners, e.g., all seven year olds; it provides a standard against with other scores are compared.

Normal Distribution: Manner in which many natural phenomena distribute themselves when measured, e.g., height, intelligence.

Percentile: A figure that indicates what percentage of the norming population lies below a certain score.

Predictive Validity: How well a test predicts scores on another test or predicts grades or some other measure of achievement.

Reliability: The probability that a test will yield the same score(s) if given again to the same learner(s).

Sampling: Selecting learners to take a test in order to establish a norm.

Standard Deviation: Square root of the variance; a measure of spread.

Standard score: A score stated in terms of the number of SDs from the mean.

Standardized Test: A test that has been "normed" on a given group.

Variance: Measure of the spread of scores about the mean.

Questions for thought and discussion

1. Could you construct a standardized test? What would you need to do in order to standardize it?
2. If you use an intelligence test to place students in fast or slow classes, what kind of validity are you assuming? In respect to what?
3. Find the mean, median, and mode of the following scores, and compare with your classmates and/or your professor.

   6, 9, 4, 18, 3, 22, 95, 3, 2, 4, 9, 4, 4, 6, 2

   Would a mean give a good idea of this distribution? A median? A variance?
4. Without calculating them, tell which of the distributions has the greatest variance?

   (a) 6, 9, 4, 5, 10, 5, 7, 4, 8

   (b) 6, 12, 3, 2, 14, 0, 3, 2, 19

   Which has the greatest standard deviation?
5. John takes a test and scores 37. The mean for the test is 40. The standard deviation is 3. What percentile is John in?

Situations calling for applications of facts and concepts

1. Suppose you find that the predictive validity of a given test is high in relation to achievement in the same subject, but the test reliability is quite low. What advice would you give to a teacher regarding its use in classes? Would you recommend it? Could it be valid if unreliable?
2. You see a statement about two groups of students which says that their scores on a given test have a positive, high correlation, and thus they are very similar. What's wrong with this statement? How would you compare the two groups? (What statistical measure(s) would you use?)

Suggested activities

1. Discuss grading practices with college teachers, high school teachers, and elementary school teachers. Note differences in techniques and philosophies, where they exist. Are any of the alternative approaches mentioned in this chapter being used?

2. Obtain an examiner's manual for some standardized test, and find the norms for different ages, grades, or types of students. An intelligence test or a general achievement test might be a good type to use. Are there tables for translating "raw" scores into standard scores, or into percentiles?

3. Find a situation where the same group of students has taken two different tests. Make a scatter diagram like Figure 15–5, and roughly estimate the correlation; is it positive or negative, high or low?

Suggested readings

If you want to study statistics, there are many texts: it is a complex field, but the elements of it are rather simple. If you want to read more about grading, the book by Kirschenbaum and others is a good start; it is well-written and interesting, and has a complete bibliography with annotations.

Bibliography

ADELSON, J. What generation gap? *New York Times Magazine,* January 18, 1970.

ALMY, M., E. CHITTENDEN, and P. MILLER. *Young children's thinking.* New York: Teachers College Press, Columbia University, 1966.

ALPER, L., B. PENCE, R. PROPP, and N. WEBB. Review of the experimental data on the effect of homework. Quoted in N. Gage and D. Berliner, *Educational psychology.* Chicago: Rand-McNally, 1975.

ALLPORT, G. W. *Pattern and growth in personality.* New York: Holt, Rinehart & Winston, 1961.

ALSCHULER, A., D. TABOR, and J. MCINTYRE. *Ten thoughts.* A booklet of the *Achievement motivation series.* Middletown, Conn.: Education Ventures, 1970.

ALSCHULER, A., D. TABOR, and J. MCINTYRE. *Teaching achievement motivation.* Middletown, Conn.: Education Ventures, Inc., 1972.

AMIDON, E. J. and J. B. HOUGH. *Interaction analysis: Theory, research and application.* Reading, Mass.: Addison-Wesley, 1967.

ANASTASI, A. *Individual differences.* New York: Wiley, 1965.

ANDERS, FRANK. If you can teach an ape to read, can you do something for my retarded child? Yes. *New York Times Magazine,* June 1, 1975.

ANDERSON, G. Effects of classroom social climate on individual learning. Paper delivered to the American Educational Research Association Convention, 1969. Mimeographed.

ANDERSON, G. and H. J. WALBERG. Classroom climate and group learning. *International Journal of Educational Sciences.* 1968, *2,* 157–180.

ANDERSON, G. J. and H. J. WALBERG. Class size and the social environment of learning. Paper presented to the American Educational Research Association, 1971. Mimeographed.

ANDERSON, R. C. Learning in discussions: A resume of the authoritarian-democratic studies. *Harvard Educational Review,* 1959, *29,* 201–215.

ASHTON-WARNER, S. *Teacher.* New York: Simon & Schuster, 1963.

Association of American Geographers and American Sociological Association. *Experiences in inquiry.* Boston: Allyn and Bacon, 1974.

ATKINSON, J. W. The mainsprings of achievement oriented activity. In J. D. Krumboltz (Ed.), *Learning and the educational process.* Skokie, Ill.: Rand McNally, 1965.

ATKINSON, R. C. and H. A. WILSON (Eds.). *Computer-assisted instruction: A book of readings.* New York: Academic Press, 1969.

AUSUBEL, D. P. Learning by discovery: Rationale and mystique. *Bulletin of the National Association of Secondary School Principals,* December 1961, 18–58.

AUSUBEL, D. P. Crucial psychological issues in the objectives, organization, and evaluation of curriculum reform movements. *Psychology in the Schools,* 1967, 4, 111–121.

AUSUBEL, D. P. *Educational psychology: A cognitive view.* New York: Holt, Rinehart & Winston, 1968.

AUSUBEL, D. P. and D. FITZGERALD. Meaningful verbal learning and retention. *Journal of General Psychology,* April 1962, 56 (2nd half), 213–224.

AYERS, A. JEAN. Improving academic scores through sensory integration. *Journal of Learning Disabilities* 1972, 5, 336–343.

AZRIN, N. H. and W. C. HOLTZ. Punishment. In W. K. Honig (Ed.), *Operant behavior.* New York: Appleton-Century-Crofts, 1966, 380–447.

BACH, J. J. and B. J. UNDERWOOD. Developmental changes in memory attributes. *Journal of Educational Psychology,* 1970, 61 (4), 292–296.

BALES, R. F. *Personality and interpersonal behavior.* New York: Holt, Rinehart & Winston, 1969.

BALES, R. F. and F. L. STRODTBECK. Phases in group problem solving. In T. L. Harris and W. E. Schwahn (Eds.), *Selected readings on the learning process.* New York: Oxford, 1961.

BANDURA, A. Behavioral psychotherapy. *Scientific American,* 1967, 216 (3), 78–86.

BANDURA, A. *Principles of behavior modification.* New York: Holt, Rinehart & Winston, 1969.

BANDURA, A. and R. H. WALTERS. *Adolescent aggression.* New York: Ronald Press, 1959.

BANE, M. J. and C. JENCKS. The schools and equal opportunity. *Saturday Review of Education,* September 16, 1972.

BANNATYNE, A. *Language, reading and learning disabilities: Psychology, neuropsycho-diagnosis, and remediation.* Springfield: Charles C Thomas, 1971.

BANUS, B. S. *The developmental therapist: A prototype of the pediatric occupational therapist.* Thorofare, N.J.: Charles E. Slack, 1971.

BANY, M. and L. JOHNSON. *Classroom group behavior.* New York: Macmillan, 1964.

BARATZ, J. C. and R. W. SHUY (Eds.). *Teaching black children to read.* Washington, D.C.: Center for Applied Linguistics, 1968.

BARNARD, K. E. and M. L. ERICKSON. *Teaching children with developmental problems: A family care approach.* St. Louis, Mo.: Mosby, 1976.

BARRON, F. *Creative person and creative process.* New York: Holt, Rinehart & Winston, 1971.

BARTON, E. J., J. K. PLEMONS, S. L. WILLIS, and P. B. BALTES. Recent findings on adult and gerontological intelligence. *American Behavioral Scientist,* November/December 1975, 19 (2).

BASKIN, S. Experiment in independent study (1956–1960). *Antioch College Reports,* No. 2, 1961.

BEACH, FRANK A. Behavioral endocrinology: An emerging discipline. *American Scientist,* March–April 1975, 63, 178–187.

BECKER, W. C. Consequences of different kinds of parental discipline. In M. L. Hoffman and L. W. Hoffman (Eds.), *Review of Child Development Research* (Vol. 1). New York: Russell Sage Foundation, 1964.

BECKER, W. C., S. ENGELMANN, and D. R. THOMAS. *Teaching 1: Classroom management.* Chicago: Science Research Associates, 1975.

BECKER, W. C., S. ENGELMANN, and D. R. THOMAS. *Teaching 2: Cognitive learning.* Chicago: Science Research Associates, 1975.

BELLACK, A. A., H. M. KLIEBARD, R. T. HYMAN, and F. L. SMITH. *The language of the classroom.* New York: Teachers College Press, 1966.

BENDER, L. *Psychopathology of children with organic brain disorders.* Springfield: Charles C Thomas, 1966.

BENNETT, N. *Teaching styles and pupil progress.* Cambridge, Mass.: Harvard University Press, 1976.

BEREITER, C. and S. ENGELMANN. *Teaching disadvantaged children in the preschool.* Englewood Cliffs, N.J.: Prentice-Hall, 1966.

BERLINER, D. C. Impediments to the study of teacher effectiveness. *Journal of Teacher Education,* Spring 1976, *27* (1), 6–13.

BERLINER, D. C. and L. S. CAHEN. Trait-treatment interaction and learning. In F. N. Kerlinger (Ed.), *Review of Research in Education 1.* Itaska, Ill.: Peacock, 1973.

BERLINER, D. C. and W. J. TIKUNOFF. The California beginning teacher evaluation study: Overview of the ethnographic study. *Journal of Teacher Education,* Spring 1976, *27* (1), 24–30.

BERLYNE, D. Curiosity and education. In J. D. Krumboltz (Ed.), *Learning and the educational process.* Chicago: Rand McNally, 1966.

BERNSTEIN, B. Language and social class. *British Journal of Sociology,* 1960, *11,* 271–276.

BERNSTEIN, B. Social structure, language and learning. *Education Research,* 1961, *3* (3), 163–176.

BERNSTEIN, E. What does a Summerhill old school tie look like? *Psychology Today,* October 1968, *2* (5), 38–41, 70.

BERTOU, P. D., R. E. CLASEN, and P. LAMPERT. An analysis of the relative efficiency of advanced organizers. *Journal of Educational Research,* 1972, *65,* 329–333.

BETTLEHEIM, B. *Love is not enough.* New York: Free Press, 1965.

BEXTON, W. H., W. HERON, and T. H. SCOTT. Effects of decreased variation in the sensory environment. *Canadian Journal of Psychology,* 1963, *46,* 95–98.

BIEHLER, R. *Psychology applied to teaching* (2nd ed.). Boston: Houghton Mifflin, 1974.

BIRCH, H. G. and L. BELMONT. Auditory and visual integration in normal and retarded readers. *American Journal of Orthopsychiatry,* 1964, *34,* 852–861.

BIRCH, H. G. and H. S. RABINOWITZ. The negative effect of previous experience on productive thinking. *Journal of Experimental Psychology,* 1951, *41,* 121–125.

BIRCH, J. W. *Mainstreaming: Educable mentally retarded children in regular classes.* Council for Exceptional Children, 1974.

BLANK, MARION. Cognitive functions of language in the preschool years. *Developmental Psychology,* 1974, *10* (2), 229–245.

BLOOM, B. S. (Ed.). *Taxonomy of educational objectives: Handbook 1: Cognitive Domain.* New York: David McKay, 1956.

BLOOM, B. S. *Stability and change in human characteristics.* New York: Wiley, 1964.

BLOOM, B. S., S. DAVIS, and R. HESS. *Compensatory education for cultural deprivation.* New York: Holt, Rinehart & Winston, 1965.

BLOOM, B. S., J. T. HASTINGS, and G. F. MADHAUS. *Handbook of formative and summative evaluation of student learning.* New York: McGraw-Hill, 1971.

BODMER, W. F. and L. L. CAVALLI-SFORZA. Intelligence and race. *Scientific American*, October 1970.

BOFFEY, PHILIP M. Return of Dr. Fox. *The Chronicle of Higher Education*, November 18, 1974.

BOND, E. A. *Tenth grade abilities and achievements.* New York: Bureau of Publications, Teachers College, Columbia University, 1940.

BORTIN, H. and RUNYON. Orthomolecular psychiatry: Niacin and megavitamin therapy. *Psychosomatics*, September/October 1970, *11* (5), 517–518.

BORTNER, M. and BIRCH. Cognitive capacity and cognitive competence. *American Journal of Mental Deficiency*, 1970, *74* (6), 725–744.

BOURNE, L. E., JR. *Human conceptual behavior.* Boston: Allyn and Bacon, 1966.

BOWER, T. G. The visual world of infants. *Scientific American*, December 1966.

BOY, A. and G. PINE. *Expanding the self: Personal growth for teachers.* Dubuque: William C. Brown, 1971.

BRAUN, CARL. Teacher expectation: Sociopsychological dynamics. *Review of Educational Research*, Spring 1976, *46* (2), 185–214.

BRONFENBRENNER, URIE. The experimental ecology of education. Paper presented at American Educational Research Association convention, 1976. Mimeographed.

BROPHY, J. E. Stability of teacher effectiveness. *American Educational Research Journal*, 1973, *10*, 245–252.

BROPHY, J. E. and C. M. EVERTSON. *Learning from teaching: A developmental perspective.* Boston: Allyn and Bacon, 1976.

BROPHY, J. E. and C. M. EVERTSON. The student attribute study: Preliminary report (abbreviated version). R & D Center for Teacher Education, University of Texas at Austin, 1976. Mimeographed.

BROUDY, H. S. and J. R. PALMER. *Exemplars of teaching method.* Chicago: Rand McNally, 1965.

BROWN, R. *A first language: The early stages.* Cambridge: Harvard University Press, 1973.

BROWN, R. and U. BELLUGI. Three processes in child's acquisition of syntax. *Harvard Educational Review*, Spring 1964, *34*, 133–152.

BROWN, R., C. CAZDEN, and U. BELLUGI-KLIMA. The child's grammar from I to III. In J. P. Hill (Ed.), *Minnesota symposia on child psychology* (Vol. 2). Minneapolis: University of Minnesota Press, 1969, 28–73.

BROWN, W. and W. HOLTZMAN. *SSHA manual, forms C and H: Survey of study habits and attitudes.* New York: The Psychological Corporation, 1968.

BRUNER, J. S. *The process of education.* Cambridge: Harvard University Press, 1960.

BRUNER, J. S. *Toward a theory of instruction.* New York: W. W. Norton, 1966.

BRUNER, J. S., J. GOODNOW, and G. A. AUSTIN. *A study of thinking.* New York: Wiley, 1956.

BRYAN, J. F. and E. A. LOCKE. Goal setting as a means of increasing motivation. *Journal of Applied Psychology*, 1967, *51*, 274–277.

BRYAN, T. and J. BRYAN. *Understanding learning disabilities.* Port Washington, L. I.: Alfred, 1975.

BURKARD, M. I. Discernment of teacher characteristics by TAT sequence analysis. *Journal of Educational Psychology*, 1962, *53*, 279–287.

BUSH, W. J. and B. D. MATTSON. WISC test patterns and underachievers. *Journal of Learning Disabilities*, 1973, *6* (4), 251–256.

BUSH, W. J. and K. W. WAUGH. *Diagnosing learning disabilities* (2nd ed.). Columbus, Ohio: Charles E. Merrill, 1976.

CAMPBELL, S. Facilitation of cognitive and moral development in infants with CNS dysfunction. *Physical Therapy*, April 1976.

CARLSON, E. *Learning through games.* New York: Public Affairs Press, 1970.

CARTERETTE, E. C. and JONES, M. H. Visual and auditory information processing in children and adults. *Science,* 1967, *165,* 968–988.

CARTWRIGHT, D. Achieving change in people: Some applications of group dynamics theory. *Human Relations,* 1951, *4,* 381–392.

CASE, R. Piaget's theory of child development and its implications. *Phi Delta Kappan,* September 1973.

CATTELL, R. B. *The scientific analysis of personality.* Chicago: Aldine, 1966.

CATTELL, R. and H. EBER. *Handbook for the sixteen personality factor questionnaire* (1957 ed.). Champaign, Ill.: Institute for Personality and Ability Testing.

CAZDEN, C. How knowledge about language helps the classroom teacher—or does it? Address to American Educational Research Association, 1976. Mimeographed.

CENTRA, J. A. and B. ROSE. Student ratings of instruction and their relationship to student learning. Princeton, N.J.: Educational Testing Service, Research Bulletin, February, 1976. Mimeographed.

CHAMBERLIN, D., E. S. CHAMBERLIN, N. E. DROUGHT, and W. E. SCOTT. *Adventures in American education: Did they succeed in college?* New York: Harper and Bros., 1942.

CHARTERS, W. W. and N. L. GAGE (Eds.). *Readings in the social psychology of education.* Boston: Allyn and Bacon, 1963.

CHOMSKY, C. *The acquisition of syntax in children from 5 to 10.* Cambridge, Mass.: MIT Press, 1969.

CHOMSKY, N. *Language and mind.* New York: Harcourt Brace Jovanovich, 1972.

CLEMENTS, S. D. *Minimal brain disfunction in children.* U.S. Dept of Public Health Services, Publication #1415, 1966, *10.*

COATES, T. J. and C. E. THORESEN. Teacher anxiety: A review with recommendations. *Review of Educational Research,* Spring 1976, 46 (2), 159–184.

COLEMAN, J. *The adolescent society.* Glencoe: Free Press, 1961.

COLEMAN, J. S., E. Q. CAMPBELL, C. J. HOBSON, J. MCPARTLAND, A. M. MOOD, F. D. WEINFELD, and R. L. YORK. *Equality of educational opportunity.* Washington, D.C.: U.S. Government Printing Office, 1966.

COLLINS, A. Processes in acquiring knowledge. In R. C. Anderson, R. J. Spiro, and W. E. Montague (Eds.), *Schooling and the acquisition of knowledge.* Hillsdale, N.J.: Erlbaum Associates, 1976.

COMBS, A. W., D. L. AVILA, and W. W. PURKEY. *Helping relationships: Basic concepts for the helping professions.* Boston: Allyn and Bacon, 1971.

Commission on Instructional Technology. *To improve learning.* Washington, D.C.: U.S. Government Printing Office, 1970.

COOPER, H.M.R., M. BARON, and C. A. LOWE. The importance of race and social class information in the formation of expectancies about academic performance. *Journal of Experimental Psychology,* 1975, *67,* 312–319.

COREY, S. M. Professed attitudes and actual behavior. *Journal of Educational Psychology,* 1937, *28,* 271.

COVINGTON, M. V. et al. *The productive thinking program.* Columbus, Ohio: Charles E. Merrill, 1972.

COVINGTON, M. V. and R. S. CRUTCHFIELD. Experiments in the use of programmed instruction for the facilitation of creative problem solving. *Programmed Instruction,* 1965, *4,* 3–4, 10.

CRAIG, R. C., W. H. MEHRENS, and H. F. CLARIZIO. *Contemporary educational psychology: Concepts, issues, applications.* New York: Wiley, 1975.

CRATTY, B. Perceptual-motor behavior and educational processes. Springfield, Ill.: Charles C Thomas, 1969.

CRUICKSHANK, D. R. Synthesis of selected recent research on teacher effects. *Journal of Teacher Education,* Spring 1976, *27* (1), 57–60.

CRUICKSHANK, W. M. *The brain injured child in home, school and community.* Syracuse, N.Y.: Syracuse University Press, 1967.

CRUTCHFIELD, R. S. Conformity and creative thinking. In H. E. Gruber, G. Terrell, and M. Wertheimer (Eds.), *Contemporary approaches to creative thinking.* New York: Atherton, 1962, 120–140.

DALE, P. S. *Language development: Structure and function.* Hinsdale, Ill.: Dryden Press, 1972.

DAVIDSON, R. J. and G. C. SCHWARTZ. The psychobiology of relaxation and related states: A multi-process theory. In D. Mostofsky (Ed.), *Behavior control and modification of physiological activity.* Englewood Cliffs, N.J.: Prentice-Hall, 1976.

DAVIS, A. and K. W. EELLS. *Davis-Eells tests of general intelligence or problem solving ability.* Yonkers, N.Y.: World Book, 1953.

DAY, H. I. and BERLYNE, D. E. Intrinsic motivation. In G. S. Lesser (Ed.), *Psychology and educational practice.* Glenview, Ill.: Scott, Foresman, 1971.

DENNENBERG, V. H. Early experience and emotional development. *Scientific American,* June 1963.

DEUTSCH, M. and C. DEUTSCH. Intelligence, heredity and environment: The critical appraisal of an outmoded controversy. *New York University Education Quarterly,* Winter 1974, 4–12.

DEUTSCH, M., I. KATZ, and A. R. JENSEN. *Social class, race, and psychological development.* New York: Holt, Rinehart & Winston, 1967.

DEWEY, J. *How we think.* Boston: D. C. Heath, 1910.

DEWEY, J. *Experience and education.* New York: Macmillan, 1963.

DILLARD, J. L. Black English. *Time Magazine,* August 1972, 46.

DIENSTHER and MUNTER. Cheating as a function of the labelling of natural arousal. *Journal of Personal and Social Psychology,* Feb. 1971, *17,* 208.

DOUGLAS, V. I. and G. MORGENSTERN. Cognitive style or cognitive ability? *Journal of Child Psychology,* 1971.

DREIKURS, R., B. B. BRUNWALD, and F. C. PEPPER. *Maintaining sanity in the classroom: Illustrated teaching techniques.* New York: Harper & Row, 1971.

DUNCAN, C. P. Recent research on human problem solving. *Psychological Bulletin,* 1959, *56,* 397–429.

DUNCKER, K. *On problem solving.* Psychological Monographs, 1945, *62,* No. 270.

DUNKIN, M. J. and B. J. BIDDLE. *The study of teaching.* New York: Holt, Rinehart & Winston, 1974.

DUNNETTE, M. D., J. CAMPBELL, and K. JAASTED. The effort of group participation on brainstorming effectiveness for two industrial samples. *Journal of Applied Psychology,* 1963, *46,* 30–37.

DURRELL, D. D. Phonics and spelling. Address to the International Reading Association, Anaheim, California, May, 1976. Mimeographed.

DWYER, F. *A guide for improving visualized instructions.* Pennsylvania State College Learning Services, 1972.

EBEL, R. L. *Measuring educational achievement.* Englewood Cliffs, N.J.: Prentice-Hall, 1965.

Educational Testing Service. *Making the classroom test: A guide for teachers.* Princeton, N.J.: Evaluation and Advisory Service of ETS, 1959.

Educational Testing Service. *Test and measurement kit.* Princeton, N.J.: Evaluation and Advisory Service of ETS, 1959.

Educational Testing Service. *Multiple choice questions: A close look.* Princeton, N.J.: Evaluation and Advisory Service of ETS, 1959.

Educational Turnkey Systems. *Performance contracting in education.* Englewood Cliffs, N.J.: Educational Technology Publications, 1970.

EKSTROM, R. B. Teacher aptitudes, knowledge, attitudes and cognitive style as predictors of teaching behavior. Presentation to American Educational Research Association, 1976. Mimeographed.

ELKIND, D. Early childhood education. *The National Elementary Principal*, 1971, *51*, 48–55.

ELKIND, D. *A sympathetic understanding of the child: Birth to sixteen.* Boston: Allyn and Bacon, 1971.

ELKIND, D. and J. H. FLAVELL. *Studies in cognitive development.* New York: Oxford, 1969.

ENGELMANN, S. *Conceptual learning.* San Rafael, Cal.: Dimensions Press, 1969.

ENGELMANN, S. and T. ENGELMANN. *Give your child a superior mind: A program for the pre-school child.* New York: Simon & Schuster, 1966.

ERIKSON, E. *Identity: Youth and crisis.* New York: W. W. Norton, 1968.

EVANS, E. D. The effects of achievement motivation and ability on discovery learning and accompanying incidental learning under two conditions of incentive-set. *Journal of Educational Research*, 1967, 60, 195–200.

FAGOT, B. L. and G. R. PATTERSON. An in vivo analysis of reinforcing contingencies for sex-role behaviors in the pre-school child. *Developmental Psychology*, 1969, *1*, 563–568.

FAKOURI, M. Achieving motivation and cheating. *Psychological Reports*, October 1972, *31*, 629.

FARNHAM-DIGGORY, S. *Information processing in children.* New York: Academic Press, 1972.

FEINGOLD, B. F. *Why your child is hyperactive.* New York: Random House, 1974.

FELKER, D. W. *Building positive self-concepts.* Minneapolis: Burgess Publishing Co., 1974.

FESTINGER, L. *A theory of cognitive dissonance.* New York: Harper & Row, 1957.

FIELDER, F. *A theory of leadership effectiveness.* New York: McGraw-Hill, 1967.

FLANDERS, N. A. *Analyzing teacher behavior.* Reading, Mass.: Addison-Wesley, 1970.

FLAVELL, J. M. *The developmental psychology of Jean Piaget.* Princeton: Van Nostrand, 1963.

FLEISHMAN, E. A. *The structure and measurement of physical fitness.* Englewood Cliffs, N.J.: Prentice-Hall, 1964.

FODOR, E. Resistance to temptation, moral development, and perceptions of parental behavior among adolescent boys. *Journal of Social Psychology*, October, 1972, 88, 155–156.

FORBES, R. H. National assessment data: Science, writing, mathematics, and functional literacy. Address to American Educational Research Association, April, 1976. Mimeographed.

FORSYTH, A. A task-first approach to research on the teaching of statistics and research methodology. Mimeographed report, furnished by author, 1976.

FOWLER, W. Cognitive learning in infancy and early childhood. *Psychological Bulletin,* March 1962, 59 (2), 116–152.

FOX, R., M. B. LUSKI, and R. SCHMUCK. *Diagnosing classroom learning environments.* Chicago: Science Research Associates, 1966.

FRANKS, C. M. *Behavior therapy: Appraisal and status.* New York: McGraw-Hill, 1969.

FRASE, L. T. Prose processing. In G. Bower (Ed.), *Psychology of learning and motivation: Advances in research and theory.* New York: Academic Press, 1975.

FREUD, A. Adolescence. In *The psychoanalytic study of the child.* New York: International Universities Press, 1958, 13, 255–278.

FREUD, S. *General introduction to psychoanalysis* (New Ed.). Garden City, N.Y.: Doubleday, 1949.

FROSTIG, M. and D. HORNE. *The Frostig program for the development of visual perception.* Chicago: Follett, 1964.

FULLER, R. Breaking down the I.Q. walls: Severely retarded people can learn to read. *Psychology Today,* 1974, 8 (5), 97–102.

FURTH, H. G. *Piaget and knowledge.* Englewood Cliffs, N.J.: Prentice-Hall, 1970.

GAGE, N., M. BELGARD, B. ROSENSHINE, N. UNRUH, D. BELL, and J. HILLER. Explorations of teacher's effectiveness in lecturing. In I. Westbury and A. Bellack (Eds.), *Research into classroom processes.* New York: Teachers College Press, 1971.

GAGE, N. L. and D. C. BERLINER. *Educational psychology.* Chicago: Rand McNally, 1975.

GAGNE, R. The acquisition of knowledge. *Psychological Review,* 1962, 69, 355–365.

GAGNE, R. Problem solving. In A. W. Melton (Ed.), *Categories of human learning.* New York: Academic Press, 1964.

GAGNE, R. (Ed.). *Learning and individual differences.* Columbus, Ohio: Charles E. Merrill, 1967.

GAGNE, R. The conditions of learning (2nd ed.). New York: Holt, Rinehart & Winston, 1970.

GAGNE, R. and N. E. PARADISE. Abilities and learning sets in knowledge acquisition. *Psychological Monographs* 1961, 75(14), Whole No. 518.

GALLAGHER, J. and M. J. ASCHNER. A preliminary report on analysis of classroom interaction. In R. Hyman, *Teaching: Vantage points for study.* Philadelphia: J. B. Lippincott, 1968.

GARDNER, L. I. Deprivation dwarfism. *Scientific American,* July 1972.

GESCHWIND, N. The apraxias: Neural mechanisms of disorders of learned movement. *American Scientist,* March–April 1975, 63, 188–195.

GETZELS, J. W. and P. JACKSON. *Creativity and intelligence: Explorations with gifted students.* New York: Wiley, 1962.

GETZELS, J. W. and H. A. THELEN. The classroom group as a unique social system. In *The dynamics of instructional groups: 49th yearbook of the National Society for the Study of Education,* Part II. Chicago: University of Chicago Press, 1960, Chapter Four.

GIFFIN, M., R. HAGIN, L. LEHTINEN, and C. STROTHER. *The educator's enigma: The adolescent with learning disabilities.* San Rafael, Cal.: Academic Therapy Publications, 1970.

GLASER, R.   Components of a psychology of instruction: Toward a science of design.   *Review of Educational Research*, Winter 1976, 46 (1), 1–24.

GLASER, R.   *Adaptive education: Individual diversity and learning.*   New York: Holt, Rinehart & Winston, 1977.

GLASSER, W.   *Reality therapy: A new approach to psychiatry.*   New York: Harper & Row, 1975.

GOLDEN, M. and B. BIRNS.   Social climate and cognitive development of infants.   *Merrill-Palmer Quarterly*, April 1968, *14* (2), 139–149.

GOOD, T., B. BIDDLE, and J. BROPHY.   *Teachers make a difference.*   New York: Holt, Rinehart & Winston, 1975.

GORDON, M.   Choice of rule-example order used to teach mathematics as a function of conceptual level and field-dependence-independence.   Report presented to American Educational Research Association, April 1976.

GOTTLEIB, J., D. GOMPEL, and M. BUDSKY.   Classroom behavior of retarded children before and after integration into regular classes.   *Journal of Special Education*, 1975, 9 (3).

GRAVES, D. H.   An examination of the writing processes of seven-year-old children.   *Research in the Teaching of English*, Winter 1975, 9 (3), 227–241.

GREENSPAN, S., A. BURKA, S. ZLOTLOW, and C. BARENBOIM.   A manual of referential communication games.   *Academic Therapy*, Fall 1975, *11* (1), 97–106.

GREENWALD, A. G., T. C. BROCK, and T. M. OSTROM.   *Psychological foundations of attitudes.*   New York: Academic Press, 1968.

GRIMES, J. W. and W. ALLENSMITH.   Compulsivity, anxiety and school achievement.   *Merrill Palmer Quarterly*, 1961, *7*, 247–271.

GRINSPOON, L. and S. SINGER.   Amphetamines and the treatment of hyperkinetic children.   *Harvard Educational Review*, November 1973, *43*, 515—555.

GRONLUND, N. E.   Personality characteristics of socially accepted, socially neglected and socially rejected junior high school pupils.   *Educational Administration and Supervision*, 1957, *43*, 329–338.

GRONLUND, N. E.   *Constructing achievement tests.*   Englewood Cliffs, N.J.: Prentice-Hall, 1968.

GROSS, M. D. and W. C. WILSON.   *Minimal Brain Dysfunction.*   New York: Brunner-Mazel, 1974.

GRUBER, H. E. and WEITMAN, M.   *Self-directed study: Experiments in higher education.*   Boulder: University of Colorado, Behavior Research Laboratory, Report No. 19, 1962.

GUETZKOW, H., C. F. ALGER, R. A. BRODY, R. C. NOEL, and R. C. SYNDER.   *Simulation in international relations: Developments for research and teaching.*   Englewood Cliffs, N.J.: Prentice-Hall, 1963.

GUILFORD, J. P.   Factors that aid and hinder creativity.   *Teachers College Record*, 1962, *63*, 380–392.

GUILFORD, J. P.   *The nature of human intelligence.*   New York: McGraw-Hill, 1967.

HAHN, C.   Eliminating sexism from the schools: An application of planned change.   *Social Education*, March 1976.

HARLOW, H. F.   The formation of learning sets.   *Psychological Review*, 1949, *56*, 132–143.

HARLOW, H. F.   Learning set and error factor theory.   In S. Koch (Ed.), *Psychology: A study of a science* (Vol. 2).   New York: McGraw-Hill, 1959.

HARLOW, H. F.   Love in infant monkeys.   *Scientific American,* June 1959.

HARLOW, H. F. and M. K. HARLOW.   Social deprivation in monkeys.   *Scientific American,* November 1962.

HARNISCHFEGER, A. and D. E. WILEY.   Achievement test scores drop: So what?   *Educational Researcher,* March 1976, *5,* 5–12.

HART, J. and B. JONES.   *Where's Hannah.*   New York: Hart Publishing Co., 1968.

HART, H. (Ed.).   *Summerhill: For and against.*   New York: Hart, 1970.

HARTSHORNE, H. and M. A. MAY.   *Studies in the nature of character, Vol. I. Studies in deceit.*   New York: Macmillan, 1928.

HASELRUD, G.   Personal communication to the author, 1974.

HAWKINS, D. and L. PAULING (Eds.).   *Orthomolecular psychiatry: Treatment of schizophrenia.*   San Francisco: W. H. Freeman, 1973.

HAWKRIDGE, D. G.   Applications of educational technology at the Open University.   *AV Communication Review,* 1972, *20* (1).

HEBB, D. O.   *The organization of behavior.*   New York: Wiley, 1949.

HEBER, R., H. GARBER, S. HARRINGONT, and C. HOFFMAN.   Rehabilitation of families at risk for mental retardation.   Unpublished progress reports, Research and Training Center, University of Wisconsin, (a) October 1971, (b) December 1972.

HEIL, L. M. and C. WASHBURNE.   Brooklyn College research in teacher effectiveness.   *Journal of Educational Research,* May 1962, *55,* 347–351.

HELD, R.   Plasticity in sensory-motor systems.   *Scientific American,* November 1965.

HENDERER, J.   Report in *Behavior Today,* May 31, 1971, 2.

HENDERSON, R. W. and J. R. BERGAN.   The cultural context of childhood.   Columbus, Ohio: Charles E. Merrill, 1976.

HENDRICKS, C. G., C. E. THORESEN, and T. J. COATES.   *Self-managing stress and tension.*   Stanford University: Stanford Center for Research and Development in Teaching, 1975.

HERRNSTEIN, R.   *IQ in the meritocracy.*   Boston: Little, Brown, 1973.

HEWITT, F. M.   *Education of exceptional learners.*   Boston: Allyn and Bacon, 1974.

HILL, K. T. and S. B. SARASON.   The relationship of test anxiety and defensiveness to test and school performance over the elementary school years: A further longitudinal study.   *Monographs of the Society for Research in Child Development,* 1966, *31* (2), Whole no. 104, 46–51, 278–290.

HILSHEIMER, G.   *Allergy, toxins and the learning disabled child.*   San Rafael: Academic Therapy Publications, 1974.

HOFFMANN, B.   *The tyranny of testing.*   New York: Collier Books, 1964.

HOLLAND, J. G. and B. F. SKINNER.   *The analysis of behavior.*   New York: McGraw-Hill, 1961.

HOLT, J.   *How children fail.*   New York: Pitman, 1964.

HORNER, M.   Toward an understanding of achievement-related conflicts in women.   *Journal of Social Issues,* 1972, *28,* 157–175.

HORWITZ, M.   Hostility and its management in classroom groups.   In W. W. Charters and N. L. Gage (Eds.), *Reading in the social psychology of education.*   Boston: Allyn and Bacon, 1963.

HUGES, M.   What is teaching? One viewpoint.   *Educational Leadership,* January 1962, 251–259.

HUNT, J. McV.   Experience and the development of motivation: Some reinterpretations.   *Child Development,* 1960, *31,* 490–504.

HUNT, J. McV. *Intelligence and experience.* New York: Ronald Press, 1961.

HUNT, J. McV. The psychological basis for using pre-school enrichment as an antidote for cultural deprivation. *Merrill-Palmer Quarterly,* July 1974, *10,* 209–248.

HUNTER, M. *Reinforcement theory for teachers.* El Segundo, Cal.: TIP Publications, 1967.

HUNTER, M. *Retention theory for teachers.* El Segundo, Cal.: TIP Publications, 1967.

INHELDER, B. *The diagnosis of reasoning in the mentally retarded.* New York: John Day, 1965.

INHELDER, B. and J. PIAGET. *The growth of logical thinking from childhood to adolescence.* New York: Basic Books, 1958.

ISAACSON, R. L. Relation between achievement, test anxiety, and curricular choices. *Journal of Abnormal and Social Psychology,* 1964, 68, 447–452.

ISAACSON, R. L., W. J. MCKEACHIE, and J. E. MILHOLLAND. Correlation of teacher personality variables and student ratings. *Journal of Educational Psychology,* 1963, 54, 119–117.

JENCKS, C. *Inequality: A reassessment of family and education in America.* New York: Basic Books, 1972.

JENCKS, C. A reappraisal of the most controversial educational document of our time. *New York Times Magazine,* August 10, 1969.

JENCKS, C. and D. RIESMAN. *The academic revolution.* Garden City, N.Y.: Anchor, 1968.

JENSEN, A. R. Individual differences in concept learning. In H. J. Klausmeier and C. W. Harris (Eds.), *Analysis of concept learning.* New York: Academic Press, 1966, 139–154.

JENSEN, A. R. Social class, race, and genetics: Implications for education. *American Educational Research Journal,* January 1968, 5 (1), 1–42.

JENSEN, A. R. How much can we boost IQ and scholastic achievement? *Harvard Educational Review,* 1969, 39, 1–123.

JENSEN, G. E. The social structure of the classroom group: An observational framework. *Journal of Educational Psychology,* 1955, 46, 362–374.

JOHNSON, D. and H. MYKLEBUST. *Learning disabilities.* New York: Grune and Stratton, 1967.

JOHNSON, L. V. and M. A. BANY. *Classroom management: Theory and skill training.* London: Macmillan, 1970.

JOYCE, B. and B. HAROOTUNIAN. *The structure of teaching.* Chicago: Science Research Associates, 1967.

KAGAN, J. Impulsive and reflective children: Significance of conceptual tempo. In J. D. Krumboltz (Ed.), *Learning and the educational process.* Chicago: Rand McNally, 1965, 133–161.

KAGAN, J. Check one: Male-female. *Psychology Today,* July 1969, 39–41.

KAGAN, J. and N. KOGAN. Individual variations in cognitive process. In P. H. Mussen (Ed.), *Carmichael's manual of child psychology* (3rd ed.) Vol. I. New York: Wiley, 1970.

KAGAN, J. and H. MOSS. *From birth to maturity: A study in psychological development.* New York: Wiley, 1962.

KATONA, G. *Organizing and memorizing.* New York: Columbia University Press, 1940.

KENNEDY, W. R. Grades expected and grades received: Their relationship to students' evaluation of faculty performance. *Journal of Educational Psychology,* 75, 6, 109–115.

KENNELL, J. H. et al. Maternal behavior one year after early and extended post-partum contact. *Developmental Medicine and Child Neurology,* 1974, 16, 172–179,

KEPHART, N. C. *The slow learner in the classroom.* Columbus, Ohio: Charles E. Merrill, 1960.

KEPHART, N. and E. ROACH. *The Purdue perceptual-motor survey.* Columbus, Ohio: Charles E. Merrill, 1966.

KERLINGER, F. (Ed.). *Review of research in education 3.* Itasca, Ill.: F. E. Peacock, 1975. Publication of AERA.

KERSH, B. Y. The motivating effect of learning by directed discovery. *Journal of Educational Psychology,* 1962, 53, 65–71.

KILPATRICK, W. H. *A sourcebook for the philosophy of education,* 1934.

KIRK, S. A. *Educating exceptional children.* Boston: Houghton Mifflin, 1972.

KIRK, S. A. and W. KIRK. *Psycholinguistic learning disabilities: Diagnosis and remediation.* Urbana, Ill.: University of Illinois Press, 1971, 1972.

KIRK, S. A. and J. J. MCCARTHY. The Illinois test of psycholinguistic abilities: An approach to differential diagnosis. *American Journal of Mental Deficiency,* 1961, 66, 399–412.

KIRSCHENBAUM, H., S. SIMON, and R. NAPIER. *Wad-ja-get? The grading game in American education.* New York: Hart, 1971.

KLAUSMEIER, H. Report delivered to the American Educational Research Association, May 1976. Mimeographed.

KLAUSMEIER, H. J., C. W. HARRIS, and W. WIERSMA, *Strategies of learning and efficiency of concept attainment by individuals and groups.* U.S. Office of Education, Cooperative Research project No. 1442. Madison: University of Wisconsin.

KLEINMUNTZ, B. (Ed.). *Problem solving: Research, method and theory.* New York: Wiley, 1966.

KLINE, P. Personality theories and dimensions. Topic 2 of the Open University Course E201, *Personality and Learning,* 1974.

KOHL, H. *The open classroom: A practical guide to a new way of teaching.* New York: Vintage, 1969.

KOHLBERG, L. Development of moral character and moral ideology. In M. L. Hoffman and L. W. Hoffman (Eds.), *Review of child development research.* New York: Russell Sage, 1964.

KOHLBERG, L. The child as a moral philosopher. *Psychology Today,* 1968, 2 (4), 24–30.

KOHLBERG, L. Psychoanalytic and cognitive-developmental approaches to moral education. AERA Paper, April 1976.

KOHLER, W. The mentality of apes (Translated by E. Winter). New York: Harcourt, 1925.

KOLB, D. A. Achievement motivation training for under-achieving high school boys. *Journal of Personality and Social Psychology,* 1965, 2, 783–792.

KOUNIN, J. *Discipline and group management in classrooms.* New York: Holt, Rinehart & Winston, 1970.

KOUNIN, J. S. and P. V. GUMP. The ripple effect in discipline. *Elementary School Journal,* 1962, 59 (3), 158–162.

KOUNIN, J. S., P. GUMP, and J. RYAN. Explorations in classroom management. In W. W. Charters and N. L. Gage (Eds.), *Readings in the social psychology of education.* Boston: Allyn and Bacon, 1963.

KOZOL, J. *Free schools.* Boston: Houghton Mifflin, 1972.

KRASNER, L. and L. P. ULLMAN (Eds.). *Research in behavior modification: New developments and implications.* New York: Holt, Rinehart & Winston, 1965.

KRATHWOHL, D. R., B. S. BLOOM, and B. B. MASIA. *Taxonomy of educational objectives, Handbook II: Affective domain.* New York: McKay, 1964.

KRAUCH, V. The hyperactive classroom. *American Education,* June 1971.

KRETCH, D. Psychoneurobiochemeducation. *Phi Delta Kappan,* March 1969, 360–375.

KRETCH, D. Don't use the kitchen sink approach to enrichment. *Today's Education,* Oct. 1970.

KULIK, J. A. and W. J. MCKEACHIE. The evaluation of teachers in higher education. *Review of Educational Research* (no. 3), F. Kerlinger (Ed.). Itasca, Ill.: F. E. Peacock, 1975, 210–240.

LAPORTE, R. E. and R. NATH. Role of performance goals in prose learning. *Journal of Educational Psychology,* 68, 3, 260–264.

LAUFER, N. W. Cerebral disfunction and behavior disorders of adolescents. *American Journal of Orthopsychiatry,* March 1962, *32,* 505–506.

LAURENDEAU, M. and A. PINARD. *The development of the concept of space in the child.* New York: International Universities Press, Inc., 1970.

LERNER, J. *Children with learning disabilities: The origins, diagnosis and teaching strategies* (2nd ed.). Boston: Houghton Mifflin, 1976.

LEWIN, K., R. LIPPITT, and R. WHITE. Patterns of aggressive behavior in experimentally created "social climates." *Journal of Social Psychology,* 1939, *10,* 271–299.

LEWIS, B. N. Course production at the Open University III: Planning and scheduling. *British Journal of Educational Technology,* October 1971, *2* (3), 189–204.

LEWIS, B. N. Course production at the Open University IV: The problem of assessment. *British Journal of Educational Technology,* May 1972, *3* (2), 108–128.

LINDSLEY, O. R. From Skinner to precision teaching: The child knows best. In J. B. Jordan and L. S. Robbins (Eds.), *Let's try doing something else kind of thing: Behavioral principles and the exceptional child.* Arlington, Va.: Council for Exceptional Children, 1972, 2–11.

LINDVALL, C. M. and J. L. BOLVIN. Programmed instruction in the schools: An application of programming principles in individually prescribed instruction. *Sixty-sixth yearbook of the National Society for the Study of Education.* Part II. Chicago: University of Chicago Press, 1967.

LIPPITT, R. and M. GOLD. Classroom social structure as a mental health problem. *Journal of Social Issues,* 1959, *15,* 40–49.

LOEVINGER, J. The meaning and measurement of ego development. *American Psychologist,* 1966, *21,* 195–206.

LOEVINGER, J. and R. WESSLER. *Measuring ego development,* 1970.

LORENZ, K. *Evolution and the modification of behavior.* Chicago: University of Chicago Press, 1965.

LORETAN, J. Alternatives to intelligence testing. *Proceedings of the 1965 Invitational Conference on Testing Problems.* Princeton, N.J.: Educational Testing Service, 1966.

LUCHINS, A. S. Mechanization in problem solving: The effect of Einstellung. *Psychological Monographs,* 1942, *54* (6) (Whole No. 248).

LURIA, A. R. *The mind of a mnemonist.* New York: Avon, 1968.

MACCOBY, E. B. and C. N. JACKLIN. *The psychology of sex differences.* Stanford, Cal.: Stanford University Press, 1974.

MACFARLANE, J. W. From infancy to adulthood. *Childhood Education,* March 1963.

MADSEN, C., JR. and C. K. MADSEN. *Teaching/discipline: Behavioral principles toward a positive approach.* Boston: Allyn and Bacon, 1970.

MAGER, R. F. *Preparing instructional objectives.* Palo Alto, Cal.: Fearon, 1962.

MAIER, N. R. F. Reasoning in humans I: On direction. *Journal of Comparative Psychology,* 1930, *10,* 115–143.

Mainstreaming: Helping teachers meet the challenge. National Advisory Council on Education Professions Development, Summer 1976, 13–15.

MANDLER, G. and S. B. SARASON. A study of anxiety and learning. *Journal of Abnormal and Social Psychology,* 1952, *47,* 166–173.

MANN, R. Mimeographed report of the "Teacher as . . ." questionnaire results, University of Michigan, 1966.

MARKLE, S. M. The psychology of the newer teaching methods. Seventh-fifth yearbook of the National Society for the Study of Education: *The Psychology of Teaching Methods.* San Francisco, 1976.

MARKLE, S. M. and P. W. THIEMANN. *Really understanding concepts, or in frumious pursuit of the Jabberwock.* Champaign, Ill.: Stipes Pub. Co., 1970.

MARKLE, S. M. and P. W. TIEMANN. Some principles of instructional design at higher cognitive levels. In R. Ulrich, T. Stachnik, and J. Mabry (Eds.), *Control of human behavior,* Vol. 3. Glenview, Ill.; Scott, Foresman, 1974, 312–323.

MARTUZA, V. R. *Applying norm-referenced and criterion-referenced measurement in education.* Boston: Allyn and Bacon, 1977.

MASLOW, A. H. *Motivation and personality,* 1954.

MASLOW, A. H. Deficiency motivation and growth motivation. In M. R. Jones (Ed.), *Nebraska symposium on motivation 1955.* Lincoln: University of Nebraska Press, 1955, 1–30.

MASLOW, A. H. Personality problems and personality growth. In C. Moustakas (Ed.), *The self.* New York: Harper & Row, 1956.

MAYER, R. E. Information processing variables in learning to solve problems. *Review of Educational Research,* Fall 1975, *45,* 525–541.

MCCLELLAND, D. Toward a theory of motive acquisition. *American Psychologist,* May 1962, *20,* (5), 321–333.

MCDILL, E. L. et al. *Source of educational climates in high schools.* Baltimore: Johns Hopkins University Press, 1966.

MCDONALD, F. J. Report on Phase II of the Beginning Teacher Evaluation Study. *Journal of teacher education,* Spring 1976, 39–42.

MCKEACHIE, W. J. Research on teaching at the college and university level. In N. L. Gage (Ed.), *Handbook of research on teaching.* Chicago: Rand McNally, 1963, chapter 23, 118–172.

MCKEACHIE, W. J. *Teaching tips.* Lexington, Mass.: D. C. Heath, 1969.

MCKEACHIE, W. J. and J. A. KULIK. Effective college teaching. In Kerlinger, F. N. (Ed.), *Review of research in education 3.* Itasca, Ill.: F. E. Peacock Publishers, 1975, 165–209.

MCKIEL, G. *The open university: Its applicability to Quebec and North America.* Report of Open College Concept Committee of Dawson College, Vanier College, and John Abbott College, Canada, 1973.

MCLEOD, J. *Dyslexia schedule and school entrance check list.* Cambridge, Mass.: Educators Publishing Service, Inc., 1969.

MEEKER, M. *The structure of intellect: Its uses and interpretation.* Columbus, Ohio: Charles E. Merrill, 1969.

MELDRUM, B. S. Childhood hypoglycemia. *British Medical Journal,* 1972, *1,* 379.

MENYUK, P. *Sentences children use.* Cambridge, Mass.: MIT Press, 1969.

MERCER, J. B. Labeling the mentally retarded. *Harvard Educational Review,* 1974, *44,* 125–141.

MERCHENBAUM, D. and J. GOODMAN. Training impulsive children to talk to themselves: A means of developing self-control. *Journal of Abnormal Psychology,* 1971, *77,* 115.

MERRILL, M. D. (Ed.). *Instructional design: Readings.* Englewood Cliffs, N. J.: Prentice-Hall, 1971.

MILES, M. B. *Learning to work in groups: A program guide for educational leaders.* New York: Teachers College Press, 1961.

MILES, M. W. and W. W. CHARTERS, JR. (Eds.). *Learning in social settings.* Boston: Allyn and Bacon, 1970.

MILGRAM, R. M. and A. NORMAN. Creative thinking and creative performance in Israeli students. *Journal of Educational Psychology,* 1976, 68, 255–259.

MILLER, G. A., E. GALANTER, and K. PRIBRAM. *Plans and the structure of behavior.* New York: Holt, Rinehart & Winston, 1960.

MILLER, G. W. Factors in school achievement and social class. *Journal of Educational Psychology,* 1970, *61* (4), 260–269.

MILLER, R. I. *Evaluating faculty performance.* San Francisco: Jossey-Bass, 1972.

MILLETT, K. *Sexual politics.* New York: Doubleday, 1970.

MINSKOFF, E. and G. MINSKOFF. Compensatory teaching. *Journal of Learning Disabilities,* April 1976.

MONEY, JOHN (Ed.). *The disabled reader: education of the dyslexic child.* Baltimore: Johns Hopkins Press, 1966.

MONTESSORI, M. *The Montessori elementary material.* New York: Schocken Books, 1973.

MORSE, H. A. and J. KAGAN. Stability of achievement and recognition seeking behaviors from early childhood through adulthood. *Journal of Abnormal and Social Psychology,* 1961, *62.*

MORSE, W. C., R. BLOOM, and J. DUNN. A study of school classroom behavior from diverse evaluative frameworks: Developmental, mental health, substantive learning, group process. *Perceptual and Motor Skills,* 1962, *14* (3), 390.

MOYER, K. E. The physiology of violence: Allergy and aggression. *Psychology Today,* July 1975, 77–79.

MURRAY, H. A. *Explorations in personality.* New York: Oxford, 1938.

MURRAY, H. A. and C. KLUCKHOHN. Outline of a conception of personality. In C. Kluckhohn, H. A. Murray (Eds.), *Personality in nature, society, and culture,* 2nd ed. New York: Knopf, 1953.

MUSSEN, P., J. CONGER, and J. KAGAN. *Child development and personality,* (4th ed.). New York: Harper & Row, 1974.

NEILL, A. S. *Summerhill: A radical approach to child rearing.* New York: Hart, 1960.

Never too old to learn. New York: Academy for Educational Development, Inc.

NEWELL, A. and H. A. SIMON. *Human Problem Solving.* Englewood Cliffs, N. J.: Prentice-Hall, 1972.

NEWMAN, H., F. N. FREEMAN, and K. J. HOLZINGER. *Twins: A study of heredity and environment.* Chicago: University of Chicago Press, 1937.

OLDS, D. Cross age tutoring and parent involvement. Doctoral dissertation, Cornell University, 1976; cited in Bronfenbrenner, 1976.

OLDS, J. and P. MILNER. Postive reinforcement produced by electrical stimulation of septal area and other regions of rat brain. *Journal of Comparative Physiological Psychology,* 1954, *47,* 419–427.

OLTON, R. M. and R. S. CRUTCHFIELD. Developing the skills of productive thinking. In P. H. Mussen, J. Langer, and M. Covington (Eds.), *Trends and issues in developmental psychology,* New York: Holt, Rinehart & Winston, 1969.

PAGE, E. B. and T. F. BREEN. Educational values for measurement technology: some theory and data. From Coffman, W. E. (Ed.), *Frontiers of educational measurement and information systems.* Boston: Houghton Mifflin, 1973.

PARELVIS, A. P. Lifelong education and age stratification. *American Behavioral Scientist,* November-December 1975, *19* (2), 206.

PASCUAL-LEONE, J. Cognitive development and cognitive style: a general psychological integration. Mimeographed, 1969.

PASCUAL-LEONE, J. A mathematical model for the transition role in Piaget's developmental stages. *Acta Psychologica,* 1970, *32,* 301–345.

PAVLOV, I. Conditioned reflexes (translated by G. V. Anrep). New York: Dover Press, 1960.

PECK, R. F. Needed research and development in teaching. *Journal of Teacher Education,* Spring, 1976, *27* (I), 18–21.

PEDDIWELL, J. A. *The saber-tooth curriculum.* New York: McGraw-Hill, 1939.

PERVIN, L. A., L. E. REIK, and W. DALRYMPLE. The college dropout and the utilization of talent. Princeton: Princeton University Press, 1966.

PHILLIPS, J. L., JR. *The origins of intellect: Piaget's theory.* San Francisco: W. H. Freeman, 1969.

PIAGET, J. *The language and thought of the child.* London: Routledge and Kegan-Paul, 1952.

PIAGET, J. *The origins of intelligence in children.* New York: International Universities Press, 1952.

PIAGET, J. *Science of education and the psychology of the child.* New York: Viking, 1971.

PIAGET, J. and B. INHELDER. *The psychology of the child.* New York: Basic Books, 1969.

PINARD, A. and M. LAURENDEAU. A scale of mental development based on the theory of Piaget. *Journal of Research in Science Teaching,* 1964, 253–260.

PINES, M. A child's mind is shaped before age 2. *Life Magazine,* December 1971. Reprinted in Dentler, R. A. and B. J. Shapiro (Eds.), *Readings in educational psychology: contemporary perspectives.* New York: Harper & Row, 1976.

POLYA, G. *How to solve it* (2nd ed.). Garden City: Anchor/Doubleday (paperback), 1957.

POPHAM, W. J. (Ed.). *Criterion referenced measurement.* Englewood Cliffs, N. J.: Educational Technology Publications, 1972.

POSTLETHWAITE, S. et al. *Audio-tutorial approach to learning through independent study and integrated experiences.* Minneapolis: Burgess Publishing Co., 1969.

POSTMAN, N. and C. WEINGARTNER. *Teaching as a subversive activity.* New York: Delacorte, 1969.

PREMACK, D. The education of Sarah. *Psychology Today,* September 1970.

PRESTON, R. C. Reading achievement of German and American children. *School and Society,* 90, 350–354.

RAMBUSCH, N. MCC. *Learning how to learn.* Baltimore: Helicon Press, 1962.

REDL, F. and W. WATTENBERG. *Mental hygiene in teaching.* New York: Harcourt, Brace & World, 1951.

REDL, F. and D. WINEMAN. *The aggressive child.* Glencoe: Free Press, 1957.

REISER, R. A. and V. S. GERLACH. *Research on simulation games in education: A critical analysis.* AERA, 1976.

REISSMAN, F. *The culturally deprived child.* New York: Harper & Row, 1962.

RING, B. C. Memory processes and children with learning problems. *Academic Therapy,* Fall 1975, *11* (1), 111–116.

RINGNESS, T. A. Affective differences between successful and nonsuccessful bright ninth grade boys. Personnel and Guidance Journal, 1965, 43, 600–606.

RODIN, M. *Can students evaluate good teaching? Change,* Summer 1973.

ROGERS, C. Personal thoughts on teaching and learning, from *On becoming a person.* Boston: Houghton Mifflin, 1961.

ROSENSHINE, B. Objectively measured behavioral predictors of effectiveness in explaining. In I. D. Westbury and A. A. Bellack (Eds.), *Research into classroom processes.* New York: Teachers College Press, 1971, 51–98.

ROSENSHINE, B. and FURST, N. The use of direct observation to study teaching. In R. Travers (Ed.), *Second handbook of research on teaching.* Chicago: Rand McNally, 1973.

ROSENSHINE, B. Recent research on teaching behaviors and student achievement. *Journal of Teacher Education,* Spring 1976, *27* (1), 61–64.

ROSENTHAL, R. The Pygmalion effect lives. *Psychology Today,* 1973, *7,* 56–63.

ROSENTHAL, R. and L. JACOBSEN. *Pygmalion in the classroom.* New York: Holt, Rinehart & Winston, 1968.

ROSENZWEIG, M. R., E. L. BENNETT, and M. C. DIAMOND. Brain changes in response to experience. *Scientific American,* February 1972.

ROTHKOPF, E. Z. and P. JOHNSON (Eds.). *Verbal learning research and the technology of written instruction.* New York: Teachers College Press, 1971.

RYANS, D. G. *Characteristics of teachers, their description, comparisons, and appraisal: A research study.* Washington, D.C.: American Council on Education, 1960.

SAMUEL, W. et al. Motivation, race, social climate and IQ. *Journal of Educational Psychology,* 1976, 68 (3), 273–285.

SANDEFUR, J. T. and R. A. ADAMS. An evaluation of teaching: An interim research report. *Journal of Teacher Education,* Spring 1976, *27* (1), 71–76.

SANDERS, F. B. An option for change in higher education. Educational Technology, September 1969.

SARASON, S. B. et al. *Anxiety in elementary school children: A report of research.* New York: Wiley, 1960.

SARASON, S. B., K. T. HILL, and P. G. ZIMBARDO. A longitudinal study of the relation of test anxiety to performance on intelligence and achievement tests. *Monographs of the Society for Research in Child Development,* 1964, *28* (7, Whole no. 98).

SATZ, P., J. FRIEL, and F. RUDEGEAIR. Some predictive antecedents of specific reading disability: A two-, three- and four-year follow up. Handout at presentation to the Hyman Blumberg Symposium on Research in Early Childhood Education, Johns Hopkins University, 1974.

SCARF, M. The anatomy of fear. *New York Times Magazine,* June 16, 1974, *10.*

SCARR-SALAPATEK, S. and M. L. WILLIAMS. The effects of early stimulation on low-birth weight infants. *Child Development,* 1973, *44,* 94–101.

SCHILD, E. O. Interaction in games. In S. S. Boocock and E. O. Schild (Eds.), *Simulation games in learning.* Beverly Hills, Cal.: Sage, 1968, 93–104.

SCHNEOUR, E. *The malnourished mind.* Garden City, N.Y.: Anchor Books, 1975.

SCHRAG, P. and D. DIVOKY. *The myth of the hyperactive child.* New York: Pantheon, 1975.

SCHMUCK, R., M. CHESLER, and R. LIPPITT. *Problem solving to improve classroom learning.* Chicago: Science Research Associates, 1966.

SCHRODER, H. J., M. J. DRIVER, and S. STREUFERT. Human information processing. In *Individuals and groups functioning in complex social situations.* New York: Holt, Rinehart & Winston, 1967.

SEARLS, E. F. *How to use WISC scores in reading diagnosis.* Newark, Del.: International Reading Association, 1971, 1975.

SEAVER, W. B. Effects of naturally induced teacher expectancies. *Journal of Personality and Social Psychology,* 1973, 28, 333–342.

SEMEL, E. *Sound order sense. A developmental program in auditory perception.* Follett Educational Corporation, 1970.

SHEEHY, G. *Passages: Predictable crises of adult life.* New York: E. P. Dutton, 1976.

SHERIF, M. et al. Experiments in group conflict. *Scientific American,* 1956, 195 (2), 54–58.

SHERIF, M. et al. *Intergroup conflict and cooperation: The Robbers Cave Experiment.* Norman: University of Oklahoma Book Exchange, 1961.

SHULMAN, L. S. and E. R. KEISLAR (Eds.). *Learning by discovery.* Chicago: Rand McNally, 1966.

SIEBER, J. Turning impulsive students into thinkers. *Report on Education Research,* February 1972, 16, 10.

SINGER, R. N. *Motor learning and human performance: An application to physical education skills.* New York: Macmillan, 1975.

SKEELS, H. M. Adult status of children with contrasting early life experiences: A follow-up study. *Monographs of the Society for Research in Child Development,* 1966, 31, (3, Whole No. 105).

SKINNER, B. F. *Walden two.* New York: Macmillan, 1948.

SKINNER, B. F. *Science and human behavior.* New York: Macmillan, 1953.

SKINNER, B. F. *Verbal behavior.* New York: Appleton-Century-Crofts, 1957.

SKINNER, B. F. *The technology of teaching.* New York: Appleton-Century-Crofts, 1968.

SKINNER, B. F. *Beyond freedom and dignity.* New York: Knopf, 1971.

SMITH, B. and M. MEUX. *A study of the logic of teaching.* U.S. Department of H.E.W., O.E., Cooperative Research Project No. 258 (7257), Urbana, Ill., 1962.

SMITH, F. J. and G. A. MILLER (Eds.). *The genesis of language: A psychological approach.* Cambridge, Mass.: MIT Press, 1966.

SMITH, F. J. and J. E. R. LUGINBUHL. Inspecting expectancy: Some laboratory results of relevance to teacher training. *Journal of Educational Psychology,* 1976, 68, 265–272.

SMITH, M. D. Learning difficulty, transfer and retention as functions of two levels of redundancy in a sequence of concept formation tasks in mathematics involving computer assistance. Mimeographed, 1970.

SMITH, M. D., G. POORMAN, and M. SCHAGRIN. Multi-media systems: A review and report of a pilot project. *School Science and Mathematics,* February, 1968, 68 (2), 96–102.

SPITZ, R. A. Hospitalism: An inquiry into the genesis of psychiatric conditions in early childhood. *Psychoanalytic study of the child,* 1945, 1, 53–74.

STALLINGS, J. A. How instructional processes relate to child outcomes in a national study of follow through. *Journal of Teacher Education,* Spring 1976, 27 (1), 43.

STAUB, E. To rear a prosocial child: Reasoning, learning by doing, and learning by teaching others. In D. J. Dephalma and J. M. Foley (Eds.), *Moral development: Current theory and research.* New Jersey: Lawrence Earlbaum Associates, 1975.

STAUB, E. The development of prosocial behavior: Directions for future research and applications to education. Prepared for Research for Better Schools, Inc., Philadelphia, Pa., April, 1976. Mimeographed.

SUCHMAN, J. R. Inquiry training: Building skills for autonomous discovery. *Merrill-Palmer Quarterly*, 1961, 7, 147–169.

SUOMI, S. J. and H. F. Harlow. Social rehabilitation of isolate-reared monkeys. *Developmental Psychology*, 1972, 6 (3), 487–496.

SUPPES, P., M. JERMAN, and D. BRIAN. *Computer assisted instruction*. New York: Academic Press, 1968.

SWANSON, R. and R. W. HENDERSON. The effects of age, televised instruction, and directed participation on the acquisition of conceptual operant behaviors, AERA, 1976.

TABA, H. and D. ELKINS. *Strategies for the culturally disadvantaged*. Chicago: Rand McNally, 1966.

TAYLOR, D. W. et al. Does group participation when using brainstorming facilitate or inhibit creative thinking? *Administrative Science Quarterly*, 1968, 3, 23–47.

TAYLOR, J. A. A personality scale of manifest anxiety. *Journal of Abnormal and Social Psychology*, 1953, 48, 285–290.

TERMAN, L. and M. OGDEN. *The gifted child grows up*. Stanford: Stanford University Press, 1947.

THARP, R. G. and R. GALLIMORE. What a coach can teach a teacher. *Psychology Today*, January 1975, 75–78.

THOMAS, A., S. Chess, and H. G. Birch. The origin of personality. *Scientific American*, 1970, 223, 102–109.

THOMAS, D. R., W. C. BECKER, and M. ARMSTRONG. Production and elimination of disruptive classroom behavior by systematically varying teacher's behavior. *Journal of Applied Behavior Analysis*, 1968, 1, 35–45.

THOMPSON, E. An experimental investigation of the relative effectiveness of organizational structure in oral communication. *Southern Speech Journal*, 1960, 26, 59–69.

THORNBURG, H. D. (Ed.). *Preadolescent development*. Tuscon, Ariz.: University of Arizona Press, 1974.

THORNDIKE, E. L. *The fundamentals of learning*. New York: Teachers College Press, 1932.

TORRANCE, E. P. Priming creative thinking in the primary grades. *Elementary School Journal*, 1961, 62, 34–41.

TORRANCE, E. P. *Thinking creatively with pictures*. Princeton: Personnel Press, 1966.

TORRANCE, E. P. and R. MYERS. *Creative teaching and learning*. New York: Holt, Rinehart & Winston, 1965.

TURIEL, E. An experimental test of the sequentiality of developmental states in the child's moral judgments. *Journal of Personality and Social Psychology*, 1966, 3, 611–618.

ULRICH, R., T. STACHNIK, and S. MABRY. *Control of human behavior*. Glenview, Ill.: Scott, Foresman, 1966.

UNDERWOOD, B. J. The representativeness of rote verbal learning. In A. W. Melton (Ed.), *Categories of human learning*. New York: Academic Press, 1964, 47–48.

UNDERWOOD, B. J. and R. W. SCHULTZ. *Meaningfulness and verbal learning*. Philadelphia: J. B. Lippincott, 1960.

VASTA, R. and R. F. SARMIENTO. Liberal grading improves evaluations but not performance. Paper presented at the meeting of the American Educational Research Association, San Francisco, April 1976.

VONNEGUT, M. *The Eden express: A personal account of schizophrenia.* New York: Praeger, 1975.

WALBERG, H. J. Class size and the social environment of learning. *Human Relations,* 1969, *22,* 465–475.

WALBERG, H. J. (Ed.). *Evaluating educational performance: A sourcebook of methods, instruments and examples.* Berkeley, Cal.: McCutchan, 1974.

WALLACH, M. and N. KOGAN. *Modes of thinking in young children.* New York: Holt, Rinehart & Winston, 1965.

WARD, B. A. and W. J. TIKUNOFF. The effective teacher education problem: Application of selected research results and methodology to teaching. *Journal of Teacher Education,* Spring 1976, *27* (1), 48–52.

WARREN, J. Evaluation and motivation: A critical analysis. Address to AERA, April, 1976.

WATSON, G. *Nutrition and your mind.* New York: Harper & Row, 1972; Bantam, 1974.

WEESNER, T. *The car thief.* New York: Random House, 1972.

WEINBERG, J. Counseling recovering alcoholics. *Social Work,* July 1973, *84.*

WEISS, R. L., S. M. SALES, S. BODE. Student authoritarianism and teacher authoritarianism seen as factors in the determination of student performance and attitudes. *Journal of Experimental Education,* 1970, 38 (4), 83–87.

WELLMAN, B. L. IQ changes of preschool and non-preschool groups during the preschool years: A summary of the literature. *Journal of Psychology,* 1945, *20,* 347–368.

WENDT, H. W. Motivation, effort, and performance. In D. C. McClelland (Ed.), *Studies in motivation.* New York: Appleton-Century-Crofts, 1955, 292–293.

WESTBURY, I. and A. BELLACK (Eds.). *Research into classroom processes.* New York: Teachers College Press, 1971.

WEXLER, D. B. Behavior modification, token economies, and the law. *California Law Review,* 1973, *61,* 81–109.

WHITE, B. L. *The first three years of life.* Englewood Cliffs, N.J.: Prentice-Hall, 1975.

WHITE, R. W. Motivation reconsidered: The concept of competence. *Psychological Review,* 1959, *66,* 297–333.

WHITING, D., M. SCHNALL, and C. DRAKE. *Automization in dyslexic and normal children.* Wellesley, Mass.: Reading Research Institute. Mimeographed.

WHORF, B. L. *Language, thought and reality.* New York: Wiley and Technology Press of MIT, 1956.

WILSON, W. and M. GROSS. *Minimal brain dysfunction: A clinical study of incidence, diagnosis and treatment in over 1,000 children.* New York: Bruner/Mazel, 1974.

WITKIN, H. A., R. B. DYK, H. F. FATERSON, D. R. GOODENOUGH, and S. A. KARP. *Psychological differentiation.* New York: Wiley, 1962.

WOLFE, D. Some theoretical aspects of language learning and language teaching. *Language Learning,* 1967.

WOLPE, J. and A. A. LAZARUS. *Behavior therapy techniques.* Oxford: Pergamon Press, 1966.

WOODWORTH, R. S. *Heredity and environment: A critical survey of recently published material on twins and foster children.* New York: Social Sciences Research Council, 1941.

WORTHEN, B. Discovery and expository task presentation in elementary mathematics. *Journal of Educational Psychology,* Monograph Supplement, February, 1968, *59* (1), Part 2.

WUNDERLICH, R. C. Treatment of the hyperactive child. *Academic Therapy,* Summer, 1973, 375–390.

ZACHARIAS, L., R. WURTMAN, and W. RAND. Study reported by R. A. Knox in an article in the Boston *Globe,* March 26, 1976.

ZAHORIK, J. A. The effect of planning on teaching. *Elementary School Journal, 1970, 71,* 143–151.

ZAJONC, R. B. *Family configuration and intelligence.* Science, 192, 227–236.

ZIGLER, E. The environmental mystique: Training the intellect. *Childhood Education,* 1970, 46, 402–412.

ZIGMOND, N. and R. CICCI. *Auditory learning.* San Rafael, Cal.: Dimensions Publishing Co., 1969.

Index